KITCHEN HINTS FROM

Heloise

KITCHEN HINTS FROM Heloise®

More Than **1,527** Time-Saving, Money-Saving, and Work-Saving Hints for Cooking, Cleaning, Shopping, and Storing

RODALE

Printed in the United States of America
Rodale Inc. makes every effort to use acid-free ♾, recycled paper ♺.

Published by arrangement with Perigee, a member of Penguin Groups (USA) Inc.

Contains materials from the following works: *In the Kitchen with Heloise* copyright © 2000 by King Features; *Heloise Conquers Stinks & Stains* copyright © 2002 by Heloise, Inc.; and *Get Organized with Heloise* copyright © 2004 by Heloise, Inc.

HELOISE is a federally registered trademark licensed exclusively to Heloise, Inc.

Cover photo by Michael Keel copyright © King Features Syndicate, Inc., and Penguin Group (USA) Inc.
Text design by Tiffany Kukec and Anthony Serge
Cover design by Anthony Serge

ISBN 1–59486–127–7 hardcover

10   9   direct mail hardcover

RODALE
WE INSPIRE AND ENABLE PEOPLE TO IMPROVE
THEIR LIVES AND THE WORLD AROUND THEM

FOR MORE OF OUR PRODUCTS
WWW.RODALESTORE.COM
(800) 848-4735

To those who like to be in the kitchen,

to those who don't but would like to be,

and to those who just don't give a fig!

Contents

Acknowledgments

They say too many cooks spoil the pot (stew) but in this case all of the "cooks" who have helped with this book made it a better "meal." Heloise Central is more than a place, it's the people who make my job appear effortless. In random order (I actually picked numbers!) Janie, Ruth, Kelly, Merry, Joyce, Cabbie, J.D. (well, the last two are our four-pawed furry friends) and as always David, my husband, who simply says "Yes dear!" sometimes with a smile and twinkle in his eye, others, well . . . you know.

Welcome to My Kitchen

In addition to the reader's hints that I receive by the thousands, I get a lot of questions about basic kitchen activities. It appears that a lot of people are lost when it comes to what I call "kitcheneering" basics. If you are one of these people, you can consider this new Heloise Hints collection to be the only textbook you'll need to get to get your degree in kitcheneering. And if you're looking for a refresher course to catch up on what's changed since you first put on an apron, this will also be your guide to remedial kitcheneering.

Most people of my mother's generation learned kitchen how-tos from their mothers. However, many of my readers tell me that, for whatever reasons, they didn't get a "domestic education" from their moms. They admit that when they are in the kitchen, all they can stir up is trouble.

If Mom didn't let you in her kitchen—or if you wouldn't have gone in anyway—this book is designed to walk you into and around the kitchen and make it easier for you to plan, prepare, and enjoy meals with family and friends or just cook for yourself.

In the early 1960s my mother's most popular book and most of her columns were about kitchen stuff. And, although it's been more than forty years since my mother began writing Heloise columns and books, readers find that many tried-and-true hints of yesterday are still useful today. Because some things never change, I've scattered some of my mother's original hints and thoughts throughout this book. Because some things do change, I've put in some updates of the old hints and provided new hints, too. One thing that definitely hasn't changed is that my mother's philosophy— "Doing it well with less work"—is still valid. In fact, the hints are even more relevant today when so many of us live on the run, juggling careers, family obligations, and housework.

Since my mother's time, there have been so

many advances in kitchen technology—new and improved appliances, revolutionary electronic and computerized gadgets, plus a lot of new information in the areas of nutrition and food safety—that I thought it was time to create this new book to help update yours and your mom's kitchen knowledge and skills.

In these pages, you'll find the traditional Heloise shortcuts and quick meals but, if you have the itch to cook something from scratch, there are recipes for that, too. After all, many people find that the cutting, chopping, and stirring that goes on in a kitchen can be a relaxing Zenlike experience. Now that's a label that would have been foreign to many of my mother's readers! With the trend toward "cocooning" for comfort in our homes instead of going out, the kitchen is again becoming the heart of the home, just as it was in Grandma's day. The difference, of course, is that the kitchen is no longer off limits to men and children. I think that just about anyone can learn to cook reasonably well and learn to enjoy the whole process of getting a meal to the table.

I have learned so much about food preparation and storage since I began writing Heloise columns and books, but just when I think there aren't any more hints about something or other in the kitchen, my readers amaze me with new and even better ideas! Heloise fans are the greatest when it comes to sending hints and recipes. One of my favorite stories is the one about Red Velvet Cake. When I published the letter from a reader asking for the recipe for old-fashioned Red Velvet Cake, and I asked my readers to respond, they sent in more than fifteen thousand recipes. (The Red Velvet Cake recipes we finally chose to publish in my newspaper column are reprinted in chapter 7.)

But kitcheneering is more than just cooking. My favorite cleaning story is a generation-gap tale about two young women who asked their local supermarket store manager where they could find that "elbow grease" for cleaning things that they'd read about in the Heloise columns. My goal in writing this book is to give you so many labor-saving Heloise Hints that you won't be using as much "elbow grease" as Mom's generation did and will have more time to enjoy family, friends, and fun things.

Technology has changed much about the way we run our lives, but there is one thing that hasn't changed about Heloise Hints: Every hint still gets researched and tested before it gets relayed to my readers. I think that my mother would have been fascinated by our ability to surf the 'Net to get the most up-to-date information from government, manufacturers, and other consumer association sources.

When my mother wrote her first kitchen book over 45 years ago, she was enthusiastic about a new product she thought would really revolutionize her readers' kitchens: tin foil. A marvel of the age, tinfoil could be used to line baking pans, wrap meat and vegetables for roasting and for storage, keep lunch-box food fresh, and do many things that the old standard wax paper could not. Today, what we now call aluminum foil is a standard feature of every kitchen—along with dozens of new products that make everything we do in the kitchen easier and safer.

I think my mother would be as thrilled with

three of today's time-saving technologies—microwave ovens, fax machines, and computer modems/e-mail—as she was with tin foil. Microwave ovens cook foods faster and save cleanup time. Fax machines let readers send me their hints and questions instantly (1-210-HELOISE). Computers bring Heloise into readers' homes whenever they want through my Web site (www.Heloise.com).SM

I like to think that my mother is smiling down at me from her heavenly cloud of nylon net when I type up the first drafts of some of my columns on her old typewriter and then send in the final drafts using e-mail. I also think that my mother would have enjoyed having a computer in her kitchen like I have in mine. I know that she would be telling a new generation of Heloise readers about the advantages of using the "net," but today, it wouldn't be her famous nylon net, it would be the Internet!

Chapter One

Your Kitchen Space and Appliances

Ergonomics in the Kitchen

Today's buzzword for organizing and selecting furnishings for the workplace is *ergonomics*. This theory holds that furniture and other equipment should be sized and arranged so that there is the least amount of stress on the worker. So why not apply workplace ergonomics principles to your kitchen? You deserve a stress-free environment whether you consider your kitchen to be a recreation station, because cooking is a hobby, or a workstation, because homemaking is your main job.

If you're building a new home or remodeling your kitchen, there are many things you can do to make your kitchen ergonomically correct, from selecting the correct height of kitchen counters and cabinet shelves to the placement of major and minor appliances. And, where you store things on and in your counters and cabinets will help you avoid unnecessary bending and stretching. Yet, even if you are not starting from scratch or doing a wholesale remodeling job, there are many ways to adapt your existing space. Here are a few ideas to consider, whatever your plans.

The *placement of appliances* should be convenient for your cooking style, but the classic arrangement in which the sink, refrigerator, and range form a triangle is usually most efficient. Even though you're used to the arrangement you now have, you might want to test other layouts at show-room kitchens in retail stores or at builders' home shows. (The selection of appliances is covered in more detail later in this chapter.)

Not all *counters* have to be the same height. Your stovetop could be lower than your sink. You'll want to see down into pots and pans but may not want to bend over to do the dishes.

Install *drawers or sliding shelves* in cabinets below the counters to avoid having to get down on all fours to retrieve items at the back on the lower shelves. (Sliding shelves are easily added to existing cabinets. Check out your local building, hardware, or closet store for storage ideas.)

The *work surfaces* should be stain and heat resistant. Aside from matters of taste and cost, you need to ask yourself what is the most practical material for your cooking style? How much time are you willing to spend on maintenance? How careful are you and the other cooks in the house? Most homes in my mother's day had laminated plastic countertops that could be damaged if you placed hot pots and pans on them without the protection of a heat-resistant mat. Also, they could be scratched by abrasive cleansers but could be made to look shiny with kitchen or furniture wax. Some of the new synthetic countertop materials, look like marble or granite but acid or heat cannot damage them. And when they become knife-scratched, they can be sanded and restored to their original finish. They are expensive but may be more practical in the long run because they are so durable. These countertops can also be custom made to include a molded sink so that you have no seams or creases to collect dirt. If you like natural materials for countertops, granite is less porous than marble, which can be easily dam-

aged by acids (for example, from fruit juices). Wood cutting surfaces, which burn and mark easily, can also harbor bacteria. The grout between tiles is also a hiding place for bacteria, even though most tile surfaces are easier to clean and more resistant to stains than wood.

✿ **HELOISE HINT:** When you need extra work space, open a drawer all the way and put a cookie sheet on it, then close the drawer until the cookie sheet fits tightly.

The *flooring* materials should be easy to maintain. Some flooring is cushioned to make long-time standing easier on your feet and back. New polyurethane finishes make wood floors in kitchens as practical as any other type of flooring. Also, new wood-look laminates tolerate a lot of abuse from spills and daily traffic. When you buy new flooring, you will find that there are several types of flooring: wood, manufactured wood, laminates, vinylsheet, vinyl tile, tile, and marble. Real wood boards and planks are great for the natural look but can be expensive, because they need to be sanded and sealed with several coats of varnish or shellac after installation. They also need to be refinished after several years, unless you use a polyurethane finish, which is fairly water resistant and durable. Manufactured wood is a thin veneer of natural wood over a base material that is factory finished instead of finished after installation. This material costs less than natural wood, and the factory-applied protective finish is often more durable than the finish applied to natural wood.

Laminates tolerate abuse extremely well, but some people think they look like fake wood;

however some of the newer products look less fake than the older ones. Prices vary, so you ought to shop around to find the best deal. Tile is durable and comes in a variety of colors and textures. The disadvantage of ceramic or clay tile is that it may crack if your house foundation shifts. If you choose a hard surface for flooring such as ceramic, terrazzo, or Mexican tiles instead of wood or cushioned flooring, take a lesson from restaurants and hairdressers: Buy a cushion-type mat and place it where you do most of your standing, such as at the sink. Marble floors are hard and need to be specially treated to prevent staining. Check the supplier's instructions for care and cleaning to avoid permanent damage to this rather expensive flooring.

Design the *lighting* in your kitchen to illuminate work surfaces clearly. Light coming from behind you, such as a single overhead fixture, will throw shadows making it difficult for you to see what you're doing. Lighting wands can be placed under cabinets (and some are even battery operated if you don't have an outlet nearby.

APPLIANCES

Like everything in our society, we have so much choice when it comes to buying kitchen appliances that it's often difficult to sort out what's what. And making a poor selection can be costly and frustrating. If you are planning to buy a new appliance for the kitchen, there are some important questions to ask: What do I want this thing to do? Am I the kind of person who likes high-tech or will simple "on" and "off" switches do just fine? If all I want to do is reheat a dish of leftovers and have a low-tech personal style, do I need a high-tech microwave with all sorts of gadgetry that will never get used? These are questions you'll answer as you do your own research.

However, remember Heloise Rule #1 when buying a new appliance: Save the manual! Manufacturers do a lot of research on their products, and you pay for that research in the price of the appliance, so it makes sense to get your money's worth by reading the manual carefully and then keeping it for future reference and troubleshooting. Keep your manuals in a file, a drawer, a binder, or any other secure, convenient place. I put them in a plastic bag with handles and hang them all together in a closet. Also keep all guarantees and warranties where you can get at them if you have any problems.

And speaking of guarantees, more often than not, when you buy an appliance, you will be asked if you want to take an extended warranty on your appliance. One factor to consider is: Would you rather pay, and can you afford to pay, the as-yet-unknown repair cost or the known cost of the extra warranty? Also, what exactly does the extended warranty cover? Will it really be a savings? It also depends on the type of appliance and its potential life. A friend of mine, whose several children helped with loading and unloading the dishwasher, doing laundry, and cleaning with other appliances, always bought extended warranties. She figured that children were more likely than adults (we hope) to have mishaps such as dropping a spoon into the dishwasher's food grinder or putting extra wear and tear on the vacuum cleaner from dragging it down the steps. However, once the children were grown and gone, she stopped buying extended warranties because she had fewer costly repairs on her appliances.

I've listed the life expectancies of kitchen appliances below. It's useful to know how long an appliance might last so that you can decide if it's worth repairing when it breaks. An appliance near the end of its life span might be cheaper to replace than to repair in the long run. Also, if your appliance has not lasted as long as the average, you might want to consider another brand when you buy a new one. If it

has lasted the maximum time, you'll want to buy that brand again, but keep in mind that manufacturers may have more than one brand name for the same appliance. You may find, for example, that Brand C is the cheaper version of Brand A, made by the same company, but with fewer frills or different features.

To help you make the best choices in appliances, I have gathered together information and hints on major and small appliances to show you what to look for and how to get the most from each.

Major Appliances

DISHWASHER

An efficiently operated dishwasher consumes less hot water and less energy than hand washing dishes—not counting the savings in human energy as well.

What to look for . . .

So many new homes and apartments are now coming equipped with dishwashers that you'll have no choice on the make, style, or size of the machine. If you are remodeling or replacing an old built-in machine, a built-in machine is the obvious choice. If you are renting where no dishwasher is installed, a freestanding machine will be your choice. If you are purchasing a machine for the first time or replacing an existing machine here are some features to consider:

- **Built-in dishwashers:** Most built-in models fit into the standard 24-inch wide space under the kitchen countertop where they will be permanently attached to the hot-water pipe

Average Useful Life Span of Major Appliances

The amount of use affects appliance life; these figures are approximated for a family of four. Some models will wear out quickly and others will last longer than average.

APPLIANCE	LIFE EXPECTANCY IN YEARS
Clothes dryer	17 to 19
Clothes washer	12 to 14
Freezer	18 to 20
Dishwasher	11 to 13
Range/oven	17 to 19
Refrigerator	18 to 20
Room air-conditioner	14 to 16
Water heater	12 to 14

and drain and get plugged into an electric socket, usually found under the sink. Some models may be more compact and narrower, but 24 inches wide is the usual opening for dishwashers. Do measure before you shop.

- **Freestanding dishwashers:** Freestanding or portable dishwashers are similar in function to built-in models, but they have a finished cabinet on wheels so that you can roll them up to the sink. Hot water gets into the portable dishwasher via a hose that clamps onto a standard kitchen faucet, which may need an adapter to allow the clamp to be attached. Accessories for attaching hoses are available where you buy the appliance. After the cycles are complete in a freestanding model, used water gets pumped from the bottom of the machine through a hose that drains into the sink. A friend of mine said that the biggest problem she had when her children first began using her portable dishwasher was that they forgot to hook the drain hose over the edge of the sink, and so the water would drain onto the floor. Now you could joke that this is one way to give the floor a good cleaning, but dishwasher detergent usually contains bleach and, combined with very hot water, it is definitely *not* a good solution for any kind of kitchen flooring. When purchasing a freestanding model, keep in mind that you will need someplace in the kitchen to store it and it takes up about as much space as a refrigerator. A small apartment kitchen might not have enough space, so measure before you shop.

Some valuable features . . .

- An **air-dry or energy-miser setting** to save you money by turning off the heat during the drying process. Hot-air drying helps eliminate spotting, but if you use a water softener, available at supermarkets, spotting is not a problem no matter how you dry the dishes. Higher priced models will have a dispenser for liquid water softener or spot-remover, but you can also buy spot-removing products that come in a plastic container that hook on the top rack of your dishwasher.

- A **delay-start function** that enables you to set the dishwasher to go on while everyone's asleep, when it is not competing for hot water with people who are showering.

- **Water-saving functions** for partial or full loads.

- A **rinse-and-hold function** that rinses partial loads while you are waiting for the dishwasher to be full enough to run through the full cycle.

- Efficient **food residue disposal**, which means you don't have to rinse dishes before putting them in the machine.

- **Quiet running**; do some research in consumer magazines or on-line before you buy to find out which brands run more quietly. Some have more insulation than others.

- **Adjustable or removable racks** that allow for different size items to fit into the dishwasher. Some top racks will adjust to hold stemware in place, and some flatware baskets have a section with a lid so that you can wash small items without having them fall to the bottom into the heating coil.

Getting the most from your dishwasher . . .

- **Dishwasher detergents:** When choosing a dishwasher detergent, don't just automatically use the brand and type that your mom used, especially if you live in a different part of the country. Some areas of the country have harder water (more mineral content) than others, and water hardness or softness affects the efficiency of dishwasher detergent and the amount of detergent needed to do a good job. Experiment to find the brand and type (gel, liquid, or powder) that works best. If you have a water softener installed in your home, you won't need to use as much detergent as you would when the water is high in mineral content. CAUTION: Never ever use regular hand dishwashing detergent in the dishwasher (see Kitcheneering Humor below).

- Dishwasher detergent can discolor **silver and some silver-plated flatware** or other silver items, and the heat of the water and drying process can damage the handles of dinner knives. Most stainless-steel flatware can be washed in the dishwasher with no bad outcome.

- **Silver- or gold-banded china and glassware** may be damaged by long-term exposure to dishwasher detergent in the machine. Hand washing is usually best for these items.

- **Prerinsing dishes:** Most manufacturers claim that you won't have to prerinse, but you can simply wipe dirty dishes with used paper napkins from the table before loading them into the dishwasher to get rid of the larger pieces of food or stuck-on sauce. The dishes will come out cleaner and the machine has to work less to dispose of the excess waste. *Note:* Whether or not you need to rinse dishes before putting them into the dishwasher depends on the efficiency of your filter/disposal system and

your personal preference. I have a friend who says that if she has to rinse the dishes before loading them, she considers the machine to be broken and in need of replacing. Also, she says, in Texas, where water shortages are a fact, rinsing is a waste of precious water.

- **Accumulated grease and gunk** at the very bottom of the dishwasher door may prevent your dishes from getting clean. This grease and gunk usually accumulates if the water supplied to your dishwasher is not hot enough to wash it away during washing cycles. CAUTION: Use a *thick* wad of paper towels to wipe away this buildup, because there might be shards of glass in the gunk if a glass has ever chipped or broken in your dishwasher. Also, the bottom edge of the door may be a bit sharp. If the gunk is too hard for wiping with paper towels or a rag, a wood ice pop stick usually makes a good and harmless scraper for this project.

- **Clogged kitchen drain pipes or sewer lines** can cause poor dishwasher results. Call your plumber! Stains from foods or minerals in the water can be removed with citric acid, a main ingredient found in powdered lemonade or citrus fruit drink, or bought in a pharmacy. Put 1 or 2 tablespoons powdered lemonade or citrus fruit drink in the detergent dispenser, *no* detergent, and run a cycle. You can also sprinkle the powder on a stain or blotch before running a cycle. Repeat if the stain persists.

- Make sure **small and odd-shaped items** are securely placed in the dishwasher racks. You can place a piece of nylon net in the bottom of the silverware basket to prevent small-handled items from poking through and possibly interfering with the rotating sprayer in the bottom of the dishwasher.

- **To prevent cups from flipping over** and collecting sediment and water, line up the cup handles and run a ½-inch dowel pin through them. Dowel pins are sold in most hardware stores.

- **Dishwashers can be used for washing things other than dishes**. For instance, those greasy, hard-to-clean metal-mesh filters used in over-the-stove vents can be run through the cycle but don't put it in with your regular dishes. (In her 1963 book, *Heloise Kitchen Hints*, my mother recommended washing glass kitchen light fixtures in the dishwasher.)

- **When you have to replace a broken dishwasher, recycle the racks as organizers** for wrapping paper and ribbons. Rolls and ribbon spools fit on the upright prongs and flat packages of tissue or gift-wrap fit in slots. Also, some old dishwashers have silverware baskets with handles that can carry flatware outside to the picnic table.

- **To repair or cover up rusted prongs** on a dishwasher rack, you can buy commercial liquid plastic products, which come in a range of colors, at appliance or dishwasher service stores.

❁ **KITCHENEERING HUMOR** ❁

A reader wrote that when she was in the hospital, her husband ran their dishwasher with liquid detergent. Her daughter arrived home to find suds bubbling and flowing from the dishwasher so fast that suds filled the kitchen and rolled out the back door, filling the porch and driveway. Her daughter's comment was "When Dad cleans, he cleans the kitchen and yard, too!"

FREEZER

As with all major appliances, the size of the available space has a lot to do with the freezer you select. Each model will have various features to suit your needs and budget in one of three basic types: chest freezers, self-defrosting upright models, and manual-defrosting upright models.

What to look for . . .

- **Chest freezers** are very efficient; cool air doesn't escape as readily when you open them as it does with upright freezers. In case of a power outage, they keep food cool longer. However, you will usually have to defrost them periodically and they take up more floor space than upright models.

- **Self-defrosting upright freezers** are probably the most popular because defrosting a freezer or refrigerator is right up at the top of the list of disliked chores. These freezers usually have wire racks or shelves for organizing food and for keeping it at eye level. Some shelves can be adjusted or removed so that you can freeze bulky foods. Other ways to organize foods include space in the door and a variety of bins or baskets that come with the freezer. Some models have a solid shelf at the top for quick freezing foods, which is colder than the rest of the freezer. This is also a good place for ice cream and ice pops, because they will keep most solid on that coldest shelf.

- **Manual-defrosting upright freezers**, like the self-defrosting models, include shelving to make organizing and finding food easier. A leading consumer magazine says that manual-defrosting models are cheaper to buy and run than self-defrosting models. However, if you don't have the time to defrost according to the manufacturer's directions, the cost won't be a factor.

Getting the most from your freezer . . .

- The time to **defrost a freezer** is when frost buildup is about ¼ inch thick. Cooling efficiency decreases when frost builds up; and when the frost is greater than ¼ inch, energy use increases, because the motor has to run more.

- **Keep food cold in a picnic cooler,** or line a laundry basket or your kitchen sink with newspapers when you are defrosting the freezer. Cover the food with more newspapers and put ice cubes on top.

- **To defrost a chest freezer,** unplug the freezer and keep the food cold as noted above. Place several large buckets of very hot water inside and shut the lid. Change the water in 15 minutes. After a couple of changes, most of the ice and water will have dropped to the bottom. Use a wet/dry vacuum or bath towels to remove it. When clean, wipe up the residue, plug in the freezer, and load it up. CAUTION: Always be careful using electrical appliances near water. Make sure the vacuum is rated "wet." A regular vacuum won't work and it's DANGEROUS if used for this purpose.

- **Even self-defrosting models need to be "defrosted" sometimes,** if only to give them a good cleaning.

- **Cleaning a freezer** (or refrigerator): A solution of 4 tablespoons of baking soda in 1 quart of warm water will clean and deodorize at the same time. Wash out the freezer, rinse, and wipe dry. If you need to scrub a stain, don't use an abrasive cleanser that will damage the surface, instead sprinkle baking soda on a wet sponge and scrub.

- **Placing the freezer in the garage or a porch** is not a good idea. The freezer's cooling system will work overtime trying to compensate for the extreme cold or heat of outdoor temperatures and won't operate as well as it would if you kept it indoors in normal room temperatures.

GARBAGE DISPOSAL

I'm told that in many places depending on codes, such as New York City, garbage disposals are illegal. The best way to find out if they are illegal in your city is to contact the city's code compliance department, which issues permits for building, remodeling, and home repairs.

What to look for . . .

The most expensive garbage disposals usually have the most power to grind heavier loads of discarded foods. For example, although they work on ordinary discarded veggies and fruits, the cheapest models may not grind up ice cubes or frozen citrus fruit hunks, which is a good and easy way to clean and deodorize the disposal. Unless you are unusually handy, you will need to have your plumber install the garbage disposal and you'll have to trust your plumber or builder to help you decide which brand will work best in your sink and for your needs.

Getting the most from your garbage disposal . . .

▪ **If you don't have an instruction manual** for your garbage disposal because it was installed before you bought your home, call the manufacturer to get one. Get the manufacturer's name and the model number from the unit; some companies will send the manual free and others may charge for it. To get the phone number, call 1-800-555-1212 and ask for the manufacturer's phone number, or your public library's business department and ask if the librarian can look up the phone number and/or address in the library's directory. Or use a Web browser to locate the company's Web site.

▪ **To banish odors** and clean off the grinder at the same time, freeze leftover lemon or lime wedges, orange peels, or other citrus fruit remnants and then run them the through the garbage disposal, followed by a lot of cold water. You can also run fresh citrus fruit waste and drops of peppermint or other extracts down the disposal to deodorize it.

▪ **If the odor persists,** the culprit could be an accumulation of gunk on the underside of the splash guard (black plastic thing). Although splash guards are inexpensive to replace, before you buy a new one, remove the old guard, if you can, and scrub the underside with hot soapy water and a brush. Check the manual that came with your disposal to see how to remove the splash guard. Usually it is attached to a ring the size of the opening in the sink and you can grab the ring and pull it up. To keep the splash guard clean, use a large round scrub brush or get a new commode brush and be sure to label it with permanent marker so it is reserved for the kitchen. Then periodically wash the inside of the garbage disposal and the underside of the splash guard with hot soapy water and dishwashing detergent. Just run hot water into the sink, add some dishwashing detergent, and scrub up and down and around with the commode brush; then rinse with clean water. If you think the detergent might run through, squirt some on the brush before cleaning.

▪ **To avoid jamming** when disposing of tough stringy matter, add other soft foods while grinding. However, I'm of the opinion that some food items should never be put down any disposal: bones; shellfish; and fibrous matter such as artichokes, asparagus, and celery stalks. Meat sinews and fibrous foods tend to get tangled up in the grinder of your disposal. Also, unless you really do a good job of flushing away meat or fish, they will cause foul odors in the disposal.

▪ **Never put grease in the disposal** because it is likely to solidify in the plumbing and may cause blockages. Also, grease that remains in the disposal or in pipes can become rancid.

▪ Most disposal manuals tell you to **never run the disposal with hot water;** use cold water and plenty of it to flush the waste all the way down and prevent odors from "burping up" into your kitchen.

▪ **If the disposal becomes jammed,** pressing the red "restart" button may do the trick. You may have to repeat the process one or twice. CAUTION: Do not put your face directly over the opening when turning on the machine. Objects may fly out and cause injury.

✿ **HELOISE HINT:** If the "restart" button doesn't work, first, turn off the machine. Then place a broom handle or very sturdy stick into the disposal and turn it counterclockwise to try to unjam the motor. Pull the stick out, run water, then turn on the machine.

▪ **If your dishwasher drains through your garbage disposal**, run the disposal for a few seconds while the dishwasher is pumping that hot soapy water through it.

MICROWAVE OVEN

The latest generation of microwave ovens has so many features, deciding which is best for you is like buying a computer. If you're going to use it just for reheating leftovers, then the buying decision will be easier because the simplest technology will do nicely. If you plan to do some serious cooking in your microwave, then you may want more elaborate timing features. Two other important things to look for when comparison shopping are price and capacity. If all you will do is heat a cup of water for tea, you don't need the size that will accommodate a roasting chicken.

What to look for . . .

▪ **The higher the voltage, the quicker the cooking, and the higher the price.** Lower wattage ovens are usually 600 to 700 watts and larger models are usually 800 to 1000 watts.

▪ **Turntables** help get uniform cooking. If your microwave did not come with one installed, you can buy a turntable in housewares departments.

▪ **Simple models** offer High, Medium, and Low and manual timer dials. Some more expensive models offer such timed cooking features as Defrost; and in addition to the usual High, Medium, and Low, they will cook Medium-High, Medium-Low, etc. Some have sensors that will cook the food until a specified temperature is reached and you can just press "Leftovers," "Frozen Food," or other buttons so that the microwave does all the calculations.

▪ **When determining the size of microwave oven that will fit on a countertop**, consider that you will need a couple of inches of space behind the oven to allow for its vents. Some microwaves can be mounted on the wall; the kit needed to do this will add to the cost but will save counter space. Built-in models require certain configurations that allow for vents; consult with the installer.

Getting the most from your microwave . . .

▪ **Keep your oven clean** because food bits and spills can alter your oven's cooking times . . . microwave ovens can't tell the difference between real food and nonedible spillover mess. *Never* scrape microwave oven surfaces with sharp utensils or harsh scrubbers; they damage the easy-clean surface. Most of the time, if you wipe out the oven with a clean soapy sponge or dishcloth, then wipe again with a rinsed sponge or cloth, followed by a dry towel, the microwave oven will sparkle.

✿ **HELOISE HINT:** Clean your oven with 2 tablespoons of either lemon juice or baking soda in 1 cup of water in a microwave-safe 4-cup bowl. Let the mixture boil in the microwave oven for about 5 minutes so that the steam condenses on the inside walls of the oven, then wipe off the walls, the inside of the door, and the door seals. CAUTION: Let the bowl set 15 minutes before opening the door.

- **To remove dried spills**, pour a puddle of water over the spill, microwave on High for 1 or 2 minutes (or pour on water before doing other normal cooking), and then wipe clean. The water will soften the spill for easy removal.
- **If a spill stains the surface of the oven**, sprinkle baking soda on a wet sponge or dishcloth and wipe, then rinse and dry. *Never* clean a microwave with harsh scouring powders or other abrasive chemicals.
- **Avoid spills** by selecting the proper size container. Or place a cheap paper plate under something that might boil over.
- **To remove odors** from a microwave, clean the oven with a solution of 4 tablespoons of baking soda stirred into 1 quart of warm water. After washing with the solution, wipe out the inside with a damp cloth or sponge. If odors remain, put 1 cup of water in a large 4-cup microwave-safe bowl and add a few teaspoons of baking soda. Cook on High for about 5 minutes. CAUTION: Don't put your face in front of the door.
- **To replace unpleasant odors with scents that makes the whole house smell good**, try this home-style "aromatherapy." Put 1 cup of water and 2 teaspoons of pumpkin-pie spice in a large microwave bowl or 4-cup glass measuring cup and heat on High until it boils. After the boiling point is reached, cook for 3 more minutes. Everyone will think you've been

baking pumpkin pies. (If you don't want to disappoint your family, you can buy a pie to have on hand when the aroma teases them into pie cravings.) You can also cook 2 teaspoons of thyme or sage to create a baked turkey aroma. Or, use your imagination and season your house with other pleasant scents.

■ A READER RECOMMENDS:
One of my readers tried several odor-removal remedies to no avail. So she put a small dish of vanilla extract in the oven, left it for a while, and it deodorized the oven without her needing to turn the microwave on.

For more on cooking in the microwave, please see chapter 7.

RANGE/OVEN

One of the problems we faced with this book is that the name of the thing on which you cook has different names in different parts of the country. We turned to our friends at the Appliance Manufacturers Association for guidance. So, here's the official word: The burners (gas, electric, ceramic, etc.) are the *range.* (Some publications also call them the *cooktop.*) The part in which you bake and roast is the *oven.* And, the whole thing together is a *stove.*

Given the choice, it seems that most traditional cooks (no matter what their age) prefer cooking with gas. But no matter what choice you make, there are some basic guidelines to consider when choosing your major cooking appliances. Consumer magazines say that free-standing stoves are the best value; built-ins usually cost more and have various configurations and combinations of ovens and stove burners that accommodate where and how they will be installed.

✿ **HELOISE HINT:** With all stoves, if you have small children, look for knobs and dials that are placed out of the children's reach at the top rather than the front of the stove. If you have a toddler, and the dials are in reach, it's safer just to take them off. Keep them in a mug or bowl beside the stove where you can get at them when you need them. It's inconvenient but safety is first!

What to look for . . .

■ **Freestanding stoves** are the most common. They have finished side "walls" so that they can be placed at the end of your kitchen counters or they will fit in a space allocated between cabinets, usually from 20 to 40 inches wide, with most widths being 30 inches. So measure the space before you shop to make sure your stove will fit.

■ **Built-in stoves, cooktops, and ovens** vary, and if you are replacing such items, measuring is absolutely necessary. Such stoves will either slide into a space between cabinets or drop into cabinets connected below the oven. The models that drop into a space will have no storage drawer.

■ If your stove has **two ovens,** such as a conventional oven or a microwave on top, the range in the middle, and the second oven below, measuring is even more important and you may need to ask how the ovens are vented to allow hot air to dissipate and whether your kitchen will accommodate the stove's venting system.

■ **Modular stoves** will have separate cooktops and separate wall ovens or dual wall ovens that can be installed at eye level beside the range or elsewhere. Buying modular stove components is the most expensive way to go and you should get advice from whoever will install them to make sure that proper installation for venting and connecting to energy sources are available.

The Range

■ Traditional cooks like **gas ranges** because, they say, they can see the flames and so they can more easily control the desired temperature. The burners are somewhat self-cleaning in that the flames will burn off some grease and gunk, but they still need occasional cleaning. Spills go below the burners and with some models, you have to remove the gas burners to clean the tray below.

■ **Electric element ranges** usually use coils, which are less expensive than flat plate elements. Electric elements will burn off minor spills, but heavy spills may go into the wells beneath the burners. Usually the range top lifts up so that you can clean under the elements.

■ **Electric ceramic cooktops** are popular with many cooks because they are so easy to clean, and new technology is making them as quick heating and as easy to regulate as gas and electric stoves. And the bonus is that you can use any kind of pot or pan on them. The early models did not allow for metal or iron pots and pans and so they were not popular because people liked to use the cookware they already had instead of buying new ceramic pots and pans. So if your mom or elder aunt tells you that ceramic cooktops are no good, you can explain that the recent models accommodate any cookware as long as the bottom is flat and not warped from misuse.

The Oven

- **Oven capacity** varies from stove to stove, and it is sometimes governed by the shelf supports that determine shelf placement. For example, if you have to remove one shelf so that a Thanksgiving turkey will fit into the oven using the lowest possible shelf placement, then you can't heat another food in the oven at the same time unless it will fit on the sides of the roaster. Some ovens are too small to put two casseroles side-by-side and still allow for proper heat circulation and baking; they may hold only smaller-size cookie sheets. Measure when you compare ovens; price does not always determine the size of the oven.

- **Timers:** Some ovens can be preset to turn on or turn off at selected times. Other ovens have a sensor that can be inserted into meats so that you can tell when the roast is done to your preference. If such features are important to you, they are worth the extra money.

- **Regular standard ovens** that have no self-cleaning or continuous cleaning features cost less. If you don't mind cleaning ovens, you can save some money, since most ovens bake and roast at about the same level of efficiency.

- **Self-cleaning and continuous-cleaning ovens** have almost eliminated the dreaded chore of cleaning. You still need to wipe out some ash at the bottom of a self-cleaning oven and wipe off the door, but this is nothing compared to the way people cleaned ovens in my mother's day.

- **Convection ovens** bake and roast foods faster than conventional ovens because they circulate the hot air inside. Formerly available only on airplanes and for restaurant kitchens, convection ovens have been available to home kitchens for several years. Sometimes you will find combination microwave-convection ovens. Check out the manual that comes with your convection oven to find out how to compare traditional oven cooking times with convection oven cooking times for the same amount of food or the same size roast.

Getting the most from your range/oven . . .

Cleaning the oven may be the single most important thing you do because baked-on grease prevents the thermostat from accurately maintaining the set temperature. Greasy ovens can smoke and spoil the flavor of foods, or the grease can catch fire and really spoil a whole kitchen and maybe the whole house! So a clean oven is a safe oven!

- Traditional gas burners have **drip trays, burner rims, and other removable parts** to clean and they must *always* be drained and dry before you replace them so that residual water won't divert the flow of gas.

❀ **HELOISE HINT:** Before replacing gas burners dry them with a hand-held hair dryer on high heat to remove moisture from all bends in the pipes.

■ **A special cleaner** is available for ceramic cooktops that will keep them shiny and bright without scratching the surface. The cleaner also helps prevent spills from sticking. However, baking soda on a wet sponge can be safely used to scrub off burned bits. Do not use abrasive cleansers, because they will scratch the surface.

■ Use **baking soda** on a wet sponge or cloth to scrub your standard oven if it's not too dirty. Rinse with wet sponge or cloth.

■ **Do's and Don'ts** for cleaning standard ovens when using commercial oven cleaners:

Do wear rubber gloves. Most commercial oven cleaners contain lye and nitrogen compounds that can cause burns.

Do have fresh air circulating; the fumes are dangerous to inhale.

Do wear protective eyewear.

Do keep children and pets away from the area.

Don't spray oven cleaners near electrical connections, heating elements, or the thermostat.

Don't spray oven cleaner on an unprotected, hot (from being lit) oven light bulb; the bulb might shatter and you will have an awful mess and risk eye damage.

■ **To scrape oven-cleaner goop** from the oven walls, use a short-handled window squeegee. When all the goop is on the center bottom of the oven, scoop it onto a piece of newspaper or brown paper bag and then discard in the garbage. Next, wipe down the inside of the oven with a wet rag and you're done.

■ When you are using commercial oven cleaner, **follow directions carefully**. Here's how you can get rid of all oven-cleaner residue so that you don't get that nasty whiff of cleaner odor the first time you heat up the clean oven:

After cleaning the oven according to the manufacturer's directions, spread a thick layer of newspapers on the oven bottom. (*Note:* for gas ovens be sure the pilot light is turned off!)

With a spray bottle, spray warm water on the top and sides of the oven walls.

Dry the inside of the oven with a clean cloth or paper towels, and then roll up the newspaper carefully and discard it.

CAUTION: Never use any kind of cleaning aid in a continuous-cleaning or self-cleaning oven.

■ The finish will be removed and then the oven will no longer clean itself. Do all wiping up with ordinary detergent and water or window cleaner. If you clean the oven racks in the self-cleaning oven cycle, they may become discolored and dull finished. If the appearance of the racks is not important to you, this is an option. If you don't clean the racks in the clean cycle, please see instructions for cleaning standard oven racks.

■ **A self-cleaning oven** provides for the removal of grease and gunk when you set a separate high-heat cycle. It must have the door locked during the cleaning cycle, and you need proper venting for the heat that comes out of the stove vents. *Never* use commercial oven cleaners in a self-cleaning oven, because they damage the surface and will prevent proper self-cleaning. A plain water-dampened sponge or paper towel will wipe up the ash that remains in the bottom of the oven after the cleaning cycle when the oven is cool. If you choose to clean the oven racks in a self-cleaning oven cycle, be aware that they will become discolored and dull finished. If the appearance of the oven racks is of no importance to you, you can leave them in the oven to get cleaned in the cleaning cycle.

■ **Wipe the edges of the racks** and the grooves in which the racks slide with salad oil after cleaning your self-cleaning oven so that the racks will slide more easily without scratching the oven walls. (Check manufacturer's instructions carefully, however.)

■ CAUTION: People like to experiment with **cleaning other greasy items in the self-cleaning cycle.** These ovens get as hot as 500 degrees F and sustain that temperature for more than 1 hour. A friend of mine tried to clean greasy barbecue grill lava briquettes during the cycle and the result was an oven full of flaming grease! When you are dealing with strong chemicals or extreme temperatures, follow the manufacturer's directions exactly and don't try to be creative!

■ **A continuous-cleaning oven gradually reduces dirt and oil** on the specially treated surface to what is usually called a "presentable" clean condition during the normal baking or broiling processes. Each time you cook, the oven burns off dirt and grease. You'll need to clean up large spills to keep the oven looking good.

■ **Oven window door:** Even with a self-cleaning oven (and wouldn't my mother have loved that idea!) the oven door doesn't always get clean. Wipe the glass window with ammonia and let it set for a few minutes. Then remove the goop with a plastic ice scraper (like those used to remove ice from auto windshields), wet rag, or strong paper towels. Wipe again with a clean wet rag or paper towels.

■ **If food baking in the oven boils over,** sprinkle a little salt on the burned gunk. In addition to killing the odors and smoke, salt makes the mess easier to wipe up when you finish baking.

■ **Avoid mess** in ovens by placing a cookie sheet or piece of foil under foods that are likely to spill over or drip a mess (like baking sweet potatoes). You may have to adjust cooking times when using a cookie sheet.

■ **Take the oven racks out into the yard to clean them.** Put them into a large heavy-duty plastic trash bag, and spray on oven cleaner or ammonia, *not both.* Close the bag tightly, and let sit overnight. The next day, spray the racks with a hose and remove remaining spots with a scrub brush. Rinse again and dry. CAUTION: Keep children and pets away from such cleaning projects and use care when opening the bag.

REFRIGERATORS

Among the best new refrigerator features to come along since my mother's day are shelves that slide in and out and shelves that contain spills. Of course, there are more glamorous and high-tech innovations, such as ice makers and water or juice dispensers, but the more of these kinds of special features on your refrigerator, the greater the price. Of the various models available, the three most popular for home use are side by side, freezer on top, and freezer on bottom.

What to look for . . .

- The **side-by-side models** are usually more expensive, but if you have limited space for the doors to open, they may be the best solution for you. The disadvantage is that they can't accommodate wide items and large platters or trays. Also, things that find their way to the back of the shelf may stay there indefinitely because it's hard to see in the back, especially in the freezer compartment, which is usually the narrower side.

- The **freezer-on-top** model is the most common type of refrigerator. It puts frozen foods at eye level but you have to bend over to get at the refrigerated foods, especially the bottom fruit or vegetable crispers.

- The **freezer-on-bottom** model places your nonfrozen foods at eye level, but you'll have to stoop over to get at the frozen ones.

- **Refrigerators with glass shelves** are usually more expensive than those with wire shelves. Glass shelves can break but they are not likely to do so with normal use. An advantage of glass shelves is that things stand upright better on them. Wire shelves are good for keeping wine bottles and similar containers from rolling around when stored on their sides. A friend of mine keeps a second refrigerator for wine, soft drinks, bottled water, and sport drinks and she made a point of getting it with wire shelves so that the bottles wouldn't roll. You decide which features are more important to you.

- Most refrigerators offer **drawers or shelves that are cooler than the rest of the refrigerator** to store meats and other things that need cooler temperatures. Fruit and vegetable drawers retain moisture better than if these foods are kept on the shelves and so they keep better and longer.

- Some top-of-the-line refrigerators have **extra storage aids** like wine bottle holders, soft drink can holders, and so forth. You have to decide if the gadgets are worth the extra cost. You may be able to find racks that fit your fridge at stores that sell wire organizer baskets and similar items.

- The most **energy efficient** refrigerators usually cost more initially but may save you money in the long run. The cost of running your refrigerator may be as much as 20 percent of your electric bill, so check it out.

Getting the most from your refrigerator . . .

- **To eliminate food odors,** wash out the refrigerator with a solution of 4 tablespoons of baking soda in 1 quart of warm water. You can also add some lemon extract or 1 teaspoon of vanilla to the rinse water for an extragood scent. Then wipe the interior to dry. If this method doesn't work set out several paper plates with dry coffee grounds on different shelves. The odors should disappear in 2 to 3 days.

- **To keep the refrigerator smelling fresh,** the tried-and-true Heloise method is to leave an open box of baking soda or a cup of fresh charcoal briquettes or activated charcoal you buy at the pet store. Change it every few months. (Deodorize kitchen and other drains with the used baking soda or recycle it for nonscratch scrubbing of the kitchen sink.)

- **Keep the gasket fresh and mildew-free** with occasional washing of mild soap and water. Do not bleach; it can cause the gasket to become brittle and crack. If the gasket is badly mildewed, try full-strength vinegar, or it may need to be replaced.

A READER RECOMMENDS:

A reader wrote to tell me that her old-model ice-maker tray would retain shards of ice and begin to overfill. When she examined the tray, she found that lime deposits were causing the problem and so, instead of buying a new tray as she had in the past, she removed the lime deposits with a 10-minute warm white vinegar soak.

- **If you are moving** and expect to have your refrigerator or freezer closed up for several days or longer on the moving van or in storage, toss in a handful of baking soda, charcoal, or unused dry coffee grounds in a cloth bag or knotted knee-high or panty hose leg. You won't be greeted by a musty odor when you open the appliance door for the first time. (This hint is a favorite among military families whose appliances are frequently placed in storage while they go to new duty stations.)
- **If your refrigerator has been in storage,** make sure that the gaskets are still good so that food is kept properly cooled. Close the door on a dollar bill; if the bill slides out easily, the gasket may need replacing because it is not sealing properly.
- If you **cover the top of the refrigerator** with plastic wrap, wax paper, shelf liner or place mat, you can just change the paper or wrap instead of scrubbing the surface to remove accumulated greasy dust.

- **Clean the painted surface of your refrigerator** or freezer with mild detergent or appliance polish only. Strong spray-on-wipe-off cleaners can ultimately remove the paint from the metal.

❀ **HELOISE HINT:** I have a system of keeping certain things in the door shelves and assigning parking spaces for specific foods on the shelves. For example, dairy products—such as butter, yogurt, and cheese—are kept on the top shelf; leftovers are kept on the second shelf, and so on. Then everyone in the house, including me, knows where to look for specific foods.

Small Appliances

Get unplugged! *Always* unplug electrical appliances for cleaning or servicing. *Never* immerse a whole appliance or electrical components in water to wash it unless the manufacturer specifically says you can do so.

BLENDER OR FOOD PROCESSOR

Blenders and food processors have made kitchen work so much easier. The cooking purist might say that all that chopping and dicing and slicing are an important parts of the processes. But if you've got to get a meal on the table fast, there's nothing like these machines—and it's impossible to make a great milk shake without a first-rate blender.

What to look for . . .

- The **capacity** should suit your needs. If you do a lot of entertaining and process mass quantities of cheese, veggies, and so forth, get a large food processor. If all you do is puree a few carrots, peas, or other veggies for your baby, a small one will do. One brand of blender comes with a 1-cup container so that you can make salad dressings or baby food and store them in the same container.

- The **power** of the motor should also suit your needs. You'll need a more powerful food processor motor if you process larger quantities of raw produce and meats or if you mix stiff bread dough. Most blenders will crush ice for smoothies and puree vegetables and fruits, and so forth.

- The **design** of either machine should allow for safe and easy access to the container or bowl. The opening, particularly in a food processor, should be large enough to accommodate the kinds of foods you are preparing. And, for example, some blender models have removable openings in the lid to allow you to add foods while the blender is going. Such openings help avoid spatters.

- **Clearly marked measurements** on the container.

❄ **HELOISE HINT:** You may want to mark the major measuring points with red nail polish on the outside of the container for easier identification.

- Many models have all kinds of **features** that you may not need but for which you are paying extra money. A larger capacity machine with basic features may be the best bet for you and may cost the same as the smaller, souped-up model. But here are some features that are worth looking for and paying for:

A **pulse feature** helps you better and more carefully control the amount of blending or processing.

An **ice-crusher mode** on blenders will make better smoothies and frozen or frappé drinks.

Multiple food processor blades for slicing, processing, or shredding and dough mixing.

Dishwasher-safe parts (the container or bowl, blades, etc.) can make clean up easier.

Getting the most from your blender or food processor . . .

- **Blenders and food processors work best if they are only two-thirds full.** Some blenders may not operate at all if they are too full. When some food processors are too full, it's difficult to remove the blade from the bowl so that you can remove the food.

- **Never attempt to slice or grate hard frozen cheese or other hard frozen foods** in your food processor or slicer. The blades may break. However a food processor will work better on harder foods, such as hard cheeses or turning peanuts into peanut butter, than will a blender. A blender works better for making milk shakes, fruit or vegetable purees, and juices.

- **To quick clean a blender or food processor,** fill it halfway with water, add a drop or two of liquid dishwashing detergent, put on the lid, run it a few seconds, rinse, and let dry. If you have a hand-held European-style blender, fill a deep bowl or large glass with water and a drop of liquid detergent, cover, whir on low speed a few seconds, rinse and let dry.

CAUTION: Handle food processor blades carefully, the serrated ones are especially sharp and can cut with just a touch from your fingers.

BREAD MACHINE

Ah, the wonderful aroma of bread baking right there in your own kitchen! Bread makers mix and bake breads from your own recipes or from mixes available in the supermarkets, and some can be set to have fresh bread waiting for you when you get up in the morning. However, they are not cheap and, before you invest in a breadmaker, ask yourself if you really will use it, considering that a supermarket bakery may be 5 minutes away.

What to look for . . .

- **Capacity:** The price often depends on the capacity of the machine, usually ranging from 1 to 2 pounds. The smallest loaves give you 8 to 10 slices of bread and the largest about 20 slices.
- Most bread machines have a **display** that tells you which stage of bread making the machine is in: mixing, kneading, baking, or done.
- Some machines have a **signal** that lets you know when to add nuts, raisins, seeds, or whatever needs adding after the machine has mixed the dough.
- Some can be **preset** to delay the start time so that the machine will start up on time automatically, giving you fresh bread when you wake up in the morning.
- A **non-stick bread pan** makes clean up easier.

Getting the most from your bread machine . . .

- **Read the manual** that came with the machine and try the recommended recipes. Also look for cookbooks specifically written for bread machines that have many more creative recipes than the manufacturers provide. It's easier to use recipes developed for machines instead of trying to adapt your favorites, and you'll get better results since others have already tested the correct proportions of ingredients.
- **Cleaning your bread machine:** Different machines have different methods; again, read that manual!

CAN OPENER (ELECTRIC)
What to look for . . .

- Some models will **mount** to the wall or the bottom of a cabinet, which helps eliminate counter clutter. With cordless models, the recharging holder is placed near a plug, and the can opener fits into the holder or base to be charged.
- Models that **leave the cut edge smooth** so that you can't cut your fingers on it is an especially good feature if you have children cooking in the kitchen, or pets.
- Some electric can openers do **double-duty as knife sharpeners** so you get a bit more function for the money.
- Make sure **hand-held models** fit your hands comfortably.

Getting the most from your electric can opener . . .

- **Always unplug** an electric can opener before cleaning.

■ **Clean cutters** on electric can openers work better. Clean the blade/cutter with a scouring pad, scrubber, or old toothbrush dipped in baking soda.

■ **Most electric can openers cannot be immersed in water** and so you need to clean and rinse them with caution. You may have to rinse off the cutter by dabbing it with a wet sponge and holding it so that the water drips away from the mechanical parts.

■ It's easier to **wipe a can opener with a damp sponge** or paper towel after each use than to wait until it has so much gunk on it that you have to scrub and scour.

COFFEEMAKER (ELECTRIC DRIP)

Although there have been significant improvements in instant coffees since my mother's day, most of us prefer to brew a full pot to get that wonderful coffee aroma while you wait.

What to look for . . .

■ **Capacity:** Most machines will make as little or as much (up to the capacity) coffee as you want, so even if a lot of people in your family don't drink coffee, you can buy a larger capacity machine that can make 10 or 12 cups for guests but still allows you to make as few as 4 cups.

■ **Automatic start** lets you program the pot to have hot coffee ready when you wake up.

■ An **automatic shut-off** prevents the glass pot from being broken if the coffee burns dry.

■ **Clear markings** on the carafe or reservoir let you see easily how much water to add.

■ **A drip stop feature** lets you remove the carafe to pour a cup of coffee before the whole amount of the water has run through. (This one's for the superbusy person who needs that jolt of caffeine immediately to get started in the morning!)

Getting the most from your electric drip coffee maker . . .

■ The manufacturer's manual tells you **how to clean the water reservoir** when hard-water mineral deposits give the coffee a bad or off taste. There are commercial products for cleaning the coffeepot but you can also clean a drip pot by running the fullest measure the pot allows of white vinegar through the cycle. Follow with a cycle or two of the fullest measure of fresh water. *Note:* The vinegar left over from cleaning the coffeepot can be stored in a jar to clean the pot again if you let the minerals settle to the bottom and use just the clear vinegar. Or clean something else with the used vinegar; kill the weeds or grass in sidewalk cracks with it, or pour it down the kitchen or bathroom drain as a deodorizer.

■ You won't have to clean your drip coffeemaker as often if you **make coffee with distilled water.** The coffee will taste better, too.

■ **If the coffee burned** on the bottom of the pot, pour table salt into the pot and let it stand for a few minutes. The burned crust will usually come loose and you can wash the pot clean. (This hint came from an office worker who used salt because nothing else was handy. That's how most hints come into being— somebody just used whatever was handy!)

■ **A READER RECOMMENDS:**
To separate flat-bottom coffee filters that are packed together, one Heloise reader recom-

mends turning the stack of filters upside down in the box and pinching off one filter at a time.

COFFEEPOT (PERCOLATOR)

Although not too many people have stove-top percolators anymore, the same hints for electric percolators apply for nonelectric ones.

What to look for . . .

▪ Look for models that have a **time/strength setting** so that you can custom brew your coffee.

▪ In my mother's day, most percolators were aluminum and they tended to get unattractive dull finishes after months of use. Now they come in **colors and stainless steel** and these finishes look better longer than the old aluminum ones. The insides may be stainless steel, too, and so they will be easier to wash with just soap and water.

Getting the most from your percolator coffee-maker . . .

▪ **To avoid getting coffee grounds into a percolator stem** when you fill the basket with coffee, hold your finger over the stem. The percolator stem must be kept unclogged and clean so that your coffee will taste good.

▪ **Clean the stem** with a small round brush made for this purpose or make a super long cotton swab by wetting the end of a wooden shish-kebab stick and twisting it in a wad of cotton.

▪ **To clean an aluminum percolator,** fill the coffeepot with water, add a handful of baking soda or 2 or 3 teaspoons of cream of tartar. Run through the full coffee-making cycle, let cool, and then scrub with a piece of nylon net.

If the pot is badly stained, you may have to repeat the process to get it shiny bright and to get good-tasting coffee again.

SLOW COOKER

In Mother's day, many households had electric roasters, which were big enough to cook a large turkey. These roasters are still available today but most have a 6-quart capacity (about the size of a roasting chicken) and they double as slow cookers. Slow cookers (or electric casseroles) let you plug in a meal in the morning before going to work so that dinner is ready when you return.

What to look for . . .

▪ **Capacity:** How much will you be cooking in your cooker? Soup or stew for four? Or will you use it for large party-size pots of beans at your barbecues? Most hold about 2 quarts of food, which is enough for a family of four.

▪ **A removable metal roaster insert** or a metal pot that just sits on the heating base is handy if you like to brown meats and/or onions on the stovetop before slow cooking.

▪ **Some models allow you to bake in them.** If you want to bake in the cooker, the temperature needs to be regulated by numbers and not merely Low, Medium, or High. Read the manual to see how convenient this may be with the cooker you are buying.

Getting the most from your slow cooker . . .

▪ **Slow cookers are great for beans, lentils, and other starchy vegetables.** You don't have to stir and watch to prevent burning at such low temperatures.

Avoid Fire Hazards

Check electrical cords for damage before you leave a cooker plugged in all day while you are gone. In fact, always check all appliance cords for safety's sake and plug all appliances directly into wall sockets. Use of extension cords for appliances is a fire hazard and can also result in temperature variations that affect cooking efficiency. Some appliances, such as electric frying pans, roasters, and slow cookers, may not heat properly when plugged into extension cords. Plug them directly into the wall socket for best results and always *unplug* when they are not in use.

■ **If your pot is ceramic,** you will have to brown the meat and onions in a frying pan when making soups and stews. Metal removable pots allow browning in the same pot in which you will simmer the food.

■ **The slow cooker is ideal for dips, cocktail meatballs, and other appetizers** that need to be kept warm on the buffet table. And in south Texas, where I live, tamales are a favorite, and they can be kept at just the right temperature in a slow cooker when you are having a "grazing" party.

DEHYDRATOR

Ideal for drying fruit, vegetables, and herbs as well as making fruit leathers, the dehydrator circulates hot air over the food, which sits on a series of trays in the machine. This machine is perfect for anyone with a large kitchen garden or who takes advantage of seasonal offerings at farmers' markets. It offers a simple alternative to canning.

What to look for . . .

■ Some dehydrators are **simple, having only "on" and "off" switches,** but others have timers so that you can set them to go off when you think the foods will be dried enough. (Experience teaches you how long certain herbs, fruits, or veggie slices take to dry.)

■ Most have a **fan to circulate the hot air** and make the foods dry faster.

Getting the most from your dehydrator . . .

■ **Home-dried foods should be stored in the refrigerator,** because they do not contain the preservatives that you find in commercially dried foods.

Drying Foods without a Dehydrator

You can dry foods in a conventional oven by placing uniformly sliced vegetables or fruits on racks on cookie sheets in a very slow oven that's 200 degrees F or less. Some microwave ovens have directions for drying foods. Some of my friends who garden and dry foods say that neither the conventional nor microwave oven works as easily as the dehydrator because you don't have to check the drying progress of foods in the dehydrator as often as you do in a conventional oven and you aren't as likely to overdry foods as you might in the microwave.

- Slices of fruits or vegetables should be **uniformly thin** so that drying will also be uniform and all will get dry at the same time.

- Some veggies will **pick up aromas** from herbs if they are dried at the same time. If you want this, it's okay to dry several varieties of garden produce at the same time.

- **Fruit leathers** can be made by drying fruit puree on sheets of plastic wrap. Add a bit of honey to the puree to make it more pliable. When the leather is translucent, you can cut the sheet in strips and roll up each strip for individual snacks. My friends who do this prefer to keep the leathers in the fridge because they don't add preservatives to the puree.

JUICER

There are a number of juicers on the market, and some go beyond the function of merely extracting juice from citrus or blending other fruits for juices. The specialty juicers can be very expensive, and you need to decide if you will really use them enough to warrant the cost. Ask yourself, Will a regular blender, which costs less, do as well for my purposes?

What to look for . . .

- Would a **less expensive** blender do the same job?

- Is the machine **easy to use**, load, add ingredients, and remove ingredients?

- If the machine is **ordered by mail,** is the seller reliable and what will you need to do if the machine is defective or stops working properly? Can it be repaired locally? If you are not familiar with the brand name, call your favorite small-appliance repairperson and ask if the machine comes into the shop often or if anybody at the shop has ever heard of it.

Getting the most from your juicer . . .

- **Try many of the recipes** from the manual that comes with the machine so that you understand the best ways to use it. Most manufacturers' recipes are simple but show off the versatility of a machine.

- **Using the general directions** for proper proportions and amounts of ingredients, try different combinations of fruits and vegetables, such as lemon-carrot juice, peppered-tomato, or tangerine-orange.

MIXER (ELECTRIC)

Whether you need a stand mixer or a handheld mixer depends on your intended use.

What to look for . . .

- **A hand mixer** may be all you need if you use it for is mixing cake batter, mashing potatoes, or whipping cream occasionally. A hand mixer is relatively inexpensive.

- If you frequently mix bread and cookie batters from scratch, you may want to spend more and get a **stand mixer**.

- The most expensive stand mixers have the **most power** and can handle the most dough or batter well; they may come with a dough hook for mixing and kneading yeast doughs. The least expensive stand mixers have less power and can handle less batter.

- **A multipurpose appliance**, which has mixer, blender, food processor, and grinder attachments may be a good solution for you if you don't already have such appliances.

Getting the most from your electric mixer . . .

- **Turn the machine off before you remove the beaters from the mixture.** It may seem obvious, but there are lots of first timers who've spent a few hours cleaning cookie dough off the walls and ceiling!

- **Avoid splatters.** I get a lot of hints on how to avoid spattering of ingredients when you are mixing. Here's one that is simple and effective. Cut a piece of wax paper big enough to cover the bowl and then make a slit for the beaters. Hold the wax paper over the bowl while you mix, until the mixture becomes frothy and is less likely to spatter. Or when you are using a hand-held mixer with a small bowl, you can make a cover with a plastic lid from an ice cream carton. Cut a slit from the edge and a hole in the center large enough for the beaters to work when they are slipped through the slit and into the hole.

- When **adding dry ingredients to wet,** always start beating slowly until the wet and dry are mixed or you will be flouring everything in sight.

- **Chocolate chips and large nut pieces** can get chopped into smaller pieces by the blades of an electric mixer. If you like larger chunks of nuts and full-size chips, you may want to stir them in by hand after mixing the batter with the mixer. Dates and large chunks of dried fruit also should be hand mixed into batter; they may even fly out of the bowl if you start up at high speed.

- It is **easier to beat shortening, margarine, or butter** if they are at room temperature as these fats are very hard right out of the refrigerator.

- **Scrape the sides of the bowl with a rubber spatula** often while you are beating batters so that all the ingredients get properly mixed in.

- **Most mixer bowls can be washed in the dishwasher;** check the manual to see if the beaters can also be washed in the dishwasher. Some stand mixers will have a plastic button on the bottom of one beater (to protect the bowl) that may not be dishwasher-safe.

PRESSURE COOKER

If your mom's pressure cooker was an object of terror because everyone worried that it might blow up, know that the new ones of today are much safer and easier to use. In fact, some new pressure cookers are programmable electric models that work like a pressure-cooking version of a bread machine.

What to look for . . .

- **A manual for operations** that has easy to understand directions, because proper use is vital for safety.

- You will find various **sizes** of pressure cookers and the largest ones (several gallons) are frequently used for pressure canning. Most are about a 4-quart size, large enough for most households.

Getting the most from your pressure cooker . . .

- **Read the manual carefully** and follow directions exactly. Too much pressure for too long can turn food into mush.

- It's important to **keep all gaskets and steam holes clean** for safest use of a pressure cooker. Especially check the steam escape holes before cooking with any pressure cooker.

■ **Don't overload the cooker.** If you are using your own recipes instead of those in the manual, compare the amounts of ingredients in your recipe with those in the manual so that you don't exceed the capacity of the cooker.

■ **Add spices and herbs toward the end of the cooking process.** Some people claim that certain flavorings become too blended and don't have enough of a zing.

■ **Pressure cookers used for canning** need to have a rack for the canning jars or some sort of perforated disk that prevents the jars from sitting directly on the bottom of the cooker, which can cause breakage from jiggling during the cooking process.

RICE COOKER

Rice cookers are handy especially if your family loves rice. The best tip I've heard from an editor is to let the rice sit for about 5 minutes in the *covered* cooker after the cooking cycle ends. You'll have fluffier rice. Most models automatically switch to a "keep warm" setting. If you're thinking that they are pretty limited in what they can do, remember that in addition to cooking rice, they can also be used to steam vegetables.

What to look for . . .

■ Some of the cookers are **attractive enough to use for serving** as well as cooking.

■ **A glass cover** is a good feature so that you can see what's happening inside.

Getting the most from your rice cooker . . .

■ **Check out recipes** that tell about adding different ingredients so that your rice will have extra flavor: raisins and a bit of sugar, nuts, or small minced bits of pepper and other vegetables.

■ **Like electric skillets, you may not be able to immerse your rice cooker.** Read that manual carefully!

SKILLET (ELECTRIC)

Electric skillets can be all-purpose cooking pans, including pots for cooking one-dish meals and ready-to-heat freezer meals. Electric skillets and electric woks can be used for the same functions.

What to look for . . .

■ **Deep-dish styles** that can be used to cook pot roasts, etc.

■ **A wide range of temperature settings** that allow you to simmer at 200 degrees F or so.

■ **Immersible** electric skillets are easier to clean; check the manual to make sure that this is possible.

■ **Nonstick surfaces** are as desirable on electric frying pans and woks as they are on the rest of your cookware.

■ **Choose a size that suits the amount of food you usually cook or fry.** The larger and deeper the wok, the less mess of spattering fat when you stir-fry. (Or reduce fat calories and stir-fry with a small amount of bouillon.)

■ With **electric woks**, as with stovetop woks, a rack that can be placed to the side of the top of the pan is handy to hold already cooked veggies or meat pieces that you don't want to overcook while other ingredients are being stir-fried.

Getting the most from your electric skillet . . .

▪ **To soak off cooked-on food,** fill the skillet about half to two-thirds full of water, add a few drops of hand dishwashing liquid and let the soapy water simmer for a while. Allow to cool before you handle it to finish the washing job.

▪ **Cleaning the outside of electric skillets** depends on the outside finish. If your skillet is colored you will have to scour with baking soda sprinkled on a wet sponge to prevent scratches. If it is aluminum you can polish it as recommended in the manual. Readers have said that they clean the bottom of a skillet that has a lot of burned on grease with oven cleaner. Follow directions listed for oven cleaner and be sure to keep the skillet away from curious children and pets. If your skillet is not immersible, take care not to get water into the electrical parts.

TOASTER
What to look for . . .

▪ If you like **toasted bagels,** do get a toaster with wide enough openings to accommodate them.

▪ A model that lets you **clean out the crumb tray easily.** Accumulated crumbs on the bottom of a toaster are a fire hazard and they affect the toaster's thermostat.

▪ **Stay-cool exteriors** are ideal, especially if you have small children

▪ **Single-slice feature:** Models with separate compartments (two or four or more!) are more economical to run if they have an optional single slice feature.

Getting the most from your toaster . . .

▪ **Keep your toaster clean** or you won't get the right shade of toasty brown, because the thermostat is reading burned black crumbs instead of the browness of your bread slice.

▪ **Line the crumb tray with foil** if your toaster has a removable crumb-catching tray. Check the manual instructions to see if this is okay.

▪ **If your toaster has to be turned upside down** so that you can shake out the crumbs, unplug it, and shake *gently.* You could dislodge wires and your toaster could become a fire hazard.

TOASTER OVEN

In addition to toasting, a roaster/toaster oven can be an energy saver for baking one or two medium to large potatoes or a small 1- to 2-pound meat loaf, and other foods. The bonus is that along with saving electrical energy, these ovens won't heat up your kitchen in the summer as much as a full-size oven does. The following energy costs were based on rates in San Antonio where I live, but the wattage use would be the same anywhere. An electric full-size oven uses 5,000 watts at a cost of 38 cents per hour; a gas oven uses 18,000 BTUs at 10 cents per hour, but an electric roaster/toaster oven uses only 1,333 watts at 8.7 cents per hour. You'll need to check with your local electric or gas company to get the cost for the wattage in your area. You save energy and money at the same time!

What to look for . . .

▪ **A continuous cleaning** toaster oven that

you need only wipe the front window or door occasionally will save you lots of personal energy.

- **Cooking sheets and pans that fit properly** usually come with the toaster oven. Just like a regular oven, things bake better when the heat can circulate.
- Some have a **timer** for toasting and broiling that prevents you from burning the food.
- You will find models with **dials that tell the temperature in numbers,** not just High, Medium, or Low and these can be used to bake small cakes as well as other foods.

Getting the most from your toaster oven . . .

- **If your toaster oven doesn't have a continuous clean surface,** it's easier to wipe it often so that you don't have to do a major cleaning of built-up gunk. Follow the directions that come with the oven to see if you can use oven cleaner on the surface or if any other cleaning method is advised. Baking soda on a damp sponge or plastic scrubber is usually safe for scrubbing most surfaces and it does cut grease.
- **Cover the bottom tray with foil** (check the manual first), and you won't have to scrub it.
- CAUTION: Take care not to touch the sides and tops of a toaster oven when it is on and never, ever store things on top of a toaster oven. The sides and tops can get extremely hot; your fingers and items placed on top can get burned. Do allow a couple of inches of space around the oven for air to circulate.
- **Aluminum foil disposable pans** are handy for broiling in a toaster oven, but do measure when you are buying pans for them; these ovens are smaller than they look.

WAFFLE IRONS

Waffle irons are a favorite when it comes to Sunday family breakfast when the whole household is present. Many have reversible grids so that they can also be used to grill sandwiches, like grilled cheese sandwiches or to fry pancakes. When I was in college, we used to make "grilled" cheese sandwiches by putting cheese between bread buttered on the *outside*, then wrapped in foil, and ironed for a few minutes with a hot iron. Still works today!

❃ KITCHENEERING HUMOR ❃

One of my editors says that her ten-year-old grandson Matthew called her up to ask, "What did the rude person eat for breakfast?" The response: "Belchin' Waffles!" So she bought him a waffle iron for Christmas for telling such a cute joke.

What to look for . . .

- **Nonstick surfaces** on the grids prevent sticking, especially if you try to use as little fat as possible in the recipe.
- The **size and shape** of the machine is a matter of personal preference. Larger waffles will have lines so that you can break up one waffle into four pieces—nice for small children.

Getting the most from your waffle iron . . .

- **Season your waffle iron**; food may stick on new or newly cleaned machines. Before using a waffle iron, grease with unsalted fat and preheat thoroughly then wipe with a paper towel before you pour on the batter.
- **To get accumulated grease off the grids,** place a nonsudsing ammonia-soaked

paper towel or napkin between the grids and let sit overnight, then clean.

- **To clean a machine with nonstick grids**, follow the manufacturer's directions.

- **Batter may work better** if you let it stand for 5 to 10 minutes before pouring it on the grids.

- **Make extra waffles**, and after they have cooled, freeze them in an airtight freezer bag. Then you can toast them for breakfast when you are in a hurry, or just eat them as a snack.

- **When adding nuts, small chocolate chips, or raisins** to the batter once it's poured onto the grids, smooth the bumps so that the pieces are buried and won't stick to the grids.

Chapter Two

Cookware, Utensils, and Gadgets

You can buy as many pots, pans, gadgets, and utensils as your pocketbook and cabinet space allows. In this chapter, I list the very basics that you need to get started in the kitchen. I've also listed a few home-style ways to care for your kitcheneering equipment. When it comes to care, however, my best advice is to first always read the packaging and promotional materials that come with your cookware, utensils, and gadgets because each manufacturer has different cleaning and care methods. Too often people just rip up the packaging and toss it away and then damage their cookware with improper use or care. It's money down the drain with no one else to blame.

COOKWARE

When selecting pots and pans for stovetop cooking, heat conduction is the most important factor. The cheapest thin aluminum or other metal pans are okay for boiling water and cooking eggs. But if you try to make pudding or sauce in a thin metal pot or try to pan broil meat in a thin metal frying pan the food will burn more easily than if you use a pot or pan with a thick or layered bottom. You will find heavy aluminum, copper-clad, and other types of pots and pans in housewares departments, and the price will match the quality. Sometimes you will save money by buying sets of pots and pans, but other times, buying a set for several hundred dollars may not be the best idea if you will use only a few pieces of the set.

If you are a novice cook, it may be a good idea to get just the basics until you know what sizes and types of pots and pans you will use.

When you shop in your favorite housewares or department store, you will find a bewildering array of nonstick finishes; again, the price will reflect the quality in most cases. For example, a nonstick surface on a cheap lightweight aluminum frying pan probably won't be as durable as the nonstick surfaces on more expensive ware, some of which allow the use of metal utensils.

Two things to consider when buying pots and pans, in addition to the actual material from which they are made, are the handles and the lids. Solid-metal handles, usually attached to frying pans, pots, and lids are usually very sturdy and durable. They also allow you to put the pan or pot into the oven. However, they will get too hot to touch in ordinary cooking so you'll need to always use a potholder, even when stovetop cooking. This can get annoying if you need to hold the pot while you stir the contents or hold the pan while you turn the meat and no potholder is handy. It can also lead to burns if you have to quickly remove a pot from the burner because it's boiling over and you do so impulsively without grabbing a potholder first! Some designs of cookware have hollow-metal handles and these stay cool while cooking on the top of the stove and still can be put into the oven. Some designs of frying pans have, in addition to the typical long handle, a second gripping handle on the other side so that you can more safely and easily lift the a pan full of food when transferring it from stovetop to oven or out of the oven. Still many

types of cookware have non-heat-conducting handles, some of which are ovenproof and some not. Some pot lids come with knobs and handles that are ovenproof and some do not. If you frequently finish off cooking foods in the oven after stovetop browning, the material from which handles and knobs are made is a significant factor. Here I go again: *Read* the labels, boxes, and promotional materials to find out what's ovenproof and what's not.

Reading the information about pots and pans with nonstick surfaces is especially important because some allow the use of metal utensils and some do not. Also the information from the manufacturer will tell you exactly how to scrub the pots and pans for best results and to preserve the finish. Most pots and pans with nonstick surfaces can safely be washed in the dishwasher. Of course, whether or not large pans will fit in your dishwasher is another issue.

■ **Heavyweight aluminum and anodized aluminum** pots and pans are very good heat conductors, and you can frequently melt cheese or chocolate in a heavy aluminum pot over a low heat without the need for a double-boiler. Prices vary greatly and often you can get good buys at discount stores or when department stores have sales.

■ **Cast-iron** skillets and pots conduct heat extremely well and can be used for roasting flat cuts of meat as well as for stovetop cooking. Cast iron is popular among cooks in the South, especially for frying and baking such specialties as cornbread. My grandmother and mother always made pineapple upside-down cake in an iron skillet, and I still do the same. (For more about cast-iron ware, see "The Care and Cleaning of Your Cookware," p. 38.)

- **Enamelware** can vary from cheap graniteware (usually blue and white) to enameled ironware which is anything but cheap. The cheap enamelware can be used to boil water or vegetables or as a coffeepot but it's difficult to fry in the frying pans because most foods will burn at only moderate temperature. Often this type of enamelware is used to decorate country-style kitchens. Enameled ironware is extremely heavy, and Dutch ovens in this material are very popular because they are so good for simmering stews and similar foods both on the stovetop and in the oven. Also, foods can be cooked and served from the same container if your service is casual and the colors work with your decor. Glass and ceramic cookware, which is safe for microwave cooking and for stovetop use, can also be used to serve at the table and to store leftovers for reheating. It saves you energy to cook, serve, store, and reheat all in the same dish.

WHAT YOU NEED

The basic start-up kitchen should include the following for cooking.

- **Glass and ceramic cookware** in 1-, 2-, and 3-quart sizes that can double as mixing bowls and casseroles.
- **A 1-quart pot** that is appropriate for solo portions of soups, stews, and other main dishes and is large enough to cook 1 cup of dry rice with 2 cups of water. (You will, however, need

Cookware and Your Health

Some people have health concerns about the various types of metals and nonstick surfaces. Here's some information, which includes guidelines from the American Institute for Cancer Research, to help you make the best decisions when choosing and using cookware (as of January 2000).

Nonstick coatings: Some nonstick coatings may abrade and chip with heavy or improper use, but the chipped-off particles have not been found to cause health problems. When you cook with pots and pans that have nonstick coatings make sure temperatures are moderate and that the pot or pan contains enough liquid. It's always best to use wooden or plastic utensils and nonabrasive cleaning materials to protect nonstick surfaces.

Anodized aluminum: These surfaces are hardened and sealed by an electrochemical process to get a nonstick, scratch-resistant surface that allows fat-free cooking. These pots and pans tend to be durable, tend to cook evenly and quickly, and don't leach materials into food.

Aluminum: Most of today's aluminum cookware has been anodized or treated with nonstick coatings. Some years ago, there was a concern about the relationship of Alzheimer's disease and aluminum cookware; but according to our references, research has shown that the high levels of aluminum in Alzheimer's patients' brains is a result of the disease and not aluminum ingestion. Cooking and storing food in uncoated aluminum cookware daily results in ingesting only a minute amount of

continued . . .

Cookware and Your Health, *continued*

aluminum, but high-acid or salty foods—like spaghetti and tomato sauce, cabbage, and sauer-kraut—may allow more aluminum to be absorbed by the food. It's not a good idea to store high-acid or salty food in aluminum containers for a long time, anyway, because it can cause the surface to pit.

Ceramics: Slow cookers and other kinds of microwave cookware and some casseroles are made of ceramics. Some glazes on ceramic cookware may carry small amounts of lead but U.S. Food and Drug Administration studies show that U.S.-made cookware doesn't exceed safety standards. However, be wary of imported ceramics, especially those from third world countries, where regulations are not so strict. They may contain unacceptable levels of lead in the glaze.

Enamel: This cookware usually has a metal base with the outside and a porcelain enamel coating on the inside. Or the outside may be coated with epoxy enamel, acrylic enamel, or polyurethane. This cookware washes well in the dishwasher, but scouring powders and steel wool may scratch the surface. Soak pans and then scrub with a nylon scrubber. Do read the manufacturer's directions for cleaning.

a larger pot to boil noodles because they tend to boil over.)

- A 3- or 4-quart pot for boiling pasta and making full recipes of soups or stews; it can double as a mixing bowl.
- A 6- or 7-inch-diameter frying pan for an egg, one burger, or one chop; use it for browning a grilled-cheese sandwich and so forth.

- A 10- or 12-inch skillet for general use.
- Look for lids that will fit over several sizes of pots and pans. You can also find lids that trap spattering grease but still allow steam to escape when you are browning foods.

Once you have the basic cookware, then you can start adding to your collection of kitchenware by getting a stockpot for soups (that you previously made in a 4-quart pot), and you can get roasting pans, covered or not, in sizes that you use everyday and big ones for Thanksgiving turkeys and entertaining. Double-boilers and steamers (a double-boiler with a perforated top pot) are also handy, but if you watch the chefs on TV, you'll see them putting stainless-steel mixing bowls on top of regular pots when the rest of us would use a double-boiler. Also, you can buy stainless-steel steamers that adjust to all pot sizes for steaming your veggies. They have a handle in the center so that you can lift out the foods and are relatively inexpensive. They are found in catalogs and housewares departments.

In addition to the basic pots and pans, the well-equipped kitchen could also include the following items for cooking and baking.

- Individual-portion-size ceramic casseroles with handles for baking or reheating meals for one in the microwave. (They are not suitable for cooking on the stovetop.)
- A 4-cup glass measuring pitcher can also be used as a mixing bowl and to boil 1 cup of water and cook foods in the microwave. A 1-cup glass pitcher works for smaller amounts.
- A 9- or 10-inch-diameter glass pie plate or glass microwave-safe and conventional

oven-safe pizza plate is good for cooking things that need to be arranged in a circle for best microwaving results, for baking in the conventional oven, as well as for serving.

- An **8-inch square and/or 9 × 13-inch rectangular, oven-safe glass or aluminum pan** is good for general-purpose baking.
- A **9 × 12-inch cookie sheet**. If you don't have a cookie sheet, bake cookies on the underside of a rectangular aluminum baking pan.
- A **jellyroll pan** (looks like a cookie sheet but with ½-inch sides) can be used for baking cookies and for baking chicken pieces with sauces; they won't let meat juices spill over.
- A **glass or metal bread loaf pan** can be used to bake quick breads, meat loaf, and casseroles.

ORGANIZING YOUR COOKWARE

There's an easy method to organizing your pots and pans (as well as utensils and gadgets) that's a simple as A, B, C. It's a technique that's been advocated by professional closet organizers for years:

Step 1: Take everything out of the cupboard and made three groupings:

A. The items used almost daily.
B. The items used for special occasions.
C. Items not used in more than a year or two (excluding those in B).

Step 2: Discard or give away items in group C. (If you are the kind of person who just can't

bear to throw anything away, my mother's advice was to put the C items in a box, put the date on it, and store it in the attic or the garage. Then, if you don't use these items for another year, the chances are that you won't use them again; give them to a charity or sell them at a garage sale.)

Step 3: Store the B items in the least accessible parts of your cabinets.

Step 4: Put the A items in the most easily accessible places.

Before returning food, pots, pans, dishes, etc. to the cabinets, wash the cabinets with a disinfectant. Check for insect activity and debug if needed; let the shelves air dry for a while, and then line shelves with the liners of your choice. (Please see chapter 9.)

Cupboard Shelf Liners

There are lots of ideas and choices for making shelf liners. Here's just a few of the good ones I've collected over the years:

- **Old shelf liners can be patterns** for cutting new ones; no need to measure.
- **Aluminum foil:** My mother liked to line cupboard shelves with aluminum foil because it reflected light in dark cabinets. When it needed cleaning, it could be wiped with a damp sponge. Most shelf paper of Mother's day was actually paper, and when it got dirty, it had to be changed—you'd have to repeat the time-consuming, tedious chores of cutting and fitting.

■ **Wax paper:** Place a sheet of wax paper under the shelf paper to prevent it from sticking to wooden cabinet shelves, especially those that have been painted or varnished.

■ **Flooring:** If you have extra flooring pieces, they will make tough liners for the shelf beneath your sink or the shelf on which you store heavy pots and pans. This material is easy to wipe clean.

■ **Miscellaneous alternatives:** You can choose any of the following and cut to fit as needed: gift wrap, old flannel-backed plastic tablecloths, old posters, last year's laminated full-year calendar, plastic or cloth placemats (especially in glass-door cabinets), butcher wrap or freezer wrap (especially the heavy-duty plasticized type).

Storing Household Cleansers

Adapt the A, B, C method to cleaners that are, in most people's kitchens, stored under the sink. Do you really use all of those products? Have some of the products become so old that the liquid in them has evaporated?

Are you storing products under the sink that could be harmful to curious children or to pets that have learned to open cabinet doors? If you have a cabinet over your kitchen sink, would it be a more convenient and safer storage place?

Would the under-the-sink cabinet be a suitable place to store tall items, such as soup pots, that don't fit in the other cabinets? Just because your mother stored all of her soaps and cleaning products under the sink, doesn't mean you must do it, too.

✿ **HELOISE HINT:** To avoid scratching the nonstick surface of pots and pans, place a cheap paper plate or round coffee filter in between each when you have to stack them in the cupboards.

THE CARE AND CLEANING OF YOUR COOKWARE

■ **To clean aluminum pots and pans:** A tried-and-true Heloise Hint is to fill the pot with water, bring to boil, and add 1 or 2 tablespoons of cream of tartar. Let simmer until the pot shines. Or if you have apple peels leftover from making pie or other dishes, toss them into the pot with water and let boil.

✿ **HELOISE HINT:** Instead of sacrificing your fingernails scraping off small stuck-on bits on pots and pans or anything else, save the little plastic squares that frequently hold bread and muffin bags shut. One reader also uses them as guitar picks! Those give-away CDs that come to us free in the mail work well, too.

■ **Pans won't turn dark** when you boil eggs or potatoes if you put a small amount of vinegar in the water. It won't affect the taste but will brighten the pan.

■ **To avoid lime buildup** in pots used to heat baby bottles or to process home-canned fruits and vegetables, or in the bottoms of double-boilers, add 1 or 2 tablespoons of vinegar to the water before boiling

■ **To get rid of burned food in a pot:**

Method 1: Remove loose bits with a spoon, pour water into the pan and return it to the burner to boil for a few minutes or allow to soak with the heat that remains in an electric burner after you turn it off. For heavy soil, add a squirt of dishwashing liquid for boiling or soaking.

Method 2: Sprinkle the burned pan liberally with baking soda, add just enough water to moisten it, then let stand for several hours and lift the burned food out.

Method 3: Soak overnight in a strong solution of dishwasher detergent and hot water; then wash as usual. CAUTION: Be sure the detergent is dissolved and *do not* use this method on aluminum; dishwasher detergent contains bleach and may discolor the pot or pan.

Method 4 (for stainless steel): Pour full-strength vinegar into a blackened or charred stainless-steel pot and let it stand for several days. Replace the vinegar with fresh vinegar and allow to stand for several more days. This method is too strong for aluminum and some other metals but has worked for stainless steel.

■ **To remove stains from nonstick surfaces,** boil a solution of 1 cup water to 2 tablespoons baking soda in a stained nonstick surface pan to remove stains. Wipe the surface lightly with cooking oil before the next use.

■ **If you have no soap pads** for scrubbing regular pans (not nonstick surfaces), sprinkle cleanser into the pot and scrub with a loosely crumpled used piece of aluminum foil.

Cast Iron

Cast-iron pots can, and do, last for generations. But they do need special care to keep them in top working order.

■ **Seasoning a new cast-iron pot:** Although some cast-iron pots are already seasoned when you buy them, if yours is not, here's how to do it:

Wash the pot with warm sudsy water, then rinse with hot water and dry well.

Slather on a thick layer of unsalted vegetable shortening over the inside and outside of both the pot and the lid.

Cover the pot with the lid, set it on a cookie sheet, and bake it in an oven at 250 degrees F for 1½ hours. Swab the shortening around occasionally with a dry cloth or paper towel to keep the surface evenly coated. CAUTION: Wear an oven mitt!

After baking, allow the pot to cool, then wipe out any excess grease and buff to a shine with a dry, clean cloth or paper towel.

■ **Old rusty iron skillets can be reseasoned:** Remove all the rust with a scouring pad, wash, dry, and season as noted above. Also, you can season and reseason iron cookware by deep-frying with it. Skillets may need reseasoning about once a year to keep them at their best.

■ **Cleaning cast iron:**

Just wash quickly in soap and hot water with a mild dishwashing liquid or run lots of hot water on it and scrub with a nylon scrubber to remove baked-on food particles. Never *soak* iron skillets in soapy water or use harsh cleansers or metal scouring pads.

After washing, rinse the pan well, place it on a burner on medium high for a few seconds to dry. *Do not* leave it on the burner for a long time; if it starts smoking, the seasoning will be removed.

Rub the pan with a light coating of vegetable oil when it is completely dry before storing.

Place a heavy paper grocery bag or paper plate or coffee filter above and below the pot if you are stacking it with others in the cupboard.

▪ **If a pot accumulates a lot of grease** on the bottom that looks like asphalt, many people like to put it into the fire of a barbecue grill after they finish cooking and let the grease burn off as the coals burn down and go out. The skillet needs to stay in the coals for about an hour. CAUTION: Let the pot cool before you touch it and don't try to rush cooling with cold water, which might crack the iron. You'll have to oil the pot before storing.

UTENSILS AND GADGETS

Visit any kitchen-supply store and you're certain to be overwhelmed by the number and range of gizmos that have been invented for the kitchen. Without a program, it might be hard to figure out what some of these things do. And if you can't tell what it is by looking at it, chances are you probably don't really need it in your basic kitchen. But of course, as I often hear from my readers, there are gadgets you just can't live without because it might make life easier. Getting back to basics, here's list of must-have gadgets for any kitchen.

▪ A good **can opener,** even if you cook from scratch. The can opener can either be electric or manual (see chapter 1 for information about electric can openers). New-style manual can openers have thick handles for easy grips; some are stainless steel and so they won't rust, and you'll find many designs that open cans more easily than the simple metal manual can openers of Mom's day.

▪ A **wire whisk** substitutes for an electric mixer, blends flour with water for gravy, and whips eggs for scrambling.

▪ Large and small **spatulas/pancake turners** for turning foods in the pan and for serving such foods as lasagna (plastic or wooden spatulas are needed for nonstick cookware). Look for the new heatproof pliable spatulas in kitchenware stores; they can be used on every type of cookware and don't melt when they touch a hot skillet.

▪ Several heatproof **plastic or wooden spoons.** You won't burn your fingers when you stir hot foods and you'll protect the surfaces of nonstick cookware.

▪ A set of **flexible rubber spatulas** in different sizes for scraping every smidgen out of a bowl or other container.

▪ A **pastry blender** does more than you can imagine. It will mash turnips or potatoes, blend crumb topping for coffeecake, chop eggs for salad, chop up boiled potatoes, and mix flour and water for gravy.

▪ A wooden-handled, **long-tined fork** for turning meats in the pan and for testing baked potatoes to tell if they are done.

▪ A **slotted spoon** for removing foods from liquids.

▪ A **spaghetti grabber** (a wooden or plastic spoon that has "fingers" on the bowl) to lift noodles, veggie hunks, and other foods out of hot liquids.

▪ A **sieve and/or a colander** for straining foods and draining noodles. Gadget departments of houseware stores also have plastic or metal pot-drainers that you can hold on the edge of the pot to drain away liquid such as water from noodles. They look like a half of a pot lid with holes. After draining, you let the noodles slide back into the pot into which you can add sauce or veggies and grated cheese. You'll save yourself the chore of washing another dish and you can drain off the liquid into another pot to reserve for other uses.

Cutting Tools

Buy the best-quality knives that you can afford. Good, sharp knives can replace any kind of cutting or chopping appliances, and if properly cared for, they can last a lifetime. Cutting knives should be washed by hand and not in the dishwasher, which can cause heat damage to the metal blade and to the handles. Before you buy knives, hold them in your hand to test if they match your grip. If you are a bit fumble-fingered, look for the new padded, fat-handled

knives and kitchen utensils. Basic kitcheneering tells us that you will be more likely to cut yourself with a dull knife than with a sharp one because of all the manipulations that go on when you are trying to cut something with a dull knife.

Your basic cutting tools should include the following:

▪ A small **paring knife** for peeling and cutting vegetables and fruit.

▪ A **French chef's knife** for chopping.

❀ **HELOISE HINT:** Instead of peeling and mincing garlic cloves, do it like the chefs do: Put the clove on a cutting board, place the broadest area of a French chef's knife flat on the clove, and give it a whack with the heel of your hand. The garlic clove will be crushed and will squirt out of the peel.

▪ A slender **boning knife** for general purposes.

Storing Knives

- Use cardboard rolls from paper towels or toilet tissue as sleeves for knife blades to protect your fingers. Flatten the roll and insert the knife. You can staple the ends and sides to get a better fit.

- Plastic ballpoint-pen tops can also protect your fingers from sharp, pointed scissors or other objects.

- To carry a paring knife safely to picnic, put it in a toothbrush holder.

- A **serrated knife** for cutting bread, tomatoes, and some meats.
- A **knife sharpener**.
- A **pizza cutter** for pizza and a whole lot of other things, such as lasagna or other flat casseroles, crusts from sliced bread, cutting refrigerated or homemade cookie dough into squares, cutting noodles if you make your own, cutting freshly baked bar cookies, and anything else that sticks to a knife when you try to cut it.
- The best **cutting board** is one that protects knives from being damaged but is still sanitary. After a board has been used for raw meat, do not use it for the cooked meat, because bacteria from the raw juices can contaminate the cooked food. So the best kind of board is one that can be washed in the dishwasher. Among the new styles of cutting boards are tray-shaped cutting boards with raised edges to keep liquids from dripping off and those that are pliable so they can fold into a funnel shape, allowing chopped foods to be poured into the pan or bowl with no mess at all. If you still prefer a wooden cutting board, you can sanitize it with 1 teaspoon household bleach in 2 cups water followed by a thorough rinsing and drying. To re-season a wooden cutting board, rub with mineral oil (rather than salad oil, it can become rancid). Let set for an hour or so, then wipe with paper towels.

MEASURING UTENSILS

Like my mother and maybe like your mother, I measure by eye and taste. But if you are a kitchen novice, it may be best to measure by spoon or cup until your eye gets trained to judge amounts of ingredients.

- **Glass containers** in 1-, 2-, and/or 4-cup sizes for liquids. The most common ones feature a spout for pouring and extra space at the top to prevent spills.
- **Plastic or metal containers** in 1-, ½-, ⅓-, and ¼-cup measures for dry ingredients that let you level off the surface with the straight back of a table knife to get an exact measure of flour, sugar, shortening, etc.
- **Measuring spoons** for salt, spices, baking powder, and baking soda also need to be leveled off to get the exact amount. Using flatware teaspoons and tablespoons as measuring spoons is not recommended because they are of so many different sizes that you won't have exact measures. Leavening agents such as baking soda and baking powder must be in the right amounts or the cake or other baked good won't rise properly.

❊ **HELOISE HINT:** Keep a freebie measuring scoop (the kind you might get in ground coffee or baby formula) in each canister of flour, rice, sugar, etc. to save washing so many measuring spoons and cups when you cook. Scoops from infant formula and other products measure 1 or 2 tablespoons.

ORGANIZING THE KITCHEN DRAWERS

Kitchen drawers can accumulate clutter faster than any other place in the kitchen. With so many interesting gadgets gathered in one place it's little wonder that most of us could never make a list of what's in the kitchen "junk" drawer before we look inside! Yet, the same organizing principle applies to the kitchen drawer that we use in the cabinets: Do you really use all that stuff? If you have six can openers, it's likely that three or four of them don't work—keep two (just in case your favorite one breaks). Put the others into the box that you will store in the attic or garage, to be checked again in 6 months to a year to see if you missed anything in it. Will you ever get around to sharpening that old paring knife or would you be better off getting rid of it? How many mixing spoons can you stir with at any time? Do you really need a half dozen?

Beyond the sort-and-discard method, there are two simple steps to start organizing your kitchen drawers:

- Make a note of the **inside dimensions**—width, depth, and height—of all your drawers.
- Check out kitchenware departments, catalogs, or specialty stores that sell **organizing racks**, bins, and dividers that will fit right in the drawers.

And here are a few more Heloise Hints and suggestions from readers:

- Use any **small container** that might work to help divide the items in a kitchen drawer: square metal candy boxes or plastic baby wipes boxes to hold oddly shaped things like tea balls, bottle stoppers, or corn-cob holders. The large plastic caps from liquid laundry detergent or short glass baby-food jars are perfect the tiniest items. One reader from Minnesota organized her kitchen drawers by recycling heavy boxes that 2-pound cheeses come in.

- When your spatulas, meat forks, and knives have the **same shape and color handles**, you have to pull the whole drawer out to find what you are looking for. A Seattle man has this solution: Just turn **the divider bin around** so that the handles point to the back and you can see immediately, what you are seeking. CAUTION: This hint works well for table flatware but sharp, pointed objects such as ice picks, kabob skewers, and sharp knives are best stored with the handles to the front of the drawer for safety's sake.

- **Corks** from wine and other bottles can be washed and then used to cover the points of knives, barbecue forks, and kabob skewers to protect your fingers when you're scooping items out of the drawer.

- Wash all those **glass jars** from jelly, olives, mayo, and pickles; remove the labels; and use the jars to store just about anything in the kitchen from food to paper clips and clothes pins. (Small spring clothes pins hold bags closed and they are cheaper than clips made specifically for that purpose.) The bonus is that you can see what's inside.

Care and Cleaning of Utensils

- **Soaking and/or scrubbing in hot soapy water** usually does the trick when you are washing kitchen utensils.
- Some utensils go into the **dishwasher**—some only in the top rack—and some do not. Some plastic utensils will melt into interesting

shapes in the dishwasher; and although I would not discourage creativity and artistic endeavors in the kitchen, misshapen spatulas, spoons, and other gadgets are not very useful! Some people put wooden utensils in the top rack of the dishwasher, but it isn't the way to clean them if you want them to last a long time. Again, read the labels and packaging to find out how to care for your utensils.

■ **To season wooden utensils:** Scrub them with hot soapy water, rinse well and let air dry, then rub them with mineral oil (not vegetable oil), allow them to set for a few hours, and wipe clean with a paper towel. Mineral oil has no taste and doesn't get rancid like salad oil does. You can also season the wooden handles of knives and other utensils with mineral oil to keep them in good condition. Do not put wooden utensils in the dishwasher.

■ If your **rubber spatula gets cracked** along the edges, you can just cut off the bad parts with kitchen shears, following the original contours of the rubber part, and you'll have a slimmer but still useful spatula that is especially good at getting the last drops out of small-mouth jars.

Chapter Three

Tableware: China, Crystal, Flatware, and Linens

In my mother's day, a bride-to-be selected her "good" china and "good" silver and then bought "everyday" china and "everyday" stainless-steel flatware. Like her mother and her grandmother before her, brides of my mother's day saved the good china and silver for special occasions, and it usually got passed on to another generation intact and like new. My mother thought this custom was silly. She liked to use all of her good china, silver, and linens. She always advised me, "Use your good china, crystal, silver, and linens or his second wife will." I take her advice and I use all of my nice things and enjoy them. Practically speaking, why save good things for your children or grandchildren who may not have the same taste as you do? If you like the designs and patterns you should be the one to enjoy them.

Here are some things about choosing, using, and caring for china, crystal, flatware, and linens—both good and everyday—that I've learned over the years.

CHINA

- **Porcelain** does not chip as readily as pottery. (Another reason to enjoy the good china!)
- **Plain white china** goes with everything and if you are putting together a household for the first time, this may be the best choice, because your tastes change as time passes and plain white can always blend in with other china colors and patterns. (Some foods look unappetizing on some colors of china to some people. A friend of mine received an everyday china set as a wedding gift that was a deep blue-green color. She said that every time she

put beets or cranberry sauce on the plates the whole dinner looked disgusting to her. She finally gave the dishes to a charity garage sale.)

- **Silver and platinum decorations** on china tend to discolor from dishwasher detergent and are best washed by hand.

- **All pieces of the china don't have to match.** If you look at designer showrooms, you'll see how china patterns, colors, and shapes are combined for an eclectic look. I know a woman who collects plates, cups, and saucers at flea markets and garage sales in designs and colors that she likes and she sets a most interesting table.

- The **lead content** of various glazes can be harmful. If you have older pieces of china and pottery that you suspect may have lead in the glaze, it may be better to use such items for decorating instead of for eating on. This applies to some foreign-made china and pottery, too. Kits are available in some hardware and housewares stores to help you test china for lead content. Check them out.

- When **stacking good dishes**, place cheap paper plates or round coffee filters in between the dishes to prevent scratches and nicks and then wrap the whole stack in plastic wrap so that the dishes will stay clean. To put a paper plate in between bowls, you can cut into the edge a couple of inches deep at intervals so that the paper plate conforms to the shape of the bowl. Also, you can buy special zippered containers for good china and glassware through catalogs or most quality china retailers.

CRYSTAL

- The **lead content** of crystal has been found to be harmful to health if it leaches into the beverages stored in the crystal. Alcoholic and acidic juices are most likely to leach lead from crystal and get consumed. Liquors should not be stored long-term in crystal decanters, even if you did get those decanters from your favorite aunt. If you want to display them you might try filling the decanters with colored water. Crystal baby bottles are best used for display; milk can leach lead from some of them—you don't want your baby ingesting lead.

- **Shapes of glasses:** If you can't afford to buy the traditional shaped glasses for each type of wine, start with the modified tulip-bowl stemware. The 8-ounce tumblers are good for mixed drinks and breakfast juice and the 12-ounce tumblers are good for soft drinks and iced tea. Although there are flat-bottomed champagne glasses, the bubbles will be appreciated more in tulip champagne stemware.

FLATWARE

Stainless-steel flatware (table knives, forks, and spoons) used to be more functional than decorative in my mother's day. But now designs are as pleasing as those for real silver flatware and the higher-quality stainless flatware is heavier and no longer feels like picnic flatware. If you are just starting out, or if polishing silver is not your hobby, you may want to buy only best-quality stainless-steel flatware and make it both your everyday and good flat-ware. On the other hand, if you like the patina of silver and can afford it, have silver and use it often. Using it frequently means that you *don't* have to polish it as often. Just wash in hot soapy water, rinse well, and dry to keep it shiny.

Cleaning Silverware

- **Clean silver** that is not too tarnished with hot, soapy water. Just wash, rinse well, and dry with a soft cloth.

- You will find various types of **commercial silver polishes** and some brands contain substances that prevent tarnishing, at least for a longer time than polishes without these additives. You will also find different forms: liquid, paste, and a can containing cotton-like fibers that are impregnated with silver cleaner. There are also polishing cloths and mitts with the polish in the fabric. Some polishes say they are for all metals, included copper and brass. Just on general principles, I would use only silver polish on my good silver. Some cleaners that also clean brass and copper could be too harsh. *Do* read the label directions on the polish. Some polishes say that you should apply polish, allow to dry and buff. Others will say that you should apply polish, rinse it off, and then buff dry. Silver-polishing cloths or mitts and the polish that comes impregnated in a cotton-like fiber are very handy for polishing large items like punch bowls and large trays as well as for things like antique clock faces that you can't rinse or when runny liquids might damage surrounding wood parts. The fiber in the can is also handy for touch-up cleaning, because all you do is pinch off a piece of the fiber, clean the tarnish, and buff.

- **The dishwasher** is not kind to silver and silver-plated flatware. Some say dishwasher detergent can discolor the silver after long-term use and the heat of the water and drying cycle can loosen knife handles. I do wash my sterling silver in the dishwasher but don't mix it with stainless pieces in the same compartment because it can damage the silver.

- **Home-style cleaning methods** may leave a dull white luster on silver and remove the dark accents (patina) in design crevices. They may also soften the cement of hollow-handled flatware. Use the following methods once in while when you are in a hurry or only for badly tarnished pieces that do not have high value.

Silver cleaner 1: Place aluminum foil in the bottom of a cooking pot. (Aluminum pots may darken if used for this process.) Add enough water to cover the silver pieces. For each quart of water, add 1 teaspoon of salt and 1 teaspoon of baking soda. Bring the solution to a boil, add the silver, and boil 1 or 2 minutes. Remove the silver, rinse well, and buff dry with a soft cloth.

Silver cleaner 2: Place a piece of aluminum foil at the bottom of the kitchen sink, fill the sink with very hot tap water, and then do the rest of the procedure described for cleaner 1.

Silver cleaner 3: Use aluminum foil, hot water, and washing soda, which has some detergent in it, and follow the same procedure as described for cleaner 2.

Silver cleaner 4: Sometimes, if there is not too much tarnish, you can wash enough of it off for respectability with regular liquid dishwashing detergent squirted full-strength on a sponge. Rinse well; shine with soft cloth.

LINENS

Today, most of us don't have the time to fuss with fancy real linen except, perhaps for special occasion. And this is one area of kitcheneering where using your good stuff means more work. But even if you don't own the real McCoy, there are lots of ways to use and care for your linens.

■ **No-iron placemats** can be made from colorful fringed terry cloth fingertip hand towels. They are easily laundered and need no ironing. The bonus is that when spills happen, the terry cloth is very absorbent!

■ **Easy iron cotton placemats** and napkins by spreading them flat on the top of the dryer while they are damp. Let the heat from the dryer "iron" them as you dry other loads of clothes. Flip the stack of napkins or placemats over at each load change so that the heat will reach all the pieces more evenly.

■ **Wash and rinse well seldom-used linens** before you store them away. Put ½ cup of vinegar in the last rinse water to eliminate soap film that may cause deterioration and yellowing of linens that are stored for long periods of time. Don't iron!

■ **To store a tablecloth,** fold it lengthwise or widthwise until it is a width that will fit on a padded pants hanger. The creases will tell you where the center of the tablecloth is and you won't waste a lot of time trying to get it to hang evenly all around all the edges.

■ **Do not iron folds in table linens** to be stored for a long time. The fabric tends to break down on the ironed folds. Also *do not* starch table linens that will be stored for a long time. Moisture can cause the starch to discolor or stain linens.

■ **To remove the folds** from a tablecloth that has been cleaned and stored, toss it into the dryer with a damp hand towel on the fluff cycle for 10 minutes or so.

■ **Fold napkins for storage** so that they are ready to put on the table and you'll save time setting the table.

■ **Old linen or cotton tablecloths** that are soft and lint-free from many washings can be cut up with pinking shears to make towels for drying glassware and crystal. Old linen or cotton placemats can serve the same purpose

■ If you discover a **stain on your tablecloth** moments before your party is to start, get creative. You can cover the stain with a trivet and then put one of the food dishes on the trivet. Or, if the stain is in the center, you can cover it with a doily, a napkin placed to look like a diamond shape, a table runner, or a small round or square tablecloth of a complementary color placed on the center of the table. Put candleholders, a centerpiece or trivet on top and it looks like you planned the table decorations to be just that way.

■ To prevent young children from **pulling on the tablecloth** and destroying the whole setting, try this reader's idea: Pull the table leaves apart at the middle or at two equal distances from each other, tuck about 1 inch of the tablecloth into the crease with a clean spatula, slide the leaves back together again to trap the cloth.

■ **Decorative board placemats** are popular in Britain and in some parts of Europe. They are used at each place setting to protect the tablecloth from stains and to protect the tabletops underneath from the heat of plates. The bonus is that they wipe clean and so laundering linens is a thing of the past, yet the table still looks good. You'll find them in upscale department and specialty stores.

■ **Protect tabletops from heat** with trivets, pads that go under tablecloths, flat thick potholders, or anything else that puts a heat barrier between the table and the hot dish. Prevention is easier that than trying to remove white marks on varnish or worse yet, scorch marks! You may have to refinish the whole table if you scorch the surface, but white heat marks can come off if you rub the mark with real mayonnaise or a pecan half, wipe off and dry, and buff with a soft cloth. Also, hardware stores sell cover sticks and pads saturated with a stain remover that come ready-to-use in a container about the size of a cold-cream jar.

■ **Tablecloth warning:** Do not lay a plain plastic, felt, or foam-backed plastic tablecloth directly on a wooden table; the plastic or foam may stick to the finish and the only solution may be to refinish the furniture. Picking up plastic sheeting that has been on the table for a while can pull up sections of varnish on some furniture. You can try to remove stuck-on foam with a plastic scrubbie, soft toothbrush, or nylon net and mineral oil.

CARING FOR AND CLEANING LINENS

Most of the questions I get when I'm on the road meeting my readers are about spots and stains. Some of the following stain-removal hints are tried and true from my mother's time and some have been updated for today's fabrics. When I get questions about spots and stains, even from my fellow passengers on an airplane, I think I should say, "If life is a stain, these are the rules!"

Here are some common stains found on table linens and the Heloise home-style ways to remove them. Be sure that you read the label on the item and use a method appropriate for the fabric. CAUTION: *Always* keep manufacturers' tags so you know the recommended laundering techniques and *always* test the stain-removal solutions on an inconspicuous place before working on a stained item. You'll find more information on stain removal in chapter 10.

■ **Alcoholic beverages:** Soak or sponge the stain promptly, using cool water. Sponge with white household vinegar. Rinse. If necessary, rub some liquid laundry detergent into any remaining stain, rinse, and launder as usual.

■ **Baby formula or milk:** Soak the item in cold water. Rub liquid laundry detergent into the stain, and then launder in the hottest water safe for the fabric, using an enzyme detergent. If a greasy stain remains, sponge the area with cleaning fluid (spot remover), launder, and check again before drying in a clothes dryer.

Heloise's Top Ten Spot- and Stain-Removal Rules

1. Get to the stain as soon as possible; the longer it sets, the more difficult it is to remove.

2. Work at the stain slowly. Some stains take time to remove.

3. Some stains are stubborn and you may have to repeat the stain-removal steps several times.

4. Try the least drastic stain-removal methods first. (Often flushing the stained area immediately with cold water will do the job.)

5. Always test a hidden area of the item before trying a stain-removal method.

6. Place a paper or terry towel beneath a stain before treating to absorb liquids as they carry the stain out of the fabric.

7. Blot soiled areas when removing a stain; rubbing spreads the stain and may damage some fabrics. (*Blot* means to dab firmly with an absorbent cloth. *Rub* means use a circular or back and forth motion to gently scrub the area.)

8. Always work from the outside to the center of the stain.

9. When using spray-type stain removers, spray the item from the wrong side first for best results.

10. Give stain removers time to work before rinsing or washing. Rushing may mean repeating the process.

■ **Ballpoint-pen ink:** Place several sheets of paper towels then place the stain facedown. Use plain rubbing alcohol on a clean cloth and dab it on the ink stain. Repeat if necessary. The ink will bleed through to the paper toweling, so change it often until as much of the ink stain as possible is removed. Rub some liquid laundry detergent directly into any remaining stain and launder as usual.

■ **Blood:** Treat the stain ASAP. Do not use hot water because heat may set protein stains.

Get the stained item into cold water and soak for 30 minutes. Then apply a prewash stain remover. If stain remains, rub it with liquid laundry detergent or bar soap. Still a problem? Make a solution of 1 tablespoon ammonia and 1 cup water and apply to the stains. Rinse and launder following care-label instructions. Check garment before putting into dryer. If the stain is still there, pour a small amount of 3 percent hydrogen peroxide on the stain (always test this on a hidden area to see if the 3 percent hydrogen peroxide affects fabric color). Launder again. Unseasoned meat tenderizer is also effective in getting rid of fresh bloodstains. Dampen the area with cold water then sprinkle on unseasoned meat tenderizer and let sit. Repeat to remove all of the stain; then the garment can be laundered.

If stain has dried, soak in warm water with an enzyme-based product. Then launder as usual.

■ **Candle wax:** Flick off as much of the hard wax as possible with your fingernail. Place paper towels on either side of the material where the wax stain is and iron on a Low-to-Medium (not High!) setting, depending on the fabric. For example, cotton and linen can tolerate higher temperature than polyester or other synthetic fabrics. Check your iron and the tags on the linens to determine the temperature. If a stain remains, apply full-strength liquid laundry detergent, let set, then wash as usual.

- **Candy (other than chocolate):** Use cold water and a small amount of liquid detergent on the stain; then rinse. If the stains are red, soak the garment in a strong laundry detergent and a bit of bleach (if it's okay for the material) or apply a prewash spray.
- **Chewing gum:** Put the item in the freezer to harden the gum, then carefully remove the gum with a dull butter knife. If any residue remains, treat the area with prewash spray or sponge cleaning fluid from the backside then "work" to break up the gum and launder as usual.
- **Chocolate:** Soak the item in cold water. Then rub liquid laundry detergent into the stain while the fabric is wet. Rinse. If a greasy stain remains in the fabric, sponge the area with cleaning fluid (spot remover).
- **Coffee/tea:** Rinse in cold water ASAP, and then rub in several drops of mild, white dishwashing liquid. Rinse well and then treat with a solution of 1 part white household vinegar and 3 parts water. Rinse again then launder as usual. Note: If you have used cream in your coffee, you may need to sponge the stain with dry-cleaning fluid.
- **Cola:** Stains can be removed from 100 percent cotton, permanent press, and cotton blends if you sponge with undiluted white vinegar within 24 hours. Then launder or dry-clean according to the manufacturer's instructions.
- **Egg:** Scrape off any residue with a dull knife; wet the stained area with cool (don't use hot water first) water, apply some liquid laundry detergent, and scrub the stain with a tooth-brush. When the stain is removed, launder in the hottest water safe for the fabric.
- **Fruit/fruit juice/berries:** Get to them as fast as you can. Try one of these methods:

> Soak the stained area in cold water for about 30 minutes. Rub liquid laundry detergent into the wet area if there are remaining stains. Launder with detergent and warm water. If there are still stains, apply hydrogen peroxide to bleach-safe fabric, then rinse well.
>
> For washable fabric, soak in cold water. If stains are still there, dab white vinegar on them and rinse. If they are stubborn, apply hydrogen peroxide to bleach-safe fabrics.
>
> For "dry clean only" fabrics (read the care label), sponge with dry-cleaning fluid.
>
> Soak in cool water; wash. If stain remains, cover area with a paste made from oxygen-type bleach, several drops of hot water and a few drops of ammonia. Wait 15 to 30 minutes; then wash as usual.

- **Ice cream:** Soak the linens in cold water, hand wash in warm soapy water, and rinse. If a greasy stain remains or if the ice cream was chocolate, sponge the stain with cleaning fluid (spot remover) and launder as usual after all of the stain is removed.
- **Ink:** An old home-style method calls for soaking ink spots in warm milk before they dry. Dried stains can sometimes be removed by rubbing in isopropyl alcohol until stain comes out. Please don't use this on highly colored material. You can also try commercial cleaning fluid (spot remover), of course.
- **Ketchup/tomato sauce:** Dab or scrape off the excess and soak the linens in cold water

for 30 minutes. Rub liquid laundry detergent or white bar soap into the remaining stain while still wet and follow by laundering in warm water and detergent. For 100 percent cotton, permanent press, or cotton blends, sponge with undiluted white vinegar within 24 hours, then launder or dry-clean according to the manufacturers' instructions.

■ **Lipstick:** First, test a hidden area of the fabric for color fastness. Immediately place the stain facedown on top of absorbent paper towels and saturate the stain with rubbing alcohol. *Dab* at the area with a cloth dipped in rubbing alcohol. You may also have good results with prewash spray. Rinse and launder as usual. Then you use a commercial spot remover or dry-cleaning fluid, if necessary. *Note:* Many newer longer-wear lipsticks need extra attention.

■ **Makeup/foundation:** Powdered or water-based makeup is nongreasy and can be removed by first dampening the area, then rubbing the stain with white bar soap. Rinse and launder as usual. Oily makeup stains can be treated with a prewash spray. Dampen the area and rub to work the stain out. Rinse and launder in the hottest water safe for the fabric after all traces of the stain are removed.

■ **Mildew:** Take the item outside and brush over the mildew stain with a stiff brush to remove mold spores. Bleachable fabrics should be soaked in a solution of 1 tablespoon of chlorine bleach to 1 quart of water for 15 minutes. Rinse and launder, adding liquid bleach to the wash cycle according to directions on the bottle. For nonbleachable fabrics, flush the stain with full-strength white vinegar or ½ cup of lemon juice and 1 tablespoon of salt. Put the item on the grass out in the sun to help "bleach-out" the mildew stain. Launder as usual after all traces of the stain are removed. *Note:* Many new white fabrics have an optical brightener "infused" into the material. The sun will turn these yellow.

■ **Mustard:** Dampen the area and rub liquid laundry detergent into the stain. Rinse, and then soak in laundry detergent and hot to warm water for a few hours. Launder with an enzyme detergent.

■ **Mystery stains:** Flush the stain with cold water. Apply prewash spray and rub into stain. Launder as usual; repeat the steps until the stain is gone. *Do not* put in the dryer until the stain is removed or you give up. These types of stains are usually soluble in water if caught in time.

■ **Oil, grease, butter, or margarine:** Greasy or oily stains require pretreatment with a prewash stain remover. Next rub liquid laundry detergent into the dampened stain. When the stain has disappeared, launder with plenty of detergent in the hottest water safe for the fabric.

■ **Rust:** CAUTION: Never use bleach on rust

Old Home-Style Cures for Kitchen Linens

- White items will come even brighter if you add 1 tablespoon of borax to the last rinse water. Dissolve the borax in some hot water and then add it to the rinse.

- Black fabrics should be rinsed in clear water to which a couple of glugs of vinegar have been added.

stains. Dampen the stain with lemon juice and sprinkle on table salt. Lay the item in the sunshine and continue to dampen the area with lemon juice until the stain disappears, then launder as usual. Look for commercial rust removers in the fabric dye section of your grocery store. *Please note:* Some whites are manufactured with optical brighteners and the lemon, salt, and sun method may not work on these, as well as on highly colored fabrics.

■ **Scorch marks:** Heavily scorched fabric cannot be returned to its original state. Try one of these removal methods but always read care labels first:

For *bleachable* fabrics: Launder with chlorine bleach.

For *nonbleachable* fabrics: Soak in enzyme detergent or oxygen bleach and the hottest water safe for fabric and then launder.

Heloise's Last-Ditch Stain-Remover Formula

For white and bleachable fabrics (no silk, rayon, etc.)

1 gallon hot water
1 cup powdered dishwasher detergent
¼ cup household liquid chlorine bleach

Mix well in a plastic, enamel, or stainless-steel container. (If this solution comes in contact with aluminum it will discolor it.) Let the garment soak in the solution for 5 to 10 minutes. If any stain remains, soak the garment a little longer, then wash as usual.

For *colorfast* fabrics: Always test a hidden area for colorfastness first then use a clean white cloth to dab 3 percent hydrogen peroxide on the scorched area to fade light scorch marks on fabrics. You may have to apply several times, but scorch marks will lessen.

For *delicate* fabrics: Rub scorch marks lightly with a clean white cloth dampened with white vinegar. Wipe with a clean, dry cloth.

■ **Sticky residue:** Residue left from gummed name stickers, price tags, etc. can be removed by carefully dabbing the area with petroleum-based prewash spray or cleaning fluid (spot remover).

■ **Vomit:** Remove any solid residue from fabric. Soak item in warm water and enzyme detergent. Launder as usual after all traces of stain are removed.

■ **Wine:** Rinse in cool water first. If the material is bleach safe, wash the fabric with bleach according to label directions. Also on bleach-safe fabrics, make a paste of powdered dishwasher detergent with a little water and scrub with an old toothbrush. After treating the spot, wash in the hottest water possible for the fabric. For 100 percent cotton, permanent press, or cotton blends, sponge with undiluted white vinegar within 24 hours, then launder or dry-clean according to the manufacturers' instructions.

❀ **HELOISE HINT:** If all fails, as it sometimes does, consider sewing or ironing on an applique design "patch" over a hopeless stain or scorch mark; it might just look like you wanted it that way!

Other Hints for Linens

Caring for your linens doesn't just mean getting the stains out. Here are some tried-and-true hints worth keeping in mind.

■ **Starching lacy items.** Grandma used a home-style sugar starch to make lacy doilies as stiff as if they were made from china. Not many of us use doilies, but the old sugar starch is still good for lacy placemats and other items. Here's how to do it:

Mix ¼ cup of water and ¾ cup of white sugar in a small pan. Stir the mixture over low heat (do not boil) until clear, not sugary. Shut off the heat and let it cool.

Wet the lacy item, roll it in a towel to remove the excess moisture, and dip it into the mixture. Squeeze out excess starch, then shape the item as you wish or flatten it on a waterproof flat surface. (People used to dry small round crocheted lace doilies over a bowl after starching them with this method; the result is a lace bowl for candies or other goodies.

Allow the item to dry and iron (if necessary) on a warm (not hot) setting. Lacy doilies don't need ironing with this starch, just smooth out on a clean flat surface and shape while wet. The top of your clothes dryer is a nice smooth surface on which to stretch out lacy items to dry. And, if you are running some dryer loads, the heat from the dryer will help iron the lace, too.

■ **To remove wrinkles from flannel-backed vinyl tablecloths:** Put the item in the dryer with a couple of damp towels, set dryer on the lowest setting. Then check the tablecloth frequently until all wrinkles are removed. Allow to lay flat while cooling to avoid more wrinkles. You can also remove wrinkles by ironing at a warm setting with a steam iron on the flannel side, *never* on the vinyl side. CAUTION: Don't place wet items or attempt to iron them on a wood table. Heat and moisture may damage the surface.

■ **When ironing embroidered linens,** it's best to do so on the wrong side, because ironing on the right side flattens the stitchery and makes make it less attractive. To really make embroidering stand out, place the item wrong side up on a terry cloth towel and then iron it.

■ **When ironing large tablecloths,** place an old bedsheet below your ironing board so that they won't pick up dirt from the floor.

■ **To avoid making floors slippery from spray starch,** put an old bedsheet on the floor or place a rug beneath your ironing board if you are spray starching items before ironing.

■ **Don't store starched linens.** Dampness in the storage area can react with the starch and cause stains or encourages mildew. Just wash and store; you can iron them when you plan to use them.

■ **Avoid ironing creases into napkins in exactly the same place after each use.** It can cause wear at the creases. When the napkins are still warm from the dryer you can finger-press them if you want them to be creased and it won't be as hard on the fabric.

■ **Roll table runners around a cardboard tube** from gift wrap to keep them from having storage creases. Roll them right side out, and they will lay flatter when you put them on the table.

Chapter Four

All About What We Cook and Eat:

Buying, Storing, Cooking, and Serving

Planning menus and shopping for food can be a challenge when you are busy with job and family obligations, but I hope that my hints on what to look for when you buy makes shopping easier. I have included some hints on eating healthfully so that you can get the best nutrition value for your food budget, too. (For more ideas for health see chapter 9.) Finally, I think that cooking and serving should be a pleasure, not a chore, and I hope that my hints will help you in this phase of kitcheneering, too. Enjoy!

BREADS, CEREAL, RICE, PASTA, AND OTHER GRAINS

Grain products such as whole grain and enriched cereals and bread have a more prominent role in our daily nutrition needs than they had in my mother's day and grains are even more important in vegetarian diets. Also, eating a starch with each meal now means a variety of grain products instead of just noodles, rice, bread, and cereals. Couscous, kasha, and wild rice are just a few of the grains that have become more common in our daily diets and are now readily available in supermarkets, not just health food stores. If they haven't become a part of your diet, try them, I'll bet you'll like them. The U.S. Department of Agriculture (USDA) tells us that grain products, such as whole grain and enriched cereals and breads, are sources of starch, protein, iron, B vitamins, magnesium, folate, and fiber. According to the USDA the average daily requirement from this food group is six to eleven servings: One serving equals one slice of bread; half of a hamburger bun or English muffin; a small roll, biscuit, or muffin; three to four small or two large crackers; ½ cup of cooked cereal, rice, or pasta; or 1 ounce ready-to-eat breakfast cereal.

Shopping

GRAINS

Whole-grain breads are usually higher in fiber than those made from refined flour but "wheat" bread does not necessarily mean *whole* wheat. You can't judge a loaf of bread by its color, because colorings may have been added to make bread look more like whole wheat. When you look at the label, it should specifically say whole wheat bread made with 100 percent whole wheat flour or other whole grain, and the whole grain should be listed first on the label. Examples of whole grains are cracked wheat, bulgur, oatmeal, whole cornmeal, whole rye, and scotch barley.

Compare labels on *cereals* for fiber, starch, sugar, sodium, and other ingredients. Bran, whole wheat, and other whole-grain cereals provide the most fiber per serving. Look for the word *whole* on the label to see if the cereal actually is made with whole grains. Sugar content can range from less than 1 percent to 55 per-

cent of the cereal by weight. Granolas and "natural" cereals may be high in calories, fat, and sugar; and many cereals are high in sodium. Many cereals say they are fortified with vitamins and minerals and provide 100 percent of the U.S. Recommended Daily Allowance (RDA) and these are usually more expensive than other cereals. The USDA says that if your diet includes a variety of foods, then cereals with 100 percent of all the vitamins and minerals you need daily are an unnecessary expense. Hot cereals, like oatmeal and other whole-grain cereals, provide the most fiber. Regular and quick-cooking types of hot cereal are much lower in sodium than instant cereals sold in individual servings.

Here is information about some of the most commonly available grains in our diets.

■ **Amaranth** is high in protein and tastes a bit like peppery sesame seeds. The seeds are very small and tend to stick to the pot when you cook with them so it's best to use nonstick cookware and nonstick spray. Many people add amaranth when cooking other grains such as quinoa or cornmeal. Follow the directions on the box for cooking.

■ **Barley** has a somewhat nutty flavor. Traditionally it's been used in stews and soups, but lately it is also served as a starch course or filler in salads. Scotch barley has more fiber and is less refined (still has the bran on) than pearl barley, which has the hull, bran, and germ removed. Barley keeps about 6 months in an airtight container in a cool cupboard. Directions and recipes for cooking barley are found on the box.

■ **Buckwheat** has a nutty flavor and buckwheat flour is a main ingredient in Japanese soba noodles and other types of noodles. Buckwheat kernels are known also as groats or kasha, which are cracked to different degrees of coarseness. Follow the box directions for the different ways to use buckwheat flour or groats (kasha).

■ **Hominy, grits, or cornmeal,** used to be a mainstay of Southern cooking but now they are appreciated in other parts of the country. Fresh corn on the cob is always a treat. Dried and reconstituted corn kernels have a nuttier flavor and can be used in various ways other than just the starchy vegetable with a meal. Add them to soups and stews. Grits and cornmeal are dried and milled corn kernels and are usually used to make breakfast grits and cornbread—both favorites of mine! The difference between regular- and stone-ground cornmeal is that the stone ground has the oily germ and is higher in fiber and mineral content.

Hominy is dried corn treated with an alkaline product and cracked into meal for hominy grits or ground into flour for masa harina, which is used to make tortillas. Whole dried white or gold hominy is available in cans, ready to heat and eat or to use in recipes.

■ **Polenta** is made by adding dry cornmeal to boiling water or stock. It is served various ways. Italians sprinkle it with Parmesan cheese before serving. Cold cooked polenta that has been molded into a roll, can be sliced, and browned in butter and then served with sauces. And now you can buy polenta in plastic tube bags, just like ready-to-use cookie dough, that's ready to use as you wish. See the package or an Italian cookbook for ideas.

■ **Millet** that is sold for food is not the same millet sold as birdseed. "People" millet has the hulls removed and is cooked like couscous for a side dish or it can be mixed with other grains, such as rice. Store it in the refrigerator to prevent its getting rancid.

■ **Oats** are familiar to most of us as oatmeal, a hot cereal that makes winter more bearable. Oats get milled and then are processed by being cut or steamed and rolled so that they will cook faster and keep longer on the shelf. The more they are processed in this manner, the faster they cook. Oat groats (also called steel-cut or Scotch oats or Irish oatmeal) are not processed as much as rolled oats and so they have more oil content and need to be stored in the refrigerator. They don't get as mushy as regular oats when cooked for cereal. Oats give a sort of sweet taste when they are added to multigrain breads.

■ **Quinoa** cooks quickly and is high in protein and minerals. It needs to be refrigerated to prevent its getting rancid. It can be used as a substitute for rice in pilafs or salads or mixed with other grains to give a nutty taste to recipes.

■ **Rice** is a staple food throughout the world. Brown rice is rice with the bran and germ still on it so that it has more fiber, vitamins, and minerals than white rice, which has been refined. Brown rice should be kept in the refrigerator and used within a month. White rice can keep a year on the cupboard shelf and cooks faster than brown rice. You will see rice identified by the length of the grain when you shop for rice. Long-grain rice is longer than it is wide and the cooked kernels will be fluffy and separate easily. Medium- and short-grained rice kernels are shaped more like an oval and contain more starch so the kernels are apt to stick together when cooked. Short-grained (sticky) rice is favored for Asian cooking. You will also find red and black rice at the supermarket, and these have more of the bran still on them so they will need long cooking times. Please read the package for cooking directions.

- **Rye** is rich in minerals and rye berries are cooked as a grain side dish; they can also be mixed with white rice for more flavor. Rye flour is more familiar to most of us than rye berries because we've had rye breads. Rye grain is also used in the making of rye whiskey. You will find many versions of rye bread: Frequently rye flour is combined with cornmeal and whole wheat flour and seeds, such as caraway, are added for extra flavor. Pumpernickel is a form of rye bread. When researching material for this book, I learned that it is named for Pumper Nickel, the Swiss baker who made it because he was trying to stretch his supply of wheat flour during a wheat shortage.

- **Triticale** is a hybrid of wheat and rye and its often mixed with wheat flour in breads. Its berries can be cooked the same way as wheat berries.

- **Wheat** is certainly one of our most familiar grains. Whole kernels that have the grain and germ still on are called wheat berries and they are very nutritious. Cooked, they are used in salads or pilafs or mixed with other grains. Cracked wheat is the result of milled wheat berries and it is either coarsely ground to be cooked like white rice or milled finely to be used in dough and batter. Bulgur is made of steamed, dried, and milled wheat berries. It doesn't need to be cooked, just softened in boiling water and allowed to stand a minute or two. Couscous is coarsely ground semolina, the hard-wheat flour used to make pasta. Most couscous has been presteamed and dried so that it cooks quickly by adding boiling water and allowed to sit for a minute or so. Wheat germ is a good fiber to add to cereals, breads, and other grain dishes. It has a lot of oil and so must be refrigerated after opening to prevent its getting rancid.

- **Wild rice** is not really rice but it is cooked the same way. Actually, most of our "wild" rice these days is cultivated instead of wild but it is still relatively expensive, and hand-harvested wild rice is more expensive than the machine-harvested grain. Kernels are partially hulled in the processing and the cooking time depends on how much processing was done; follow the instructions on the container.

PASTA

Whether you call it pasta or noodles, it's a basic food in our American diet. And the Italians have given pastas poetic and descriptive names. Fresh pasta is usually made from unbleached all-purpose flour and dried pasta is usually made with durum semolina flour. Both flours are moistened with eggs, water, or wine and may have seasonings, herbs, or pureed vegetables, like spinach, added. The rule of pasta, whether you buy it fresh or dried, is to always cook it in lots of boiling water, which is about 6 quarts to 1 pound of pasta and add 1 tablespoon of salt for each 3 quarts of water. If you cook too much pasta in too little water it's likely to stick together and cook unevenly. Overcooking pasta is also a no-no because it gets too mushy. Pasta is best cooked to *al dente* which means "to the teeth," or firmly to the bite. Here are a few of the more popular pastas, along with substitutes and cooking times.

- **Capellini** (angel hair) is a fine, thin, long pasta that cooks in just 2 to 4 minutes. It is best served with light sauces or tossed with fresh herbs and oil. You can substitute vermicelli or spaghettini.

- **Conchiglie** (shells) looks like conch shells and comes in different sizes. It cooks in 8 to 20 minutes and is often put into soups, casseroles, and salads in addition to being served with sauce. Substitute ziti, penne, fusilli, or orecchiette.

- **Farfalle** (butterflies or bowties) looks like little bowties. It cooks in 9 to 12 minutes and is often served with sauces or primavera (with vegetables). Substitute shells, short fusilli, sedani, or penne.

- **Fettuccine** (ribbons) is a flat, long pasta, sometimes found as a roll of noodles. It's a favorite with cream (Alfredo) and other sauces. It cooks in 7 to 9 minutes and you can substitute tagliatelle.

- **Filled pastas** include the popular ravioli, capelletti, and tortellini. Cook them gently so that they don't fall apart; they are usually done when they float to the top. Capelletti or tortellini is made from fresh pasta that is rolled flat and then cut into rounds; filling is placed in the center and then the rounds are folded in half and the edges sealed. The half-circle is then bent and the ends are twisted together to hold the filling in. Tortellini are usually filled with meat and capelletti are filled with cheese or other fillings. Ravioli are squares with filling between two layers; cook like capelletti or tortellini. All can be served with sauces or in consommé for soup that's also the whole meal.

- **Fusilli** (corkscrews) comes in long and short forms, and the short ones are good for "mac and cheese." The others are used with sauces and in casseroles. Cook the long fusilli for 8 to 12 minutes and the short for 10 to 15 minutes (the short are thicker). You can substitute penne, bigoli, bucatini, sedani, medium shells, farfalle, or rotelle.

- **Gnocchi** (dumplings) is served with various sauces. Potato gnocchi cooks for 6 minutes and semolina gnocchi is baked for 25 minutes. Because these are not really noodles, substitutions are not recommended.

- **Lasagna** is the favorite pasta to use when cooking for a crowd. It's easy to make and some of the new lasagna noodles need not be boiled first but can be put into the casserole with sauce and cheeses in a one-step procedure. When cooked before use, lasagna is boiled 9 to 15 minutes. An old Italian cookbook in my collection says that in Italy a mother would make lasagna as wide as her children's mouths opened.

- **Linguine** (little tongues) are long, slightly flattened noodles that can be served with various sauces; they cook in only 5 to 8 minutes.

- **Orzo** looks like very long, large grains of rice and it's especially good in soups. It cooks in 10 to 13 minutes.

- **Penne** looks like old-fashioned quill pens; it is hollow pasta that holds sauces as well. It cooks in 10 to 15 minutes, and you can substitute shells or short fusilli.

- **Spaghetti** (little strings) is so versatile and can be served with a variety of sauces. In dry form it cooks in 7 to 8 minutes.

- **Vermicelli** (little worms) is a long, thin noodle that is often served with lighter sauces, such as garlic and oil; it cooks in only 4 to 6 minutes. You can substitute capellini.

- **Ziti** is a hollow short tube that holds sauce well. It cooks in 12 to 18 minutes. You can substitute rigatoni or penne.

- **Asian noodles** are usually made with wheat flour and come in several thicknesses and shapes. Also popular are several types of rice flour noodles. Japanese soba noodles are made from buckwheat flour. The very popular Japanese ramen noodles are the same as the Chinese egg noodles called mein.

- Some **German noodles** are different from Italian noodles. For example: Germans have potato dumplings (balls of mashed or sieved potatoes thickened with egg and flour) and spaetzle (egg dumplings made from a flour, egg, and water batter) that are cooked by dropping spoonfuls into boiling broth. Special spaetzle makers are sold in gourmet cooking stores; they look like a hand grater with a hopper attached; you put the batter in the hopper and work it back and forth over the grater so that the little spatzle fall into the soup or broth.

❃ KITCHENEERING HUMOR ❃

A friend of mine who lived in Germany for a few years said she bought a spaetzle maker and made spaetzle once and only once. It seems she didn't much care for standing over a boiling pot of steaming water—said it cleared her sinuses but frizzed her hair and fogged her glasses.

Grain, Rice, and Noodle Mixes

There are many types of grain and pasta mixes available. They can be used as side dishes or main dishes if you add meat or other protein. Sometimes it is more costly to use mixes with packaged seasonings than it is to make up your casseroles, pilafs, pancakes, biscuits, breads, and cakes from scratch, but the convenience may be well worth the extra cost. Your time and energy have to be considered. Also, if you don't keep a lot of seasonings, spices, herbs, and so forth on hand you'll need to buy all these things (and replace them often so that they are always fresh) so that you can make recipes from scratch, which may end up costing you more money than if you use mixes. Convenience foods used to be too salty to be healthy, but now many food companies provide low-salt versions of their mixes.

Storing

When I buy raw cereals, flour, rice, and certain other packaged foods, I put them into glass jars to prevent bug traffic from one food to the other. I save the cooking instructions and put them into the jar or tape them on the outside. Big gallon pickle jars make my favorite canisters.

❃ **HELOISE HINT:** If you store foodstuffs made from grain, especially flour and cornmeal, in the freezer for at least 7 days after bringing them home, any visible or invisible infestations will be destroyed and you won't have to share your groceries and cupboards with uninvited crawly guests.

■ **Whole grains**, such as brown rice and millet, will not store as long as refined grains, such as white rice and pearl barley. Grains that are higher in oil content, such as quinoa and wheat germ, can become rancid quickly and should be stored in the refrigerator as soon as you buy them or certainly after you open the container. It's best to buy other whole grains in amounts you will use in about 1 month and then store them in tightly covered jars in the cupboard or sealed in freezer-quality plastic bags either in the refrigerator or the freezer. If grains have an odor before you cook them or a bitter taste after you cook them, they are spoiled or rancid.

■ The National Food Safety Data Base recommends storing **cornmeal** in the refrigerator, especially in the summer.

■ **Cooked grains** can usually be stored in the refrigerator for 3 days. They may keep a few days longer when cooked in water instead of cooked with stock or other ingredients.

■ If you don't eat **bread** fast enough to prevent it from getting stale or moldy, double-bag the loaf, with a bag from a previous loaf. Close the bags tightly with twist ties or a spring clothespin and store in the freezer. When you remove a serving of bread, try leaving the heel plus one or two slices frozen together on the end to protect the remaining slices from drying out. To thaw frozen bread slices, either toast or zap in the microwave (10 to 20 seconds per one or two slices on Low or the Defrost setting). Commercially baked bread keeps about 3 months in the freezer. For unbaked frozen bread dough, check the label for storage instructions.

■ Make batches of **pancakes** or **waffles** larger than you need for one meal. Prepare as usual but cook the extras until done but not totally browned. Cool on racks. Put the pancakes into a freezer-safe bag or container, separated with wax paper, and freeze. To serve, heat in the microwave oven for about 1½ minutes on Medium or heat in a toaster.

■ Store **pasta** in well-sealed containers to prevent insects from getting into these foods. Please see the section on general storage hints.

■ **Cereal** will keep fresh longer if you seal the inside bags tightly with a spring clothespin or twist tie. Or keep in airtight containers.

■ Store **uncooked rice** in a well-sealed container to prevent infestation by insects. **Cooked rice,** covered tightly, keeps about 1 week in the refrigerator.

■ Keep **soup/oyster crackers** in a well-washed and dried plastic quart or gallon-size jug with a lid. You'll have a handy pouring container and airtight storage to keep the crackers fresh.

Cooking

BREAD BAKING

Baking bread and setting dough to rise can present challenges but there are many solutions. Readers have sent me lots of ideas based on their experience and I am happy to share the best of these with you here.

■ Put the rack into your **microwave oven** (if your oven has one) and place a pan of very warm water on the bottom of the oven and the bowl with the dough to rise on the rack. Cover with a clean dishtowel. *Do not* turn on the microwave for this. If your microwave has no rack, use a cake-cooling rack or place a container of very warm water beside the bowl of dough. The microwave provides a draft-free environment, which is ideal for the dough to rise.

■ Preheat your **conventional oven** to warm for just 5 minutes, turn it off, and leave the door closed. Cover the bowl of dough with a clean dishtowel and pop it into the oven. The temperature should stay about right if you don't open the door too often.

■ Turn the **oven light** on. It will usually maintain just enough low heat to allow the dough to rise.

■ Place a **pan of hot water** in the oven on a lower shelf and place the dough in the covered bowl on the rack above it. Change the water if it cools off.

■ Heat a **slow cooker** to only its lowest warm setting. Place the dough in the container and cover loosely with a clean dishtowel. Unplug the cooker and let the dough rise.

■ Put the dough where the **sun** will shine on it, cover the bowl loosely with a clean dishtowel. Let solar heat do the work.

■ Turn the **clothes dryer** on for a few minutes, turn it off, set the bowl of dough on the floor of the drum and close the door. (Be sure to let people know that the dryer is being used for bread raising by posting a big sign on the door.)

❀ KITCHENEERING HUMOR ❀

A reader tried the dryer method noted above. Instead of just putting the bread dough into the dryer on the drum, she put a cookie sheet in and balanced the dough bowl on it. But she forgot to turn the dryer off and so when she closed the door, the drum revolved one full turn before she could stop it. The good news was that drum rotated so quickly that the dough bowl and cookie sheet didn't even move and ended up exactly as they had begun. So, she suggests that an unbreakable stainless-steel bowl would be the best for this hint, just in case you get a science-class demonstration of centrifugal force right there in your laundry room.

BREAD CRUMBS AND STALE BREAD

■ To make **bread crumbs** if you don't have stale bread, grate frozen bread; it gets "crummy" more easily than fresh, unfrozen bread.

■ As a **bread crumb substitute,** seasoned croutons are a tasty alternative to plain bread.

❀ **HELOISE HINT:** Crush commercially packaged croutons with a potato masher in the bowl that you'll use for mixing meat loaf or in a shallow dish or plate you'll be use for dipping the meat to be breaded.

■ Other **bread crumb substitutes:** unprocessed bran, wheat germ, crushed dry corn flakes, or other nonsugared packaged breakfast cereal.

■ **Stale bread** (especially cinnamon-raisin bread) makes good bread pudding. Almost any variety old bread that's been dried, cubed, and oven toasted makes good croutons or, if crushed, interesting bread crumbs.

✿ **HELOISE HINT:** To crush dried bread, put it into a sturdy plastic bag, expel the air, place it on the countertop and crush with a rolling pin.

■ Bread that's **stale but still soft** can be pushed into greased muffin cups, baked until toasty, then used as an eggcup for your poached eggs.

■ **Stale bread** makes good French toast or, when cut into cubes and dipped in beaten egg or egg substitute, "egg cubes." Egg cubes are basically French toast in pieces. Cut the bread into squares, add them to the beaten egg or egg substitute as you would with French toast, stir, then fry stirring them occasionally so that the cubes aren't one big mass. The cubes are quick and easy to make and children like them because the pieces are small.

■ **"Quick cookie" treat:** Dip days-old bread slices into sweetened condensed milk, then in flaked coconut, and then place on a baking sheet. Toast in a hot oven until the bread is hot and the coconut is brown.

■ Use **day-old French bread** to make bread pudding. Or slice stale French bread, bake it until brown and hard, sprinkle it with your favorite grated cheese, and melt the cheese in the oven for a few minutes. Float the crispy, cheese bread slice in a bowl of any kind of soup. Or make croutons for salads, soups, or snacks by baking French bread cubes in a 275 degree F oven for 30 to 45 minutes or until golden brown and crunchy. For flavorful variation, drizzle cubes before baking with a spiced butter mix-

ture. (Butter mixture for one-half loaf of French bread is one stick of butter or margarine, 1 teaspoon of minced basil—fresh is best—and two cloves of minced garlic.) Place the cubes in a roasting pan, drizzle spiced butter mixture over all and bake as directed above. Store in a tightly sealed plastic container or jar. Or for a quick breakfast or light supper, cut stale bread into cubes; mix with beaten eggs and fry in a small amount of butter or margarine as you would with French toast. Serve with or without syrup.

■ Flavor **the dipping for French toast** with a dash of vanilla or other flavored extract, or a bit of chocolate syrup.

OTHER BREAD HINTS

■ If you are limiting the bread you eat, you can make **thin toast** by first toasting a slice of bread then carefully cutting it horizontally through the soft middle with a serrated edge knife. The toasted sides will hold the bread together and guide your knife for easy cutting. Put sandwich filling on the untoasted sides for a whole, but skinny, bread sandwich or spread the pieces with fruit preserves.

■ **Cinnamon toast variation:** For something new, mix a bit of instant coffee with the cinnamon and sugar for coffee toast. Or try mixing in granulated orange drink with the sugar to sprinkle on your buttered toast.

■ For a different **topping for pancakes or French toast,** heat up chunky-style applesauce with 1 or 2 teaspoons of cinnamon and spoon it on to add the nutrition of fruit instead of just sugar from syrup. Or sprinkle with powdered sugar or drizzle with a maple and chocolate syrup mix.

■ **Pancake fun:** When you make pancakes, put the batter in a cake decorating tube (or pour with a spoon if you are handy) and then make faces or write names with the pancake batter; cook as usual. Or instead of one large round pancake, make squiggles, critters (one larger, plus one smaller circle with two ear dots and a tail can be any critter), or just large initials of the pancake lovers.

■ **Squirt bottle for pancakes:** Put pancake batter in a clean squirt bottle, such as one from ketchup, then you can squirt batter into the pan with ease, especially if you are making silver-dollar pancakes for children. In fact, if you are a slow starter in the morning, you can make the pancake batter the night before and store it in the squirt bottle so it will be ready to use in the morning.

■ **Keep pancakes or waffles warm** in a bun warmer until the whole batch is cooked, then you can serve everyone at once, including the pancake maker, who often ends up eating alone.

■ **Pancakes for small children:** To avoid sticky messes, cut up the pancakes or waffles and add the syrup before serving them and serve in soup bowls instead of plates.

■ **Quick dumplings:** Flour tortillas cut into strips or bite-size pieces and then dropped into hot broth to cook for a few minutes can substitute for homemade dumplings. Or cut canned home-style or buttermilk biscuits into quarters and drop them into hot broth.

GRAINS AND OATMEAL

■ Before cooking **bulk purchased grains**, you should put them in a fine mesh sieve and rinse with cold water to let the chaff and other debris to wash off or come to the surface. Then pick them over with your fingers to remove any remaining debris such as tiny stones or twigs. Grains sold in boxes are usually clean and ready to cook.

■ **Reheat cooked grains** in the microwave or in a pot on the stove:

In the **microwave**, spread a single serving on a microwave-safe plate, cover with plastic wrap and microwave on High for 1 to 2 minutes. To heat more than a single serving in a bowl, sprinkle the surface lightly with water, cover with plastic wrap, and microwave on High for about 1½ minutes per cup of food. Stir before serving.

To reheat in a **pot on the stove**, put a small amount of water in the pot, plus 1 or 2 tablespoons of water and the grain; simmer, covered, over medium heat until it's the proper serving temperature. You can also use bouillon instead of water to reheat grains for added, fresher flavor.

■ **Oatmeal:** Add fresh or dried chopped fruit; nuts; chocolate, peanut-flavored, or butterscotch chips; or crumbs from the bottom of the box of dry cereals to make oatmeal crunchier and to add different flavors. The old favorite additions are brown sugar, cinnamon, raisins, applesauce, honey, and molasses.

■ **Oatmeal granola in yogurt:** Add a little dry instant oatmeal (let it set a few minutes) to fruited or regular yogurt to add extra fiber. It won't look pretty but it tastes good, especially if you add a few chopped nuts as well.

RICE

- To make **rice cereal treats** with less mess, cover the mixture in the pan with clear plastic wrap. Then, press the mixture down into the pan with your hands. The top will be smooth and your hands won't get sticky.

- **Rice cakes** can be the base for quick meals.

> **Spread them** with margarine and sprinkle with cinnamon and sugar or spread them with peanut butter and jelly.
>
> **Make them Mexican:** Spread on refried beans, a bit of sour cream, top with grated Cheddar or Monterey Jack cheese, and then heat in the oven for a few minutes.
>
> **Make them Italian:** Spread with Italian sauce; top with some mozzarella, provolone, and/or Parmesan cheese; and heat until the cheese melts.

- To **keep rice from sticking** to the pot while cooking, spray the inside bottom and sides of the pot with nonstick vegetable spray before adding the water or rice.

- **Never-fail rice:** You don't really need any special pot for cooking rice. Follow the directions on the package. The usual way is to measure out 2 cups of water to 1 cup of regular white rice. When the water comes to boil, add the rice, about ¼ teaspoon of salt, and 1 teaspoon of butter, margarine, or oil. Stir, lower the heat to simmer, and let cook on low heat for 20 minutes. Brown rice is cooked the same way, except that you need 2½ cups of water to 1 cup of rice and it needs to cook for 40 minutes. Wild rice, which is a tasty grain that's not truly rice but is served as rice, is often blended with rice or other grains, so the best advice is to follow the directions on the package.

✿ **CLASSIC HELOISE HINT FOR INSTANT RICE MAKEOVER:** My mother suggested adding frozen peas, in an amount appropriate to the amount of rice, to the boiling water. Bring the water back to a boil, add the instant rice, stir once, cover, and cook for the time recommended on the box. The peas will put some green and some crunch into the rice. For extra color, add about five drops of yellow food color to the water before you add the rice; the whole dish will look buttery delicious without the calories of butter.

- Enliven **leftover rice** with bacon bits, bell peppers, peas, onions, cut celery, or other veggies as you heat all in a frying pan. Then add one or two eggs or egg substitute mixed with soy sauce to taste for a quick lunch.

PASTA

- **Colored noodles:** My mother added ten drops of yellow food color to one box of plain noodles as they cooked to make them look more appetizing. No butter, egg, or cheese calories added, she said! For holidays or just for fun, add a few drops of food color to the cooking water for macaroni and other noodles and you'll have colors appropriate to the holiday, the favorite colors of a birthday child, or just fun colors instead of blah white noodles. To make multicolored pasta for a festive dish, cook pasta as usual, and then separate into portions and color each portion as desired. A nonmessy way to do this is to put a few drops of food color in a jar, add cooked macaroni, cover, and shake until all the noodles are the desired color. You can buy colored pasta, but the colors won't be bright (if that's what you want) and may not be the colors you need for a particular holiday: pink or yellow for Easter; red and green for Christmas, orange for Halloween, and so forth.

▪ If you **make your own noodles**, let the dough rest for about 20 minutes after you roll it out so that it gets slightly dry before you cut it, the noodles will be easier to handle. For easiest cutting, cut the noodles into strips with a disk-type pizza cutter.

▪ **Lasagna shortcut:** You don't have to cook the noodles before assembling lasagna. Layer the hard, uncooked lasagna noodles in the pan with the other ingredients and then increase the amount of sauce and cheese slightly to provide more liquid; bake as usual. You may want to experiment a time or two before you do this for guests to find out how much more sauce is needed for this method; sauce amounts in individual recipes vary so the increased amount of liquid will vary.

▪ **Avoid boil overs and stuck pasta** by greasing the inside rim of the pot or spray with nonstick spray before putting the water in to boil. Also spray the colander so that draining pasta won't stick to it.

❀ **CLASSIC HELOISE HINTS FOR NOODLES:** Here's my mother's method for no-burn, cooked-just-right noodles:

1. Bring 2 to 3 quarts of water to a *rolling boil,* add salt, and then add macaroni slowly so the water continues to boil. Stir quickly with a spoon so that the hot water touches all of the macaroni.

2. Put the lid on the pan, give the lid a twist to seal, then turn off the burner and allow the lid to remain on the pot for 20 minutes. *Do not* lift the lid to peek inside during that 20 minutes.

3. After 20 minutes, remove the pan from the stove, pour the macaroni into a colander to drain off the water, and serve. If you are not serving the noodles immediately, rinse with cold water to prevent overcooking. Then you can reheat the noodles with a brief bath in hot water to serve.

▪ You might want to make **extra noodles** to store in a zipper bag to add to soups and casseroles or just to reheat with a bit of butter or olive oil, garlic, optional vegetable bits, and cheese for a quick meal.

▪ **A READER RECOMMENDS:**
Add browned meat, kidney beans, and chili powder to leftover tomato sauce for instant chili con carne.

▪ Make a "**spaghetti dog**" by using leftover pasta sauce on hot dogs. Sprinkle on some shredded Parmesan or Romano cheese and you'll have the Italian answer to the chili dog.

▪ **Save leftover spaghetti sauce** in a small plastic freezer bag, expel all air, flatten the bag-o'-sauce, and freeze it flat. (Flat freezing saves freezer space and allows the food to thaw more quickly!) The next time you need a bit of sauce you can easily thaw it in heatproof container of hot water and then put it on pasta, or just dump it on the hot noodles, which will melt the sauce!

- To **prevent steam buildup** while a sauce cooks and the boil-over mess on the stove, let some steam escape by putting a wooden toothpick between the pot and its lid.

Serving

BREADS

- Serving **frozen breads:** If you freeze sliced bread or rolls because you don't eat them fast enough, frozen bread slices thaw in the microwave if you toss them in, thaw on High for 10 to 20 seconds for one slice or one small roll. If you freeze bagels or English muffins for the same reason, slice them before freezing them so that they will be easier to pry open if the centers don't thaw completely in the microwave.

- To **heat soft dinner rolls** before serving, wet your hands under the faucet and then flick the droplets off your fingers over the rolls before you seal them in foil for reheating in a conventional oven. Those few drops of water will help add moisture and prevent the rolls from getting too dry while they heat.

- **Cereal** eating can be a drippy mess when kids are just learning to feed themselves. If your child likes yogurt, mix dry cereal with vanilla or fruited yogurt instead of milk. It sticks to the spoon and the extra nutrition sticks to the ribs, too. Low-fat yogurt and milk are about equal in calories per amount.

- **Leftover hot dog or hamburger buns** can be transformed into quick garlic bread. Spread with margarine or olive oil, sprinkle with garlic salt or garlic powder, and toast under the broiler until slightly browned. You can also sprinkle on other herbs, such as oregano, marjoram, or parsley, for added color and flavor.

- **Open-faced bagel sandwiches** need not be only lox and cream cheese. Try cream cheese and other lunch meats for variety, especially when you need something different for lunch.

- **Pita sandwiches** are popular. Substitute pita breads for plain old sliced bread to add variety to lunches. If you are putting such sandwiches in the lunch box, remember that if the filling is too drippy, the pita will get soggy and fall apart. If the sandwich is for an adult or older child, you could put the filling in a margarine tub so that it could be put into the pita just before eating.

CEREALS AND PANCAKES

- **Hot cereal on the run:** There are no kitchen police to tell you that your cereal must be in a bowl. If you are in a hurry, you can put hot cereal in a cup, add enough warm milk so that you can "drink" it. This is also a good way to serve cooked cereal in a less messy way to a child.

- I get lots of hints on how to **prevent sugar from sinking to the bottom of the bowl.** One reader suggested dissolving the sugar in the milk before pouring it on the cereal, but the easiest way is to pour milk on the cereal first, then sprinkle on the sugar. The sugar granules will stick to the moist cereal.

- **Cereal saver:** Make a custom blend of different cereals by mixing all the last few ounces of cereal left in the boxes into one "cereal surprise."

- **Cereal snack:** When children prefer to eat cereals that have the nutritional value of a cookie, mix the sweet favorites with real-food cereals and serve them as snack.

POPCORN

▪ **Edible popcorn serving cups** can be used to hold nuts or small candies instead of using paper party treat containers. Make a recipe of popcorn balls using a mix sold for that purpose. Instead of forming balls, shape the popcorn ball mix over the bottoms and sides of glasses that have been well greased with margarine. After the mixture hardens, remove the cups from the glasses and fill with goodies. You could also use small glass custard cups for this purpose.

▪ **Gourmet popcorn** is easy: Sprinkle popcorn with seasoned salts, salt-free herb blends, dry salad dressing mixes, taco or chili seasoning mixes, or grated hard cheeses (such as Parmesan, Romano, and/or Cheddar). You can take the powdered Cheddar from macaroni and cheese dinners for this if you can't find powdered Cheddar. Save the noodles for a casserole.

✿ **HELOISE TOOTHSAVER HINT FOR SERVING POPCORN:** Put popcorn into resealable plastic bags after it's cooled. Cut a small hole in the corner of the bag and give the whole thing a good shake so that unpopped kernels fall out of the hole. There'll be no surprises to your bridgework when you bite down!

TORTILLAS

▪ **Tortillas**, especially flour ones, can substitute for hot dog buns or other rolls when you are serving sausage or wieners. To soften a tortilla so that it wraps around a sausage, heat it in the microwave for 20 seconds on High. CAUTION: It will be hot, so handle with care.

▪ **Tortilla finger sandwiches** are easy to make from flour or other soft, fresh tortillas. Spread a fresh tortilla (one that is soft and easy to roll or one that has been softened in the microwave and cooled slightly) spread with a filling, roll up, chill in the refrigerator, then cut crosswise into 1-inch pinwheel finger sandwiches. If the pinwheels want to unroll, secure them roll with a toothpick. (Colored ones are nice and safer, too, because they will be noticed more easily.) Here are some suggested fillings, or use any combination you like, just as long as there is some binding agent like cream cheese or guacamole to serve as a "glue" for the pinwheel and everything is sliced thinly so you can roll up the tortilla:

Cream cheese mixed with herbs or spices.
Cream cheese, a thin slice of ham, thin slice of cheese, and a lettuce leaf.
Guacamole sauce applied in a thin layer, very finely shredded head lettuce or a leaf of leaf lettuce.

RICE AND PASTA

▪ Use a **measuring cup to scoop rice** out of the pot. It makes a nice compact shape and you'll know exactly how much you are eating if you are counting your carbohydrates.

▪ **Leftover ravioli or tortellini** make a great addition to soup. Or just cook some in the soup. Ravioli and tortellini, fresh or dried, will fall apart when cooked too long, so if you are adding them to soup, leave them in the soup pot just long enough to heat through.

■ **Easy-to-eat-spaghetti:** Serve with a table-spoon so that you can twirl long pasta with your fork against the bowl of the spoon. Try teaching children the twirling technique (they'll need to master it some time to keep up appearances at important corporate dinners) but it's okay to cut long pasta for the sake of your sanity.

DAIRY

Dairy products are such a versatile addition to any menu for people of any age, and their use ranges from beverages to main dishes to desserts. If you don't like to drink milk, there are plenty of alternatives with yogurt, cheese, and recipes made with dairy products.

Shopping

The USDA reminds us that dairy products are good sources of calcium and protein. You will find a broad range of calorie and fat content in the different products, and for nutrition's sake, you need to read labels carefully and compare serving sizes with the calorie counts of different brands of products. Labels will also tell you the sodium and calcium content in milligrams so that you can compare these ingredients, too. The calcium, calorie, and fat contents listed here are average; specific brands may have different counts.

CHEESE

Cheese making is the way farmers have dealt with their surplus milk ever since humans kept herd animals. The process is simple. A sub-stance called rennet gets added to milk, which causes the milk to divide into two parts: curds and whey. Whey is the remaining liquid and the curd is the semisolid stuff we call cheese. If the curd is fresh, then it is used as cottage cheese, cream cheese, ricotta, and so on. If the curd is fermented, it becomes either soft cheese (such as Camembert) or hard cheese (such as Cheddar or Parmesan). Each cheese-making region has its own variations of basic types of cheese, and so cheese eating is an adventure in tasting and testing.

Natural cheeses made with part skim milk are lower in fat than those made with whole milk. Low-moisture mozzarella made with part skim milk has 80 calories and 5 grams of fat, and 205 milliliters of calcium per ounce. Natural Swiss cheese has 105 calories and 8 grams of fat, and 270 milliliters of calcium, per ounce; natural Cheddar has 110

USDA Recommended Daily Servings for Dairy Products

One serving equals 1 cup of milk, 8 ounces of yogurt, 1½ ounces of natural cheese, or 2 ounces of process cheese.

Two servings from entire group daily for most people.

Three servings for women who are pregnant or breast-feeding and for teens.

Four servings for teens who are pregnant or breast-feeding.

Cheese Classifications

Cheeses are classified as *very hard* (for grating), *hard, semisoft, or soft* and as *ripened* or *unripened*. The storage times vary, with very hard cheeses keeping longer than very soft ones.

The following are classified as *ripened cheeses*.

- *Very hard:* Asiago, Parmesan, Romano, sapsago, and Spalen.
- *Hard:* Cheddar, granular or stirred curd, caciocavallo, Swiss, Emmentaler, and Gruyère.
- *Semisoft:* brick, Muenster, Limburger, Port-Salut, Trappist, Roquefort, Gorgonzola, blue, Stilton, and Wensleydale.
- *Soft:* Bel Paese, Brie, Camembert, cooked, hand, and Neufchâtel (as made in France).

The following are considered *unripened* cheeses, they are also *soft* cheeses:

- Cottage
- Pot
- Baker's cream
- Neufchâtel (as made in the United States)
- Mysost
- Primost
- Fresh ricotta

calories, and 9 grams of fat, and 200 milliliters of calcium per ounce. Some natural cheeses have been aged longer and so they are generally dryer. Harder, dryer cheeses are best grated before being melted for sauces or recipes. Some examples of aged, dryer natural cheeses are aged Cheddar, Parmesan, and Romano.

Processed cheeses, such as American cheese, have a lower melting point than natural cheeses, allowing them to melt more easily and faster. They are softer and creamier and so they need only be cut into cubes before melting for a sauce recipe. Process American cheese, cheese food, and cheese spreads are lower in calcium and higher in sodium than most natural cheeses. Process American cheese food has 95 calories, and 7 grams of fat, and 175 milliliters of calcium per ounce; process American cheese spread has 80 calories, 6 grams of fat, and 160 milliliters of calcium per ounce.

Here are just a few of the most popular cheeses:

- **Brie:** If you have noticed that the brie we have in the United States is not the same as the brie served in France, where it originated, your taste buds are right. Brie needs to be made with unpasteurized milk, but our laws prevent importation of cheeses made from unpasteurized milk, unless they have been aged for 60 days. Unfortunately, brie aged that long would not be edible anymore so French cheese makers either preserve the brie in a can or make it with pasteurized milk; either way, it changes the flavor.
- **Camembert:** This strong flavored cheese with its solid outer surface and runny insides is said to have been a favorite of Napoleon. Now it's a favorite with all sorts of people. It should always be served at room temperature to take advantage of the runny center. Brie is served the same way and is often put into a pastry crust

and baked. (And yes, you can eat that moldy looking outside of these aged soft cheeses.)

■ **Cheddar:** Originally made in Cheddar, England, this cheese has a sharp, tangy flavor. The longer it's aged, the sharper, tangier the flavor. Very sharp Cheddar crumbles and grates easily. Milder cheddars, sometimes called Cheshire or American cheeses, are usually used for sandwiches.

■ **Cottage Cheese:** Usually made from skim milk, cottage cheese is fresh and unfermented and is just about everyone's favorite diet food. Although low-fat cottage cheese is very low in fat, it is also relatively low in calcium and high in sodium compared to other dairy products: ½ cup of low-fat cottage cheese has 80 calories, 1 gram of fat, and 70 milliliters of calcium; ½ cup of creamed cottage cheese has 110 calories, 5 grams of fat, and 65 milliliters of calcium. Low-fat ricotta, which some people use interchangeably with cottage cheese in some recipes, has 170 calories, 10 grams of fat, and 335 milliliters of calcium in ½ cup. You will find large- and small-curd cheese, and in some parts of the country, it's available with added vegetables and/or fruits to make it more interesting to eat. The size of the curd is a matter of taste as is the choice of creamed or dry cottage cheese. Usually the creamed versions have more calories.

Cottage cheese can be pressed through a sieve or pureed in a blender or food processor to make a creamy base for dips or for use in making cheesecakes.

For a tasty diet lunch, try mixing about 1 cup of cottage cheese (any kind of your choice) with one large red apple (cut into ½-inch or larger cubes) and one or two stalks of celery (sliced). Serve on a big leaf of lettuce, or in a bowl with red carrots or raisins.

To make cottage cheese look better and to add flavor, add grated carrot and/or chopped chives or green onion tops.

Mix cottage cheese with canned pineapple chunks; you can also add grated carrot to this mixture.

Ricotta cheese is the best for lasagna, but cottage cheese can usually be used as a substitute. You should "drain" it to remove some liquid.

Ricotta cheese can substitute for cream cheese in some dips and as a spread on bagels.

■ **Cream cheese:** Cream cheese is fresh, unfermented cheese that is ideal as a base for spreads, frosting, crusts, and dips. You will also find regular, low-fat, and nonfat versions of cream cheese. Not all recipes for dips and cheesecakes will work if you substitute the low-fat or nonfat versions for the real thing. You may want to experiment with your favorite recipes to see if they will have the same or similar enough taste and texture when made with the substitutes. Also experiment with different brands of low-fat and nonfat cream cheese because some have a more acceptable taste and texture than others. Cream cheese is available already mixed with herbs and spices, ready to spread on crackers and toast.

Regular cream cheese has 100 calories and 10 grams of fat per ounce (2 tablespoons).

Plain, light cream cheese has 70 calories and five grams of fat per ounce (2 tablespoons).

Plain, nonfat cream cheese has 30 calories and no fat per ounce (2 tablespoons).

■ **Edam:** This Dutch cheese is mild and flavorful and distinguished by its bright red rind. At room temperature, it's spreadable. When used on a cheese board, it's attractive if you don't remove all of the rind so that the red color distinguishes the Edam from other similar-looking cheeses. Carefully cut through the rind, leaving about one-third to one-fourth of the cheese still covered. You can always pop off the remainder of the rind as the cheese is eaten.

■ **Feta:** Usually made from goat's milk, feta is popular in salads and in a variety of dishes. It has a creamy texture and strong flavor.

■ **Mozzarella:** Most familiar to pizza lovers, this soft, mild cheese melts well and gets a stringy texture. Originally it was made from buffalo's milk but today most of our mozzarella is made from cow's milk.

■ **Parmesan:** Named for the village in which it was first produced, Parmesan can be a sliced cheese if it is not fully aged. But most of it is fully aged and grated to be used in sauces and to top casseroles, pizza, pasta, and other dishes.

■ **Provolone:** Usually pear-shaped, this white cheese has a slightly smoky taste, which distinguishes it from Mozzarella cheese, which is the same color but is much milder.

■ **Roquefort:** The monks of the Roquefort region of France, who originated this cheese, used only ewe's milk. Roquefort cheese is known for its blue veining and pungent, sharp taste. Americans are fond of Roquefort bits in salads and in salad dressing.

■ **Stilton:** This is a strong-flavored, blue-veined aged English cheese. Try serving it with apples or tangerines, walnuts, and Port wine for a special dessert after a hearty meal.

■ **Swiss:** A nutty-flavored, pliable textured cheese with holes that form during the fermenting process, Swiss cheese is as good for eating as it is for cooking. Aged or imported Swiss cheeses, such as imported Gruyère or Emmentaler, often have a stronger flavor than everyday domestic types.

MILK

You will find more than just regular, skim, and low- or nonfat milks in the dairy case. Some milk is fortified with vitamin D and other nutrients; some have the lactose removed for those who are lactose intolerant. This milk comes in several forms, with 70 to 100 percent of the lactose removed and in low and nonfat versions also. I'm a big fan of the fat free version, it tastes "sweet" and rich like "real" milk. You'll need to read those labels to get information on the different brands and types of milk.

Here I've listed the food values of cow's milk, which is the most frequently purchased type of milk. Values are for 1 cup.

■ **Skim:** 90 calories, 1 gram of fat, and 315 milliliters of calcium.

■ **Low-fat (1 percent):** 105 calories, 2 grams of fat, and 315 milliliters of calcium.

■ **Low-fat (2 percent):** 125 calories, 5 grams of fat, and 315 milliliters of calcium.

■ **Whole:** 150 calories, 8 grams of fat, and 290 milliliters of calcium.

- **Buttermilk:** Buttermilk used to be the end product from churning cream into butter, but now specially prepared lactic acid cultures are added to pasteurized fresh skim milk and then the mixture is allowed to develop until it has the proper consistency and flavor, before it is cooled and bottled or boxed. When used in recipes, buttermilk adds a zesty flavor.

- **Cream:** Cream is made from the fat that rises to the top of nonhomogenized milk.

> **Whipping Cream** (heavy cream) contains at least 36 percent milk fat and is the richest. **Light whipping cream** contains 30 to 36 percent butterfat. Unwhipped cream is added to sauces and soups and is used to make ice cream. Whipped, it is used to garnish desserts and coffees.
>
> **Light cream** (coffee cream or table cream) is 15 to 18 percent butterfat and cannot be whipped. It's used in coffee and in some recipes.
>
> **Half-and-half** is a mixture of cream and milk with 10 to 18 percent butterfat. It can be used in coffee or tea and substitute for cream in some recipes.

- **Sour milks and creams:** These products are good for sauces and baking and include buttermilk, sour cream, crème fraîche (like English clotted cream), clotted or Devonshire cream, and yogurt.

- **Goat's milk:** Goat's milk is whiter and richer tasting than cow's milk. Its nutritional content is about the same, except that goat's milk usually contains more fat than cow's milk and isn't usually available in low-fat versions. People who are lactose intolerant or who are allergic to cow's milk need to avoid goat's milk as well.

MILK PRODUCTS

- **Frozen desserts**, such as sherbet, sorbet, and frozen yogurt are lower in fat than most ice cream and tofu-based frozen desserts. The lower fat content may not change the calorie count though, because many are high in sugar. *Do* read labels to compare before you buy.

- **Sour cream:** Sour cream, sometimes called cultured cream or Devon-style cream, is made from pasteurized, homogenized sweet cream of about 18 percent butterfat. A lactic acid culture is added to the milk, and the mixture incubates until the proper flavor and consistency have been attained. Then it is cooled and packaged. Rich in the protein, minerals, and vitamins found in milk, it adds a special zesty taste to recipes for sauces and dips and is used as a topping for various soups (add a dollop to float on top of a spicy soup just before serving for a cool taste), and for other foods, such as baked potatoes. Sour cream can be found in various forms: Regular, light, nondairy, and nonfat. The following nutritional information is for 2 tablespoons of sour cream:

> **Regular:** 60 calories and 5 to 6 grams of fat.
> **Light:** 40 calories and 2.5 grams of fat.
> **Nondairy:** 50 calories and 5 grams of fat.
> **Nonfat:** 20 to 35 calories and 0 grams of fat.

- **Yogurt:** Yogurt is a cultured milk with a custard consistency made by added specially prepared cultures to milk and then allowing the mixture to incubate under controlled conditions until the proper flavor and consistency are achieved. In the process, lactic acid inhibits the growth of certain bacteria, and so while being processed, yogurt is kept at 110 degrees F for about a half day while the milk sours and the lactic acid increases. After the process is finished, the yogurt is refrigerated. Some sources claim that live acidophilus (lactobacillus) in yogurt has certain health benefits; others say the amount available in one serving of yogurt is not significant enough to make a difference. I think that if you like yogurt, eat it as a nutritious food and enjoy! Yogurts vary widely in fat content; choose one made with skim or low-fat milk. Read labels to compare serving sizes with calorie counts. If you add your own fruit, you'll be getting less sugar than if you eat yogurt to which fruit is already added. Generally speaking, the nutritional content of 8 ounces (1 cup) is as follows:

Plain lowfat: 145 calories, 4 grams of fat, and 415 milliliters of calcium.

Flavored low-fat: 195 calories, 3 grams of fat, and 390 milliliters of calcium.

Fruited low-fat: 230 calories, 2 grams of fat, and 345 milliliters of calcium.

Fruited whole milk: 270 calories, 7 grams of fat, and 335 milliliters of calcium.

✿ **HELOISE HINT:** Plain regular yogurt (not low-fat, etc.) can sometimes substitute for sour cream in certain recipes.

Storing

CHEESE

▪ Cheeses should be **stored in the refrigerator.** Store sliced cheese in its original film wrapper. Wrap other cheeses with plastic wrap. Processed cheese, cheese food, and spreads sold in sealed jars or packages keep without refrigeration but must be refrigerated after opening. Aged cheeses generally last longer than soft cheeses, because they have less water to encourage the growth of spoilage-causing bacteria.

▪ **Moisture can cause cheese to mold.** Some people place a few sugar cubes in a zipper bag with the cheese. When the cubes get soggy in a few days, replace them. To prevent mold formation on large hunks of cheese, the traditional way is to wrap the cheese in a piece of cheesecloth (what else!) that has been moistened with vinegar; that's moistened, not dripping wet. Place the wrapped cheese in a plastic bag and into the refrigerator. The vinegar won't affect the cheese's taste, and you may have to sprinkle more vinegar on the cloth

---

Storage Times for Dairy Products

The following optimum storage times for dairy products are provided by the USDA.

Milk: 5 to 7 days.

Cottage cheese: 5 to 7 days.

Cheese, hard: several months.

Cheese, processed: 3 to 4 weeks.

Cream, in the carton: 1 week.

Evaporated milk, opened can: 1 week.

Ice cream (sherbet): 1 month in the freezer.

every now and then if you are going to store the cheese for several weeks.

▪ **Surfaced-ripened cheese:** Some cheeses like Camembert and Brie look moldy even when they are not. To make sure these cheeses are suitable for eating, they should pass the sniff test. If they have even a hint of the odor of ammonia, they are past their peak for eating. Don't buy them and don't eat them. My sources say that it is a cheese-seller's myth that the ammonia scent is okay.

▪ **Ripened cheeses** usually keep longer than unripened cheeses, so you can buy enough to last for several weeks. Most soft unripened cheeses are perishable and so it's best to buy only as much as you'll consume in a short time.

▪ **Freeze** some types of cheese but those like Cheddar may crumble after freezing, making them suitable for casseroles and salad toppings, but not good at all for sandwich slices.

MILK

▪ **Condensed milk** can be stored unopened in the cupboard for 15 months. Once opened, it must be refrigerated and will keep for 1 week in its original can.

▪ **Milk cubes:** If you live alone or just don't use a lot of milk within the "use by" date, pour some of the milk into an ice-cube tray, cover with plastic wrap and freeze. After the cubes are solid, store in a freezer safe plastic bag—then you can add "milk" and cool your coffee or tea at the same time! The cubes can also be used for cooking and baking. Just put the cubes into a microwave-safe, glass measuring cup and defrost in the microwave oven.

▪ **Dry powdered milk:** If you find yourself often throwing away milk because it sours before you can drink it all, try powdered milk. It has a long shelf life and when mixed with cold water, it can be palatable on cereal or in cooking.

❀ **HELOISE HINT:** If you mix up a quart or so of powdered dry milk and let it sit overnight in the refrigerator in a covered jar or pitcher, it will taste better.

Cooking

CHEESE

▪ **Cheese cooking:** Generally speaking, softer cheeses will melt to a runny consistency and harder cheeses will melt but not get runny unless thinned with milk or other liquids. For example, if you are making a cheeseburger or casserole, a soft processed cheese put on top and then heated or broiled will melt and drizzle down the sides of the burger or cover the top of the casserole, whereas a hard aged Cheddar or Parmesan will melt but will stay just about where you put it and form a firm topping. Choose the cheese to get the effect that you want.

▪ **Cheese leftovers** can be melted with skim milk (canned or fresh) to make a cheese sauce for vegetables or noodles or to make a cheese dip. The more different kinds of cheese, the more interesting the flavor. When melting cheese in a sauce, do it in a heavy pot or double-boiler, over low heat, and stir constantly to prevent the cheese from getting lumpy or stringy.

▪ **Grilled cheese sandwich:** Try this no-mess, no-frying, quick method for making a grilled cheese sandwich: Toast two slices of bread in the toaster, put cheese in between, heat in the microwave on Medium to High for 20 to 30 seconds, depending on the type of cheese and microwave wattage.

❀ **HELOISE HINT:** To keep the toast crisp, when making a grilled cheese sandwich in the microwave, put the sandwich on a paper towel or cheap paper plate before zapping; either one will absorb moisture.

▪ **Grating cheese:** Many people have a habit of abusing one or more fingers when they grate cheese on a grater. To prevent the pain, wear a thimble on the finger(s) that get grated with the cheese. If you are grating very hard Cheddar, Parmesan, or Romano cheeses, try using the shredding part of the hand grater instead of the part that makes the cheese into a more powdery texture. You'll get a better impression of the flavor when such cheeses are not sawdust textured.

▪ **Flavored cream cheese:** Perk up your breakfast by sprinkling flavored fruit gelatin on cream cheese after you've spread it on your English muffin, bagel, or toast.

MILK AND MILK PRODUCTS

▪ **Creamer for coffee:** No coffee cream? Use a spoonful of sweetened condensed milk—you'll get sugar and cream together.

▪ **Low-fat coffee creamer:** Combine nonfat dry milk powder with low-fat liquid milk. Store in the refrigerator and shake before pouring.

▪ **Dry powdered milk:** There are so many uses for dry powdered milk. You can add it to instant pudding mixes and use water instead of fresh milk.

❀ **HELOISE HINT:** I like to add a spoonful of powdered milk to my coffee instead of dry coffee creamer and sometimes, to get extra calcium, I stir a spoonful of dry milk into regular skim milk. It tastes richer, too!

▪ **Buttermilk:** Dip chicken, meats, vegetables, and other foods for deep-frying in buttermilk before breading; it's an especially good hint for folks who can't eat eggs, which are usually used for breading dips. Many people who cook game birds like to soak them in buttermilk before frying or baking because it takes away that gamey flavor. Soak quail, dove, or other small game birds in buttermilk for an hour or so (or overnight) in the refrigerator, then roll in seasoned flour, and fry. (You can use regular milk for soaking, but buttermilk does a better job of removing the gamey taste. Also, substitute buttermilk for regular milk when making biscuits, cornbread, cakes, and other baked goods to get a richer flavor.

▪ **Milk substitute:** If you're out of milk and your friendly neighbor is not home, you can usually complete a dish by mixing nondairy creamer with a little water as a milk substitute. But not for souffles!

▪ **Yogurt "cream cheese":** Strain plain yogurt through a coffee filter set up in a strainer sitting over a bowl and refrigerate overnight. By morning the liquid will have separated from the solids. Mix the solids (the "cheese") with fruit, honey, wheat germ, vanilla, or a bit of sugar for flavoring; then spread on whole-grain toast or bagel for a nutritious and tasty, low-cholesterol breakfast. Yogurt "cheese" can also be used as a substitute for cream cheese in some recipes and I like to add herb seasonings for a different low-fat dip/spread. The liquid part that is left, the whey, is rich in nutrients and can be added to soups or stews.

Serving

CHEESE

- **Cut cheese** with ease using dental floss (unflavored). Grasp each end of a long piece of floss, hold it taut, and slice away. Floss works for cheesecake and other cakes, too!

- **Garnish cheese with fruit.** Bunches of red and green grapes can be placed beside cheeses when serving them; they enhance the cheese flavors, too. And just like wines that come from grapes, strong red grapes taste better to some people with stronger flavored cheese like Cheddar and white grapes taste better to some people with lighter flavored cheeses like Swiss or Emmentaler. And consider serving cheese with fruit instead of crackers. For example, Cheddar, Stilton, and Swiss taste delicious with apple slices. Leave the skins on the apples for more color and dip the slices in an ascorbic acid solution made with water and a product sold in supermarkets to keep fruits fresh when freezing them. (Follow directions on the container.)

- **Dips and spreads:** Cottage cheese processed in a blender until smooth can substitute for sour cream or cream cheese in many types of dips and spreads. Plain yogurt also makes a good substitute for sour cream or cream cheese in dips and spreads. You can thin cream cheese with plain yogurt to make it more dipable or spreadable.

- **Serve cheese at room temperature.** Cheese tastes the best at room temperature, but when you have a large hunk of cheese, instead of putting the whole hunk out to get to room temperature, which is the best for serving and flavor, cut off only the amount you expect to eat. Being taken in and out of the refrigerator and left on the table dries out the cheese and speeds up spoilage.

- **Meat loaf:** Put something extra in meat loaf—put half the mixture into the pan, add a layer of mozzarella or other cheese, then put the remaining half into the pan. Top with Italian sauce for extra flavor.

MILK AND MILK PRODUCTS

- **Chocolate milk—good to the last drop:** Pour some milk into the chocolate syrup container when you have just a bit left in the bottom and shake. You'll use up every last good drop of syrup.

- **Colored milk:** When children decide that they hate milk, try stirring in a few drops of food color—their favorite color—into the milk.

- **Flavor yogurt** with fruit, jam, vanilla, or other flavoring (about ½ teaspoon per cup according to your taste). Vanilla yogurt is a delicious, low-cal, and nutritious dressing for sliced fruit. I have a dieting friend who adds plain cocoa, vanilla, and sweetener to nonfat yogurt when she gets a craving for chocolate ice cream. It's neither ice cream nor pudding, but she says it stops her craving.

▪ **Whipped topping:** While purists will quibble over this, whipped topping can substitute for high-calorie whipped cream most of the time, and the bonus is that you can keep a tub of it in the freezer for emergency dessert toppings or topping gelatin desserts.

MEAT AND MEAT ALTERNATIVES

Meat was the foundation for most people's meals in my mother's day, unless budgets were tight, but now healthy eating means focusing more on vegetables and/or carbohydrates as the central point of a meal. Also, many people have adopted a vegetarian lifestyle for various reasons. Meat, poultry, and fish, however, are still a good sources of protein, iron, zinc, and B vitamins, and probably the most expensive part of a meal, so shopping wisely and storing them properly is a pocketbook as well as a health issue.

The USDA recommends two to three servings daily from the entire group; amounts should total 5 to 7 ounces of cooked lean meat, poultry, or fish daily. Count ½ cup of cooked beans, or 2 tablespoons of peanut butter as 1 ounce of meat.

Shopping

Whatever the type of meat, the tenderest parts of the animal are those that did the least moving around; those parts are also more expensive. For example, fillets of beef, pork, and lamb are the tenderest parts of the animal. When you see the T-shaped bone of beef steak, lamb, or pork chops, you will notice that at one side of the T-bone there is a roundish-shaped section that is not the full length of the T-bone and at the other side is a larger section that goes the full length of the bone. That smaller round-shape is the fillet (tenderloin) and, with beef, it is often sold in individual portions separately without the bone, as in filet mignon (fillet wrapped with bacon). The fillet (tenderloin) can also be cut from the whole rack of T-bones of beef and pork, and sold for broiling whole instead of for broiling individual portions.

The fat content of meat varies greatly and fat marbled through the meat makes it juicier. If you are cutting back on fats, however, you can trim the fat when you cook the meat. In addition to the grades of meat (listed), you will also see labels that have a "yield" number that tells the proportions of lean to fat, and on some labels you will see a percentage of fat listed. The more bone or fat in the cut of meat, the fewer servings you will get from it. So the least amount of fat and bone gives you the most value of meat for your money, even if the price per pound is more than for bone-in meats.

When you buy trimmed meat without bones, you need to allow ¼ to ⅓ pound per serving;

this includes ground beef, lamb, or veal; boneless roasts; briskets; steaks; stew meat; flank steak; tenderloin; and variety meats. When meat has some bone—steaks, chops, ham, rib roasts—you need to buy about ⅓ to ½ pound per serving. When meat has many bony sections, you need to buy ¾ to 1 pound per person; for example, when buying spareribs, short ribs, lamb shanks, shoulder cuts, or hocks (leg parts).

Meat is graded according to federal standards for tenderness, juiciness, and flavor, and there are six grades of meat. The two grades that you are most likely to see at the market are Choice and Good. Meats are aged in refrigerated warehouses for various periods of time, which allows them to develop full flavor and tenderness.

- **Prime** has the most marbling of fat and is the most tender, juicy, and flavorful and thus is the most expensive meat. However, it is rarely seen at the market and is usually bought by restaurants, hotels, and dining clubs.
- **Choice** has less marbling than Prime but is still tender and juicy; it can be dry-roasted or broiled.
- **Select** has less marbling than Choice but is still tender and juicy; it can be dry-roasted or broiled.
- **Good** is leaner and less expensive than Choice but is also less juicy and less flavorful. Good is best cooked with moist heat (braised, pot roasted, stewed) or oven roasted.
- **Standard** is the lowest quality meat and is usually dry and not very flavorful; it should be cooked with moist heat only (stews, soups, pot roasts).

- **Commercial/Utility** is meat from old animals, which is very tough and usually used for soups.
- **Kosher:** The K for kosher means that the animal has been ritually slaughtered and is being sold, as required by Jewish law, within 72 hours of slaughter. If you want to be sure meat is fresh, look for the K.

The leanest cuts of meat include the following:

- **Beef:** round, loin, sirloin, and chuck (arm) steaks or roasts, especially Select grade cuts.
- **Chicken and turkey:** both are leaner choices than other meats, especially light meat (breast).
- **Lamb:** leg, loin roasts and chops, and foreshanks.
- **Pork:** tenderloin, center loin roasts and chops, ham.
- **Veal:** chops, loin roasts, and sirloin.

Storing

The USDA has provided the following optimum storage times for meats:

Cooked meats and meat dishes: 3 to 4 days.
Cured and smoked meats (frankfurters, bacon, sausage, and whole ham): 1 week. (Storage time applies to opened or nonvacuum-sealed packages; note freshness date information of unopened vacuum-sealed packages.)
Gravy and broth: 1 to 2 days.
Ground meat, stew meat, poultry, and variety meats: 1 to 2 days.

Luncheon meats: 3 to 5 days.

Roasts, steaks, and chops: 3 to 5 days.

To freeze bacon so that you can remove only one or two strips at a time, try these methods:

- Roll up each strip, place the roll on a cookie sheet, cover, and pop it all into the freezer for a few hours. Then put the bacon rolls into a freezer bag for storage. When it's time to cook the bacon, take out one or two rolled strips, as needed, and microwave them on High for 15 to 20 seconds or until done.

- Lay out a long piece of plastic wrap or wax paper on the counter; place a strip of bacon at one end, roll, place another strip on top with the end of the wrap separating the strips, roll again, and continue until all the strips are rolled up and separated by a thickness of plastic wrap or wax paper. Then put all in a freezer-safe bag and freeze.

- If the bacon strips are lean on one side and very fatty on the other cut the strips so that you have the lean, meaty parts of the bacon for meals. Then cut the fatty strips crosswise into small pieces and put them into a freezer bag and save to **render** (see chapter 6) when you need fat for browning meats. Pieces of fatty bacon can also be used for **barding** or **larding** (see chapter 6).

❊ **HELOISE HINT:** To separate strips of bacon quickly, take the whole "flat" as it comes from the store and roll it up across the strip lines, the strips will be easy to peel apart.

Cooking

Specific information about techniques for cooking meats is given in chapters 6 and 7. Here are some general hints for meat cooking:

- Add **salt** at the end of the cooking time; whether it is by dry or moist heat methods. Salt tends to draw juices from the meat, and if added too soon will make the meat dry and tough. Rub meat with garlic or other herbs and spices to flavor it during the cooking time, and salt it at the end of the cooking time.

- To **tenderize tough meats**, you can marinate them in vinegar, wine, lemon juice, buttermilk, or yogurt. Other techniques include pounding with a wooden or rubber mallet or the flat side of a cleaver or pounding with a special mallet that has diamond-shaped points of two sizes. Enzyme-type meat tenderizers are available in the spice section of the supermarket. These will tenderize the meat, but if left on too long before cooking they tend to make the texture rather grainy, so use these just before cooking. Usually the directions tell you to sprinkle the tenderizer on the meat and then poke the meat with a fork to let the enzyme get into the meat, and then cook.

- When **shaping ground meat** into meatballs or meat loaf, handle it gently, otherwise it will become too packed and will be rubbery after it is cooked. A fork works well to mix meat loaf and meatball mixtures.

- The best **test for doneness** of any meat or poultry is a meat thermometer. When using a meat thermometer, poke the thermometer into the center of the meat away from fat or bone, keeping the top of the thermometer away from the heat source. If you don't have a thermometer, roasts and steaks can be poked with a finger; the meat should feel soft but resilient. Whole roasted poultry is usually done if the leg or wing feels loose when you jiggle it. Thick roasts and whole poultry can be poked with a fork to find out if the juices run clear (it's done) or bloody (not done), but poking the meat and releasing the juices is not a good idea, because you want the juices to remain in the meat. *Note:* Poultry and pork should always be cooked to well done.

■ Unstuffed **frozen poultry** should be thawed before cooking, and for food safety concerns the thawing must take place in the refrigerator, not on the counter. It's important to note that a Thanksgiving turkey of 14 or more pounds will probably take two days to thaw in the refrigerator and a large bird of 18 to 20 pounds may take 4 days to thaw. Don't forget to thaw it on time! To quick-thaw frozen poultry, leave it sealed in its original plastic wrapper and place it in cold water for 2 to 7 hours, depending on the size, changing the water often (when it turns to room temperature) to keep the thawing process going. Cook immediately after thawing.

■ When **roasting whole poultry,** place the bird on a rack in a roaster, with the breast side up. Some people like to place a piece of cheesecloth which has been dipped in unsalted butter or vegetable oil over the whole bird and then remove the cloth ½ hour before the bird is done. You can also roast the bird in an aluminum foil tent or roast the bird uncovered in a roasting pan. To roast a bird, put it into a pre-heated 450 degree F oven and then reduce the heat immediately to 350 degrees F (or to 325 degrees F for large birds). After the first ½ hour of cooking, baste the bird every 10 minutes with pan drippings. Roasting the bird in a tent lets you avoid basting the turkey so often, and you can remove the tent before the last ½ hour of roasting so that the skin can brown. Generally, poultry roasts for 20 to 25 minutes per pound for birds up to 6 pounds and about 15 to 20 minutes per pound for larger birds. If you are roasting a turkey that's more than 16 pounds, allow about 15 minutes per pound. The internal temperature of a done bird should be 180 to 185 degrees F.

■ Even if you select **lean meats,** cooking and extras added at the table can add fats. The USDA recommends that you trim the fat from meat and remove the skin from poultry. For healthiest eating, broil or bake instead of frying meat, poultry, and fish. Go easy on sauces, gravies, and dressings. Avoid adding excess salt during cooking and at the table.

✿ **CLASSIC HELOISE HINT FOR BACON:** My mother used to fry a whole pound of *bacon* at once, drain it on paper, and store it in a wide-mouthed glass jar in the refrigerator so it was handy to pop in the broiler whenever she wanted some for breakfast or in a BLT for lunch. *Update:* Today she would cook the bacon in a microwave. She also would cut off about a ½ inch from each end of the bacon while the slices were still together, fry the bits and store them in the freezer so they were handy for sprinkling on salads, vegetables, and casseroles. She said our family would never miss having less than a whole bacon strip and she was right.

- To avoid lumpy **gravy**, blend a little of the thickening agent (flour, cornstarch, or arrowroot) with a little hot liquid (water, bouillon, or milk) to make a paste and then stir the paste into the rest of the hot liquid. Or pour some liquid into a clean empty jar with a tight-fitting lid. Add the flour or cornstarch, screw on the lid, and shake until completely blended. Add the mixture to casseroles, soups, gravies, sauces, etc. (Sprinkling paprika into gravy as it thickens will give it a nice warm, brown color and won't affect the taste unless you add too much of it.)

- To **avoid spattering grease** when you turn a fried patty over in the pan, place one pancake turner on top and another on the bottom, and slide the patty back into the pan.

- When you are **grinding leftover meat** to make a spread, you can get the last bits out of the grinder by grinding a slice of bread last; it will push the meat out. You can wash away the remaining bread from the grinder.

- To **make broth for cooking dried beans** and flavoring other vegetables, put the bone with leftover ham still on it into a large pot and cover with water. Bring to a boil, and boil until all the meat falls off. Cool and skim off the fat. Divide the ham bits and broth into portion-size containers and freeze. For extra flavor, toss in some celery leaves, onion, and other flavors of your choice.

- If you don't have a rack for **roasting meat**, substitute an aluminum pie pan from a frozen pie. Place the pan on a cutting board and punch a few holes in the bottom with an ice pick. Then turn it upside down and place it in the roaster. You can bend it to an oval shape if it doesn't fit the roaster's bottom. The bonus is that this rack is disposable if it gets too crusty to wash easily. Or take that last strip of aluminum foil that gets left in the box and is too narrow to wrap anything and roll it into an S, then place the S foil rack in the roaster. Or just crumple up a piece of heavy-duty foil; it can be a rack for lighter pieces of meat, such as chicken parts.

- When making **pot roast or stew**, substitute noodles for potatoes. Add more liquid than usual; when the roast or stew is done, add the noodles and cook them in the meat juices; they will take on nice brown color and will thicken the juice to automatically make gravy.

❀ **CLASSIC HELOISE HINT FOR MEATBALLS:** Instead of browning meatballs in a skillet on top of the stove, my mother put them into a large greased skillet and placed them in the oven, uncovered, to bake at 350 degrees F for 35 to 45 minutes, depending on how brown she wanted them. Sometimes she dusted the meatballs with flour first and then when they were put into spaghetti sauce, the flour helped thicken the sauce and helped the sauce stick to the meat.

MEAT LEFTOVERS

Roasts and other leftovers are really pre-cooked convenience foods, and when you have a hectic schedule, having leftovers is a real blessing. Generally speaking, adding a fresh ingredient, such as browned onions, garlic, vegetables, bouillon, new spices, or herbs will make leftovers taste like new.

- Cube leftover meats and mix with noodles or rice and salad dressings for a luncheon salad.
- Slices of meat in leftover sauce or gravy or gravy made from a mix can be served over leftover rice or noodles or on bread for open-faced sandwiches.
- Either slice leftover meat for sandwiches or grind it up to make sandwich spreads by adding commercial sandwich spread or mayo and chopped carrots, celery, mushrooms, olives, or other vegetables for filler.
- Cube the remains of stew meat, potatoes, and carrots; add the cubes to some onions browning in a bit of butter or oil; and brown all together for roast meat hash. If you have some leftover gravy or sauce, it's even better.
- Need to put a little color into leftover gravy? Add a touch of ketchup, which will also put some tomato flavor into the recycled meal. Or add a tablespoon of low-salt soy sauce or Worcestershire, depending on your taste and the type of meat served.

FISH AND SEAFOOD

According to the American Heart Association, fish is low in sodium and generally contains less saturated fat than red meat and about the same or slightly less cholesterol. So fish is a slightly better choice than lean red meat in a cholesterol-lowering diet and is a much better choice than fatty meat. Any fresh or frozen fish is a good choice and so is tuna (either canned in water or canned in oil and then rinsed). Shrimp, lobster, crab, crayfish, and most other shellfish are very low in fat but when you compare them by weight to poultry, meat, or other fish, some have more sodium and cholesterol. Some fish have omega-3 fatty acids, which may help lower the levels of some types of blood fats. Fish high in omega-3 fatty acids include Atlantic and coho salmon, albacore tuna, mackerel, carp, lake whitefish, sweet smelt, and lake and brook trout.

Shopping

- **Caviar:** The names of caviar—such as beluga, sevruga, osetra, and sterlet—tell you which type of sturgeon produced the roe (fish eggs). Caviar tins are also labeled with the name of the district where the fish was caught and when you see the word **Malosol** on the label, it means that the caviar is only slightly salted. **Malosol** comes from the Russian words **malo** ("little") and **soleny** ("salted").
- **Crab:** Crabs should move when touched.
- **Fish:** Look that fish right in the eye! If fresh, the eyes should be clear and bulge a little. Only a very few fish, such as walleye pike, have naturally cloudy eyes. Flesh should be firm and shiny whether it's a whole fish or fillets. If you can, press the fish with a finger. If it leaves an indentation, the fish is not fresh. Dull flesh can mean old fish. There should be no darkening around the cut edges of the fish (edges of fillets or edges where the head has been removed from the whole fish) or brown or yellowish discoloration, especially if these areas look dry or too mushy. Ask to have the fish

rinsed under cold water and then smell it. Fresh fish should have no ammonia or fishy smell.

- **Frozen fish:** Do not buy packages that are open, torn, or crushed on the edges. Avoid packages stored above the frost line of the store's freezer. If the package has a transparent wrapper, look for signs of frost or ice crystals, which means that the fish may have been stored for a long time or thawed and refrozen. There should be no evidence of drying out, such as white or dark spots, discoloration, or fading of red or pink fleshed fish.

- **Lobster:** Lobster tails curl under their bodies when *carefully* picked up if they are fresh and healthy.

- **Seafood, cooked: Do not** buy cooked seafood—such as shrimp, crabs, or smoked fish—if they're displayed next to raw fish. They could be cross-contaminated.

- **Shellfish:** The shells of hard clams, mussels, and oysters should be closed or should close if their shells are tapped. Necks of steamer clams should twitch when their shells are tapped.

Storing

- **Caviar:** Caviar needs special care because it is highly perishable. It should be removed from the refrigerator 15 minutes before eating and the lid should be removed only at the last moment. Unopened, a container of fresh caviar may be stored in the refrigerator for up to 4 weeks.

- **Clams, mussels, and oysters, live:** Store in the refrigerator, keeping them damp by covering them with a clean damp cloth, moist paper towel, or washed lettuce leaves. *Do not* place them on ice or allow freshwater to come in contact with them and *never* put them in an airtight container, which will kill them. Keep freshly shucked oysters, scallops, or clams in their shells and store in the refrigerator at about 32 degrees F, preferably with ice around the package.

- **Crabs and lobsters, live:** Store live lobsters and crabs in the refrigerator in moist packages (moist seaweed or damp paper strips) but not in airtight containers, freshwater, or saltwater. Lobsters should remain alive for about 24 hours.

- **Fish:** Take the following steps to ensure that fresh fish stays in top form until you can get it into the pan!

Before refrigerating, remove the fish from its original wrappers, rinse under cold water and pat dry with paper towels. Wrap with plastic wrap and place on a plate (to catch any drips) and then refrigerate as soon as possible; keep it at 32 to 37 degrees F.

If you are to keep fish more than 24 hours, place it on a cake rack in a pan, fill the pan with crushed ice, and cover tightly with plastic wrap or foil. Rinse the fish daily, cleaning the rack and changing the ice. If the fish gets a strong fishy or ammonia smell, throw it out.

If you want to keep fish more than 2 days, first, rinse it under cold water and pat it very dry with paper towels. Wrap it tightly in plastic wrap and then in aluminum foil and put it into the freezer. Use the fish within 2 weeks. Always thaw frozen fish in the refrigerator.

Cooking

■ **Ready to eat:** You will know that fish is cooked when the juices run clear and the flesh is flaky when cut with a fork.

■ **Breaded fish:** When preparing ready-to-cook breaded fish in the oven or microwave place the fish pieces on a rack and the bottom side won't get soggy.

■ **Fish herb blend:** Basil, bay leaf, French tarragon, lemon, thyme, parsley, fennel, sage, and savory are all good herbs to flavor fish.

■ **Steaming:** Before steaming fish, place it on a large flat-bottomed coffee filter. Then you can lift out the fish whole instead of in a bazillion crumbled pieces. Fish steamers with racks that lift out are very helpful but most people don't have them and use other types of pans.

■ **Microwave:** To get even cooking, place the thickest parts of the fish pieces toward the outside, cook a few minutes, then, take the fish out of the microwave and cut a small slit in the thickest part to test for doneness. When the flesh starts looking barely opaque, remove the fish from the microwave. It's important to let the fish stand 1 or 2 minutes to let it finish cooking. It's best to undercook fish slightly because it continues to cook when removed from the microwave oven.

❀ **HELOISE HINT:** When cooking in the microwave: Unless the fish is crumb coated, cover with wax paper or plastic wrap to retain moisture while it cooks.

■ **Shellfish:** The best advice is to cook shellfish before eating. Eating mollusks (clams, mussels, and oysters) raw used to be considered safe for most people, except for those with specific health problems. But as this book is being written, the FDA and other sources are warning people that they may become ill from raw shellfish. Among those who may be at risk without knowing it are people who drink only two or three alcoholic drinks daily or who have low stomach acid, such as people who take antacids regularly. These people should not eat raw mollusks, even when the mollusks come from a reputable restaurant or fish dealer. Mollusks like oysters and mussels draw in certain harmful bacteria from their environments even when they are harvested from clean waters.

■ **Shrimp:** When boiling or grilling shrimp, do not overcook. Except for the very large prawns, shrimp will cook in about 3 minutes. When shrimp are cooked they turn pink and curl up to form a C. If they form an O, they may be overcooked.

■ **Odor on hands:** Apply lemon or lime juice and wash.

Serving

■ **Caviar:** Serve caviar in its original container in a bed of crushed ice, using a nonmetal utensil. In the United States, caviar is usually seved with toast points (small crackerlike triangles of thin, white toasted bread or crackers) and can be accompanied by dishes of minced hard cooked eggs, (whites and yolks separated), minced onion, lemon wedges, unsalted butter, sour cream, and sometimes capers. Ice-cold vodka served straight or chilled champagne is a perfect complement.

- **Crab or shrimp:** When you serve peel-your-own shrimp or crack-your-own crab, give each person a flat-bottomed coffee filter for discarded shells. Or serve shrimp Gulf Coast tavern style: piled on a table that has been covered with several layers of newspapers. After the feast is over, you can just roll up the mess inside the newspapers and toss it into the garbage. *Note: Do* take the garbage out ASAP. Left overnight, the smell from old shells is worse than anything you can imagine!

- **Drawn butter:** Use a small egg cup, the kind used to hold hot eggs served in the shell, to hold butter for dipping.

- **Lemon wedges** and lemon halves are the traditional garnish and seasoning for seafood. My mother wrapped her lemon halves with her famous yellow nylon net tied with a green ribbon instead of cheesecloth. When you eat shrimp, crab, or lobster, you can use that lemon wedge for sprinkling on the food. When you finish the feast, you can use the same lemon to rub the odor off your hands.

- **Lobster:** When serving boiled whole lobster, a nut cracker is handy for cracking the shells and an olive fork will help you get the meat out of corners if you don't have a seafood fork made for that purpose.

🏵 KITCHENEERING HUMOR 🏵

When one of my editors was new to Gulf Coast crawfish boils, she was asked to bring her own crackers to a party. "Why would they want us to bring our own soda crackers?" she wondered. Then she decided she'd just eat crawfish and forget the crackers. When she got to the party, she also got some smarts about crackers: Everyone had brought their own shell cracker!

EGGS

An egg yolk contains cholesterol. But egg whites contain no cholesterol and are an excellent source of protein. Egg substitutes are over 90 percent egg whites and can be used for cooking and in most recipes.

Shopping

- **Egg safety:** Because you can't always tell a good egg from a bad one by smell, taste, or looks, precautions suggested by the FDA consumer magazine are listed in this section. Although the precautions are especially important for the elderly, the very young, and anyone with a weakened immune system, the FDA suggests that everyone should follow these warnings to minimize health risks.

- Egg safety: According to the American Egg Board, because eggs lose quality rapidly at room temperature, buy AA- or A-graded eggs from refrigerated cases only. Then, get the eggs home quickly, refrigerate immediately, and keep them at 40 degrees or lower until you're ready to use them.

Buy only Grade A or better eggs.

Do not buy eggs that are cracked or leaking. Open the carton to check the eggs before you buy them.

CAUTION: Never leave eggs or egg-containing foods at room temperature for more than 2 hours—and that includes the preparation and serving (but not cooking) times. If you are **refrigerating** a large amount of a hot egg-rich dish or leftovers, *do* divide it into several smaller shallow containers so that it cools quickly.

■ **Egg color:** Brown and white eggs have the same nutritional value, but, if you are planning to hard-cook some of the eggs, you may want to buy one color to use as raw eggs and the other for hard-cooking so it's easy to tell the difference.

Storing

❀ **CLASSIC HELOISE HINT:** My mother bought brown eggs one week and white ones the next week to make sure she used the older eggs first.

■ Store **fresh eggs** in their original cartons, in the main section of the refrigerator and not in the egg section of the door, which can be warmer than the rest of the fridge and subject to vibration every time the door is opened and closed. Fresh eggs can be stored in their cartons in the refrigerator as long as 5 weeks.

■ **Hard-cooked eggs in the shell** can be stored 8 to 10 days.

■ **Egg whites** in a covered container or egg yolks covered with water can be kept 2 to 4 days in the refrigerator.

■ **Freezing eggs:** Although eggs cannot be frozen in their shells, raw whole eggs, whites, and yolks and hard-cooked yolks can be frozen.

■ Here's the "scoop" according to the American Egg Board.

■ To freeze raw whole eggs, beat them just until blended and pour into a freezer container that can be tightly sealed. Label the container with the number of eggs and the date they were frozen.

■ To freeze the whites only, separate the whites from the yolks, making sure that no yolk gets into the whites. Pour whites into a freezer container that can be tightly sealed. Label the container with the number of egg whites and the date they were frozen.

■ To freeze egg yolks, beat together and add either ⅛ teaspoon of salt or 1½ teaspoons of sugar or corn syrup for each four yolks. Put them into a tightly sealed freezer container labeled with the number of egg yolks and the date they were frozen. In addition to the date and number of yolks, note on the label whether you've added salt or sugar so you'll know if they can be used for main dishes or baking.

■ **Thaw frozen eggs** overnight in the refrigerator or under cool running water. Yolks and whole eggs should be used as soon as they're thawed; thawed whites will have better volume when beaten if they are kept at room temperature for about thirty minutes. Use thawed frozen eggs only in dishes that are thoroughly cooked.

■ **Storing food made with eggs:** Creams, custards, meringue pies, and other foods with custard fillings—including cakes, cream puffs, and eclairs—should *not* be kept at room temperature. Cool slightly and then refrigerate. When these yummy foods are taken on picnics please be sure to keep them in a cooler. Salads and sandwiches made with salad dressings containing eggs or milk products are best refrigerated.

- **Stuck eggs:** If there are eggs stuck to a carton, soak the carton in lukewarm water, just long enough for the UNCRACKED eggs to loosen. Once you are able to remove them from the carton, refrigerate or cook them immediately. **CAUTION:** *do not* ever use cracked eggs, even if they are not leaking! Eggs can easily get contaminated when cracked.

Cooking

SAFETY

- Review recipes to see if it's possible to **substitute** pasteurized eggs or egg substitute for regular eggs.
- **Avoid serving or eating foods that contain raw eggs.** Caesar salad, Hollandaise sauce, homemade ice cream, homemade eggnog, and homemade mayonnaise can carry **Salmonella.**

Safest Egg Cooking Times

Scrambled: 1 minute at 250 degrees F.

Poached: 3-5 minutes in boiling water.

Fried: 1-2 minutes at 250 degrees F or until "done" the way you want them on one side then turn egg and cook for 30-60 seconds more on other side.

Boiled: 7 minutes in boiling water.

- Be aware that **lightly cooked foods** containing eggs, such as soft custards and French toast, can be risky for **people in high-risk groups** such as the elderly, the very young, and people with a weakened immune system.
- **Cook eggs thoroughly** until both yolk and white are firm and not runny for greatest safety.
- **Wash hands** with hot, soapy water; wash and sanitize utensils, equipment (like blenders), and work areas before and after they are in contact with eggs and uncooked egg-rich foods.
- **Discard the egg** if any shell bits fall into it.
- When cooking **scrambled eggs in batches,** make the batches no larger than 3 quarts. Hold for serving at 140 degrees F or hotter, such as on a steam table.
- **Do not** add a batch of just-cooked scrambled eggs to leftover eggs held on a steam table; put the new batch in a clean serving container.

HOW TO HARD COOK AN EGG

The American Egg Board suggests these steps:

1. Gently put the eggs in a single layer into a deep saucepan that has a cover.
2. Add water so it covers the eggs by 1 inch, cover the pan, place over high heat, and let the water come to a boil. (*Boil* is defined the point at which large, breaking bubbles form in the water.) After the water is boiling, turn off the heat (remove the pan from the burner if you have an electric stove).
3. Let stand 15 to 17 minutes, uncover the pan, and run cold water over the eggs until

they are cool, about 5 minutes. Remove the eggs from the pan and refrigerate.

✿ **HELOISE HINT:** When boiling eggs, add a few drops of food coloring and vinegar to the water so you'll know which eggs are boiled when you look in the fridge. You can celebrate Easter any time of the year; it's your house!

To peel a hard-boiled egg, tap the egg on all sides on the countertop, roll the egg gently between your hands to crackle the shell, and start peeling at the large end of the egg. Hold it under cool running water to help get the shell off quickly.

CAUTION: *Do not* microwave whole eggs in the shells; they will explode.

HOW TO SCRAMBLE AN EGG

1. Beat 1 egg and 1 tablespoon of milk with a fork or wire whisk until well mixed.
2. Melt butter or margarine in a small skillet or spray it with nonstick spray and heat over medium heat. If using margarine or butter, roll the pan so that the bottom is covered.
3. When the skillet is hot, add the egg mixture and push it around the pan with a pancake turner until it looks cooked but is still shiny. The eggs will continue to cook while standing, so don't overcook them.

To make **microwave scrambled eggs**, beat the egg (and milk if desired) in a small, microwave-safe bowl until well mixed. Cover with a paper towel or plate and cook on High for about 1 minute. Stir and check for doneness about every 30 seconds and remove when the egg puffs up around the sides of the dish. Let stand a minute or so to finish cooking. Don't overcook!

HOW TO POACH AN EGG

Here's the best way to poach an egg. Oil, or spray with nonstick vegetable spray, a pot that will hold enough water to be twice the depth of the egg. Put in enough water to be twice the depth of the egg, add a dash of salt, and bring the water to a full, rolling boil. While the water boils, break an egg into a small bowl. *Note:* It is easier to break the egg into a bowl and then slide the egg from the bowl into the water than it is to plop the egg directly from its shell; also the yolk is less apt to break. When the water is boiling, swirl it with a spoon and slide the egg gently into the "whirlpool" center of the boiling water. Reduce the heat to simmer. You can either simmer the egg in water for about 4 minutes or take the pot off the heat and let the egg sit in the water for about 8 minutes. The white should be firm and the yolk should be soft if you've done it properly. Repeat the process for each egg.

✿ **HELOISE HINT:** One of my editors tells me that a favorite light energy lunch for skiers in Austria is bouillon with a raw egg poached in it. Make a cup of bouillon with boiling water in a pot and drop an egg into it, let it simmer for about 4 minutes or let it stand covered for 5 to 8 minutes to let the egg cook. It will look something like Chinese egg drop soup.

To lift poached eggs out of the hot water, get a potato masher—the kind made with a round disk that has punched-out holes, slide the disk under the egg and lift. You'll get all of the egg but the water will drain off.

MORE EGG HINTS

■ **Egg sizes:** When a recipe doesn't specifically say which size egg to add, always use a large egg, because that is the recipe standard. If you don't have large eggs, the American Egg Board recommends the following substitutions:

Egg Equivalents

LARGE	MEDIUM	SMALL
1	1	1
2	2	3
3	3	4
4	5	5
5	6	7
6	7	8

■ **Egg substitute in an "egg-mergency":** If you are making a recipe that requires several eggs, you may be able to substitute a mixture of 1 tablespoon of regular cooking oil and 2 tablespoons of heavy cream for one egg. However, all this does is replace missing liquid. Because eggs usually have a specific function in a recipe such as binding, thickening, or emulsifying, leaving out an egg can affect the recipe outcome. If you use this substitution in recipes for baked goods, for example, that call for just one or two eggs, the recipe is likely to flop.

✿ **CLASSIC HELOISE HINT FOR EGG SUBSTITUTE:** In her 1966 book *Heloise's Hints for Working Women,* written before commercial egg substitute was available, my mother gave her recipe for homemade egg substitute. She separated the yolks from the whites, and for each egg white, she added two drops of yellow food color. Then she directed: "Stir the droplets of coloring among the egg whites with a fork. Do not beat them or put them in a blender unless you want solid-yellow scramble eggs." The point of stirring with a fork is to have part white and part yellow scrambled eggs as if you had scrambled a whole egg. Mother liked lots of salt and pepper on her substitute scrambled eggs and sometimes she topped them with hamburger relish. Today she would have topped them with salsa. She also suggested that if you put the egg whites into a blender with some baking powder and food color, the mixture would be fluffy like an omelet and all one color.

■ **Leftover egg whites or yolks:** Save egg whites for meringues. Save yolks for custards, sauces, or to add to scrambled eggs. Cooked eggs, especially those leftover Easter eggs that are not too old can become egg salad or be chopped and added to tuna, chicken, or potato salad. If you have used egg whites in a recipe, poach the leftover egg yolks; let them cool; put them through a sieve; and then use to garnish soups, salads, and appetizers.

■ **Leftover eggnog:** Moisten bread for bread pudding with leftover eggnog. Just add some raisins and a bit of cinnamon to the nog and bread (leftover raisin bread is extra good), bake, and enjoy!

QUICHE AND VARIATIONS

Here's a simple basic quiche recipe.

MAKES 4 SERVINGS

6 ounces sliced bacon, cooked until medium
    crisp, drained of fat on a paper towel

1 partially baked 9-inch pie shell (see chapter 7)

3 ounces Swiss or Gruyère cheese, cut into thin
    slices or shredded

3 eggs

1½ cups milk

½ teaspoon salt

⅛ teaspoon pepper

⅛ teaspoon nutmeg

Preheat the oven to 400F.

Place the bacon into the bottom of the pie shell and sprinkle with the cheese. Beat the eggs until fluffy (usually a light lemon yellow color means you've beaten the eggs enough) and then beat in the milk, salt, pepper, and nutmeg.

Place the pie plate on the oven shelf and pour in half of the milk and egg mixture. Close the oven and let bake for about 2 minutes to set. Then add the remaining liquid. Bake for 25 to 30 minutes. When done (a knife inserted in the middle should come out clean), remove from the oven. Serve hot or cold.

VARIATIONS: Add grated cheese, chopped almonds, or ground pecans to the crust recipe. Substitute ham or Canadian bacon for the regular bacon.

SERVING

▪ **Salad:** When making egg salad or adding eggs to tuna or other salad, grate the eggs to save time and to get a finer diced texture. Use the large holes in the grater. You won't have big hunks of egg falling out of a sandwich or spoiling the appearance of your salads. To make egg slices, use an egg slicer (this is also a handy gadget for slicing other soft foods, such as mushrooms).

▪ **Deviled Eggs:** Serve deviled eggs in miniature paper cupcake liners. They won't slide around on the serving plate and will be easy to pick up if you're serving a buffet. *Note:* if you don't have any paper cupcake liners, cut a small slice off the bottom of the egg white half to make a flat surface, and the eggs will stay in place without rolling over.

❀ **HELOISE HINT:** To carry deviled eggs to a potluck buffet, wash and dry a plastic foam egg carton to make a carrier or line an egg carton with small cupcake liners to hold the eggs.

VEGETABLES

Vegetables are always at the top of my shopping list. Raw, steamed, stir-fried, however you cook them, vegetables please the eye and palate and are an excellent source of nutrients and fiber. In addition to being important in preventing many diseases, vegetables will fill you up if you are trying to lose weight without adding a lot of calories to your diet. Of course, if you smother the veggies with heavy sauces or dollops of butter or other fats, they won't be low-cal anymore!

The USDA recommends three to five servings daily from the entire group; one serving equals 1 cup of raw leafy vegetables, ½ cup of other vegetables (cooked or chopped raw), or ¾ cup of vegetable juice.

Shopping

Generally speaking, if you look at the cut end of any vegetable and it is brownish and/or dried out, that vegetable has been on display for a long time. Granted, produce managers can go around making fresh cuts, but they aren't likely to get to all of the vegetables on display so, although it is not foolproof, this is still a good rule of thumb. Here's how to judge the best quality of some popular and some formerly exotic vegetables.

■ **Anisa, anise** (sweet fennel): Usually in season during cool weather, anise has fernlike green foliage that looks something like fresh dill weed with a thick white bulb. Chop the greens for seasoning and steam the white flesh as a side dish. Watch for fresh, green foliage and crisp-looking bulbs for the best sweet licorice flavor. This vegetable is more popular in Europe than in the United States, but it's becoming more available and more of us are eating it in this country.

■ **Asparagus:** Look for tight compact "leaves" on the head of the stalk; opened ones or those with yellow showing are old. Also look at the cut end of the stem; the fresher the cut, the fresher the asparagus.

■ **Avocado:** Once called alligator pears in some parts of the country, avocados come mainly from California and Florida. The difference between avocados from these two regions is, to some folks, like the difference between ice cream and ice milk. Florida avocados are usually twice as big as those from California and have a lower calorie count, like ice milk. The California avocados have a more nutlike flavor and richer, creamier flesh. To **test for ripeness**, put the avocado in the palm of your hand. A Florida avocado is ready to serve if it yields to slight pressure. A California avocado needs to ripen one more day after this test. To **ripen avocados** in half the natural time, put them into a brown paper bag with a tomato and then put the bag in the warmest part of the house. The natural ethylene gas from the avocado and tomato plus the warmth will speed up ripening.

■ **Broccoli** should be firm, green, and not yellow or budded with yellow flowers. Some broccoli has a slightly purple cast to the buds, and this is a mark of quality.

■ **Cabbage:** The outer leaves should look fresh and crisp and the cut end should not be brown.

■ **Celeric** (knob celery) is usually sold in bunches with three knobs and green tops attached. Celeriac is eaten as a cooked vegetable or raw in salads. Buy smaller ones, because larger knobs tend to be woody.

■ **Kale** is a curly-leafed member of the cabbage family that tastes much like cabbage when cooked. Buy crisp, dark green or slightly blue leaves. Wilted, limp, or yellow leaves is a sign of age. Pink, purple, or white-heated kale is usually ornamental and considered too expensive for eating.

■ **Kohlrabi** looks like pale green beets but it grows above the ground. Buy kohlrabi that is the same size as beets, about 3½ inches in diameter, to avoid getting a woody, overly mature one. It should look crisp. If the leaves are wilted and yellow, don't buy.

• **Mustard greens, spinach, Swiss chard, and other green leafy vegetables** should look and feel crisp. If the stem ends are brown, the vegetable has not been cut recently; the fresher looking the cut end, the fresher the veggie. This is especially evident with head lettuce, romaine, bok choy, and similar green vegetables. Mustard greens should have dark or light green leaves, which may have a bronze cast. Swiss chard should have crisp green leaves and reddish stems. Spinach should be a rich green.

• **Peppers,** either sweet or hot, come in many sizes, shapes, and colors. All peppers tend to turn from green to red, or even yellow or purple, as they ripen. Generally, the smaller and more pointed the pepper, the hotter it is. You need to be able to identify peppers to tell which are hot and which are sweet, but some supermarkets have charts that show you how hot each pepper is. Some types of hot peppers are chili, jalapeño, cayenne, pulla, and serrano. Bell and Anaheim (poblano) are sweet peppers.

• **Potatoes** that are soft, bruised, cracked, wrinkled, sprouting eyes, or greenish looking should be avoided. Buy the best type for your needs. Here are some of the popular varieties and their properties.

Russet Burbank potatoes are large, oblong tubers with dark, rough skin. They cook up fluffy and make great mashed potatoes and French fries. Idaho russets are favorites for baking.

California and White rose are all-purpose long, oblong potatoes with thin, smooth skin. They're best for roasting, boiling, steaming, and pan frying.

Round reds or whites, which are sold immediately after harvesting and without being stored, are called "new" potatoes. They are best for boiling in their thin skins.

Yukon golds have become very popular lately. They are small with good texture and a deliciously different taste. They can be boiled with the skins and served like new potatoes or used in a variety of recipes.

• **Head lettuce:** Select firm, relatively heavy heads with crisp-looking leaves and a fresh stem end.

• **Salad greens:** Serving just head lettuce is a so-so salad these days when so many delicious greens are available. Combine them for variety. Here are descriptions of just a few greens and some suggestions for salad dressings:

Belgian endive, with its long, small, pale green, spear-shaped leaves, tightly packed in a firm head, is pleasantly bitter and best mixed with other strongly flavored greens. It can also be stuffed with cream cheese or other filling to make hors d'oeuvres.

Bibb has soft, green broad leaves. Its delicate taste is enhanced by a mild dressing.

Boston has green outer leaves with yellow-green inner leaves. It's milk buttery flavor is best enhanced by mild salad dressing.

Curly endive (chicory or frisee) has a somewhat bitter flavor. Its leaves are large, lacy, and fringed. The outer leaves are darker in color and have a stronger taste. Mix with some milder greens and serve with a strong-flavored salad dressing.

Gourmet blends, (mesclun) are also available in most supermarkets and are made up of a mix of various greens. These blends are usually made up of small-leaf varieties, including arugula, endive, radicchio, curly endive, and other greens of different textures, shapes, and shades.

Red leaf is usually a large head of frilly green leaves with reddish tips. It also has a delicate taste and is best with a subtle dressing.

Romaine has long green leaves with a pale green to whitish crunchy rib. This is the green used for Caesar salad.

Rugula (arugula) is a dark, bitter-sharp green popular in Italian cooking. It is often found in salad mixes.

Watercress leaves are small and dark green and have crisp stems. Its strong peppery taste is good when teamed with other pungent greens.

- **Shallots** are members of the onion family with a taste that is somewhere between a sweet onion and garlic. They have light purplish red skin and range in size from a giant olive to a small plum. Use shallots whenever you want a more delicate flavor than you can get from onions or garlic. They are especially good for seasoning fish dishes.

- **Summer squash** is harvested before full maturity while the rind and seeds are still tender and edible and its flesh is thin and string free. The most popular summer squashes are green zucchini, yellow, crookneck, and discus-shaped white squash. Select only those that are small and firm and avoid squash with soft ends or a rubbery texture.

- **Winter squash** are distinguished by hard rinds. The most common varieties include acorn (dark green or orange and green, and shaped like an acorn, of course), buttercup (oval and dark green with whitish stripes), butternut (long, tubular, and creamy tan in color), hubbard (one of the largest squashes, bumpy all over and in various colors), spaghetti (smooth yellow outside and stringy spaghetti texture inside), and turban (brightly colored with rounded lumps on one end).

Storing

Fresh vegetables will keep from 1 to 7 days in the refrigerator's crisper drawer. It's best not to wash vegetables before storing them, because excess moisture can cause spoilage. A dry sponge in the bottom of the vegetable crisper will also absorb excess moisture and help preserve vegetables stored there. Cooked, leftover vegetables placed in a covered container and canned vegetables in the original can or other covered container will keep 3 days in the refrigerator. Unopened nonacid canned vegetables will keep in a cool temperature of about 70 degrees F for 2 to 3 years. Acid foods, such as tomatoes and all fruits, are safe for about 18 months.

CAUTION: If you see rust or any discoloration on a can at the seam or anywhere else or if the can bulges at either end; throw out the can without opening it. *Never taste or handle such food!* Discard spoiled food carefully so that children and pets cannot get at it. If you open a can of food and it smells spoiled or looks discolored, flush it down the garbage disposal or toilet to prevent children, pets, or other animals from eating it. Do run lots of water down the disposal to wash away the spoiled food.

Most vegetables do not freeze well in their raw state and cannot be eaten raw when unfrozen. Lettuce, cabbage, onions, peppers, celery, and carrot sticks will lose crispness and get limp and/or tough, but you can use them for soups, stews, and casseroles. Most vegetables need to be blanched in boiling water for several minutes before freezing to prevent deterioration. The exceptions are onions and bell peppers, which can be frozen (cleaned and chopped) for future use in recipes. Garden tomatoes can be blanched and frozen whole in a zipper bag for use in cooking only.

- **Avocados:** Do not ripen in the refrigerator. Refrigeration will make the flesh turn black. You can freeze pureed but not whole or cut avocados.
- **Carrots** will keep in cool, dark place or in the refrigerator crisper for several weeks. Once cleaned, they should be kept in a tightly covered container in the fridge. They need not be immersed in water if they were dripping wet when you put them into the container.
- **Celery:** Keep whole stalks in a plastic bag in the crisper drawer of the refrigerator. Save leaves for seasoning soups and stews. To have instant celery sticks for snacking, cut off the bottom to release the stalks, wash, and then

stand individual full-length stalks of celery in a wide-mouth container that's as tall as the stalks with about 2 inches of water in the bottom. Or cut stalks into smaller lengths, wash, and put in a tightly covered container as described for carrot sticks. Or dice the celery, cook until tender in a bit of water, then cool. Divide into portions for adding to soups and stews, put into freezer bags or containers, and freeze.

- **Salad greens:** If you wash salad greens before storing them in the refrigerator instead of washing them just before serving, then they will keep better if they are allowed to drain either in a colander or on paper towels.

CLASSIC HELOISE HINT: My mother suggested putting a head of lettuce into a bowl covered with water and storing it in the refrig-

Fresh Vegetable Storage

The following optimum storage times are recommended by the USDA.

Beans (snap or wax), cauliflower, celery, cucumber, eggplant, green peppers, salad greens, and tomatoes: 1 week.

Beets, carrots, parsnips, radishes, rutabagas, and turnips: 2 weeks.

Broccoli, Brussels sprouts, greens (spinach, kale, collards, etc.), okra, green onions, peas, and summer squash: 3 to 5 days.

Cabbage: 1 to 2 weeks.

Corn: eat as soon as possible.

erator. *Update:* Now we believe that storing lettuce immersed in water leeches vitamins from it, so simply refrigerating lettuce wrapped with the remnants of the water from washing should do the trick.

▪ A READER RECOMMENDS:

Wrap damp washed lettuce firmly in a paper towel and store in a sealed plastic bag in the fridge.

- **Dried peas, beans, or other legumes** can be stored indefinitely if stored in a tightly covered container and in a dry place.
- **Mushrooms** should be stored in the fridge unwashed; they become slimy sooner if stored wet. Make sure they're dry and then put them into a paper, not plastic, bag. Paper bags let them breathe so that they will stay fresh longer.
- **Onions** may be stored whole in a cool, dry place. They do not need to be refrigerated.

❊ **HELOISE HINT:** A clean cottage cheese container can be recycled for storing chopped onions.

- **Potatoes** are best stored in a dark, cool, and well-ventilated place; but don't leave them in the plastic bags in which they are sold. The bags prevent good air circulation. Potatoes need to be cooked before freezing. CAUTION: According to the National Potato Board, potatoes that are exposed to artificial or natural light will turn green. However, those that have turned slightly green are acceptable to eat, but always remove the green skin before cooking or eating.

- **Summer squash** (zucchini, crookneck, and white) should be stored in the refrigerator for 3 to 5 days.
- **Winter squash** (acorn, buttercup, turban, butternut, hubbard, and spaghetti) may be kept for 3 to 6 months in a cool dry place but not in the refrigerator, unless they are cut.

Preparing, Cooking, and Other Hints

Vegetables lose valuable nutrients along with their appearance and taste if you boil the heck out of them, as was not uncommon in my mother's day. Today, we can enjoy vegetables prepared in a wide range of healthful and delicious ways. Steamed vegetables keep their shape, color, and nutrients better than boiled. Grilled vegetables are a wonderful alternative, especially for the summer. Just drizzle a bit of olive oil and add a few herb flakes. In the winter, do the same thing by roasting vegetables in the oven. Try combining different vegetables for a whole new taste. One cookbook author wrote that anything that is cooked in water, will taste better cooked in bouillon or wine. This certainly applies to vegetables. Flavored vinegars can also perk up boiled or steamed vegetables, especially greens. Add just a dash or so of balsamic or other flavorful vinegar as the veggies cook.

- **Beets:** My mother had the easiest way to peel beets. She would put them in a pan of water, leaving the root and ½ inch of the stem on the beet. Bring the water to boil and boil for 30 to 45 minutes. The cooking time depends on the size of the beets; small ones will take less time than larger ones. Remove the beets from the stove and place them, still in the pot, in the sink and run cold water over them. When the beets are cool enough to handle, cut off both ends of the beet—stem and root—and the peel will slip right off.

A READER RECOMMENDS:

A Texas reader says she buys Texas-size jugs of sweet pickles (gallon or half gallon) and then when the pickles are gone, she adds a can of drained cooked beets, a cinnamon stick, and a few whole cloves and microwaves all until it is warm. After the beets and juice cool, she puts it in the refrigerator and in 2 or 3 days, she has great pickled beets.

- **Broccoli:** After you remove the flower ends of the broccoli, slice the stems thinly and toss them into a green salad or add them to stir-fry veggies for extra crunch and food value. You can also peel the stalks and cube them for stir-fry dishes.

- **Celeriac** (knob celery). If the greens are fresh, they can be used to flavor soup. Celeriac is easy to peel after cooking. If served raw, sprinkle it with lemon juice because it discolors when cut.

- **Corn on the cob, grilled:** Pull off the corn shucks, boil the corn for about 5 minutes, and grill it over the hot coals in the barbecue pit for several minutes. Alternatively, you can grill it still in the husk: Pull the husk back from the top of the cob and remove the silk. Re-wrap the cob. Soak in cold water for 2 or 3 minutes, drain, and put on the grill. The cob can also be shucked, wrapped in foil, and grilled. Grilling the corn in the husk or wrapped in foil doesn't give the same caramelized flavor as grilling the cob bare.

- **Cucumbers:** When your garden produces more cucumbers than any human can eat in salads or pickles, try cooking the cucumbers. Peel them, cut into quarter-size slices, and simmer in chicken broth for about 5 minutes. Drain, add a bit of butter and pepper and you have a tasty veggie dish. If you are cutting calories, cook in skimmed chicken broth and flavor with diet margarine.

- **Garlic:** A garlic **bulb** is composed of several garlic **cloves**. It's important to know this because if a recipe calls for two garlic cloves (or buds) and you use two garlic bulbs, you'll certainly shock the taste buds of everyone who eats what you cook. Garlic can be roasted whole and unpeeled; the flesh is then squeezed out of the cloves to use in a recipe. To peel raw garlic, smash the clove with the side of a large, wide-bladed knife, cut off the stem end, and press the flesh out. You can slice it, chop it or put it through a garlic press, depending on your recipe.

- **Green leafy vegetables:** The simplest way to prepare mustard greens, spinach, Swiss chard, kohlrabi leaves, and others is first to wash them well to remove any sand and then to put them in a heavy bottomed pot, large deep sided pan, or a wok. Do not dry the leaves, because the water clinging to them is usually enough liquid for cooking. Cook over medium heat, tossing gently all through the process, for just a few minutes until they lose only a bit of their texture. Season and serve.

■ **Hot peppers:** Wear rubber gloves when handling hot peppers to protect your skin. Some say the seeds cause them to be hot and others say it's the veins that are hottest, especially in serrano peppers. *Never* rub your eyes with your hands after handling hot peppers—it really, really hurts!

■ **Leeks** look like very large green onions, but they have a distinctive mild taste. They are most frequently used to flavor soups and stews, but they can also be poached or grilled as a vegetable side dish.

■ **Mushrooms:** To get perfectly sliced mushrooms quickly, cut the stems level with the caps, then place each mushroom in an egg slicer stem side up.

■ **Onions, raw and crisp:** When you'll be needing raw onion slices for garnish on burgers or in salads, cut the slices the day before, put them in a glass jar, fill with cold water, cover, and refrigerate. Change the water once or twice if the onions seem strong. Drain on paper towels before using.

■ **Onions, French fried:** Dip onion rings in a batter made from prepared pancake mix and deep fry.

■ **Onion peels:** For extra flavor, toss onion peels and leftover hunks on the coals when you barbecue.

■ **A READER RECOMMENDS:**
One reader rubs sugar on his hands to remove the odor from peeling and chopping onions. Or rub your hands on the chrome faucets of your kitchen sink to remove onion odors. A stainless steel table knife works, too.

Classic Heloise Hints for Onions

• When grating an onion my mother's hint was to leave the head or root end on after peeling to serve as a handle while you grate the onion. It will protect your fingers. *Update:* Now we can grate or chop onions in a food processor, following the manufacturer's directions for proper speed and technique.

• My mother suggested wearing rubber gloves when cutting onions to keep the odor off your hands. Rubber gloves are a good idea for people whose skin is sensitive to foods. *Update:* Disposable plastic gloves are cheap and are easy to slip on to protect your hands while preparing food.

• My mother's hint for peeling was that if you did not plan to use a whole onion, just slice what you needed without peeling the onion first. The dry peel protected your hands from onion odors and protected the unused section from drying out! Just slip off the peel right before using.

■ **Onion substitutes:** French onion soup will substitute for onions in some recipes and will a add rich flavor, too.

■ **Onion tops:** Snipped green onion tops can substitute for chives in many recipes and on baked potatoes. You can snip them with kitchen shears and freeze the ones you don't use for future recipes.

■ **Peas, beans, and other legumes:** When cooking dried peas or beans, adding sugar, salt, or meat to them *during cooking* can cause them to stay hard. Cook in plain water for best results.

✿ **CLASSIC HELOISE HINT:** One of my mother's readers tested cooking dried beans—one pot with salt and the other without. She found that cooking dried beans with salt made them hard. My mother duplicated the test in her kitchen with the same result, so she recommended adding salt after the beans are completely cooked and tender. Many cooks disagree, it's up to you!

■ **To cook dried legumes in a slow cooker** if you don't want to soak them overnight, place them in enough water to cover, bring to a boil and then let simmer for 10 minutes on the stovetop. Drain and put the legumes into the slow cooker. For each pound, add 6 cups of water. Cook on low for 8 to 12 hours. Season once the legumes are tender.

■ **To cook dried legumes on the top of the stove,** follow the directions on the package. Generally, you need to soak the beans overnight in three times the volume of water to one part of beans. If you don't soak them overnight, bring the beans and water to a boil, turn off the heat, cover tightly, and let sit for 2 hours. Then simmer the beans, partially covered, adding water if necessary, for about 2 hours or longer, depending on how soft you want them.

■ **Quick pickles:** If you like fresh deli-style pickles (refrigerated type), save the jar and contents when the pickles are finished. You can cut up cucumbers and put them in the jar with the

Heloise Hints for Avoiding Onion Tears

Like my mother, I get a lot of questions and hints from readers on how to avoid onion tears. Here are just a few ideas:

• My mother recommended storing onions in the fridge for a few days; they are less apt to induce tears when you cut them cold. Alternatively, you can put them in the freezer for 30 to 45 minutes before slicing. **CAUTION:** Do not leave onions in the freezer too long, or they will be mushy. If you forget and do freeze the onions, you can still cook with them later.

• Wear swimming goggles. Lots of readers have written and even sent photos to tell me that this is their preferred and foolproof method for avoiding tears. Such a sight!

• A home economist wrote to my mother saying that if you turn on a burner of your gas stove while cutting onions, you won't cry. And this idea worked!

• Cut and chop a lot of onions at one time and get the misery over with. Then freeze the ready-to-use onions in clean margarine containers for future cooking. They may not have good consistency for using raw once thawed but they work fine for cooking.

• Hold a wooden match, toothpick, or piece of bread between your front teeth while you cut onions so that you are forced to breathe through

continued . . .

your mouth instead of your nose. One of my mother's books said that breathing through your mouth keeps the onion odor from reaching your tear-producing glands. *Update:* Now we know that chopping or slicing onions releases a gas called propanethiol S-oxide, which reacts chemically with the water in your eyes to form sulfuric acid. Tears are your eyes' defense against the acidic irritation, and some people are more bothered by onion gas than others. However, the more onions you cut, the more tolerance you build up to the gas, which may or may not be good news!

pickling liquid. Let season for a day or two in the refrigerator, and you'll have another jar of fresh pickles!

❄ **CLASSIC HELOISE HINT FOR PIMIENTOS:** Because one seldom uses a whole can or jar of pimientos in a recipe, my mother used to wrap each leftover pimiento separately and freeze it so she'd always have a single one handy to put color into a recipe.

▪ **Potatoes, baked:** Because you already have the oven on, bake extra potatoes for future meals (see chapter 7). Use the extras for potato soup, which will be delicious with the baked flavor. Save the skins for broiling with cheese and/or salsa. If you like to eat baked potato skins, try this: Salt the potato skins with coarse

salt after the potatoes are washed and still dripping wet. Then bake on the oven rack as usual.

▪ **A READER RECOMMENDS:**
One Heloise reader says she cuts potato baking time in half by placing potatoes on the oven rack and then putting an iron pot or pan over them.

❄ **CLASSIC HELOISE HINT FOR POTATO GRAVY:** My mother used to sprinkle instant potatoes into hot meat juice and then swish around a few times. She had quick and lumpless gravy with a bit of nutrition added.

▪ **Potato salad in a hurry:** Cut potatoes into hunks before you boil them. Cook and drain and pour your favorite dressing mixture over potatoes while they are hot or heat the dressing mixture and the potatoes will absorb more of the flavor.

❄ **HELOISE HINT:** Although cooks in my mother's day peeled potatoes for most recipes, today many cooks leave the skins on to get the extra nutrients, flavor, color, and texture.

▪ **Shallots** can be used instead of onion and garlic to give a lighter taste to any recipe, but they can become bitter if overcooked so be sure to sauté them until just clear and not browned.
▪ **Summer squash** can be cut crosswise or into matchsticks and stir-fried or steamed for side dishes. Add some chopped bell pepper, a bit of onion, and a dash of Balsamic vinegar. Try grilling, brushed with salad oil and sprinkled with herbs.

❀ **CLASSIC HELOISE HINT:** My mother liked to French fry sweet potatoes. She would prepare and fry raw sweet potatoes the same as white potatoes.

▪ **Tomatoes:** To thaw and peel frozen tomatoes at the same time, just run warm water over the tomato; you can peel the skin off easily. Wait a few minutes and you'll be able to cut off the stem ends and cut the tomatoes into pieces with a French chef's knife. Then toss the tomatoes into stews, soups, and other recipes.

▪ **Winter squash** is easy to bake in the microwave. Usually you need to cut it in half, scoop out the seeds, put the cut side down on a microwave safe dish, add about ¼ cup of water, and cook on Medium covered with plastic wrap for about 12 minutes, depending on the size. However, these squashes will taste even better if you bake them in the oven when you are roasting meat. Prepare as for the microwave and bake uncovered at 325 to 350 degrees F for 30 to 45 minutes, depending on the size.

❀ **HELOISE HINT:** A serrated grapefruit spoon is the best tool when you want to remove the seeds from tomatoes or squash before cooking. Also use it to scoop out pulp from cooked squash for serving as a side dish and to remove baked potato pulp from the skin for twice-baked potatoes.

▪ **Zucchini:** If you grow zucchini in your garden, you will probably have a surplus. Grate the zucchini in a food processor, pack the pulp in freezer bags in portions for making zucchini bread or other baked goods later in the year.

LEFTOVERS

▪ **Store leftover vegetables** in a tightly covered container in the freezer and continue to add all leftovers and their cooking water until you have enough to make vegetable soup. To flavor, brown onions, add bouillon or stock, and your favorite herbs/spices to the mix. Simmer at least 20 to 30 minutes to blend the flavors.

▪ **Add leftover cooked vegetables** to salads or sandwich spreads or just arrange them on top of a plain lettuce salad and add dressing.

▪ **Brown leftover potatoes** with onion and egg or egg substitute for a hearty breakfast or light supper. You can add diced red and/or green bell peppers to make this dish more attractive. And, if you like, put some salsa on top.

▪ **Fry leftover mashed potatoes** flavored with your favorite cheese for breakfast or as a side dish.

▪ **Make "veggie puppies"** instead of hush puppies. Mash leftover starchy vegetables and add egg, leftover egg yolks or egg substitute, and some crumbs to thicken; then deep-fry like traditional hush puppies.

▪ **Fry leftover mixed vegetables,** such as corn, peppers, potatoes, peas, and beans with some onion, garlic, and other seasonings to make vegetables hash.

Serving

▪ **Corn on the cob:** If you butter a slice of bread and then use the buttered bread to butter corn on the cob, it's less drippy. Or put the pat of butter on your plate, add salt and pepper to it and spread all on the corn at the same time.

■ **Cheese:** Instead of cheese sauce, simply sprinkle shredded Parmesan or Cheddar on vegetables just before serving. Easy and tasty, without much effort.

■ **Colors:** To perk up vegetables, sprinkle on chopped parsley, basil, oregano, paprika, or other colorful compatible-flavored fresh herbs or spices just before serving. You can also put some diced red, yellow, and green pepper pieces in a small bowl, add a small amount of water, and cook in the microwave for 2 minutes or so on Low to Medium. Then sprinkle the bits over green beans, broccoli, or cauliflower at serving time.

■ **Dip dish:** When serving carrot, celery, and other fresh veggie sticks, hollow out a red cabbage or remove the top and seeds from a bell pepper (red or green) to make a "dip dish." A hollowed-out cabbage can also hold shrimp cocktail sauce and you can spear some of the shrimp with toothpicks and stick them into the cabbage (like antennae) for extra decoration.

■ **Green leafy vegetables** will come to life if you add a dash of Balsamic vinegar just before serving.

■ **Herbs mix:** Add basil, parsley, or savory to vegetables to cook a minute or so before serving to add new flavor. Experiment with your favorite herbs and eating vegetables won't get monotonous.

■ **Salad, make ahead:** To prevent salad from becoming soggy, put the desired dressing in the bottom of the salad bowl, layer in tomatoes and other vegetables and then add lettuce, spinach, or other greens. Put the prepared salad in the refrigerator and toss just before serving.

■ **Salad bar:** To encourage family salad eating, acknowledge that not everyone will like the same ingredients in a salad and serve salads like restaurant salad bars. Offer sliced mushrooms, carrots, beets, celery, chopped green onion, olives, garbanzo beans (chickpeas), kidney beans, sprouts, radishes, etc. in the cups of muffin tins served beside a large bowl of greens. Offer several types of salad dressings. Let family members make custom salads. Cover the muffin tin with plastic wrap after dinner to store leftovers in the fridge for the next day or two. Foods like celery, radishes, and carrot shreds will keep fresher for the next day if you put a wet, not drippy, paper towel on top before wrapping.

■ **Salad toss:** Tear greens into a large plastic bowl with a tight-fitting lid. Add dressing, give it a few shakes and no more tossing and bruising the lettuce.

■ **Vegetable pot luck:** When taking vegetables to a pot-luck dinner, one reader puts the hot vegetables—for example, Brussels sprouts—into a wide-mouth half-gallon thermos. They are still steaming hot several hours later when they are poured into the serving dish.

FRUIT

Fruit can be a snack, a dessert, or a delicious addition to other foods. There are many ways to add fruit to your daily diet. You can add bananas or raisins to your morning cereal. Dried fruits such as raisins, dates, figs, and others make easy and tasty additions to baked goods, salads, and other recipes. Or simply serve fresh fruit such as sliced apples or whole strawberries with a dip instead of crackers and chips for snacks or appetizers.

The USDA recommends two to four servings daily; one serving equals one whole fruit, such as an apple, banana, or orange; ¾ cup of fruit juice; half a grapefruit; a melon wedge; ½ cup of berries; ½ cup of cooked or canned fruit; or ¼ cup of dried fruit

Shopping

All the fruit that you buy—from the common apple to the most exotic tropical variety—should look fresh and crisp, be firm but not hard, and have no bruises or very soft spots. When you buy fruit such as berries in boxes, check to make sure the bottom ones aren't all squashed or rotten. Here's some helpful information and hints for your next visit to the supermarket or local fruit stand.

▪ **Apples:** Buy the right variety for the job. Some apples are good for eating out of hand and others are better for baking and pie making. Others like Granny Smith, are popular for both eating and cooking.

Apples can be stored in a plastic bag in the hydrator for 1 to 3 weeks depending on the variety or type of apple. Check the apples frequently for signs of rotting and discard the "bad apple." Here are a few of the most commonly available apples and their general uses. Many thanks to the International Apple Institute for this information.

Cortland: Juicy and tangy; used in pies, sauces, and cider; good for drying.

Fuji: Crisp, sweet, and tart; good for eating out of hand.

Gala: Crisp, sweet, and tart; good for eating out of hand and drying.

Golden Delicious: Yellow skin; juicy and sweet; good for eating out of hand; used in fruit salads and cider.

Granny Smith: Crisp and tart; white flesh with green skin; used in pies and sauces; good for baked apples.

Jonathan: Crisp and tart; good for eating out of hand; used in sauces, pies, and cider.

McIntosh: Juicy, spicy, and tart; good for eating out of hand; used in sauces and cider.

Red Delicious: Crisp, juicy, and mildly tart; good for eating out of hand; used in cider.

Rome beauty: Crisp, juicy, and mildly tart; good for baking and drying; used in cider.

Winesap: Very juicy, crisp, and firm; yellowish flesh with red skin; good for eating out of hand; used in sauces and cider.

▪ **Banana:** Slightly green bananas will ripen at home. If the bananas are yellow, a few brown spots are okay, but don't buy very bruised bananas because they could already be too overripe to eat.

▪ **Berries:** There are a wide variety of berries available for cooking and eating raw. Here are some of the most common and their properties:

Blackberries: Deep purple-black with a sweet-tart taste; many seeded; good raw or cooked in pies and preserves.

Blueberries: Deep blue with a dusky hue; tart; very popular addition to pies, pancakes, and muffins, good raw with cream.

Cranberries: Bright red, hard, and very acidic; most often used in cooking and baking around Thanksgiving and Christmas; ideal for relishes and sauces, and in pies and puddings.

Currants: Small, red, and tart; often used in cooking, fresh or dry.

Gooseberries: Green grapelike berries; good raw; usually made into jam or pies.

Lingonberries: Red and tart; cooked in sauces or jams; recently noted for their healthful properties.

Raspberries: Red, black, or golden yellow; sweet; good raw; used in pies, jams, and puddings.

Strawberries: Perhaps the most popular berry; plump, red, and sweet; the seeds are on the outside; good raw; cooked in a wide variety of preserves, sauces, pies, and other desserts.

▪ **Grapefruit:** Yellow or pinkish skin with pale or pinkish flesh; should be heavy and firm. Eat raw in halves or sections. Halves can be sprinkled with brown sugar and grilled lightly.

▪ **Grapes:** Among the many popular varieties are cardinal (dark red), concord (black), muscadine (green, russet or black, sweet and juicy) and Thompson (sweet, green, seedless). Most grapes are eaten raw but many, especially the smaller seedless varieties can be used in baking or in sauces.

▪ **Guava:** Light green or yellow, these plum-shaped fruits are available from December to February and are usually made into jelly. The flesh inside is white to dark pink, and unless they are tree ripened, they will be very tart.

▪ **Kiwi** (kiwifruit): Buy firm fruit and let it ripen at room temperature for about a week. When a kiwi is about as soft as a ripe plum, it is ready to eat. **Note:** If a kiwi at the store is already soft, it may be bruised and ready to rot instead of ready to eat. Usually, kiwi from California is available from May through November; New Zealand kiwi is available from November through May.

▪ **Kumquat:** Buy firm, orange fruit, never green, because they won't ripen to an acceptable flavor. They are very tart and have lots of seeds, so are usually made into marmalade. They are not a very popular eating fruit. Store them in the refrigerator. The peak season is December to May.

▪ **Lemon:** Lemons should be firm and heavy with a smooth skin. Old lemons or those that have been stored improperly are bumpy, bruised, or wrinkled.

▪ **Lime:** This sour, green citrus fruit is popular as a garnish and is used in cooking. Like lemons, they should be firm, but not hard, and heavy with a smooth skin.

▪ **Loquat:** These look like small fuzzy apricots and they have three or four pits. Even when in peak season—mid-March to May— they are very expensive.

▪ **Lychee** (lychee nuts): Fresh and dried lychees are sold in Asian communities as gifts. This rather expensive fruit is about as big as a golf ball and has a rough, tough, inedible skin, which fades from strawberry color to dusty pink after picking. The light green flesh surrounds an inedible nut. The edible part of one lychee is about equal to the flesh of two or three grapes.

■ **Mango:** Mangoes can range in size from a few ounces to 4 pounds. Some types are very fibrous and stringy. Usually the flat, kidney-shaped varieties are the most fibrous and sour. The three popular types of mangoes in this country are Haden (yellow skin with a red cheek when ripe), Kent (large with a green skin with a reddish cheek), and Keitt (large with a green skin; may have a red cheek). Although they are in season from January through September, their peak is May to July. Tree-ripened mangoes are the sweetest and imported mangoes are usually ready to eat when bought at the market. Florida mangoes are picked hard and need a week at room temperature to ripen.

■ **Melons:** Usually, if a bit of stem is still attached to the melon, it means that the fruit was picked before it was ripened. Since some melons don't ripen after picking, look for a dent where the stem was, which indicates that the melon was ripe when it was picked. Almost all ready-to-eat melons should have a fruity scent; and you should choose the ones they feel heavy for their size. They should have no cracks, mold, or soft spots other than at the ends, which should have a slight give when you press them. Some say that if you shake a cantaloupe and can tell that the seeds are moving inside, the melon is ripe; but if it has soft spots on the rind, it may be too ripe or even rotten. Others say that when you can tell that the seeds are moving inside of any melon, it is

too ripe. The only melons that ripen after picking are those with smooth rinds, such as honeydew. You can hasten ripening by placing the uncut melon in a brown paper bag until it is ripe. Melons, such as cantaloupe, with webbed skin should be ready to eat when you buy them.

■ **Orange:** Oranges and other citrus fruits (grapefruit, lemons, limes) should feel heavy relative to their size. For example, if you pick up a large orange, perhaps one that's the size of a small grapefruit, and it feels lighter than it should for its size, when you peel it, you'll probably find a very thick peel and not much flesh inside. Look for an orange with a thinner skin and more pulp.

■ **Papaya:** Papayas are usually light green when harvested; they ripen to golden yellow. The flesh inside is yellow or orange-pink. Buy firm, pale green or pale yellow fruit and ripen it at room temperature. It's better not to refrigerate them. They are in season year round. When you buy papaya, don't forget to buy some limes. They are delicious when sprinkled with fresh lime juice.

■ **Passion fruit:** This fruit is about as big as an egg with an inedible, withered skin that ranges from purple to red-gold. Its flesh is yellow and can be eaten out of hand or used in puddings or pies.

■ **Pears:** Pears are one of the few fruits that have to ripen after being picked, so you can buy them at any stage of green and keep them until they are ripe. You can refrigerate pears but not in sealed plastic bags, which causes the centers to become brown. Here are a few of the most commonly sold pears:

Anjou: A winter pear with white flesh and bland flavor; good for eating out of hand; used in cooking; keeps up to 7 days.

Asian: Large, yellow, and apple shaped; very white crisp flesh; best for eating out of hand.

Bartlett: Golden skin; sweet and juicy; good for eating out of hand; used in cooking, canning, and drying; keeps up to 8 days.

Bosc: Russet skin; juicy beige flesh; good for eating out of hand; used in cooking and drying; keeps up to 7 days.

Comice: Roundish shape; sweet; good for eating out of hand; used in desserts; keeps up to 7 days.

Seckel: Small; green to a maroon "blush" skin; the sweetest; used in desserts. Keeps up to 7 days.

■ **Persimmon:** Ripe persimmons look like shiny, acorn-shaped, deep orange tomatoes. Domestic persimmons are available from October to January and Chilean ones are sold in the spring. The old wives' tale about freezing unripe persimmons so that they will be ripe and edible when they thaw is true. And the other truth is that if you ever eat an unripe persimmon, you will never forget how tightly your lips puckered from the tartness! Buy firm, colorful persimmons and ripen them for several days at room temperature. When the skin is shriveled (blistered skin is not yet ripe), and has lost its color, the fruit can be eaten. The skin can also be eaten, if you wish.

■ **Pineapple:** Buy the largest pineapple in the display that is firm and shows some color. Some people like to press on the bottom to test

for a little give to the touch. Pineapples are available year round from Hawaii and Latin America. Read the tags to see where the pineapples have been grown. Usually, Hawaiian pineapples are sweeter and juicier because Latin American pineapples are picked while too green to have reached their full sugar content.

■ **Prickly Pear:** This fruit of the cactus is not really a pear, although it is more or less pear shaped. Most are deep red, but some are pale yellow, orange, or pink. Buy large fruit, ripen at room temperature, and then refrigerate before serving. Most prickly pears in the market have been singed to remove the barbs. The other challenge to eating this fruit, in addition to its skin, is the very seedy pulp. The seeds are edible but hard to chew.

■ **Star fruit** (carambola): When cut crosswise, this fruit look like a five-pointed star. Most come from Hawaii and the Caribbean islands, although some are grown in the U.S. mainland. The deeper the yellow color of the fruit's waxy-looking edible skin, the less tart the fruit will be. Eat them raw, float them in punch, or use them make jam and jelly. The peak season is from September to January.

■ **Watermelon:** Some say that if you look at the underside of a watermelon, the yellower the patch on which the melon rested, the sweeter the melon, because it had more time to ripen on the vine. The only way to be absolutely certain of a watermelon's ripeness is to buy one that's been cut in half or quarters. Sometimes, melons that are sold at roadside stands have been in the sun too long and will be almost mushy, as if cooked. (This happens with tomatoes, too.) Ask to have the watermelon plugged so that you can see what's inside.

Storing

For best preservation of quality, most fresh fruit keeps about 5 days in the refrigerator crisper drawer, but there are exceptions, which are noted below. Canned and cooked fruits in covered containers will keep about 1 week in the refrigerator. Unopened canned fruit keeps 1 to 2 years on the shelf. Dried fruit keeps about 6 months. (Some storage information was given in the last section.)

■ **Store apples** without washing in a crisper or moisture-resistant wrap that has breathing holes. *Don't* store apples and carrots in the same crisper drawer of the refrigerator. Apples give off ethylene gas, which will make carrots bitter.

Fresh Fruit Storage

The USDA says to ripen fruit at room temperature and to store them in the refrigerator for the following times.

Apples: 1 month.

Apricots, bananas, grapes, nectarines, peaches, pears, plums, and watermelon: 3 to 5 days.

Berries and cherries: 2 to 3 days.

Cranberries and melons (except watermelon): 1 week.

■ **To freeze raw apples** use with this simple method: Peel, core, and slice the apples. Sprinkle with lemon juice or ascorbic acid (which is sold at supermarkets for home freezing and canning) to keep them from turning brown. Store in freezer containers or plastic freezer bags in specific-use quantities, such as 1-, 2-, or 3-cup packs for recipes.

■ **Bananas** need not be refrigerated. If you want to prolong the storage time by refrigerating bananas that have become ripe enough to eat, the skins will get dark but the inside will be good for about 2 weeks.

■ **To ripen green bananas,** store them in a plastic bag.

■ **Overripe bananas** can be frozen and then used for banana bread or other baked goods.

■ **Berries and cherries** will keep about 3 days in a crisper or moistureproof wrapping.

■ You can **freeze cherries.** According to the Northeast Cherry Growers, here's how: Put them into a large colander to rinse well, pat dry then pit. Pack into freezer-safe plastic bags. They can be stored for 6 to 12 months under normal freezer conditions.

■ **Citrus fruit** keeps about 1 week at room temperature and 2 weeks in the refrigerator crisper or in a plastic container with a tight-fitting lid.

■ **Fresh-squeezed fruit juice** will keep about 3 to 4 days in a covered container.

■ To keep **lemons and limes** on hand, freeze whole or in wedges in a sturdy plastic freezer bag. When you need one, jut take it out of the bag, microwave it for a few minute or two on Medium; let stand on the counter for 10 more minutes before using it as you wish.

❀ **HELOISE HINT:** Save used hunks of limes or lemons, freeze them, and then let them go through the disposal to clean and remove odors when needed.

▪ **Pineapple** can be stored in the refrigerator for 2 to 3 days if you wrap it below the crown in plastic. If you remove it from the shell and slice it, it can be kept in an airtight container for 3 to 4 days. It's best to eat pineapple as soon as possible after buying it.

Cooking

▪ **Jams, Jellies, and Spreads:** Some of the commercially produced brands are sugar-free or have greatly reduced sugar content. *Read those labels!*

Jam is fruit (or vegetables, like chutney) which has been cooked and pureed into a soft and thick consistency.

Jelly is made from fruit juice or clear liquid and syrup or sugar. It's called jelly because the cooked mixture gels.

Fruit spreads are usually smooth and thick and made from fruit pulp and spices.

▪ **Applesauce:** When you cook apples for applesauce, leave on the skins of red-skinned apples, such as Cortland or McIntosh, then press them through a sieve or run them through a food mill to mash the sauce and remove skins and seeds. *Note:* Food mills are sold in cookware departments or shops.

▪ **Candied fruit peels:** Wash and dice the fruit peels to the appropriate size. (You can collect peels as you eat the fruit and store them in the freezer until you have pieces from about four each of oranges, lemons, and grapefruit.) In a large heavy bottomed pot, over low heat, boil 2 cups of sugar, 1 cup of water, and ¼ cup of corn syrup for 30 minutes. Add the peels and cook for 45 to 60 minutes, or until all the syrup is absorbed. Watch carefully in the last few minutes to avoid burning. Then sprinkle some sugar—about as much as you'd see on a sugared doughnut—on wax paper, lay the peels on it, and toss to coat. Or put the sugar in a paper bag or bowl and toss to coat. Allow to air-dry for a couple of days on wax paper. The advantage of tossing the peels on wax paper is that you can just leave them on the wax paper to dry. The candied fruit peels will keep indefinitely in the refrigerator.

▪ **Dried fruit** is a good snack for eating out of hand. Whenever a recipe calls for raisins, you can usually substitute the same amount of other dried fruit, although large fruit pieces may need to be cut smaller so that the pieces are better distributed throughout the dough. Dried fruit can be marinated with wine or brandy and kept in the refrigerator until they absorb the liquid, then put over ice cream for a delicious dessert.

▪ **Cut up dried fruit** with this simple method: Spray kitchen scissors blades with nonstick cooking spray and then snip fruit into small bits to make the job faster, easier, and safer than using a knife.

▪ **Remove identification stickers** from fruit without damaging the skin: Place a small piece of transparent tape over the sticker and it will pull the sticker right off.

▪ **Squeeze the juice** out of lemon or lime halves with a nutcracker.

- **Perk up a glass of water** with slices of lemon or lime.
- **Remove odors** from your hands with lemon or lime pieces.
- **Freeze lemon or lime juice cubes** to add to your iced tea. And, to avoid spilling the juice when carrying trays to the freezer, put the trays in the freezer first, and fill them with a turkey baster.
- **Quince** is usually made into jelly. Follow the directions given by the manufacturers of jelly-making pectin products.
- **Rhubarb:** Only the stalk is edible; the leaves are poisonous. Because rhubarb is bitter, it is cooked (poached, stewed, or baked) with sugar.
- **To stew rhubarb:** Cut up 1 pound of rhubarb into small pieces and place in a heavy pot with a couple of tablespoons of water and ½ to 1 cup of sugar. Simmer for about 20 minutes. (Add strawberries in the last few minutes of cooking to get a delicious sweetness.) Remove from the heat, cool, and then chill. Serve plain or with ice cream.

❀ **CLASSIC HELOISE HINT FOR CLEANING STRAWBERRIES:** My mother had a way of getting the sand off strawberries without bruising them: Fill a pan or sink half full of water (deep enough for the berries to float), put the strawberries into the water and then toss them lightly with your fingers. Use the cold water faucet or use a spray attachment to let the strawberries tumble themselves. Soon you'll see sand in the bottom of the pan. Remove the strawberries with your fingers, drain the pan or sink, and repeat the process as needed until the berries are free of grit. This may sound like a lot of trouble but if you have ever crunched sandy strawberries, you will want to try this method.

- **The zest of citrus fruit** is only the very outside colored part of the skin, *not* the whole peel or rind. You can remove the zest with a potato peeler, a grater, or a special zester tool available in kitchenware departments. Or simply scrape it with a sharp knife. Don't include any of the white part of the peel, because it is extremely bitter and will ruin the flavor of your recipe.

Serving

- **Grate apples for salad or other raw dishes** if you or a family member can't bite apple chunks because of dental problems.
- To make **banana ice pops,** freeze peeled bananas, then dip them in chocolate syrup and refreeze until the syrup hardens. If you put the bananas on a clean ice pop stick, they will be less messy to eat. Or cut peeled bananas into quarters and put peanut butter on the cut sides, wrap in plastic wrap, and freeze.
- Make **banana ice cubes:** Slice ripe bananas into 1-inch hunks, freeze, and then use them instead of ice cubes and malt to froth up blender milk shakes.
- For **faster mixing of frozen juice concentrates,** break up the frozen juice hunks with a potato masher. Or plan ahead: Before you go to bed, dump the frozen juice concentrate into a container, add the required amount of water, and put the container in the refrigera-

tor. In the morning, the juice will be thawed and you need only shake or stir.

■ To make **tasty fruit treats**, pour juice or the liquid from canned fruit (light syrup is best) into molds or paper cups, add an ice pop stick, and freeze. (To catch the drips when eating ice pops, slit the lid of a clean margarine or yogurt tub, poke the stick through the slit, and the plastic lid will catch the drips.)

■ **To prevent a grapefruit half from rocking** while you eat it, cut a thin slice off the bottom and it will rest more securely on the plate.

■ **Sprinkle peeled and cut kiwi with lime juice** to eat as is. Of use it for dipping in chocolate fondue. If you like yogurt, then kiwi and any kind of berries mixed with vanilla-flavored low-fat yogurt is a tasty and fairly low-cal dessert.

■ To serve **mango,** peel and remove flesh from the large seed in the middle, arrange the pieces on a plate and sprinkle with fresh lime juice.

❀ **HELOISE HINT:** Some mango seeds will grow into a houseplant tree. Just press the flat side of the seed into the dirt in a pot, just until the seed is just covered, and keep moist.

■ Peel and seed **papaya** and serve with a sprinkling of lime juice.

■ Cut off the top and bottom of **prickly pear** and then cut the fruit from end to end so that you can peel off the inedible skin.

■ **Freeze grapes or banana chunks** for sweet cold snacks.

■ If you have **slightly bruised fruits,** cut off the bad parts and make fruit salad or fruit pies. Or add to a tuna or chicken salad—apples and grapes are really delicious in salads!

■ **Make orange cups:** Cut the fruit in half, remove the pulp for whatever recipe you are making, and use the rind as a container for flavored gelatin or other dessert.

SWEETS, DESSERTS, AND BAKED GOODS

Whether it's dessert at the end of a good meal or an afternoon pause to pick up your spirits, sweets, desserts, and baked goods are a treat and home-baked goods are a special treat. Just the aroma from something baking in the oven warms the heart and tells you that you are home. In fact, potpourris that mimic the aromas of baked goods, such as vanilla and cinnamon, are often simmered in houses that are for sale to make them smell pleasant and comfortable to prospective buyers.

Shopping

Although you can buy virtually any type of baked goods in most supermarkets, a lot of people still enjoy making desserts at home. The types of ingredients that you consider as basics varies according to the type of baking you will do. For example, if you always use cake and other ready mixes, all you need to keep on hand are the ingredients that you add to the mixes, such as oil (or applesauce as a substitute for oil), eggs or egg substitute, and either ready-made frosting or ingredients for frosting (powdered sugar, vanilla, and butter or margarine). When you are shopping for ingredients, check your recipe first or take the recipe with you to the store to make sure you buy all the ingredients you will need. Also, check individual ingredients. For example, chocolate chips have a chocolate chip cookie recipe right on the bag so you have your shopping list for ingredients automatically made out for you.

The following ingredients are needed for most baked goods:

- **Flour**: wheat, whole wheat, cake, or self-rising.
- **Leavening agent**: yeast, baking powder, or baking soda. (If you bake with self-rising flour, you don't need to use leavening agents, but substituting it for flour and baking powder or soda may not work in all recipes.)
- **Sugar**: brown, granulated, or powdered. (*Note:* some artificial sweeteners are not suitable for baking. Read labels to find out if your favorite sugar substitute can be used for baking.)
- **Fat**: shortening, butter, margarine, or oil.

These are ingredients that flavor baked goods:

- Vanilla is basic but you may want to flavor with other **extracts** such as almond, brandy, rum, etc.
- Various **spices** such as cinnamon, ginger, allspice, nutmeg, and pumpkin pie spice (or a mixture of these).
- Baking **chocolate** squares, cocoa, and chocolate chips (milk or bittersweet).
- **Other chips** such as butterscotch, peanut butter, or toffee.
- **Dried fruits**, such as dates, raisins, apricots, prunes, figs, apples, and mixed dried fruits.
- **Nuts** such as pecans, walnuts, almonds, and peanuts.
- Shredded **coconut**.

For decorating cookies and frosted cakes:

- Colored **sugars**, cinnamon hearts, confetti candies, and chocolate shot (Jimmies).
- **Food color** for tinting frosting and other foods.
- Colored **frosting** in tubes, ready for decorating.

Ready-mades for short-cut baking:

- Cake, cookie, bread, and quick bread mixes. (Quick breads do not use yeast as a leavening agent and include banana, cranberry, and date-nut breads, which use baking powder and/or soda to make them rise.)
- Frozen cakes, ready to thaw and eat.
- Tubes of refrigerated cookie dough, ready to slice and bake or freeze to keep on hand for times when you want fresh cookies without the mess.
- Tubes of refrigerated sweet and dinner rolls.
- Frozen or ready-made pie shells from pie dough or crumbs (graham or chocolate cookie crumbs).
- Frozen pies ready to thaw and eat or ready to bake and eat.
- Phyllo dough (pastry dough that is layered with butter to make a crisp, rich crust).
- Frozen bread and rolls, ready to bake or ready to let rise and then bake.

Storing

- **Freezing cake:** It's best to freeze cakes before frosting or filling, because fillings can make the cakes soggy. To freeze layers without frosting, wrap the cake in several layers of plastic wrap as soon as it's thoroughly cooled and place in a carton or other container to prevent crushing. Cakes do not freeze completely solid. To thaw, leave in the wrapping to prevent moisture from forming on the cake surface. Large cakes may take 2 to 3 hours at room temperature to thaw; a single cake layer may take about 1 hour; cupcakes, about 30 minutes. Unfrosted cakes may be kept frozen up to 3 months, but frosted cakes are best stored only 1 or 2 months. If you freeze a cake after frosting, do so *before* you wrap it to avoid messing up the frosting. Wrap with plastic wrap, and then place it in a heavy carton or other protective container.

- **Canister substitute:** Recycle plastic 1-gallon milk jugs by cutting an opening in the front of the jug and cutting off the *front* top half of the jug 1 or 2 inches below the neck, so that the handle and upper part of the jug supporting the handle and the lower half of the jug are left intact. Then you can put bags of flour or sugar into the remaining bowl of the jug. The bags won't tip or spill and you'll have an easy handle for pulling them out of the cupboard.

- **Chocolate for cooking:** Heat, light, and odors can ruin chocolate. Chocolate should be kept wrapped and stored in a cool, dry place. Some people feel better if they keep it in the refrigerator, but the cupboard will do, just so it's not near a heat source like above the stove. Chocolate will usually last for about 1 year, but if you notice a flavor or texture change, then the chocolate has lived past its shelf life.

- **Chocolates for eating (or not!):** Although it sounds like something that could never happen, it is possible to have more chocolate than you can eat in a reasonable time. (Of course, it depends on your definition of *reasonable time*!) The good news is that you can freeze chocolate in plastic freezer bags or in an unopened plastic-wrapped box. In fact, many people like to freeze those extra Valentine or holiday chocolates and take them out one at a time or in the amount that they want to allow themselves on any given day.

▨ A READER RECOMMENDS:

One Heloise fan has her children put all extra candy, like from Halloween and birthday parties, into a "candy bank" to save for a rainy day. Then when they are cooped up in the house, they can have a treat from the bank. She says it teaches delayed gratification and the value of saving for a rainy day.

- **Custards and cream pies:** Custards, custard sauces, and cream-filled pies or cakes should be stored on the coldest shelf of the refrigerator and kept only 2 to 3 days.

- **Ice cream:** Recycle 1-cup yogurt containers with lids to store individual portions of ice cream. This avoids a mess when children help themselves and helps dieters who suffer from container eating or who are tempted to eat the whole thing.

- **Marshmallows:** It really is easy to keep

Equivalent Measure for Baking Ingredients

Butter, margarine or shortening: 1 ounce = 2 table-spoons; ¼ pound = ½ cup or 1 stick; ½ pound = 1 cup; 1 pound = 2 cups.

Cheese: 1 pound American = 5 cups grated; one 3-ounce package of cream cheese = 6⅔ table-spoons.

Chocolate: 1 square = 1 ounce = 3½ tablespoons dry cocoa plus 1 tablespoon butter.

Crumbs: graham crackers: 9 coarsely crumbled or 11 finely crumbled = 1 cup; small vanilla wafers: 20 coarsely crumbled or 30 finely crumbled = 1 cup.

Eggs: 12 to 14 egg yolks = 1 cup; 8 to 10 egg whites = 1 cup.

Flours: all-purpose: 1 pound sifted = 4 cups; cake: 1 pound sifted = 4½ cups; graham: 1 pound unsift-ed = 3½ cups; cornmeal: 1 pound = 3 cups.

Fruits and nuts: 1 lemon = 3 to 4 tablespoons of juice; 1 orange = 6 to 8 tablespoons of juice; one 15-ounce package of seedless raisins = 3 cups; ¼ pound shelled nuts = 1 cup chopped (for most nuts).

Rice: 1 pound = 2⅓ cups raw.

Sugar: granulated: 1 pound = 2½ cups; confection-ers': 1 pound unsifted = 4 cups; confectioners': 1 pound sifted = 4½ cups; brown dark, firmly packed: 1 pound = 2¼ cups; brown, light: 1 pound = 2⅓ cups.

marshmallows fresh and unstuck. Put marsh-mallows in a freezer-safe plastic bag or a plastic container with a tight-fitting lid and store them in the freezer.

- **Flour:** Flour should be stored in airtight containers. Whole wheat flour, especially, is best stored in the refrigerator or freezer to maintain best quality.

- **Sugar:** Store sugar in a clean and dry recy-cled plastic milk jug. It won't attract bugs or get hard and lumpy, and the jug is easier to handle than a bag. Also, you'll be able to see how much is left in this free, recycled canister.

- **Shakers for flour and sugar:** Keep large shakers of flour and sugar handy on the kitchen counter so you won't have to haul out the can-isters when you need just a sprinkle or so of either one. A shaker of flour is used to dust the counter to roll dough and for drenching meat before browning it. Sugar can be sprinkled on baked goods and hot cereals.

Cooking

- **Batter beating:** To avoid spatters when beating batters, make an oblong-shaped hole that's large enough to insert the two beaters in the center of a clean shower cap or plastic bowl cover. Place the cap over the bowl; insert the beaters (rotary hand beater or electric mixer) and beat away. You can also make a cover for the bowl from plastic wrap, wax paper, or foil, but the elastic from the shower cap holds the cover in place.

- **Brown sugar substitutes:** Although it won't have the same texture as store-bought brown sugar, you can substitute the following mixture in a pinch. Mix together 1 cup of granulated sugar with 4 tablespoons of dark molasses. Mix with a fork to make sure the molasses is evenly distributed. *Note:* Molasses is one of the ingredients used in manufacturing brown sugar; the amount added determines light or dark brown sugar. You can substitute dark for light or light for dark brown sugars in recipes, but the dark will have a stronger flavor because it has more molasses.

■ A READER RECOMMENDS:

One reader added a couple of heaping tablespoons of cottage cheese to her corn muffin recipe when she was out of buttermilk and said the taste was richer and the leftover muffins stayed moist when they were reheated.

■ **Cookies from a cake mix:** To boxed cake or dry muffin mix, add two eggs and ½ cup of vegetable cooking oil. You can also add raisins, nuts, or coconut. Mix well. With a teaspoon, drop spoonfuls of batter on an ungreased cookie sheet, about 2 inches apart. Bake at 350 degrees F for 8 to 10 minutes. Cool and enjoy!

■ **Extra moist cake:** Substitute an equal amount of club soda for water when you make a German chocolate cake from a mix and you'll get an extra moist and tasty cake.

■ **Football-shaped cake:** Grease and flour a roaster pan as you would a regular cake pan. After baking, take the pan out of the oven, place it on a warm, wet towel. The cake will slide right out. To decorate: Color coconut with brown food color to cover the cake icing and make "laces" with black licorice.

■ **Heart-shaped cake:** If you don't have heart-shaped cake pans, bake a two-layer cake as directed on the package, except bake one 8-inch square layer and one 8-inch round layer. To assemble: Cut the round layer exactly in half across the diameter. Place the square layer on a doily-covered cookie sheet or tray in a position that lets you add the cut diameter-sides of the round layer on either side of the top corner to form a heart. Frost to cover the seams between cake pieces. Decorate with Valentine candies or decorator frostings.

■ **Cutting unfrosted cake layers:** Instead of a knife, cut cake layers with a long piece of thread or dental floss held taut; it will be less messy and will be very even.

■ **Preventing dome-shape layers** for most cakes: Try baking the cake at 250 degrees F for 1 hour and 20 minutes or until done. Often baking at too high a temperature makes the cake rise too fast.

■ **Cake leftovers:** Although it's hard to imagine leftover cake in most households, when you are cooking for one or two, you may have leftover cake! Here are a couple of ideas:

Break the cake into pieces and layer with slightly softened ice cream; freeze and slice for a new dessert. You can drizzle chocolate sauce or an appropriate liqueur over each serving. Try coffee-flavored liqueur over chocolate ice cream and angel food cake, or chocolate liqueur over chocolate mint chip ice cream and any cake, or orange liqueur over vanilla ice cream and cake.

Prepare one package of cooked chocolate pudding mix as directed; cool. Whip 1 cup of whipping cream with ⅓ cup of confectioners' sugar, and fold into cooled pudding. Cut up one layer of a 9-inch cake (white, yellow, or chocolate) into 2-inch squares and line the bottom of an 8-inch-square baking dish. Pour the pudding over the cake and sprinkle with ¼-½ cup of chopped nuts (optional). Chill several hours in the refrigerator before serving. Serves four to six.

■ **Odd-shaped cakes:** If you need to measure the batter capacity of an odd-shaped pan, such as hearts, lambs, bells, stars, etc., to determine the amount of batter, fill the pan with water, pour the water into a large measuring container and then note the amount of this water. Fill the pan with batter equal to *half* the amount of water that filled the pan.

■ **Cake pan substitute:** Substitute stainless-steel mixing bowls for cake pans. See "odd-shaped cakes" (above) for directions.

■ **Cake tester** (for doneness): Out of toothpicks? Substitute a long thin piece of uncooked spaghetti. It will keep you away from oven heat so you can test long distance and is especially handy for angel food or other deep cakes.

■ **Canned cake frosting** isn't only for cakes; you can frost baked rolled-out cookies with it, too. If you need colored frosting, add a few drops of food color to white canned frosting.

■ **Greasing cake pans:** Keep a plastic sandwich bag in the shortening can so that you can poke your hand into the bag, grab some shortening and grease the pans with the same bag over and over. Saves time and recycles the bag!

■ **Stuck in the pan:** If you forget and let the cake get completely cooled before turning it out so that it's stuck in the pan, put the pan into a warm oven briefly to soften the shortening used to grease the pan. When the pan bottom gets warmed, remove it from the oven and turn the layer out immediately onto a cooling rack.

■ **Avoid flour dust on the bottom of cake layers:** Instead of sprinkling flour on the greased pan to prevent sticking, sprinkle some of the mixed dry ingredients of the recipe or some dry cake mix. Tap the excess back into your mixing bowl and proceed as usual.

■ **Cake decorating:** Here are some quick and different ideas to keep in mind:

Spaghetti drawings: Cook very thin spaghetti until pliable, rinse in cold water, drain, and cut to desired lengths. In a bowl, gently stir several drops of food color into the spaghetti and let sit while you decorate the rest of the cake. Blot each strand to catch drips of color then use the colored spaghetti to make shapes. You can draw Easter bunny whiskers and mouths, and more!

Black frosting: Add blue food color to chocolate frosting until you get the desired blackness.

Decorating bag: Cut the corner out of the bottom of a plastic sandwich or storage bag, slip in the decorating tip, fill the bag with frosting, zip close, and decorate like a pro.

Substitute for chocolate drizzle: Instead of making drizzle icing, cut a chocolate bar into thin pieces, put them on top of the cake while it's still warm and you'll get near-instant drizzles.

- **Cake frosting made easy:** If you have trouble frosting a crumbly cake because the icing lumps up and the crumbs keep sticking to the knife, put the cake into the freezer until it is firm, and then put the icing on the cake!

- **Double-good cake frosting:** If you like chocolate peanut butter cups, add about 1 tablespoon of peanut butter to chocolate frosting; it's delicious! You could even make a stretch and say you're adding nutrition with the peanut butter as well as flavor!

- **Chocolate dipping:** When dipping pretzels, crackers, cookies, etc. in melted chocolate, place one or two pieces on a potato masher, dip into the melted chocolate, withdraw and let excess chocolate drip back into the cooking pot. Place on wax paper or a rack to cool.

- **Melting chocolate:** If you let the boiling water touch the bottom of the top pot of a double-boiler while you are melting chocolate, the chocolate will scorch and get hard and gritty. Cooking the chocolate too fast or in a too lightweight of a saucepan also can make it gritty. I like to melt chocolate in a heavy saucepan over very low heat and stir often. I stir with a spatula so that the whole pan is scraped in a few swishes. You can also melt chocolate in the microwave; follow the directions for your microwave or those on the chocolate package.

- **Cocoa cans:** Some cocoa cans have openings too small for measuring utensils. So sift the whole 8-ounce can of cocoa into a 2-pound clean plastic margarine tub with an airtight lid. Then you can scoop with any measuring utensil and the cocoa won't get lumpy.

- **Cookie baking:** When you make dozens of cookies at a time, use a large melon baller to measure the cookie dough onto cookie sheets. The cookies will be uniform and will be done at the same time.

- **Cookie time-saver:** Flatten cookies that you roll into a ball, like peanut butter cookies, with a potato masher.

✿ **HELOISE HINT:** To keep peanut butter cookies from sticking to your fork when you criss-cross the tops to flatten them, use a plastic fork; batter doesn't stick to the plastic. Or coat a metal fork with a light spritz of cooking spray.

- **Chocolate chips:** When making chocolate chip cookies, reserve a teaspoon of the chips when you mix the dough. When you get to the last spoonfuls of batter, which usually don't have too many chips, you can add the reserved chips and make those last cookies as good and chocolatey as the first ones.

- **Cookie crumbs:** Recycle cookie crumbs from the bottom of the cookie jar and add them to bread pudding.

- **Cookie cutters:** Plastic seasonal cookie cutters come in many shapes and colors. Use them for holiday napkin rings after the baking is over.

■ **A READER RECOMMENDS:**
One reader saves time rolling and rerolling cookie dough with this hint: When cutting out cookies, leave enough space between each cut cookie to make "crazy cookies" with the weird shapes left behind by the cookie cutters. Children can use their imaginations to decide what the cookies could be.

- **Cookie decorating:** After preparing cookie dough and cutting out the cookies with cutters, place the cookie cutter around the cutout cookie before sprinkling on colored sugars or sparkles. The cutter keeps the sprinkles from being scattered about. This hint is especially good if you are making cookies with children.

- **Cookie dough freezing:** Make a double batch of cookies and freeze cookie dough logs so that they are ready to slice and bake when you get a serious case of the munchies.

- **Cookie monster trick:** If you are trying **not** to eat cookies because you are avoiding sugary things, fill your cookie jar with low-sugar, dry cereal. It's not a rich chocolate treat but cereal is still a great snack!

- **Calorie counting:** Cut a few calories from chocolate chip cookies by substituting ½ cup mini-chips for 1 cup of regular-size chips. Few cookie munchers will notice.

- **Cookie repair:** Cookies too brown on the bottoms? Rub the brown off with the coarse side of your vegetable slicer/grater.

- **Fat substitute:** Substitute vegetable oil for butter or lard in recipes. You will need one-third less vegetable oil. For example, 2 teaspoons of vegetable oil substitutes for 1 tablespoon or solid shortening (1 tablespoon equals 3 teaspoons).

- **Bread flour vs. all-purpose:** There is a difference. Bread flour has a higher protein content than all-purpose flour. The higher the protein content, the more elastic the dough becomes and the better the volume and texture; therefore, the flour is more manageable, especially for novice bread makers. The amount of protein may vary from brand to brand of bread flour, so if you are just learning to bake, make a note of the brand of flour that gives you the best results.

- **Frosting, a quick substitute:** A few minutes before removing cupcakes from the oven, top each with a marshmallow and let bake until the marshmallows are melted and slightly brown and you'll have instant frosting. Or the minute you remove cupcakes or cookies from the oven, place a square of chocolate (from a candy bar) on top, let melt, and give the chocolate a few swirls with a table knife or spatula.

- **Gelatin** will mix more quickly and easily if you sprinkle powdered gelatin over the boiling hot water instead of adding cold water to the gelatin.

- **Graham cracker crumbs:** When you need to crush graham or other crackers, put them into a large plastic zipper bag, release the air, seal, and then crush them with a rolling pin.

❁ KITCHENEERING HUMOR ❁

One of my readers likes to wear wooden clogs. For crumbs, she puts crackers or stale bread in a plastic bag and walks on it. She says it is fast and more fun than a rolling pin.

- **Ice for homemade ice cream:** Freeze water in empty quart milk cartons overnight. With a hammer, strike all four sides of the frozen carton a couple of times. Open the top and the crushed iced drops neatly into the ice cream maker. About 5 quarts of ice with a layer of rock salt added after each one is enough for the average ice cream machine.

- **Marshmallows:** One large marshmallow equals ten small ones.

■ **Muffin tin greasing:** If you don't have nonstick spray or paper liners for the cups of your muffin tin, here's a less-mess way to oil them: Pour about ¼ cup of oil into one of the muffin cups, then dip a waded-up paper towel into the oil. Rub the other cups with the towel, reoiling it as you go.

❀ **HELOISE HINT:** Keep a clean shoehorn in the kitchen to lift muffins out of the tin without tearing them.

■ **Oil dispenser:** Wash a squirt bottle from mustard or mayo and you'll have an oil dispenser.

■ **Cracking nuts:** Freeze Brazil and other hard-shell nuts before cracking. If freezing doesn't work for pecans, try placing them in a microwave-safe bowl, add enough water to cover and heat on High for about 3 minutes. Remove the pecans from water and let them cool. The shells should crack easily.

■ **Nut chopper:** Put shelled nuts into a sturdy plastic bag and crush them with a meat mallet or wooden potato masher or rolling pin. *Note:* If you use a meat mallet, use the side because the teeth will poke through the plastic bag and make a mess.

■ **Nut alternative:** If you or a guest can't eat nuts or you just don't have any, substitute the same amount of rice cereal in the recipe.

■ **Nut substitute:** You can substitute walnuts for pecans in pecan pie and other pecan recipes. The taste won't be the same but walnuts are delicious, too.

■ **Sugar shaker:** Use a salt shaker to sprinkle the sugar on cookies hot from the oven. (Colored sugar may need a sugar shaker with large holes.)

■ **Sugar coloring:** Put 1 cup of granulated sugar in a glass bowl or measuring cup, add a few drops of food color and mix well until the color is distributed evenly. Darken the color by adding a drop or two more of food color. Let dry and store in a sprinkle top bottle for decorating cookies and cakes.

■ **Confectioners' sugar substitute:** Mix 1 cup of granulated sugar and 1 tablespoon cornstarch in a blender at high speed until it is a fine powder. *Note:* As with most substitutes, the consistency and texture of the dish may be slightly altered.

■ **Sugar, baking with less:** In most recipes, you can replace half the sugar in a recipe with half heat-stable diet sweetener.

■ **Sweet and sugar substitutes:** You can't substitute corn syrup or honey for sugar when baking because sugar is a dry ingredient so it adds bulk as well as sweetness. If you substitute corn syrup for honey, you'll need to add a bit more because it isn't as sweet as honey.

■ **Cut the fat!** Fruit puree as a substitute for fat in recipes is now available at the supermarket; follow the directions on the jar.

■ **Sugar replacements:** If you have to limit your sugar intake, try other flavorings:

Add cinnamon, vanilla, or other extracts to your coffee.

Add vanilla or fruit (dried or fresh) to plain nonfat yogurt.

Sprinkle cinnamon on a baked apple or applesauce.

Sprinkle pumpkin pie spice mixture on sweet potatoes along with a sprinkle of butter substitute.

Add chopped dried fruit to your cereal.

■ **Pie baking:** To keep juice from boiling over and out of a fruit pie, make the top crust large and put it on loosely, pushing it back toward the center of the pie. Then seal the edges as usual. The loose crust will expand with the steam and the juice will stay in the pie. *Note:* As always, you still need to cut a few slits into the top crust to let steam escape while the pie bakes.

■ **Two-fruit pies:** If you want to make two different fruit pies at the same time, try this hint from one of my mother's readers: Place a circle of pastry in a 12-inch pie pan. Put filling in half of it and fold the other half of the dough over to the outer edge of the pan, crimp the edges together. It will look like a large fried pie. Then roll out the second pastry circle, fit it into the same pan with the wide part against the other pie and pour in the other filling. Fold over the top half to the other edge of the pan, seal. Cut stem vents in each section and bake as usual.

■ **Chocolate-bottom pies:** After baking the shell for a chocolate or other custard or pudding pie, sprinkle pieces of a broken-up chocolate bar or chocolate chips on the bottom of the crust and then add the hot custard or vanilla pudding. The hot pudding melts the chocolate and you'll have a chocolate bottom pie. You can shave a few curls of chocolate off the chocolate bar to save for a garnish on the top of the finished and cooled pie.

■ **Leftover pie crust:** Roll out leftover pie dough and brush lightly with margarine or butter. Sprinkle with brown sugar and roll it up. Slice into pinwheels about 1 inch wide and place on a cookie sheet. Bake them in the oven while the pie is baking. They will take about 15 minutes to get golden brown, depending on the temperature used for baking the pie.

■ **Meringue:** Making a meringue-topped pie intimidates many cooks but readers have sent many good hints on how to top pies with perfect meringues:

Egg whites should always be room temperature before beating them for meringue, and you need to use a minimum of three egg whites for each pie.

After the egg whites are beaten stiff but not dry, sprinkle ¼ teaspoon cream of tartar and a dash of salt on top and beat slightly. Then slowly add 3 level tablespoonfuls of sugar for each egg white in the bowl, beating all the while.

Food Safety Note: In my mother's day the cook would taste the meringue and if grains of sugar could be detected, you would need to beat the egg whites longer, but today's cooks are discouraged from tasting any raw eggs to avoid the possibility of *Salmonella.* So you may want to pinch some of the meringue with your fingers; if you have a light touch you may be able to feel sugar grains in the meringue.

When you top the pie with meringue, *always* have the meringue touching the edges of the pie crust; it prevents shrinking.

Put the pie on the middle shelf of the oven (not the top), so that it will brown evenly and the points or swirls of meringue won't get burned.

When the meringue is almost as brown as you want it, turn off the oven, and open the door slightly so that the meringue cools slowly; this prevents the meringue from cracking or splitting.

Never set the pie to cool where cold drafts can get at it because it must cool *slowly*.

- **Light versus dark brown sugar:** The only difference between light and dark brown sugars is the amount of molasses added by the manufacturer. Each can substitute for the other, but because the dark brown sugar has more molasses added, the recipe will have a bit more molasses flavor.

- **Soften hardened brown sugar:** Many cooks put a slice of fresh bread or a slice of fresh apple in with the brown sugar to soften it overnight.

❀ KITCHENEERING HUMOR ❀

Told by an experienced cook to use a piece of bread to soften brown sugar, a novice cook complained that she'd put a slice of bread on top of the brown sugar to soften it without success. So the experienced cook checked out the sugar to see what had gone wrong. "See," the novice cook said, "I put the bread on top." It was on top of the canister, not inside with the brown sugar!

- **Measuring syrup, molasses, or honey:** Avoid a mess when measuring sticky ingredients by first spraying the measuring cup or spoon with plain cooking spray—the sweetener will slide right out and clean-up is a breeze.

- **Crystallized honey** will recover if you microwave it for a few seconds (uncovered) on High or let the jar of honey sit in very hot water for a while. Store on the shelf—not in the refrigerator—to avoid this problem.

- **Slippery whipping bowls:** When you whip cream or toppings, the mixing bowl won't slip and slide across the counter if you place a damp washcloth under it before turning on the mixer.

- **Syrup substitute:** If you run out of pancake syrup, mix 1 cup of brown sugar and ½ cup of water in a saucepan. Bring mixture to boil, let simmer for about 15 minutes. *Don't* let it boil again or overcook. Add 1 teaspoon or so of maple flavoring to suit your taste and serve. Or if you've run out of syrup for your pancakes or waffles, add a little water and a dab of butter to fruit jelly and heat over low heat for a short time. You'll get delicious fruit syrup.

- **Whipped cream/topping:** Add a sprinkle of allspice, cinnamon, or nutmeg and a drop of vanilla extract to whipped cream or topping to make it extraspecial.

- **Whipped topping substitute:** Whip a couple of egg whites until stiff, add a drop of vanilla and sugar to taste, then whip until foamy and dollop onto desserts.

Serving

- **Overbaked brownies:** If you overbake brownies, place them in the microwave on Low for a few seconds right before eating and they'll be nice and soft.

■ **Birthday candle holders:** Miniature marshmallows or small gumdrops will hold birthday cake candles on a cake. You can poke the candles directly into the marshmallows but you'll have to poke a hole into the gumdrops before inserting the candle. If you have the time, you can make candle holders from maraschino cherries that have been dipped into heavy syrup, then rolled in finely chopped nuts, or just drain the cherries on a paper towel to remove drips and roll them in confectioners' sugar to make birthday cake candle holders.

■ **No-mess lunch-box cakes:** Slice a piece of frosted sheetcake in half (lengthwise) then "fold" the two pieces so that the icing is in the center (fold the tops to center). The icing won't stick to the plastic wrap.

■ **Mail-order cookies:** Save tall potato chip cans so that you can stack cookies in them for mailing.

■ **Soften ice cream for scooping:** Zap the carton in the microwave on Low or Defrost. Depending on the power of your microwave, a pint takes 10 to 15 seconds, a half gallon 30 to 45 seconds. Experiment to find the right amount of time, but remember to let it sit for a minute or two before zapping again, since the ice cream will continue to "cook" after being removed from the oven.

■ **Gelatin molds:** Get a perfect mold by first oiling the pan with a neutral-flavored oil, such as canola, or with nonstick vegetable spray. After the gelatin is set, place it in a pan of hot water for 2 or 3 minutes, or until it loosens, lift the pan out and dry the bottom of the mold to avoid drips on the serving plate. Place a plate on top of the mold, and turn it upside down. Or put the mold upside down on the serving plate and apply a hot, wet towel to it.

■ **Stubborn gelatin:** Try inserting a thin knife point at the very edge where the gelatin meets the side of the mold to let some air in and break the suction holding the mold in.

■ **Lettuce bed for gelatin:** After loosening the mold as noted above, place lettuce leaves on top of the gelatin with the leaves folded down around the edges of the mold, then place the serving plate, upside down, over the lettuce. Hold the mold and plate firmly, turn the whole thing over so that the mold is on top and the plate is on the bottom, with lettuce in between. Shake the mold gently in a circular motion while holding the plate and mold in place. The salad should drop down and be centered on the lettuce.

■ **Ice cream cone drips:** To prevent drippy messes from that hole that seems to appear *after* you have put ice cream into the cone, put a small marshmallow into the cone *before* you scoop in the ice cream; then, if the ice cream melts, the marshmallow will serve as a plug to prevent drips from the cone's bottom.

■ **Ice cream cones cups:** Serve children's healthy snacks, such as dry cereal, small crackers, and raisins, in an ice cream cone.

■ **Ice cream sticks:** Here are some ideas for using recycled ice cream sticks.

Use them to stir coffee on the go.
Use them to level dry ingredients when measuring.

Take them to picnics for spreading mustard, mayo, and ketchup.

Use them to scrape mud or other gooey stuff from shoes.

Make ¼-inch marks on them and use them in the garden when planting seeds or bulbs.

Use them to make identifying sticks for plants.

Use them to spread glue, paste, grout, or paint.

Let kids use them for all sorts of construction projects.

■ **Dispensing jams and jellies:** Spread jams and jellies neatly with a squeeze bottle, like a recycled ketchup or mustard bottle. This is an especially good hint for households with children. Little hands can't always deal with a knife or spreader. If the squeeze bottle doesn't let enough jelly out, you can cut a bit more off the nozzle tip to make a larger hole.

BEVERAGES: COFFEE, TEA, BEER, WINE, AND SPIRITS

We've all been told since our childhood to drink eight glasses of water every day and this is a healthy practice. But we humans do not exist on water alone. We also like variety in our beverages and tastes vary. We all know someone who can't start the day without a cup of steaming coffee but we also know people who get their caffeine from cola drinks in the morning instead of coffee. And we have as many coffee and beer snobs as wine snobs these days because more and more varieties of all beverages are available in supermarkets—no more driving around town to find a special vintage or brew in a gourmet shop. Having so many choices so readily available can make shopping for beverages bewildering. I hope this section helps you when you make a beverage run to either the supermarket or the liquor store.

Coffee

SHOPPING

Coffee came to North America with the Dutch when New Amsterdam was settled in 1660. By the time the British took over the city and renamed it New York, coffee drinking had replaced beer for breakfast. (Yes, beer was the beverage of choice in our country's early days!) The first coffee houses were more like taverns and were places to socialize and to conduct business. But coffee was a rich person's beverage; tea was the most popular hot beverage for the majority. Then in 1773, when King George of England put a tax on tea, the American colonists revolted. The citizens of Boston, dressed as Native Americans, boarded English merchant vessels and emptied their entire tea cargoes into the ocean, and this event, known as the Boston Tea Party, was the beginning of our American love affair with coffee.

Just like wine tasters seek out the bouquet or tannin or fruity flavors in their wines, coffee connoisseurs have certain terms for the flavors of different coffees. I've listed them here so that you can impress your friends at the coffee houses with your coffee savvy and so that you can pick the brews you enjoy without having to abuse your tongue with flavors that you don't like. The information is adapted from *The Book of Coffee* by Jack Baxter.

- **Acidity:** This refers to a sharp and pleasant taste that's neither sweet nor sour and doesn't always mean a degree of acidity in the beans.
- **Body:** When coffee is on your tongue, there should be a pleasing aroma and the flavor should be rich. Thin watery coffee is said to lack body.
- **Harsh:** An unpleasant raw weedy taste, but many coffee drinkers like a hint of harsh in their brews.
- **Winy:** A taste occurring when beans have been fermented, it is a somewhat gamey taste.

Aside from the famous and popular Kona coffee from Hawaii, most of the coffees we drink in the United States are grown in other parts of the world. Here's information from *The Book of Coffee* about the world's coffees.

- **Angolan** coffee has a strong flavor, and is mostly robusta (harsh).
- **In Brazil** the favored bean is Bourbon Santos, which is smooth and sweet with a medium body. Santos arabica is usually a medium roast and regular grind for brewing by the jug method (see below). Santos robusta is usually finely ground for filter brewing and used primarily as a blend with other coffees.

- **Cameroon** coffee is 70 percent robusta (harsh) and 30 percent arabica (mellow and sweet) and is usually a dark roast and fine grind for filter brewing; it is also blended with other coffees.
- **Colombia** produces arabica coffee, and the Medellin type has less acidity than most Colombian coffees and a rich flavor. Usually Medellin coffee is a medium to dark roast and coarsely ground for percolators.
- **Costa Rica** produces arabica coffee that is mild with a nutty flavor; it is rich and full bodied.
- In the **Dominican Republic**; Santos Domingos coffee has good body and a pleasant sweet flavor.
- **Ecuador**'s coffee has a sharp, woody flavor and is usually blended with other coffees to get more body.
- **El Salvador** produces arabica coffees; the top two grades are mildly flavored with good acidity and body.
- **Ethiopia's** Hawar coffee is best known. It has a winy, smooth, and strong flavor and excellent aroma. The arabica is usually a medium roast and coarsely ground for percolator brewing. It is also traditionally used for Turkish coffee.
- **Guatemala** coffees are arabica, and the best are Antigua and Coban, which have good zesty flavors.
- **Haiti** is known for its mellow, mildly sweet, and full-bodied aromatic coffees.
- **Hawaiian** coffee is very familiar to Americans, and Kona is the most well known. It is full bodied with a strong and mellow flavor.

■ **In India**, Mysore is the best known coffee; it has a rich, strong flavor with good body. The Monsoon Malabar arabica is usually a dark roasted fine grind for filter brewing and may be blended with other coffees. It is considered especially good for after-dinner drinking.

■ **Indonesian** coffee includes Java, which is heavy bodied with a thick mellow flavor; it is blended with Yemeni-Java. Other Indonesian beans include Celebes and Sumatra.

■ **Jamaica** is best known for Blue Mountain coffee, which has a very sweet, mellow flavor with an excellent aroma. It's usually a medium roast and ground fine for filtered coffee. It is best drunk black.

■ **Kenya**'s arabica coffee has a mild, smooth taste and a fine aroma. The arabic is a medium roast and regular ground for the jug brewing method (see below). The Peaberry arabica is a medium roast, and coarse grind for percolators and general purpose.

■ **Mexico** produces arabica coffee varieties, including Coatepec, Jalapa, and Pluma, which tend to have a sharp taste with a good aroma.

■ **Nicaragua** coffees have a biting acidity with good body. They are usually medium roasts and regular grinds for the jug brewing method (see below).

■ **Peru**'s Chanchamayo has a mild, slightly sweet flavor and very good body.

■ **Puerto Rico** produces a sweet, full, rich-flavored coffee with a full body that tastes like a French roast or a blend of French and Italian dark roast.

■ **Tanzania** produces arabica coffee with a rich, mellow taste and delicate body.

■ **Venezuela**'s Maracaibo coffee has a rich, mellow, and slightly sweet and winy taste with a light body and light aroma.

■ **Yemen**'s Mocha coffee is almost chocolate flavored. (**Mocha** is the name usually used for coffee-chocolate combination favors.)

STORING

If you find yourself with a lot of coffee in any form, such as the holidays when you get a lot of food gift packs, it can be frozen (put coffee in a freezer safe plastic bag to protect the flavor and moisture content for at least 6 months). Do not attempt to grind frozen whole beans in a home grinder; take out what you need and wait a while, 30 or so minutes, until the beans are thawed. Ground coffee can be used right from the freezer; it will thaw sufficiently while you prepare the water and the rest of the pot. Instant coffee must be kept dry in a tightly sealed container or it will become a nasty tasting lump and *always* spoon it out with a clean dry spoon to keep moisture out of the granules.

BREWING

Today, most supermarkets offer custom coffee grinding or you can buy special grind coffees in cans on the shelf. You can also buy whole beans and grind them in a home coffee grinder. The type of brewing method determines whether you want coarsely or finely ground coffee beans. Generally, coarser and regular grinds are used for the jug method in which the coffee is actually in the water (Turkish coffee is an exception.) or for percolators in which the water runs through the coffee repeatedly; fine grinds are usually for drip and espresso and similar brew methods in which the water passes through coffee contained in mesh baskets, with or without filters.

■ **Jug method:** The oldest, simplest brewing method involves heating a jug or pot with hot water, you pour the water away and put the measured coffee amount into the pot, then add hot water and thoroughly stir. Allow to brew or infuse for 3 to 5 minutes. Strain the coffee to serve without disturbing the grounds, which will have settled in the bottom of the pot.

■ **Plunger or cafetiere brew:** Prewarm the pot, add medium ground coffee, and add hot water. Let the coffee infuse for 4 minutes and depress the plunger carefully.

■ **Vacuum brew:** A vacuum pot is really two pots that fit into each other; you put cold water into the bottom pot and then put the other pot on top, creating a seal that also makes a vacuum. Then put coffee into the top half and put the whole thing on a burner. When the water boils, it will rise up through the top bowl's funnel and mix with the coffee. Stir and let infuse for 1 to 4 minutes. When the pot is removed from the burner, the vacuum that forms in the lower pot will cause the brewed coffee to filter back down into the bottom pot.

■ **Neapolitan flip:** Popular in Italy, this coffee maker has two containers with a coffee basket in the middle. You fill the bottom container with water, fill the basket with finely ground coffee, screw on the top container upside down. Place the coffee maker on the burner. When the water boils, remove the pot from the heat and flip it over to let the hot water run through the coffee grounds into the top pot, which then becomes the bottom pot and server.

■ **Filter coffeemakers:** One of these is the typical cone-shaped plastic coffee basket that you line with a filter and that fits either on a pot or a single cup or mug. You put the coffee basket on the pot or mug, add finely ground coffee to taste, boil water, pour it into the coffee basket and let it drip down. Automatic filter coffee makers operate on the same principle, but the machine heats the water in its well and lets it seep through a filter-lined coffee basket, which contains regular or finely ground coffee; the brewed coffee collects in the pot, which is kept warm on a heater. From what I've seen, this is the most popular method of brewing coffee these days.

■ **Percolator:** Percolators come in stovetop and electric models, and the method is the same for both. Pour in the required amount of cold water then insert a stem that holds the coffee basket. It is best to line the basket before adding the regular ground coffee to taste. Put on the lid, which has a small glass knob that allows you to see if the water is perking. Plug in the electric pot or place the nonelectric pot on the stove. Electric models will time the brew automatically and most have a high, medium, low strength setting so that they brew to your taste. Stovetop models need to be timed after the pot starts to perk, usually 6 to 8 minutes. Percolated coffee will get stronger with less coffee in less time than dripped coffee, because the water goes through the coffee many times as it bubbles up and then goes through the basket.

■ **Turkish coffee:** If you don't have a special, usually brass, pot (called an *ibrik*) for

Dos and Don'ts for All Coffeepots

Don't reuse coffee grounds.

Don't boil coffee.

Do wash coffeepots thoroughly after each use to prevent a rancid taste.

Do start with fresh, clean, cold water.

Do use the proper amount of coffee, which is usually 2 teaspoons per cup but can vary according to taste.

Do use the proper grind for the method you choose for brewing.

Do drink the coffee while it's fresh; coffee that's been on a heater too long takes on a life of its own. But then you knew that!

Turkish coffee, you can use any pot. Put the amount of sugar that you like into the pot, add water, and bring to boil over low heat. Add very finely ground coffee, stir, and put back on the burner. When liquid reaches a frothy boil, remove the pot from the burner and stir gently. Repeat this step twice. At the final boil, add 1 teaspoon of cold water to help settle the grounds. To serve, pour a bit of froth into each demitasse cup so that everyone gets some froth and then pour the rest. It's best to make only 3 cups at a time. This coffee is for the true coffee lover, it is meant to be sipped and you can also add spices of choice, such as cinnamon, which

may make it necessary to boil it more than twice to get full flavor.

- **Espresso:** You will find many types of espresso machines, most of which will be pricey but they all work on the principle that pressure in the machine caused by the water boiling at extremely high temperatures produces steam that is then forced through coffee grounds, making a strong brew. If you have no espresso machine, you can make espresso with an Italian "Moka" type pot, some of which have a little man drawn on the side. You put cold water in the bottom, insert the stemmed coffee basket which has been filled with very finely ground coffee, screw on the top part and put the pot on the burner. You will hear a gushing and sputtering of water as the water goes from the bottom pot, through the coffee, and into the top part of the coffee maker. Remove the pot from the burner when the water rises. This pot has a rubber washer to make the seal, which should be replaced periodically.

- **Instant coffee:** Boil water, add coffee to taste in the cup and according to the brand's directions, add water, stir gently, or use a small whisk to briskly stir for a little added *umph,* and it's as good as it will get. Instant coffee is better tasting than it was in my mother's day, especially the freeze-dried instants, but most coffee lovers prefer any style of brewing to instant.

COFFEE MAKING

A READER RECOMMENDS:

One clever reader found that if she puts a small amount of water in the filter holder of her drip coffeepot after the filter is in place, and rolls the water around, the filter sticks to the sides of the filter holder. Then, when you add ground coffee, the dampened filter prevents grounds from falling into the pot.

■ **Flavored coffee:** Add a sprinkle of cinnamon to the ground coffee before brewing. Or add a drop or two of almond, vanilla, or other extract to the ground coffee. For mocha, add chocolate syrup or cocoa mix to the brewed coffee. Flavoring your own coffee is less expensive than buying it, and you can control the intensity of the flavor.

■ **Coffee filter packs:** You can make your own coffee filter packs if you measure the amount you usually use for a pot and put it into a coffee filter which has been placed in a large margarine tub. Then layer coffee filters with coffee in them until the tub is full. Seal to keep the coffee fresh. You'll have the filter packs ready to go when you make the next several pots of coffee.

■ **Coffee cone filter substitute:** When you run out of 1-cup filter cones, you can fold a regular filter in half, then in half again. Open one side and you have a cone. *Note:* Usually, ordinary filters cost less than filter cones so this is a money saver hint, too.

■ **Gourmet instant coffee:** You can make your own gourmet coffees with these directions: Blend the ingredients listed below in a blender or food processor until powdered. Substitute appropriate amounts of artificial sweetener for sugar and powdered creamer for powdered milk, if you wish. To serve, put 2 rounded teaspoons of coffee into a cup filled with hot water.

Orange coffee: Blend ½ cup of instant coffee, ¾ cup of sugar, 1 cup of powdered milk, and ½ teaspoon of dried orange peel.

Mocha coffee: Mix ½ cup of instant coffee, ½ cup of sugar, 1 cup of coffee creamer, and 2 tablespoons of cocoa.

Cinnamon coffee: Blend ½ cup of instant coffee, ⅔ cup of sugar, ⅔ cup of powdered milk, and ½ teaspoon of cinnamon.

■ **Iced cappuccino:** According to the Specialty Coffee Association of America, you can make iced cappuccino by pouring one shot of freshly brewed espresso over ice and adding 3 ounces of cold milk. Spoon foamed milk on top, sweeten to taste.

■ **Heat your coffee mug** by placing it on top of the drip coffeemaker when it starts brewing. It will warm up enough to keep your coffee hot longer as you sip it and enjoy!

■ **Thermos-warm:** If you keep your coffee in a thermos instead of on the heater, it will stay hot without getting stronger and you'll have a tastier late-morning pick-me-up cup of coffee! Some people who are slow starters in the morning, make a pot of coffee before retiring and store it in a thermos so that their first eye-opener cups are ready as soon as they wake up. Believe it or not, if you heat the thermos with hot water before adding the coffee, the coffee will be drinkable.

■ **Two pots—fast:** If you need two pots of coffee quickly when you have guests, pour the first pot into a thermos as soon as it's brewed so that you can start the second pot immediately. This hint is especially good if you need one pot of "caf" and one pot of "decaf." **CAUTION**: Always rinse a thermos with hot water to heat it before pouring in hot coffee, and if you have time, let the hot water stay in the thermos while the coffee is brewing. Heating up the thermos before filling it prevents breaking the glass insert and the coffee will stay hot longer in a heated thermos.

▪ **Coffeepot safety**: If you don't have a coffeepot that shuts off automatically, and you have a problem remembering to unplug the pot when you've finished with it, here's a good safety hint: Make it a habit to plug a night light into the same socket with the coffeepot when you start the coffee. Turn off the night light when you switch off the pot. The extra light will call your attention to the pot, even when you are just passing through the kitchen.

Tea

Chinese legends say that tea was discovered by accident in 3000 B.C.E. by Shen Nog, the same mythical person who is said to have discovered herbal medicine. It seems that Shen Nog was boiling water outdoors one day when some leaves from a tea plant fell into the water. He liked the flavor and found that it had medicinal value. Through the centuries tea has been an aid to meditation in Asia and a social and comfort beverage everywhere else. Chinese and Japanese tea ceremonies ritualize tea drinking. Formal teas were popular in my mother's day, although coffee was served on one end of the tea table and tea on the other to accommodate nontea drinkers. Purists say that tea should

never ever be in bags because bags give the tea a paper taste. Some British tea drinkers are horrified by the American practice of dunking tea bags up and down to hurry the brewing along. Some folks like their tea black, and others like it with milk, sugar, or lemon; and so serving tea requires serving some accompaniments, including a second pot of hot water to add if the tea is too strong.

❀ KITCHENEERING HUMOR ❀

One of my tea-drinking editors tells this story about a trip to Ireland where she ordered tea in a major Dublin hotel lobby restaurant. The waitress brought the teapot, hot water pot, milk pitcher, sugar bowl, little bowl of lemon slices, teacup, saucer, and spoon and a small plate of biscuits (cookies to Americans). When all these things were placed on the little round tea table my editor's husband had no space left for his coffee. The waitress looked sympathetically at the husband, balancing his coffeecup and saucer on his knee and said in her lilting Irish brogue, "These tea drinkers are a messy lot, aren't they."

Here are some tea terms and information adapted from *All the Tea in China,* by Kit Chow and Ione Kramer. Like coffee and wine, tea quality is judged by several criteria.

▪ **Color**: Tea that has been properly made will be clear, never muddy. Black tea will have a reddish color, oolong will have an orange-brown color, and green tea will be yellowish green.
▪ **Aroma**: Because they have been fermented, black and oolong teas usually have more

aroma than green teas, but green teas can also have a special aroma.

- **Flavor:** Taste should be smooth and fresh without sharpness or bitterness.

Here are some tea types and terms.

- **Assam** tea comes from Assam, in northern India and has a heavy, dark flavor. It's the base for Irish breakfast tea.
- **Black tea** is processed by oxidation/fermentation. Tea leaves are spread out to wither; then rolled or not rolled (depending on the type of tea), and spread out in a cool place to allow fermentation or oxidation, which activates enzymes that produce essential oils and tannin. The leaves are then fired or stir-fried to stop the enzyme action, sterilize the leaves, and stop fermentation. After the leaves are about 80 percent dry, they are allowed to finish drying over charcoal or wood fires. Finally, they are sifted according to size, and some teas are blended.
- **Broken grade** is usually sold in tea bags; these leaves have been crushed into small pieces so that the tea flavor can be released quickly.
- **Caravan** is a blend of Chinese Lapsang Souchong and Indian black teas.
- **Chrysanthemum tea** is made of dried pale yellow blossoms. It is brewed like tea and usually used medicinally.
- **Congou** was originally the general name for nonbroken black tea leaves, but now it is also used for broken black tea.
- **Country greens** was originally a term for all Chinese green teas other than those from certain provinces, it now means any Chinese green tea.

- **Darjeeling** is sometimes considered the "champagne" of teas. It grows in Darjeeling in northern India and is a type of black tea.
- **De-enzyming** is a process of steaming, pan frying, or baking tea leaves to deactivate the enzymes and remove the raw green taste from it.
- **Dust** is the finest siftings from tea.
- **Earl Grey** is a blend of Indian and Chinese black teas flavored with oil of bergamot, which is made from Canton orange peel. It gets its name from Charles Grey, the second Earl Grey, who was British prime minister from 1830 to 1834 and who allowed this family blend to be sold to the public.
- **English breakfast** tea was originally the name of Chinese black tea used in the United States; today it is a blend of black teas, usually from India and Ceylon.
- **Green tea** comes from the same leaf as black tea but is processed differently. It is not oxidized/fermented like black tea.
- **Hyson** was originally the name for a Chinese green tea; this term is now used to describe the earliest, most tender leaves.
- **Irish breakfast** tea has a malt flavor and is thick and whitish, as if it had milk added. When this tea cools, the caffeine and tannin sink to bottom and a milky film rises to the top, a process that's called creaming down.
- **Jasmine** tea is enriched with jasmine flowers, which are layered with tea leaves and processed to remove moisture so that the flowers don't mold. Finding jasmine flowers in the tea doesn't always mean it's of high quality because the flowers are removed from better quality tea after the proper scent is achieved. Both green and oolong teas can be scented with jasmine.

- **Lapsang Souchong** is a black tea which is smoked to give it a smoky flavor.

- **Pekoe** was originally the name of the white down cover on certain types of leaves and buds, but now it refers to a certain size of leaf-bud sets and is not related to quality. Orange pekoe used to mean an orange blossom scented tea, but now it just refers to the appearance of the leaf-bud set.

- **Pinguey** is a large general category of teas from China, which includes black and green teas. In the United States most of this tea is black; the most famous is green gunpowder tea.

- **Twankay** is a Chinese green tea.

- **Young Hyson** is a term for younger, tender leaves and is also used for Chinese green tea.

- **Yunwu tea** is an extremely tender, high-grade Chinese green tea.

- **Oolong** is fermented about half as long as black tea.

SHOPPING

- **Tea Portions:** When you buy tea, the number of tea bags per pound tells you how strong the tea is. Most teas are sold with 200 bags to the pound; if you usually get 1 to 2 cups per bag from such a tea, then you get 4 cups per bag from a tea that has 150 bags per pound and may need two bags for 1 cup if the tea has more than 200 bags per pound. Some premium loose tea leaves need only a scant teaspoon for a 3-cup pot. You need to experiment with a new type or brand of tea to see how strong you want it.

- **Herbal tea:** When you buy herbal teas, *do* read labels carefully to be sure you don't buy herbs to which you are allergic or herbs that

The Perfect Cup

Here are the seven simple steps to a perfect cup of tea.

1. Bring a kettle of fresh cold water to a full boil.

2. While you wait for the water to boil, warm the teapot with hot water (hot from the tap will do) letting it stand until you are ready for the next step. *Note:* Pot size should relate to the number of cups you are brewing. The smaller pots full make a better flavor than larger pots that are only half full.

3. When you see the water about to boil, empty the teapot and add the recommended amount of tea or number of tea bags per cup. Generally it's 1 teaspoonful of tea or one tea bag for each cup. When brewing more than six cups, most people add an extra spoon or bag "for the pot." (If you are brewing tea to ice, allow three tea bags or spoonfuls for two glasses of iced tea.)

4. Pour the boiling water into the pot and cover. My dear friend Sue's mother, Mrs. Marie Carey, always said "bring the teapot to the kettle not the other way to keep the water at a full boil."

5. Allow the tea to steep for 3 to 5 minutes, according to taste.

6. Rinse cups with hot water. Pour tea into the cups through a strainer (if you are using loose tea) and serve.

7. Strain off the remaining tea into another heated pot if you are going to let the tea sit for any time (or remove the tea bags) to avoid overbrewing.

might affect certain medical conditions. For example, many herbal teas contain caffeine, which you may be trying to avoid. Some contain chicory and other herbs which are mild laxatives and that could cause distress if you drank too much. Some herbs, such as tonka beans, sweet clover, borage, and comfrey are coumadins (substances that prevent blood clotting) and could be dangerous to some people when consumed in excess.

■ **Taste testing:** A good way to test teas for taste is to buy the combination boxes of tea bags offered by almost all manufacturers; they usually have three or four flavors or blends in each box. The special flavors also come in decaf or regular, if caffeine is a problem for you.

■ **Instant tea:** Most of the people I know who use instant tea, use it for iced tea, but it can be used to make hot tea, too. It's so quick and easy and you can buy it with lemon, sweetened, or plain so that you can add whatever you like.

■ **Canned tea:** Canned or bottled gourmet specialty teas are also available and are a real benefit at parties for those who don't drink carbonated or alcoholic beverages; ice some of them down for yourself and your guests. Also, there is no rule that I know of that says you can't heat canned or bottled tea if you wish.

❋ **HELOISE HINT:** If your iced tea is cloudy after refrigeration, add 1 cup of hot water to about 1 quart or so of tea and it will usually clear up. It will be slightly diluted so add less ice.

BREWING AND COOKING

▇ READERS RECOMMEND:

BEST HOT TEA HINTS

- A reader from Ohio says he finds this recipe extra satisfying for the aroma of country harvest as well as for its taste. Brew peppermint tea in a 2-cup teapot. Add 1 teaspoon grape jelly, and then float a ½-inch complete cross-cut section of fresh apple and let steep for about 10 minutes. (Winesap or Jonathan apples are suggested for their tartness.)
- A Houston reader strips lengths of orange peel with her potato peeler and freezes them. Then when she makes a cup of hot tea, she puts a couple of strips of orange zest into it.
- A North Carolina reader likes to recycle old hard candies that have become soft in their wrappers by dropping them into hot tea. Instead of buying flavored teas, she has in-house flavors and she doesn't need to add sugar!
- A Nebraska reader puts extra zest into orange spiced tea by adding warm orange juice as others would add milk. She adds a bit of sugar and a sprinkling of nutmeg and cinnamon.
- A Houston reader soaks pitted whole prunes in brandy or rum for 15 days or more and adds a prune to each cup of hot tea. Sounds interesting!
- A Maryland reader makes instant hot tea with instant iced tea mixes.

❋ **HELOISE HINT:** I like to stir my herbal or other teas with a cinnamon stick. I reuse the stick for several cups of yummy lightly spiced hot tea.

■ **"Drip" tea:** If you don't drink coffee, you can still use your coffee maker to brew tea. Unfortunately, this method doesn't allow you to use boiling water to get a really first-rate brew, but it's a fine alternative. Here's how.

Single serving: Drop a tea bag into the brewing basket and add 2 cups of water, then brew like coffee.

For a pot using tea bags: Measure the amount of water needed into the coffee maker tank, put the appropriate number of tea bags in the carafe, turn it on, and you'll have hot tea before you can find some cookies to go with it. Make iced tea with the leftovers. *Note:* Let the bags steep for at least 3 to 5 minutes for fullest flavor.

For a pot using loose tea: If you prefer loose tea, sprinkle tea leaves into a coffee filter in the brewing basket as you would ground coffee. Try the same amount of cut tea leaves that you would brew in a teapot or just experiment to get the right amount for desired strength and flavor.

■ **Microwave tea:** You can shortcut the seven-step method outlined earlier by first boiling the water in microwave-safe pot. Then add tea (loose or bag), brew for 4 minutes with the pot covered with a tea cozy (padded cover), and serve. **CAUTION**: When making a single mug of tea (or coffee) by the microwave method, if you add the tea bag within a second or two after removing the cup from the microwave oven, the water is likely to bubble over or even "explode" because of the microwaves' action in the cup. Wait a few seconds and put the cup where spillovers won't burn you.

■ **Tea for a crowd:** You can prepare tea concentrate for a large crowd ahead of time. Here's how to make enough tea for forty to fifty cups:

Bring 1½ quarts of fresh, cold water to a rapid boil.

Remove the water from the heat and immediately add ¼ pound loose tea. Stir to immerse the leaves and then cover the pot.

Let stand 5 minutes. Strain into a teapot or other heatproof covered container until ready to use.

■ **To make hot tea from the concentrate:** Bring a kettle of fresh water to a boil. Add boiling water to the concentrate in proportions of about 2 tablespoons of tea concentrate to each cup of water. You can prepare the tea in a pot or in individual cups. **To make iced tea from the concentrate:** Follow the same procedure for hot tea but add 50 percent more tea to allow for melting ice—that is, use 6 tea bags or 6 teaspoons of tea for four glasses of iced tea.

■ **Instant iced tea:** When mixing instant iced tea, or fruit flavored beverages, mix the flavor crystals in a heatproof container in a bit of very hot water until they are dissolved and then add the cold water. You will get a better flavor because all of the crystals will have dissolved completely.

■ **Sinking tea bags:** When you are using tea bags with tags, wrap the tag around the pot or cup handle to prevent it from falling into the water. You won't have that paper taste and you won't have burned fingers from fishing the tag out of the water. Or cut an L-shaped slit in the tag, starting at the bottom edge and then when you make a cup of tea, open the slit and hook the tag on the cup lip. Or clip the tags to the edge of the cup with a spring clothespin.

- **Sun tea:** Using any kind of tea you like, put the appropriate number of tea bags—about one tea bag for each ¾ cup of water—into a quart or gallon glass container. Fill the container with fresh cool water, cover, and place it on a sunny patio or doorstep where it will be safe from curious pets and children. Depending on the weather, you'll have tea by noon or certainly by tea time at 4 o'clock.

HERB TEAS

- **Making your own herb teas:** CAUTION: Do not experiment with unfamiliar herbs when making homemade tea blends. Some herbs are actually poisonous (for example, some ferns) and others (like some mints) have medicinal properties that could interact with certain medications and could be harmful to people with certain health conditions.

- **Drying herbs for tea:** To dry herb leaves for tea, cut the branches just as they mature or flower; hang for about a week in an airy, shady place; and then crumble dried leaves into airtight jars. To make tea from dried leaves, steep in boiling water. To make 1 cup of tea, place a few leaves in a cup, pour boiling water over them, and add honey and lemon juice to taste.

- **Freezing herbs for tea:** If you want to have fresh herbs for tea, instead of drying the leaves, brew a concentrate and freeze it in cubes so that you can thaw one cube for a cup of hot tea or add melted cubes to lemonade. To steep, mash the leaves, cover with hot water, allow to steep for a day or so, strain the fluid, and freeze in cubes.

- **Tea infusion:** To make a tea infusion, strip the leaves from the stems and chop, measure twice as much water has you have chopped leaves, and add leaves to the water when it boils. Boil for 5 minutes, let cool, and strain into a jar for storage in the fridge For a cup of tea, add twice as much boiling water as infusion and sweeten to taste with honey, adding lemon if you wish.

- **Mint tea:** Choose larger leaves or pinch off leaf clusters at the stem end (instant pruning), drop a handful or so into a quart of boiling water, steep for 10 minutes, strain, and serve. To dry mint leaves for tea, cut the branches before they bloom, hang in a shady place until dry, strip the dried leaves off the stems, and store in an airtight jar.

- **Lemon-mint tea:** In a teapot, pour 2 to 4 cups of boiling water over three to five tea bags. Cover and let steep for 5 minutes. Remove the tea bags and add 3 tablespoons of lemon juice and 1 to 2 tablespoons of finely cut fresh mint. (If you use dried mint, use half the amount because it is stronger.) Sweeten to taste with honey, brown sugar, or other sweetener.

- **Frozen concentrate for mint tea:** Dried mint tea is not as tasty as fresh mint tea. One way to get the fresh mint flavor is to brew a frozen concentrate for mint tea. To a pint of boiling water, add about 2 cups coarsely chopped mint leaves and stems, return the water to boil, remove from heat, cover, and let cool for 1 hour. Strain the liquid and freeze in ice cube trays. After the cubes are frozen, you can release them from the trays and save them in a re-sealable plastic bag. For tea, heat a cube with enough water to make 1 cup or add cubes to other teas, punches, or soups. For a special treat, freeze a block of mint concentrate (with a nice sprig or two in the middle for decoration) and let it float in the punch bowl.

OTHER TEA HINTS

■ **Tea ice cubes:** Freeze leftover tea (or coffee) in cube trays so that when you chill your tea or coffee, you won't dilute the flavor. You can also poke in a few mint leaves or lemon or lime slices into the tea ice cubes to add flavor to your drinks.

■ **Barbecue with tea:** Some cooks say that if you toss some tea leaves on the briquettes when you grill, you will get a new taste treat in the meats.

■ **Tea dye:** Strong tea solutions can be used to dye white fabric so that it looks antique. My mother used this hint to turn white slips into beige!

STORING

Tea is considered a fragrant herb. Whether or not you buy loose tea or tea bags, tea should be stored in a container with a tightly fitting lid. Tea bags hold dried tea leaves but do not protect the flavor unless individually wrapped and sealed in plastic or foil. In addition to a tight-fitting lid, tea should be kept from light and heat.

Beer, Wines, and Spirits

SHOPPING

Shopping for *beer* has become as complicated as shopping for wine. It's more than regular or light beer, it's lagers, stout (stronger flavors and darker colored beers), and ales (lighter in color and flavor), as well as specialty beers that have fruity flavors, flavors from different grains (like wheat), and on and on. Even nonalcoholic beers are available in various types and flavors, including dark, full-flavored lagers. If you are having guests, it's best to include regular and light beers along with the nonalcoholic beers and, if your budget allows, a local beer and a specialty or imported beer.

Champagne: Portions per Bottle Size

Split: ½ pint; 1 to 2 glasses.

Pint: ⅛ gallon; 2 to 3 glasses.

Quart: ¼ gallon; 5 glasses.

Magnum: 2 quarts; 10 glasses.

Jeroboam: 4 quarts; 21 glasses.

Rehoboam: 6 quarts; 31 glasses.

Methuselah: 8 quarts; 41 glasses.

Salmanasar: 12 quarts; 62 glasses.

Balthazar: 16 quarts; 83 glasses.

Nebuchadnezzar: 20 quarts; 104 glasses.

Tastes are very subjective and not as much is written about beer tasting as about wine tasting, but drinking boutique or specialty beers has become the thing to do. It is all a matter of taste—yours.

In France, all sparkling wine labeled **Champagne** must come, by law, only from the Champagne region of France, whereas American vintners are not prevented from calling their sparkling wines champagne. German sparkling wine is called *sekt,* and in Italy, sparkling wine is called *spumante.* Champagne is meant to be consumed within a short period of time. So, don't buy champagne to keep and store for 5 or 10 years unless you have a wine cellar and it's a very special vintage. If you are buying champagne for the near future, it's better to buy bottles of less than magnum size. They last longer.

Fortified wines are wines to which some alcohol is added at some point in their production so that they generally contain 17 to 21 percent alcohol by volume. Examples of these wines are Sherry, Port, Madeira, and Marsala. Vermouth and some other aperitif wines are both fortified and flavored with herbs. The taste ranges from very dry to very sweet, and fortified wines are not usually served with a meal but are served before or after a meal, or at other times of the day.

Sparkling wines include Champagne and other sparkling, bubbly, Champagne-type wines made in most countries in various ways.

The term **table wine** generally refers to all wines containing 14 percent or less alcohol. They are usually served with a meal but can be enjoyed any other time, too.

Reading Wine Labels

Like Idaho potatoes or Louisiana oysters, most wine names are place names that tell you where the wine came from. Here are some examples: Chablis, Sauternes, Pommard, Piesport, Valpolicella, Barolo, Tokay, Châteauneuf-du-Pape, Bernkastel, and Saint-Emilion are names of European villages; Beaujolais, Rioja, and Chianti are specific districts in France, Spain, and Italy, respectively.

The label will also tell you the grape(s) used to make the wine, and different grapes are grown in different areas, such as Cabernet Sauvignon in Bordeaux, Pinot Noir and Chardonnay in Burgundy, the Nebbiolo in northern Italy, and Riesling in the Rhine and Moselle of Germany. Some labels will combine the village name and the grape, such as Bernkastler Riesling and Cabernet de Maribor. Some vineyards label their wine with just the grape's name or with a place name that is so well known that it's become a generic term to describe a type of wine (for example, California Chablis, Spanish Burgundy, Chilean Sauternes, and Australian Moselle).

And if that's not confusing enough for you, some wines get fantasy names that don't relate to the geography or the grape. Here are some examples: Larima Christi (tears of Christ), which can come from several places in Italy, and Liebfraumilch (milk of the Blessed Mother), which originally came from only a specific vineyard in the Rhine Valley but is now a name for many wines from the Rhine Valley.

Bad Wine

Every now and then you will get a bottle of bad wine and you should be able to get a refund or exchange from the store. Here are some ways to tell if wine has gone bad.

- *Mold* growth under the foil capsule or a small amount of sticky seepage around the foil may not always mean that the wine is bad.

- Red wine can look *cloudy* if it has been shaken up; such wine may need a day or two standing upright to let the sediment settle. Do decant it before serving. When white wines or young red wines are cloudy, they have not been made properly or have spoiled. Don't buy such wines.

- If you smell or taste *vinegar* in wine, the cork has leaked; it's bad. Some people use wine that has turned for marinating meat or as salad vinegar.

- When white wine (especially sweet ones) has been chilled for an excessive time, *white crystals* may be found in the bottom. There will be no change in the wine unless it has been chilled for several weeks.

- When you find *white flecks of sediment* in white wine, it spoils the appearance but probably not the flavor. Strain and decant it before serving.

- Old or improperly stored white wines may take on a *brownish tinge*. Some sweet white wines are purposely allowed to mature, because it adds to the flavor.

Judging Wine Tastes

When all is said and done, and when all is sipped and swallowed, wine appreciation is a matter of taste—yours—so tasting is the best way to find out what you like. Here are some ways to learn about wine and wine tasting.

- Attend wine tastings at stores that sell wine; they are usually held when a vintner or a wine merchant is promoting specific wines.
- Attend wine tasting charity benefits; here in San Antonio, where I live, our public television station, as many do, sponsors wine tastings as a fund-raiser.
- If you are traveling in wine country, such as California, France, Italy, or Germany, do a wine tour.
- And don't forget to tour your own state's wineries. Recently, states like Texas, where folks thought good wine couldn't be produced, have been winning ribbons at international tastings. Be adventuresome!

Judge wine according to the following criteria.

- **Color:** Whether red or white, good wine should be bright, free of cloudiness or suspended bits, and have the hue of that specific wine. For example, Moselles are pale gold with a touch of green, white Burgundies are a richer gold, and Beaujolais are purple-red. Red wines usually get lighter in color as they age and white wines usually get a deeper gold color when they age. You can best see the color and hue of the wine if you tip the glass to one side and look at the outer edge of the wine against a white cloth or background. Looking down into the glass won't work because the wine's depth will make the color deeper.

- **Bouquet:** About 80 percent of the sense of "taste" is based on your sense of smell. For you to enjoy the wine's aroma, an 8-ounce wineglass should be filled only about halfway and should be tapered so that the bouquet gets concentrated. Fill the glass halfway, swirl the wine so that more of its surface is exposed to air and more bouquet is released, then sniff. Better wines will give you the bouquet of their grapes. For example, a Moselle with smell flowery and fragrant, a Beaujolais will have a fruity smell, and a red Bordeaux or California Cabernet Sauvignon may have a deeper, more complex bouquet. Generally, younger wines have fruitier bouquets and older wines have a more refined and subtle character. Bad wine can smell "corky," cheap wines can often give a sort of prickly sensation in the nose caused by excessive addition of sulfur dioxide, which is used to stabilize wines. Sometimes wine will smell musty, sour, or vinegary; the latter is an indication that the wine is too acidic.

- **Taste:** Because your taste buds can tell only salt, sour, bitter, and sweet—and these tastes are sensed on different areas of your tongue—you need to let wine rest on your tongue for a moment so that you can separate the different tastes. It's at this point that professional tasters will whistle in air or slurp the wine to let more air through it and release the flavor. Slurping is not always a good idea at a dinner party but a friend of mine, who likes to appreciate every mouthful says she can get the same effect of slurping if she lets the wine stay on her tongue for a while, then swallows it in increments, slowly, and then slowly inhales and exhales through her mouth with her lips just slightly open. She says the aftertaste is so delightful—it's like enjoying each mouthful twice. It should be noted that not everyone's taste buds record sweet, sour, salt, and bitter the same way; so what is sweet to me may be slightly sour to you and what is bitter to you may be a pleasant bite of tannin to me. Tasting wine is so subjective that you just have to make up your mind yourself. When you have a party, it's always best to offer white, red, and rosé wines so that everyone can get something he or she likes.

MORE ON WINE

- **Carbonation in wine:** Still wines can have a slight amount of tingly carbonation, which may be the intent of the winemaker. In a light young wine, it can be pleasant, but in other wines, it may cause an unpleasant flavor.

- **Aging red wine:** Some red wines may lose their flavor if aged too long, others just get better!

- **Inexpensive wines:** Often inexpensive wines are blends of various grapes and are grown in places where the quality is about the same every year because the vintners grow hardy grapes that consistently produce high yields. In the great wine regions of the world, such as France and Germany, greater risks are taken to grow less hardy, high-yielding grapes and so, depending on the weather, there will be great or poor years. Since wine drinking is a matter of personal taste and good wine depends on grape-growing conditions and the wine maker's skills, for many years, American wines were snubbed by serious wine drinkers. However, in recent times, some wines from various parts of the United States have been getting better quality marks than some European wines at international tastings. Most people say that you should never buy the cheapest wine in any category because the cost of bottling, corking, and other aspects of production are the same for all wines, it's the contents that affect the price; and because you will be paying for all the production costs anyway, you may as well add some more money to your purchase and get something good to drink.

- **Wine journal:** Keep dated records of where and when you bought your wine. Note any comments about taste so that you'll know what to buy next time. I have a friend who soaks labels off wine bottles and files them in envelopes marked "bad" or "good" or "wow" as a guide for the future.

STORING

- Unpasturized **beers** must be stored in the refrigerator but most beers are better off stored in the fridge anyway so that they are ready to drink. Most beer sold in bottles and cans is pasteurized to prevent spoilage during transport and storage, while draft beers (in the keg) and certain other beers are not; many people say that unpasteurized beer has a better taste. Pasteurized beers will keep for several weeks in a cool place, but if you have had some beer for a long time, like a couple of months, and you plan to serve it to company, it's best to check, since it may have gone flat. Most people buy what they need for a few weeks and have no problem with beer that has gone flat.

- **Champagne** is ready to drink when you buy it and need not be saved for aging. Also, do not store champagne in the refrigerator. Purists

say that champagne can absorb odors from other foods in the refrigerator over a long periods of time. In addition, in cold temperatures, the cork will eventually shrink, allowing the bubbles to escape and the champagne to go flat. Store champagne in a cool, dark place on its side. Place it in the refrigerator or in a bucket of ice water for at least two hours before serving.

- **Wine** that is capped instead of corked is wine that is ready to drink when you buy it. Wine that doesn't need aging or that you will drink soon can be stored standing up for a short time, but wine that is to be aged should be stored lying on its side to keep the cork damp so that no air can reach the wine. If you buy a case of wine, the whole case can be placed on its side in a cool place for storage. Or insert wine into cabinets to hold stored wine bottles on their sides. *Note:* Wine can breathe through the cork, so cellar odors can be absorbed by the wine. Also wine rests better in the dark, and it doesn't like vibrations, especially if it is an aged wine. Store wine away from laundry machines or other vibrating equipment.

- **Storage temperatures for wines:** Most oenophiles (wine experts) say that the ideal temperature for a wine cellar is between 55 and 60 degrees F, with 45 to 70 degrees F being the outer limits. Keeping the temperature constant is even more important than the exact temperature. The best humidity level is 75 percent. Humidity prevents the corks from drying out, allowing the wine to evaporate or spoil. However, too much humidity will allow fungus to grow. If you are moving during very hot or very cold weather, you will need to insulate the wines. My sources say that when moving at any time of the year, wrap the wine bottles in about a 1-inch thickness of newspaper for shipping. Once the wines have been moved, let the bottles rest undisturbed for at least a month before they are opened.

■ **Storage racks:** You can make your own wine racks if you don't have commercial ones:

Construct a concrete-block "student bookcase" by layering blocks with sturdy boards and then stacking wine bottles, which have been inserted into mailing tubes, on the shelves.

Stack clay tubular drain tiles against a cool cellar wall to hold wine bottles. The tiles can be supported on the sides of this wine rack if they are placed wall to wall or within a bookcase or other sturdy frame.

Fit two sturdy pieces of wood, which have been fitted with grooves so that they are joined diagonally to form an X, into a square cabinet and then insert wine bottles in the spaces.

COOKING

■ **Beer:** Substitute beer for wine as the liquid in stews and you'll get delicious, rich sauce.

■ **Champagne:** Many cooks claim that it is a waste to cook with expensive sparkling wine because cooking kills the bubbles. A fine sauce can be made equally well with good-quality dry white wine. Save the bubbly to celebrate the dinner!

■ **Wine and spirits:** Although it's true that you can cook with any old wine, most chefs agree that a good wine makes for a superior dish and that if you wouldn't consider drinking the wine, you shouldn't consider cooking with it either.

Cooking wines sold specifically for that purpose have other ingredients, such as salt or MSG, added to make them undrinkable as is, which is required by law. So most serious cooks prefer to use real wine or other spirits because of their superior taste. The story is that salt was added to cooking wine in households of the past to prevent the cook from drinking it.

Whiskey, beer, sherry, and other liquors can be used to flavor various dishes in addition to those dishes you flavor with white or red wines. Also, if you don't have red wine to flavor a dish, try a dash or two of best-quality Balsamic vinegar.

If you are adding sherry to soup, add it just before serving time (about 1 teaspoon of sherry per cup of soup) so that the taste doesn't evaporate. New Orleans chefs serve sherry with that city's famous turtle soup and it's added at the table.

When you are bored with vegetables, try steaming them with a couple of tablespoons of white or red wine or a bit of sherry or balsamic vinegar instead of plain water. Greens, such as spinach and chard especially, benefit from this extra flavor.

Not all foods benefit from cooking with wine. Very acidic foods like vinegar, citrus, tomatoes, and pineapples may give wine an off-flavor; so will artichokes, asparagus, chocolate, and onions. The sulfur in egg yolks also gives an off-flavor. If you have marinated meats in wine and then need to brown them before cooking, dab the meat with a paper towel, drippy wet meats don't brown well, and the liquid may spatter when you put the meat in the pan. Bring the marinade to a gentle boil for 2 minutes and strain out the solidified meat juices if you want a clearer stock to add to the meat after it's browned or to use for sauce.

When you plan to flambé a dessert, such as bananas Foster or cherries jubilee, the higher the proof (alcohol content) the more easily the sauce will ignite. For best results, preheat the alcohol to about 130 degrees F, add it to the food, and touch the match to it as soon as you can. If you wait too long to ignite the alcohol, it will get absorbed by the food and may not light up.

■ **Substitutes for cooking with alcohol:** If you don't keep alcoholic beverages in your home, you can still use recipes that require them as ingredients. If a recipe calls for 1 or 2 tablespoons, you can usually consider the wine, sherry, or other alcohol as an optional ingredient and omit it. If more than 2 tablespoons are required, you will need to substitute some other liquid because the recipe may end up being too dry. For savory dishes, substitute chicken broth for white wine. For a fruity flavor or for sweetened foods or desserts, you may be able to substitute apple, pineapple, or orange juice for alcoholic beverages. You can also substitute nonalcoholic wines and beers in recipes. Some alcoholic beverages, such as rum or brandy, are available as extracts and so you can try combining the number of drops recommended on the bottle with enough water to match the amount of water required by the recipe.

Basic Liquor Bar

Most people will consume two or three drinks during the first 2 hours or so of a party and less after that. To avoid serving too much liquor to people with empty stomachs, limit the cocktail hour to just that: no more than 1 hour from the guests' arrival time to the time for serving dinner.

If your budget is tight, consider serving jug wines or punch (alcoholic or nonalcoholic) along with soft drinks. And, by all means, always include nonalcoholic beverages for nonimbibers and for the designated drivers in each group.

• *Hard liquor:* Do be sure that whoever tends bar measures hard liquor with a jigger of 1½ ounces so the drinks are uniform and guests won't get startled by a drink that makes their eyes water! You will get twenty-two 1½-ounce drinks from a liter-sized bottle (33.8 ounces).

• *Basic bar for entertaining* (in addition to red, rosé, and white wine or champagne): Include vodka, gin, Scotch, a blended whiskey, a Canadian whiskey, bourbon, rum, vermouth, a cream sherry, Port wine, and beers (regular, light, nonalcoholic), and after-dinner liquors (créme de menthe, Kahlua, brandy, etc.).

• *Mixers:* Include tomato and fruit juices, such as orange juice, ginger ale, club soda, mineral water, tonic water, bitter lemon, and soft drinks.

• *Important Note:* If you are cooking for someone who must not have alcohol, our updated information is it's *not true* that all of the alcohol in alcoholic beverages, such as wine or liquors, evaporate when food is cooked or heated; some still remains in the food or sauce whether the food is baked, stewed, roasted, boiled, flambéed, or whatever.

SERVING

• **Beer:** In this country we serve our beer icy cold, but in Europe they prefer it to be nearer to room temperature, that is 70 degrees F or so. Serious beer drinkers say that beer glasses should be washed and then rinsed several times in hot water to remove all traces of suds and then allowed to dry naturally. They claim that any vestige of detergent or any lint from a dishtowel will adversely affect the beer foam. Some beer drinkers prefer icy mugs (stored in the freezer and removed just before pouring beer into them), others prefer pilsner glasses (long, V-shaped glasses), and others just pop open the flip-top lid of a can and say "Prozit!" Some Mexican beers are traditionally served in the bottle with a small piece of lime perched on top with the idea that you will rub the lip of the bottle with the lime and drop it into the bottle so that you can enjoy a bit of lime taste with each sip. Some German beers are served with a thin slice of lemon floating in the brew. As with all beverages, it's a matter of taste.

• **Champagne:** The only time to waste Champagne by spraying it out all over the room is when you are on a football team that wins the Super Bowl, and if it is good Cham-

pagne, that still seems like a waste! The best way to open a bottle of Champagne is as easy as 1, 2, 3:

1. Place a clean napkin or tea towel over the cork and upper portion of the bottle is exposed. This protects you and others if the bottle breaks or cork pops! It also keeps the heat of your hand from the narrowest point on the bottle where there's the most pressure.
2. Remove the foil and then the wiring, usually 7 twists, keeping the bottle pointed away from you and not at anyone else. The cork could pop out once the wiring is removed.
3. Hold the cork in one hand and *twist the bottle* gently away from the cork. If the cork doesn't ease out, you'll have to carefully push it away from the bottle with your thumb. Sometimes running warm water over just the neck of the bottle will help. If you keep the bottle at a 45-degree angle during the procedure, more of the Champagne's surface will be exposed to the atmosphere and, therefore, the Champagne will be less likely to have pressure built up at the bottle neck with less likelihood of an explosion.

• **Wine:** Although there are glass shapes for white (tulip) and red (bowl-shape) wines, a simple tulip-shaped wineglass can do for all wines. Colored glass does not allow you to see the color of the wine, but if you and yours are drinking it without judging it or just don't care, colored glassware may be okay. Pottery wine servers are interesting, but you can't see the wine in them either; again, if you don't care, that's okay. Traditionally in Germany, amber-brown stemmed wineglasses are used to serve white wines because the amber color enhances the color of white wine. Green stemmed glasses are used to serve red wine, because the contrasting green and red enhances the red wine color. Most restaurants use clear, plain neutral stemware.

■ **White versus red wine:** The rule of white wine with fish and poultry and red with red meat is no longer followed strictly. Wines are being matched to foods according to acidity and other factors, so it's best to ask someone who knows wines and how they might taste with the food you are serving, or taste the wine yourself to see if you like it.

■ **Wine temperatures:** Generally, white and rosé wines are served chilled (2 hours in the refrigerator or 15 or 20 minutes in a large ice bucket that allows the bottle to be covered with ice/ice water should do it). Red wines are usually served at room temperature, however when this rule was made, *room temperature* meant rooms without central heating that were cooler than about 70 degrees F. If your rooms are warmer than that or if it is summer, it may be advisable to cool down a light red wine such as Beaujolais, California Burgundy or Bardolino, by putting it in the fridge for about 20 minutes or so. A complex red wine should never be chilled, nor should you warm a red wine near a fire or oven. Red wines should be allowed to stand upright for 1 or 2 hours before serving to let any sediment settle and then some should be allowed to stand opened for

½ hour before serving so the wine is allowed to breathe and develop its bouquet. If you think the breathing phase isn't necessary, notice that the second glass of wine that you have in a restaurant usually tastes better than the first, which usually is poured right after the waiter opened the bottle.

■ **Wine portions:** A 1-liter bottle contains about ten 3-ounce portions of wine. Usually, a 7- or 8-ounce tulip glass that can be used to serve any type of wine, is filled halfway. Expect a 750-milliliter bottle of table wine to provide about eight 3-ounce servings and plan on an average of two servings per person.

■ **Liquor portions:** A liter-size bottle of liquor contains 33.8 ounces or about twenty-two 1½-ounce jiggers. The liquor is then usually added to about 4 ounces or so of mixer, plus ice. Mixers list the number of servings on their labels so figure you will need at least two or three servings per guest. If you are serving canned beer or soda, each person will have at least two or three, so buy accordingly. If you are buying large bottles of soda or mixers, you will find the number of servings inside listed on the label.

■ **To frost a beverage glass** swirl half a glass of water in the bowl of a wine glass, until interior is completely wet. Pour the water out, and place the wine glass in the freezer for about one hour. To frost a glass for a margarita cocktail, moisten the rim of a chilled glass with lime (lime juice is in the cocktail) and dip it into salt.

■ **Big ice cubes** that last much longer than the usual size, can be made in clean margarine tubs or other plastic containers. Float these giant ice cubes in punch or use them in wide-mouth thermos jugs. You can even freeze fruit pieces or slices, maraschino cherries, strawberries, grapes or a few mint leaves in them for added color in a punch bowl.

- **Cool punch:** When you're serving cold punch or eggnog, make ice cubes from a portion of the drink mix so that you can cool it without diluting.

✿ **HELOISE HINT:** When adding carbonated beverages to juice in the punch bowl for a party, refrigerate both liquids so that the punch is cold from the start and won't melt the ice so quickly. It's most important to chill the carbonated beverage; chilled carbonated beverages won't spurt out of the bottle like warm ones often do, which could be a mess if you open the bottle at the table. Put the juice in the bowl first, add ice, and then add the chilled carbonated beverage just before serving.

HERBS AND SPICES

According to *Simon & Schuster's Guide to Herbs and Spices*, edited by Stanley Schuler, spices come mainly from tropical countries and herbs grow in temperate regions and are easily cultivated. Both herbs and spices are considered "aromatic" plants and both groups have been considered medicinal at one time or other. Herbs are generally added toward the end of the cooking period to prevent their aroma from cooking away. Some spices, such as cinnamon or pepper can scorch in cooking so they, too, are added at the end of the cooking period. Some of the items listed in this chapter are neither herbs nor spices but are traditionally found on shelves near them because they are used for cooking and baking.

Shopping

When shopping for dried herbs and spices, buy only amounts that you will use in a short time. Having a year's supply in a huge container won't be a bargain if you use so little that the herb or spice loses its flavor and has to be discarded. When an herb that is supposed to be green takes on a gray cast, it could be past its prime. Don't buy it! And if it's already on your shelf, it's time to replace it.

REFERENCE GUIDE TO HERBS, SPICES, AND SEASONINGS

I have marked with an asterisk (*) those items that could be considered basic to every kitchen. However, some items may not be basic to your kitchen. For example, if you never ever bake anything, you won't need leavening agents or baking spices. If you do Mexican cooking, cumin is a basic; if you cook Italian, oregano is a basic.

- **Allspice** is found in many baked goods, it is also used in Jamaican jerk and barbecue. In Polish cuisine it is called kubaba and used whole in soups and pickling.
- **Anise** provides the sweet licorice taste found in cooking, sausages, and sauces. It is popular in Mediterranean cuisine. Star anise, a Chinese spice shaped like a star, has a stronger and sweeter licorice flavor than anise seeds. It is used in pickling, curry, stir-fry, barbecue, and baking.

- **Annatto** is essential to South American, Caribbean, Mexican, and Spanish cooking. It adds a red color and pungent flavor in rice or polenta, fried chicken or fish, and braised pork or beef for enchiladas.

- **Arrowroot*** thickens clear glazes for fruit pies and clear gravies, especially in Chinese stir-fries of seafood and poultry.

- **Baking powder*** is a leavening agent that makes batters rise when they are baked.

- **Baking soda*** is a leavening agent that makes batters rise when they are baked.

- **Basil** flavors tomato dishes and fresh tomatoes, chicken, fish, pasta dishes, stews, salads, and vegetables. If you grow it fresh, you can put a few basil leaves in your sandwich instead of lettuce. When cooking with basil, add it in the last 10 minutes to get maximum flavor.

- **Bay leaves*** are usually bought dried; they flavor soups, roasts, poultry, and spaghetti sauce and can make salt-free foods more appealing. Use about two or three leaves for a roast and two per quart of liquid in soups. *Always* remove the leaves before serving or put the leaves in a tea ball so they don't get lost in the food. Dried bay leaves can cause choking.

- **Bouillon*** (cubes, powder, or liquid) can make a cup of soup any time you want one and will flavor other foods. Do consider regular bouillon to be a salt substitute and reduce or eliminate salt in recipes when you add it. You will also find low-salt bouillons in the diet section of your supermarket.

- **Capers** are little, tart pickled flower buds from the caper tree. They are are slightly salty and are often served with smoked fish, eggs, and tomatoes.

- **Caraway** is added to rye bread, cabbage dishes (sauerkraut and coleslaw), pork, cheese sauces, cream soups, goose, and duck. It was used by the Greeks to calm upset stomachs and to season hard-to-digest foods. In Germany, a caraway liqueur called Kummel is served with heavy meals.

- **Cardamom** seed, with its lemon-ginger taste, is popular in baked goods, especially in Scandinavia.

- **Celery seed*** (or flakes) is used wherever you want celery flavor; add it to soups, stews, sauces, and casseroles.

- **Charnushka** (nigella sativa) is favored in Armenia, Lebanon, Israel, and India; it is also called black caraway. New York bakeries top Jewish rye with these tiny, black, smoky-flavored seeds.

- **Chervil** is a delicate, sweet herb that flavors vegetables, potato or egg salads, and fish. It resembles parsley when fresh. A friend of mine makes a delicious cream cheese dip/spread for crackers by combining about five sprigs of minced fresh chervil and two or three minced shallot cloves with a tub of cream cheese (thin with a couple of tablespoons of yogurt to make it spreadable) and then chilling it overnight.

- **Chive*** flavors omelets and chicken broth and tops baked potatoes, vegetables, and salads. It is available freeze-dried and often you can find it growing in a small box so that you can keep it on a sunny windowsill and have fresh chives when you want them. Cut fresh chives with kitchen scissors.

- **Cilantro** (chinese parsley)* is the leaf of the coriander plant and is common in Mexican foods, such as tacos, guacamole, and salsa.

It can also season salads, curries, soups, and stews.

- **Coriander** seed has a light lemon flavor and is best used to season foods that cook for longer than 1 hour (such as roasts), or foods cooked for short times at high temperatures, (such as pan-fried, broiled, or grilled meats).

- **Chili peppers*** are used in various foods of many countries and are ranked by their hotness. The heat, flavor, and color of chili peppers can vary from crop to crop, depending on the weather and other growing conditions. Here are approximate heat ratings in Scoville units.

PEPPER	RATING	UNITS
Sweet Bells, Sweet Banana, and Pimento	0	Negligible
Mexi-Bells, Cherry, New Mexica, New Mexico, Anaheim, and Big Jim	1	100–1,000
Ancho, Pasilla, Española, and Anaheim	2	1,000–1,500
Sandia and Cascabel	3	1,500–2,500
Jalapeño, Mirasl, Chipotle, and Poblano	4	2,500–5,000
Yellow Wax and Serrano	5	5,000–15,000
Chile de Arbol	6	15,000–30,000
Aji, Cayenne, Tabsco, and Piquin	7	30,000–50,000
Santaka, Chiltecpin, and Thai	8	50,000–100,000
Habanero and Scotch Bonnet	9	100,000–350,000
Red Savina Habanero and Indian Tezpur	10	350,000–855,000

- **Chinese five spice** is called for in many Chinese recipes. You can buy this spice blend ready mixed; it is a combination of cinnamon, star anise, anise seed, ginger, and cloves, or other similar combinations that can include fennel seed, szechuan peppercorns, or cassia.

- **Cinnamon*** is in the inner skin of the cassia tree bark; it is used in stick and ground forms in cocoa, coffee, curry, dessert sauces and syrups, baked goods, rice dishes, and other foods from many countries.

- **Cloves*** are used to sweeten the flavor of baked goods; it is also popular for pickling and barbecuing. Whole cloves are used to stud hams, and they will bring out the beefy flavor of beef stew.

- **Cream of tartar*** is a white powder that stabilizes delicate foods such as meringue toppings and other baked egg white products. It can reduce discoloration of boiled vegetables (add ½ teaspoon to the cooking water), it will remove discoloration on aluminum cookware if you boil cream of tartar in water in the pot, and when made into a paste, it cleans copperware.

- **Cumin*** provides a pungent flavor to Indian, Mexican, Asian, northern African, Middle Eastern, and Latin American cooking; it is used by Americans mainly in chili.

- **Curry*** is a blend of several spices. Different ethnic cuisines feature different combinations of spices, so that the curry of India, for example, does not taste exactly like the curry of Egypt. Some of the spices commonly found in curries are pepper, turmeric, coriander, cumin, cardamom, fenugreek, ginger, nutmeg, fennel, cinnamon, cloves, and saffron.

- **Dill** (seed and weed) is found in northern and eastern European cuisines. Dill seed flavors fish and, of course, pickles. Dill weed is lighter in flavor than the seeds and is added to dishes made with white sauces, such as potato salad, sour cream dips, and salad dressings; it also flavors poultry and omelets. Dill weed is popular in German and Scandinavian cooking.

- **Fennel** seed is found in Italian sausages, and ground fennel is used in Italian tomato sauces and for pork roasts. The English use it for fish dishes; and in folk medicine, it is used as a digestive aid.

- **Garlic*** —fresh, granulated, and powdered—is used in all cuisines. To substitute dry garlic for fresh, use ¼ teaspoon for each garlic clove required in a recipe or about ½ teaspoon per pound of poultry, steak, chops, or fish (see also the vegetable section of this chapter).

- **Ginger*** is used primarily for baking in the United States. It flavors Asian and Indian meats, seafood, and vegetables, as well as chicken soup, roast chicken or pork, sautéed vegetables, and grilled steak.

- **Gumbo file*** is powdered sassafras leaves and is used to thicken and flavor Cajun and Creole seafood soups and stews.

- **Horseradish**—a peppery white root—is usually bought as a ready-made sauce to flavor meats, seafood cocktail sauces, and other dishes.

- **Juniper** is an aromatic berry used to flavor game meats, such as venison, squab, pheasant, and rabbit; it lessens the wild flavor and adds tartness. It is especially important in German recipes for sauerbraten, goose, and beef stews.

- **Lemongrass** is a Southeast Asian herb that is also used in India and China. It flavors soups, sauces, and stir-fries and its lemon flavor goes well with ginger, garlic, and curries.

- **Mace** is made from the lacy covering of the nutmeg's outer shell, and is often used to flavor doughnuts, hot dogs, and English fruit cakes. It can be found in pumpkin pie mix and barbecue sauce.

- **Marjoram** is related to oregano and is used in Polish, Italian, Mexican, and French cuisines. It is best added near the end of the cooking time. Use it in tomato sauces, vegetables, salad dressing, and in place of basil or oregano in chicken and pasta dishes. It is a main flavoring in Polish sausage.

- **Mint** comes in many varieties, including peppermint and spearmint. It is used to make jellies and to flavor salads, beverages, and desserts. In the Middle East it flavors tabouli, vegetables, and other dishes.

- **Monosodium glutamate (MSG)** is a flavor enhancer found mainly in Chinese and Japanese cooking. It is also used in soups, sausages, seafood, and salad dressings.

- **Mustard seed** is most often used for pickling, canning, and sausage making and in vegetarian dishes of Asia and Africa. It can be added to barbecue sauce and marinades. Try sprouting it for use in salads and sandwiches.

- **Nutmeg*** is the ground kernel of the fruit of nutmeg trees. It is sprinkled on top of baked goods and cocoa in Europe and is used to flavor cream sauces for noodles. It is also used in sausages and syrups and to flavor fresh fruit.

- **Onion powder*** is sprinkled on roasts, baked meats, and chops and is added to salad dressings and vegetable dishes. Use ½ teaspoon of onion powder to equal to ¼ cup of freshly chopped onion.

- **Oregano*** is available in two types. The Mediterranean oregano has a sweeter, milder flavor than the Mexican oregano. Mediterranean oregano is best for Italian spaghetti sauces, Greek salads, and Turkish meats. Both should be added at the beginning of cooking, such as when browning onions or meat for spaghetti sauce or chili, to give the herb a chance to blend in with the other ingredients.

- **Paprika*** comes in hot and sweet varieties. Hungarian sweet paprika is the favorite spice for goulash, for baked chicken, and for adding color and a sweet flavor to a variety of dishes and sauces. In the United States, it is often sprinkled on potato salad and deviled eggs to give a dash of appetizing color. Some varieties are a bit hot, so you want to be carefully when choosing this spice to get the right level of sweet or hot for your cooking.

- **Parsley*** is best used fresh in soups and stews, with vegetables, in bread stuffing for poultry, and of course, as a garnish. Many people believe that parsley is a good breath freshener, so they eat the parsley that garnishes their restaurant meals instead of pushing it to the side of the plate to be discarded. Because it is easily grown in the garden, you can have fresh parsley handy; and it will do fine grown in a pot.

- **Poppy seed** is used in baking, to top breads and rolls, in muffins and cake, and in fruit salad dressing, in the United States. In India, it flavors lentil and rice dishes. It has a high oil content, so it is best stored in the refrigerator or freezer during hot weather.

- **Peppercorns*** season almost any food, and freshly ground pepper has more flavor than already ground pepper. There are several varieties of peppercorns.

Black: Available as Telicherry (large, premium grade) and Malabar (small).

White: Ripened on the vine and then soaked in water until the black shell comes off; provide a hotter flavor than black peppercorns; sometimes mixed with black pepper of added zest; used in Southeast Asian and eastern European cuisines for soups, grilled meats and poultry, and light colored dishes.

Green: Harvested before they mature; often soft enough to crush between your fingers; may be mixed with other peppers; used in poultry, vegetable, and seafood dishes.

Pink: Actually berries that look and taste like peppercorns; used to flavor many foods, including poultry, fish, salads, and seafood.

Sichuan: Berries used to flavor Chinese cuisine; used whole in soups; used crushed in poultry and pork dishes.

- **Pickling spice** is a combination of many spices, including bay leaf, clove, whole peppercorn, and chilies.

- **Rosemary**, when fresh, looks like it should be a pine branch Christmas decoration. It adds a strong minty flavor to pork, lamb, poultry, fish, and other dishes. Use a sprig of rosemary to brush oil on your barbecue meats. Try crushed rosemary with potatoes—boiled or mashed—for a special treat. Or sprinkle rosemary on your garlic bread before heating.

Rosemary sprigs can also be used to make herb oils and herb vinegar. It complements thyme, garlic, tomato, and many other flavors. If you grow it in your garden, cut a bouquet of rosemary, put it in a vase and you'll have a room freshener that doesn't smell like medicine or fake flowers.

■ **Saffron** is very expensive and once you learn how it is harvested, you'll know why. Saffron is the red stigma of the fall-flowering crocus, and there are only three threads of saffron in each flower. The threads are carefully removed by hand; to produce 1 pound of saffron, it takes one acre of flowers, about seventy thousand crocus flowers. Because it is so expensive, powdered saffron is often mixed with turmeric (another spice that colors foods), and so to get your money's worth, it is better to buy saffron only in the thread form. Saffron comes from various parts of the world, each of which claims its saffron to be the best. It flavors and colors Indian, Spanish, and northern European dishes, especially rice dishes. We are most familiar with saffron as the main spice for Spanish Paella. In a bind, you can substitute turmeric for saffron if you are the type of cook that can accept substitutions. Normally, you use a small pinch of saffron, crushed between your fingers, to about 1 cup rice in a recipe.

■ **Sage*** is a favorite herb for flavoring poultry, poultry dressings, pork, and sausages. It is also a good addition to beef and game dishes.

■ **Salt*** is sodium chloride and some brands contain added iodine. Ordinary table salt has some starch added to prevent it from sticking together, but Kosher and sea salt do not and so should be kept in an airtight container to prevent their clunking together. Also, these two salts are usually found in a coarse grind, and believe it or not, you will get better flavor with less salt when you use a coarser grind to season foods, especially meats and French fries.

■ **Savory** has a flavor between thyme and mint with a bit of pepper. It seasons beans, poultry, pork, beef, and vegetables. Put it in stews and soups.

Herbal Combinations

Unless otherwise noted, use equal parts of each herb listed.

Barbecue: Cumin, garlic, hot pepper, and oregano.

Eggs: Basil, dill weed, garlic, and parsley.

Fines herbes: Parsley, chervil, chives, and French tarragon (may add a small amount of basil, fennel, oregano, sage, or saffron).

Fish: Basil, bay leaves (broken), French tarragon, lemon thyme, and parsley (may include fennel, sage, or savory).

Italian: Basil, marjoram, oregano, rosemary, sage, savory, and thyme.

Poultry: Lovage, marjoram (two parts), and sage (three parts).

Salad: Basil, lovage, parsley, and French tarragon.

Tomato sauce: Basil (two parts), bay leaves, marjoram, oregano, parsley (may include celery leaves or cloves).

Vegetables: Basil, parsley, and savory.

■ **Sesame seed** is the beige-colored seed that's sprinkled on top of breads and rolls and used in some cereals. It can also flavor chicken, fish, and salads, especially in Indian and Asian dishes. Black sesame seed is used in Chinese and Japanese cuisine.

■ **Shallots** have a flavor between onion and garlic, but milder and sweeter. They are good flavor enhancers in poultry, veal, salads, eggs, and soups. One ½-teaspoon dried shallots equals about one clove garlic.

■ **Tarragon** is a favorite flavoring for poultry, fish, and other French dishes; we know tarragon mainly as a flavoring for vinegar to use in salads.

■ **Thyme** flavors poultry, pork, fish, soups, and roasts. When Simon and Garfunkel sang about parsley, sage, rosemary, and thyme they not only had a pretty song but also they were giving us a pretty good combination of herbs for cooking.

■ **Turmeric** puts the yellow in curry powders and prepared mustard. It is also used in pickling and Indian cooking.

■ **Vanilla*** is found in whole bean and extract forms. It flavors ice cream, baked goods, custards, and sugar. Put a whole vanilla bean into a tightly covered jar of confectioners' sugar, let it sit for a week or so, and you'll have delicious vanilla sugar to sprinkle on pound cakes, cookies, and other foods.

■ **Yeast** is a leavening agent that is usually used in bread doughs. You will find granulated (dry) yeast on store shelves and yeast in cubes in the refrigerated sections of the store. There is also yeast recommended for bread machines. Follow the directions on the label for use.

Storing

Although you'll find many spice shelves installed above or beside kitchen ranges in decorating magazines, this is one of the worst places to store dried herbs and spices, which need a cool, dry, dark place to keep their potency. Stored above a stovetop, they will be subjected to steam and heat and, just as if they were in direct sunlight, they will discolor and lose flavor. The older the dried herb or spice, the more you will usually need to get the proper flavor in your recipe. For this reason, it's best to buy smallest amounts available so that you can buy fresh ones often.

The classic way to *keep salt from clumping* is to put a few grains of dry, uncooked rice in the shaker. Some people put crushed crackers in with the salt to keep it free flowing. Another solution is to make a dome by putting a glass fruit jar upside down over the salt shaker when the weather is damp so that the moisture from the air doesn't get into the shaker.

Cooking

■ **Add Spice to Your Life, and Life to Your Spice:** Pour spices into your hand or a spoon first instead of sprinkling them directly from the container over steaming foods because they absorb the steam and deteriorate faster, not to mention getting all clumped up.

■ **Bouquet garni:** This is a mix of one bay leaf, two parts parsley, and one part thyme. The herbs can be wrapped in cheesecloth or the parsley can be wrapped around the thyme and bay leaf. **CAUTION**: Bay leaves *do not* soften when they are cooked; pieces of bay leaf are a serious choking hazard.

❀ **HELOISE HINT**: When using whole herbs and spices (like peppercorns, cloves, and bay leaves) in soups and stews, put them in a mesh or perforated metal tea ball; that way they can easily be removed before serving the dish. Plus you don't have to worry about any one biting into a hard spice or choking on a piece of bay leaf.

■ **Herb butter**: To one stick of unsalted butter, add 1 to 3 tablespoons of dried herbs or 2 to 6 tablespoons of finely chopped fresh herbs, ½ teaspoon of lemon juice, and white pepper to taste. Combine the ingredients and mix until fluffy. Pack in covered container and let set in refrigerator at least 1 hour. Try one of the combinations listed on page 148.

■ **Herb vinegar**: Heat any type of vinegar, depending on your preference, in an enamel pan and pour it into a vinegar bottle; add one or several culinary herbs to taste. Do not let the vinegar boil. Let the mixture steep for 2 weeks before using.

■ **Salt alternatives**: If you must avoid salt, try a commercial substitute, lemon juice, or other herbs and spices to perk up your taste buds.

❀ **HELOISE HINT**: Here's a homemade salt substitute. Mix 5 teaspoons of onion powder; 1 tablespoon each of garlic powder, paprika, and dry mustard; 1 teaspoon of thyme; ½ teaspoon of white pepper; and ½ teaspoon of celery seed. Combine and store in an empty clean, dry spice jar in a cool, dry place.

❀ **KITCHENEERING HUMOR** ❀

A Texas reader's mom was teaching her to make enchiladas. As they prepared the chili gravy, she handed her mom the chili powder. Her mom poured and stirred and poured and stirred but somehow the gravy never looked right. Then they discovered that the reader had given her mom paprika instead of chili powder. The moral of the story, of course, is to read those labels when you cook. Imagine if her mom were making Hungarian goulash and had added lots of chili powder to it instead of sweet paprika!

■ **Making a spice bag**: If you don't have any cheesecloth from which to make a spice bag for mixtures such as bouquet garni, put the spices in a metal tea ball or put them in a single-cup coffee filter and wrap them up or staple the filter closed.

▮ **A READER RECOMMENDS:**
One reader said she emptied a tea bag, replaced the tea with spices and then stapled it shut and tossed it into the stew.

FATS AND OILS

Although we are told to avoid consuming excessive amounts of fats and oils, we still need to have some fat in our daily diet because without them certain nutrients cannot be used by our bodies.

Shopping

When you buy fats and oils for cooking, health is always a consideration these days. The USDA recommends avoiding too much fat, saturated fatty acids, and cholesterol. Eating too much fat, especially saturated fatty acids, causes higher blood cholesterol levels in many people, which increase the risk of heart disease. Cholesterol is a fat-like substance found in foods of animal origin (egg yolks, meat, poultry, fish, whole milk, and dairy products). Foods of plant origin (fruits, vegetables, grains, nuts, seeds, dry beans and peas, and vegetable oils) have no cholesterol.

The USDA tells us that all fats are mixtures of three types of fatty acids—saturated, monounsaturated, and polyunsaturated— which differ in the amount of hydrogen they contain. Saturated fatty acids contain the most hydrogen, and polyunsaturated contain the least. Liquid oils tend to be higher in polyunsaturated fatty acids than partially hydrogenated fats like shortenings, stick margarine, and others. Hydrogenation is the process that makes vegetable oils solid at room temperature. When you read labels look for monounsaturated or polyunsaturated fatty acids. When labels don't specify which oil is in the product, manufacturers may vary the type of oil they put into it according to availability and cost, and so they may use coconut, palm,

and palm kernel oils, which are high in saturated fats.

Meat fat, poultry fat, butter, cream, lard, cocoa butter, coconut oil, palm kernel oil, and palm oil contain large amounts of saturated fatty acids. Olive oil, peanut oil, and canola oil contain large amounts of monounsaturated fatty acids. Safflower, soybean, corn, sunflower, cottonseed, and sesame oils contain large amounts of polyunsaturated fatty acids.

Taste is also a factor in selecting oils for cooking. Oils like canola, corn, and sunflower are fairly neutral tasting and so won't change the taste of a recipe. Peanut oil has a slightly sweet taste and is good for stir-fries and for beef fondue. Peanut oil also tolerates high temperatures, so it's good for deep frying. Olive oil adds its distinctive flavor to meats, Italian foods, salads, and other recipes.

BUTTER AND MARGARINE

The natural color of **butter**, pale to deep yellow, depends on the breed of cow and what the cows ate, so manufacturers add dyes to make the butter color consistent; salt is also usually added. Because the amount of salt varies from one brand of butter to another and in different areas of the country, most chefs cook with unsalted butter to get consistent flavor in recipes. When salted butter is used for cooking, you may have to adjust the amount of salt added to a recipe.

Whipped butter is just that—butter to which air has been beaten in. It spreads better and melts more quickly than unwhipped butter but it is not convenient for baking and other recipes. You need to increase the volume of butter called for in a recipe to account for the air in the whipped butter. Usually, you need to increase the amount of whipped butter by one-third or more. It's really better to use regular butter in recipes.

Butter granules are to butter as powdered milk is to liquid milk. They are made mostly of dehydrated buttermilk solids, with the fat removed and various ingredients added to keep the granules from caking; they are one way to get butter flavor without the fat. Butter granules work best if sprinkled on hot, moist foods, such as steamy baked potatoes and cooked vegetables. You will find several brands at the store. Some give directions on how to mix the granules with hot water to form liquid "butter" and this liquid can be used as you would melted butter for flavoring. However, you can't fry with the liquid. An easy way to make a liquid butter with granules that come in individual packets is to heat a ½ cup of water in the microwave in a glass microwave-safe measuring cup until hot (not boiling), add a packet of granules, stir, and pour over whatever food needs a butter flavor.

Choose **margarine** that lists a liquid vegetable oil on the label as the first ingredient. The softer the margarine, the less saturated fat in it. Stick margarine is harder and, therefore, contains a fair amount of saturated fat; liquid margarine has the least amount of saturated fats, and tub margarine has less saturated fat than stick and more than liquid or pourable margarine. Stick margarine is easier to measure for baking, because one stick equals ½ cup; in some baking recipes, it is a better substitute for

butter than tub margarine. Some tub margarine and some low-fat or nonfat varieties of margarine cannot be used for baking or frying because they have ingredients other than just fat (water, milk solids, etc.), making them unsuitable for many recipes and for pan frying. However, they can be used to flavor foods and for spreads. You will find information on the margarine's label to tell you if it can be used for frying or in baked goods. If no information is available on the label, stick to stick margarine for baking and frying.

VEGETABLE OILS

The healthiest vegetable oils are those that are monounsaturated, because they decrease the amount of low-density lipoproteins (LDL; the bad cholesterol) in the body. However, this does not mean that you should consume oil for that purpose; oils are fats and need to be counted as such when considering your total daily fat intake. Also note that some oils on the market are combinations of more than one oil so you need to read the labels. The American Heart Association recommends the following oils: safflower oil, soybean oil, sunflower oil, corn oil, sesame seed oil, canola oil, olive oil, and oil-based salad dressing. Oils recommended for occasional use only are peanut oil and vegetable shortening. Not recommended because of the saturated fats in them are butter, shortening, bacon, salt pork, suet, lard, chicken fat, meat fat, coconut oil, palm kernel oil, and palm oil.

According to the book *Kitchen Science* by Howard Hillman, knowing the smoke point of oil is important because when an oil smokes, it begins to decompose, and each time you deep-fry with an oil, its smoke point gets lower. So if you buy an oil with a high smoke point, you will be able to reuse it for deep-frying. Smoke points for oils vary according to brand, but here are some oils and their average smoke points to help you:

Safflower	510 degrees F
Soybean	495 degrees F
Corn	475 degrees F
Peanut	440 degrees F
Sesame	429 degrees F
Olive	375 degrees F
Vegetable shortening	375 degrees F

Cool and strain used oil, then refrigerate it. You can tell when an oil should no longer be fried with if smoke appears on the oil surface before the temperature reaches 375 degrees F, the proper temperature for deep-frying. Other signs are a stale, rancid, or burned taste. Even if you don't deep-fry foods, knowing the smoke point will help you choose the right oil for other stovetop cooking, such as stir-frying at high temperatures. Be sure to also read about clarified fats, discussed below.

Some oils for **deep frying** include corn, sunflower, canola, cottonseed, grapeseed, and pure olive oils. Some oils for **cooking and salad dressings** include grapeseed, corn, sunflower, canola, and safflower oils. Some oils for **special salads or pastry making** include the stronger flavored walnut, hazelnut, pecan and pistachio oils. These oils should be purchased in small bottles because they tend to get rancid faster than other oils and so you should buy an amount you will use up quickly.

Substituting oil for solid fats is not always a good idea because they have different properties when used for baking, however, if you substitute oil for butter in a recipe, reduce the amount by 15 to 20 percent.

OLIVE OIL

Olive oil is good for any type of use in the kitchen from frying to salad dressings. Buying olive oil is more complicated than in my mother's day. There are so many different types and brands, not to mention prices! According to my sources, there are no nutritional differences between the types of olive oil. All are good choices because the monounsaturated fat does not raise blood cholesterol and studies suggest that olive oil does not promote cancer development the way some other fats may. However, the calories add up just as quickly, so we need to use all oils in moderation.

The largest producers are Spain, Italy, Greece, Portugal, and Tunisia. I had the thrill of visiting Crete in 1998, where 80–90 percent of its olive oil is considered high quality. The Cretan olive oil that we enjoyed during our stay was delicious and I can't wait to go back and indulge in some more! It's amazing that this beautiful little island produces close to 100,000 tons of olive oil per year. Since only 5,000 to 10,000 tons gets exported to the United States, if you are lucky enough to find some, buy it! You won't be sorry.

The different types of olive oil have different intensities of color, flavor, and aroma, all of which are affected by the growing conditions of the olive trees and the stage of pressing of the olives. Most quality olive oils come from the first pressing. Later pressings will have more of the olive skin and seed flavor because more pressure was needed to get the oil out. The term **cold pressed** means that no or almost no heat was used to remove the oil, giving it a better taste than oils processed with heat.

- **Virgin oil** is unrefined oil from the first pressing of the olives. If a virgin oil is bright emerald green and gets even greener when you heat it in the pan, it may have been artificially colored. Experiment with different brands of oils to find the taste that you like; oils are like wines and so personal taste is a factor when choosing one brand over another.
- **Extra-virgin oil** has a medium color and a very distinct olive oil flavor. The most expensive olive oils are the extra-virgin oils. Most do not exceed acidity of 1 percent and are cold pressed and may be unfiltered, which means you may find bits in the bottom of the bottle.
- **Extra-light oil** has been refined to remove color and flavor, and so you can use it like other vegetable oils.
- **Light oil** does not mean fewer calories or less fat. It can be pure olive oil or a mixture of pure olive oil and any other unsaturated oil.
- **Pure oil** is the most commonly found olive oil in supermarkets. It contains no colorants and is generally yellow golden. It is usually in between extra-virgin and extra-light in color and flavor and is good as an all-purpose oil.

OTHER FATS

- **Lard** is rendered pork fat and is used for baking and frying. Since it is from an animal source, it is a saturated fat. However, many cooks still prefer to make pie crusts with lard because they say it makes the crusts crispy and flakey. Also many cooks prefer to deep-fry with lard because the crispy bits on fried foods like chicken and potatoes are crispier if lard is used. If you substitute lard for butter, use 15 to 20 percent less lard.
- **Shortening**, like margarine, is made up of oils that have been hydrogenated (artificially hardened). Look for those that have hydrogenated oil listed as the second ingredient, not the first. Shortening is frequently used as a substitute for butter in cookies, other baked goods, and general cooking.
- **Suet** is meat fat. It is used in some recipes to flavor and to fry or brown meats and/or onions.
- **Spray-on oils** and nonstick sprays have many uses in the kitchen. They keep foods from sticking to pots, pans, and baking dishes. They also save calories when used instead of fat for browning foods on the stove and for pan frying. You will find these products in various flavors: butter, olive oil, garlic, roasted garlic, and so on. Do spray racks before cooking meats as well as the pans and cleanup will be easy whether you wash by hand or just put the items in the dishwasher. Most are considered to add zero calories when used according to directions, if you are counting such things.

Storing

- **Butter** keeps in the refrigerator for 1 to 2 weeks; in the freezer for 9 months.

- **Margarine** keeps 4 to 6 months in the refrigerator. Look for the "Use By" date stamped on the container.
- Most **vegetables oils** will store on the shelf; but some, like walnut oil, say on the label that you should refrigerate them. So read those labels!

❀ **HELOISE HINT:** Use cleaned and appropriate size lids from margarine, yogurt, or potato chip containers as coasters for bottles of oil in the cupboard. The lids will collect drips so you don't have to clean the whole messy cupboard shelf so often.

- **Olive oil** doesn't need refrigeration but if you have stored it there, it will get thick and cloudy. However, it's not ruined; it will lighten up again if you let it get back to room temperature. Olive oil, stored on the shelf, in a cool, dark place, protected from light, will keep longer than other edible oils. You can buy most olive oil in a can, which helps it keep longer. Since these cans are usually large, you can transfer a quantity to a glass bottle or dispenser for easier use.

❀ **HELOISE HINT:** If you buy olive oil in large cans, you can put it in a clean recycled plastic ketchup or mayo squeeze container for less mess squirting when you need some oil.

- **Olive oil with garlic:** Some people like to flavor their olive oil with a few cloves of garlic. **CAUTION:** The International Olive Oil Institute says that jars of garlic in oil should not be stored in the refrigerator for more than

24 hours. When garlic is kept in oil, bacteria that may be on the garlic can grow due to the lack of oxygen. The longer the garlic stays in the oil, the higher the risk of food poisoning. Although the chances of getting bacterial growth are low, it *can* happen and this is a word to the wise.

- **Lard and suet:** These fats are usually rendered from pork. Lard is generally sold unrefrigerated, but it will keep better if you store it in the refrigerator; it can be frozen.
- **Shortening:** Shortening can be kept several months or more if you store it in the refrigerator.
- **Peanut butter:** Best kept refrigerated, peanut butter keeps about 6 months unopened and 2 months after opening.

❀ **HELOISE HINT:** If you buy natural peanut butter, meaning the type that has no other added ingredients, you will need to stir in the peanut oil into the solids before putting it into the refrigerator. Store the jar on its side in the cupboard for a day or so to make this task easier. A friend of mine, trying to cut fats from her diet, poured off the oil and discovered that the remaining peanut solids didn't spread at all; the oil is necessary for spreadability!

- **Fat and oil substitutes:** As this book is being written several fat and oil substitutes, some of which claim to lower cholesterol when eaten, are being introduced to the market. Some of these products may produce unpleasant side effects in some people. Others are recommended for use as spreads but not for baking or frying. We really have to read those labels!

COOKING
Clarified Fats

Clarifying fats that have been used for deep-frying means removing burned food particles and other impurities. To clarify used fats, heat them slowly with several slices of raw potato—about four slices per cup of fat. After the potato slices are browned, strain the fat into a container, and store in the refrigerator.

❄ **HELOISE HINT:** To avoid spattering grease when you deep-fry or are making beef fondue at the table, always drop a couple of white potato slices or cubes (about ½-inch dice) into the grease while you fry. They will help prevent spatters.

❄ **CLASSIC HELOISE HINT FOR HARD BUTTER:** When your butter or margarine is hard as a brick, this hint from my mother is still good: Shave off thin curls from a firm or frozen stick of butter or margarine with a vegetable peeler. The curls will be soft enough to spread almost instantly. Or fill a bowl with boiling water, pour out the water and quickly turn the hot bowl upside down over the butter dish. The butter will soften without melting.

You will get a more delicate flavor if you fry foods in clarified butter. The milk solids in butter burn more quickly than the fat does. To make clarified butter, heat 1 pound of butter over low heat until it is completely melted. It will foam and bubble at first. When it begins to sizzle,

most of the white foam will have disappeared. This is the time to remove the butter from the heat. Do not let the milk solids get brown, because this will change the delicate flavor of the clarified butter. Skim off the white froth that remains on top. Then pour the butter into a large heatproof glass measuring cup and let it stand for 5 to 10 minutes. The pale gold milk particles will sink to the bottom of the cup and the top layer will look clear and oily. Pour off the clear oily butter and use this for frying. You can store what you don't use in the refrigerator. Save the milk solids to reheat and flavor vegetables as you would beurre noisette (French for "light brown butter"); it is an instant butter sauce.

❄ **CLASSIC HELOISE HINT FOR FRYING WITH BUTTER:** When pan frying with butter, my mother always put a bit of vegetable oil in the bottom of the skillet before adding the butter. That way the butter would brown gently without burning.

More Cooking Hints

■ **Measuring stick butter or margarine:** Before you remove the wrapper from a stick of butter or margarine, score the stick on the measurement lines provided, then you can still get a measured dose when you need it without messing up a measuring utensil. Or simply cut through the stick at the appropriate measure, and wrap the rest in plastic for storage.

■ **Measuring solid shortening:** The water-displacement method makes it a less-mess thing. If you need ½ cup of shortening, fill a 1-cup measuring cup with ½ cup of water, then add dollops of shortening until the water level reaches

1 cup. Drain off the water and shortening comes right out without the need for scraping.

■ **Recycle the wrapper:** When you unwrap a new stick of butter or margarine, fold the wrapper, butter sides in, and store in a zipper bag in the freezer. Then when you need to grease a pan, pull out a wrapper, grease the pan, and toss the wrapper into the trash. *Note:* If each of us used disposable items twice whenever possible, we would benefit the environment by reducing the amount of trash in our ever-decreasing landfill spaces.

■ Fresh oil gives the best flavor for **deep-frying** foods. Usually, bits of breading, cracker meal, or other coating on the foods, will fall to the bottom of the deep fryer and get burned, which, in turn, gives the fat a burned taste. Change the oil in a deep fryer often. If you are frying several batches of deep-fried foods, use two pans; pour off the clear oil from the first pan into the other so that you can discard the burned crumbs from the bottom (see also Clarified Fats, above). *Do be careful when handling hot oil!* Many cooks prefer to deep-fry foods in canola oil, which gives no flavor at all to the foods, or in peanut oil, which is also a light oil that tolerates high temperatures. Peanut oil is the choice of most cooks for fondue pots.

■ **Shortening substitute:** If you wish to substitute vegetable oil for butter or lard in other foods besides bread and desserts, you will need to experiment with your recipes to get the right amount. As a rule, you use one-third less oil. For example, 2 teaspoons of vegetable oil replaces 1 tablespoon of solid shortening. But if you are counting fat grams or calories, remember that even if good vegetable oil is low in cholesterol, it is still a fat and so the number of fat grams and calories will remain the same, but the saturated (bad) fats will be replaced by unsaturated (good) fats.

Serving

■ **Butter pats:** While the butter or margarine stick is still cold, slice it into individual pats with an egg slicer. Pats are easier and less messy at the table, and if you are counting fat calories, you'll know exactly how much butter you're using. Store extra pats in an airtight container so you won't need to measure your allowed portions for a while.

■ **Margarine squeeze containers:** Well-washed margarine squeeze containers can be used to serve a variety of oils and other foods like syrups, mustard, salad dressings, and steak sauces. Be sure to *write on the outside* what's on the inside!

■ **Olive oil:** Serve olive oil in a saucer or sauce dish at the table and use it instead of butter for dipping bread. You can also add your favorite spices, such as freshly ground peppercorns; cayenne, other hot ground peppers, or pepper flakes; dried onion or garlic bits; or any other palate pleaser.

Chapter Five

Shopping for and Organizing Your Food

SHOPPING FOR FOOD

The best place to start shopping is in your kitchen. Take an inventory of what you have in the cupboards and in the refrigerator. If you have your food well-organized (discussed later in this chapter) then this chore won't be so hard. As you plan your menus for the week and write up your shopping list, you should know what you have on hand (especially dated items) and what you'll need to buy.

• **Inventory:** Every time you use something and when you get to the bottom of a bulk item like flour, salt, sugar, or cereal, write it on a posted list.

A READER RECOMMENDS:

A Virginia reader keeps a 3 × 3-inch pad of stick-on note paper on the refrigerator door (remove the back sheet and stick the pad on the fridge) so that when she runs out of something, she can write it on the pad. When she's ready to go shopping, she just takes the top note and sticks it on her wallet. When she gets to the store, she sticks it to the handle of the grocery cart for easy reference.

❀ KITCHENEERING HUMOR ❀

One reader apparently sat on one of the many stick-on notes she writes to herself as reminders to pick up this or that. While she was shopping, someone tapped her on the shoulder and pointed out that there was something stuck on the seat of her trousers. Much to her embarrassment, in big, block letters the note read: "LARD!"

- Make up a **preprinted shopping list**. With a home computer it's easy to make up lists and customize them to your own needs. You can organize your list by types of items or follow the layout of your supermarket. I've given you a sample shopping list on p. 163.

- **Menu planning:** Make up menus for all meals for each day of the week—and don't forget Saturday and Sunday. Compare what you need with what you've got on hand and your shopping list will write itself. (If you plan to try new recipes, make sure to check them first so you'll get all the ingredients.)

- **Specials and coupons:** Before you finalized your menu, check grocery ads to see what's on special that week and what discount coupons are available.

- **Planned leftovers:** Plan meals with an eye to what's on sale or what you can buy in bulk, then cook accordingly to use the leftovers. Rice or noodles can be a side dish one day and used in a casserole the next.

Coupon Shopping and Other Money-Saving Tips

Take pride in being able to stay within your budget. Instead of looking at careful shopping as a horrible chore, view it as a game. I have a friend who likes to see if she can save 10 percent of the total bill when she uses coupons to shop for staples. But coupons save money only if you use them to get discounts on items that you will actually use.

- **Clip coupons** for items that you may need in the future and note the expiration date. If you organize coupons by category, you may wish to keep the earliest expiration dates at the front.

- **Organizing coupons:** You can buy specially designed coupon organizers or simply use old envelopes. (You can write your shopping list on the back the envelope!) Or, use an old checkbook cover with the to-be-used coupons in one side pocket and the coupons for the items you've found and placed into your shopping cart in the other side pocket.

▪ **A READER RECOMMENDS:**
One reader clips together all coupons that correspond to items on her shopping list with a magnetic clip and hangs it on the refrigerator beside her shopping list.

- **Avoid shuffling through your coupons** by putting a "C" beside each item on your shopping list that has a coupon.

- **Impulse shopping:** Stores are designed to promote impulse buying. Recently, I read that the number of impulse purchases is about the same whether you have a shopping list or not. Remember that the most expensive items are placed on shelves that are at eye level; the idea is to get you to grab the first thing that you see. (Bending down to the bottom shelf or stretching to see what's on the top is also good exercise!)

- **Too many quick trips:** It used to be that people shopped daily for fresh goods, but nowadays, the reality is that the more trips you make to the supermarket, the higher the incidents of impulse shopping.

- **Unit pricing:** Most supermarkets now feature "unit pricing" labels on the shelves.

Look carefully to compare the unit prices of various items. In my mother's day, there was no law requiring unit pricing and so you had to figure out for yourself the cost per ounce. Even though the math is now done for you, make sure that you are comparing ounces to ounces, or whatever the unit may be for different brands. (Today, most items do not have individual price labels, which is something of a pain, so you have to make sure that the shelf label corresponds precisely to the item you are buying.)

■ **Convenience foods** cost more and many are high in fat, sugar, or salt. Also, many convenience foods are overpackaged and so you'll be adding to our landfill problems as well as subtracting from your budget.

■ **Eat first:** Don't shop when you are hungry or you'll be tempted to buy just about anything that looks good.

■ **Kids in the cart:** If you have to take children shopping, let each child pick one item only. If they get a case of the "gimmees" you can say that they had a chance to choose.

How Much to Buy

Most recipe amounts are measured by volume and most foods are sold by weight. Here are some equivalents to help you know how much of some common foods to buy:

Apples: 1 pound equals about three medium or 3 cups sliced.

Bananas: 1 pound equals about three medium or 2½ cups sliced.

Butter or other fats: 1 pound equals 2 cups; 1 stick equals ¼ pound or ½ cup.

Candied fruit and peels: ½ pound equals 1½ cups cut up.

Cheese, American Cheddar: 1 pound equals 4 cups grated.

Cheese, cottage: 1 pound equals 2 cups.

Cheese, white cream: a 3-ounce package equals 6 tablespoons; ½ pound (8 ounces) equals 16 tablespoons or 1 cup.

Chocolate, unsweetened: ½ pound equals eight 1-ounce squares.

Coconut, shredded: 1 pound equals 5 cups.

Coffee, ground: 1 pound equals 80 tablespoons.

Cream, whipping: 1 pint equals 2 cups or 4 cups whipped.

Dates: 1 pound whole equals 2¼ cups; 1 pound pitted equals 2 cups; 1 pound chopped equals 1¾ cups; 1 pound finely cut equals 1½ cups.

Eggs: sizes vary but usually two medium eggs equal ⅓ cup; two large eggs equal ½ cup; three medium eggs equal ½ cup; three large eggs equal ⅔ cup.

Flour, sifted: 1 pound all-purpose equals 4 cups; 1 pound cake equals 4½ cups; 1 pound whole wheat equals 3½ cups, 1 pound rye equals 4½ to 5 cups.

Lemon: 1 medium equals 2 to 3 tablespoons juice and 1½ to 3 teaspoons lightly grated rind.

Marshmallows: 16 large equal ¼ pound; ¼ pound equal 4 ounces; 38–40 large equal a 10-ounce bag; ten small equal one large.

Nuts, whole shelled: 1 pound almonds equals 3½ cups; 1 pound pecans equals 4 cups; 1 pound peanuts equals 3 cups; 1 pound walnuts equals 4 cups. *Note:* 1 cup whole shelled nuts yields 1 cup minus 1 teaspoon

Numbered Can Sizes

In my mother's day, many recipes called for can sizes in numbers instead of the measured amount of the canned food. Because many of us use Grandma's or Mom's recipes, here are the equivalents of size numbers to weight.

CAN SIZE	WEIGHT
No. 1	10 to 12 ounces
No. 300	14 to 16 ounces
No. 1½ or 303	1 pound, 17 ounces
No. 2	1 pound, 4 ounces; 1 pint, 2 fluid ounces
No. 2½	1 pound, 12 ounces to 1 pound, 14 ounces
No. 3	3 pounds, 3 ounces; 1 quart, 14 ounces
No. 10	6 pounds, 2 ounces; 7 pounds, 5 ounces

CAN SIZE	MEASURE	EXAMPLES OF FOOD
8 ounces	1 cup	Fruits and vegetables
10½ ounces	1¼ cups	Condensed soups, meat, and fish
12 ounces	1½ cups	Corn
1 pound (16 ounces)	1¾ cups	Pork and beans, baked beans, cranberry sauce
16 to 17 ounces	2 cups	Fruits, vegetables, ready-to-serve soups
1 pound, 4 ounces (20 ounces, (18 fluid ounces)	2½ cups	Juices, fruits, ready-to-serve soups
1 pound, 13 ounces (29 ounces)	3½ cups	Fruits, vegetables, pumpkin, sauerkraut, and tomatoes
3 pounds, 3 ounces (46 fluid ounces)	5¾ cups	Fruit and vegetable juices, whole chicken, pork and beans

coarsely chopped and ⅞ cup finely chopped nuts.

Orange: one medium equals ⅓- to ½-cup juice and 1 to 2 tablespoons lightly grated rind.

Raisins: one 15-ounce package equals 3 cups whole or 2¾ cups chopped or 2½ cups finely cut.

Sugar, brown: 1 pound equals 2¼ cups firmly packed.

Sugar, granulated: 1 pound equals 2 cups.

Sugar, confectioners': 1 pound sifted equals 3½ cups.

Canned foods are labeled in ounces. Here are the cup measures for some common can sizes.

ORGANIZING YOUR FOOD

My mother's words of wisdom for organizing a kitchen were, "Let's get our homes clean; get rid of all the clutter. We spend most of our waking hours in the kitchen. So keep it simple."

When my mother was writing her newspaper column in the 1960s, "housewives" (as they were called then) did spend most of their "waking hours in the kitchen" but now, we need to organize our kitchens because we have so little time to spend there, unless we want to or we have the time to spare. In the first part of this book we saw how simple and rewarding it can be to get your cookware and other nonfood

SHOPPING LIST

BREADS, CEREALS, AND PASTA:
Breads
  Sliced
  Specialty
  Rolls
Cereals
  Dry
  To cook
Cereal snacks
Crackers
Chips, tortillas, snacks
Rice
  White
  Brown
Pasta
Other

FRESH FRUITS:
Apples
Bananas
Cherries
Grapes
Grapefruit
Oranges
Lemons
Limes
Peaches
Pears
Plums
Melons
Other

FRESH VEGETABLES:
Artichokes
Asparagus
Avocado
Broccoli
Cauliflower
Carrots
Celery
Corn
Corn-on-the-cob
Cucumbers
Green beans
Green onions
Lettuce
Mushrooms
Onions
Peas
Peppers
Potatoes
Squash
Sprouts
Sweet potatoes
Tomatoes
Zucchini
Other

FROZEN FOODS:
Artichokes
Asparagus
Broccoli
Carrots
Corn
Corn-on-the-cob
Cauliflower
Green beans
Peas
Mixed vegetables
Fruit
Breakfast foods
Dinners
Pizza
Ice cream
Ice treats
Juices
Pastry
Other

DAIRY CASE:
Butter
Margarine
Cheese
  Cream
  Cottage
  Grated/shredded
  Sliced
Eggs
Milk
  Whole
  2%
  1%
  Skim
  Buttermilk
  Cream
Yogurt
Other

MEAT COUNTER:
Bacon
Beef
Chicken
Luncheon meat
Pork
Sausage
Turkey
Seafood
Other

SWEETS:
Cookies
Cake
Sweet rolls

Other

GROCERIES:
Canned fruit
Canned vegetables
Tomato products
Soups
Canned tuna
Canned meat
Other canned goods
Cooking/salad oils
Shortening
Nonstick spray
Vinegar

BEVERAGES:
Coffee
Tea
Soda
Beer
Wine
Bottled water
Juices

HERBS, SPICES, AND BAKING SUPPLIES:
Baking powder
Baking soda
Flour
  All-purpose
  Bread
  Whole wheat
  Other
Sugar
  White
  Brown
  Confectioners'
  Substitutes

Other
Cornmeal
Gelatin
Spices
  Pepper
  Salt
  Other
Condiments
  Catsup
  Mustard
  Mayo
  Pickles
  Olives
  Salad dressings
  Bottled sauces
  Other
Peanut butter
Jams and jellies

GENERAL MERCHANDISE:
Pet food
Deodorant
Shampoo
Toothpaste
Vitamins
Cosmetics
Laundry detergent
Fabric softener/sheets
Dishwasher detergent
Liquid dish detergent
Other cleaning
  supplies

MISCELLANEOUS:

items in order. The same principles are even more important when it comes to food. Getting organized is the first step to making your time in the kitchen enjoyable.

For more hints on storing food safely, see chapter 9.

In the Cabinets: Color Me Beautiful

"A place for everything and everything in it's place" may be an old-fashioned idea, but my mother's system for organizing canned, boxed, and other nonperishable food in the kitchen cabinets is as time-saving and up-to-date as any computer technology—and I still use it.

To make finding what I want quick and easy, I arrange all food shelves by color: green, red, orange, yellow, and white. And to keep your kitchen helpers from unorganizing the color

---

Food Storage by Color (for nonperishable canned or boxed items)

Green shelf: peas, green beans, asparagus, pickles, etc.

Red shelf: beets; cranberries; pimientos; cherries; tomatoes; tomato sauce, puree, and paste; etc.

Orange shelf: yams, carrots, peaches, etc.

Yellow shelf: corn, pineapple, mayonnaise, etc.

White shelf: apples and applesauce, pasta, sauerkraut, white beans, canned white potatoes, etc.

---

storage system, either mark the green, red, etc. shelves with corresponding color markers or labels, or write "green" or "red" on plain labels stuck to the front of the shelves where those foods are stored. Copy the abbreviated color-code chart shown below and tape it to the inside cabinet door, so everyone knows the plan. Color coding the foods also lets you tell at a glance what you need from each color group when you make your shopping list.

A Perfect Ten

While there is no perfect method for organizing that suits everyone's needs and space, in addition to the color code for grouping foods my mother also devised the "Ten-Shelf" system, which worked well for her. She didn't mean for the numbers of shelves to be taken literally, because the item groupings could be on parts or divisions of a shelf according to the shelf space and configuration available in your storage cabinets or pantry. While some kitchens do have a floor-to-ceiling pantry cupboard, which could have ten shelves, mother's point was that often-used items should be placed more conveniently than seldom-used ones and arranged in color groups so that everyone in the house knew where to find things. Using the number system to indicate groupings rather than strict placement, here are the bare bones of my mother's system that you can adapt for your own needs.

1. The top shelf, or least accessible space, was reserved for canned meats and fish for the days when Mother needed a quick meal.

This was the place for canned stews and pastas, tamales, canned sausage, and anything that could be a meat substitute, like some kinds of beans.

2. Dried and boxed goods—such as biscuit mix, boxed custards, rice, and so forth—that were not used daily could be placed above or below the optimum level for accessibility.

3. The Green Shelf included some of the most-often used items, so it was at eye level.

4. The Red Shelf also had often-used items and so was readily accessible.

5. The Orange Shelf.

6. The Yellow Shelf.

7. The White Shelf.

8. Condiments such as catsup and steak sauces were kept together at a level that was above or below the optimum accessibility level, since they weren't the most frequently used. Although the condiment shelf could have included mustard and mayonnaise (before they were moved to the refrigerator, once opened), my mother kept her mustard and mayo on the Yellow Shelf because it was easier to tell the male members of our family how to find these two "yellow" condiments. (My mother claimed that men couldn't find anything in a kitchen! Times have changed and there are now a lot of men who really know their way around the kitchen!)

9. Spreads, or anything that goes on a piece of bread such as honey, jellies, jams, preserves, etc.

10. Cereals were put on the most convenient shelf, where my brother and I could easily reach them when we were small.

More Heloise Hints for Storing Foods

▪ One reader nails her **breadbox** to the underside of the kitchen cabinets to save counter space. (If you use this hint, make sure you don't cover the vent holes that allow air circulation. If your bread frequently goes moldy, punch more holes in the box to increase the circulation.)

▪ Storing food in tightly **sealed canisters** prevents insects from getting into them and if the foods have insects from the market, canis-

Storing Herbs and Spices

Bear in mind that a spice rack hung above the stove looks cute and may be convenient, but it's a disaster when it comes to preserving the flavor of dried herbs and spices. These items need to be kept in a cool, dry, dark place and *not* subjected to the steam and heat of your stove or light from a window. And, although it seems like compulsive behavior, it really is easier to find your dried herbs and spices if you line them up alphabetically or at least by categories in your cupboard or pantry. Use small risers (available in notions catalogs or in specialty departments and shops) to maximize the space on the shelf and so you can see each box or jar clearly. You might consider storing spices on the same shelf as other condiments. The amount of space you need depends on how extensive your collection is.

ters prevent them from getting into other foods. (You can also put boxes of foods into appropriately sized zipper bags to keep insects out—or in.)

■ **Coffee cans can be recycled as canisters.** You can cover them with adhesive shelf paper to match your shelf liners or decorate them with stickers that indicate what's inside.

■ **Panty hose** can be washed and recycled for storing various foods. Put onions in the legs, making a knot between each onion and hang in a cool dry place. This allows the air to circulate and prevents rot from spreading from one onion to the next as it does when onions are stored in a bin. (You can also put frozen food boxes into panty hose and they won't stick to each other.)

In the Refrigerator and Freezer

The goal for organizing food in your refrigerator and freezer is to avoid having such a hodgepodge that you can't find what you want and that your leftovers become scientific research on different types of molds. I think of shelves as assigned parking spaces for specific foods. Although there are preset places for many items—the crisper, dairy section, or meat keeper, depending on your model—I always put certain things on the top, middle, or bottom shelves or on the doors. For instance, I try to keep leftovers together on the same shelf and in the front so that they don't get lost. Dairy products, such as butter, yogurt, and cheese are kept on the top shelf; leftovers are kept together on the second shelf; and so on.

■ **Adjust the shelves** in your refrigerator or freezer, if that is an option. Most adjustable-shelf refrigerators have suggested arrangements in their manuals. Experiment to see what is most convenient for you instead of leaving everything as it was when delivered.

■ **Place items in the freezer section so that they don't block the cold airflow,** which usually comes from the top rear of the freezer. If you block the airflow, it can cause the refrigerator section to get colder than you've set the temperature for and can actually freeze some items in the refrigerator. Naturally you may not realize that foods, especially vegetables and fruits, are getting frozen in the refrigerator and when you want to use them, they may have alternately frozen and thawed and become mushy.

■ **Label everything:** Keep a roll of white masking tape and a marker handy to make labels for everything that you store in the fridge or freezer. Or you can write directly on some frozen food packages with a marker or grease pencil, but others may have too slick a surface to write on and so masking tape or labels may stick on better. If you have a label maker in your computer, make labels with the months of the year so that you can stick them on food items as you store them.

❧ **KITCHENEERING HUMOR** ❧

A reader tells us that one time, a couple of hours after dinner, her husband said he'd like to snack on some leftovers. "They're in a cottage cheese container," she told him as he headed to the kitchen. About twenty minutes later, her husband returned looking perplexed; he said he couldn't find the leftovers he was look-ing for. "*Everything* is in cottage cheese contain-ers," he said, sighing.

- **Use clear jars or containers with clear lids,** for storing leftovers; it helps everyone see what's stored in the fridge. If you use plastic containers that are not clear, label each before it goes into the fridge or freezer.
- **Wipe the bottoms of condiment con-tainers** such as ketchup and mustard, before replacing them in the refrigerator, you won't have so many unsightly drip rings to clean up.

✿ **HELOISE HINT:** Freeze leftovers in the shape of the pot in which you plan to heat them. Line the pot with plastic wrap or foil, put in the leftovers, cover with the remaining wrap and freeze. After the food is frozen, remove the pot so that you can use it as usual.

- **Freeze soups and stews and other sim-ilar leftovers in sealable plastic bags** lying flat in the freezer. Stacked flat bags take up less space than bulging round bags that result when you stand the bags up on end.
- **Use plastic or wire mesh baskets to** hold categories of food in the freezer; then you can just lift out a basket to get at the items in it or to get at the items below the basket.

▪ **A READER RECOMMENDS:**
One Heloise reader keeps her chest-type freez-ers from becoming a jumble of food by mark-ing paper grocery sacks according to contents, such as vegetables, beef, chicken, and so on and then storing foods in the freezer in their labeled paper sacks. Plastic bags work, too. Then all you have to do is lift out a category of food instead of digging through the pile. But some people think this system is too much trouble and prefer stacking plastic or wire bas-kets.

- **Tape a sheet of paper to the freezer door** to record the dates that items were placed in the freezer and to serve as an inventory sheet to let you know what's in and what's run out. An alternative is to attach a sheet of paper that will be a shopping list; write down what you need when the last package of whatever is used. Of course, you will have to train your family to help with an inventory, but that's a whole other problem.

Chapter Six

Cooking Terms and Techniques

Now that we've found a place for everything, and everything's in its place, it's time to put all this preparation to the test. But before you put a pan to the flame, it's a good idea to get familiar with a few basic terms and techniques. And for those of you who've been toiling in the kitchen for a while, here's a chance to brush up on your basic kitcheneering techniques and terms, and pick up a few new pointers along the way.

COOKING METHODS

All cooking methods fall into two general categories: dry heat and moist heat.

Dry-Heat Cooking

Dry-heat cooking includes baking, grilling/barbecuing, broiling, deep-frying, microwaving, pan-frying/broiling, sautéing, roasting, and toasting, because these techniques do not have you cover the pot or pan, which keeps the moisture in.

Baking and roasting are essentially the same dry-oven heat process, although each term is usually used for specific kinds of food. We speak of baking a cake, cookies, bread, fruit, or casseroles. And for some reason, we also bake some meat, such as ham and fish or meats that are cut up, as with chicken pieces. Baking appears to be used for foods that have been assembled, although not exclusively. We speak of roasting a large piece of meat, a whole

Cooking Meats with Dry Heat

Meats for dry-heat cooking are usually those that are well marbled (fat layers in the meat itself that looks like marble grain) or that have a layer of fat on the outside, such as a rump roast or poultry, which has fat under its skin. Other ways to get fat into meats so that they will remain juicy include *larding* (inserting solid fat into slits cut into the meat either by poking it in with your fingers or "sewing" it in with a larding needle) and *barding* (wrapping solid fat around the meat before cooking, such as wrapping a slice of bacon around a beef filet mignon).

bird, or vegetables (when not in a casserole or other recipe). Generally, roasting implies that the food is cooked uncovered.

Broiling is cooking meat or other foods over or under direct heat from a flame (gas stove or outdoor grill) or coils (electric). Most foods are broiled 3 to 6 inches from the heat source to the highest or thickest part of the food to be broiled. Meat broiled too close to the heat source may dry out on the outside without being properly cooked on the inside. If it's too far from the heat source, it may not get a good color, or desired crispy surface. When you broil foods in a conventional, indoor oven, it's best to leave the oven door ajar to get the crusty texture desired in broiled foods. If the oven door is kept closed, the meats will be more like roasted than like broiled.

Deep-frying/French frying is the cooking of foods in deep hot fat until they are brown and crisp. *Note:* After you deep-fry the meat or fish, make French-fried potatoes in the same oil. Cooking potatoes will clarify the oil for re-use. Also, you will have fewer spatters of oil if you float a piece of potato in the oil during the frying process; as the potato piece gets brown, remove it and add a fresh piece.

Barbecue (as a noun or a verb) refers to food that is prepared with a spicy marinade or sauce and most often cooked on a grill. (Although vegetables can be cooked on the grill, most people generally reserve the term *barbecue* for meats.) Most foods are grilled when the coals are medium-hot—when you can see a red glow in a few places through a layer of gray ash. However, when a slow fire is needed, such as for roasts or large birds, you should wait until the coals have a *thick* layer of gray ash and almost no red visible. If you are flavoring the food with hickory, mesquite, or other woods, soak the wood chips at least 1 hour before cooking.

❀ **HELOISE HINT:** To create two cooking temperatures on the grill, pile more coals on one side than the other. Then you can sear or quick-cook foods on the hotter side—the one with more coals—and slow-cook foods on the not-as-hot side.

Here are some outdoor grilling safety hints:

Never use a charcoal grill indoors.
Always place the grill away from dry grass, bushes, or other combustibles.
Do close any windows near your barbecue; smoke may get into the house and set off a smoke alarm.
Never add starter fluid to hot or even warm coals; flare-ups are dangerous.

Do not light charcoal with kerosene, gasoline, alcohol, or other volatile fuels; an explosion can result!

Do not wear loose-fitting aprons, flowing sleeves or any other article of clothing that could brush across the grill and catch fire. Prevent burns while tending the grill by using heat-resistant cooking mitts and long-handled utensils.

With an open grill, douse flare-ups with a spray bottle filled with water (or a child's squirt gun). You need to spray the water gently so that food won't get covered with loose ashes.

With a covered grill, flames will die down when you place the lid back on the grill.

❉ HELOISE HINT: If you don't have a covered grill, you can make a foil tent from heavy-duty broiler foil. Cut off two 4-foot lengths of heavy-duty foil. Lay one sheet on top of the other, dull sides out. Fold together along one long edge, making first a ½-inch fold, then a second ½-inch fold. Open up the foil. You should have one big sheet securely fastened down the center. Halfway along each long and short side, make a deep tuck. The foil should peak in the center to make a pyramid-shaped tent, shiny side in. Stabilize the tent by turning up 1 inch all along the bottom edges. Some people think it's easier to make the folds on all the edges before you make the tucks. Whatever works for you is best.

Pan frying or broiling is to cook foods in an uncovered skillet in a small amount of fat. Generally, pan-broiling means that you first spray the pan with nonstick spray or just cook the meat on a very hot iron skillet, with the only fat being that which cooks out of the meat. For pan-frying you usually add some fat to make the meat juicier. Also, when pan-broiling, you pour off the fat as it melts from the meat; when pan-frying, you let the fat stay in the pan as the meat cooks. *Note:* To prevent spatters when pan-frying or pan-broiling foods always blot off any excess liquid before putting the food into the fat, and slide the food gently into the fat instead of dropping it in.

Sautéing is to brown quickly in a small amount of oil or fat.

Roasting can be done either covered or uncovered. If you want a crisp skin on poultry or if you want other meats to have a rich brown color, roast them uncovered. Covering a roast will keep the steam inside and the meat will

Grilling Temperatures

Hot: Coals are barely covered with gray ash. You can hold your hand near the grill for only about 2 seconds. The actual temperature is 375 degrees F or higher.

Medium: Coals glow through a layer of gray ash. You can hold your hand near the grill for only 3 or 4 seconds. The temperature is 300 to 375 degrees F.

Low: Coals are covered with a thick layer of gray ash. You can hold your hand near the grill for 5 to 7 seconds. The temperature is 200 to 300 degrees F.

cook faster but will not be as brown or crisp. When roasting covered meats, lower the temperature by 25 degrees F if you want to keep the same timetable as you would have with an uncovered roast.

To prevent meat that is roasting uncovered from drying out, you will probably need to baste it every 15 to 30 minutes with the liquid or juices from the bottom of the pan or with additional liquid, which should be heated or at least at room temperature. Cold liquids will affect the cooking process by cooling the surface of the meat. Also, when roasting meat uncovered, the roast should be placed on a rack so that all sides of the meat will cook evenly. Allowing the roast to sit in liquids will make the bottom of the roast cook to a mushy texture before the top is done.

✿ **HELOISE HINT:** Place three or four whole stems of washed celery across the bottom of a roasting pan to serve as a roasting rack. At serving time, you can garnish the meat with the roasted celery. It won't be pretty because it will be roasted but it will be tasty.

Toasting is browning foods, usually bread or bread products, by direct heat either in the oven or in an electric toaster.

Moist-Heat Cooking

Moist-heat cooking includes braising, broiling, poaching, simmering, steaming, stewing, and pressure cooking. Cooking by moist-heat methods is preferred for meat that is not natu-

rally tender and for plant foods that have tough fibers.

Braising, primarily of meat, involves two steps: browning in hot fat (shortening, oil, butter, margarine) on the stovetop, then simmering in a covered pot or pan, either on top of the stove or in the oven in a small amount of liquid. It is better to simmer foods in the oven because oven heat more uniformly surrounds the meat and so all parts of it receive the liquid and consistent temperature. You won't have to turn the meat frequently, as you would when simmering on top of the stove. (See chapter 7 for my foolproof and delicious Swiss steak.)

Poaching is simmering a food in liquid that is kept just below the boiling point. Eggs and fish are the most commonly poached foods.

Pressure cooking is a fast cooking method that cooks and steams foods under pressure from a sealed pot. Older ones have weight placed over a steam vent in the lid, newer ones don't. CAUTION: Follow the instructions that came with the pressure cooker *exactly as written*. These cookers, although improved in design since my mother's day, can cause serious accidents and burns, if improperly used.

✿ **CLASSIC HELOISE HINT:** My mother wrapped different vegetables separately in foil packets, as if for baked potatoes. Then she cut an X in the top and folded the point back to make a little "bowl" for each one, and poked a small hole in the bottom; then, she'd put the bowls on the grate of the pressure cooker. Steaming vegetables this way saved nutrients and flavor, and she could store any leftovers in the same foil packets.

Update: This method could be adapted for a regular nonpressurized vegetable steamer or a homemade steamer consisting of a colander placed over a couple of inches of water in a Dutch oven. It's an especially good idea if you are cooking for one and like to have variety without lots of pots to wash!

Simmering means cooking in liquid at a temperature that's below the boiling point. The liquid should be moving gently, with bubbles forming just below the surface.

Steaming, which is usually done with vegetables, means cooking over boiling water, using a colander or some other perforated heat-resistant container to hold the food above the water. You can also steam foods in a pressure cooker or in the top of a double-boiler.

❀ **HELOISE HINT:** Put a metal jar lid or a few marbles into the bottom of the double-boiler, the rattling sounds will warn you when the water is getting too low.

Stewing, like braising, is a means of cooking tougher cuts of meat at a low slow boil to make them tender and juicy. Follow the same directions as for braising, but you can add more liquid to the pot at the beginning. The benefit of moist-heat, slow cooking is that you can use meat from older animals, which is more flavorful.

❀ **HELOISE HINT:** When browning meats, dusting the surface with flour prevents the meat sticking to the pan and helps make better gravy. To brown unfloured meat, dab the surface of the meat with a paper towel to remove any liquids; you'll get a better brown color and the fat in the pan won't spatter as much.

MISCELLANEOUS COOKING TERMS

I have tried to list the cooking terms you may find in recipes or on restaurant menus for several types of cuisine, and I've included other useful information for novice as well as experienced cooks.

- **Á la King:** Food prepared in a rich cream sauce.
- **Á la mode:** French for "in the manner of." When used with desserts, it means "with ice cream."
- **Al dente:** An Italian term for cooking pasta so that the teeth (dente) can feel it. Pasta should not be overcooked.

❀ **KITCHENEERING HUMOR** ❀
Some people tell me that the way to test pasta, especially spaghetti, is to toss a strand of spaghetti at the refrigerator or wall, if it sticks, it's just right. I don't think it's actually the best way, but it certainly could be fun if you're with people who have a sense of humor!

- **Amandine:** French, meaning "with almonds."
- **Antipasto:** Assorted Italian appetizers, such as peppery sausage, canned pimiento, sardines, anchovies, and pickled vegetables.
- **Aspic:** A clear, savory jelly made with

gelatin or from meat bones that's used in molds to garnish cold dishes.

- **Au beurre:** French, meaning cooked with or in butter.

- **Au gratin:** French for a creamed dish that has a topping of buttered crumbs or crumbs mixed with cheese that's been broiler or oven browned.

- **Bain-marie:** A French cooking utensil that's similar to a double-boiler. It has one part for heated water, and another pot that sits in the heated water to keep its contents warm.

- **Bard:** To cover meat or game with sliced bacon, salt pork, or other solid fat.

- **Baste:** To drizzle or spoon fat or liquid from the pan over food that is roasting, broiling, or on the barbecue.

- **Batter:** A semiliquid mixture of flour, water, milk, and eggs that can be a coating for food to be fried. It is also the mixture of ingredients for cakes, cookies, waffles, or pancakes.

- **Beat:** To combine foods or to incorporate air into them such as in eggs or egg whites by blending or whipping with a spoon, whisk, electric mixer, or rotary hand beater/mixer.

- **Beurre manie:** French, for small balls of flour and butter blended together, which are added to thicken the gravy of stews or soups.

- **Beurre noir:** French for butter that's been heated until it is dark brown (black). It is added as flavor to sauces.

- **Bind:** To add liquid, beaten eggs, cream, or other ingredients to make a mixture of dry ingredients hold together.

- **Bisque:** Usually a thick creamy soup, but it can also be a frozen cream dessert.

- **Blanch:** Blanching reduces the strong flavor or color of foods by immersing them for a short time in water that is off the fire but at the boiling point. Blanching is used to stop enzyme actions of vegetables before freezing them so that they won't deteriorate during the storage time. Blanching nuts in hot or boiling water loosens the skins for removing. Fruits, including tomatoes, are usually blanched in boiling water and then plunged them into ice water to make the skins easy to peel off.

- **Blaze or flambé:** A dramatic serving technique in which you pour warmed brandy or other liqueur over food and set it aflame. Bananas Foster, the famous New Orleans dessert, is an example of this technique.

- **Blend:** Combining ingredients by mixing them with an electric mixer, whisk, or other implement until they are smooth.

- **Boil:** Liquid is considered boiling when bubbles are breaking the surface. Boiling food is cooking it in liquid that is at a boiling temperature, 212 degrees F for water.

- **Bone:** To bone fish, meat, or poultry, you remove the bones with a special, short, sharp pointed boning knife. *Note:* If you have meat, fish, or poultry boned at the supermarket, ask to take the bones home to make stock.

- **Bouillon:** A clear, strained soup/stock made from beef, veal, or poultry and cooked with vegetables and seasonings.

- **Bouillon cube:** A dehydrated, concentrated cube of bouillon used to add flavor to sauces and other recipes. Bouillon also comes in powdered and liquid forms.

- **Bouquet garni:** A small bundle of herbs used to flavors stews, sauces, soups, sauces, and other recipes. Usually it's composed of three to four sprigs of parsley, one or two small stalks of celery, one leak, one bay leaf, one or two springs dried thyme, all tied together with a clean cotton string.

- **Brine:** A strong solution of salt and water used to pickle vegetables and other foods.

- **Brochette:** Also called a shish kebab, a brochette is made of small pieces of meat, vegetables, fish, chicken, etc. threaded on a long metal skewer and then cooked under broiler heat or on a grill.

- **Brown:** To seal in juices of meat or other foods by cooking them in a little fat at high heat in a skillet or by placing them under a broiler or in the oven until they are golden brown in color. When the instructions say to "brown the top" of a casserole or an au gratin dish, you usually place the dish under the broiler and watch it carefully.

- **Brûlé, brûlée:** French for "burned." A famous New Orleans dessert, crème brûlée is a custard dessert topped with caramelized sugar.

- **Brush:** To spread a light coating of butter, sauce, or other liquid on the surface of meats or other foods with a pastry or other brush.

🌸 **HELOISE HINT:** You can wash some pastry brushes in the dishwasher to get them clean or you can keep a buttered pastry brush in a zipper bag in the freezer ready for greasing pots and pans.

- **Caramel:** A liquid burned sugar used for color and flavor. Caramelized sugar is used most frequently in candy making and is the brown color on flan, a custard dessert popular in Mexico and other countries.

- **Chill:** To store in the refrigerator or on ice until cold but not frozen.

- **Chop:** To cut into small pieces with a food processor, knife, or other chopper. Also a cut of veal, lamb, mutton, and pork.

- **Choux paste:** A cream puff pastry that's cooked in a saucepan over heat before being shaped.

- **Clarified butter:** Melted butter that has been strained or skimmed. Used in some sauces and to avoid burning when frying foods. Also called drawn butter.

- **Clarify:** To heat a cloudy liquid such as aspic, bouillon, or soup stock by heating it gently with a raw egg white. Stir the liquid until it's clear, and then strain through a fine sieve or cheesecloth.

- **Coat:** To dip a food in flour, crumbs, or other mixture before frying.

- **Cocottes:** Small dishes, like ramekins, which are used for baking.

- **Combine:** In a recipe, this means mix two or more ingredients together

- **Compote:** A dish of sweetened and cooked fruits.

- **Consommé:** Clarified bouillon or soup stock.

- **Core:** To take out the seed center of fruits or vegetables while leaving the remainder intact, as in coring an apple for baking.

- **Court bouillon:** A stock used to poach fish and make fish sauces made with white wine, water, herbs, fish bones, and/or vegetables.

- **Cream:** When baking, to cream means to work in or beat shortening, butter, or other fat until light and fluffy, with or without adding sugar or flour.

- **Crisp:** A cooking technique in which bread, crackers, or dry cereals are heated in the oven for a few minutes to freshen them. Also, a method to restore the texture of vegetables by covering them with ice water for a short period before serving. Crisps are fruit desserts with a crispy crumb topping, as in apple or rhubarb crisp.

- **Croquettes:** Foods that have been ground or chopped finely, mixed with some sort of binding ingredient, like eggs or a sauce, formed into various shapes, dipped in crumbs or flour, and then deep-fried.

- **Croute:** French for the pastry or crust with which food is wrapped or topped.

- **Crumble:** To break (usually bread) into small pieces or crumbs with your fingers.

- **Cube:** Cut foods into small square bits.

- **Cure:** A method for preserving meats with salt, liquid, smoking, or other means. Hams, jerky, and some sausages are good examples of cured meats.

- **Cut against the grain** (roasts, hams, poultry breasts): **Grain** refers to the lines you see on pieces of meat, roasts, and the breasts of poultry. To cut against the grain means to cut at right angles to these lines to get slices that are easier to chew. Cutting with the grain gives a piece of meat that will seem tough, even if it has been cooked it properly.

- **Cut-and-fold:** A method for blending mixtures with liquids. The action is to cut into the mixture with a spoon or spatula held sideways to combine the ingredients, then lift the mixture from the bottom and fold it over the top until the mixture is properly blended. The most commonly folded ingredient is beaten egg whites. You fold gently rather than stir so that you keep them fluffy.

- **Cut in:** Usually a direction given for making pastry and pie dough, it means to combine shortening or other fat with flour and dry ingredients with a chopping motion. The best tool is a pastry blender, but if you don't have one, you can use two table knives or two metal spatulas.

- **Deglaze:** After meat has browned in a pan, the dark bits that cling to the pan can be used to make sauces or gravies. To deglaze the pan means to add hot liquid to it and stir until the bits are loosened and the browning dissolves. *Note:* Adding *hot* liquid prevents spattering. Also, pouring very cold liquid onto a hot pan can warp the pan's bottom. Warped pans won't heat evenly and properly on ceramic/glass cooktops and some electric stovetop burners.

- **Devil:** In a recipe, deviled means that hot seasonings or sauces are added to flavor the food.

- **Dice:** Like cube, dice means to cut foods into small square pieces. For example, you would dice onions to add them to meat loaf or potato salad.

- **Dilute:** To make the flavor weaker or the mixture thinner by adding liquid.

- **Dissolve:** To become liquid or to melt.

- **Dot:** When a recipe says dot, it means to sprinkle small pieces of butter or other garnish over the top of a mixture before cooking or baking.

- **Double-boiler:** A two-part pot in which the slightly larger bottom pot is used to boil water, which in turn, heats the contents of the smaller top pot, which has a lid. In my mother's day, the double-boiler was also a "fifth burner" on the stove. She would cook one vegetable, for example, carrots, in the bottom pot and heat a can of peas at the same time in the top pot; two vegetables cooked on the same burner!

- **Dough:** Usually referring to bread, dough is a spongy mixture of flour and other dry ingredients with liquid. The difference between dough and batter is that batter can be stirred easily, whereas dough is thicker.
- **Drain:** Strain liquid from solid foods.
- **Draw:** To remove the entrails (inner organs, etc.) from poultry, game, etc.
- **Drawn butter:** See *clarified butter*.
- **Dredge:** To coat foods before cooking with flour, sugar, or some other dry mixture.
- **Drippings:** The fat that melts from meats while it cooks and runs into the bottom of the pan is called drippings. Drippings mixed with a thickening agent (such as flour or cornstarch) and a liquid (such as water, bouillon, or wine) make gravies and sauces.
- **Dust:** To lightly sprinkle a food with flour, sugar, or other dry mixture as in to dust the top of a cake with confectioners' sugar.
- **En papillotte:** Originally, this meant "baked in paper." At one time, cooks baked certain foods in oiled paper sacks, but today, it can also mean baked in foil.
- **Essence:** Just as perfume "essence" is more strongly scented than cologne, essence in cooking means a concentrated stronger flavor.
- **Fat:** When a recipe calls for fat, it can be butter, margarine (not diet margarine), lard, vegetable shortening, oils, or fat rendered

(melted) from meats. Different fats will have different melting points and flavors so some are more appropriate for some recipes than other fats. Cholesterol-conscious people will choose vegetable oils over animal fats whenever possible. However, many cooks believe that animal fats, such as butter, lard, and drippings, make the foods cooked with them crisper than when the same foods or recipes are made with vegetable fats.

- **Fillet/filet:** The act of removing bones from meat or fish and the resulting piece of boned meat or fish.
- **Filter:** To strain the liquid through several layers of cheesecloth or a special paper filter. For example, you would filter (strain) out the juice of grapes to make jelly instead of mashing the fruit and making jam or preserves with pulp and juice combined.
- **Flake:** To flake (fish, for example), you gently separate hunks of the meat from each other into thin pieces with a fork or pair of forks.
- **Flambé:** See *blaze*.
- **Fold:** To gently lift a mixture with a spoon in an overlapping movement from one side of the bowl to the other, using an up and over motion. This direction to fold in is often found in recipes using separately beaten eggs and egg whites. The gently folding motion allows you to mix dry ingredients into whipped ingredients (egg whites, whipped cream) without mashing out the air bubbles. The result of properly folding in ingredients is fluffy product.
- **Fondue:** A cheese or meat dish cooked at the table in a fondue pot that is kept hot with a

sterno heater or an electrically heated fondue pot.

- **Forcemeat:** This word is not commonly used in this country but it means a seasoned stuffing, that's been finely minced, pounded, ground, or combined in a food processor and cooked separately to be served as a garnish.

- **Frappé:** French for "frozen" used to described lightly frozen fruit or vegetable juices served as appetizers or beverages served over cracked or shaved ice or blended in a blender.

- **Freeze:** To chill a food in the freezer compartment until it is solid.

- **Fricassee:** Usually chicken or veal that has been stewed in a cream sauce with seasonings and white wine, brown sauce, or stock. It is considered a braising method of cooking.

- **Frizzle:** To fry in hot fat until the edges of the food curl.

- **Frost:** To coat; two things to frost are cakes and the rims of a beverage glass for presentation.

- **Garnish:** To decorate a prepared dish for presentation with pieces of other foods.

- **Glacé:** A French word for iced, glazed, or frozen foods.

- **Glacé de viande:** French for a glaze of meat. Reducing brown meat stock to a jelly-like consistency makes the concentrated flavoring for sauces and other dishes.

- **Grate:** Either rubbing foods over a grinder/grater or running them through a blender or food processor until they are in very small bits.

- **Gravy:** Pan drippings, flour or cornstarch, seasonings, and milk, cream, or stock, cooked in the pan in which meat, fish, or poultry was cooked.

- **Grill:** To cook over or under direct heat.

- **Grind:** To make food into a fine consistency by putting it through a chopper, grinder, food processor, or blender.

- **Grease:** When a recipe says to grease the pan, it means to rub the inside of the pan, mold, or baking dish with some form of fat to prevent the food from sticking to the container as it cooks. The fat leftover in a pan after meat is fried is also grease, and some grease, such as bacon grease, can be clarified by filtering and then stored in the refrigerator for a second use as flavoring or for frying.

- **Hang:** When meat or game is aging in a cool refrigerated place, it is said to be "hanging."

- **Hors d'oeuvres:** French for "appetizers."

- **Ice:** Obviously this means frozen water, but you also *ice* a cake or cookies with frosting. Ice can also be a smooth, frozen, fruit juice dessert made without milk. Some ices are used as a "palette cleansers" in between courses of an elaborate dinner. These can be made from fruit, but some are flavored with herbs, such as mint or rosemary.

- **Icing:** Cake or cookie frosting.

- **Infusion:** When tea, coffee, or herbs are steeped in boiling water, the liquid strained from them is called an infusion.

- **Julienne:** Foods cut into thin strips. You will frequently see julienne of carrots, green beans, zucchini, and other vegetables served at restaurants as the vegetable with your entrée; it is often so pretty that it is also the garnish.

■ **Knead:** To work dough, usually bread-type dough, with your hands, usually on a floured surface, to make it smooth and spongy and to thoroughly mix in extra ingredients such as raisins, sugar/cinnamon mixtures, nuts, and herbs. The motion is a folding backward with the fingers and pressing forward with the heel of your hands.

■ **Lard:** Fat rendered, usually from hogs. Lard, as a cooking method, means to insert thin strips of bacon, salt pork or suet (meat fat) into lean meat so that it will be moister when it cooks. Larding can also mean to lay strips of fat such as bacon or salt pork over lean meats before they are roasted.

■ **Leaven:** To lighten a mixture. Leavening agents include yeast, baking powder, and eggs.

■ **Line:** When a recipe says line the pan, it means to cover the inside of the pan or dish with paper or foil, or with pastry crust, or crumbs.

■ **Liquor:** The liquid juice from shellfish is call liquor and often shellfish recipes will tell you to add the liquor at some point when cooking a sauce.

■ **Marinate/macerate:** You marinate meats and you macerate fruits and vegetables. Regardless of the word you use, the idea is to add extra flavor by letting the food sit for several hours or days in an appropriate liquid, and in the case of meats, an acidic marinade (citrus juice, vinegar, or wine) acts as a tenderizer, too.

❉ **HELOISE HINT:** When you marinate or macerate food, you won't need as much liquid if you put the foods into a zipper bag, add the liquid, push out all the air, and seal. As a precaution, place the bag in a bowl or on a large dinner plate to prevent accidental spills.

■ **Mash:** Reduce to a pulp using a potato masher, fork, or other implement.

■ **Mask:** To cover a food completely with sauce, mayonnaise, gelatin, etc. *Note:* The trend in my mother's day was to mask foods as noted here, but today many restaurants put the sauce on the plate, place the food on top, then garnish with other foods or herbs for a more attractive presentation.

■ **Melt:** To heat a food until it is liquefied. *Note:* In my mother's day, a double-boiler or very heavy bottomed aluminum pot was use to melt cheese or chocolate, but today we can do this in the microwave with less mess and less possibility of scorching or burning.

■ **Mill:** A small hand mixer, chopper, or grinder. The term also applies to the process of beating hot chocolate and other milky drinks to a froth with a whisk.

■ **Mince:** To chop very finely or to put through a chopper, food processor, or blender until finely chopped.

■ **Mirpois:** A French term for a combination of finely chopped and sautéed vegetables, most often carrots, celery, and onions, added to a casserole or dish in which you will be braising meat or poultry.

■ **Mix:** As a verb, means to blend ingredients by stirring or by using an electric mixer, food processor, or blender. As a noun, mix refers commercially prepared cake, pastry, or casserole products that already include the dry ingredients.

■ **Moisten:** To add *small* amounts of the liquid as by the tablespoon.

■ **Mortar and pestle:** The bowl-shaped container and the heavy blunt instrument used to crush spices, herbs, etc. by hand instead of in a blender or food processor. They are most often made of wood, marble, stone, or ceramic.

■ **Mold:** To shape food such as ice cream or gelatin mixtures in a pan or dish.

■ **Mousse:** A light, creamy, often whipped or frozen dessert. It can also be a jelled mixture of finely ground fish, ham, chicken, or other meat combined with cream and served either hot or chilled.

■ **Mull:** To heat liquid, usually juices, wine, or cider, with sugar and spices.

❀ **HELOISE HINT:** In a large microwave-safe bowl, you can mull and serve cider or wine for Wassail in the same container.

■ **Oven terms and temperatures:**

Slow = 200 to 275 degrees F.
Moderately slow = 300 degrees F.
Moderate = 325, 350, 375 degrees F.
Moderately hot = 400 degrees F.
Hot = 425 to 450 degrees F.
Very hot = 475 to 525 degrees F.

■ **Organically grown:** According to the Tufts University Health and Nutrition Letter (May '99), organically grown fruits and vegetables, are those farmed without pesticides, herbicides, and fungicides. They are healthier for our planet because they keep toxic chemicals out of the soil and away from humans and animals, but they have not been shown to be more nutritious than other produce.

■ **Parboil:** To boil food until partially cooked.

■ **Pare:** To peel, as in to remove the skin of fruits and vegetables with a small knife or parer.

■ **Paste:** As a culinary term, a mixture— generally of flour and water—used to bind ingredients or thicken sauces. Ground foods such as nuts or fruits or a combination of nuts and fruits with sugar is also called paste.

■ **Pastry:** A mixture of flour, shortening, salt, and water used for pie shells, tarts, and turnovers.

■ **Pastry bag:** A cone-shaped bag with a hole in the small end for various metal tips used to shape dough, soft foods (like mashed potatoes and other vegetables), whipped cream, frosting, etc.

❀ **HELOISE HINT:** To make a disposable pastry bag, cut a small hole in the corner of a strong food-storage plastic bag, such as a zipper bag, insert the metal tip, and fill with the food to be shaped. You can also make a cone-shape from several sheets of wax paper. If the food you are shaping is hot, wrap a towel around the pastry bag to protect your hands.

■ **Pâté:** Cooked and seasoned liver paste.

■ **Peel:** See *pare*.

■ **Pickle:** As a verb, to preserve foods in brine (salt) or vinegar. As a noun, a vegetable or fruit that has been preserved by pickling.

■ **Pinch:** If ever a measurement reflected a cook's enthusiasm for spices, it's the term pinch. Officially, it is about $\frac{1}{16}$ teaspoon or as much as the cook takes up between the thumb and forefinger.

▪ **Pipe:** The method of shaping or decorating foods using a pastry bag.

▪ **Pit:** As a noun, the seed or stone in a fruit; as a verb, to remove the fruit's seed or stone.

▪ **Pizzaiola:** An Italian word that means "pizza style."

▪ **Pound:** In addition to being a weight, it also means to tenderize meat with a mallet or to grind herbs and spices with a pestle.

▪ **Prick:** When used in a pastry recipe, to pierce the surface with a fork or sharp knife to make vents to let steam out.

▪ **Puree:** To pulp foods to a smooth consistency, or paste, in a blender or food processor or by forcing them through a food mill.

▪ **Ragoût:** A rich brown stew.

▪ **Ramekin:** A small individual-size baking dish.

▪ **Reduce:** To cook the liquid, such as wine or stock, until it is about half the original quantity and very concentrated.

▪ **Render:** To fry, simmer, or otherwise heat meat until the fat melts and can be strained away.

▪ **Rice:** When used as a direction in a recipe, rice means to force a food, such as boiled potatoes, through a sieve or ricer.

▪ **Roll out:** When you need to roll out a batch of cookie dough or pastry, first flour the surface (or sugar it for some cookies), place the dough on the surface and flatten gently with a floured rolling pin. *Note:* Always roll gently and try to handle dough and pastry as little as possible to prevent it from getting tough.

✿ **HELOISE HINT:** If you place some wax paper or plastic wrap on the surface before rolling it out, you can easily lift up the pastry and put it into the baking pan.

▪ **Roux:** A mixture of butter and flour cooked to a smooth paste until it is either just thickened, or thickened and lightly browned; it is used to thicken sauces and stews.

▪ **Scald:** To heat a liquid, most often milk, to just under boiling when tiny bubbles begin to form around the edge. To scald other foods means to pour boiling water over them.

▪ **Scaloppine:** An Italian word meaning "pieces," most often refers to the cut of meat such as chicken or veal.

▪ **Scallop:** As a cooking term, to bake in a cream sauce, under a crumb or a crumb-cheese topping.

▪ **Score:** To cut gashes into the meat surface, such as when you score a tough cut like flank steak, or to cut gashes into the fat edging of hams, chops, and other cuts of meat to prevent them from curling up as they cook.

▪ **Scrape:** In my mother's day, vegetables like carrots and potatoes were usually peeled or scraped to remove the outer skin. Today, we preserve the nutrients in vegetables and get more fiber in our diets by cooking most vegetables with their skins and eating the skins along with the pulp.

▪ **Sear:** To brown the surface of meat at a high temperature so that the juices are kept inside.

▪ **Season:** Add salt, pepper, and other seasonings, either according to the recipe or to taste.

▪ **Seed:** To remove seeds.

▪ **Shred:** Slice into small strips, as in shredding meat or poultry as an ingredient in Chinese stir-fry recipes, or by pressing vegetables through a grater.

■ **Sieve:** A wire mesh strainer used to strain or to rice cooked foods.

■ **Sift:** To shake flour or other dry ingredients through a sieve or sifter.

■ **Singe:** To burn hairs off the skin of plucked poultry.

■ **Skewer:** See *brochette*. *Note:* If using wood skewers for barbecue or shish kebab, soak them before threading the meat on them so that they don't char and burn.

■ **Skim:** To remove the fat or other floating matter from the top of cooking liquid using either a spoon, a strainer spoon (with slots or holes in it), or a skimmer (a long-handled, shallow-bowled spoon with small holes in the bowl). Skimming helps to clear the stock of a soup or stew. Alternatively, the stock can be chilled first so that the solid fat that rises to the top can be easily removed. Some people remove the fat from soup or stew by tossing ice cubes on the surface. This works if the ice gathers the fat before it melts and you can scoop it up quickly; otherwise the ice dilutes the sauce or soup.

■ **Sliver:** To cut into very small, thin pieces.

■ **Soak:** To cover food with a lot of liquid to soften it.

■ **Spice:** Seasoning (see chapter 4).

■ **Spit:** A metal rod on which poultry or meat is placed for barbecuing or roasting.

■ **Steam:** A method of cooking foods in which the foods are put into a colander or perforated steamer over boiling water.

■ **Steep:** To heat food in water kept just below the boiling point so that you can extract juices, flavor, and color.

■ **Sterilize:** Usually used in canning or preserving. Cans or jars, with or without food in them, are placed in boiling water, steam, or dry heat to kill bacteria.

■ **Stir:** To blend ingredients with a spoon or other utensil using a circular motion.

■ **Stock:** The liquid that is strained from cooked meat, fish, poultry, or vegetables.

■ **Strain:** To puree foods through a sieve or to remove liquids from solid foods.

■ **Stud:** To stick cloves or other flavorings into foods.

❋ **HELOISE HINT:** It is easier to stick cloves into the less fatty part of a ham if you first make a hole with an ice pick, toothpick, or other pointed tool.

■ **Stuff:** To fill the cavity of poultry with minced, chopped, seasoned ingredients. You can also stuff flat pieces of meat by rolling them around the stuffing (seasoned filling) and fastening with skewers or string.

■ **Suet:** The hard fat that surrounds certain cuts of meat.

❋ **HELOISE HINT:** To get extra flavor in stews or soups, cut the suet into small cubes, fry until crisp in the pot in which you will cook the meat. Remove the cubes and drain on paper towels. Use the melted fat to brown onions and the meat. When you serve the soup or stew, sprinkle a few of the crispy suet cubes on top as a garnish. Not low-cal, but very tasty!

■ **Tenderize:** To make meats tender by pounding them with a mallet, marinating them in acidic liquids, or sprinkling with commercial tenderizers.

■ **Thicken:** To give a liquid more body by adding flour, cornstarch, potato starch, cream, eggs, or grated cheese.

❀ **HELOISE HINT:** Casserole too soupy? Can't thicken it the usual way with a starch? Try crumbling nacho chips into it for a Mexican "Dry" soup.

■ **Thin:** See *dilute*.

■ **Toss:** To combine ingredients very lightly with two forks or a fork and spoon, as in a salad or crumb mixture.

■ **Trim:** To cut away parts of meats and vegetables that you don't want to use. With meat, it usually means cut off excess fat or dangling ends before cooking.

❀ **KITCHENEERING HUMOR** ❀

There's an old story about a family that always trimmed the end of the holiday ham before baking it. One day, a daughter asked her mother why she cut off the end of the ham. "I don't know," her mom replied, "My mother always did it." Then the girl asked her grandmother why she cut off the ham end and she said the same thing. So the girl asked her great-grandmother why everyone cut off the ham end and great-grandma said, "I don't know why they do it, but I had to cut off the end so the ham would fit in my roaster." The lesson, of course, is that doing things just because that's the way

they were always done does not always make sense!

■ **Truss:** To tie the wings and legs of poultry with skewers or string so that the bird holds its shape while roasting. Trussing a

---

Measuring Equivalents

WEIGHTS AND MEASURES

3 teaspoons = 1 tablespoon

4 tablespoons = ¼ cup

5 tablespoons plus 1 teaspoon = ⅓ cup

8 tablespoons = ½ cup

12 tablespoons = ¾ cup

16 tablespoons = 1 cup

2 tablespoons = 1 liquid ounce

1 cup = 8 fluid ounces

2 cups = 1 pint

4 cups = 1 quart

2 pints = 1 quart

1 quart = 32 fluid ounces

4 quarts = 1 gallon

OTHER DRY MEASURES

4 ounces = ¼ pound

8 ounces = ½ pound

8 quarts = 1 peck

4 pecks = 1 bushel

---

turkey for a holiday meal used to be more of a chore in my mother's day but now the legs are tucked into the bottom of the bird so neatly that trussing isn't always necessary.

- **Whip:** To blend ingredient vigorously as in incorporating air into egg whites, cream, or gelatin mixtures to increase the bulk and make them fluffy.

- **Work:** When applied to dough, to knead or mix slowly.

- **Zest:** The skin of citrus fruits (limes, lemons, and oranges) used to flavor desserts, drinks, and other recipes. To obtain the zest, grate only the colored part of the skin, which contains the flavorful oils; the white part beneath the skin will be bitter.

MICROWAVE COOKING

The microwave oven is one of the most popular time-savers in today's kitchens and one I think would have thrilled my mother. Yet some people still use their microwave ovens only for heating up and re-heating foods and beverages. This is unfortunate because a microwave oven can do so much more once you learn to use it properly. Overcooking causes most micro-cooking failures. After you get past thinking that everything must be cooked longer than the directions say to make sure a food is really done, you'll have fewer bouncing "rubber" meatballs and unchewable "hockey-puck" chicken breasts. Some foods, vegetables for example, keep their color better and don't get overcooked as easily when microwaved. Also, cooking in, serving or eating from the

same dish is one of the major advantages of less-mess micro-cooking. The most important guide for cooking with your microwave is the information that came with it. Cooking times relate to wattage and different appliance brands have different models; so if you consult the manufacturer's directions, you'll have more success with your microwave cooking.

Microwave Precautions

- **Test for microwave-safe dishes:** Microwave-safe materials include glass, ceramic, pottery, special microwaveable plastics, and paper. Most new containers indicate if they are suitable for microwaving. Containers that are not microwave safe can crack during cooking and also can cause burns because they get too hot and don't cool off as quickly as micro-safe dishes do. Here's how to test a cup or dish:

Pour a cup of water in a glass measuring cup and place it in the microwave, then put

Test to Determine Wattage

Pour exactly one cup tap water into a microwave safe 2-cup glass measuring cup. Microwave on High uncovered until the water begins to boil.

IF WATER BOILS IN:	YOUR WATTAGE IS:
Less than 3 minutes	600 to 700
3 to 4 minutes	500 to 600
More than 4 minutes	Less than 500

the dish or mug you want to test next to the measuring cup.

Close the door and turn the power on High for one minute.

If the water in the measuring cup is hot and the dish is cool, then the dish is microwave safe.

If the dish is hot, it is NOT safe to cook with it in the microwave.

Note: Never use dishes with silver or gold trim or any metal parts in the microwave. It can cause arcing, which is a fire hazard. Most microwaves can tolerate small strips of aluminum foil but this information *must* be in your microwave booklet. It's safer not to put any metal in the microwave.

▪ **Baby bottles** should not be warmed in the microwave. The bottles can feel cool to the touch on the outside even when the milk or other fluid inside is hot enough to scald a baby's mouth. Microwaving mother's milk tends to destroy nutrients.

▪ **Canning** in the microwave is not safe; it does not ensure the killing of harmful organisms. Follow the canning instructions for each particular food: hot water bath or pressure cooker.

▪ **Deep-fat frying** in the microwave is a fire hazard.

▪ **Eggs** in the shell may explode when steam builds up and the result can be a damaged oven.

▪ **Heat susceptor packaging:** When you microwave foods in heat susceptor packaging, observe the following:

Don't microwave the product any longer than instructed on the package; the temperature may get too high.

Don't eat foods, such as popcorn, if the package has become very brown or charred—signs that the food may have been overheated.

Don't re-use containers with heat susceptors or remove the susceptors for cooking other foods.

▪ **Jars for heating:** Most instruction booklets tell you to *never* heat foods or liquids in jars, even if they are glass canning jars, because they can break because of the microwave action on the curved shoulders at the top. I have not had this happen but, as the old saying goes, it's better to be safe than sorry.

▪ **Popcorn** should be cooked only in microwave-safe containers or prepackaged microwave bags, according to the package directions. Kernels can scorch and catch fire if cooked in nonsafe containers, such as brown paper bags. Reheating popcorn is a fire hazard.

▪ **Potatoes:** If you don't pierce the skin with a fork to let steam out as the potatoes cook, they may explode when you open the door and cause eye injury or serious burns.

▪ **Stuffed poultry** (turkey, chicken) doesn't always cook completely, and the result could be food poisoning.

▪ **Printed plastic bags** should not be used to cover food for microwaving. The paint on the wrapper may not be food grade.

Basic Microwaving Techniques

To adapt your recipes to microwave cooking, find a similar dish in the cookbook that came with your microwave oven to determine cooking time, dish size, and proportions of ingredients to use. Directions on microwave frozen meals and in microwave recipes give a range of times for cooking because microwave ovens vary according to wattage. If your microwave oven is less than 600 watts, you may need to add time or cook for the maximum time suggested. For in ovens with less than 500 watts, best results are obtained with use of High or maximum power, even when directions say 50 percent power. High on ovens with less than 500 watts is equal to 50 percent of the power from 600- or 700-watt ovens.

Also, a microwave oven will work best if it is the only appliance plugged into an electrical circuit; competing with other appliances reduces available wattage.

If you are unsure of the *time* required to cook a food, cook the lesser time suggested by the recipe first; you can always cook a little longer, but once you overcook foods like meat or some vegetables, they will be tough and stringy. Overcooking is the major cause of poor results because we just can't believe how fast a microwave can cook.

If you add a *large amount of liquid* to a dish, it lengthens the cooking time. Usually, you need to reduce the amount of liquid to about half that used in conventional recipes. Also, if the container is sealed in plastic wrap, very little liquid will evaporate. *Note:* When you reduce the amount of liquid in a recipe, you need to also reduce the amount of salt.

Food cooks more slowly *in a deep container* than it does in shallow ones. Shallow containers expose more food surface to the microwaves and so more food cooks at the same time. *Round or oval containers* allow foods to cook more evenly than square or rectangular ones in which the corners may get overcooked and dried out before the centers are done. *Straight-sided containers* are better than slanted ones because they keep food at a more uniform depth, thus allowing it to cook more evenly. Food on the edges of sloped containers tends to cook faster and may overcook before the center is done. *Ring-shaped containers* are best for foods like cakes that can't be stirred during cooking because the open center allows microwaves to contact the food from all sides as well as top and bottom; cooking is more uniform. Also, veggies and some other foods are best made in a microwave-safe ring mold or bundt pan container. Microwave-safe plastic pans are available in housewares departments.

❋ **HELOISE HINT:** To make your own ring pan, place a glass ovenware custard cup, microwave-safe water glass or preserving jar in the center of a microwave-safe round casserole of a suitable diameter.

Prevent spillovers by using cooking containers that are two to three times the volume of the ingredients. Milk, creamy mixtures, and some cereals, like oatmeal, are particularly prone to bubbling up quickly and overflowing.

❋ **HELOISE HINT:** A 4-cup microwave-safe glass measuring cup is a good cooking container, and it automatically measures the amount so you can determine the cooking time.

Tie microwave *cooking bags* with dental floss, *never* with metal twist-ties, which can cause arcing sparks that can damage your oven. CAUTION: Always open cooking bags and pot lids away from you to prevent steam burns.

Look for *browning wraps* in supermarkets and housewares departments of other stores. They help you crisp and brown foods.

✳ **HELOISE HINT**: "Painting" foods with Worcestershire sauce, soy sauce, or other sauces enhances the appearance of microwaved foods, too.

Some microwave instructions say that when you place *several dishes* in an oven at the same time, you should place one in the center and the others around it in a circle. Always *arrange food* so that the thicker pieces or thicker ends are to the outer edge and the thinner pieces or ends are toward the center. If you cook in a round dish, you'll do this automatically.

If your microwave oven didn't come with a *built-in rotator,* you can buy a manual one in a housewares or department store. You won't have to stir as often, and foods cook more evenly when on a rotator. Mark your microwave-safe dishes with a dot of red fingernail polish; then when you place the dish in the microwave, make it your habit to center the mark at "12 o'clock" so that if you have to give it a quarter or half turn during cooking, you'll know how much of a turn you've made. Or put a wooden toothpick under the front of the dish, then move it with the dish as you rotate it so that you can tell at a glance how often the dish was turned. For

example, start with the toothpick at 6 o'clock, move it to 9; then 12, and so on.

You can add most *seasonings* as usual when microwave cooking your favorite recipes. But, don't sprinkle salt on food; the crystals reflect microwaves and cause uneven cooking; instead, dissolve salt in liquid, mix it into the food or, better, add it just before serving. Microwaving makes pepper more intense; it's better to use it sparingly and add more after cooking, to taste. Although dried herbs and pepper flavors get intensified in microwave cooking and need to be reduced, fresh herbs need to be increased to get the intensity you'd get in conventional ovens. Garlic cooks out quickly, so you need to increase the amount you'd use in conventional cooking.

Wine and other alcohol flavors are usually unstable in microwave cooking You need to increase the proportion of wine in cooking liquids to get the flavor you want.

If you crumple *wax paper* slightly before covering food containers, the paper won't blow off when you turn on the microwave.

✳ **HELOISE HINT**: Save landfill space. Buy a microwave cooking lid where cooking equipment is sold. These plastic covers are generally dinner-plate size in diameter and have steam escape holes in the top and/or sides. CAUTION: Like all lids, open away from your face to avoid steam burns.

General Hints for Better Microwaving

• **Melt baking chocolate** squares right on the paper in which the squares are wrapped so there is less cleanup and less danger of scorching them.

- **Grilling:** Microwave foods before grilling to partially cook them and speed up barbecue time. Also, grilling extra food and storing it in the freezer can provide quick microwave reheat meals when time is short.

> Microwaving meat will help it stay moist in addition to getting it cooked faster. Cook meat about three-quarters of the way done and then finish it on the grill to give it that great barbecue flavor.
>
> Try grilling extra steaks, chops, hamburgers, and chicken; wrap and freeze quickly. Then, when you want barbecue but don't want to fire up the grill, pop the frozen foods into your microwave oven to defrost and heat.
>
> Bake potatoes, corn-on-the-cob, and onions according to directions for your microwave oven, then wrap them in foil and put them into the coals for 10 to 15 minutes to reheat.

- **Frozen vegetables** can often be heated in their own containers. Follow the manufacturer's instructions.

- **Café au lait** (coffee with boiled milk): Heat milk in a (microwave safe) mug in the microwave oven and then pour hot coffee into the boiled milk. It's not New Orleans' famous Café du Monde but it's a pretty good make-do. You can also heat milk in a glass measuring cup to add to coffee. *Note:* Canned skim milk will give you a rich taste without the fat calories.

- **Hot cereal:** Most manufacturers now provide package instructions for cooking single portions of cooked cereal in the bowl—no mess and no pot to clean up!

- **Fish:** When cooking fish, place the thickest parts toward the outside, cook a few minutes, than then take the fish out of the microwave and cut a small slit in the thickest part. When the flesh starts looking barely opaque, remove the fish from the microwave. *Note:* Then let it stand a 1 or 2 minutes and it will finish cooking. Unless the fish is crumb coated, cover it with wax paper or plastic wrap to retain moisture. It is best to undercook fish slightly because it continues to cook when removed from the microwave oven. As with other foods, you have to allow for residual cooking time.

- **Foil-covered frozen foods:** Some products are packaged in foil and are safe for *some* microwave ovens *under certain conditions.* Check the cookbook for your microwave to make sure your oven won't be damaged by sparks arcing from the foil. Or, if you can't find instructions about foil in your manual, call the manufacturer's consumer line that should be given in your manual. You may be able to get an 800 number for the manufacturer by calling 1-800-555-1212, the 800 information number.

- **Heating plates:** If the plates/dishes are microwave safe, you can heat them in your microwave oven. If you're not sure, test one plate first to make sure it is microwave safe.

- **Paper plates:** Keep a cheap white paper plate in the microwave to absorb spills and another to cover the dish with.

- **Toast nuts:** Put about 1 cup of shelled nuts in a microwave-safe dish and toast on High for 1 to 2 minutes.

- **Vegetables:** Since microwaves cook from the outside in, when placing vegetables such as broccoli or cauliflower on the cooking dish, place them in a circle with the stem ends toward the outer edge so that the tender "flower" end won't get overcooked before the tougher stem end is done.

Microwave Reheating Hints

Check the manual that came with your microwave to get specific times and settings for reheating foods. Microwaves vary greatly in wattage and so the times given here for commonly microwaved foods are approximate. When in doubt, use the lowest setting and least amount of time; otherwise you'll make the food item hard, dry, and overcooked. The settings here are approximate for a 600-watt microwave; you will need less time with higher wattage, and more time will less wattage. If your microwave has only High, Medium, and Low settings, Low, Warm, and Defrost are probably similar to each other. Reheat and Roast may be similar to Medium. High is, of course, the highest setting on any microwave. For best results, check your manual.

- Baby food (one 4-ounce jar): in the original jar with lid removed; Reheat, 20 to 30 seconds.
- Bacon (four slices): between paper towels; High, 4 to 4½ minutes.
- Buns and rolls (two at room temperature): on a paper plate or towel; Reheat, 10 to 15 seconds.

- Butter, to soften (½ cup at refrigerator temperature): in glass or pottery; Warm, 1½ to 2 minutes.
- Chicken (nine pieces, fried, room temperature): in a fast food paper box; Reheat, 6 to 7 minutes.
- Chocolate, to melt (1-ounce square): in 1-cup glass measure; High, 2 minutes.
- Coffee (1 cup): in glass or pottery cup (without metal trim); High, 1 to 1½ minutes.
- Eggs (two scrambled with 3 tablespoons milk and 2 teaspoons butter): in a glass or pottery bowl; Roast, 2 to 2½ minutes.
- Hamburger (1 pound): thaw in original plastic wrap; Defrost, 8 to 10 minutes.
- Hamburgers/sandwiches (two at room temperature): on a paper towel or napkin; Reheat, 30 to 45 seconds.
- Hot Dogs (two at refrigerator temperature): wrapped loosely in a paper towel or napkin; Reheat, 1 to 1½ minutes.
- Potatoes (four baked): pierce skin; on oven bottom, no plate; High, 10 to 12 minutes.
- Rice (1 cup cooked at refrigerator temperature): in a covered glass casserole; Reheat, 1½ to 2 minutes.
- Sauce (1 cup, sweet or savory without sensitive ingredients at refrigerator temperature): in wax paper–covered glass casserole or 2-cup glass measure; Reheat, 3½ to 4 minutes. (*Note:* Fatty sauces heat faster.)
- Soup (two bowls): in glass or pottery serving bowls; Reheat, 7 to 8 minutes.
- Spaghetti (one 16-ounce can): in a 1-quart covered glass casserole; Reheat, 3 to 4 minutes.
- Frozen dinner: follow directions on package.

■ Vegetables (one 16-ounce can, undrained): in a 1-quart covered glass casserole; Reheat, 3 to 4 minutes.

To avoid burning your lips or tongue, when reheating coffee or tea, wait a while to let the liquid get "calm" before you take that first sip, or stir first.

Bread products that are heated too long become tough and dry. It only takes a few seconds, usually 15 or 20 seconds on High is enough for one serving. Prevent soggy bottoms on sweet rolls or pastries by placing them on a paper towel or paper plate (real paper, not foam or plastic). *Note:* you can re-use a paper plate a few times if the bread product is not greasy. *Dry bread products* can be rescued by putting a cup of water in the microwave next to the bread or pastry to provide moisture. Or put the roll or pastry in the microwave, run some water over your fingers and flick some drops off your fingers and on to the bread before zapping it for a few seconds.

When reheating *fried chicken,* the meat will stay moist and tender and the coating crisp if you heat it in the microwave for 1 minute on High; then finish heating it in a conventional oven at 400 degrees F for 5 minutes.

Recycle frozen dinner trays and plates from frozen dinners to *take leftovers to work* and heat them up in the microwave. CAUTION: If the package directions warn against re-use of the container discard after the first use.

Instead of frying *tortillas* before filling them, microwave them for about 20 seconds. If you are just heating one tortilla, you can just toss it into the microwave as is. If you are heating a stack, you'll need to put them in a covered container or wrap them in a damp paper towel for heating.

Defrosting Foods in the Microwave:

Because microwaves vary in their wattage and availability of different settings, it is best to check with the manual that came with your microwave. The following are just general hints for thawing foods in the microwave.

■ **Remove all twisties** from food bags and close the bags with a rubber band.

■ Place food in a **flat glass baking dish** to catch drips.

■ **Use a Defrost setting** to thaw (for some microwaves, this would be a Low setting) fish or meat weighing up to 4 pounds, ground meat weighing up to 2 pounds, and poultry weighing 4 pounds or less.

■ **Use a High/Roast setting** to thaw large roasts weighing 4 pounds or more, ground meat weighing 2 pounds or more, and poultry weighing more than 4 pounds. Thaw 1 minute per pound on High, then 2 minutes per pound on Roast.

■ If **turning** is specified on your microwave's thawing directions, start thawing whole poultry breast-side up; for other foods, start thawing with the thickest side up.

■ Food will be **icy in the center** when removed from the microwave. If you try to thaw meats, fish, or poultry totally in the microwave, you are likely to begin cooking the edges of the foods.

- There will be a **standing time** after thawing in the microwave to complete the thawing, usually about 5 minutes for a 1-pound chunk of food and longer for larger chunks of food, for example, 45 to 60 minutes for a 4- to 5-pound roast.

- When thawing **whole poultry**, remove the loosened giblets before the standing time and save them for gravy or broth.

Chapter Seven

Recipes

My mother started collecting recipes long before the beginning of her *Heloise* newspaper column and books. And I have continued that tradition with the help of friends, colleagues, professional associations, and, of course, my wonderful readers. What I'm offering in the following pages is probably the single biggest collection of these recipes assembled to date. It's certainly an eclectic collection. You'll find lots of familiar dishes, some unusual concoctions, and some "classic" Heloise recipes.

If you've been collecting your own recipes—from magazines, friends, or from TV chefs—you might want to create your own collection. Buy an inexpensive binder and plastic sheet protectors from an office supply store or a binder-style photo album with magnetic pages and tabbed dividers. Sort your recipe clippings into the usual categories and insert. Use a loose-leaf binder so you can insert pages wherever you wish. You can even include the pictures published with the newspaper or magazine recipes. Keep the cookbook near your reading or TV chair so that you can file each recipe as you clip it to avoid those messy piles of recipes. Or tape recipes to index cards with nonyellowing transparent tape and file the cards in a loaf-size plastic bread container, which holds much more than the usual file box.

But even creating your own cookbook might not be the solution to keeping track of all the recipes that we read in cookbooks. I know that most of us have lots of cookbooks and it's frustrating when you go to find a favorite recipe and end up leafing through a dozen books. So, here's a Heloise Hint for finding your favorites recipes: Write on an index card the recipe name, the title of the cookbook, and page number, and file the recipe card in a recipe box under the appropriate category.

But recipes are more than just formulas for making food. For many of us, our favorite recipes are a record of family traditions. Your family might enjoy the meals you make with the recipes in this book—or your other favorites—but if you want to create something really special, create your own cookbook! You could write your favorites in a special notebook or type them up and insert them in a loose-leaf binder. (A binder allows you, or the recipient of this gift, to add recipes.) This personal collection makes a great gift for a young couple just setting up house.

In addition to the recipes, this chapter also includes two important sections: "Cooking with Planned and Unplanned Leftovers" and "Heloise to the Rescue: Food Repair, Substitutions, and Other Hints to See You Through a Food Crisis." These features are what Kitcheneering is all about—ways to make your time in the kitchen easier and more enjoyable.

Many of the following recipes are from different decades, parts of the United States, other countries, and in the "voice" of the author. Some of the recipes are very old and really a verbal, or as told to. In fact, you can almost "hear" my mother's voice in many of them. Please read the recipe *twice* before starting, and have all of the ingredients out so you won't have to stop halfway through! We have done our best to bring some of the ingredients up to date. For example, a can of corn or a box of cake mix, means a average size can which can be 13½ to 16 ounces, or an average size box of cake mix, 18 to 18½ ounces.

SOUPS

EGG-DROP CHICKEN SOUP
A very filling Chinese favorite.
MAKES 4 SERVINGS.

4 chicken bouillon cubes

4½ cups water

4 ounces cooked chicken, shredded

½ cup finely shredded carrot

½ teaspoon dried parsley, crumbled

1 teaspoon soy sauce

2 eggs, lightly beaten

4 teaspoons sliced scallions (for garnish)

Dissolve the bouillon cubes in the water in a large saucepan over medium heat. Add the chicken, carrot, parsley, and soy sauce and bring to a boil, stirring occasionally. Cook for 5 or 6 minutes, then slowly dribble the eggs into the boiling soup, stirring constantly until the eggs have cooked. Sprinkle each serving with scallions.

CHICKEN SOUP
This Jewish comfort food may not actually cure your cold but it will certainly make you feel better.

1 slice breast of beef flanken (flank)

1 beef knee bone, split

Water, salted, to cover

Small bunch of fresh curly parsley, tied with a thread

1 (4½-pound) chicken and giblets, quartered, with wings and legs disjointed

4 stalks celery, leaves and all, cut into halves and scraped

1 knob celery, pared and quartered

1 large petrushka (root parsley) with leaves,
    pared and washed well

4 large carrots, scraped and cut in half lengthwise

2 large onions, quartered

Salt

White pepper

Chopped fresh dill (for garnish)

Place flanken and bone in a 2-quart saucepan and cover with salted water. Boil uncovered for 10 minutes and remove from the range. Strain in a colander and rinse the meat with cold running water. Place the remains aside on a paper towel and throw out. Put the parsley in a container covered with cold water and refrigerate. Place the chicken, giblets, flanken, bone, and all the vegetables into a 6-quart saucepan. Fill with water and bring the meat and vegetables to a boil; lower the heat and simmer covered for 1 hour, then add salt and white pepper to taste. Drain the parsley and add it to the soup. Cook, covered, until done. Top each serving with some dill.

NOTE: Can be served with Matzo Balls (recipe below).

MATZO BALLS
Recipe of Mrs. Solomon J. Jacobson, San Antonio.

2 eggs

1 cup boiling water

2 tablespoons shortening (chicken fat is
    preferred for its flavor)

Salt and pepper

1 cup matzo meal

Large pot of boiling water

Beat the eggs lightly in a medium bowl. Add 1 cup boiling water, shortening, salt, and pepper. Mix in the matzo meal. Refrigerate several hours or overnight. Shape into balls and drop into a large pot of boiling water. Keep your hands moist while forming the balls to prevent the dough from sticking. Cover the pot and boil for about 20 minutes. Do not uncover pot during this time. The balls will have puffed up while boiling. Remove them from the water and put them into the chicken soup.

CHICKEN AND DUMPLINGS SOUP
Here's a quick lunch of comfort food.
MAKES 2 SERVINGS.

1 can chicken noodle soup or chicken broth

2 cups baking mix

⅔ cup milk

Bring the soup to a boil in a medium saucepan. Meanwhile, combine the baking mix with the milk and blend well (or use your favorite dumpling recipe). Spoon the dough into the boiling soup; cover lightly and reduce the heat to a simmer. Cook for 12 to 15 minutes.

NOTE: When you are spooning the dough into the boiling soup, dip the spoon into the hot broth after each spoonful to prevent the dough from sticking to the spoon.

"GOLDEN" CHICKEN AND NOODLE SOUP

*Kelly Golden Moravits's family recipe is very old
and doesn't have exact measurements. In fact, when
you measure the milk to add to the noodle mixture,
you measure it in half of the empty eggshell!*

MAKES 4 SERVINGS.

2 eggs
2 half shells full of milk
Pinch of salt
Enough flour to make a dough
1 whole chicken
Water to cover
2 carrots, chopped
2 stalks of celery, chopped

Crack the eggs into a bowl and then measure in the milk. Add the salt and enough flour to make a dough (the dough should be a little sticky). Roll out the dough on a floured counter or cutting board. Let dry for 4 to 6 hours. The dough may be too sticky to cut before that amount of time. When the dough is more manageable, cut it into thin strips (¼ to ½ inch wide, depending on your taste).

In the meantime, cook the chicken in a large covered pot with enough water to cover until done. When fully cooked, remove the chicken and debone it. Skim all the fat off the broth and put the deboned chicken back in. Add the carrots and celery. Cook until tender. Add the noodles and cook for 15 to 20 minutes or until done.

CHICKEN TORTILLA SOUP

*Fellow Texan Merry Clark, now a New York
editor, loves to cook for crowds. She has introduced
her friends with faint-hearted taste buds to the joys
of hot, spicy food. Here's her version of tortilla soup.*

MAKES 12 SERVINGS.

12 corn tortillas
2 onions, chopped
½ cup olive oil
½ cup tomato puree
4 quarts rich chicken stock
2 cups diced cooked chicken
2 tablespoons chopped fresh cilantro
Dash each of cayenne pepper and Parmesan
   cheese (for garnish)

Cut the tortillas into strips and fry in ¼ inch oil over medium-high heat until crisp (just like tortilla chips). Drain on paper towel and set aside.

Sauté the onion in ½ cup oil in a soup pot over medium-high heat until tender. Add the tomato puree and stock. Add the chicken, cilantro, and tortillas. Cook over medium heat for about 1 hour. Top each serving with a sprinkle of cayenne and Parmesan cheese.

MEXICAN MEATBALL SOUP

*This south-of-the border soup is tasty but
low in fat!*

MAKES 8 SERVINGS.

½ pound lean ground beef
4 teaspoons chopped, fresh parsley
½ teaspoon black pepper
1 garlic clove, minced

1 teaspoon dried oregano, crushed

5 tablespoons chopped fresh cilantro

2 tablespoons long-grain rice, uncooked

1 egg white

6 beef bouillon cubes

6 cups water

2 teaspoons light cooking oil

1 medium onion, finely chopped

1 cup peeled and diced tomatoes

2 cups diced celery

4 cups peeled and sliced carrots

1 cup fresh or frozen corn kernels

4 tablespoons fresh cilantro, chopped

Mix the beef, parsley, pepper, garlic, oregano, 1 tablespoon of the cilantro, the rice, and egg white in a medium bowl. Form into small meatballs, no larger than 1 inch in diameter.

Dissolve the bouillon cubes in the water in a bowl or pan to make beef broth, and set aside. Heat the oil in a large saucepan over medium-high heat and add the onion. When soft, add the tomatoes, celery, carrots, and broth. Bring to a boil and drop in the meatballs. Reduce the heat and add the corn; then simmer gently for 25 to 30 minutes. Stir in the remaining cilantro just before serving.

BEEF MINESTRONE

Served with crusty bread, this soup will feed a houseful of hungry people for a weekend lunch or supper and it won't take hours to prepare.
MAKES 8 LARGE OR 12 SMALL SERVINGS.

1 teaspoon cooking oil

½ cup minced onions

¾ pound lean ground beef

2 garlic cloves, minced

½ pound fresh green beans, sliced into 1-inch pieces

2 (14½-ounce) cans whole tomatoes

4 beef bouillon cubes

4 cups water

2 cups shredded cabbage

1 cup diced zucchini

½ cup peeled and diced carrots

2 (8-ounce) cans cannellini beans (white kidney beans), drained

4 ounces vermicelli, uncooked, broken into 1- to 2-inch pieces

Salt and pepper

Grated Parmesan cheese (for garnish)

Heat the oil in a large saucepan over medium-high heat and add the onions, ground beef, and garlic. Cook until the meat is brown, stirring frequently. Remove from the heat and drain, then blot any remaining fat in the pan with paper towels. Return the meat mixture to the pan.

Add the green beans and tomatoes, including the liquid. Dissolve the bouillon cubes in the water and pour into the pan. Stir thoroughly and bring to a boil. Reduce the heat, cover, and simmer for 15 minutes.

Now add the cabbage, zucchini, and carrots. Add the cannellini beans to the mixture together with the vermicelli. Season with salt and pepper to taste. Return to a boil, reduce the heat, and simmer until the vermicelli is cooked (test with a fork), 15 to 20 minutes. Sprinkle Parmesan cheese on top of each serving.

HEARTY VEGETABLE BEEF SOUP

MAKES 4 SERVINGS.

1 (10½-ounce) can unsalted chicken broth

½ cup water

2 cups frozen mixed vegetables for soup

1 (16-ounce) can whole tomatoes, broken up

1 cup cooked and diced beef

1 teaspoon dried thyme, crushed

Dash of pepper

¼ teaspoon salt

1 bay leaf

2 ounces narrow-width noodles, uncooked
   (about 1¼ cups)

Heat the broth and water in a medium saucepan over medium-high heat. Add the vegetables, tomatoes, meat, and seasonings. Bring to boil, reduce the heat, and boil gently, uncovered, for 15 minutes. Add the noodles and cook until they are tender, about 10 minutes. Be sure to remove the bay leaf before serving. (Bay leaf, if swallowed can choke a person if it gets stuck, so always remove it!)

NOTE: If using already cooked noodles, simmer the soup for 20 minutes, then add the noodles and heat through, about 5 minutes.

REFRIGERATOR SOUP

This is my idea of a quick soup and great for moms who come home from work and need to create a healthy, hearty meal in a hurry. It's so simple. Just open your refrigerator door, pull out leftovers, any vegetables from the bin, dibs and dabs of leftover rice or squash, meat or chicken cut in bite-sized pieces and put it all in a saucepan and add water and some beef or chicken bouillon. Then season with your favorite spices and simmer for a few minutes. Your family won't even recognize those leftovers!

GRANNY'S COUNTRY-STYLE BEEF SOUP

This German-American recipe comes from Elleen Gooding who lives on a farm and processes her own meat. This is her way of using all parts of the meat, even the bones. It makes a delicious and healthy meal and can be easily altered to your own taste. This is good served with cornbread.

MAKES 6 TO 8 SERVINGS.

1 large soup bone

8 cups water

8 ounces tomato sauce

⅓ cup rice, uncooked

4 large garlic cloves, minced

1 large onion, cubed

1 cup cubed carrots

1 cup cubed celery

1 large potato, cubed

1 small summer squash (zucchini or yellow),
   cubed

2 teaspoons salt or to taste

¼ teaspoon pepper

1 teaspoon sugar

4 to 6 ounces medium egg noodles, uncooked

In a 6- to 8-quart pot boil the soup bone in the water and tomato sauce for 4 to 6 hours (depending on size). Add more water, if necessary. Add the remaining ingredients, except the noodles, and boil for 20 minutes. Add the noodles and simmer for 15 minutes.

QUICK-AND-EASY HEARTY VEGETABLE-BEEF SOUP

This recipe comes from the USDA's Shopping for Food and Making Meals in Minutes Using the Dietary Guidelines.

MAKES ABOUT 4 SERVINGS.

10½ ounces unsalted chicken broth

½ cup water

2 cups frozen mixed vegetables for soup

1 (16-ounce) can tomatoes

1 cup cooked and diced beef

1 teaspoon dried thyme, crushed

Dash of pepper

¼ teaspoon salt

1 bay leaf

2 ounces narrow noodles, uncooked (about 1¼ cups)

Heat the broth and water in a large saucepan over medium-high heat. Add the vegetables, tomatoes, meat, and seasonings. Bring to a boil, reduce the heat, and simmer gently, uncovered, for 15 minutes.

Add the noodles; cook until tender, about 10 minutes. Be sure to remove the bay leaf before serving.

TESS AVERNA'S WONTONS FOR SOUP

My secretary, Joyce Buffolino, loves it when her mother, Tess, makes this soup. Make these ahead of time and store in the freezer.

MAKES ABOUT 34 WONTONS.

1 10-ounce package (frozen) spinach, chopped

Pat of margarine or bit of oil

1 15-ounce container whole or skim ricotta cheese

¾ cup diced mozzarella cheese

1 package wontons wrappers

Sauté the spinach in a medium saucepan over medium heat with a pat of margarine until cooked. Then drain. Put into a bowl along with the ricotta and mozzarella cheeses. Mix thoroughly.

Place a wonton wrapper on a working surface. Put a teaspoon or so of the mixture in the middle of the wrapper. Wet the edges of the wrapper and press together in a triangular shape.

Place the wontons flat on wax paper, cover, and freeze. Then store in a freezer-safe, zipper-type bag.

To use fresh: Add as many wontons as desired to the soup you've prepared and freeze the rest. *To use frozen:* Do not thaw; drop frozen into the soup and simmer about 15 minutes or until done (taste the edges).

NOTE: Packaged wontons can be bought in the fresh vegetables department in most large supermarkets. They are found in the refrigerated section.

ITALIAN PASTA SOUP

Janie learned this soup from her mother, Jo Mulrenan. The secret ingredient in this pasta soup is hot dogs—an ingredient you probably have on hand (particularly if you have children). Hot dogs get gobbled up so fast that you may not think of using them in soups. Your kids will love this.

MAKES 8 TO 10 SERVINGS.

3 (16-ounce) cans stewed tomatoes

2 (16-ounce) cans cannellini beans (white kidney beans)

4 cups water

2 stalks celery, sliced

1 small onion, diced

2 carrots, sliced

Pinch *each* of sweet basil, oregano, parsley, garlic powder, pepper, and salt

3 to 6 hot dogs, sliced

1 cup elbow macaroni, uncooked

In a large pot, heat the stewed tomatoes and beans over medium heat. Add the water. Stir in the celery, onion, and carrots. Sprinkle with the seasonings, adjusting the amounts to taste. Bring to a boil, lower the heat, and simmer until the vegetables are cooked, about 1 hour. Add the sliced hot dogs and simmer an additional 15 minutes. In another pot, cook the macaroni according to the package directions until firm but not overcooked. Rinse and drain. Add to the soup, stir, and serve.

TORTELLINI AND BEAN SOUP

Here is a soup recipe from my dear longtime friend Judy Hill Moorhead. She made this for our annual (college girlfriends) "Girls Health Weekend" and we request it every year!

½ pound dry kidney beans or 2 (16-ounce) cans, drained

1 bay leaf

Sprinkle of garlic powder

¼ pound sliced regular bacon or pancetta (a type of unsmoked bacon), cooked, bacon drippings reserved

Water

1 onion, diced

2 garlic cloves, minced

4 cups chicken broth

2 cups beef broth

1 (29-ounce) can crushed tomatoes

¼ teaspoon dried basil, crushed

¼ teaspoon dried oregano, crushed

¼ teaspoon black pepper

9 ounces cheese tortellini

2 cups fresh spinach, chopped fine

¼ cup Parmesan cheese (for garnish)

Cook ½ pound kidney beans with bay leaf and garlic. Fry bacon or pancetta.

In bacon drippings, sauté onion and garlic cloves until golden brown.

Add the chicken broth, tomatoes, beef broth, basil, oregano, black pepper, and salt and simmer.

Add the tortellini and the kidney beans, cook 20 minutes. Add the spinach and cook 10 minutes.

Garnish with ¼ cup Parmesan cheese.

VARIATION: To make vegetarian, Judy omits the pancetta or bacon, chicken and beef broth. She uses vegetable broth, bean "juice," and vegetable juice. She also adds parsley and increases other spices.

CREAMY CAULIFLOWER-CARROT SOUP

MAKES 6 SERVINGS.

1 tablespoon cooking oil

1 cup chopped onions

1 pound carrots, peeled and diced

12 ounces cauliflower, broken into small pieces

4 chicken bouillon cubes

4 cups water

6 tablespoons nonfat dried milk powder

1 teaspoon ground cumin

Dash of ground nutmeg

Salt and pepper

1 scallion, finely chopped

In a large saucepan, heat the oil, and add the onion, carrots, and cauliflower pieces. Cover the pan and cook over medium heat for 5 to 10 minutes, stirring at intervals. In a bowl or pan, dissolve the bouillon cubes in 3 cups of the water, then stir in 4 tablespoons of the dried milk. Pour this mixture over the vegetables and add the cumin, nutmeg, and salt and pepper to taste. Cover and bring to a boil, then lower the heat and simmer for 20 minutes or until the vegetables are cooked.

Strain the vegetables and return the liquid to the saucepan. Puree the cooked vegetables with ½ cup of the liquid and the remaining 2 tablespoons of dried milk until the consistency is smooth and even. Pour the pureed vegetable mixture back into the saucepan and stir in the scallion. Add a little of the remaining water if the consistency is too thick; stir, reheat, and serve.

HARVEST SQUASH SOUP

Any winter squash, such as butternut, pumpkin, or acorn, or a mixture of different varieties, can go into this delicious soup. For extra flair, serve pumpkin soup in the pumpkin shell.

MAKES ABOUT 8 SERVINGS.

2 tablespoons cooking oil

1 large onion, chopped

¼ teaspoon dried thyme, crushed

¼ teaspoon ground mace

3 pounds winter squash, peeled and cut in chunks

1 pound new potatoes, peeled and cut in chunks

1 pound parsnips, peeled and cut in chunks

4 chicken bouillon cubes

4 cups water

1 teaspoon hot pepper sauce

Salt and pepper

Mace (for garnish)

Heat the oil over a medium heat in a large saucepan and add the onion, thyme, and ¼ teaspoon mace. Cook, stirring frequently, for about 5 minutes. Then add the squash, potatoes, and parsnips. Cook over medium heat for about 30 minutes, stirring occasionally, until the vegetables start to soften.

Mix the bouillon cubes in the water in a bowl or pan to make chicken broth. Pour the broth over the vegetable mixture and add the hot pepper sauce and salt and pepper to taste. Bring to a boil, then cover, lower the heat, and allow to simmer for another 30 minutes. The vegetable chunks should now be completely cooked.

Tip the mixture into a blender container, a portion at a time, and puree until smooth. Use the bowl or pan used for mixing the broth to hold the soup until you have pureed all the vegetable mixture, then return the mixture to the saucepan and reheat. Sprinkle each portion with a pinch of mace before serving.

RED PEPPER SOUP

This soup is tasty and pretty, too!
MAKES 8 SERVINGS.

4 chicken bouillon cubes

4 cups water

1 tablespoon cooking oil

4 cups chopped onion

8 large red bell peppers, seeded and chopped

1 tablespoon wine vinegar

Salt and pepper

8 parsley sprigs

Dissolve the bouillon cubes in the water in a bowl or pan to make chicken broth. Heat the oil in a large saucepan over medium-high heat, add the onion and sauté for about 5 minutes until translucent. Add the broth and red pepper and bring to a boil, stirring occasionally. Reduce the heat, cover, and simmer for 15 to 20 minutes.

Pour the pepper mixture into a blender container, a portion at a time, and puree until smooth. Use the bowl or pan used to mix the broth to hold the soup until you have pureed all the mixture, then return the mixture to the saucepan and reheat over medium heat. Add the vinegar and salt and pepper to taste. Stir thoroughly and make sure the soup is piping hot before serving. Top each portion with a sprig of parsley.

SOUTHWESTERN VEGETABLE LENTIL SOUP

This soup's flavor is complete when served with cornbread.
MAKES 8 SERVINGS.

1 tablespoon cooking oil

2 cups chopped onions

½ cup chopped celery

¾ cup peeled and chopped parsnips

¾ cup peeled and chopped carrots

6 cups water

½ pound dried lentils

4 vegetable bouillon cubes

1 teaspoon chili powder

1 teaspoon ground cumin

1 (14½-ounce) can whole tomatoes

1 teaspoon hot pepper sauce

1 jalapeño pepper, seeded and sliced *

Heat the oil in a large saucepan over medium-high heat, add the onion and sauté for about 5 minutes until translucent. Add the celery, parsnips, carrots, water, and lentils. Crumble the bouillon cubes into the pan. Stir in the chili powder and cumin and bring to a boil, stirring frequently. Reduce the heat, cover, and simmer for 30 minutes. Add the tomatoes, including the liquid, the hot pepper sauce, and sliced jalapeño pepper. Stir well and simmer for another 45 minutes or until the lentils are tender.

Wear rubber gloves.

TOMATO SOUP

Use fresh or canned tomatoes for this soup.

1 quart tomatoes, peeled

Pinch of baking soda

1 quart hot boiled milk

Salt and pepper

3 tablespoons butter

¼-½ cup cracker crumbs (optional)

Cook the tomatoes in a saucepan over medium heat until they are soft. After cooking, strain off the seeds and mash any remaining lumps. Then bring the tomatoes to a boil and add the baking soda. Then add the milk and salt and pepper to taste. Last, add the butter. Heat through and serve with cracker crumbs if desired.

NOTE: You can cheat and start with a large can of tomato juice. The whole tomatoes make a tastier soup, but the juice is faster.

QUICKIE FRENCH ONION SOUP

If your vegetable bin is brimming with extra onions that you don't seem to be using up quickly enough, here's a way to use them. Select as many onions as you want.

Onions

Oil or beef bouillon

Instant onion soup mix

Water

Grated cheese (for garnish)

Peel, slice, and sauté the onions in a large frying pan for a few minutes in oil or beef bouillon until brown. Put the cooked onions into a medium saucepan.

Add several packages of soup mix and the specified amount of water per package. Simmer until ready to eat. Top with grated cheese.

MARILYN'S GARDEN CHEDDAR SOUP

2 carrots, peeled and sliced

2 small zucchinis, halved and sliced

2 tomatoes, peeled and cut into wedges

1 celery stalk, sliced

1 cup sliced Portobello mushrooms

1 onion, halved and sliced

2 garlic cloves, minced

4½ cups beef broth

1½ cups tomato juice

1 tablespoon fresh basil, minced

½ cup dry red wine

½ teaspoon salt

½ teaspoon pepper

2 tablespoons fresh parsley, minced

1 cup shredded Cheddar cheese (for garnish)

In a stockpot, add first nine ingredients and heat to boiling. Reduce the heat and simmer covered for 30 minutes or until the vegetables are tender.

Stir in the basil, wine, salt, pepper, and parsley just before serving. Sprinkle top of each serving with Cheddar cheese.

MEME'S POTATO SOUP

Ruth Schmidt's beloved grandmother Lillian R. Graves shared this very old recipe from the late 1800s. Ruth called her grandmother "Meme," so this soup is appropriately named.

MAKES 4 SERVINGS.

4 medium potatoes, cubed

1 small onion, chopped

1 tablespoon shortening

1 cup water

2 cups milk

¾ teaspoon salt

Dash of pepper

Cook the potatoes, onion, shortening, and water in a large pot over medium heat until the potatoes are soft. Add the remaining ingredients and simmer for 20 to 30 minutes.

VEGETABLE CHOWDER WITH BEER AND CHEESE

Fred Griffith is a longtime friend and was co-host of Cleveland's Morning Exchange *TV show that ended its twenty-seven-year run in September 1999. He and his wife, Linda, authors of* Onions, Onions, Onions *and* Cooking Under Cover, *share a creamy, thick, and cheesy vegetable chowder that is perfect for a cold day. Serve it with warm bread and a big salad for a satisfying supper.*

3 tablespoons unsalted butter

⅔ cup diced yellow onion

2 carrots, scrubbed and sliced into thin disks

2 cups thinly sliced zucchini

1 cup thinly sliced yellow squash

½ cup corn kernels

½ cup peas

½ cup coarsely chopped red bell pepper

1 teaspoon dried thyme, crushed, or 2 teaspoons fresh, chopped

3 tablespoons unbleached flour

1 quart hot milk

1 cup beer

3 cups shredded Cheddar cheese

Kosher salt and freshly ground white pepper

2 teaspoons Worcestershire sauce

Fresh dill (for garnish)

Melt the butter in a soup pot over low heat. Add the onion and carrots, cover tightly, and braise over very low heat for 10 minutes. Add the remaining vegetables and thyme. Stir well, cover, and cook over very low heat for 5 minutes. Sprinkle evenly with flour and cook for 2 minutes more, stirring constantly.

Slowly add the milk, stirring gently until the mixture has thickened. Stir in the beer. Cover and cook over low heat until mixture begins to simmer, about 5 minutes. Then add the cheese, stirring until it is melted. Season with salt, pepper, and Worcestershire sauce. Serve in heated bowls. Sprinkle the top with dill.

HELOISE'S ECONOMICAL CORN CHOWDER (1960)

1 medium sized potato

1 medium sized onion

1 large can of cream style corn

1 cup of canned milk

2 slices of cooked and chopped bacon

Salt and pepper

Dice the potato and onion and cover with a little more water than necessary (about an inch). When cooked add corn and milk. Add bacon and season with salt and pepper. If too thick, add more water or milk.

GAZPACHO

This cold soup makes a super starter for a summer meal or is great with crusty bread for a satisfying lunch.

MAKES 6 SERVINGS.

3 cups peeled, seeded, and chopped tomatoes

1½ cups tomato juice

1 cup peeled, seeded, and chopped cucumber

½ cup seeded and chopped green bell pepper

½ cup chopped onion

1 (4-ounce) can diced green chilies, drained

1 garlic clove, minced

2 tablespoons Balsamic vinegar

¼ to ½ teaspoon hot pepper sauce, to taste

Salt and pepper

6 small mint sprigs (for garnish)

Mix the tomatoes, tomato juice, cucumber, bell pepper, onions, green chilies, and garlic in a large bowl. Transfer portion by portion to a blender container and blend until smooth, pouring the puree into another bowl until all the mixture has been processed. Stir in the Balsamic vinegar, and the hot pepper sauce (to your hot "taste"); season with salt and pepper to taste.

Cover and chill well, for at least 2 to 3 hours. Serve in individual bowls with a sprig of mint on top.

FRESH TOMATO AND BASIL SOUP

I've collected hundreds of recipes for tomato soup and I'm working my way through trying them all. This one is delish! It can be served cold or hot.

MAKES 4 LARGE OR 6 SMALL SERVINGS.

3 vegetable bouillon cubes

3 cups water

2 pounds tomatoes, peeled and sliced

3 garlic cloves, sliced in half

3 fresh basil leaves

4 tablespoons finely chopped fresh parsley

1 tablespoon virgin olive oil

Salt and pepper

4 to 6 parsley sprigs (for garnish)

Dissolve the bouillon cubes in the water in a bowl or pan to make vegetable broth. Pour a little broth into a large saucepan and add the tomatoes, garlic, basil, and parsley. Cook over medium heat, stirring frequently, until the garlic is cooked through, then remove and discard all but 2 half cloves. Pour the tomato mixture into a blender container and puree on medium speed until the consistency is smooth.

Return the puree to the saucepan and add the remaining vegetable broth and the olive oil. Stir throughly and simmer gently until the soup has reduced a little in volume and thickened. Season with salt and pepper to taste. Serve hot or cover and chill for 2 to 3 hours. Before serving, garnish each bowl with a sprig of parsley.

NOTE: When served hot, this soup is extra delicious served with a few fingers of whole wheat toast floating on top of each portion.

AVOCADO SOUP

If you like guacamole, you'll love this cold soup.
MAKES 6 SERVINGS.

2 medium ripe avocados
2 cups light sour cream
2 teaspoons lemon juice
½ teaspoon hot pepper sauce
2 cups water
2 teaspoons chicken bouillon granules
6 small mint sprigs (for garnish)

Peel the avocados, remove the pits, and slice. Put the slices in a blender container with the sour cream, lemon juice, hot pepper sauce, and water; crumble the bouillon granules on top. Blend on medium speed until smooth and evenly colored. Pour into bowls and chill in the refrigerator for at least 2 hours. Garnish with mint sprigs and serve.

DOUBLE BERRY SOUP

Cool fruit soups can be a first course or dessert. Some versions of this recipe add blueberries to the mix; a West Coast variation includes kiwi. Choose your fruits for this soup by what is in season for best taste and economy.
MAKES 6 SERVINGS.

1 cup orange juice, unsweetened
2 cups cranberry-raspberry drink
1½ cups plus 3 tablespoons water
½ orange rind (white pith removed), cut into
   quarters
2 tablespoons cornstarch
2 cups sliced, fresh strawberries

2 cups fresh raspberries
¼ cup strawberry or raspberry schnapps
   (optional)
6 small mint sprigs

Mix the orange juice, cranberry-raspberry drink, and 1½ cups of water in a large saucepan (not aluminum); add the orange rind (be sure to remove as much of the white pith as possible). Bring the mixture to a boil, reduce the heat, and simmer for 2 or 3 minutes.

Thoroughly mix the cornstarch with the remaining 3 tablespoons of water in a cup and slowly stir this into the juice mixture. Keep the saucepan over the heat and stir constantly until the mixture is clear and thickens. Remove from the heat; take out and discard the orange rind.

Add the strawberries, raspberries, and schnapps (if using) and stir thoroughly. Pour into a bowl; cover and chill for at least 2 to 3 hours before serving. Garnish with mint sprigs.

SPARKLING PAPAYA SOUP

My fellow syndicated newspaper columnist and friend Jeanne Jones, who writes the "Cook It Light" newspaper column, focuses on light cuisine. She's full of ideas and is the author of over thirty-two cookbooks. Here's an original soup idea from her cookbook Healthy Cooking for People Who Don't Have Time to Cook.
MAKES 4 SERVINGS.

2 large ripe papayas, peeled and cut into large
   cubes
¾ cup plain low-fat yogurt (nonfat won't work),
   divided
¼ cup freshly squeezed lime juice

¼ cup mild-flavored honey (such as clover honey)

1 cup sparkling water, divided

4 mint sprigs (for garnish)

Place the papayas, ½ cup of the yogurt, the lime juice, and honey in a food processor, reserving some of the papaya for garnish. Process until smooth. Add ½ cup of the sparkling water and continue processing until blended. Keep chilled until ready to serve.

Just before serving, add the remaining sparkling water and mix well. Garnish each serving with several papaya cubes, 1 tablespoon of yogurt, and a mint sprig.

NOTE: Each serving contains approximately 193 calories; 1 gram fat, 2 milligrams cholesterol, and 37 milligrams sodium.

VARIATIONS: In a flash! Make this soup ahead of time and add the sparkling water just before serving.

Spin off: Blend leftover soup with crushed ice for a great drink.

CREAM SOUP, GENERIC BASE

You can cut calories and fat by cooking with nonfat dried milk powder instead of whole milk.

MAKES 4 TO 6 CUPS.

1 cup nonfat dried milk powder

1 tablespoon dried onion flakes

2 tablespoons cornstarch

2 tablespoons chicken bouillon powder

½ teaspoon dried basil, crushed

½ teaspoon dried thyme, crushed

¼ teaspoon black pepper

Mix all the ingredients and store in an air-tight container.

SOUP

2 cups cold water

½ cup main ingredient

To make soup: Add the water to the mix in a large saucepan and stir constantly over medium heat until thick. Add the main ingredient of your choice—mushrooms, for example—and cook until done. If the soup is too thick, add more water and stir thoroughly over medium heat.

Add other seasonings of your choice.

SALADS AND SIDES

SINFUL SEVEN LAYER DIP

This colorful dip is easily taken to bring-a-dish parties and is almost a meal by itself. You need to use a glass pan, preferably a 9 × 13-inch baking dish, so that people can see that they should dip to scoop some of the bottom layer.

1 (14–16-ounce) can pinto beans, mashed (see Note 1)

2 or 3 avocados, mashed with 1 teaspoon vinegar or lemon juice (see Note 2)

1 pint sour cream

1 bunch green onions, diced

1 (16-ounce) bottle of mild or hot picante sauce (salsa)

2 cups grated cheese, such as longhorn Cheddar

2 fresh tomatoes, cubed

Tortilla chips for serving (see Note 3)

Spread the beans on the bottom of a 9 × 13-inch baking dish. Spread the mashed avocados on top. Spread sour cream on top of avocados. Sprinkle on a layer of diced green onions. Spread a layer of picante sauce. Sprinkle a layer of grated cheese. Sprinkle the tomatoes on top as a garnish. Serve with tortilla chips for dipping.

NOTES: (1) Substitute a can of refried beans. (2) Substitute ready-made guacamole dip. (3) For an extra garnish put triangular tortilla chips into the dip—either in a design or at random.

HELOISE CHINESE BEETS

A Heloise classic, this is one of my most requested recipes. My mother brought this home with her from China when my parents lived there in the late 1940s.

6 cups cooked, sliced beets, or 3 (16-ounce) cans sliced beets
1 cup sugar
1 cup vinegar
2 tablespoons cornstarch
24 whole cloves
3 tablespoons ketchup
3 tablespoons cooking oil (optional)
1 teaspoon vanilla extract
Dash of salt

Drain the beets, reserving 1½ cups of the beet liquid. Place the beets in a medium saucepan with the reserved liquid and the remainder of the ingredients. Mix well; then cook for 3 minutes over medium heat, or until the mixture thickens. Let it cool, then store in the refrigerator.

PEA SALAD

This simple add-on or main-dish salad keeps in the fridge so you can make it the day before or the morning of, if you wish.

1 (14-ounce) can baby peas, drained
2 hard-boiled eggs, peeled and chopped
¼ cup grated sharp cheese
2 tablespoons finely chopped onion
Mayonnaise to bind
Salt and pepper to taste

Mix all ingredients together, adding enough mayonnaise to moisten. This salad will keep in the fridge for a couple of days in an airtight container.

HELOISE'S COLE SLAW

This slaw is better if made a bit ahead of time so that all flavors have time to blend together; it's a good party dish.

1 head cabbage (about 2 pounds)
Ice water to cover
2 ounces vegetable oil
1 ounce vinegar, lime juice, or lemon juice (not all three)
½ teaspoon prepared mustard
¼ teaspoon celery salt
1 ounce mayonnaise
Salt and pepper to taste
Dash of paprika

Shred the cabbage and soak in the water for 30 minutes. Meanwhile, mix together the remaining ingredients. Drain the cabbage and mix in the dressing. Refrigerate until ready to use.

COLE SLAW WITH YOGURT

½ cup nonfat yogurt

1 small sweet pickle, minced

2 tablespoons minced green onion

1 teaspoon lemon juice

⅛ teaspoon pepper

1 cup shredded cabbage

⅓ cup shredded carrot

Combine the yogurt, pickle, onion, lemon juice, and pepper in a bowl. Mix in the cabbage and carrot, making sure the yogurt mixture is evenly distributed and all of the cabbage and carrot gets well coated. Chill before serving.

NOTE: You can buy packaged shredded cabbage and carrots at some supermarkets and salad bars.

MOTHER'S POTATO SALAD

My mother's potato salad is still a reader favorite. Note that this is a "to taste" recipe. My mother didn't measure ingredients; she just added them to taste. I like to serve this on a lettuce leaf and make a meal of it but it can also accompany a meal.

Potatoes, boiled in their jackets

Enough mayonnaise to moisten

Bit of vinegar

Celery salt, to taste

Savory salt, to taste

A nice amount of chopped pimiento

Dash of pepper

Some chopped eggs

Several stuffed olives (optional)

Bit of chopped onion (optional)

Dab of prepared mustard

Sprinkle of paprika (for garnish)

Peel and dice the cooked potatoes and place them in a large bowl. Mix the mayonnaise, vinegar, celery salt, savory salt, pimiento, and pepper together and pour over the warm potatoes. Add the eggs, olives (if using), onion (if using), and mustard, and mix all ingredients well. Sprinkle with a bit of paprika before serving for color.

HELOISE'S HOT POTATO SALAD
(1959)
MAKES 4 TO 6 SERVINGS

2 pounds small white potatoes

Boiling water

½ cup diced bacon

¾ cup minced onion

1½ teaspoons flour

4 teaspoons sugar

1 teaspoon salt

¼ teaspoon pepper

¼ to ⅓ cup vinegar

½ cup water

2 teaspoons snipped fresh parsley

1 teaspoon celery seeds

½ cup sliced radishes

Celery leaves

About 1 hour before serving, cook the potatoes in their jackets in a saucepan with 1 inch of boiling water. When tender, peel and cut into ¼-inch slices. (Large potatoes peeled and cut into chunks will do fine.)

In a small skillet, fry the bacon until crisp.

Add ½ cup of the onion and sauté until just tender, not brown.

In separate bowl, mix the flour, sugar, salt, and pepper. Stir in the vinegar and ½ cup water until smooth. Add to the bacon and stir on simmer until slightly thickened.

Pour this hot dressing over the hot potatoes. Add the remaining onion, and the parsley, celery seeds, and radishes. Serve lightly tossed and garnished with the celery leaves.

LEFTOVER MASHED POTATO PATTIES

Good for that last "feed 'em well before they go" hearty brunch you serve your guests before they leave after a fun weekend!

1 cup mashed potatoes
½ cup flour
2 tablespoons baking powder
2 beaten eggs
½ teaspoon salt
Pepper

Combine all of the ingredients, adding pepper to taste. Form into pancake-size patties. Fry in oil on both sides till golden brown.

QUICK POTATOES À LA HELOISE

My mother concocted this one day to use up some juice from a canned ham. Since it requires cooked meat and canned potatoes, you can have all the ingredients ready the day before and put them all together long before any guests arrive.

Juice from a canned ham, or beef or chicken bouillon cubes dissolved in water
Salt and pepper

1 tablespoon cornstarch or flour
1 (14½–16-ounce) can small whole potatoes
1 small onion, very thinly sliced
¼-½ cup grated cheese to cover potatoes
1 stalk celery, thinly sliced (optional)
Leftover bits of meat (optional)

Preheat the oven to 325 degrees F.

To the ham juice, add the salt and pepper to taste and the cornstarch; stir. Slice the potatoes with an egg slicer and layer them into an oven-proof large casserole, alternating with the onion, celery (if using), and meat bits (if using) until the casserole is full. Pour the juice mixture over all and top with cheese. Bake until bubbly and hot.

HELOISE'S PEKING DOUBLE-BAKED STUFFED POTATOES
(1948)

Mother called these Peking potatoes and some folks call them stuffed potatoes. Whatever the name, they're terrific because you can make them ahead of time and freeze or refrigerate until you're ready to reheat them!

Baking potatoes
Milk to moisten
Drop or two yellow food color
Bit of margarine
Salt and ground pepper
Cheese, your choice (see Note)
1 onion (see Note)
Garlic juice or salt, to taste (optional)
Chopped chives (for garnish; optional)
Sliced tops of green onions (for garnish; optional)
Chopped pimientos (for garnish; optional)
Grated Parmesan cheese (for garnish; optional)

In conventional or microwave oven, bake the potatoes until done. Cut each one in half, scoop out the centers with a spoon and place pulp in a mixing bowl. Mash while *dry*. (I used my beater for this, but a potato masher will do.) Add a little milk to moisten, yellow food color, margarine, and salt and pepper to taste.

Grate the cheese and raw onion using coarsest holes of the grater or food processor. Add the cheese, onion, and garlic (if using) to the mashed potatoes and stir well with a fork. Do *not* beat or use the mixer or masher for this. Then fill each baked potato half-shell with this mixture, place in a baking dish, cover with clear plastic wrap so that you can see what's inside, and freeze.

To serve: Thaw and heat until thoroughly warm. After rebaking the potatoes and just before removing them from the oven, sprinkle on any garnish you wish.

If you like garlic, add the optional garlic juice or salt before filling the shell or sprinkle the garlic on top before reheating the potatoes. Chopped chives, green onion tops, pimientos, and grated Parmesan cheese are colorful garnishes for these delicious potatoes.

NOTE: If you bake extra potatoes when you are oven cooking a meal, you can use them for this recipe without heating up an oven just for one cooking project. And baking potatoes in the microwave will just take a few minutes, saving you time and energy.

POTATO LATKES

This recipe is from Mrs. A. H. Gans, San Antonio, and was printed in The Melting Pot, Ethnic Cuisine in Texas.

MAKES 4 TO 6 SERVINGS.

4 large potatoes
1 small onion, grated
4 tablespoons flour
1 teaspoon salt
¼ teaspoon pepper
2 eggs, beaten
½ cup oil or schmaltz
Sour cream or applesauce (for topping)

Peel the potatoes and grate. Drain off any excess liquid. Add the onion, flour, salt, and pepper to the potatoes. Fold in the eggs and mix well. Heat the oil in a heavy skillet over medium-high heat. Drop the batter in by tablespoons and brown each pancake on both sides. Serve hot with sour cream or applesauce.

HELOISE'S CHENTU POTATOES
(1959)

The amounts of the ingredients can be varied, because the potatoes may be different sizes. Naturally, bigger ones take more seasoning.

MAKES 16 SERVINGS.

8 medium baking potatoes
1 very big onion
½ stick margarine
1 pinch of garlic salt (optional)
Salt and pepper
Hot water
1 pound cheese
3 egg whites

Bake the potatoes until well done. Keep the oven on. Slice the potatoes lengthwise, remove the insides with a spoon, and place in a mixing bowl. Save the potato jackets. Grate the biggest onion you can find and add it to the potatoes. Add the margarine, garlic (if using), and salt and pepper to taste.

Mash the potatoes until smooth. I use electric mixer. Do *not* add milk. This will ruin your potatoes. Use *water*. Hot water from the tap should be added until the mixture is very thin but not runny.

Grate the cheese using the medium holes on the grater. Beat the egg whites until they stand but are not stiff. Do not add these two ingredients until potatoes are *nearly cold*. After the potatoes are cool, add the egg whites, folding them in gently. Add the cheese and mix well. Stuff the potato jackets with the mixture. Place in a hot oven and bake at 350 degrees F for 10 minutes.

CHEF'S SECRET SWEET POTATOES

Mother got this recipe from a hotel chef who wanted to stay anonymous so nobody would know he used canned sweet potatoes. These tangy, delicious spuds require no peeling or precooking!

1 (1-pound, 13-ounce) can or 2 (1-pound) cans
    sweet potatoes, liquid reserved
½ cup firmly packed brown sugar
1 lemon, thinly sliced, seeds removed
12 whole cloves
1 cup water

Drain the potatoes, pouring the liquid into a medium saucepan. Add the sugar, lemon, cloves, and water. Boil until a thin syrup is formed.

Cut the potatoes in half and add to the saucepan. Allow to boil for just a few minutes.

HELOISE'S FRIED RICE
(1948)

My mother got this recipe when she lived in China in 1948 while my father was stationed there and it's one of my favorites! Cook the rice the day before or in the morning.

MAKES 4 TO 6 SERVINGS.

1 cup rice, uncooked
2 cups water
4 to 5 slices bacon
3 or 4 eggs
3 or 4 green onions (scallions), chopped, tops
    and all
Leftover bits of pork, beef, or ham, chopped into
    small pieces (optional)
Soy sauce

Cook the rice in the water according to the package directions and cool. It's better if it's had a chance to dry out a bit. Brown the bacon in a heavy skillet over medium-high heat until crisp. Remove the bacon, reserving the drippings, and turn down heat. Slightly beat the eggs and pour them into the hot bacon drippings. Add the rice and onions; mix together. Crumble the bacon and add it with the meat (if using). Mix. Add soy sauce until the rice is as brown as you like it. Stir well and cook on low heat 15 to 20 minutes.

SOUTHWESTERN VEGGIE RICE

This is a microwave oven recipe that goes well with chicken fajitas or barbecue dishes.

MAKES 8 TO 10 SERVINGS.

3 tablespoons salad oil

1 large onion, chopped

2 garlic cloves, minced or pressed

1½ cups rice, uncooked

2 chicken bouillon cubes

2 cups boiling water

⅛ teaspoon cayenne pepper

½ teaspoon salt

10 ounces frozen mixed peas and carrots, thawed

1½ cups peeled, seeded, and chopped tomatoes

Heat the oil in a 3-quart microwave-safe casserole on High for 2 minutes. Add the onion, garlic, and rice. Cook uncovered on High for 3 minutes until the onion is limp and the rice is opaque. Stir once. Dissolve the bouillon cubes in the water and add to the onions along with the cayenne and salt. Cover tightly and cook on High for 4 to 7 minutes or until the liquid begins to boil. Reduce the power to Medium, and cook for 10 to 12 minutes, or until most of the liquid is absorbed and the rice is tender. Let stand covered for 5 minutes. Stir in the peas and carrots and tomatoes.

Rice Cakes

Packaged rice cakes can be the base for quick meals, especially if you are counting calories. If you've previously thought rice cakes were too bland, try them again! Here are some recipes from the Rice Council for cooking with rice cakes. The recipes each make 4 servings. If 2 servings would be a full meal for you, just use half of the ingredients.

MEXICAN RICE CAKES

4 rice cakes

¼ cup refried beans

¼ cup picante sauce (salsa)

⅓ cup shredded Cheddar cheese

¼ cup sliced jalapeño peppers

Preheat the oven to 400 degrees F.

Place the rice cakes on a baking sheet. Spread the refried beans evenly on each rice cake; top with picante sauce, cheese, then with the jalepeños. Bake for 10 minutes. Serve immediately.

Microwave Method: Cook uncovered on High for 1½ minutes; rotate after 1 minute.

PIZZA RICE CAKES

4 rice cakes

⅓ cup pizza sauce

¼ cup *each* sliced ripe olives, diced green pepper, and sliced mushrooms

⅓ cup shredded mozzarella cheese

Preheat the oven to 400 degrees F.

Place rice cakes on baking sheet. Spread the pizza sauce evenly on each rice cake; top with remaining ingredients. Bake for 10 minutes. Serve immediately.

BAKED RICE

This recipe from the Rice Council saves energy—yours and electricity, too. Bake the rice at the same time you're baking a chicken or other meat.

I cup rice, uncooked
2 cups boiling water
I tablespoon butter or margarine
I teaspoon salt

Preheat the oven to 350F.

Combine the ingredients in a greased large casserole. Stir. Cover with a tight-fitting lid or heavy-duty foil. Bake 25 to 30 minutes, or until the rice is tender and the liquid is absorbed.

NOTE: If the oven is hotter than 350F, the rice will take less time to cook.

CONFETTI RICE

Go ahead and play with this recipe by adding other meat bits; chopped green, red, or yellow peppers; and some onions.

MAKES 1 SERVING.

2 slices bacon
I cup cooked rice, cooked in chicken broth
I (4-ounce) can sliced mushrooms, drained
⅓ to ½ cup cooked green peas
2 tablespoons diced pimientos
I to 2 teaspoons chopped chives
Salt and pepper

In a skillet, cook the bacon over medium-high heat until crisp. Drain off the fat. Add the remaining ingredients to the skillet and heat thoroughly.

GREEN CHILIES AND RICE FRITTATA

This is favorite of mine and is so easy and quick.

MAKES 1 SERVING.

About 2 tablespoons finely chopped onions
I tablespoon butter or margarine
2 eggs
2 tablespoons milk
Dash of salt
¼ teaspoon Worcestershire sauce
I drop hot pepper sauce (optional)
½ cup cooked rice
I ounce canned chopped green chilies, undrained
¼ medium tomato, chopped
2 tablespoons grated Cheddar cheese

In a skillet over medium-high heat, cook onions in the butter until tender. Beat the eggs with the milk and seasonings.

Stir in rice, chilies and tomato. Pour into the skillet. Reduce heat to medium-low. Cover; cook until top is almost set, about 5 minutes. Sprinkle the cheese, cover, remove from the heat. Let stand until the cheese melts.

MRS. MARY PROSSER'S PINTO BEANS

From The Melting Pot, Ethnic Cuisine in Texas.

I pound dried pinto beans
⅛ pound salt pork
3 quarts water
I onion, chopped
I teaspoon oil
2 teaspoons salt
I teaspoon baking soda
2 teaspoons chili powder

Wash the beans to remove any rocks and grit. Add the beans and salt pork to the water in a large pot and cook over high heat until tender. Lower the heat and add the remaining ingredients. Simmer gently for 1½ hours.

BOOTLEG BEANS À LA HELOISE
(1950s)

3 strips bacon

1 small onion, chopped

1 (15-ounce) can pork and beans in tomato
    sauce

1 tablespoon packed brown sugar

2 to 3 tablespoons ketchup

Fry the bacon in a medium saucepan over medium-high heat until almost crisp. Add the onion and continue frying until the onion starts to brown. Pour off almost all of the grease. Add the remaining ingredients. Stir to mix well, cover, and simmer until heated through.

VARIATIONS: If you'd like you could mix cooked bacon with the remaining ingredients and place in an ovenproof baking dish. Bake at 300F for 1 hour, or until hot and bubbly.

ELENA'S CABBAGE PIE
(1959)

CRUST

2 cups sifted flour

1 teaspoon onion powder

⅛ teaspoon salt

⅔ cup salted butter

4 to 6 tablespoons ice water

Softened butter (for rolling)

Grilled Vegetables

If you cook the side dishes on the grill at the same time you're grilling the meats, your vegetables get extra flavor and you save energy—mostly yours, because you have no extra pots to clean! Here's how to grill some common vegetables.

- *Bell peppers:* Cut into quarters, remove the seeds, and grill skin-side down for 12 to 15 minutes until tender.

- *Corn-on-the-cob:* Soak the corn in the husks in cold water for 30 minutes. Peel back the husks but do not remove. Do remove the corn silk. Pull the husks back over the cobs and twist closed. Cook on the grill for about 15 minutes, until the husks start to brown or the corn is tender.

- *Eggplant:* Cut off ends and slice into ¼- to ⅓-inch slices. Brush with some oil and cook until brown, 5 minutes per side.

- *Mushrooms:* Cut the stems level with the caps. Brush on olive oil and cook until tender and brown; about 2 minutes per side.

- *Potatoes:* Baking or new potatoes are best for the grill. Slice between ¼-inch and ½ inch thick. Place the slices on foil squares and dot with butter or drops of olive oil. Sprinkle with herbs (try minced garlic, chives, parsley, and rosemary). Seal the foil into packets and cook on the grill until tender.

- *Potato skins:* Bake whole potatoes in a microwave or conventional oven until tender. Cut in half lengthwise and scoop out the centers, leaving about a ¼-inch shell. Cut each shell in half lengthwise again. Brush both sides with butter and sprinkle on salt

continued . . .

FILLING

5 cups chopped cabbage, cut into ½-inch pieces
   (see note)
¼ cup butter
½ teaspoon salt
¼ teaspoon pepper
⅛ teaspoon dried oregano, crushed
1 tablespoon sugar
Pinch monosodium glutamate
¼ cup undiluted consommé
2 hard-boiled eggs, chopped medium fine

Make the crust: Sift the flour, onion powder, and salt together and cut in the butter with two knives or a pastry blender. Add the water a little at a time until the mixture will hold together.

Roll out on a lightly floured board into a rectangle about ¼ inch thick. Spread lightly with a small amount of softened butter, fold and roll again. Repeat two more times. Divide the dough into two parts and chill in the refrigerator until the filling is done.

Make the filling: Melt the butter in a large skillet over medium heat. Add the cabbage and cook about 3 minutes, tossing occasionally. Add the remaining ingredients, except the eggs, and cook until cabbage is cooked but not soft. Remove from the heat and cool.

When the mixture is cool, add the eggs and stir well.

Finish the pie: Preheat the oven to 450F. Roll out one part of the dough and line a pie tin. Fill the crust with the cabbage mixture. Roll out the other half of the dough and place on top, pinching the edges to seal. Cut steam vents in the top crust. Bake for 15 minutes. Reduce the heat to 350F and continue baking until brown,

Grilled Vegetables, continued

and pepper. Cook on the grill until crisp. About 4 minutes per side.

- *Red onions:* Peel and cut the onions in half, brush with oil, and cook until brown, about 10 minutes per side. Brush with more oil while the onions cook.

- *Zucchini:* Trim the ends and slice lengthwise into ½-inch-thick strips. Brush on oil and cook until brown and tender, 4 minutes per side.

about 30 minutes. Serve hot or cold. This can be kept in the refrigerator.

NOTE: Use a small cabbage and be sure to omit the hard core.

HELOISE'S HUMDINGER OF A SALAD

I cook like my mother did—without exact measurements—so please tolerate my "to taste" ingredient amounts. This salad tastes better if it can stay in the fridge for a few hours, but it can be eaten immediately if you're in a hurry. It sure does stretch a can of tuna, chicken, or turkey.

3 celery stalks
10 to 12 black olives
1 can tuna, chicken, or turkey, 6 ounces or larger
1 hard-cooked egg, diced
1 (2–4-ounce) small can sliced mushrooms (see
   Note)
Salt and pepper, to taste
Dashes of celery salt, to taste
1 to 2 tablespoons prepared hot mustard, or to
   taste

Mayonnaise or salad dressing to bind
Leaf lettuce, washed and separated
Sweet paprika (for garnish)

Slice the celery stalks very thin and on the diagonal instead of chopping them and place in a medium bowl. Slice the black olives, using any amount you like, and add to the bowl. Mix in the tuna, egg, mushrooms, and seasonings. Add the mustard and enough mayonnaise to bind the ingredients. Mix together.

Arrange the lettuce on a serving platter and mound the salad on top. Sprinkle with a dash of paprika for extra color.

NOTE: Use the cheapest brand of sliced mushrooms for this recipe.

HEARTS OF PALM AND ARTICHOKE SALAD

Slightly rewritten from Good Food, Good Friends. *This is a good salad to take to a potluck dinner. Halve the ingredients to make salad for two.*

MAKES 4 SERVINGS.

1 (14-ounce) can hearts of palm, drained and sliced
1 (14-ounce) can artichoke hearts, drained and cut in half
1 medium head radicchio, torn
1 bunch watercress, torn
¼ cup creamy buttermilk salad dressing
Pepper

In a large bowl, gently toss together the hearts of palm, artichoke hearts, radicchio, and watercress. Pour dressing over all, tossing gently to coat. Season with pepper to taste. Cover and chill until serving time.

10-MINUTE BEEF SALAD WITH CURRY DRESSING

National Livestock and Meat Board offers this zesty salad. Feel free to adjust the ingredients to have more of whatever you like; for example, if you like to fill up on lettuce, just use half of the meat and all of the other ingredients.

MAKES 2 SERVINGS.

6 ounces thinly sliced cooked beef, cut into ½-inch strips
2 cups torn leaf lettuce
¼ cup shredded carrot
2 tablespoons raisins
2 tablespoons *each* reduced-calorie mayonnaise and plain low-fat yogurt
½ teaspoon curry powder, or to taste
1 teaspoon lemon juice

Place the beef, lettuce, and carrot in medium bowl. Toss lightly; sprinkle with the raisins. Cover tightly and chill. Combine the mayonnaise, yogurt, curry powder, and lemon juice. Cover tightly and chill. To serve, pour the dressing over salad and toss.

NOTE: Ingredients may be halved to make 1 serving.

SALAD BAR VEGETABLE MEDLEY

This recipe is adapted from the FDA's booklet Shopping for Food and Making Meals in Minutes Using the Dietary Guidelines.

MAKES 2 SERVINGS.

1 tablespoon water
½ pound or 2½ cups mixed salad bar vegetables (see Note)

¼ teaspoon dried marjoram, crushed

I tablespoon reduced-calorie French or Italian
    salad dressing

Heat the water in a frying pan over medium-high heat. Add the vegetables; sprinkle with marjoram. Cover and cook 5 minutes or until the vegetables are crisp-tender. Drain, if necessary. Toss the vegetables with the salad dressing.

NOTE: The vegetable pieces should be fairly similar in size. Try broccoli and cauliflower florets, carrot slices, green pepper strips, sliced celery, mushrooms, and zucchini slices.

WALDORF SALAD
(1959)

½ cup diced pineapple

2 cups diced apples

I cup chopped celery

½ cup broken nut meats

½ cup diced oranges

½ cup diced bananas

½ cup diced marshmallows

5 cherries, diced

¼ cup whipped cream

Mix the ingredients together and chill until served.

GELATIN
(1960)

The olive topping gives this dish a professional look and adds red and green to contrast with the purple.

I (3-ounce) package grape gelatin

¾ hot (not boiling) water

I cup grape juice

1½ cups coarsely chopped purple cabbage

½ apple, grated

I carrot, grated

I cup sliced stuffed green olives

Lettuce leaves (for serving; optional)

Mayonnaise (for serving; optional)

Mix the gelatin in the water and stir until dissolved. Add the juice; set aside to cool. Mix the cabbage, apple, and carrot with the cooled gelatin mixture and place in the refrigerator to set. (You can use a mold if desired.)

When set, top with the olives. Serve as is or place on a lettuce leaf and top the gelatin with a drop of mayonnaise.

HELOISE'S STUFFED AVOCADO
WITH CRABMEAT
(1960)

MAKES 1 SERVING.

½ avocado

3½ ounces crabmeat

I tablespoon Romano cheese

I tablespoon bread crumbs plus extra for topping

I teaspoon chopped fresh parsley

I pat of butter

Chopped green onion (tops included)

Preheat the oven to 325F.

Remove the seed from the avocado. Cut a thin slice from the bottom of the avocado so that it will sit firmly on the plate. Mix the crabmeat, cheese, bread crumbs, and parsley. Fill the hollow of the avocado with the mixture, piling it into a rounded peak but keeping it within the outside shell. Sprinkle with some extra bread crumbs and top with the butter. Place on a sheet of foil and bake for 10 to 15 minutes. Sprinkle with chopped green onion before serving.

PASTA-VEGGIE SCRAMBLE

This is for egg lovers on cholesterol-lowering diets.
MAKES 2 SERVINGS.

½ cup halved thin zucchini slices (about 2 ounces)

⅔ cup chopped green onions with tops

⅓ cup julienned red bell pepper

2 whole eggs (or egg substitute)

4 egg whites

2 tablespoons grated Parmesan cheese

1 teaspoon garlic salt

¾ teaspoon Italian seasoning

⅛ teaspoon cayenne pepper

4 ounces fettucini or linguine, cooked and drained

4 cherry tomato halves

Spray 10-inch omelet pan or skillet with nonstick cooking spray. Add the zucchini, onions, and bell pepper. Cover and cook over medium heat until the zucchini is crisp-tender, about 3 minutes.

Meanwhile, beat together the eggs, egg whites, cheese, and seasonings. Pour over the vegetables. Add the fettucini and tomatoes. As the egg mixture begins to set, gently draw an inverted pancake turner completely across the bottom and sides of pan. Continue until eggs are thickened but still moist. Do not stir constantly. Serve immediately.

HELOISE'S ORIENTAL NOODLES

Here's a way to use up leftover fresh and cooked vegetables and leftover cooked noodles. Thin pasta noodles (spaghetti, linguine, or vermicelli) work best, but go ahead and use flat noodles if that's what you have in the fridge. I've listed some ideas, but use whatever you have on hand. All amounts are "guesses," it's whatever you have on hand.

Cooking oil

½ cup cooked leftover vegetables

½ cup cooked leftover meats, cut into bits

½ cup celery, bok choy, or Chinese cabbage

½ cup chopped green, red, and/or yellow bell pepper

2 green onions, chopped

½ to 1 cup leftover noodles

Up to 1 cup bouillon or broth

Soy sauce

Sesame oil (optional; see Note)

Heat some cooking oil in a large frying pan over medium-high heat; add the cooked vegetables and meats and cook until brown; add the fresh vegetables and stir-fry until crisp-tender. Add the noodles along with more oil, if necessary. Heat through, adding bouillon if the mixture is too dry for your taste. Stir in the soy sauce and sesame oil to taste and serve.

NOTE: Sesame oil comes in hot and mild forms. If this is your first experience with hot sesame oil, use just a drop to begin with—it really is hot!

VEGETABLE PANCAKES

MAKES 4 SERVINGS

½ cup finely shredded carrot or zucchini

½ cup finely shredded potato

I tablespoon minced onion

⅛ teaspoon salt

Dash of pepper

I teaspoon *each* butter and olive oil

2 tablespoons plain yogurt

¼ teaspoon grated lemon peel

Combine the carrot, potato, and onion; pour off any liquid. Stir in the salt and pepper. Heat the butter and oil in large nonstick frying pan over medium heat. Spoon 4 equal portions of vegetable mixture into frying pan and flatten with a spatula. Cook 4 to 6 minutes, turning once. Meanwhile combine the yogurt and lemon peel. Garnish the pancakes with the lemon-yogurt mixture before serving.

HELOISE'S DUSTY RICOTTA
(1979)

Substitute cocoa or carob powder for the espresso to make a wonderful triple-chocolate treat.

I pound ricotta cheese

½ cup confectioners' sugar or sugar substitute to equal ½ cup

2 tablespoons rum or brandy or ¼ tablespoon rum or brandy extract

I or 2 tablespoons instant espresso (see Note)

Espresso powder or cocoa (for garnish)

Mix the ricotta, sugar, rum, and espresso in a medium bowl. Whisk until thoroughly blended. Put into small serving bowls or pretty sherbert glasses. Chill well. Dust with dash of instant espresso and cocoa just before serving.

NOTE: Substitute 1 tablespoon cocoa or carob powder. Or use the cocoa or carob in addition to the espresso.

SANDWICH FIXINGS

SAUSAGE BISCUITS

This is an easy recipe for breakfast biscuits or for serving at a brunch or cocktail party.

I can refrigerated biscuits

I pound lean ground pork or lean pork sausage

½ cup commercial barbecue sauce

¼–½ cup Cheddar cheese, shredded

Preheat the oven to 375F.

Press one biscuit into each cup of a muffin tin, forming a cup with the biscuit.

In a skillet over medium-high heat, brown the pork; drain. Stir in the barbecue sauce. Spoon the mixture into the biscuit cups. Top with some shredded cheese and bake for about 20 minutes.

HELOISE'S PIMIENTO CHEESE SPREAD
(1960s)

Another of Mother's favorites, this recipe uses the cheapest kind of boxed soft cheese.

I pound boxed soft cheese

I cup mayonnaise

½ cup super-finely chopped sweet or sour pickles

4 ounces cheapest pimientos on your shelf

OPTIONAL INGREDIENTS

Juice from 1 jar of pimientos

4 ounces chopped stuffed salad olives

Chopped onions, to taste

Grate the cheese coarsely using the large openings of a grater or food processor. Now, the fun part: Layer the ingredients as if you were making lasagna. Place a large piece of wax paper or plastic wrap on the counter. Put down a layer of grated cheese, then mayonnaise, pimientos, and a handful of pickles. Use a spatula to fold it over and over, starting from the bottom. Repeat the process, folding again and again until you have used all of the ingredients.

I divide this up into two batches. Put the mixture in jars, seal well, and pop into the fridge.

VARIATIONS: If you want a thinner gooey spread, add the juice from one jar of pimientos and mix well. Vary the spread by adding chopped salad olives and/or onions.

PINEAPPLE CREAM CHEESE SPREAD

The reader who sent me this recipe says it's better than an ice cream cone "if you want to lose yourself." Delicious!

8 ounces softened cream cheese

1/3 cup undrained crushed pineapple

1 teaspoon vanilla

Dash of salt

Sugar (to taste; optional)

Sourdough or French bread

Mix all ingredients thoroughly and spread on fresh bread.

RAISIN TAPENADE

This recipe comes from the California Raisin Advisory Board.

MAKES 4 SERVINGS.

FILLING

1/2 cup pitted ripe olives

1/4 cup golden raisins

1 garlic clove

2 tablespoons chopped fresh basil or 2 teaspoons dried basil, crushed

1 tablespoon drained capers

2 tablespoons olive oil

1 teaspoon red wine vinegar

1/4 teaspoon pepper

SANDWICHES

4 large crusty sandwich rolls

4 lettuce leaves

1/2 pound sliced Jarlsberg or Swiss cheese

2 small tomatoes, sliced

1/2 cup drained roasted red peppers

Make the filling: In a food processor, blend the olives, raisins, garlic, basil, and capers. Add the olive oil, vinegar, and pepper; pulse to combine.

Make the sandwiches: For each sandwich, halve a roll horizontally; spread each cut side with 1 tablespoon filling. Layer the bottom half with one lettuce leaf, 2 ounces of the cheese, 1/2 of a sliced tomato, and 2 tablespoons of the red pepper. Cover with the top of roll, cut side down.

HELOISE'S OLIVE NUT SANDWICH SPREAD

One of my favorites, this makes a great lunch when spread on a lettuce leaf (to save bread calories), and it can be a delicious make-ahead spread for party finger sandwiches.

6 ounces softened regular or low-fat cream
 cheese
½ cup regular or low-fat mayonnaise
½ cup chopped pecans
1 cup sliced salad olives (the jar will say "salad
 olives" and is filled with bits & pieces of
 olives and pimientos)
2 tablespoons juice from the olive jar
Dash of pepper (But no salt!)

Mix all the ingredients well. This spread will keep in the fridge for weeks.

HOT OPEN-FACED TOMATO AND CHEESE SANDWICH

This recipe came from a disabled reader who, because she lost the use of her left side, had to learn new and easier ways of one-handed cooking. It's a nice spur-of-the-moment lunch for when your neighbor drops by.

Tomatoes, sliced
Zucchini, sliced
Onion, sliced
1 pound ground beef
English muffins or bread slices
Slices mozzarella or Cheddar cheese

Mix the tomatoes, zucchini, onion, and ground beef, then cook mixture in microwave until beef is done, about 15 minutes on medium. If you can't slice the veggies, you can easi-ly "chop" them with a pizza cutter or some types of potato mashers after they are cooked.

Divide the mixture into single portions. Reserve one portion for the day's meal and pour the remainder into zipper-type freezer bags to freeze for other meals.

To serve: Toast the English muffins; pour the thawed tomato mixture on a muffin half, top with a cheese slice, and microwave until the cheese melts.

10-MINUTE ONION 'N' PEPPER BEEF STEAK SANDWICHES

Here's a recipe from the National Livestock and Meat Board.

MAKES 2 SERVINGS.

2 teaspoons vegetable oil
1 small onion, cut into ¼-inch wedges
1 medium jalapeño pepper, cut crosswise into
 rings (see Note)
1 small garlic clove, minced
8 ounces beef round tip steaks, cut ⅛ to ¼ inch
 thick
⅛ teaspoon salt (optional)
2 Kaiser rolls, split
¼ cup chopped tomato

Heat the oil in large nonstick frying pan over medium-high heat. Add onion, jalapeño pepper, and garlic; stir-fry 3 to 4 minutes or until lightly browned. Remove from the frying pan; reserve. Add the beef to the frying pan and cook over medium-high heat 1 to 2 minutes, turning once. Do not overcook. Season with salt (if using). Place equal amounts of beef on the bottom half of each Kaiser roll. Top with equal amounts of the reserved onion mixture and then the tomato.

NOTES: (1) To reduce the heat, remove the membranes and seeds. (2) Be sure to wear rubber gloves when handling jalapeño peppers, and don't rub your eyes!

MAIN DISHES

HELOISE'S ORIGINAL ITALIAN SPAGHETTI SAUCE
(1960s)

This makes a large pot of sauce. You can freeze the leftovers, if there are any left from this favorite!

¼ cup olive oil

½ cup butter

I cup finely chopped onions

I pound ground beef

4 strips bacon, finely chopped

4 garlic cloves, chopped fine

3 tablespoons finely chopped fresh parsley

I bay leaf, crumbled

I tablespoon salt

Black pepper

I teaspoon crushed red pepper

2 ounces red wine

2 (15-ounce) cans of whole tomatoes or tomato sauce

I (4-ounce) can of tomato paste

I cup water

I carrot, finely chopped

Heat olive oil over low heat in a pot large enough to hold all the ingredients. Add the but-ter and simmer until melted. Add the onions and sauté until lightly browned. Add the ground beef and bacon; sauté until browned, stirring occasionally. Add the garlic, parsley, bay leaf, salt, black pepper to taste, and red pepper. Cook over low heat for 10 minutes. Add the wine, cover and steam for a few minutes more.

Add the tomatoes, tomato paste, and water. Bring the mixture to a boil and add the carrot.

Quick Pasta Sauce

To get a traditional Italian tomato-based sauce that tastes like it's been cooking for hours, my mother put all the raw ingredients for the sauce—tomatoes, onions, seasonings, etc.—into the blender and pureed them on high for about I minute, until thoroughly mixed. The mixture becomes white and foamy; the sauce will settle down after a few minutes of cooking. She added a dollop (an unmeasured amount, perhaps a couple of tablespoons) of bacon grease for added flavor, but you can leave out the bacon grease if you are watching your fat intake. Put the sauce in a large saucepan and simmer over medium heat for 50 to 60 minutes.

Mother sometimes added little meatballs to this sauce. She made them one-bite size and placed them on a foil-lined cookie sheet and put them under the broiler to sear in the juices. The meatballs have to be turned frequently so that they brown evenly. Mother added the meatballs and the meat juices to the sauce near the end of the cooking time, letting them simmer in the sauce for about 5 minutes. She then covered the pot, removed from the heat, let it stand about 10 minutes before serving over noodles.

Cover and cook over very low heat for 1 hour, stirring occasionally. Serve over your favorite cooked pasta.

PEPPERONI MUSHROOM "PIZZA"
MAKES 4 SERVINGS.

1½ cups cooked rice
1 egg, beaten
½ cup (2 ounces) shredded Cheddar cheese
½ to ¾ cup tomato sauce
¼ teaspoon dried basil, crushed
¼ teaspoon garlic powder
¼ teaspoon ground oregano
1 tablespoon grated Parmesan cheese
1 cup shredded mozzarella cheese, divided
2 ounces pepperoni, thinly sliced
½ cup sliced mushrooms
1 tablespoon snipped fresh parsley

Combine the rice, egg, and Cheddar cheese. Press into buttered (or sprayed) microwave-safe 12-inch pizza pan or 10-inch pie pan. Cook uncovered on Medium for 2 minutes. Combine the tomato sauce, basil, garlic powder, and oregano. Spread over the rice crust. Sprinkle with Parmesan cheese. Layer ½ cup mozzarella cheese, pepperoni, and mushrooms. Top with the remaining mozzarella cheese and the parsley. Cook uncovered on Medium for 7 minutes. Let stand 5 minutes.

To make in a conventional oven, bake the rice crust at 400F for 4 minutes. Layer on the toppings as directed and bake for 8 to 10 minutes.

5-MINUTE FRANKFURTER PIZZAS
Here's an easy recipe from the National Livestock and Meat Board.
MAKES 1 TO 2 SERVINGS.

1 English muffin, split and toasted
1 tablespoon pizza sauce
2 beef frankfurters
1 slice mozzarella cheese (1 ounce), cut in half
⅛ teaspoon dried oregano, crushed

Place muffin halves on a paper plate. Spread the cut sides with equal amounts of pizza sauce. Carefully make 5 crosswise cuts into the frankfurters, spacing them ¾ inch apart and cutting almost through. Arrange 1 frankfurter in a circle on each muffin half; cover with a half slice of cheese. Sprinkle with the oregano. Microwave on High for 1 minute.

HOLIDAY HAM
MAKES ABOUT 20 SERVINGS.

Heloise's Cornbread Dressing (see opposite)
1 (12- to 14-pound) fully cooked ham
¼ cup firmly packed brown sugar
1 (6-ounce) can pineapple juice
1 tablespoon Dijon mustard
1 fresh pineapple, peeled and cut into ½-inch slices

Preheat the oven to 325F. Prepare the cornbread dressing. Remove the bone from the ham. Spoon the dressing into the ham bone cavity and reshape the ham around the dressing, tying a string around the dressing and another string around the ham to hold the shape. Set aside any remaining dressing.

Put the ham on rack in roasting pan, fat side up. Make diagonal diamond slashes ½ inch deep in the fat side of ham. Place an ovenproof meat thermometer in the middle of the lean meat and cook for 18 to 20 minutes per pound, or until the thermometer reads 140F.

About 1 hour before the ham has finished cooking, prepare the glaze. In a small saucepan, combine the brown sugar, pineapple juice, and mustard. Stir over medium heat until the sugar dissolves. This makes enough glaze to baste the ham two or three times while it is still cooking.

Put the remaining cornbread dressing in a greased casserole. Bake with the ham 30 to 45 minutes.

Remove the cooked ham from the oven and let sit for 20 minutes before carving. Meanwhile, place the pineapple slices on a cookie sheet and broil until light brown. Place around the carved ham on the serving platter.

HELOISE'S CORNBREAD DRESSING

This dressing may be used with any turkey recipe, either cooked separately or as a stuffing.

MAKES 10 SERVINGS.

1 cup broth (see Note 1)
6 to 8 slices stale bread, torn into pieces
1½ cups packed crumbled cornbread
1 stick butter or margarine
½ cup chopped celery
½ cup to 1 cup chopped onion
2 eggs, beaten
¾ teaspoon salt
½ teaspoon pepper
1 teaspoon poultry seasoning
1 tablespoon dried sage, crumbled

In a large bowl, pour the bouillon over the bread pieces and cornbread.

Heat the butter in a small skillet over medium-high heat. Sauté the celery and onions until tender. Add them to the bread mixture along with the eggs, salt, pepper, and seasonings. Mix well.

NOTES: (1) Make broth by cooking the giblets and neck in water with seasons, use canned chicken broth, or chicken bouillon. (2) To cook separately, place the dressing in a buttered casserole and bake at 350F for about 30 minutes.

CARIBBEAN BARBECUED PORK

MAKES 6 SERVINGS.

1½ pounds boneless pork steaks
1 large red onion, thinly sliced
¾ cup lime juice
1 teaspoon salt
¼ to ½ teaspoon cayenne pepper

Trim excess fat from the pork. Place the pork and onions in a nonmetal baking dish. Combine the lime juice, salt, and cayenne; pour over the pork; cover and refrigerate for several hours.

Preheat the grill.

Remove the steaks from the marinade, brushing off the onion. Cook over hot coals, 3 inches from the heat, for 8 to 10 minutes, or until thoroughly cooked, turning once. Heat the onions and marinade to boiling and serve with the cooked pork.

HAM PIE WITH CHEESE BISCUIT TOP

MAKES 4 TO 6 SERVINGS.

3 tablespoons minced onion

4 tablespoons chopped green bell pepper

4 tablespoons butter or margarine

6 tablespoons flour

1 (10½-ounce) can condensed chicken soup

1⅓ cups milk

1⅓ cups diced ham

1 tablespoon lemon juice

Cheese Biscuit Top (see below)

Preheat the oven to 450F. Butter a casserole dish.

Place the onion and bell pepper in a medium or large saucepan. Soften in the butter over medium heat; do not brown. Add the flour and blend until frothy. Then stir in the soup and milk; cook until thick and smooth. Add the ham and lemon juice, remove from heat, and pour into prepared dish.

Arrange the cheese biscuits on top of the ham mixture to make a crust. Bake for 20 minutes, or until the biscuits are golden brown.

CHEESE BISCUIT TOP

1½ cups ready-made biscuit mix

½ cup grated cheese

6 tablespoons milk

Combine the biscuit mix, cheese, and milk to make a medium soft dough. Place the dough on a floured board and roll into a thick layer. Cut the biscuits with biscuit or doughnut cutter.

BARBECUED APRICOT-GLAZED HAM

1 (16-ounce) can unpeeled apricot halves

¼ cup packed brown sugar

4 teaspoons vinegar

2 teaspoons prepared mustard

½ teaspoon ground cinnamon

1 (5- to 7-pound) fully cooked boneless ham

Whole cloves

Watercress (for garnish)

Preheat the grill.

Drain apricots, saving ¼ cup syrup. Set 6 apricot halves aside for garnish. In a blender, blend the remaining apricot halves, the saved syrup, brown sugar, vinegar, mustard, and cinnamon. Score the ham with shallow cuts in a diamond pattern and stud with cloves. Insert a meat thermometer near center of ham.

Arrange the coals around a drip pan; test for medium heat. Place the ham on the rack over the pan, cover and grill for 1¼ hours. Brush the ham with the glaze and grill about 15 minutes more or until the meat thermometer registers 140F. Before serving, brush the ham with the glaze again; garnish with apricot halves and watercress.

HELOISE'S BARBECUED SPARE RIBS
(1960)

1 tablespoon fat

¼ cup chopped onions

½ cup water

2 tablespoons vinegar

1 tablespoon Worcestershire sauce

¼ cup lemon juice

Salt and pepper to taste

2 tablespoons packed brown sugar

1 teaspoon chili powder

¼ teaspoon paprika

Preheat the oven to 400F.

Heat the fat in a medium saucepan over medium heat. Sauté the onion until tender. Add the remaining ingredients, except the ribs, and simmer for 20 minutes.

Cut between the ribs and place in large pan. Cover lightly with aluminum foil and bake for 15 minutes. Reduce the heat to 350F, remove the foil, and pour the sauce over the meat. Bake 1 hour. Baste with the sauce frequently.

SLOPPY JOES

This recipe is for either ground beef or ground turkey. If using ground turkey, you can give the dish a beefier taste by adding beef bouillon to the turkey while it's browning in the pan.

MAKES 4 TO 6 SERVINGS

1 pound ground beef or turkey

1 tablespoon vegetable oil

1 (14-ounce) can vegetable soup, undiluted (see Note)

Ketchup, barbecue sauce, or steak sauce, to taste

Optional ingredients, to taste: chopped onion, chopped green bell pepper, minced garlic, Worcestershire sauce, soy sauce, 1 tablespoon or so of dried onion soup mix

French bread or hamburger buns

In a large frying pan, brown the meat in oil over medium-high heat; stir in the remaining ingredients, except the bread. Reduce the heat and simmer 10 to 20 minutes until the flavors

have blended and the sauce has thickened. Serve on French bread.

VARIATION: Try this spooned over a hot baked potato.

NOTE: Substitute dried mixed vegetables and bouillon for the soup.

MRS. M'S BEEF BURGUNDY STEW

This is an easy party dish that can be served with or without snails as an appetizer and accompanied by a simple green salad with a vinegar-and-oil dressing, crusty French bread for dipping in the wine sauce, and a robust Burgundy wine. Dessert can be cheeses and fruit—European style.

½ pound salt pork, sliced about ¼ inch thick and cut 1-inch squares

2 dozen small white onions (see Note 1)

4 pounds lean chuck beef, cut into 2-inch cubes

1 tablespoon flour (optional)

Pepper

1 to 2 garlic cloves, crushed

1 piece orange peel, fresh or canned

1 bouquet garni made up of 2 small bay leaves, 1 thyme sprig, 1 small sliver of nutmeg or mace, 4 parsley spigs, and ½ teaspoon marjoram or oregano (see Note 2)

½ (24-ounce) bottle dry red table wine, heated (see Note 3)

1 cup tiny button mushrooms, browned in butter (see Note 4)

Chopped fresh parsley (for garnish)

Bread slices, browned in butter or plain croutons (for garnish)

Put the salt pork bits into a heavy pan or Dutch oven, preferably cast iron. Brown over medium-high heat until crisp; remove the pork bits to drain on paper towels. Leave the melted fat in the pan. Sauté the onions in the fat until golden brown. Remove the onions and reserve. In the same fat, brown the meat pieces. Stir frequently with a wooden spoon so that the meat browns well on all sides. (Be sure to use a pan that's big enough to prevent crowding and to allow the proper browning of the meat.)

Return the salt pork bits to the pan, sprinkle them with the flour (if desired). Sprinkle the meat liberally with pepper, or to taste. Add the garlic, orange peel, and bouquet garni. Pour the wine over the meat; it should just barely cover the meat pieces. Cover tightly and cook over very low heat on the top of the stove or in a slow oven (150F to 300F.) for about 3 hours. If too much liquid evaporates, you can add a bit more hot wine or stock, but do not add too much or the result will be too soupy. About 15 or 20 minutes before serving, add the browned onions and place the mushrooms into the center.

At serving time, sprinkle the top generously with the parsley and add the browned bread.

NOTES: (1) Use well-drained canned onions if fresh aren't available. (2) Tie up in cheesecloth or use a tea ball. (3) Use a robust-flavored wine. (4) May substitute canned browned-in-butter mushrooms, undrained. (5) If you choose the oven method, cook the stew in a heavy casserole, that you can bring to the table for easier serving.

MRS. YU'S BEEF AND PEA PODS
(1950s)

This scrumptious recipe came from a friend of my mother's, Mrs. Byung P. Yu, and it's a favorite of Oriental food fans.

MAKE 4 TO 6 SERVINGS.

2 tablespoons dry cooking sherry
2 teaspoons sugar
4 to 6 tablespoons soy sauce
2 tablespoons cornstarch
¼ to ½ teaspoon powdered ginger
2 pounds round beef roast, sliced thin
5 tablespoons salad oil
2 (10-ounce) packages frozen pea pods or
    Italian green beans
Water
Cooked rice

Combine the sherry, sugar, soy sauce, cornstarch, and ginger in a medium bowl. Add the meat and toss to coat with the sauce. Let stand for at least 30 minutes. Heat 2 tablespoons of the oil in an electric skillet, blazer, or chafing dish. Add the pea pods and cook just until hot and still crisp, about 2 minutes. Spread in a single layer on a platter.

Drain the marinade. Add the remaining oil to the skillet and sauté the beef. Turn to cook evenly, about 5 minutes. Combine the peas and the beef and warm. Place in a serving dish.

Add a small amount of water to the skillet with the drippings. Heat and pour over the beef and pea pods. Serve with hot rice.

HELOISE'S PEKING ROAST
(1948)

Use any cut of beef roast, even the least expensive, and the result will be fork-tender meat with a delicious gravy.

MARINADE:

1 (3- to 5-pound) beef roast
Garlic slivers (optional)
Onion slivers (optional)
1 cup vinegar
Water to cover

TO COOK:

Oil
2 cups strong black coffee
2 cups water
Salt and pepper

If desired, use a sharp knife to cut slits into the roast and insert slivers of garlic and onion to taste. Put the meat into a bowl and slowly pour the vinegar over it. Add enough water to cover the meat. Cover with plastic wrap and refrigerate 24 to 48 hours, basting the meat occasionally with the vinegar mixture.

Before cooking, drain the meat. Heat enough oil to cover the bottom of the pot over medium-high heat in a heavy pot—cast-iron Dutch oven is best. Add the meat and brown until very dark on all sides. Pour the coffee over the meat and add 2 cups of water. Cover. Reduce the heat and cook slowly for approximately 6 hours. You may need to add more water at some point, so check it once in a while. Add only a small amount of water at a time. About 20 minutes before serving, add salt and pepper to taste.

MEAT AND POTATOES IN A PAN

This works best in an iron skillet. The more well done you cook the meat, the less tender it will be; but the tenderizer will help prevent toughness and shrinkage.

MAKES 1 SERVING.

1 (1½- to 1-inch-thick) steak or chop (pork, lamb, or veal)
Meat tenderizer
Vegetable spray
1 baking potato, sliced thin (see Note)

Sprinkle the meat with the meat tenderizer, according to the package directions. Allow the tenderizer to work as directed (may take up to 15 minutes).

Meanwhile, spray a large iron skillet with vegetable spray and heat over medium-high heat. Place the potato slices around the perimeter of the pan, leaving room for the meat. Let the potatoes begin to brown while the pan is heating.

When the potatoes begin to cook, add the meat. Cook 4 to 6 minutes, or until the meat juices bubble up and show on the surface of the steak. Turn to pan-broil the other side, spraying the pan with vegetable spray, if needed. For rare, turn as soon as the juices show; for well-done, turn when the juices appear cooked (grayish and opaque). Serve immediately with the potatoes.

NOTE: You can zap the potatoes in the microwave to heat them up before adding them to the pan; this will speed up the browning process.

TEXAS BARBECUED BRISKET

Brisket is a favorite party barbecue meat in Texas and traditionally it's mesquite smoked.

MAKES 15 TO 18 SERVINGS.

1½ to 2 pounds mesquite wood chunks

Water to cover

¾ cup water

¼ cup Worcestershire sauce

2 tablespoons cider vinegar

2 tablespoons cooking oil

2 garlic cloves, minced

½ teaspoon instant beef bouillon granules

½ teaspoon dry mustard

½ teaspoon chili powder

¼ teaspoon ground red pepper

1 (5- to 6-pound) beef brisket

½ cup ketchup plus more as needed

¼ to ½ cup packed brown sugar

2 tablespoons butter or margarine

Soak the wood chunks in enough water to cover for at least 1 hour before cooking.

In a small bowl, mix the ¾ cup water, Worcestershire sauce, vinegar, oil, garlic, bouillon granules, mustard, chili powder, and red pepper to make the cooking sauce. Set aside ½ cup of this sauce.

Preheat the coals in a covered grill. Drain the wood chunks. Arrange the coals around a drip pan and test for slow heat. Place about one-quarter of the wood chunks on top of the coals. Place brisket fat-side up on the rack over the drip pan and brush with the sauce; cover the grill. Cook for 2½ to 3 hours or until tender, brushing with the cooking sauce every 30 minutes and adding more dampened wood chunks as necessary.

Meanwhile, make the table sauce. In a small saucepan, combine the reserved ½ cup of cooking sauce with the ketchup, brown sugar, and butter. Heat the mixture through and add more ketchup as needed to achieve the desire consistency. To serve, slice the brisket across the grain and pour on the table sauce.

DAVID'S MESQUITE SMOKED TEXAS BRISKET

My husband, David, gets raves for his South Texas Dilly Digs Brisket. Please read the whole "recipe" thoroughly before you start.

1 beef brisket, 8 to 12 pounds, 2 to 4 inches thick (*not* corned beef)

10 to 20 cloves of garlic, peeled

¼ cup of all-purpose Greek seasoning (contains 13 spices)

To prepare the beef:

1. Make deep cuts into the brisket with a paring knife.
2. Place cloves all the way into the cuts.
3. Liberally sprinkle brisket with Greek seasoning.

To cook the meat, you'll need:

an outdoor smoker

charcoal

mesquite wood, soaked in water until thoroughly wet

To cook the brisket:

1. Pour a pile of charcoal in the smoker. Light and let coals turn gray/hot.
2. Place mesquite wood over the charcoal to smother the coals, so they smoke a lot, but there's no flame.
3. Put brisket—fat-side down—on grill

away from the fire/charcoal/wood. Never place meat directly over the fire.

4. Smoke the brisket for 2 hours. Do not turn the meat.

5. Take meat out and immediately wrap brisket tightly 2 times in extra heavy aluminum foil. Put in oven on a cookie sheet at 250F for 2 hours.

6. Remove from oven and let sit (still wrapped in foil) 30 minutes to one hour before serving. This allows the meat to "firm up" and the "juice" to be absorbed.

To serve:

Cut meat across the grain into thin slices.

Serve the way we do here in San Antonio with pinto beans, potato salad, cole slaw, crisp sliced white/yellow onions, sliced dill "hamburger" pickles and old-fashioned white bread.

Put on some country music and you are all set!

SLOW-AND-EASY BARBECUED BRISKET

This recipe has a long cooking time but a very short preparation time so it's nice for parties because the chef gets more time to visit with the guests as it cooks.

MAKES 30 SERVINGS.

1 teaspoon salt

1 teaspoon pepper

1 teaspoon paprika

2 (9-pound) pieces beef brisket (not corned beef)

2 cups ketchup

1 tablespoon sweet relish

1 tablespoon margarine

½ teaspoon liquid smoke

1 tablespoon Worcestershire sauce

Preheat the grill.

Mix the salt, pepper, and paprika together and sprinkle on the brisket. Cook slowly over low heat coals for 4 to 6 hours, adding a few briquettes every hour or so to maintain the temperature.

To make the sauce, bring the remaining ingredients to a boil in a small saucepan. Add salt, pepper, and paprika to taste. Serve over the sliced brisket.

NOTE: While meat cooks on the grill, you can grill vegetables, too (see p. 215).

SANTA FE SHORT RIBS

MAKES 6 SERVINGS.

Unseasoned meat tenderizer

6 pounds lean beef short ribs, cracked

1½ cups dry red wine

3 tablespoons olive or salad oil

1 small onion, chopped

2 garlic cloves, minced or pressed

1 teaspoon salt

½ teaspoon pepper

1 bay leaf

½ cup red chile salsa

Apply the tenderizer to ribs according to the package directions; then place the ribs in a large heavy-duty plastic bag. In a bowl, stir together the wine, oil, onion, garlic, salt, pepper, bay leaf, and salsa. Pour over the meat in the bag; seal the bag securely and shake. Put the bag in a shallow baking pan and refrigerate for at least 4 hours or until the next day, turning occasionally.

Preheat the grill. Drain the ribs (save the

marinade for basting) and place on a lightly greased grill 4 to 6 inches above a solid bed of medium coals. Cover the grill and cook, turning and basting occasionally with the marinade, until the meat near the bone is done to your liking, 30 to 40 minutes for medium-rare; cut to test.

15-MINUTE FRENCH HERB PATTIES

The National Livestock and Meat Board developed this recipe.

MAKES 2 SERVINGS.

½ pound lean ground beef
¼ teaspoon pepper
¼ teaspoon dried rosemary, crushed
¼ teaspoon dried thyme, crushed
1 tablespoon butter
2 small onions, sliced and separated into rings
1 tablespoon Dijon-style mustard
Salt (optional)

Shape the ground beef into 2 patties, each ½ inch thick. Combine the pepper, rosemary, and thyme; gently press into both sides of the patties. Melt the butter in a small nonstick skillet over medium heat. Add the onions; cook 6 to 8 minutes, or until transparent and tender. Stir in the mustard. Divide the onions evenly between 2 plates; keep warm.

Place the patties in the same pan; cook 4 minutes. Pour off the drippings. Turn the patties and continue cooking 4 minutes, or to the desired doneness. Season with salt (if using). Place the patties over the onions.

NOTE: You can freeze one patty, uncooked, to have for another meal. Freeze the uncooked

onions, too, if desired. Thaw the patty in the refrigerator and cook as directed. Cook the onions straight from the freezer; do not thaw.

15-MINUTE MINI BEEF LOAVES WITH YOGURT DILL SAUCE

Here's a recipe from the National Livestock and Meat Board. Serve this with assorted veggies.

MAKES 2 SERVINGS.

BEEF LOAVES

8 ounces lean ground beef
2 tablespoons dry bread crumbs
½ small onion, minced
1 tablespoon milk
1 egg, slightly beaten
1½ teaspoons prepared horseradish
¼ teaspoon dried dill, crushed
¼ teaspoon salt
Paprika (for garnish)

YOGURT DILL SAUCE

¼ cup chopped seeded cucumber
¼ cup plain yogurt
1 teaspoon minced onion
⅛ teaspoon dried dill, crushed
⅛ teaspoon garlic powder
Salt (to taste; optional)

Combine the beef loaf ingredients in a medium bowl, mixing lightly but thoroughly. Divide the mixture into 2 equal portions; shape into small loaves. Arrange the loaves in microwave-safe dish. Sprinkle each loaf lightly with paprika. Cover with wax paper; microwave on High 4 to 4½ minutes, rotating the dish one half turn after 2 minutes. Let stand 5 minutes.

Meanwhile, combine all the ingredients for the sauce in a small bowl. Spoon over the mini loaves before serving.

SWISS STEAK

If you want baked potatoes with this dish, be sure to put them in the oven about 30 minutes before you put the meat in.

1 round steak
Flour for dusting
2 tablespoons oil or fat
1 medium onion, sliced
Dried herbs of your choice
1 to 2 carrots, sliced (optional)
½ cup water, bouillon, or wine
Salt and pepper

Preheat the oven to 350F.

Lightly dust both sides of the steak with flour. Heat the oil in a large ovenproof skillet over medium heat. Add the steak and brown on both sides. Top with the onion, herbs, and carrots. Add the water and sprinkle on salt and pepper to taste. Cover and put the pan in the oven to braise for about 30 minutes, or until the meat is tender.

VARIATIONS: For a different flavor, top the meat with an envelope of dried French onion soup mix or vegetable soup mix.

ROAST BEEF HASH

This recipe is from the National Livestock and Meat Board.

MAKES 4 SERVINGS.

1 tablespoon oil
1 cup chopped green, red, or yellow bell pepper
½ cup chopped onion
1 pound cooked beef, cut into ½-inch pieces
½ pound all-purpose potatoes, peeled and cut into ½-inch pieces
½ teaspoon black pepper
½ cup prepared brown gravy

Heat the oil in a large frying pan over medium-high heat. Sauté the bell pepper and onion for 3 minutes. Add the beef and potatoes; stir in the black pepper and gravy. Cook over medium heat 12 to 15 minutes until potatoes are cooked, stirring occasionally and pressing down with a spatula near the end of cooking time to brown the potatoes.

VARIATIONS: Make this with deli roast beef and leftover boiled or baked potatoes. If you don't have any canned gravy on hand, you could add ketchup or barbecue sauce for a different flavor. This is really a recipe that you can play with!

ITALIAN STIR FRY

Here's a quick recipe from the National Livestock and Meat Board.

MAKES 2 SERVINGS.

8 ounces beef round tip steaks, cut ⅛ to ¼ inch thick
1½ teaspoons olive oil
1 garlic clove, crushed

Salt and pepper
1 small zucchini, thinly sliced
½ cup cherry tomato halves
2 tablespoons bottled Italian salad dressing
1 cup hot cooked spaghetti
Grated Parmesan cheese

Cut the beef crosswise into 1-inch-wide strips; cut each strip crosswise in half.

Heat the oil in a large nonstick skillet over medium-high heat; cook and stir in the garlic 1 minute. Add the beef and stir-fry 1 to 1½ minutes. Season with salt and pepper to taste. Remove the meat with slotted spoon; keep warm.

Add the zucchini to same skillet; stir-fry 2 to 3 minutes or until crisp-tender. Return the beef to the skillet with the tomatoes and dressing; heat through.

Serve the beef mixture over hot pasta; sprinkle with Parmesan cheese.

❀ **HELOISE HINT:** Too often new cooks are afraid to adjust recipes. Playing with a recipe often yields something better than the original, so feel free to be creative with any recipe in this or any other book! You are cooking for *you*!

10-MINUTE BEEF TENDERLOIN STEAKS WITH BLUE CHEESE TOPPING

A tasty recipe from the National Livestock and Meat Board.

MAKES 2 SERVINGS.

1 tablespoon cream cheese
2 teaspoons crumbled blue cheese
2 teaspoons plain yogurt

1 teaspoon minced onion
Dash of white pepper
2 (4-ounce) beef tenderloin steaks, cut 1 inch thick
1 garlic clove, halved
¼ teaspoon salt, divided
1 teaspoon chopped fresh Italian parsley (for garnish)

Preheat the broiler.

Thoroughly combine the cream cheese, blue cheese, yogurt, onion, and pepper; reserve.

Rub each side of the steaks with the garlic. Place the steaks on the rack in a broiler pan so the surface of the meat is 2 inches from heat source. Broil the first side 5 to 6 minutes. Season with half of the salt. Turn; broil the second side for 3 to 4 minutes. Season with the remaining salt. Top each steak with half of the reserved cheese mixture. Broil an additional 1 to 2 minutes. Garnish with the parsley and serve immediately.

NOTE: Salting meat lightly prevents loss of juices. You can always add more salt after the meat is cooked.

VARIATION: If cheese is not your type of steak topping, you can use any other sauce.

10-MINUTE ANTIPASTO-ON-A-STICK

A pretty dish from the National Lifestock and Meat Board.

MAKES 1 SERVING.

2 slices (about 3 ounces) cooked lean beef, cut into 1-inch strips
1 cup torn romaine lettuce
3 ripe olives pitted

2 small cherry tomatoes

2 (¾-inch) cubes provolone cheese

2 marinated artichoke heart quarters, drained

2 tablespoons Italian dressing

Roll up the beef strips (pinwheel fashion). Arrange on the lettuce along with the olives, tomatoes, cheese, and artichoke hearts. Pour the dressing over the top. Refrigerate several hours or overnight.

VARIATIONS: For an easy bag lunch, string the meat and veggies on two bamboo skewers. Place the lettuce and dressing in separate carry-along containers. Transport in an insulated bag. To serve, remove the antipasto from the skewers and arrange on top of lettuce. Pour the dressing over the top.

CREOLE ROAST

2 to 2 ½ pounds beef tenderloin

I tablespoon Worcestershire sauce

I tablespoon snipped fresh parsley or ½ to I
    teaspoon dried parsley flakes, crumbled

½ teaspoon salt

½ teaspoon black pepper

¼ teaspoon celery seeds

⅛ to ¼ teaspoon ground red pepper

⅛ teaspoon onion powder

⅛ teaspoon garlic powder

⅛ teaspoon ground cloves

Trim off any excess fat and rub the meat with Worcestershire sauce. Combine the remaining ingredients and sprinkle the mixture over the meat and rub it in. Cover the roast and let stand at room temperature for 1 hour or overnight in the refrigerator.

Norwegian Meatballs

Here's a different way to make meatballs. Season the ground meat with ginger and nutmeg to taste. Form into small meatballs and brown well in butter or margarine. Remove the meatballs from the pan and make a flour gravy from the drippings. Return the meatballs to gravy and simmer until done. Serve with mashed or boiled potatoes. To make the gravy even more delicious, add a bit of sour cream to the gravy at the very last minute before serving.

Preheat a covered grill. Arrange the hot coals around a drip pan; test for medium heat above the pan. Insert a meat thermometer near the center of the roast and place it on a grill rack over the drip pan but not over the coals. Cover the grill and cook until the thermometer registers 140F for rare (about 45 minutes), 160F for medium (about 55 minutes), or 170F for well done (about 1 hour).

SPICY SWEDISH MEATBALLS

2 cups bread crumbs

½ cup milk

8 ounces ground beef

8 ounces spicy sausage meat

½ teaspoon onion powder

½ teaspoon Tabasco sauce

I teaspoon garlic salt

I teaspoon soy sauce

½ teaspoon monosodium glutamate (optional)

I (5-ounce) can sliced water chestnuts, chopped

Jelly or Wine Sauce (see p. 236)

Preheat the oven to 350F.

Mix the bread crumbs and milk in a large bowl. Add the remaining ingredients and mix well. Roll the meat mix into 1½-inch balls and place on an ungreased cookie sheet, close together (they shrink when cooked so you can really crowd them). Bake about 30 minutes, until well done and golden brown. Remove from the oven and drain on paper towels. Transfer to a serving dish and pour the Jelly or Wine Sauce over the meatballs.

JELLY SAUCE

1 cup grape jelly
1 cup cocktail sauce (shrimp sauce)

Combine the grape jelly and cocktail sauce in a medium saucepan. Cook over a low heat, stirring constantly, until bubbling. Remove from the heat.

WINE SAUCE

1 cup consommé
1 cup Burgundy or Port wine
2 tablespoons cornstarch
½ cup water

Combine the consommé and wine in a medium saucepan and bring to a boil over medium heat. Mix the cornstarch and water and gradually add to the hot liquid. Cook until clear and thickened. Immediately remove from the heat.

Marinade for Beef, Veal, or Lamb

Here's a marinade that will tenderize cheaper cuts of meat. Use before grilling, roasting, or broiling.

1 cup dry white or red wine
¼ cup cider vinegar
1 cup salad oil
2 teaspoons salt
½ teaspoon pepper
⅛ teaspoon dried tarragon, crushed
1 bay leaf, crushed
½ teaspoon dried thyme or marjoram, crushed
1 large garlic clove, finely chopped

Combine all ingredients in medium bowl.

To use, marinate the meat for about 4 hours, turning it from time to time. For safety, marinate the meat in the refrigerator for most of the time. But about 1 hour before cooking, let the meat stand at room temperature (either in or out of the marinade).

For added flavor include a sliced onion, a large sliced carrot, and/or some celery ribs.

BARBECUED MEAT LOAF

8 ounces ground lean beef
8 ounces ground lean veal
8 ounces lean pork
4 ounces diced Swiss cheese
1 medium onion, chopped
2 eggs, beaten
2 tablespoons chopped sun-dried tomatoes, packed in oil, drained if desired

⅔ cup dried bread crumbs

1 cup milk

¾ teaspoon salt

Pepper, to taste

Preheat the grill to medium.

In a large bowl, mix the meats, cheese, onion, eggs, and tomatoes. Stir in the bread crumbs, milk, salt, and pepper to taste. Avoid handling the meat too much or the meat loaf will be heavy. Spoon the mixture into a 9 × 5-inch loaf pan and place the pan inside another larger loaf pan for insulation. Put the pan on the rack 4 to 6 inches from the coals. Cover the grill and open the vents. Cook for 90 minutes or until a meat thermometer inserted in center registers 160F. You may have to add more briquettes after 45 minutes to maintain a constant temperature. Carefully remove the pan from the grill to a carving board. Cover with foil and let stand for about 10 minutes, this is very important. Place on a warm platter and serve immediately. Or allow to cool completely and store wrapped in foil in the refrigerator until ready to serve.

HELOISE'S TAMALE PIE
(1959)

This recipe can be made a day ahead and stored in the refrigerator. It also freezes well. This is a family favorite that I updated by adding chopped green chiles to the cornmeal mix.

2 large onions, chopped

2 pounds ground beef

2 14- to 16-ounce canned tomato sauce

2 teaspoons chili powder

Salt and pepper

2 (4-ounce) cans sliced black olives, drained

3 cups yellow cornmeal

Preheat the oven to 350F.

In a large frying pan over medium-high heat, sauté the onions and beef. Add the tomato sauce and chili powder and season with salt and pepper to taste. Add half of the olives. Simmer for about 30 minutes.

Cook the cornmeal as directed on the package. Spread one half of it on bottom of large flat greased pan with sides. Spread the meat mixture over this and top with the remaining cornmeal. Dot the top with the remaining olives. Bake 30 minutes.

GRANDMOTHER'S OLD-FASHIONED TURKEY DRESSING
(1960)

1 can (10-12 count) biscuits, baked

1 recipe baked yellow cornbread (1 box)

1 large loaf bread, sliced and toasted

1½ cups chopped onions

2 cups chopped celery

1 cup chopped celery tops

1 tablespoon dried sage, crumbled

1 tablespoon poultry seasoning

1 cup water

1 cup turkey drippings

Salt and pepper to taste

1 egg, beaten

Preheat the oven to 300F.

Break all breads into small pieces and put into a big pot. Set aside.

Turkey and Sauce Variations

MAYONNAISE METHOD

Rub the turkey thoroughly all over with mayonnaise before cooking. Make an aluminum foil tent over it and cook at 325F for the calculated time. Remove the aluminum during the last 20 or 30 minutes, and the turkey will roast to a gorgeous golden brown. It will be not only delicious looking but also especially moist and tender.

PEANUT AND PAPRIKA METHOD

Baste the turkey with peanut oil and then rub all over with paprika. Place it in a roasting pan and make an aluminum foil tent as described above. Cook at 300F to 325F, removing the foil at the end to brown. The turkey will be exceptionally succulent.

PEACH SAUCE

If you don't like cranberries, here's a substitute for the holidays.

  1 can peaches
  Water, as needed
  ½ cup sugar
  ½ teaspoon ground nutmeg
  1 (3-ounce) box lemon gelatin

Drain the peaches, saving the syrup in a measuring cup. Puree the peaches in the blender and set aside. Add enough water to the syrup to make 1 cup of liquid. Pour the liquid into a medium saucepan and add the sugar and nutmeg. Bring the mixture to a boil, and boil for about 1 minute.

Empty the gelatin powder into a large bowl and stir in the hot liquid until the gelatin dissolves. Add the pureed peaches, and pour into a mold. Chill until set.

NOTE: If you are limiting your sugar intake, substitute diet gelatin and peaches packed in light syrup or omit the sugar.

Put all the remaining ingredients, except the egg, in a saucepan. Bring to a boil and boil 10 minutes, or until the celery and onions are tender. Pour over the broken bread and toss. Add the egg and mix lightly again. Spread the dressing on a greased cookie sheet with sides and bake for 30 minutes.

ROASTED TURKEY

  1 (12-pound) turkey
  5 tablespoons dry mustard
  2 tablespoons Worcestershire sauce
  2 tablespoons olive oil
  1 tablespoon vinegar
  Salt and pepper
  2 celery stalks
  1 bunch parsley, rinsed
  1 onion, halved
  2 slices bacon
  1 stick butter, cut into small pieces
  1 piece cheesecloth soaked in olive oil
  2 cups rich chicken stock

The day before cooking, rub the turkey inside and out with a paste made from the mustard, Worcestershire sauce, oil, vinegar, and salt and pepper to taste. (For a larger turkey, proportionally increase the amounts given.)

Preheat the oven to 300F.

Just before roasting, place the celery, parsley, and onion inside the bird. Lay the bacon across the breast. Insert small pieces of butter between the drumsticks and the body. Place the cheesecloth over the turkey; then put the bird in a roaster and add the stock and roast for 20 minutes per pound. Baste several times while roasting. Remove the cheesecloth during the last 30 minutes to brown.

NOTE: Roast 18 minutes per pound for a 15- to 18-pound turkey and 15 minutes per pound for an 18- to 20-pound bird.

EASY-DOES-IT CHICKEN

Buy whole chicken legs (drumstick and thigh) and bake several so that you can have leftovers for another meal or two. Save energy by putting a couple of sweet or baking potatoes in to bake with the chicken.
MAKES 4 TO 6 SERVINGS.

4 to 6 chicken legs (drumstick and thigh)
Barbecue sauce (see Note)

Preheat the oven to 375F.

Cover a pizza or jelly roll pan (looks like a cookie sheet with sides) foil. Spray the foil with nonstick vegetable spray. Put a rack on the foil, if you have one, to let the fat drain away. Place the chicken pieces, skin side up, on the rack or in the pan. Drizzle with barbecue sauce to taste.

Bake 45 to 60 minutes, depending on the size of the chicken.

NOTES: (1) Feel free to use whatever sauce you'd like (for example, Jamaican jerk sauce) or use a favorite spice blend instead (for example, Cajun, Mexican, or Italian). (2) You can make this dish with frozen chicken, just be sure to allow for extra baking time.

TURKEY LOCO

This method cooks the turkey on the grill, leaving the rest of the stove free for other dishes.
MAKES 12 TO 16 SERVINGS.

1 (10- to 12-pound) turkey
About 4 limes, cut into halves
About 4 teaspoons dried oregano, crushed
Salt and pepper

Remove the neck and giblets from the turkey and discard any large lumps of fat. With poultry shears or a knife, split the turkey lengthwise along one side of backbone. Pull the turkey open; place, skin side up, on a flat surface and press firmly, cracking the breastbone slightly until bird lies reasonably flat. Rinse and pat dry.

Preheat the grill.

Before cooking, squeeze 1 or 2 lime halves and rub the juice over turkey; sprinkle with the oregano and add salt and pepper to taste.

Barbecue the turkey by indirect heat, placing it, skin side up on a grill above a drip pan, not the coals. Cover and cook for 1½ to 2 hours, until a meat thermometer inserted in the thickest part of the thigh (not touching bone) registers 185F, or until the meat near the thigh bone is no longer pink (cut to test). Every 30 minutes, squeeze 1 or 2 lime halves and rub the juice over the turkey.

To serve, place the turkey on a platter. Cut off the legs and wings and slice the meat from the breast and thighs.

TASTY TURKEY TETRAZZINI

MAKES 6 SERVINGS.

⅔ cup mayonnaise

⅓ cup flour

½ teaspoon celery salt

Dash of pepper

2 cups milk

7 ounces spaghetti, broken into thirds, cooked and drained

2 cups cooked turkey, chopped

3 ounces Parmesan cheese, grated

1 (4-ounce) can mushrooms, drained

2 tablespoons chopped pimiento

2 cups fresh bread cubes

3 tablespoons margarine, melted

Preheat the oven to 350F.

Mix the mayonnaise, flour, celery salt, and pepper in a medium saucepan over low heat. Gradually add the milk, stirring constantly, over low heat until thickened. Add the spaghetti, turkey, 2 ounces of the cheese, the mushrooms, and pimientos; mix gently.

Pour the mixture into a 2-quart casserole dish. Toss the bread cubes with margarine and the remaining cheese, then sprinkle over the casserole for a topping. Bake for 30 minutes, or until lightly browned.

Batter-Fried Chicken

My mother had a terrific method for batter-fried chicken that works well with pork chops, fish, and veggies, too. She soaked the chicken pieces in salted water for a few hours, then she shook off the excess water and immediately rolled the chicken in unseasoned flour. It's less messy if you put the flour in a plastic bag and then shake the pieces in it. Then Mother placed the pieces on wax paper and put them in the refrigerator for at least 1 hour and sometimes overnight.

When Mother fried the chicken, she put a few drops of yellow food color in the oil. The result was golden-fried chicken (or chops), just like the restaurants make. If you have no food color, you can put some paprika into the flour and you will still get a pretty color.

If you are concerned about the fat from deep-fat frying, try this method. Deep-fry the larger pieces quickly until they are browned but not cooked. Then put the pieces on a rack in a baking pan and put into a 325F to 350F oven to finish cooking. Then deep-fry the smaller pieces until brown and place them in the oven, too, to finish cooking, usually about 20 minutes, depending on the size of the pieces. This will give you crispy chicken, but most of the fat will have dripped off into the bottom of the pan.

BAKED PINEAPPLE CHICKEN

Serve this chicken over rice and add a salad.

1 chicken, cut up, or equivalent in parts

Paprika

Garlic powder

Onion powder

2 to 3 tablespoons (low-sodium) soy sauce

1 (20-ounce) can chunk pineapple, juice packed

Preheat the oven to 350F. Spray a casserole dish with nonstick spray.

Place the chicken pieces in the casserole. Sprinkle with paprika, garlic powder, and onion powder to taste. Add the soy sauce to the juice from the pineapple and mix; then baste the chicken with the mixture. Pour the pineapple over the top. Bake for about 1 hour.

BAKED ITALIAN CHICKEN
Serve with a salad on the side.

1 chicken, cut-up or equivalent in parts
1 (8-ounce) bottle nonfat (or regular) Italian
   salad dressing
1 onion, sliced
4 medium potatoes, sliced

Preheat the oven to 350F. Spray a casserole dish with nonstick spray.

Place the chicken in the casserole and cover with the Italian dressing. Top with the onion and potatoes. Bake for about 1 hour, or until done.

BAKED BARBECUE CHICKEN
If you don't like barbecue sauce, sprinkle the chicken with your favorite seasoning salt instead and bake as directed. Bake potatoes (white or sweet) at the same time and add a salad to make a meal.

1 chicken, cut up, or equivalent in parts
1 bottle barbecue sauce

Preheat the oven from 375F to 400F. Spray a foil-covered cookie sheet with nonstick spray.

Place the chicken on the cookie sheet. Drizzle with your favorite barbecue sauce. Bake for about 1 hour.

GRILLED CHICKEN FAJITAS
MAKES 4 TO 6 SERVINGS

2 pounds boneless chicken breasts
Fajita seasoning to taste (see Note)
1 (8-ounce) bottle Italian dressing
½ cup white wine
1 onion, thinly sliced and sautéed until soft
12 flour tortillas, warmed

Sprinkle the chicken breasts thoroughly with the fajita seasoning. In a large bowl, combine the dressing, wine, and chicken. Marinate overnight.

Preheat the grill.

Remove the chicken from the marinade and grill over hot coals for 5 to 8 minutes per side, depending on thickness; do not overcook. Baste with the marinade. Slice the chicken into lengthwise strips and place on a hot platter. Scatter the onion on top. Serve with the tortillas.

NOTE: Packets of fajita seasoning are available at most supermarkets.

CHICKEN FAJITAS
Serve Southwestern Veggie Rice (p. 213) as a side dish.
MAKES 6 SERVINGS.

1 pound skinned and boned chicken breast
Juice from 1 lime
1 garlic clove, minced
¼ teaspoon dried oregano, crushed
¼ teaspoon chili powder
¼ teaspoon ground cumin
1 small green bell pepper, sliced
1 small onion, sliced

6 (8-inch) flour tortillas
1 medium tomato, chopped
Sliced lettuce

Cut the chicken into thin strips. Place in a 3-quart microwave-safe casserole. Combine the lime juice with the garlic, oregano, chili powder, and cumin; then pour the mixture over the chicken. Allow to stand 20 minutes at room temperature or cover and allow to marinate overnight in the refrigerator. Add bell pepper and onion to the chicken. Microwave on High, uncovered, for 6 to 10 minutes or until the chicken is tender, stirring once. Heat the tortillas by layering them between paper towels; microwave on High 45 to 60 seconds, or until heated.

To serve, place some chicken mixture on a tortilla and top it with tomato and lettuce.

Fold up the tortilla and enjoy!

CHICKEN TAMALE

This may be made ahead and refrigerated until you are ready to put it in the oven.

MAKES 6 TO 8 SERVINGS.

3 tamales cut into bite-size pieces
1 cup canned tomatoes diced well drained
1 (14-ounce) can whole-kernel corn
1 cup chopped or sliced ripe olives
½ cup chili sauce
1 tablespoon olive or salad oil
1 tablespoon Worcestershire sauce
2 cups chunked cooked chicken (equal to
    1 large stewing hen)
1 cup grated cheese

Preheat the oven to 350F.

Mix all the ingredients except the cheese, and place in a large casserole dish. Sprinkle the cheese on top and bake for 1 hour.

SAN ANTONIO TACO CASSEROLE

This is a good way to use leftovers!

Grease (or spray with nonstick spray) a casserole dish, put a bit of salsa on the bottom, then add torn-up tacos or taco chips, and layer with leftover taco meat, and/or beans, cheese, peppers, and more salsa. Bake until hot, then cover with sour cream and olives and chopped lettuce before serving. This is one of those "non-recipes" we all keep in our heads—there's no set amount or even set number of ingredients, only what you have on hand as leftovers or in cans in the cupboard.

PAN-BROILED BONELESS CHICKEN BREASTS

Serve these as is or place in a hamburger bun for a hot sandwich.

garlic cloves, thinly sliced

skinless, boneless chicken breasts

cup Italian-flavored or plain dried bread crumbs (optional)

1 teaspoon olive oil or margarine, as necessary

Spray a frying pan with nonstick spray and heat over medium-high heat. Add the garlic slices to the bottom of the pan. Roll the chicken in the bread crumbs (if using) and place in the pan on top of the garlic. Spray the top of the chicken with nonstick spray to keep it moist. Cook until brown; turn and cook the other side. If the chicken looks too dry, add a teaspoon of olive oil. Sauté just until done; if overcooked, the chicken will be dry and stringy.

VARIATION: Top with a bottled sauce of your choice.

CHICKEN ITALIANO

Serve with yellow squash and a tossed green salad with creamy Italian dressing and garlic toast to make an easy company meal.

MAKES 6 SERVINGS.

12 chicken pieces, 2½ to 3 pounds total

1 (1⅜-ounce) envelope onion soup mix

1 (10¾-ounce) can condensed cream of mushroom soup

½ cup dry sherry or chicken broth

1 cup drained canned tomatoes

3 cups hot cooked rice

Preheat the oven to 375F.

Place the chicken pieces in a buttered or sprayed 9 × 13-inch baking dish. Sprinkle with the soup mix. Blend mushroom soup and sherry. Pour over the chicken. Add the tomatoes. Cover with foil and bake for 1 hour, or until the chicken is tender. Serve over the rice.

ONE-POT CHICKEN, POTATOES, AND PEAS

MAKES 2 SERVINGS.

1 teaspoon oil

1 cup chopped onion

1 cup diced potato, cut into ½-inch cubes

1 garlic clove, minced

1 teaspoon chopped fresh parsley plus extra (for garnish)

2 tablespoons chopped celery

1 cup water

1 bay leaf

⅛ teaspoon dried thyme, crushed

Pepper, to taste

1 cup canned peas

2 (3-ounce) skinless, boneless chicken breasts, halved

Heat the oil in a heavy large skillet over medium heat and add the onion and potato; cook, stirring, until they begin to brown. Then add the remaining ingredients, except the chicken and peas. Stir and bring to a boil. Place the chicken in the sauce, reduce the heat to simmer. Cover and cook for about 12 minutes. Then add the peas and continue to simmer until the liquid is reduced, about 5 minutes or so. To serve, place one chicken breast on each plate and spoon the sauce over the top. Garnish with parsley.

HELOISE'S OVEN-FRIED CHICKEN
(1960)

This is an easy recipe that produces greaseless, crispy, delicious chicken. Best of all, the pan needs no washing! I generally use thighs for this recipe.

1 single serving package of nonsugared corn flakes
1 package chicken
¼ cup milk or about ½ cup
Salt and pepper

Preheat the oven to 350F.

Crush the corn flakes. Dip the chicken in the milk and then in the corn flakes. Place in an aluminum foil–lined pan, sprinkle well with salt and pepper to taste. Bake 1 hour.

NOTE: Use any other herbs or spices you'd like.

HELOISE'S SESAME BAKED CHICKEN
(1960)

1 cup flour
1 teaspoon baking powder
2 teaspoons salt
¼ teaspoon pepper
¼ cup chopped pecans
2 tablespoons sesame seeds
¼ teaspoon paprika
1 egg, beaten
½ cup milk
1 frying chicken, cut up
1 stick butter

Preheat the oven to 400F.

Combine the flour, baking powder, salt, pepper, pecans, sesame seeds, and paprika. In another bowl combine the egg and milk and mix well. Dip the chicken into the egg mixture then into the flour mixture.

Melt butter in the oven-safe dish that chicken is to be baked in. Coat the chicken on both sides with this butter. Place the chicken in the dish, skin side down. Bake for 30 minutes. Then turn the pieces skin side up and bake for 30 minutes more.

GARLIC SHRIMP
MAKES 6 SERVINGS.

¾ cup (1½ sticks) butter or margarine
10 large garlic cloves, minced
2 tablespoons lemon juice
1 teaspoon cayenne pepper
36 large shrimp, uncooked, peeled, and deveined, tails left intact
Rosemary sprigs

Preheat the grill.

Melt the butter in a small saucepan and simmer for 1 minute; add the garlic, lemon juice, and cayenne pepper and mix. Soak skewers in water. Thread the shrimp on wooden skewers and brush with seasoned butter. Grill the shrimp for about 3 minutes, or until pink. Turn and grill for about 1 minute, or until opaque, basting with the butter mixture. Serve on a bed of fresh rosemary sprigs.

SHRIMP DIJON

Serve this over rice.

2 pounds shrimp, fresh or frozen, or
   1 ½ pounds peeled and deveined
¼ cup butter or margarine
1 medium onion, thinly sliced
¼ cup flour
1 ½ cups milk
2 tablespoons Dijon mustard
¼ teaspoon ground nutmeg
½ teaspoon salt
⅛ teaspoon pepper
1 (6-ounce) package cream cheese, softened

Clean the shrimp if necessary and let thaw on paper towels. Heat the butter in a large frying pan over medium heat. Add the shrimp and onion and sauté for 3 minutes; do not brown. Sprinkle a little flour into the pan, thinning the "mixture" a little bit with the milk, to avoid lumping. Add the mustard, nutmeg, salt, and pepper and cook for 3 to 5 minutes. Stir in the cream cheese until blended, warm through, but *do not boil*.

HELOISE'S NEW ORLEANS SHRIMP CREOLE
(1959)

Serve this over steamed rice.
MAKES 6 TO 8 SERVINGS.

3 pounds shrimp
1 tablespoon butter
1 large onion, chopped
2 ½ cups diced tomatoes
Salt and pepper to taste
2 bay leaves
4 stalks celery, chopped

1 garlic clove, minced
1 thyme sprig, minced
Dash of cayenne pepper

Boil the shrimp until cooked (they should look pink) and remove the shells.

In a large saucepan, melt the butter over medium-high heat. Add onion and brown. Add the tomatoes and their juice; cook 5 minutes, stirring thoroughly.

Add the remaining ingredients, except the shrimp, cook 10 minutes; then add the shrimp. Cook another 10 minutes.

HELOISE'S HAWAIIAN CURRIED SHRIMP
(1959)

Served with rice and condiments.

6 tablespoons butter
1 medium onion, finely chopped
2 teaspoons finely chopped fresh ginger
6 tablespoons flour
1 ½ teaspoons salt
2 to 3 teaspoons curry powder
2 cups milk
1 cup coconut milk
3 cups cooked shrimp

Melt the butter in a large saucepan over medium heat. Add onion and ginger, and cook slowly until transparent. Add the flour, salt, and curry powder and blend thoroughly. Add the milk and coconut milk, stirring constantly. Cook slowly until thick and smooth. Add the shrimp and heat through.

GRILLED SWORDFISH WITH MUSTARD SAUCE

8 (½-pound) swordfish steaks, about 1 inch
    thick
¼ cup lemon juice
5 tablespoons Dijon mustard
¼ cup (½ stick) butter or margarine
Mustard Sauce (see below)

Preheat the grill.

Rinse the fish and pat dry. Brush with lemon juice and spread the mustard on one side. Dot with butter. Grill the fish, mustard side up, for about 20 minutes, or until just opaque; do not turn. Arrange the fish on plates, mustard-side down. Spoon on the mustard sauce and serve.

MUSTARD SAUCE

6 tablespoons butter or margarine, melted
3 tablespoons lemon juice
2 tablespoons Dijon mustard

Heat the butter, lemon juice, and mustard in a small saucepan and mix thoroughly.

HELOISE'S SALMONETTES
(1960s)

This is a Heloise classic. Be sure to watch the salmonettes closely when you deep-fry them; they brown fast! They also disappear fast!

1 (14-ounce) can salmon or tuna
½ cup flour
1 egg, slightly beaten
Pepper (optional)
1 heaping teaspoon baking powder
¼ cup liquid from the salmon or tuna
Oil for deep frying

Drain the salmon, reserving ¼ cup of the liquid. Put the salmon into a mixing bowl, breaking it apart well with a fork. Add the flour and egg; then add pepper to taste (if using), and mix well. Add the baking powder to the reserved liquid and beat well with a fork until foamy. Pour this back into the fish mixture and stir until blended.

Use 2 teaspoons to form the patties. Scoop out the mixture with one of spoons and use the other to push the mixture into a deep-fryer that is half full of hot oil. After they are brown (watch 'em, it doesn't take long!), drain on a paper towel and serve.

HUEVOS CASAS
MAKES 1 SERVING.

1 egg
1 teaspoon water
1 tablespoon shredded low-moisture, part-skim
    mozzarella cheese
1 (7-inch) corn tortilla
2 tablespoons prepared salsa or taco sauce
Shredded lettuce

Spray a 7- to 8-inch omelet pan or skillet with a light coating of vegetable spray. Heat the pan over medium-high heat until just hot enough to sizzle a drop of water. Break and slip the egg into the pan. Immediately reduce the heat to low. Cook until the edges turn white, about 1 minute. Add the water. Cover the pan tightly to hold in the steam. Cook 3 minutes. Sprinkle with the cheese; re-cover the pan, and continue cooking to the desired doneness. Place on the tortilla on a plate and put the egg on top. Top with salsa and lettuce. For ease in eating, lap the edges of the tortilla over the egg to form a roll.

VARIATION: To cook in the microwave, omit the water. Put the egg into a lightly greased pie plate, saucer, or custard cup. Gently prick the yolk with the tip of knife or a wooden pick. (*Note:* If you don't prick the yolk it may explode!) Cover with plastic wrap. Cook on 50 percent power just until the egg is almost the desired doneness, 2 to 2½ minutes. Sprinkle with the cheese. Let stand, covered, until the desired doneness, 30 to 60 seconds. Meanwhile, put the tortilla on a microwave-safe serving plate. Cook on High until warm, 15 to 30 seconds. Top with the egg, salsa, and lettuce.

EGGS PARKHURST

MAKES 1 TO 2 SERVINGS.

½ cup (4 ounces) low-fat cottage cheese
¼ teaspoon Worcestershire sauce
1 (4-ounce) sliced mushrooms, drained
1 (2-ounce) jar chopped pimientos
2 tablespoons chopped green onions with tops
    or 2 teaspoons instant minced onion
2 hard-cooked eggs, wedged
Hot cooked noodles

Place the cottage cheese and Worcestershire sauce in blender container. Cover and blend at medium speed until smooth. Pour into a small saucepan. Stir in the mushrooms, pimientos, and onions. Gently stir in the eggs. Cook over low heat just until heated through. Ladle over noodles.

VARIATION: To make in the microwave, combine the mixture in a small microwave-safe bowl and cook on High for 2 to 3 minutes, stirring each minute.

EGGS IN POTATO NESTS

MAKES 2 SERVINGS.

2 tablespoons chopped tomato, well drained
1 tablespoon finely chopped green onions with
    tops or 1 teaspoon instant minced onion
3 slices canned sliced jalapeño peppers, drained
    and chopped
2 servings prepared instant mashed potatoes
2 eggs
1 to 2 tablespoons shredded Monterey Jack
    cheese.

Preheat the oven to 375F. Grease a pie plate. Stir the tomato, onion, and jalapeño peppers into the mashed potatoes. Press the mixture into the pie plate with a spoon, shaping it into 2 nests with each center about 2½ inches in diameter. Break and slip 1 egg into each nest. Sprinkle with the cheese. Cover with foil or another pie plate. Bake 12 to 18 minutes or until the eggs are the desired doneness.

VARIATION: To bake in the microwave, be sure to prick the yolks with tip of knife or a toothpick before sprinkling with the cheese. Cover with plastic wrap and cook on High 3 to 4 minutes or until the eggs are the desired doneness.

EGGS FU-YUNG

This recipe is adapted from the USDA's Shopping for Food and Making Meals in Minutes Using the Dietary Guidelines.

MAKES 2 SERVINGS.

EGG MIXTURE

2 eggs

1 cup fresh bean sprouts

⅓ cup cooked and diced chicken or beef

1 or 2 ounces canned mushrooms, stems and
   pieces, drained

1 teaspoon instant minced onion

1 teaspoon oil

SAUCE

⅓ cup water

1 teaspoon soy sauce

½ tablespoon cornstarch

Beat the eggs with electric mixer or whisk until very thick and light, about 5 minutes. Fold in the bean sprouts, chicken, mushrooms, and onion. Heat the oil in a medium frying pan over moderate heat. Pour the egg mixture by ½ cupfuls into the pan. Brown on one side; turn and brown on other side. Keep warm while preparing sauce.

Mix the sauce ingredients in small saucepan until smooth, cook over low heat, stirring constantly, until thickened. Serve the sauce over the egg patties.

MICROWAVE OMELET

MAKES 1 SERVING.

1 teaspoon butter

2 eggs

2 tablespoons water

⅛ teaspoon salt

Dash of pepper

Fillings of your choice (optional)

In a 9-inch microwave-safe pie plate, cook the butter on High until melted, about 45 seconds. Spread to coat the bottom of the plate. Beat together the remaining ingredients until blended. Pour into the plate. Cover tightly with plastic wrap. Cook on High 2 to 3 minutes, rotating one-quarter turn each 30 seconds. Do not stir. When center is set but still moist, fill, if desired. (It's better to fill the omelet when it's slightly underdone. The heat retained in the eggs completes the cooking.) With a pancake turner, fold the omelet in half or roll and slide from pie plate onto serving dish.

NOTE: To make a tender, easily rolled microwave French omelet the secret is to have a tight-fitting cover. Trapped steam helps it cook evenly; no need to stir. For more information, see "Microwave Cooking" on page 184.

BARBARA'S SAUERKRAUT HORS D'OEUVRE LOAF

When this loaf was sampled, even people who said they dislike sauerkraut liked this dish. Many thought it was made with crabmeat.

1 (1-pound, 4-ounce) can sauerkraut
2 cups grated sharp Cheddar cheese
2 tablespoons chopped onion
2 tablespoons chopped pimiento
3 tablespoons chopped green bell pepper
1 hard-cooked egg, chopped
¼ cup mayonnaise
½ teaspoon salt
½ cup crushed corn flakes or dried bread crumbs
1 (8-ounce) package cream cheese, softened
   (for topping)
Sliced stuffed olives and sliced pimiento (for
   garnish)
Crackers (for serving)

Drain and chop the sauerkraut, squeeze as dry as possible. Mix all the ingredients, except the cream cheese, and press the mixture into a greased large loaf pan or several small molds. Chill overnight. Remove from mold and frost with the cream cheese, which has been softened to spreading consistency. Garnish with olives and/or pimiento and serve with crackers.

APPETIZERS, SAUCES, SUBSTITUTES, AND MORE

EDAM CHEESE SPREAD WITH WINE

1 large Edam cheese (at room temperature)
1 teaspoon parsley

1 teaspoon pimiento
2 teaspoons sherry
2 teaspoons minced onion
1 tablespoon mayonnaise
1 teaspoon Worcestershire sauce

Carefully slice the top from the cheese approximately 1 inch from the top. Scoop out the cheese up to ½ inch from the rind. Combine cheese and other ingredients in a large bowl. Blend well with a mixer and return mixture to shell. Refrigerate for several hours or overnight. Serve as an hors d'oeuvre with breads, crackers, or water biscuits.

FAST SHRIMP SPREAD

Serve with crackers or bread.
MAKES ABOUT 2 CUPS.

8 ounces cream cheese, softened
½ cup mayonnaise
4 ounces tiny cocktail shrimp, drained and
   rinsed, preferably fresh
2 tablespoons seafood cocktail sauce
½ cup finely chopped onion
⅛ teaspoon garlic salt

Thoroughly mix the cream cheese and mayonnaise until well blended. Mash or chop the shrimp and add to mixture; stir in remaining ingredients. Refrigerate until needed. Serve at room temperature.

PINEAPPLE-ALMOND CELERY STALKS

You can also use this spread on bread or crackers.
MAKES ABOUT 4 CUPS.

2 (8-ounce) cans crushed pineapple
8 ounces cream cheese, softened
4 cups shredded sharp Cheddar cheese
½ cup mayonnaise-style salad dressing
1 tablespoon soy sauce
1 cup chopped natural almonds, toasted
½ cup finely chopped green bell pepper
¼ cup minced green onion or chives
Celery stalks

Drain the pineapple. In a large bowl, beat the cream cheese until smooth and thoroughly mix in the Cheddar cheese, salad dressing, and soy sauce. Stir in the pineapple, almonds, bell pepper, and onion. Keep refrigerated until needed. To serve, fill the celery stalks with the spread and serve at room temperature.

FIESTA TEXAS CAVIAR

This is a yummy appetizer that can be served with triangular tortilla chips (my favorite!).

1 large jar medium or hot picante sauce
2 (16-ounce) cans black-eyed peas, drained
1 (16-ounce) can white hominy, drained
1 cup diced green bell pepper
1 cup chopped white onion
1 cup chopped fresh tomato
½ cup finely chopped fresh cilantro
¼ cup seeded and chopped jalapeño peppers (see Note)
1 cup chopped green onions including the green tops
1 tablespoon sugar

1 tablespoon salt
2 tablespoons pepper
2 tablespoons ground cumin

Mix all the ingredients together well. Marinate in the refrigerator for 24 hours before serving.

NOTE: If you don't care for hot tasting food, leave out the jalapeño peppers.

JAMAICAN BARBECUE SAUCE
(1963)

Mother got this recipe from a hotel chef in Jamaica. It's so good it can be used on anything, not just meats.
MAKES 1¾ PINTS.

1½ cups cider vinegar
4 teaspoons lemon juice
3 tablespoons Worcestershire sauce
2 teaspoons packed brown sugar
1 tablespoon prepared mustard
¾ teaspoon salt
½ teaspoon flavor enhancer (monosodium glutamate/msg)
1 cup ketchup
1 tablespoon liquid smoke
1 teaspoon garlic powder
1 teaspoon cayenne pepper
½ cup tomato puree

Mix all ingredients together well. Pour into a quart jar, cover, and refrigerate until you're ready to use it. It keeps well several weeks in the refrigerator. Just heat and use when needed.

STEAK SAUCE

This recipe from a budget-conscious reader tastes surprisingly good for being so simple to make.

1 cup Worcestershire sauce
1 cup ketchup

Mix. Store in the fridge. Use on any meats.

RED CHILI SAUCE

Serve this sauce with meats, put on a baked potato, or dip raw veggies into it.

MAKES ⅔ CUP.

½ cup sour cream
2 tablespoons mayonnaise
1 tablespoon chili powder
½ teaspoon ground cumin

Mix all ingredients in a blender until smooth. Refrigerate in a small container for up to 5 days.

DENVER BREW

This is a barbecue sauce for meats.

MAKES 1⅓ CUPS.

1 cup dark beer
¼ cup vegetable oil
2 tablespoons plus 1½ teaspoons Dijon
   mustard
2 garlic cloves, minced
½ teaspoon salt
¼ teaspoon pepper
¼ teaspoon sugar

In a medium bowl whisk all ingredients together. Use immediately or pour into a con-tainer with a tight-fitting lid. Cover tightly; refrigerate up to 7 days. Use when barbecuing meats or baking chicken parts.

PICO DE GALLO

This is best made fresh and eaten the same day, but you can refrigerate it for a day or two. Serve with grilled meats or as an appetizer dip for tortilla chips.

MAKES 1½ TO 2 CUPS.

1 cup coarsely chopped tomato
¼ cup coarsely chopped onion
1 tablespoon finely chopped fresh cilantro
2 or 3 serrano peppers, minced
½ teaspoon salt

Stir together the tomato, onion, cilantro, and peppers. Add the salt and mix well.

CILANTRO SAUCE

MAKES ABOUT ¾ CUP.

1 cup loosely packed cilantro sprigs
¾ cup coarsely chopped green onions with tops
2 tablespoons lemon juice
2 jalapeño peppers, seeded and coarsely chopped
¼ teaspoon ground cinnamon
¼ teaspoon ground cloves
¼ teaspoon ground cumin
¼ teaspoon ground turmeric
¼ cup olive oil

In a food processor fitted with the metal blade, combine all the ingredients, except the olive oil, until finely chopped, stopping occa-sionally to scrape down the bowl. With the processor running, slowly add olive oil to make a thick paste.

Teriyaki Recipes

These recipes came straight from my mother's old yellow newspaper columns from the late 1950s, when our family lived in Hawaii. I can still see the palm trees swaying and smell those yummy teriyaki sauces on the shrimp or chicken.

FAVORITE TERIYAKI SAUCE

1 button garlic
1 tablespoon brown sugar
½ teaspoon ginger
½ teaspoon pepper
1 tablespoon sesame oil
2 tablespoons water
¼ cup soy sauce

Mash garlic with sugar to fine pulp then mix the remaining ingredients.

HELOISE'S EASY TERIYAKI SAUCE
(1970s)

5 ounces soy sauce
2 ounces sesame oil
3 cloves of crushed garlic
1 teaspoon ginger
1 teaspoon dry mustard
1 tablespoon molasses

Just throw it together in a bowl and away you go.

TEXAS SAUCE

MAKES 2 CUPS.

½ cup salad oil
2 tablespoons lemon juice
2 tablespoons vinegar
1 tablespoon packed brown sugar
2 teaspoons salt
¼ teaspoon pepper
¼ teaspoon dried oregano, crushed
¼ teaspoon cumin seeds
1 teaspoon chili powder
¼ cup chili sauce
1 tablespoon prepared mustard
2 tablespoons Worcestershire sauce
½ cup beef broth or ½ bouillon cube
    dissolved in ½ cup water
Dash or two of hot pepper sauce
¼ cup chopped onion

Mix all the ingredients in blender. Pour into a saucepan and simmer slowly for 30 minutes. You can make this sauce several days in advance and store in refrigerator.

SALSA, PICANTE SAUCE

This salsa is yummy on eggs, tacos, and even tuna salad.

1 small garlic clove
1 small onion
3 jalapeño peppers*
1 teaspoon chopped fresh cilantro
1 large can of whole tomatoes
2 teaspoons lime juice
Salt and pepper

Finely chop together the garlic, onion, jalapeño peppers, and cilantro. Add the tomatoes, lime juice, and salt and pepper to taste. Chop until all ingredients are mixed and the tomatoes are partially liquefied but lumpy. Refrigerate for 2 or 3 hours and enjoy.

*Wear rubber gloves.

SWEETENED CONDENSED MILK SUBSTITUTE
You may not think this is as good as the real thing, but it does nicely in a pinch.

- 2¼ cups dried milk
- ¼ cup warm water
- ¾ cup granulated sugar

Mix together milk, water, and sugar in a blender and mix until smooth. Use 1⅓ cups to equal one can of sweetened condensed milk.

HELOISE'S NO-SALT SPICE SUBSTITUTE
This salt substitute will help you avoid salt in your diet and still enjoy flavorful foods. Use it on meats or vegetables. Please note it uses onion and garlic powders, not salts.

- 5 teaspoons onion powder
- 1 tablespoon garlic powder
- 1 tablespoon paprika
- 1 tablespoon dry mustard
- 1 teaspoon thyme
- ½ teaspoon white pepper
- ½ teaspoon celery seeds

Mix all ingredients and store in a tightly covered container in a cool, dark place. Never store spices near the stove even if it is convenient—they lose their zip.

HELOISE'S SEASONED SALT
This substitutes for commercial seasoning salts. Aside from saving money, making your own spice mixtures lets you add the spices you like and leave out those you don't like.

- 1 cup salt
- 2 tablespoons onion powder
- 1 teaspoon garlic powder
- 1 tablespoon celery seeds, well ground
- 2 teaspoons paprika
- 1 teaspoon chili powder
- ½ teaspoon cayenne pepper
- 1 teaspoon dried parsley flakes, well ground

Mix all ingredients together well. Store in any jar with a lid. Put in a salt shaker for table use.

PUNGENT SALT SUBSTITUTE

- 3 teaspoons dried basil, crushed
- 2 teaspoons dried savory, crushed (summer savory is best)
- 2 teaspoons celery seeds
- 2 teaspoons ground cumin seeds
- 2 teaspoons dried sage, crushed
- 2 teaspoons dried marjoram, crushed
- 1 teaspoon dried lemon thyme, crushed

Mix all ingredients well. Make a powder using a mortar and pestle, if you have one. Or put in a plastic bag, expel the air to make it flat, then crush the mixture using a rolling pin.

HELOISE'S SPICY SALTLESS SEASONING

1 teaspoon ground cloves
1 teaspoon black pepper
1 teaspoon coriander seeds, crushed
2 teaspoons paprika
1 tablespoon dried rosemary, crushed

Mix ingredients in a blender. Store in an airtight container.

PUMPKIN PIE SPICE
MAKES ENOUGH FOR 1 PIE.

½ teaspoon ground cinnamon
¼ teaspoon ground ginger
⅛ teaspoon ground allspice
⅛ teaspoon ground nutmeg

Mix all ingredients.

NOTE: Double or triple the ingredients and store in a labeled container.

HELOISE'S CINNAMON SUGAR MIXTURE
MAKES 3½ CUPS.
(SEE NOTE 1)

3 cups sugar (see Note 2)
½ cup ground cinnamon

Place in a large bowl and use a large fork or wire whisk to mix thoroughly. If you like a more spicy taste, use more cinnamon.

Store mixture in a clean jar with a tight fitting lid. Use the mixture for cinnamon toast, baked apples, or any other baked dish. I love to sprinkle some in oatmeal, or yogurt.

NOTES: (1) 3½ cups is a lot so you can half the recipe using 1-½ cup sugar and ¼ cup cinnamon. (2) I sometimes use 1 cup sugar substitute and 2 cups regular sugar.

TACO SEASONING MIX
Makes the equivalent of one envelope.

2 teaspoons chili powder
Salt, pepper, and onion powder, to taste
Dash of dried oregano, crushed.

Mix all ingredients well.

BREAD-AND-BUTTER PICKLES
MAKES 6 PINT JARS.

4½ pounds pickling cucumbers
1 pound white onions
½ cup pickling salt
3 cups packed brown sugar
3 cups cider vinegar
1 cup water
1½ tablespoons mustard seeds
1 teaspoon ground turmeric
½ teaspoon celery seeds
½ teaspoon ground cloves

Wash the cucumbers and remove 1/16 inch from the blossom end, then cut into ¼-inch slices. Thinly slice the onions. In a large bowl thoroughly mix the onion and cucumber with the salt. Let stand for 3 hours, pour off accumulated liquid and rinse well in cold water.

Meanwhile, sterilize six pint jars and start heating water in the water bath canner.

Combine the remaining ingredients in a 4-quart saucepan and bring to a boil, stirring occasionally. Add the drained cucumber and onion slices to the vinegar mixture and bring back to a boil. Immediately fill the hot sterilized jars with the mixture, leaving ½ inch headspace. Seal the lids after releasing any trapped air bubbles. Process in a boiling water canner for 5 minutes. Allow to cool and check the seals before storing.

GARLIC DILL PICKLES

5 pounds pickling cucumbers (3 to 4 inches long)
4 cups water
3 cups white or cider vinegar
¼ cup pickling salt
½ teaspoon crushed red pepper
32 garlic cloves
16 dill sprigs

Sterilize eight pint jars and start heating water in the water bath canner.

Wash the cucumbers and cut ¹⁄₁₆ inch from the blossom end. Mix the water, vinegar, salt, and red pepper in a 3-quart saucepan and bring to a boil. Split the garlic cloves and put 2 pieces and 1 dill sprig in the bottom of each hot sterilized jar. Pack the cucumbers in the jars, leaving just a bit more than ½ inch of headspace and top each with 2 more pieces of garlic and another sprig of dill. Fill the jars with the hot vinegar mixture, leaving ½ inch of headspace. Use a plastic spatula to release trapped air bubbles. Put on the lids and process in a boiling water canner for 10 minutes. Allow to cool and check the seals before storing.

HELOISE'S GREEN TOMATO PICKLE RELISH
(1961)

6 pounds green tomatoes
4½ pounds onions
½ cup pickling salt
3 pints cider vinegar
1 small red bell pepper, chopped
1 tablespoon minced garlic
1½ pounds brown sugar
1 teaspoon celery seeds
1 teaspoon table salt
1 tablespoon whole cloves
1 stick cinnamon

Slice the tomatoes and onions thinly and place in layers in a large glass baking dish, sprinkling pickling salt in between each layer. Let stand overnight, drain, and rinse with cold water.

Sterilize 8–10 pint jars and start heating water in the water bath canner.

Heat the vinegar to boiling in a 4-quart saucepan, add the bell pepper, garlic, sugar, celery seeds, and table salt and stir until the sugar is dissolved. Spoon in the tomato and onion slices. Tie the cloves and cinnamon stick in a cheesecloth bag and immerse in the saucepan. Bring the mixture to a boil and simmer partially covered until the tomatoes are translucent, up to 1 hour. Remove the spice bag, spoon the mixture into the hot sterilized jars, seal and process in the boiling water canner for 5 minutes.

PARSLEY DRESSING FOR FRESH TOMATOES

This dressing will keep in the refrigerator for 2 weeks so it can really be made ahead. Serve ice cold over a platter of chilled, peeled, sliced tomatoes.

2 cups fresh parsley
½ cup chopped fresh chives (see Note)
I cup sweet pickles, drained
2 garlic cloves
Salt and pepper
½ cup olive oil
½ cup red wine vinegar
¼ cup tarragon vinegar

Put the parsley, chives, pickles, garlic, and salt and pepper to taste through the food grinder twice, using the small blade. Save any juices that escape.

Mix in the remaining ingredients, including the juice leftover from the grinding. Keep in a covered jar at room temperature for 24 hours, then refrigerate.

NOTE: Cut the chives very fine, scissors work best.

CELERY VINEGAR

I quart finely chopped celery or 4 ounces
   celery seeds
I quart white or cider vinegar
I tablespoon white sugar
I tablespoon salt

Put the celery into a glass container. Heat the vinegar, sugar, and salt to boiling; immediately pour it over the celery. Let the mixture cool, cover, and let stand 2 weeks. Strain and bottle.

SPICED VINEGAR

Useful for flavoring salads and other dishes.

I quart cider vinegar
½ ounce celery seeds
⅓ ounce dried mint, crushed
⅓ ounce dried parsley, crushed
I garlic clove
3 small onions
3 whole cloves
I teaspoon whole peppercorns
I teaspoon grated nutmeg
I tablespoon sugar
I tablespoon brandy (optional)
Salt to taste

Put all ingredients into a glass container; cover and let stand for 3 weeks. Strain and bottle.

SNAILS (ESCARGOTS)
BUTTER FOR SNAILS

FOR 50 SNAILS, USING CANNED SNAILS

50 canned snails
¾ pound unsalted butter
2 teaspoons shallots, chopped
4 garlic cloves, crushed to a fine paste
Salt and pepper to taste
¼ cup white wine
About ¼ cup dry, finely ground unflavored
   bread crumbs
Nutmeg (optional)

Preheat the oven for broiling. Place canned snails in a strainer, drain off liquid and discard, rinse snails gently in cold water, let drain while you prepare the snail butter.

Cream together butter, shallots, garlic, and salt and pepper in a sauce pan large enough to accommodate the snails. Heat over low heat until butter melts. Add snails and wine, and heat gently over LOW heat for about 5 minutes. If you have snail shells, put a snail in each shell, add butter mixture to fill the shell, put the shells (open side up) in individual oven-safe dishes or dishes especially made to hold snail in shells. If you have no shells, put the snails into snail dishes or ramekins (or ceramic dishes or flat shells) for individual servings.

Pour on the butter-wine mixture. Sprinkle the tops of shells, snail dishes, or ramekins with a very, light layer of dry bread crumbs and, if desired, a dash of nutmeg on each serving. Place shell dishes or ramekins on a cookie sheet for easy handling and broil just until the butter bubbles and the bread crumbs are lightly browned, about 5 minutes. Serve immediately with crusty French bread to sop up the butter sauce. This butter mixture can be used also for shrimp and other seafood.

APPLE JELLY

A reader who cooks for a diabetic husband came up with this recipe. It does have natural sugar in it, so diabetics must be sure to figure this into their carbohydrate and calorie counts of the day.

1 quart apple juice
4 tablespoons artificial sweetener
2 tablespoons lemon juice
2 packages unflavored gelatin

Mix all ingredients in saucepan and boil gently for 5 minutes. Let cool, pour into containers and refrigerate.

HELOISE'S FAVORITE CINNAMON BUTTER

This recipe yields a delicious and delightful "sinful butter" to spread on toast or rolls at brunch or lunch.

MAKES 20 OUNCES.

½ pound butter or margarine
3 tablespoons cinnamon
½ pound confectioners' sugar

Mix all ingredients well with an electric mixer. Store it in an airtight plastic container and keep refrigerated.

Apricot Preserves
1974

Buy one 8-ounce package of dried apricots, get out ½ cup of sugar and half of a fresh lemon. That's all it takes.

Put 4 cups of water in a pot, throw in the package of apricots and add the sugar. Slice the lemon into extremely thin slices and then chop it into tiny pieces. Add to pot and give a quick stir. Set the timer for 30 minutes and cook slowly over a medium fire without a lid.

After about 20 minutes, when the dried fruit is all welled up, take your potato masher (yep, you heard right) and give them a quick mash, but not so good that you don't leave some pieces in there. The chunks are what make it taste like Grandma's homemade stuff. Stir slightly.

When the 30-minute bell goes off, stir again and see if it's thick enough. If so, turn off the heat; if not cook a wee bit longer. Let sit until it cools to room temperature and then put it in jars. That's all there is to it. I keep mine in the rear of the refrigerator.

JELLIED PEACH SAUCE

1 13- to 16-ounce large can peaches
Water as needed
½ cup sugar
½ teaspoon ground nutmeg
1 (3-ounce) box lemon gelatin

Drain the peaches, saving the syrup. Puree the peaches in the blender.

To the reserved peach syrup, add enough water to make 1 cup of liquid. Pour into a medium saucepan and add the sugar and nutmeg. Bring the mixture to a boil and let boil for about 1 minute.

Empty the box of gelatin into a bowl and stir in the hot liquid until the gelatin is dissolved. Add the pureed peaches and pour into a mold. Chill until set.

BREADS

HELOISE'S FAVORITE BISCUIT OR PANCAKE MIX

I like this mix because it's less expensive than the store-bought kind and keeps well in the cupboard. It stays fresh longer if stored in the refrigerator. Make a batch and then impress your house guests with your delicious breakfast biscuits or pancakes!

8 cups all-purpose flour
⅓ cup baking powder
2 teaspoons salt
8 teaspoons sugar (optional)
1 cup shortening
Milk

Mix all the dry ingredients together. Using a pastry blender, cut in the shortening until the mixture resembles coarse meal. Store in a well-sealed container in the pantry or fridge.

To make biscuits, use ⅓ cup milk for each cup of mix. Bake at 450F for 12 to 15 minutes.

To make pancakes, add enough liquid for the batter consistency desired.

BAKING MIX

MAKES ABOUT 8 CUPS MIX.

3 cups whole wheat flour
3 cups all-purpose flour
3 tablespoons baking powder
1½ teaspoons salt
¾ cup nonfat dry milk
¾ cup vegetable shortening

Mix the dry ingredients thoroughly. Cut in the shortening with a pastry blender, mixer, or two forks until fine crumbs are obtained and the shortening is evenly dispersed. Store, tightly covered, in the refrigerator. Use within 3 months for biscuits or muffins as directed.

BISCUITS

MAKES 8 BISCUITS.

⅓ cup water
1½ cups Baking Mix

Preheat the oven to 425F.

Stir most of the water into the mix. Add rest of water as needed to make a dough that is soft but not sticky. Shape the dough into a ball. Pat or roll the dough into a rectangle about 8 x 4 inches; cut into eight pieces. Place on an ungreased baking sheet. Bake until lightly browned, about 15 minutes.

APPLESAUCE MUFFINS

MAKES 8 MUFFINS.

1½ cups Baking Mix
1 tablespoon sugar
½ teaspoon ground cinnamon
1 egg white, slightly beaten
½ cup unsweetened applesauce
¼ cup water

Preheat the oven to 400F. Grease muffin tins.

Stir baking mix, sugar, and cinnamon together. Mix the egg white, applesauce, and water thoroughly; add to the dry ingredients. Stir until barely moistened (the batter will be lumpy). Fill the muffin tins two-thirds full. Bake until lightly browned, about 20 minutes.

EVERYONE'S FAVORITE BEER BISCUITS

These melt-in-your-mouth biscuits are favorites with my readers and I get many requests for this recipe.

1½ tablespoons sugar
6 ounces warm beer (see Note)
2 cups commercial biscuit mix

Dissolve the sugar in the beer and add it to the biscuit mix. Mix the dough according to directions on the box and bake them following the baking instructions on the biscuit mix box.

VARIATIONS: If you make your biscuits from scratch, just add beer instead of the liquid

called for in the recipe. Be sure to add the amount of sugar listed above. Do not, however, substitute beer for milk.

NOTE: Use nonalcoholic beer, if desired.

HELOISE'S ANGEL BISCUITS
(1960s)

This recipe makes biscuits that really are as light as angel wings and fluffier than Heloise's famous nylon net!

1 package dry yeast
¼ cup warm water
2½ cups flour
1 teaspoon baking powder
1 teaspoon salt
⅛ cup sugar
½ cup shortening
1 cup buttermilk

Preheat the oven to 400F. Grease a baking sheet.

Let the yeast dissolve in the warm water and set aside. Mix all the dry ingredients together as listed. Cut the shortening into the dry mixture until it resembles coarse meal. Stir in the buttermilk and yeast mixture. Thoroughly blend the mixture. The dough can be refrigerated or can be kneaded lightly. (After removing the dough from the refrigerator, it should be allowed to rest at room temperature to allow it to rise.)

Roll the dough out on a floured board. Cut out the biscuits with a biscuit cutter. Place the biscuits in the prepared pan and allow the dough to rise a little before baking. Bake them for 12 to 15 minutes.

ENGLISH TEA "BISCUITS"

In England, a small cake is called a biscuit.
I found this tea cake recipe to help a reader
who was hungry for them.

1 cup sugar

2 eggs

1½ cups milk

1 heaping teaspoon baking powder

¼ cup butter

Flour to make a stiff batter

1 pint of fresh fruit or berries, drained
   (optional)

Preheat the oven to 400F.

Combine all the ingredients. Bake on a cookie sheet until golden brown and serve while warm with afternoon tea.

IRISH BREAD
(1959)

1 cup prepared biscuit mix

¼ cup seeded or seedless raisins

1 teaspoon caraway seeds

¼ cup plus 2 tablespoons milk

Butter (for serving)

Preheat the oven to 450F.

Mix all the ingredients together (except butter) quickly and lightly and put in a well-greased 6-inch skillet. Bake about 12 minutes. Cut into wedges and serve quickly with lots of butter.

SOURDOUGH STARTER
(1961)

Use a glass jar or crock.

1 cake yeast or 1 package of dry yeast

1 cup lukewarm water

1 teaspoon sugar

2 cups flour

Beat all the ingredients to a smooth batter. Cover loosely and set in a warm place to ferment. Stir several times a day while this is working. In about 3 days, your sourdough starter should be ready.

NOTE: Never keep the starter in a metal container, and don't leave a metal spoon in it and always use a glass or crockery jar.

SOURDOUGH MUFFINS

½ cup whole wheat flour

1½ cups white flour

½ cup melted shortening

½ cup sugar

½ cup canned whole milk

1 egg

1 cup raisins

1 teaspoon salt

1 teaspoon baking soda

Sourdough Starter

Preheat the oven to 375F. Grease muffin tins.

Mix all the ingredients, adding enough sourdough starter to make the mixture moist and hold together like ordinary muffins. Stir only enough to blend. Bake for about 30 minutes. These bake slower than ordinary muffins.

Sourdough Bread

When you plan to make sourdough bread, you need to increase the volume of the basic starter the night before. Here's how. Add 6 cups of flour and 3 cups of water to the fermented batch of starter (original) and let set overnight. The reason is that you will need 1 quart of this "New" starter for the bread and you will want to save some.

MAKES 4 LOAVES.

1 quart Sourdough Starter (new)
1 quart lukewarm water
¾ cup sugar
2 tablespoons salt
6 tablespoons shortening, melted
12 cups flour

Preheat oven to 375F

Mix in the order given, adding the flour last. Use enough of the flour to make dough that can be handled. Knead until smooth and elastic. Shape into a ball.

Place in a greased bowl, cover with a clean dish towel (not terrycloth), and let rise. This will take longer than yeast bread. Knead down again and let rise once more until it doubles in size. Punch dough down and turn out onto lightly floured surface. Divide into 4 round balls and let rest for 10 minutes. Place on greased baking sheet. Flatten each ball slightly and make a criss-cross slash on top of each loaf. Cover, let rise until each loaf is nearly double in size. Bake in preheated 375F oven for about 30 to 35 minutes.

MATZO MEAL PANCAKES
(1961)

Serve these pancakes with sour cream, jelly, or a dusting of plain sugar.

1 cup matzo meal
1 cup very warm milk
1 teaspoon sugar
¼ teaspoon salt
4 eggs, separated
Butter or margarine (for frying)

In a medium bowl, mix the matzo meal and milk. Add the sugar, salt, and beaten egg yolks. In a separate bowl beat the egg whites until stiff. Fold gently into the matzo mixture. Heat the butter in a large frying pan over medium-high heat.

Drop the batter by spoonfuls into the hot butter. Cook until golden brown on one side. Turn and brown on the other side. They will have a pretty lacy edge.

NOTE: These can be fried in deep fat or shallow fat. I have also made them like regular pancakes, but they are much better when fried in at least ⅛ inch of shortening.

HELOISE'S LIGHTER PUMPKIN BREAD
(1970)

If you use ½ cup more pumpkin you'll get a stronger flavor.

MAKES 2 SMALL LOAVES.

1⅔ cups regular or whole-wheat flour
  (or ½ each type)
10 to 12 packets (about 2 tablespoons) artificial
  sweetener (the kind you can cook with) or
  1¼ cups sugar (see Note 1)

1 teaspoon salt

1 teaspoon baking soda

1 to 2 teaspoons *each* of allspice, ground cinnamon, and ground nutmeg

½ cup chopped nuts (optional; see Note 2)

2 eggs, slightly beaten

½ cup salad oil

1 cup (half of one 12-ounce can) pumpkin

Preheat the oven to 350 F. Grease and flour 2 small loaf pans.

Sift the dry ingredients and add the nuts. In a separate bowl, mix the eggs, oil, and pumpkin; add to dry ingredients. Pour into the prepared pans. Bake for 50 or 60 minutes.

NOTE: (1) I sometimes use half sugar and half sweetener. (2) May substitute bran, wheat germ, or sesame seeds.

"OFFICE" MONKEY BREAD

Everyone in the Heloise office loves this easy to make bread.

½ cup margarine or butter

⅓ cup granulated sugar

⅓ cup firmly packed brown sugar

¼ cup finely chopped nuts

1 tablespoon ground cinnamon

3 (12-ounce) cans buttermilk biscuits

Preheat the oven to 375F. Coat the inside of a bundt pan with cooking spray or butter.

Melt the margarine in a pot or bowl. Mix the sugars, nuts, and cinnamon in a separate bowl.

Open 1 can of biscuits, separate, and cut each into 4 sections. Next roll each quarter into a ball and then put each one into the sugar

mixture to coat. Place the balls in the bundt pan in a single layer; drizzle a little melted butter evenly over the top. Repeat with the other 2 cans of biscuits.

Sprinkle the remaining sugar mixture over the top and bake for 30 to 35 minutes.

Be sure to let cool for a minute or two before turning the bread onto a plate and carefully removing the pan. If you leave the monkey bread in the pan much longer, it will stick and be hard to remove.

CAKES, PIES, AND DESSERTS

COLD OVEN CAKE

Many readers shared this recipe with me. It gets its name from being started in a cold oven, then baked as usual.

MAKES 1 TUBE CAKE.

¼ pound (1 stick) butter or margarine

1 cup shortening

3 cups sugar

5 eggs

3¾ cups flour

¼ teaspoon salt

½ teaspoon baking powder

1 teaspoon vanilla extract

1 teaspoon lemon extract

1 cup plus 1 tablespoon milk

Grease and flour a tube pan. Cream the butter, shortening, and sugar. Add the eggs, one at a time, beating well. Sift the dry ingredients and add to creamed mixture. Fold in the vanilla, lemon extract, and milk. Pour the batter

Angel Food Cake and Ice Cream

Here's a make-ahead and keep-on-hand dessert that you store in the freezer. You need 1 angel food cake (baked from mix or store-bought), 1 gallon of ice cream (any flavor), and syrup or a flavored liqueur to complement the ice cream.

Slice the angel food cake into three layers with a thread (it works more neatly than a knife). Let the ice cream soften a bit. Now, working as quickly as you can, scoop or slice the ice cream so that you can layer ½ to 1 inch of ice cream between the cake layers as you stack them and then put a layer on top of the cake. Frost the sides of the cake with the remaining ice cream. It may be very soft by now so you may have to use your hands to press slabs of ice cream to the sides of the cake.

Wrap the cake with plastic wrap and rush it to the freezer to get solid. Then add an extra wrap of aluminum foil. The cake will keep several weeks in the freezer.

At serving time, allow the cake to soften for 5 to 10 minutes at room temperature to make slicing it easier. Serve as is or top with a drizzle of chocolate syrup or a liqueur. If you're feeling fancy, drizzle the "topping" in a design on the plate before you place the cake on it. Some good combinations are vanilla ice cream cake with crème de menthe, chocolate ice cream cake with kahlua, and strawberry ice cream cake garnished with fresh strawberries.

into the prepared pan and place in a COLD oven. Turn oven on to 325F and bake for 1½ to 2 hours.

NOTE: The basic ingredients for this cake are those of a pound cake. Recipes sent to me used a variety of flavorings (including rum, butter, butternut, and coconut) which you could substitute for the lemon flavoring, according to your own taste.

WAR CAKE

This old recipe was developed around 1918 during World War I to compensate for shortages of milk, butter, and eggs—it's milkless, butterless, and eggless. What a treat for someone allergic to dairy products or eggs! And one of the best parts of this dark, heavy cake is that you mix it all in one pan—no fuss and hardly anything to wash.

MAKES 1 TUBE CAKE.

2 cups packed brown sugar
2 cups hot water
2 teaspoons shortening
½ to ¾ cup raisins
1 teaspoon *each* of salt, ground cinnamon, and ground cloves
3 cups flour
1 teaspoon baking soda dissolved in 2 teaspoons hot water

Preheat the oven to 350F. Grease a tube pan.

Mix the brown sugar, hot water, and shortening in a medium saucepan. Add the raisins, salt, cinnamon, and cloves. Mix and boil for 5 minutes after it first bubbles. Remove from the stove and let cool completely (very important).

After the mixture is cool, add the flour and baking soda mixture. Mix well. Pour into the prepared pan and bake for 1 hour.

NO-MIX CHERRY-PINEAPPLE NUT CAKE

This is the easiest cake recipe I've ever seen for the holidays or any other time when you have too little time. You make it in the pan—no messy mixing bowls! I have also seen this recipe called the Better-Than-Sex Cake.

MAKES 12 SERVINGS.

1 (20-ounce) can crushed pineapple in heavy syrup
1 (21-ounce) can cherry pie filling
1 (2-layer size) package yellow cake mix
1 (3-ounce) can (1 cup) chopped pecans
½ cup (1 stick) butter or margarine, chilled

Preheat the oven to 350F. Grease a 9 × 13-inch baking pan.

Spread the pineapple with its syrup evenly in the prepared pan. Spoon the pie filling evenly over the pineapple. Sprinkle the dry cake mix evenly over the fruits, then sprinkle the chopped nuts over all. Slice the butter into thin slices, then put the pieces evenly over the top. Bake for 50 minutes or until golden. Serve warm.

CHRISTMAS RAINBOW POKE CAKE

This favorite isn't just for Christmas! It can be enjoyed anytime you want a pretty dessert. There's no rule that says you can't substitute different but compatible gelatin flavors to get different colors.

1 (double-layer) package white cake mix
1 (3-ounce) packet raspberry gelatin
2 cups boiling water
1 (3-ounce) packet lime gelatin
8 ounces nondairy whipped topping, thawed
Green and red gumdrops (for garnish)

Prepare the cake mix as directed on the package, baking it in two 9-inch round pans. Cool about 10 minutes in the pans before removing and allowing to cool on a wire rack. Clean and dry the pans.

Place the cake layers, top sides up, back into the clean pans and prick each layer with a wooden-handled utility fork at ½-inch intervals.

Dissolve the raspberry gelatin in 1 cup of the boiling water in a bowl and spoon over one cake layer. Repeat with the lime gelatin, spooning it over the other cake layer. Refrigerate both layers for 3 to 4 hours. Remove the layers from the pans by dipping in warm water for 10 seconds, then inverting them over a plate; shake gently to loosen. Sandwich the layers together using 1 cup of the whipped topping. Frost the cake with the remaining topping and refrigerate. Decorate the top with flattened gumdrops cut into holly leaf and berry shapes for Christmas.

CHOCOLATE SAUERKRAUT SURPRISE CAKE

This cake is moist and tasty and you'll want to give it a try. Don't tell anyone what the "surprise" is until after they have tasted it.

MAKES 1 CAKE.

1½ cups sugar
⅔ cup shortening or butter
3 eggs
1¼ teaspoons vanilla extract
¼ teaspoon salt
½ cup cocoa
2¼ cups flour
1 teaspoon baking soda

1 teaspoon baking powder

1 cup water or beer

½ to ⅔ cup chopped sauerkraut, rinsed, and
  drained well

Frosting

Preheat the oven to 375F. Grease and flour a
9 × 13-inch baking dish or two 9-inch cake
pans.

Cream together the sugar and shortening.
Add the eggs, and mix well. Then add the
vanilla, salt, and cocoa.

In a separate bowl, sift together the flour,
baking soda, and baking powder. Alternating,
add the dry ingredients and the water to the
cocoa mixture. Mix, then fold in the sauerkraut
by hand.

Bake for 35 to 45 minutes, or until a toothpick inserted into the cake comes out clean. Let
cool and frost it with your favorite kind of
frosting, although sour cream or cream cheese
icing is simply delicious!

Quick version: Add ½ to ⅔ cup chopped sauerkraut, rinsed, drained, to a boxed chocolate
cake mix. (Follow the package directions for
mixing the cake and then add the kraut.) The
cooking time may be a little longer, so test for
doneness.

STRAWBERRY GELATIN CAKE

MAKES ONE 3-LAYER CAKE.

1 (18.25-ounce) box white cake mix

1 box (6-ounce) strawberry gelatin

½ cup oil

½ cup water

4 whole eggs

½ small box frozen strawberries

Strawberry Icing (see below)

Preheat the oven to 350F.

In a large bowl, mix the cake mix and
gelatin together well. Add the oil, water, and
eggs and beat until smooth. Add half of the
strawberries and half of the juice (keep the rest
for the icing). Pour the batter into 3 greased
round cake pans and bake for 1 hour or so.

STRAWBERRY ICING

1 box confectioners' sugar

1 stick butter or margarine

½ small box frozen strawberries

Mix well and spread on the cooled cake.

EASY CHOCOLATE TOMATO SOUP CAKE

*This version has no added spice. Frost this cake
with Cream Cheese Icing (p. 267).*

MAKES 1 CAKE.

1 (18- to 18.25-ounce) box chocolate cake mix

1 (10¾ ounce) can undiluted tomato soup

1 teaspoon baking soda

2 eggs

Put the dry cake mix in a large bowl and add
ONLY ingredients listed here. Mix until blended. Bake according to cake mix directions.

Red Velvet Cakes

In 1995 a reader requested a recipe for Red Velvet Cake when she lost all her recipes in a home fire. Our wonderful readers responded. We received over 15,000 red velvet cake recipes!

This cake is easy and fun to create. It is one of the most delicious desserts that can be presented and will fit into any dining atmosphere. Here are some of the variations we received along with some delicious frostings.

RED VELVET CAKE

MAKES 1 LARGE LOAF CAKE OR ONE 3-LAYER CAKE.

4 (0.5-ounce) bottles red food color

3 tablespoons cocoa

½ cup solid vegetable shortening

1½ cups sugar

2 eggs

1 teaspoon vanilla extract

2½ cups sifted cake flour

1 teaspoon salt

1 cup buttermilk

1 tablespoon vinegar

1 teaspoon baking soda

Preheat the oven to 350F.

Mix the food color with the cocoa and set aside. Beat the shortening with the sugar; add the eggs one at a time, mixing after each addition. Add the food color mixture and vanilla. Alternately add the flour, salt, and buttermilk, beating well. Stir in the vinegar and baking soda. Pour the batter into a greased large loaf pan or 3 small layer pans. Bake for 30 minutes, or until done.

OLD-FASHIONED ICING

Here's a good frosting for red velvet cakes.

MAKES ENOUGH TO FROST 1 CAKE.

½ cup butter

½ cup white shortening

1½ cups sugar

3 tablespoons flour

⅔ cup milk

2 teaspoons vanilla extract

Pinch of salt

1 teaspoon lemon juice

Cream together the butter, shortening, and sugar until it is not grainy. Add the flour, one spoonful at a time, beating well after each addition. Add the milk and beat; add the vanilla, salt, and lemon juice. Turn mixer on high and beat 12 minutes, or until smooth and creamy.

QUICK RED VELVET CAKE

MAKES 1 CAKE.

1 (18.25-ounce) box yellow cake mix

5 eggs

½ cup oil

1 cup low-fat or regular buttermilk

2 tablespoons cocoa

2 ounces red food color

In a large bowl, combine the cake mix with the eggs, oil, buttermilk, cocoa, and food color. Check the directions on the cake box to see how long you need to beat the ingredients together before baking. Bake according to cake box directions.

RED VELVET POUND CAKE

MAKES I TUBE CAKE.

3 cups sugar
½ cup butter
¾ cup solid shortening
1 tablespoon vanilla extract
1 (0.5-ounce) bottle red food color
7 eggs
3 cups unsifted flour
1 teaspoon baking powder
¼ teaspoon salt
½ cup cocoa
¾ cup milk
Cream Cheese Icing (see below)

Preheat the oven to 275F. Grease and flour a large tube pan.

Cream the sugar, butter, shortening, vanilla, food color, and eggs in a large bowl. In a separate bowl, stir the flour, baking powder, salt, and cocoa together. Add them a cup or so at a time alternating with the milk. Mix well. Pour the batter into the prepared pan and bake for 1½ hours, or until done.

Turn out of the pan to cool. The cake should be *cool* to the touch before icing, if the cake is too warm, the icing will melt and make a mess. Prepare the Cream Cheese Icing and frost the cake.

CREAM CHEESE ICING

1 (8-ounce) package cream cheese, softened
½ stick butter, softened
½ box plus 2 tablespoons confectioners' sugar
1 teaspoon vanilla extract

Cream together all ingredients until smooth and spreadable.

LIGHT VELVET CAKE

This lighter and lower-calorie version comes to us thanks to Jeanne Jones. Jeanne's version uses no red food color; I like to add 1 or 2 bottles to make the cake red!

MAKES ONE 8-INCH LAYER CAKE.

2½ cups unbleached flour
1 teaspoon baking powder
2 teaspoons cocoa powder
1 teaspoon baking soda
½ teaspoon salt
1 cup sugar
1 egg plus 2 egg whites
1 cup canola oil
1 cup buttermilk
1 teaspoon white vinegar
1½ teaspoons vanilla
½ cup chopped walnuts, toasted (see Note)
Ricotta Cheese Frosting (see below)

Preheat the oven to 350F. Spray three 8-inch round cake pans well with nonstick vegetable spray.

In large mixing bowl mix the flour, baking powder, cocoa powder, baking soda, salt, and sugar. In separate bowl, combine the egg and egg whites, oil, buttermilk, vinegar, and vanilla. Pour the liquid ingredients into the dry ingredients and mix well. Stir in ¼ cup of the nuts.

Pour the batter into the prepared pans and bake for 25 to 30 minutes, or until the cake springs back when gently touched with the finger.

Allow to cool. Prepare the frosting and then the cake. Sprinkle with the remaining nuts.

NOTE: To toast walnuts, place them in a single layer in a jelly roll pan and bake in a 350F oven for 8 to 10 minutes.

RICOTTA CHEESE FROSTING

2 cups part-skim ricotta cheese
½ cup Neufchâtel cheese
6 tablespoons sugar
1 tablespoon vanilla extract

Blend all the ingredients in a blender or food processor fitted with the metal blade until smooth.

HELOISE'S TOMATO SOUP CONVERSATION CAKE

This recipe came from my mother's column of September 17, 1959. She called the cake Conversation Piece. Here's the recipe for you to give a try, and you'll see that it certainly can start a conversation.

MAKES ONE 10-INCH SQUARE CAKE.

½ cup solid shortening

1 cup sugar

1 cup chopped nuts

1 teaspoon baking soda

1 (10½-ounce) can tomato soup

1 cup raisins

1½ cups flour

1 teaspoon baking powder

OPTIONAL INGREDIENTS

1½ teaspoons ground nutmeg

2½ teaspoons ground cinnamon

1 teaspoon ground allspice

½ teaspoon ground cloves

Conversation Cake Icing (see below)

Preheat the oven to 375F. Grease a 10-inch square cake pan.

Cream the shortening and sugar in a large bowl. Stir in the tomato soup (undiluted) and then mix in the rest of the ingredients, except the icing, one at a time. Cream well after each addition.

Pour the batter into the prepared pan and bake for 45 minutes.

When cake is done, remove it from the oven. Loosen the edges with knife. Turn onto cake rack and let cool. Prepare the icing and and frost the cake.

CONVERSATION CAKE ICING

1 (3-ounce) package cream cheese

1 teaspoon vanilla extract

1 cup confectioners' sugar

¼ cup chopped nuts

Place the cheese in a small bowl and let it soften at room temperature. Add the vanilla and sugar. Mix well. Spread the icing on the cooled cake. Sprinkle it with the chopped nuts.

CHERRY SOUR CREAM NUT CAKE

This recipe comes from Mrs. Rosamond Hill who was my dear friend Judy's mother. It's a Hill family favorite in Del Rio, Texas, and I'm sure it will be yours, too!

MAKES 1 TUBE CAKE.

2 sticks butter or margarine

2 cups sugar

3 eggs

1 teaspoon vanilla extract

2 teaspoons almond extract

1 pint sour cream

3 cups flour

1 teaspoon baking soda

½ teaspoon salt

1 cup chopped maraschino cherries

1½ cups chopped nuts

Cherry Icing (on the next page)

Preheat the oven to 325F. Grease and flour a tube pan.

Cream together the butter and sugar. Add the eggs, beating well. Mix in the extracts and sour cream. Then mix in the flour, baking soda, and salt. Stir in the cherries and nuts. Pour the batter into the prepared pan and bake for 1 to 1½ hours.

Prepare the icing and frost the cooled cake.

CHERRY ICING

½ box confectioners' sugar

Cherry juice—enough to make sugar smooth
  and spreadable

Drop of vanilla extract

Mix well and spread on the cooled cake.

HELOISE'S CARROT CAKE
(1960)

MAKES 1 LAYER CAKE.

1 cup sugar

¾ cup salad oil

1½ cups flour

1 teaspoon baking powder

1 teaspoon baking soda

1 teaspoon ground cinnamon

¼ teaspoon salt

1 cup grated carrots

2 eggs

½ cup chopped nuts

Filling (see next column)

Golden Sauce (see next column)

Preheat the oven to 375F.

Mix the sugar and oil in a large bowl. Sift the dry ingredients together and combine with the sugar mixture. Add the carrots and mix well. Then add the eggs one at a time, beating well after each addition. Add the nuts and blend well. Pour the batter into a greased round cake pan and bake for 35 to 40 minutes; test for doneness.

After cake is cool, slice it horizontally to make two layers. Prepare the filling and spread (on a cut side) between the layers. Reassemble the cake. Prepare the sauce and pour over the whole cake.

FILLING

1 (6-ounce) container whipping cream (see Note)

3 eggs

2 tablespoons cornstarch

½ cup sugar

1 tablespoon butter

1 teaspoon vanilla extract

Pinch of ground cinnamon

Mix the ingredients in the top of a double-boiler as you would a custard.

NOTE: May use a 5-ounce can of evaporated milk.

GOLDEN SAUCE

1 cup sugar

⅓ cup flour

⅓ teaspoon salt

2 cups boiling water

½ cup carrots, grated

½ cup lemon juice

2 tablespoons grated orange rind

⅓ cup butter

Mix the sugar, flour, salt, and water in a medium saucepan. Cook over medium heat until clear. Add the remaining ingredients. Cook, stirring constantly, for 20 minutes.

STRAWBERRY-WALNUT BLACK-BOTTOM PIE

This recipe is from the Walnut Marketing Board.

MAKES 6 TO 8 SERVINGS.

⅔ cup half-and-half

1 (6-ounce) packet semisweet chocolate
   pieces

3 eggs, separated

¾ cup chopped walnuts

1 (9-inch) pie shell, baked

2 pints strawberries, washed and stemmed

2 teaspoons lemon juice

1 (3.04-ounce) envelope unflavored gelatin

¼ cup cold water

¼ cup sugar plus extra for the berries (optional)

Heat the half-and-half in a large saucepan over medium heat. Stir in the chocolate; beat smooth with wire whisk. Remove from heat; whisk in the egg yolks, one at a time, mixing until well blended. Return to heat. Cook, stirring, 1 to 2 minutes longer. Cool; mix in the walnuts. Pour into the pie shell and chill until set, 2 to 3 hours.

In electric blender or food processor puree 1 pint of the berries with the lemon juice (you need about 1⅔ cups puree). Soften the gelatin in the water in a small saucepan and warm over low heat to dissolve completely, then stir into the berry puree. Chill until the mixture begins to set. Meanwhile, beat the egg whites until foamy. Gradually beat in the sugar, beating to form soft peaks. Fold into the thickened berry mixture. Pour over the chocolate-walnut layer; chill until set. Slice the remaining berries; sweeten if desired. To serve, spoon the sliced berries over wedges of pie.

SHOO-FLY PIE

It seems that this pie originated in Pennsylvania Dutch country. While baking numerous pies on a daily basis in large outdoor ovens, pioneer women were constantly "shooing" flies away from the pies. Other accounts suggest the name is a distorted version of the German word scufli, *a reference to crumbs. The pie was a popular one among early settlers of this country because it could be made from available staples, such as molasses, brown sugar, and flour.*

MAKES 3 PIES.

1 cup molasses

1 cup boiling water

1 teaspoon baking soda

4 cups unsifted flour

1 cup firmly packed brown sugar

¾ cup lard

3 (9-inch) pastry shells, unbaked

Preheat the oven to 350F.

Mix the molasses and boiling water in a large bowl. Cool slightly, then add the baking soda. While the mixture is cooling, combine the flour, sugar, and lard to make crumbs.

Pour the molasses mixture into the crusts, top with the crumbs and bake for about 25 minutes.

MOCK PECAN PIE

MAKES 8 SERVINGS.

1 cup cooked unseasoned pinto beans (see
   Note)

1½ to 2 cups sugar

4 ounces butter or margarine

4 eggs, well beaten

2 tablespoons molasses or dark corn syrup

3 teaspoons vanilla extract

½ teaspoon salt

1 (9-inch) pie shell, unbaked

½ cup chopped pecans

Whipped cream or nondairy whipped topping
   (for serving)

Preheat the oven to 350F.

Drain and mash the beans thoroughly. In a medium bowl, cream the sugar and butter. Add the eggs, molasses, vanilla, and salt. Mix in the beans. Pour into the pie shell and sprinkle the chopped pecans on top. Bake for 45 to 60 minutes, until firm or a knife inserted into the center comes out clean. Serve with the whipped cream.

NOTE: Use canned beans or start from dried beans.

MOCK APPLE PIE
(1959)

You'll swear this delicious pie really has apples in it.
MAKES 1 PIE.

Pastry for a double-crusted 9-inch pie

2 cups water

1¼ cups sugar

2 teaspoons cream of tartar

20 whole soda crackers

Butter (for dotting)

Ground cinnamon (for sprinkling)

Preheat the oven to 375F. Line the bottom of a 9-inch pie pan with pastry.

In a medium saucepan, boil the water, sugar, and cream of tartar. Add the soda crackers and boil only 1 minute. Spoon gently into the pie shell. Dot the top with butter and sprinkle on the cinnamon to taste. Cover the pie with the top crust and cut vents in it. Bake 35 minutes. Let the pie cool completely before cutting so it can firm up.

NEVER FAIL PIE CRUST
(1959)

This makes a crisp, crunchy crust that's always good. Sift the dry ingredients before measuring.
MAKES ENOUGH FOR A 1-CRUST PIE.

2¼ cups flour

¾ cup shortening

1 teaspoon salt

5 tablespoons cold water

Mix the flour and shortening with the salt. Blend with a fork until the size of peas. Add the water. Roll between wax paper.

HEALTHY PIE CRUST

This recipe is from the University of Texas's Lifetime Health Letter.
MAKES ENOUGH FOR A 1-CRUST, 9-INCH PIE.

1½ cups sifted flour

½ teaspoon salt

1 teaspoon vanilla extract

⅓ cup canola oil

¼ cup (or less) ice water

Combine all ingredients except the water with a fork, pastry blender, or in a food processor fitted with the steel blade. Add enough water to work the mixture into a ball. Refrigerate for 1 hour or more before rolling out on a well-floured board. Place in a 9-inch pie pan; trim the edges and flute the crust. If you need a baked shell, prick with a fork and bake for 10 to 15 minutes at 425F.

FUNNEL CAKES

They'll melt in your mouth and are best if eaten while still warm.

Oil for deep frying

2 eggs

1½ cups milk

2 cups flour

1 teaspoon baking powder

½ teaspoon salt

Powdered sugar (for topping)

A deep fryer is best, but if you don't have one, use a heavy deep pan. Pour oil to a depth of 2 inches and let it get very hot, but not so hot that it smokes or burns.

Mix the eggs, milk, flour, baking powder, and salt. Pour the batter through a funnel into the hot oil, moving it in a circular motion, then in a crisscross one, until you have made a cake about the size of a large doughnut. The little cakes cook quickly so watch them carefully.

When lightly browned, remove them from the oil and drain on paper towels. While hot, dredge them in the powdered sugar or if you prefer, sprinkle it over the tops of the cakes. (You can use a large-holed kitchen salt shaker or shake the sugar through a sieve.)

Short-Cut, No-Bake Desserts

CHEESECAKE

Mix one average size package of vanilla pudding according to the package directions. Add 1 (8-ounce) package of softened cream cheese and mix until well blended. Pour the mixture into a ready-made graham-cracker pie crust and refrigerate until set. Top with your favorite canned pie filling and serve. Keep the leftovers in the refrigerator.

CHERRY-CHOCOLATE DESSERT

One reader combines equal parts of cherry pie filling and chocolate pudding for a quick dessert—a sort of Black Forest pudding or parfait.

CRANBERRY FLUFF

A quick and pretty holiday dessert!

MAKES 6 SERVINGS.

1½ cups finely chopped raw cranberries

1 cup miniature marshmallows

¼ cup sugar

½ cup mayonnaise

1½ cups finely chopped apple

¼ cup chopped walnuts

⅛ teaspoon ground cinnamon

Combine the cranberries, marshmallows, and sugar in a large bowl. Stir lightly. Cover and chill before gently mixing in the remaining ingredients.

RASPBERRY FLUFF

1 (3-ounce) packet raspberry gelatin

1 cup boiling water

1 (12-ounce) package frozen raspberries

1 pint raspberry sherbet

1 cup whipped cream or nondairy whipped
    topping, thawed

Pour the gelatin mix into a large glass or metal bowl. Stir in the boiling water until the gelatin is dissolved. Put the frozen raspberries into the hot gelatin and separate with a fork. Add the sherbet and blend. Put in the refrigerator and allow to cool and solidify for approximately 1 hour. Fold in the whipped cream and mix well. Chill for several hours or overnight.

COOKIE, CANDY, AND SWEETS

ONE, TWO, THREE NO-BAKE FUDGE COOKIES

2 cups sugar

½ cup butter

Pinch of salt

½ cup milk

4 tablespoons cocoa

½ cup peanut butter

2 cups rolled oats

1 teaspoon vanilla extract

½ cup chopped nuts

Mix the sugar, butter, salt, milk, and cocoa in a medium saucepan and bring to a boil. Boil 1 minute. Remove from the heat and add the remaining ingredients. Mix well. Drop by tea-

spoonful onto wax paper–covered cookie sheets. Let cool. Store in tins.

NO-BAKE CHOCOLATE SANDWICHES

Golden buttery round crackers

1 cup peanut butter

8 to 12 ounces white chocolate, almond bark
    chocolate, or chocolate chips

Spread half the crackers with peanut butter. Place the remaining crackers on top, making sandwiches.

Melt the chocolate in the top of a double-boiler. Dip the sandwiches into the chocolate to coat. Hold the sandwiches with tongs or balance them on a grate-like potato masher for dipping. Place the sandwiches on wax paper–lined cookie sheets and let harden. Store in a tin.

NOTE: Place the cookie sheets in the refrigerator to make the chocolate harden faster.

CANDY CANE COOKIES

These cookies are great for Christmas.

MAKES 24 COOKIES.

1 cup butter

1 cup confectioners' sugar

1 egg

1 teaspoon vanilla extract

2½ cups flour

Red food color

1 cup candy canes, crushed into small pieces

Preheat the oven to 350F.

In a large bowl, mix together the butter, sugar, egg, and vanilla. Then stir in the flour to make a dough. Divide the dough in half and add a few drops of red food color to one half and mix well. Take 1 teaspoon of each dough and roll into strips about 4 inches long and ¼ inch thick. Twist the strips around each other and form into candy cane shapes on an ungreased cookie sheet.

Bake 15 to 20 minutes. Remove from the oven. While the cookies are still warm, sprinkle some of the crushed candy canes on each one.

SNOWBALL COOKIES

Now you can have snowballs any time of the year!
MAKES ABOUT 30 COOKIES.

1 cup butter or margarine (not diet), softened
1 cup confectioners' sugar
2 cups flour
2 teaspoons vanilla extract
¼ teaspoon salt
2 cups chopped pecans

Combine the butter and ½ cup of the sugar in a large bowl; using an electric mixer, blend on medium speed until fluffy. Mix in the flour, vanilla, salt, and nuts. Chill the dough in refrigerator until firm enough to work with.

Preheat the oven to 350F. Grease cookie sheet sheets.

Roll spoon-sized portions of the mixture into balls and place in the prepared pans approximately 2 inches apart.

Bake for 15 to 18 minutes, or until golden brown. Remove from the oven and roll the warm cookies in the remaining powdered sugar. Allow to cool, then roll once again in the sugar.

BROWNIES FROM A CAKE MIX

1 egg
¾ cup water plus more as needed
½ cup chopped pecans (optional)
1 (18.25-ounce) box devil's food cake mix

Preheat the oven to 350F. Grease a 13 × 9-inch pan.

Mix the egg, water, and nuts in a large bowl. Add the dry cake mix; stir well. If the batter needs more water, add a teaspoonful at a time; don't add too much because the batter should be thick. Be sure not to overmix.

Pour into the prepared pan, being sure to smooth the top evenly. Bake for 20 to 25 minutes for chewy brownies; if you like them a little drier, bake a few minutes longer.

COOKIES MADE FROM A CAKE MIX

Choose any flavor cake mix you'd like. Feel free to add nuts, raisins, or chocolate chips.

1 (18.25-ounce) box cake mix
2 eggs
½ cup vegetable oil

Preheat the oven to 350F.

Mix only the above ingredients in a large bowl until blended. Drop the batter by spoonfuls onto an ungreased cookie sheet about 2 inches apart. Bake for 8 to 10 minutes. Cool.

HELOISE'S TOFFEE COOKIES
(1960)

2 cups sifted cake flour
½ teaspoon cream of tartar
½ teaspoon baking soda
½ teaspoon salt
1 cup packed brown sugar
½ cup vegetable oil
1 egg, beaten
1 teaspoon vanilla extract
¼ cup water
1 cup chopped nuts

Mix the flour, cream of tartar, salt, and baking soda and sift. In a separate bowl, cream the sugar and oil. Add the egg, vanilla, and water to the sugar mixture; blend well. Gradually blend in the dry ingredients, adding the nuts last. Shape the dough into a roll. Wrap in wax paper and chill for several hours or overnight.

Preheat the oven to 375F.

Cut the dough into thin slices and place on a greased cookie sheet about 1 to 2 inches apart. Bake 8 to 10 minutes.

VINEGAR TAFFY

We used to make this candy when I was a child. It doesn't sound sweet but it's really yummy, not to mention the fun of pulling the candy. Try it at a Christmas tree decorating party, summer pool party, or other casual gathering. Be sure to "butter" your hands before pulling the taffy so that it won't stick to you!

3 cups sugar
½ cup vinegar
1 cup water
2 tablespoons butter or margarine (not diet)
1 teaspoon vanilla extract
Butter, to grease the platter and your hands
    while pulling taffy

In a medium saucepan, mix the sugar, vinegar, and water. Stir well. Cook over low to medium heat until the mixture reaches the hard crack stage on a candy thermometer. Add the butter and vanilla; mix. Pour the mixture onto a buttered platter and let it cool enough so that you can handle it.

Now the best part: Butter your hands and pick up a blob of candy, then pull it, the more people to pull, the better, and the more you pull, the whiter the candy gets. When you have pulled it enough and have the right consistency, cut the taffy into small pieces with butter-greased scissors (easier than using a knife).

BUTTERMILK PECAN PRALINES

I use a 6- to 8-quart pot for this because the mixture foams to great heights while cooking.

1 cup buttermilk
2 cups sugar
1 teaspoon baking soda
1 tablespoon butter or margarine (not diet)
1 teaspoon vanilla extract
2 cups pecan halves

Pour the buttermilk into a very large pot, stir in the sugar and baking soda until dissolved. Cook over medium heat, letting it bubble until it turns brownish in color and reaches the soft ball stage (about 235F) on a candy thermometer. (If you don't have a candy thermometer, test the candy by dropping a small amount into cool water and work with it to see if it forms a soft ball.) While cooking, you will need to stir constantly so the mixture won't stick.

At soft ball stage, remove the pot from the heat and add the butter, vanilla, and pecans. Return to the stove and heat the mixture until it becomes glossy and starts to crystallize. On wax paper or a greased baking sheet, quickly spoon out the candy into little patties. I like to use 2 iced tea spoons about 2 inches in circumference. You can decorate each patty by placing a pecan half on it while it's still warm.

Let them cool and store in an airtight container. If the candy starts to turn sugary and hardens too fast, return the pot to the heat for a few minutes, then spoon it out again.

NOTE: The cooking stages are crucial to the outcome of this candy. Overcooked, it's very sugary; undercooked, it won't be firm. That's why a candy thermometer is so important. It takes the guesswork out of candy making.

LONE STAR CANEFEST PRALINES

This recipe comes from my friends at Imperial Sugar, in Texas, during the Lone Star State's 1986 sesquicentennial. It's slightly different from my other praline recipe.

MAKES TWENTY 2-INCH CANDIES.

2 cups granulated sugar
1 teaspoon baking soda
1 cup buttermilk
⅛ teaspoon salt
2 tablespoons butter or margarine
2½ cups pecan halves

In a 3½-quart heavy saucepan, combine the sugar, baking soda, buttermilk, and salt. Cook over high heat about 5 minutes or to 210F on a candy thermometer. Stir often and scrape the bottom of the pot; the mixture will foam up. Add the butter and pecans.

Over medium heat, continue cooking, stirring constantly and scraping bottom and the sides of the pot, until it reaches the soft ball stage (235F) on a candy thermometer.

Remove from heat and cool slightly, about 2 minutes. Beat with a spoon until thick and creamy. Drop from a tablespoon onto a sheet of aluminum foil or wax paper. Let cool.

SHORT-CUT MAPLE-NUT CANDY

Although nothing replaces sugary smooth buttermilk pralines, this recipe is a tasty substitute and is a good way to use up leftover ready-made frosting.

MAKES 6 DOZEN CANDIES.

1 (16-ounce) tub ready-made vanilla frosting
¾ teaspoon maple flavoring
½ cup toasted chopped pecans

Heat the frosting and maple flavoring in a 2-quart saucepan until thin. Stir in the pecans. Drop the mixture by level teaspoonfuls onto a wax paper–covered baking sheet. Refrigerate until set, about 4 hours. Store in the refrigerator.

HELOISE'S FUDGE

This yummy fudge will make you forget about counting calories. This is best stored in the fridge—if it doesn't disappear as soon as it's cool enough to eat!

4½ cups granulated sugar

1 (12-ounce) can evaporated milk

3 (6-ounce) packages chocolate chips

1 (10-ounce) package miniature marshmallows

½ cup butter or margarine

1 teaspoon vanilla extract

2 cups chopped nuts

Mix the sugar and milk in a large, heavy saucepan and slowly bring to a rolling boil. Let this mixture boil for 8 minutes. Remove the saucepan from the heat and add the chocolate chips, marshmallows, and butter. Mix only until the chips and the marshmallows are melted. Add the vanilla and nuts and blend. Spread the mixture in a large ungreased pan; let it cool and enjoy!

LILLIAN'S EASY PEANUT BRITTLE

This recipe, in response to a reader's request, came from one of my assistant's grandmother, Lillian R. Graves. Ruth smiles when she talks about how yummy this is.

1 cup sugar

1 cup light corn syrup

2 cups raw shelled peanuts

1 teaspoon baking soda

Pinch of salt

Bring the sugar and corn syrup to a boil in a large saucepan. Add the peanuts. Stir constantly and cook until the mixture turns light brown in color. This is a very important phase of making peanut brittle. You want to make sure it has a good color!

Remove the pan from the heat and add the baking soda and salt. Pour the mixture into a thin layer on wax paper and let it cool. Then just break into bite-size pieces and enjoy.

MATTHEW'S MICROWAVE FUDGE

1 pound confectioners' sugar

½ cup cocoa

¼ teaspoon salt

6 tablespoons butter or margarine

4 tablespoons milk

1 tablespoon vanilla extract

1 cup chopped pecans or walnuts

Butter a 9 × 5-inch loaf pan.

Combine all the ingredients, except the nuts, in a microwave-safe bowl. Microwave on High until all the ingredients are melted and smooth. Stir periodically. When the mixture is smooth, remove from the microwave and stir in the nuts.

Spread the candy into the prepared pan and allow to cool completely before cutting into bite-size pieces.

SIMPLE CANDIED CITRUS FRUIT

This delicious Christmas treat can be enjoyed all year round! It keeps indefinitely in the fridge.

Peels of 4 lemons, 4 oranges, and 4 grapefruits

1 cup water

¼ cup corn syrup

2 cups sugar plus extra (for sprinkling)

Wash and dice the peels. Slowly bring the water, corn syrup, and sugar to a boil in a medium saucepan; then simmer for 30 minutes over low heat. Add the peels and cook for 55 to 60 minutes, or until all the syrup has been absorbed.

Lay out a large piece of wax paper and sprinkle it liberally with sugar. Put the candied peels on the wax paper and toss to coat with sugar. Let it sit for 1 or 2 days to dry. Store in the refrigerator.

NOTE: You can wash and dice the peels as you collect them and freeze them in a freezer-safe container. When you have enough peels, you can make this recipe.

Easy Kids' Treats

BANANA POPS

Poke frozen treat sticks or the handle end of plastic spoons into bananas and freeze them for a half day or less. Have some handy at a birthday party for the child who can't eat dairy or cake.

RICE CEREAL TREATS

Instead of making rice cereal treats the conventional way by melting miniature marshmallows and butter and so forth, try this no-cook-at-all recipe. Mix the rice cereal with marshmallow cream—no butter necessary except to grease the pan and your hands so you can press the mixture into the pan.

EASIEST EVER DELICIOUS DOUGHNUTS

The store brand biscuits are just as good and more economical than name brands for this quick-and-easy treat for a coffee party, a brunch, or a late-night snack.

MAKES 10 DOUGHNUTS.

Oil for deep-frying
1 (10 count) can refrigerator biscuits
Confectioners' sugar or sugar-cinnamon
    mixture (for topping)

Heat enough oil to cover the doughnuts. Shape or cut each biscuit into a doughnut shape. (Or just break each one in half and shape into balls for doughnut holes.) Drop the doughnuts into hot oil and cook until golden brown. Don't cook them too fast or you'll have a doughy, gooey center.

Drain on a paper towel and roll in the sugar. These taste best when still warm.

NOTE: If you use granulated sugar, you can prevent a mess by dropping the doughnuts into a brown paper bag along with the sugar. Shake, remove from the bag, and let cool slightly on paper towels.

ELEPHANT EARS

You don't need the memory of an elephant to make this easy tasty treat. These are great to make for a brunch. Enjoy, and don't even think about the calories!

MAKES 10 PASTRIES.

½ cup ground cinnamon
1 cup white sugar
1 8-ounce (10 count) can cinnamon buns (found
    in the dairy case)

Preheat the oven to 375F. Line cookie sheets with foil.

Mix the cinnamon and sugar together and spread it evenly on a sheet of foil or wax paper. Remove one cinnamon bun from the can and lay it on the sugar and cinnamon mixture. Using a rolling pin, roll the cinnamon bun out thin, turning it often so it absorbs as much sugar and cinnamon as possible. The finished diameter should be 6 to 8 inches when you finish. Place on the prepared pan. Repeat for the other buns.

Bake on the center rack or as close to the center as possible. Check them often so they don't scorch or overbake—they are very thin.

Cinnamon Candy Gelatin Salads

CINNAMON-RASPBERRY

1 (3-ounce) package raspberry gelatin
1 cup boiling water
3 tablespoons red cinnamon candies
1 cup applesauce

Dissolve the gelatin in the water along with the candies. Add the applesauce and place in mold if desired. Refrigerate until set.

CINNAMON-LEMON

1 (6-ounce) package of lemon gelatin
3 cups boiling water
1/4 cup red cinnamon candies
2 cups applesauce
1/2 cup chopped nuts (optional)
1/2 (12-ounce) container whipped topping

Dissolve the gelatin in the water along with the candies. Let cool slightly and stir in the applesauce and nuts (if using). Chill until nearly firm. Fold in the whipped topping and spoon into a mold. Refrigerate until firm.

CINNAMON-CHERRY

MAKES 6 TO 8 SERVINGS.

1 (3-ounce) package cherry gelatin
1 cup boiling water
1/4 cup cinnamon candies
1 (1 pound, 1 ounce) can applesauce
1 tablespoon vinegar

Dissolve the gelatin in the boiling water along with the candies. Stir in the applesauce and vinegar. Pour into a mold and chill until firm.

BEVERAGES

EGGNOG

The American Egg Board and the USDA suggest that any form of raw eggs should not be eaten, so here's an update for an old standby. My recipe for eggnog is not only ideal for the calorie conscious, it also eliminates the worry of using raw eggs and is a delicious holiday treat!

HELOISE'S LOWER CALORIE EGGNOG

MAKES 4 SERVINGS.

3 eggs
3 tablespoons sugar or artifical sweetener
   equivalent, or to taste
Pinch of salt (optional)
3 cups skim or low-fat milk
1 to 2 tablespoons powdered milk (See Note)
3 tablespoons bourbon extract or to taste
3 teaspoons vanilla extract
Dash of nutmeg or cinnamon (for garnish)
4 cinnamon sticks (optional)

In large saucepan, beat together eggs, sugar or sweetener, and salt, if desired. Stir in 1½ cups milk and powdered milk.

Cook over low heat, stirring constantly, until mixture is just thick enough to coat a metal spoon and reaches 160F. Remove from the heat and stir in the rest of the milk and vanilla.

Refrigerate until thoroughly chilled. Before serving, garnish with a dash of nutmeg or cinnamon, and a cinnamon stick for stirring.

Chocolate Extract Coffee

For my morning treat, I add chocolate extract to my coffee. Serve this anytime or when you and a friend take an afternoon coffee break.

For 1 cup: Add 2 drops of extract (or to taste) to a mug of coffee.

For 8 cups: Add ½ teaspoon of extract to the pot.

For 24 cups: Add about 1½ teaspoons of extract to the pot.

You can substitute cocoa for the chocolate extract.

NOTE: Use coffee creamer to make a richer drink.

HELOISE'S HOT COCOA

Made in a jiffy, this cocoa will warm you and your guests on a cold winter's day. Top with whipped cream or ice cream for a special treat. It's also a terrific mix for campers or for gift giving.

MAKES ABOUT 3¼ CUP DRY MIX
(16–20 SERVINGS).

HELOISE'S HOT COCOA MIX

2 cups powdered milk
¼ cup cocoa
1 cup confectioners' sugar (see Note 1)
Dash of salt
⅓ cup powdered nondairy creamer (optional; see Note 2)
1 to 2 tablespoons malted milk powder (optional)

Combine the dry mix ingredients thoroughly and store in a tightly covered container.

To serve, spoon about 4 tablespoons of the mix (or to taste) into a mug. Fill with boiling water and mix well.

NOTES: (1) May use an equivalent amount of sugar substitute. (2) This makes for a richer mix.

VIENNA COFFEE MIX

½ cup instant coffee granules

⅔ cup granulated sugar (or an equivalent amount of artificial sweetener)

⅔ cup powdered milk or powdered coffee creamer

½ teaspoon ground cinnamon

Easy Coffees

COFFEE OLÉ

You'll love how easy this is! Make a regular cup of coffee and add a little extra milk (regular or skim) and 1 tablespoon of powdered skim milk. Add sugar (or artificial sweetener) to taste. Put this mixture in the blender and blend until foamy. Then microwave, in a microwaveable-safe cup for a few seconds and enjoy a steaming cup of delicious coffee.

COFFEE AU LAIT

Make a delicious cup in an instant. Simply heat 1 to 2 ounces of milk (regular or skim) in a large microwave-safe mug then pour hot coffee into the boiled milk. Canned skim milk makes this drink especially good and saves a few fat calories, too.

Combine the dry mix ingredients and blend well. Store in an airtight container.

To serve, put 2 rounded teaspoons of the mix into an 8-ounce cup and add boiling water, stirring well.

SPICED COFFEE MIX

For added flavor, sprinkle each serving with ground nutmeg.

DRY MIX

1 cup instant coffee powder

4 teaspoons dehydrated lemon peel

4 teaspoons ground cinnamon

1 teaspoon ground cloves

Combine the dry mix ingredients and blend well. Store in tightly covered container.

To serve, put 1 rounded teaspoon of the mix into a coffeecup. Stir in boiling water.

NOTE: Use this mix to make iced coffee.

SPICED TEA MIX

6 (2-inch-long) cinnamon sticks

1 teaspoon whole cloves

1 whole nutmeg

2 cups tea leaves

2 tablespoons dried grated orange peel

2 tablespoons dried grated lemon peel

Wrap the cinnamon, cloves, and nutmeg in a double thickness of cheesecloth. Crush with a mallet. Place in a medium bowl. Add the tea and orange and lemon peels. Mix well. Store in an airtight container.

To serve, boil water. Rinse out a teapot with some boiling water; then spoon in 1 teaspoon of the mix per serving. Add boiling water. Let steep 2 to 5 minutes and strain into teacups.

ANISE AND LEMON TEA MIX

MAKES 2½ CUPS MIX (40 SERVINGS).

3 tablespoons anise seed
2 cups tea leaves
½ cup grated dried lemon peel

Blend the dry mix ingredients thoroughly. Store in an airtight container.

To serve, mix 1 teaspoon tea with 6 to 8 ounces boiling water. Let steep for 5 minutes. You may want to taste-test the amounts. Sometimes I make it stronger when I need a real "lift."

FRIENDSHIP TEA MIX

This is an often asked for Heloise recipe and it is such a nice gift.

2½ cups powdered orange-flavored breakfast drink
1¾ cups powdered instant tea (not sweetened)
2 to 2½ cups sugar to taste
1 small package lemonade mix (makes 2 quarts)
1½ teaspoons ground cloves
1½ teaspoons ground cinnamon

Blend together all dry mix ingredients. Store in a tightly sealed jar.

To serve, use 1 to 2 teaspoons mix per 6 to 8 ounces hot water.

Ginger Tea

Make your own ginger tea by putting a small piece of fresh peeled ginger in the pot along with any flavor tea. Try this with a small piece of candied ginger.

VARIATIONS: To make a sugar-free version, use sugar substitute, diet powdered orange drink, and sugar-free lemonade. You can blend it in the blender to make it smooth and creamy looking. This version is more concentrated so use less mix (about 1 teaspoon to 6–8 ounces hot water.)

CREAMY MINUTE COCOA

MAKES 1 SERVING.

4 teaspoons hot chocolate mix
½ to 1 teaspoon nondairy creamer (any flavor)
Sugar or artificial sweetener to taste
Boiling water

Place the dry ingredients into a mug. Fill with the water and stir.

Citrus Drinks

When you have lemons and/or limes and a juicer, you can make lemon or lime juice ice cubes to store in freezer trays or in zipper bags after they are frozen. One cube makes a glass of lemonade or limeade; sweeten to taste.

COOKING WITH PLANNED OR UNPLANNED LEFTOVERS

Leftovers are the original precooked convenience foods. In fact, it's a good idea to plan leftovers by cooking extra amounts of rice, noodles, and meats. You will find some ideas for serving leftovers in this section. One good principle to follow when serving leftovers is to add a fresh ingredient to give the food a whole new taste. Add freshly browned onions or garlic, new vegetables, some bouillon and/or complementary new spices or herbs. Also, don't always serve the same thing with the same leftovers. For example, don't always make hot turkey or beef sandwiches with leftover roast turkey or beef. Instead, look in cookbooks for recipes that list among the ingredients, cooked beef or turkey (or chicken, since chicken and turkey recipes can be switched).

Coffee Creamer Ideas

LOW-FAT COFFEE CREAMER

Save money by making your own low-fat coffee creamer. Just combine a little nonfat dry milk with low-fat liquid milk. Store in the refrigerator and shake before using.

COFFEE CREAMER SUBSTITUTE

If you run out of coffee creamer, try a spoonful of sweetened condensed milk. It replaces both the cream and the sugar.

- **Buttermilk:** Dip chicken, meats, vegetables, and other foods for deep-frying in buttermilk before breading; it's an especially good hint for folks who can't eat eggs, which are usually used for prefrying dips. Also, substitute buttermilk for regular milk when making biscuits, cornbread, cakes, and other baked goods.

- **Cheese:** You can melt leftover bits of cheese with canned skim milk and have a delicious cheese sauce for vegetables or noodles. Or make a cheese dip. The more kinds of cheese, the more interesting the flavor.

- **Egg yolks:** If you needed egg whites for a recipe, poach the leftover egg yolks, let cool, put through a sieve and then garnish soups, salads, and appetizers.

- **Eggs:** Save egg whites for meringues or fruit whips. Save yolks for custards, sauces, or to add to scrambled eggs. Cooked eggs, especially those leftover Easter eggs can become egg salad or can be chopped and added to tuna, chicken, or potato salad.

- **Eggnog:** Moisten bread for bread pudding with leftover eggnog. Just add some raisins and a bit of cinnamon to the nog and bread (leftover raisin bread is extra good), bake and enjoy!

- **Family buffet:** When you have accumulated several meals of leftovers, serve a "family buffet" to get them eaten up. One reader wrote that she makes a joke of buffet day by posting a menu on the fridge that has the name of a very famous restaurant in her city printed on top with the "choices du jour" listed below.

- **Meat, cold:** Any leftover meat can be sliced for sandwiches or ground up to make sandwich spread. Just add commercial sandwich spread or mayo and chopped carrots, celery, mushrooms, or other vegetables for filler. Cubed meats can be mixed with noodles or rice and salad dressing for a luncheon salad.

■ **Meat, hot:** Heat meat slices in leftover sauce for hot open-faced sandwiches or to serve over leftover rice or noodles. Add some onion, garlic, mushrooms, and/or complementary herbs to change the flavor of the sauce. Layer leftover meat with noodles and other vegetables add sauce, top with cheese, and you have a casserole. To make this casserole look better, add a layer of peas and/or red or green bell peppers. If you have a lot of sauce, but not much meat, supplement the meat with canned chickpeas, beans, or other vegetable proteins and cut the meat into small pieces.

■ **Soup stock:** Save the necks and backs of poultry or the bones cut off steaks and chops to make your own soup stock. Add herbs and seasonings to make the stock tasty. You can then freeze the stock in cubes in a freezer bag. They'll be handy to toss into dishes you want to season. The bonus is that when you make your own stock, you can accommodate any special diet needs, such as eliminating salt or fat.

■ **Vegetables:** Here are some good ideas for leftover veggies.

Store bits of leftover vegetables in a tightly covered container in the freezer. Add leftovers and their cooking water until you have enough to make vegetable soup. To enhance the flavor, add browned onions, bouillon or stock, and your favorite herbs or spices. Simmer at least 20 to 30 minutes to blend the flavors.

Add leftover cooked vegetables to salads or sandwich spreads or just arrange them on top of a plain lettuce salad and add dressing.

Cut or dice leftover potatoes, brown them with some onion, and add eggs or egg substitute for a hearty breakfast or light supper. You can add diced red and/or green bell peppers to make this dish more attractive. I like to put some salsa on top.

Fry leftover mixed vegetables—such as corn, peppers, potatoes, peas, and beans—with some onion, garlic, and other seasonings to make a vegetable hash.

HELOISE TO THE RESCUE: FOOD REPAIR, SUBSTITUTIONS, AND OTHER HINTS TO SEE YOU THROUGH A FOOD CRISIS

Throughout this book, I've included lots of Heloise Hints and Reader Recommendations that will save you time, money, and hassle in the kitchen. But this section features the most often requested first-aid kitchen tips for when things go wrong—as they inevitably do.

■ **A runny casserole** can be quickly thickened with dry instant potatoes, crushed tortilla or potato chips, or grated or shredded cheese. For example, crushed tortilla chips would go with a Mexican-type casserole; grated Parmesan cheese would go with an Italian-flavored casserole; potato thickeners would be fairly neutral.

❀ KITCHENEERING HUMOR ❀

A friend of mine was preparing a zucchini squash side dish for a large group of relatives. The dish got very runny, and so she added crushed corn chips; then because the corn chips made the dish too bland, she added various spices; then because it was still too thin, she added some leftover shredded Cheddar cheese; and then to make it look better, she topped the casserole with sliced cheese, crushed tortilla chips, and some chopped jalapeño peppers. Finally she browned the top of the dish under the broiler. Everyone raved about the dish and asked what was in it. "I have no idea," was all she could say.

- **Salvage a salty soup or stew** with a dash of instant mashed potatoes or by adding cut up peeled raw potatoes. Potatoes tend to absorb salt.

- **Revive limp celery stalks** in ice cold water in a tall container. They will keep in the refrigerator for a day or two.

- Pour a small amount of confectioners' sugar into a bag of **stuck-together marshmallows** and shake it so that the sugar coats the marshmallows. Most of the marshmallows will separate but you may need to work on the stubborn ones. Once coated with the sugar, the marshmallows won't be sticky anymore.

- So you planned mashed potatoes and instead, you overcooked them to **mushed potatoes.** Wash three or four potatoes, poke with holes, pop them into the microwave and cook till done. Then peel them and add them to the overdone potatoes. Whip up briefly to blend.

HELOISE'S HANDY INGREDIENTS SUBSTITUTIONS

Here are some common ingredients substitutions (see chapter 4)

WHEN A RECIPE CALLS FOR;	YOU CAN SUBSTITUTE;
Baking powder (1 teaspoon)	½ teaspoon cream of tartar plus ¼ teaspoon baking soda
Bread crumbs (1 cup)	¾ to 1 cup cracker crumbs or nonsugar cereal crumbs
Buttermilk or sour milk (1 cup)	1 cup whole milk plus 1 tablespoon fresh lemon juice or white vinegar. Stir, then let mixture set 5 to 10 minutes
Cayenne pepper (⅛ teaspoon)	4 drops hot pepper sauce
Cornstarch for thickening (1 tablespoon)	About 2 tablespoons white flour
Cream Cheese (1 cup)	1 cup low-fat cottage cheese blended with ¼ cup margarine
Unsweetened chocolate (1 square)	3 tablespoons unsweetened cocoa plus 1 tablespoon shortening or cooking oil

WHEN A RECIPE CALLS FOR;	YOU CAN SUBSTITUTE;
Egg (1 whole large)	2 egg whites plus 1 tablespoon vegetable oil for baking cookies, cakes, etc.
Self-rising flour (1 cup)	1 cup of all-purpose flour plus 1 tablespoon baking powder or 1 cup all-purpose flour plus 1 teaspoon of bicarbonate of soda and 2 teaspoons cream of tartar
Whole milk (1 cup)	½ cup evaporated milk plus ½ cup water or 1 cup water with ⅓ cup nonfat powdered milk
Onion (1 small)	1 teaspoon onion powder or 1 tablespoon dried minced onion
Sugar, granulated (1 cup)	1¾ cups powdered sugar
Tomatoes, canned (1 cup)	About 1⅓ cups fresh cut-up tomatoes, simmered 10 minutes
Tomato juice (1 cup)	½ cup tomato sauce plus ½ cup water

Chapter Eight

Entertaining and the Holidays

One of my favorite stories is about the cook—and I know one—who emerged triumphantly from the kitchen carrying the Thanksgiving turkey on a platter and, as all the guests "oohed" and "ahhed" in anticipation of the feast, she tripped and sent the turkey sliding across the floor. Calmly, she scooped the turkey back on the platter and said, "No problem, I'll just take this turkey back into the kitchen and get the other one." Of course, there was no "other one," but who would dispute that on Thanksgiving Day? Kitchen disasters happen, but point of this chapter is not just to anticipate entertaining catastrophes but to avoid them and make every celebration a time to enjoy friends, family, and the special memories and joys that each holiday or special occasion brings.

I receive a lot of letters, especially during the Christmas, New Year, and Hanukkah seasons that say, "I wish you could give my mother a hint" or "Why can't someone else take a turn now and then" or "My in-laws have been upset with me since last year because I did (or didn't) do what they wanted or expected." Too many us forget that holidays and special occasions are times for families and friends to get together instead of get torn apart. Although you can't always avoid disasters, I've come up with three basic rules to make every occasion more enjoyable for you and your guests:

▪ **Rule #1: Plan ahead!** Whether it's who will host an event, when and where it will happen, or how you are going to pull off having 50 people for dinner in your two-bedroom bungalow, everything depends on planning. I've included in this chapter a party timeline that you can adapt to any situation from a simple dinner party to the most elaborate celebration.

- **Rule #2: Keep it simple.** This might not always be easy to follow, especially if you want to put on an impressive affair, but there are ways to simplify the process, beginning with Rule #1. This chapter includes ideas to simplify your life both in planning and in food preparation. And I also pass along ideas from readers that have helped make their party plans easier and more fun.

- **Rule #3: If someone offers to help, accept it willingly.** But also be prepared to give specific guidelines. When a guest asks if he or she can bring something, look at the list you've drafted (see how important Rule #1 can be!) and suggest something from that list: a relish tray, extra ice, a dessert, or a side dish or whatever that person wants to bring. And, of course, when your event is in full swing, be prepared to accept a guest's offer to help. Whether it's filling the ice bucket, lighting the candles, putting dishes on the table, or helping clean up, many people have a better time if they are participating in the party by doing something. Remember, though, a guest is a guest and you shouldn't *expect* a guest to pitch in. One reader told me that he doesn't expect his guests to do the dishes after a dinner party, and he doesn't expect to do them at someone else's house—although he always offers.

From preparation and shopping to organizing and serving, from party themes to clean up, these are just some of the hundreds of holiday and entertaining hints sent in by my readers. I'm passing a few of my favorites on to you so

Here's a Thanksgiving Day poem Dorothy Gormick sent us in 1987 that I think says it all.

Lord, we humbly ask thy blessing,
On the turkey and the dressing.
On the yams and cranberry jelly,
And the pickles from the deli.
Bless each and every calorie.
Let us enjoy Thanksgiving dinner,
Tomorrow we can all get thinner.
For all thy help along the way,
We're thankful too for all our dear ones,
For all the far away and near ones.
Although we may be far apart,
We're together in my heart.
Keep us in thy loving care,
This is my Thanksgiving prayer.

P.S.: Anyone who wishes may help with the dishes!

that you too can have a "Happy *Every* Holiday" throughout the year. I've also included some simple gifts from the kitchen that will make any occasion special, because these come from the heart of your home.

GETTING ORGANIZED

A READER RECOMMENDS:

A California reader labels cardboard file boxes according to holidays and/or seasons and stores everything for the respective season: decorations, table linens, baking pans, idea books, stickers, stationery, rubber stamps, etc.

Also, when she gets new ideas or clips information about specific holidays during the year, she just put them into the appropriate box.

The Party Timeline: Countdown to a Great Hassle-Free Event

Now, as soon as you decide to have a big party, make a guest list, because the number of people will govern the other decisions you will make, such as location, food, and beverages. The bigger the party, the sooner you have to start actively planning.

- Book a facility if you are not going to have the party at home.
- Get the invitations printed and mailed. (For big events, invitations go out 4 to 6 weeks before the event.)
- Book a caterer, if you are hiring one (see section below).
- Arrange for the rental of tables, chairs, or other equipment (see below).
- Arrange for music or other entertainment, if any will be provided.

DAY 14 (TWO WEEKS BEFORE THE EVENT)

- If you have young children, **hire a sitter** or arrange for a sleep-over tradeoff with friends' parents.
- **Plan your menu** and make two shopping lists: one for perishables and one for nonperishables.

How to Work with a Caterer

Never assume what a caterer can, or is willing to do. The following checklist will save you a lot of anxiety on the day of your event. Make sure the caterer comes to see the location for the event. And, as with all contracted work, have everything in writing.

If you book a caterer many months or a year ahead, as you would for a wedding, it's a good idea to call about 2 to 4 months before the event to confirm that you are still on the books. And, of course, do call when you have the number of guests who have responded.

- Write down clearly all details about the food and beverages and how they will be served.
- Ask about the price per person and if the price will change if you furnish the wine, a special dessert, or whatever else you want to take responsibility for.
- Find out when the caterer needs the final guest count and if last-minute guests be accommodated. Ask if you will be billed for no-shows; the answer is usually yes.
- Determine fees for bartending and food service.
- Be clear on who will supply the tableware, serving dishes, punch bowl, ice buckets, serving utensils, warming trays, chafing dishes, etc. And if you are using disposable plates, napkins, and cups, find out who is responsible for buying them.
- Ask who will furnish table linens and centerpieces.
- Determine the schedule for serving.
- Find out how much of the cleanup the caterer will be responsible for.
- Ask about the leftovers—are they yours or will the caterer take them after the party is over?

Buy nonperishables items now; don't risk the store being out of an essential the day before your party. Nonperishables include all bottled beverages; all bottled, canned, and frozen food items; and all disposable plates, cups, glasses, tableware, and napkins.

Order all special-cut meat from the butcher, if you can, to be ready the day before or of the party.

■ **Check your dishes**, glasses, flatware, serving pieces, coffee maker, and anything else you can think of. Make a list of what you have on hand and what you will need to purchase or rent (see below).

DAY 7

■ **Do heavy cleaning** such as floor waxing, carpet shampooing, brass and silver polishing, and washing crystal or china. It'll all be done when you need your energy for cooking.

■ **Make a list** of the chores you really need to do. For example, do you really need to wash windows for a nighttime party when nobody will see them? Who really cares if you scrub every nook and cranny with an old toothbrush? Would you rather focus on food instead of house cleaning?

✿ **CLASSIC HELOISE HINT:** My mother always reminded readers that the most successful party-givers she knew just flicked a feather duster over the furniture and replaced all bright light bulbs with lower-wattage or colored bulbs. Why do a major housecleaning before the party when you'll just have to do it all over again?

DAY 1

■ **Check all of your lists** to make sure you have everything you need.

■ **Get out the serving dishes**, trays, and bowls to make sure they are clean and ready to use. *Note:* To avoid a possible mess, pretest the capacity of serving casseroles or bowls by filling them with water measured according to the recipe's amount.

■ **Arrange the serving dishes** on the table to make sure they will all fit and that you will have enough trivets or other hot dish protection for your table. (You will also want to make sure that the arrangement of furniture works if you are serving buffet style.)

■ **Look at your table linens** to see if they need ironing or, for some permanent-press cloths, a spin in the dryer with a damp towel to fluff out wrinkles (see also chapter 3).

■ **Buy most perishables.** Some vegetables, meats, fruits, etc., will be certainly keep for 24 hours, but some breads and rolls (such as French bread or specialty rolls) may not and will need to be bought the day of the party.

■ **Cut, chop, slice, dice,** marinate (meats), macerate (vegetables), cook, and do anything else to the food that can be done the day before.

DAY 0

If you have done all of the possible advance preparations for a party, on the actual day of the party, you have only the last-minute details to deal with. I think it's important to make some time for yourself on today so that you aren't so tired that you don't have a good time at your own party. So try to start the day pleasantly if you can by having a nice, quiet breakfast before you tend to the last-minute things. (Ha!)

Get dressed and ready at least ½ hour before the guests are suppose to arrive, you don't want to get caught in your bathrobe (as I once was) by an early arrival.

Things to Beg, Borrow, or Buy

Food, drink, and how you serve them are the primary components of any party or dinner. You'll probably have lots of staples in the pantry or liquor cabinet, but chances are you'll have to do special shopping for a party. And depending on how often and how you entertain, you may not need to acquire much. But most of us need a few extra things when it comes to entertaining.

Food Amounts

Although it depends on the occasion, how early your serve the food, and how hungry your guests are, there are a few rules of thumb for estimating the amount of food you need.

- **Dips:** 1 quart of dip, such as crab or broccoli, will make about 150 teaspoon-size servings.
- **Meat:** 1 pound of cooked lean meat provides about thirty-two ½-ounce slices for small sandwiches.
- **Chicken:** One 3½- to 4-pound chicken makes chicken salad for about 70 small triangular sandwiches.
- **Cheese:** A ½-ounce slice of cheese is enough for one small sandwich.

- **Bread:** A 20- to 24-ounce loaf of sandwich bread has about 25 slices and will make 52 small, triangular closed sandwiches.
- **Ham:** A 6- to 8-pound ham with a bone will serve 18 to 24 people for a buffet or 12 to 16 people for dinner; an 8- to 10-pound ham without a bone will serve 24 to 30 people for a buffet and 16 to 20 people for dinner.
- **Roast:** Boneless meats, such as a rolled rib roast, are calculated at about ¼ pound per person before cooking, yielding about 3 ounces per serving after they are cooked.
- **Ribs:** Meats with a lot of bone, such as barbecue ribs, can vary greatly according to how meaty or bony the slabs are; one slab of baby back ribs may serve only three people but a regular slab of ribs may serve four to six people.
- **Vegetables:** Generally, ½ cup is considered one serving. For example, ¼ pound of fresh green beans or ½ cup of canned green beans equals one serving.
- **Potatoes:** Serve one medium baked potato per person; for creamed or mashed potatoes, plan on 6 to 8 pounds of potatoes for twenty-five ½-cup servings.
- **Rice:** One serving is about ¼ cup cooked.
- **Noodles:** Count on about ½ cup cooked noodles per serving.
- **Salad:** For a green salad, one head of lettuce makes about six servings, not calculating the amount of other veggies you may add, such as cucumbers, celery, carrots, or tomatoes.
- **Nuts:** A 12-ounce can of nuts should serve 20 to 25 people.
- **Candies:** ½ pound of small candies serves about 25 people.

Beverages Service and Amounts

See chapter 4 for specific information on stocking your bar for a party.

- **Champagne:** Will you be serving the champagne as just a toast (one glass per guest) or as a cocktail drink (average of 2 or more glasses), or with the dinner (2 glasses per person)? Chapter 4 includes a chart that lists how much champagne is in each size bottle.

- **Wine:** When calculating your dinner wine, expect a 750-milliliter bottle of table wine to provide about eight 3-ounce servings, and you can count on an average of two servings per person. The same size bottle of dessert wine will provide about ten 2½-ounce servings and you can expect one or two servings per person of this wine, too.

- **Punch:** There's more to serving punch than just having the ingredients (juices, sparkling waters, liquors, etc.). Count on forty servings per gallon of punch.

  Ice block with or without garnish frozen in it.
  Garnishes including oranges, lemons, other fruit slices, maraschino cherries, and edible flowers.
  Punch bowl and ladle.
  Punch cups or 4- to 6-ounce glasses (may be disposable).

- **Tea and coffee:** Loose tea or tea bags; decaf and/or regular coffee; plus the accompaniments, including milk and coffee cream, lemon, mint leaves, and sweeteners (sugar, honey, artificial sweetener). A pound of coffee brews 50 cups.

Serving Needs

Usually, to think green means that you use disposable plates in areas where water conservation is a priority and nondisposables in areas where limited landfill space requires people to decrease trash output. If you don't have enough china and flatware for a party but still want to avoid creating a lot of trash, buy sturdy plasticware that can be washed and reused. Some plastic flatware can even survive the dishwasher! You may need to buy, borrow, or rent what you need so it's a good idea to review the following list at least 2 weeks before the event:

Plates: hors d'oeuvres, dinner, salad, bread and butter, and dessert.
Bowls: soups, flat bowls for pasta, and/or bowls for dessert.
Bowls, platters, and/or compotes for serving the courses.
Flatware: knives, forks (dinner, salad, dessert), and spoons (soup, tea/coffee).
Glasses: Wineglasses, cocktail glasses, punch cups, glasses or mugs for beer and soft drinks, and water glasses.
Cups and/or mugs for hot drinks.
Serving utensils: large serving spoons, serving spatulas, relish spoons and forks, large meat forks, carving knives, salad servers, butter knives, cheese and spread servers, pie servers, and cake knives.
Warming trays and chafing dishes. (*Note:* Plan where you will plug in electric warming trays, chafing dishes, and coffee makers; cords should not dangle where they will trip

people, and plugging too many appliances into one circuit may blow fuses or trip circuit breakers.)

Tablecloths, placemats, napkins (for appetizers, the meal, and dessert plus extras for messy foods like barbecue), bread cloths, and doilies.

Centerpieces.

Trivets to protect the table from hot dishes.

Water or juice pitchers and coffee and tea servers.

Food Service

Timing is all. You can have the best food in the world, but if you don't have a plan for serving, you'll end up in a confused state. The simplest way to avoid anxiety is the tried-and-true Heloise way—make a list. Whether or not you have a caterer, you'll want to have a complete list of everything you will serve and when it is to be served. You may also wish to create a corresponding timeline to tell you when to prepare, assemble, and/or cook (with temperatures and times included) items as needed. Don't forget the garnishes and condiments, which may have been pushed to the back of the refrigerator during your preparation for the party. This list gives you both the food and the serving dishes you'll need altogether. You don't want to be scrambling at the last minute looking for the perfect dish to serve that gorgeous soufflé you've just spent hours preparing.

- **Hors d'oeuvres**
Hot
Cold
Crudités/dip
Serving dishes and utensils

- **Entrée(s)**
Casseroles
Meat/Fish
Sauces
Garnishes
Serving dishes and utensils

- **Side Dishes**
Starch
Vegetable(s)
Salad
Serving dishes and utensils

- **Rolls/Breads**
Butter/margarine
Other toppings (roasted garlic, olive oil, etc.)
Heat before serving?
Serving basket or dishes or bread board/ spreaders

- **Desserts**
Garnishes (whipped cream, fruits, mint leaves, chocolate shavings)
Serving plates, bowls, and utensils; extra napkins

- **Cheeses**
Crackers
Crisp breads
Garnish (grapes, parsley)
Cheese board, plate, spreaders, knife, toothpicks for cubes, small dessert plates

- **Nuts:**
Serving dish

Small spoon for scooping
Small napkins

- **Mints or Chocolate Treats**
Serving dish, bowl, or plate

Themes and Variations

Just in case you're running out of ideas to make some occasion extraspecial, here are a few themes, recipes, and other hints to make your next party a night to remember.

GENERAL PARTY HINTS

If several people are bringing videotapes, cassettes, or CDs to your party, cut down on confusion by keeping a list of who brought what or by sticking a note on the protective container with the owner's name on it. If you are a lender to such a party, put an address label on the container or the item itself or make note of what you took to the party.

If you have drawing software on your computer, you can make all sorts of creative party invitations. If you design your invitation to be a trifold "brochure" you can seal it with a colored "sticky dot" from a stationery or office supply store, and you won't even need an envelope.

Check all invitations twice to make sure you've given your guests all the information they need: Use the reporters' guide of "who, what, when, where, why, and how." Tell guests who is hosting the party; what kind of party it is (brunch, luncheon, dinner, buffet, outdoor barbecue, or other event); when (date, time), where (address and directions, if necessary), and

why the party is being held (birthday, anniversary, other occasion, or just for fun); and how to dress (casual, black tie).

Be aware that there is a generational and regional difference in the interpretation of the word *casual*. In some parts of the country, casual means that the proper expected dress is business suits or a sport coat and slacks for men and similar business wear for women, but in other parts of the country and to some people under thirty or so, casual means "beachwear" or shorts, tank tops, and sandals for guys and gals. Lately, I've heard of invitations that say "nice casual" to let all generations know that men and women can dress comfortably but not quite so casual as beachwear.

❀ KITCHENEERING HUMOR ❀

A parent holding a multigenerational wedding rehearsal dinner at a family-style bar and restaurant planned to put *casual* on the invitations so that the guests would know not to wear cocktail attire or coats and ties. But the wise bride-to-be said, "Better not, or your son's friends will come in shorts, T-shirts, and workout clothes because that's casual to them." Out of the mouths of babes come words to the wise!

To give good directions to your party site, copy a section of the city map and highlight the streets on the route to the party. This is especially important if the location is off the beaten path.

Not everyone knows what *R.S.V.P.* means (an abbreviation for *repondez s'il vous plaît*, which is French for "Please respond"). If this is true in your circle of friends, you may want to put "Please respond, regrets only" or "Please call {number} if you can join us." If you receive an invitation that has R.S.V.P. on it, do your host a favor and respond. When hosts don't have a true number of guests, they can end up paying caterers for meals that go uneaten or if the hosts are doing the cooking, they end up with too many leftovers or worse yet, not enough food! *Note:* Many invitations to formal catered parties and weddings have an acceptance card with a stamped envelope to make responding easier. Please use them if you are the guest!

If you have hired a caterer, let the catering servers do their work and don't hover over them. If you've hired a good caterer (one whose work you have seen at other parties) then you should be enjoying your own party.

Take a hint from commercial party rooms. If you are having a summer party, make the house cooler than you would normally have it so that after all the people arrive and doors get opened and closed often, it will still be comfortable indoors. In the wintertime, set your thermostat a bit lower (meaning less warm) than normal. Run ceiling fans if you have them. A room full of people tends to warm up. (You could say that it's all that hot air conversation. *You* could but I won't!)

Preparing your house for a party sure can put the spotlight on everything that is worn out or in need of serious cleaning. If you can't get the repairs done a week before a party, it may be better just to cover up what's wrong and then fix it after the party. And, if you have damage after a party, check with your homeowner's insurance: The repair costs may be covered. Some insurance companies require that a representative see the broken chair leg or cigarette burn on the sofa so do call the company before you get estimates for repairs.

When you are serving coffee at a casual stand-up dinner party, mugs are a good choice because they don't spill as easily as teacups and disposable cups do. Provide napkins and set out coasters to serve as saucers and hope that people use them. (This hint came from a caterer.) If possible, serve after-dinner coffee from its own place, such as a small table or buffet. Then you can set up the cups/mugs, sugar, sweetener, and cream pitcher ahead of time (fill the cream pitcher as the guests are eating the main course so the cream isn't out of the fridge too long).

✿ **HELOISE HINT:** Many people think that marble tops on furniture are impervious like glass, but anyone who owns marble-topped furniture knows that it is easily stained nad etched by beverages, especially alcoholic and citrus ones. If you own marble-topped furniture, put an extra thick layer of paste wax on it before the party and, if possible, strategically place a thick decorative table runner on it to protect the marble and to prevent unpleasant memories of the party from getting etched into furniture.

If you are serving jug wines at your party, it will be less messy and easier to pour if you put some in a cocktail pitcher or smaller decanter. Often during the holidays wines are sold in 1-liter decanters that you can wash and recycle for this purpose.

Need a super-size ice bucket to hold decanters or wine or liter champagne bottles? Look in restaurant supply houses for large decorative plastic salad bowls that can double as punch bowls or ice buckets. Just about anything can serve as a cooler to hold canned or bottled beverages and ice. I've seen people use antique bathtubs, metal washtubs, plastic baby bathtubs, wading pools, kitchen or bar sinks, and plastic-lined garden barrel halves—anything that holds melting ice without leaking will do. One reader said she lined her clothes washer with bathtowels and then put in canned beverages and ice. The bonus was that the water from melted ice just drained away.

If you keep the cooler outside, it doesn't matter if it leaks or if condensed moisture drips, but if you have a makeshift cooler inside, moisture may condense on the outer surface and damage the floor or at least make it a slippery hazard. To protect your floor and your guests, first put down a plastic garbage bag, folded shower curtain or plastic tablecloth. Cover this with a towel or rug. Place the cooler on top. The towel will catch the drips and the plastic will save your floor.

At a large party, where plasticware is the only choice for wine and champagne, you may want to consider serving wine in 4- to 6-ounce plastic cocktail or punch cups instead of plastic stemware, which tends to tip and spill. Champagne does need to be served in stemware, and you can find tulip-shaped disposables, which are better for serving champagne than the flat-bowled plastic stemware.

If you live alone and you are cooking for the party yourself, arrange for single friend to help you host the party and serve as a bartender. It's really difficult to do it all alone. And, of course, anytime anyone you invite to the party asks, "Can I bring anything," say, "Yes!" And if you are fussy about all the food matching, say, "Yes, the theme is Italian [or whatever], I'd love an Italian [cheese, appetizer, wine, whatever]." And, if someone brings a wine or food that absolutely won't go with what you are serving, say "Oh that looks so good, I think I'll save it as a treat for myself tomorrow while I'm recovering from this party!"

Seasonal or party decorations for your door are easy if you buy either a grapevine or straw wreath at a craft store. As each season approaches you can remove the old bows and decorations and put on new ones for the next season or holiday. For example, pastel ribbons, plastic eggs, and bunnies for Easter; green bows and shamrocks for St. Patrick's Day; red, white, and blue bows and American flags for Memorial Day or Fourth of July; orange and black bows and small plastic bugs for Halloween; orange ribbons and multicolored fall leaves for Thanksgiving; and red and green bows and ornaments for Christmas. To get inspiration, copy ready-made wreaths you see in stores or catalogs.

Keep children busy while they wait for party dinners by having them make place cards for the table. They can decorate them with appropriate holiday designs (or designs of their choice). These can become treasures to take home, especially for doting grandparents.

BIRTHDAYS

Many catalogs sell birthday plates that say that the person being honored is special. If you don't have a store-bought birthday plate, you can make the birthday honoree feel special by using a family heirloom plate or flatware or some other piece of tableware that's reserved just for the birthday guy or gal. Let the honoree sit at the head of the table on his or her special day. Family traditions are part of the glue that holds families together.

One of my mother's readers had a great idea for a children's birthday party. Instead of candles on the cake, she put one colored toothpick on the cake for each guest. She taped a number on each toothpick so that it looked like the toothpicks were flags. Then, after the cake and ice cream were eaten, each child got a prize to match the number on the toothpick he received. The toothpick flags could also be a way of distributing door prizes at a luncheon, brunch, or other adult group event.

Make a balloon money tree centerpiece and gift. One family just plain ran out of ideas for what to give their eighty-year-old mom. So they made her favorite cake, which had an angel food cake base with a hole in the center. From the center of the cake, they floated a tree of eight helium-filled balloons—one for each decade of age. Each balloon held money for her to use as she pleased on taxi fares, dinners with her friends, and so forth. With the help of her grandchildren, she popped the balloons and got her special gift.

Make the party cake ahead of time when you aren't so rushed and freeze it. On the day you need the cake, thaw it, frost, and decorate.

For very young children or toddlers, substitute cupcakes for a single cake and put a candle on each one. That way each child gets to blow out a candle. This is a real peacemaker for very young children who don't understand why the birthday child is the only one who blows out candles. Try making cupcakes in flat-bottomed cup-shaped ice cream cones so that small children can eat the cake with less mess. Here's how: Fill the cones two-thirds full with batter and put in muffin tins for easy handling; bake according to the original recipe. Frost and decorate as usual. You can use different flavors of cake batter and colored cones for an even more colorful look. This is a good picnic party idea as well as a birthday idea.

If you have the courage, for a young child's birthday or even an adult birthday for people who are creative, bring out the cake iced but not decorated and let the guests draw on it with tubed decorative frosting and add jelly beans and other candy decorations. Layer or sheet cakes will do but you could also provide cupcakes or cookies to decorate.

If you want to decorate sheet cakes just like the bakeries do, you can find all sorts of sports figurines and other items at craft shops. Just be certain that they are safe for use with food; you wouldn't want paint flecks to fall into frosting or any other harmful bits to fall off decorations and get eaten.

If a birthday gift is just too big to wrap with traditional paper, wrap it in a paper birthday party tablecloth. Try recycling the shiny helium balloons you get on holidays to use as gift wrap. Carefully slit the edge of the balloon to make an opening large enough to insert the gift, then realign the open edges and tape them shut with transparent tape. Or tie the open end with crinkle gift ribbon and make a curly pompon. If you wrap gifts in the colored comics section of the Sunday newspaper, you'll be recycling and saving money at the same time.

If you have no gift wrap but you have several colors of plastic wrap, try this. Layer two or more colors and clear wrap, then place the gift in the center and bring up the edges and fasten with a twist tie. You can cover the twist tie with crinkle gift ribbon and make a curly pompon to finish the wrap. This is a good way to give a food gift such as a stack of cookies or a mound of candy.

No gift card? Cut one from the gift wrap or cut the front from an old greeting card and write on it. If you spilled coffee on the gift card's envelope or otherwise spoiled the envelope you could wrap the card with gift wrap or a colored paper that coordinates with the wrap.

If you have publishing software on your computer or if you are writing a note to an elderly person with failing eyesight, make the print extra large.

BABY SHOWERS

Baby showers used to be for women only but now they often include the dad-to-be. Consider having a couples baby shower.

Baby shower games could include a diapering contest to see who can diaper the fastest; to make it interesting, substitute balloons for the baby. An interesting game is to provide a basket of nursery aids—such as thermometer, diaper pin, baby wipes, aspirator, medicine dropper, baby bottle, pacifier, and various small toys—and ask the guests if they can give alternative uses for the items.

Create a baby pool. Have guests make guesses about the baby's birth date and time of birth and give a prize to whoever is closest when this information is known.

Winter Celebrations

CHRISTMAS

▪ **Christmas food centerpiece:** This idea for an edible "Della Robbia" centerpiece tree or wreath to lay flat as a centerpiece is easy to make with ordinary supplies from a craft store or florist. You'll need a 12-inch plastic foam cone or 12-inch-diameter wreath, parsley, sticky gum and florists stickpins, strong toothpicks (multicolored are best), purple and green grapes, stuffed olives, cherry tomatoes, radish roses, a miniature treetop ornament if using a cone or a bow if making a wreath. Cover the cone or wreath with the parsley, sticking it on with florist stickpins. Put some sticky gum on the bottom of the cone or wreath to make it adhere to a round serving plate. Now decorate by sticking toothpicks through the parsley and deep into the cone or wreath; then impale grapes, olives, tomatoes, and radishes on the individual picks. Top the tree with a miniature star or attach a bow or bows to the wreath with a toothpick or florists pin to finish your centerpiece.

▪ **Pinecone potpourri** is easy to make. Put some pinecones into a plastic bag, add a few drops of cinnamon or other fragrant or Christmas-scented oil (usually sold in small containers at craft and gift shops), and then shake well, leave overnight or longer. You can also give these scented cones as gifts.

■ **Gift wrap, if you're on a budget,** can be any kind of plain paper decorated with stenciled Christmas motifs. Or run a squiggle of glue down the package and sprinkle red and green glitter on it. If you use glitter, put your paper in a box that has at least 4-inch sides so that the glitter will fall into the box and not make a mess.

■ **Christmas gifts from the heart and hearth** are always welcome.

■ **Christmas ornaments** are gifts that will remind your friends and family of your thoughtfulness. I enjoy decorating with things given to me by friends.

■ **Save red or green bows** from gifts and floral arrangements that you receive throughout the year and use them to decorate anything in the house that is not moving! On second thought, you could put one on the dog if your dog will stand for such a thing!

■ **Santa's footprints** can be trailed through the house from the fireplace and back to it. Cut two foot shapes from paper to make a stencil. Place the stencils on the floor and sift flour over them. Carefully pick up the food stencils, shake off excess flour into a bag, and then move them to the next step sites. In the morning your child will see where Santa tracked the "ashes" or snow from your fireplace the tree, and back again to the fireplace. Flour vacuums up easily. If you substitute baking soda for the flour, you'll be deodorizing your carpets at the same time.

■ **Live Christmas trees** are sold throughout the country with the idea that you can decorate them for Christmas and then, after the holiday, plant them in your yard. Note that it's best not to keep a live tree in the house for more than 2 weeks. Keep the tree outdoors and well watered until just before Christmas, then place it indoors where it can get plenty of sunlight but not in front of an unshaded, south-facing window. It should also be away from heaters, fireplaces, or other locations where it can get extreme changes of temperature. Temperature changes can cause the tree to drop needles. You can also keep a Norfolk pine tree as a houseplant and then decorate it each year for a permanent Christmas tree.

■ **Instead of the usual Christmas fare** of turkey or ham, consider making a meal themed to your family's ethnic origin. One of our favorites is a South Texas Ranch breakfast—ham, bacon, sausage, eggs, fresh tomatoes, cream gravy and biscuits!

■ **Red and green foods:** Serve colorful Christmas meals by using appropriately colored foods.

Fill a wooden bowl with red Delicious and green Granny Smith apples and use as a centerpiece.

Add diced red and green bell peppers to rice, potatoes, and noodles.

Put red cherries and green grapes in red gelatin or green celery and diced red apples in green gelatin.

Garnish dishes with parsley and pimientos or chives and paprika.

Add diced red bell peppers to your green beans.

Blanch long thin strips of red bell peppers

and use them to garnish asparagus or whole green beans so that it looks as if the green vegetables were tied into a bundle with a red string.

■ **A children's Christmas candle salad** is so easy to make that the children can do it. Place a flat lettuce leaf on a small plate. Then place a ring of canned pineapple on the lettuce leaf. Then insert about a 2-inch long piece of banana into the hole of the pineapple ring so that it's standing up and looks like a candle in a holder. Put a blob of nondairy whipped topping on the top of the banana candle to look like wax is dripping down, and then put a maraschino cherry on top of the whipped topping to be the flame. If some of the red juice drizzles down, it looks even more flame-like. You might want to dip the banana pieces into the canned pineapple juice after you cut them so that they don't turn brown.

OTHER WINTER CELEBRATIONS

Hanukkah (also spelled Chanukah) is a Jewish holiday that's celebrated any time from late November to late December, depending on the phases of the moon. The menorah (nine-candle candelabra) is the main symbolic decoration. Traditionally, a game is played with a spinning top called a dreidel and presents are opened each night of the eight days of celebration. Foods can include latkes (potato pancakes), challah, sweet wine, honey pastries, and other foods featured in the kosher sections of food stores. A Sabbath meal might include gefilte fish, chicken broth with dumplings, noodles, rice and barley, and boiled or roasted chicken.

Kwanzaa is an African-American holiday that is celebrated during the last seven days of December. Decorations reflect Kwanzaa's principles. For example, fruits and vegetables signify the product of unified effort; a straw placemat reminds one of the reverence for tradition; an ear of corn represents each child in the family; a communal cup is used for the libations ceremony; and a seven-branched candleholder represents the African continent and the peoples of Africa. Foods are traditional African, Caribbean, and regional African-American dishes, featuring such foods as okra, plantain, sweet potatoes, barbecued meats, candies, and other desserts such as sweet potato pie.

For a **Valentine's Day** mixer party, cut cheap valentines in half and give the halves to guests as they enter. Their dinner companions are their valentines' other halves. If you need to group guests at a Valentine's bridge party, buy a pack of cheap children's valentines that includes at least four copies of each design. Have each guest draw a valentine from a basket. Then assign four people with matching designs per card table.

When giving roses to your Valentine's Day sweetheart, remember that the color of the roses has a specific meaning. Pink roses symbolize perfect happiness and sweetheart. Red roses symbolize love. Yellow roses symbolize friendship. White roses symbolize innocence and purity.

Spring Celebrations

ST. PATRICK'S DAY

March 17 is the day to wear a shamrock and green clothing even if you're not Irish. It's fun to serve green beer and green foods, such as lime gelatin salad, and Irish staples like corned beef and cabbage. One of my favorite memories is Mother making green pancakes!

EASTER

Try coloring eggs the old-fashioned way. Instead of using commercial egg dyes use yellow or red onion peels to tint them yellow-beige or pinkish, or boil with spinach or turnip tops to make them green. Cook with fresh beets to make them red. The colors will be softer and homey, just right to display in a natural fiber basket with real straw or raffia. When using commercial egg dyes, you can let the eggs drip dry in an old egg carton. Just poke holes in each of the egg cups so that the drips can run out, and put the carton on a thick pile of newspapers to absorb the drips. Make sure that there is plastic under the newspaper or that it is on a surface that won't get damaged if some dye seeps through.

Recycle green plastic strawberry baskets by putting Easter grass in them. You can also a lace ribbon through the holes near the top of the basket; tie with a bow. If you have no grass to make up an Easter basket, substitute a fluffed-up skein of green rug yarn and then you can recycle the yarn to tie up Christmas presents. Instead of Easter baskets, put candies and other goodies in useful containers, such as sand pails, bike helmets, sun hats, and so forth.

After the holiday, use the baskets to hold small gardening tools and gloves, craft supplies, or the remote controls for your TV. Or paint them and use them for containers for gifts, such as toiletries. Paint the basket to match your bathroom and use it to store rolled up washcloths and/or decorative soaps.

PASSOVER

Passover is one of the most dramatic Jewish observances of the year. This week-long holiday begins with the Seder, a ritual family dinner that includes prayers, songs, and narratives. Foods may include gefilte fish, chopped liver, chicken soup, baked chicken, potato cakes, kugels, tea, sweet red wine, macaroons, and fruit compote. Matzo is eaten throughout the holiday as a reminder of the unleavened bread baked by the Jews before their flight from Egypt.

Summer Celebrations

MEMORIAL DAY

Memorial Day is usually the first holiday of the summer and the traditional day to bring out your white summer clothing. It's a time for picnics and barbecues and going to the beach if your climate and geography allows. If you can't go to the beach, have a beach party in your backyard.

INDEPENDENCE DAY

Fourth of July is usually celebrated outdoors, at the beach, at the park, or in the backyard. Decorate with American flags. Stick them into centerpieces with red and white flowers. Place red, white, and blue runners made from ribbon or crepe paper rolls down the length of your picnic table. Freeze a marachino cherry in each ice cube of the tray to brighten up drinks. Decorate a sheet cake to look like a flag by frosting the cake with whipped topping, making blue stars with blueberries and red stripes with strawberry halves.

Autumn Celebrations

LABOR DAY

Labor Day is traditionally the end of the summer season and is usually celebrated with picnics, and barbecues. Because it is also harvest time in some parts of the country, grill squash, corn, and other garden vegetables while you grill the meats.

Rosh Hashanah (the Jewish New Year) and **Yom Kippur** (the Day of Atonement) represent a time for spiritual renewal and for taking stock of your life. At the Rosh Hashanah dinner, it's traditional for each person to dip a piece of apple in honey to ensure a sweet year. Yom Kippur is a day for fasting, repentance, and seeking forgiveness. After sundown, families gather and break the fast with a variety of traditional foods.

HALLOWEEN

All Saint's Eve is celebrated on October 31 and is traditionally a children's holiday, but there is no rule that says adults can't celebrate it, too. You can draw spiderwebs on windows with a black felt-tip, nonpermanent marker.

Add a few plastic spiders by suspending them from the curtain rod with fishing line. The marker will come off easily with window cleaner. Cut silhouettes of witches, arch-backed cats, or pumpkin faces from black construction paper to tape over your porch light or to put in windows to scare those hobgoblins that fly by during this spooky night.

Be creative with the jack-o-lanterns that you carve. They can smile, pout, or have any other expression that you like. To scoop out the pulp quickly and easily, use an ice cream scoop. Sprinkle the inside of the pumpkin with nutmeg and cinnamon and when the candle burns, your pumpkin will smell delicious. Instead of carving a face into your pumpkin, try drawing on the face; then after Halloween is over, the pumpkin meat inside will still be good to cook for pies and pumpkin bread.

Yucky games are the rule for **Halloween parties**. Put oddly shaped and yucky things like fake rubber bugs, faucet washers, plastic toys, rubbery plastic fishing worms (no hooks), cooked rice or oatmeal, or gelatin into several non-see-through containers and have children put their hands inside to guess the contents— pretend that they are witches' eyeballs, tarantulas, and spell-casting scary things.

If you don't want to give sweets to trick-or-treaters, give small toys or gift certificates for cold drinks at fast-food or convenience stores if your city's businesses offer them.

THANKSGIVING

Thanksgiving is the peak of fall holiday celebrating and fall leaves are the base for decorating along with dried gourds and dried corn of all colors, which can be used in centerpieces. Try heaping gourds and corn in a wooden salad bowl and fill in the gaps with fall leaves from your yard.

Keep children busy while they wait for Thanksgiving dinner by having them make paper-bag turkeys. Draw a turkey head with neck in profile on both sides of a piece of brown paper-bag (or cut a picture out from a magazine or coloring book). Next, stuff a lunch-size brown paper bag with a ball of crumpled newspaper, filling the bag about half full, to make the turkey's body. Tie the bag shut with a piece of string or fall-colored yarn so that the open end of the bag flares out to become the turkey's tail. With glue or clear tape, attach the head/neck to the stuffed bag and you have a squatty, sitting turkey.

Although turkey, cranberries, stuffing, sweet potatoes, and pumpkin pie are traditional, if your family doesn't like these foods, they might not feel as if they have something to be thankful for. Make foods that everyone likes and everyone will be thankful, including the cook, because who likes to make food that people don't like? Especially something as time-consuming as a Thanksgiving dinner.

Other Events

- **Family reunion:** Have each member of the family bring a favorite recipe and then put them all together to make a family favorites cookbook that celebrates family unity. Also, have each family member write down a favorite remembrance about family holiday traditions and then read them out loud. The remem-

brances can be put together so that the stories of all the generations can be saved for future generations.

- **Going-away party:** For a farewell party, hold a potluck. Ask the guests to write down the recipes for the foods they brought so that the person who's leaving can take the food memories to his or her new location.

- **Gourmet dinner group:** Form a gourmet group in your neighborhood. One group I know had monthly dinner parties in which the host would choose a theme (Italian, Chinese, Mexican, Cajun) and each guest brought a favorite food in that "flavor," either home-made or store-bought. The host would coordinate the menu and each guest's food came with all the needed serving trays, implements, warming dishes, and so forth. After dinner, the dirty dishes with any leftovers was put into a big plastic garbage bag so that it could go back home with the guest who brought it.

- **Heloise's birthday (April 15):** When you go to your post office to mail your income tax return why not send me a little gift of your favorite hint. I'm always looking for new ones to share. Mail them to Hints from Heloise, P.O. Box 795000, San Antonio, TX 78279, or Fax to 1-210-HELOISE.

POTLUCK PARTIES

You can have a potluck dinner or party for just about any occasion. Here are a few hints to make it easy to organize and enjoy.

- **Potluck cookie parties** can be fun. Limit the guests to twelve and ask each guest to bring thirteen dozen cookies, divided. One dozen goes on a tray for that day's party along with the other guests' cookies. The other dozens are placed in containers or zipper bags containing one dozen each. Then each guest takes home one dozen each of twelve different types of cookies. This is a really terrific idea to do a couple of weeks before Christmas. Then each person has a variety of cookies to serve during the holidays but had to bake only one type!

▪ **Potluck for singles:** If you live alone and get weary of cooking for yourself, try this party. Have a potluck dinner for all your friends who are in similar circumstances (and anyone else who might like to come). Ask each person to bring enough food for six (casseroles, noodle salads, other salads, etc.) and then have plenty of plastic bags and other containers handy so everyone can take some leftovers home for the next day's meal.

▪ **When you carry a casserole** to a potluck affair, you can put it into an appropriately sized paper or plastic grocery bag, or a box lined with a newspaper to insulate the bottom and to help catch any drips. If the dish has no lid, place plastic wrap over the top and sides, heat on High in the microwave for a couple of minutes and the plastic wrap will have a tight seal that avoids a mess. This hint is good even when the dish has a lid; many lids leak.

▪ **To keep a casserole hot,** put a folded towel in the bottom of a small foam ice chest and cover the casserole with another folded towel. It should stay warm for about 1 hour. CAUTION: Food should *not* stand for more than 2 hours between preparation and eating and should be kept at 185F or should be chilled and then heated to that temperature before serving.

▪ **To transport a casserole,** or any other dish of food, safely, be sure the lid is on securely, wrap in newspaper or put into a heavy paper bag, then set on a piece of carpet padding (rubber or waffle pads used to keep throw rugs from slipping) on the floor of your car or in the trunk.

▪ **Put a self-sticking address label** on the dish and the lid that you take to a party. If you forget to take your container home, it can be easily returned to you.

▪ **Pick up some old containers** at a garage sale that you can use for potluck dinners—then you won't have to worry about having them returned.

Gifts from the Kitchen

The recipes given here are quick and easy to make, so you can give them as gifts to a party host or to friends for any occasion. Package the food in a pretty container or jar, if you have one. Be sure to attach an instruction tag to the container that identifies the food and includes any necessary information about refrigeration, shelf life, serving ideas, or how to use it. Do be considerate of the recipient's dietary restrictions and concerns. Highly spiced or sugared food is not appropriate for everyone. Don't forget to review chapter 7, which also includes great gift recipes and mixes.

If you send perishable food gifts through the mail or other delivery service, be aware of safe food guidelines. To make sure, call the USDA Meat and Poultry Hotline at 1-800-535-4555.

When you order foods to be sent, find out how perishable they are, how protective the packaging is, and when the expected delivery date will be. Don't send food to someone's office; if it arrives over the weekend, it may be spoiled by the time the recipient gets it.

• **Edam cheese spread with beer:** Let a large Edam cheese reach room temperature. Carefully cut the wax off the top and scoop out the cheese, leaving a shell behind. Combine the cheese with 1 cup of room temperature beer. Then blend in ¼ cup of butter, 1 teaspoon of caraway seeds, 1 teaspoon of dry mustard, and ½ teaspoon of celery salt. Spoon the mixture into the cheese shell and refrigerate for several hours or overnight. This cheese can be served as an hors d'oeuvre with breads, crackers, or water biscuits.

• **Fiery hot basting sauce:** Combine 2 cups of cider vinegar, 1 tablespoon of Worcestershire sauce, 1 tablespoon of pepper, 1 tablespoon of hot pepper sauce, and ½ tablespoon of salt, or to taste. Mix well and allow to stand for at least 1 hour at room temperature. Makes 2 cups. Store in the refrigerator.

• **Heloise's diet refrigerator strawberry jam:** Note that you can use any fresh fruit instead of the strawberries, if you prefer. In a medium saucepan, mix ¾ to 1 cup of cubed fresh fruit, ½ teaspoon of lemon juice, ⅛ to ¼ cup apple juice (depending on preferred sweetness), and ½ to 1 teaspoon of fructose or sugar substitute. Taste for sweetness. Heat over medium heat for 3 to 4 minutes. Then sprinkle 1 to 2 teaspoons of unflavored gelatin over the mixture and stir until it is completely dissolved. Pour into a jar and chill until firm. This fresh jam keeps in the fridge for 1 to 2 weeks. Because it has no preservatives added, it is best to make only small batches as you need them.

• **Heloise's favorite low-cal grape jelly:** In a saucepan, mix 2 cups of unsweetened grape juice, 1 cup of water, ½ cup uncooked tapioca, and artificial sweetener to equal 3 cups of sugar. Let the ingredients sit for 5 minutes to allow the tapioca to soften. Bring mixture to a boil over medium heat, and boil for 1 minute. Skim off any foam, pour into sterilized jars, and seal. Refrigerate.

• **Herb mixes:** Chapter 4 includes some great ideas for creating custom herb blends.

• **Fruit vinegar:** Place ½ cup of fresh, washed and stemmed, strawberries or other berries in a large clean jar. Pour in white vinegar to cover. Cover the jar and let stand at room temperature for 1 week before using. You can remove the fruit or leave it in; if you leave the fruit in, the vinegar will continue to mellow and become stronger. Use in any recipe calling for a fruit vinegar.

• **Festive tricolor popcorn:** Make this recipe for gifts or parties. For each color you'll need 8 cups of popped popcorn, ⅓ cup of butter or margarine, 3 tablespoons of light corn syrup, ½ cup of packed light brown sugar or granulated sugar, and 1 (4-serving-size) package of flavored gelatin. Preheat the oven to 300F. Line a large jelly roll pan with foil. Put the popcorn in a large bowl. Mix the butter and corn syrup in a medium saucepan and warm over low heat. Stir in the sugar and gelatin; bring to a boil over medium heat and then reduce the heat and simmer for 5 minutes.

Immediately pour the syrup over the popcorn and toss to coat well. Using two forks, spread in a single layer in the prepared pan and bake for 10 minutes. Let cool and break up into small pieces. Repeat twice more using different colored gelatins. Package each color in a separate plastic bag. To serve, layer in large bowls. Store in an airtight container.

■ **Pomander balls:** To put a wonderful fragrance throughout your home during the holidays or any other time, stick rows of whole cloves into oranges or apples. When each fruit is *completely* covered with cloves so none of the fruit is showing, allow to dry in a cool place for several weeks. After the fruit has dried completely, make a mixture of one part orris root (available at drugstores) and one part mixed spices, such as cinnamon, allspice, nutmeg, and mace. Coat the fruit with this mixture and leave for 2 weeks. Then shake off any excess and tie each fruit with strips of ribbon. Make a loose ribbon at the top for hanging. Put the pomanders in closet or anywhere else in your house.

■ **For a wedding shower:** Collect favorite family recipes from grandparents, aunts, uncles, sisters, brothers, friends, write them on index cards and arrange them in a file or in an album according to appetizers, main dishes, desserts, and so on. Or wrap kitchen gadgets in new dish towel or apron and hold them closed with chip-bag clips or colored spring clothespins, add a bow made from two colored scrubbies held together with chenille pipe cleaners.

More Hints for Entertaining

■ **Allergies:** When you learn that a friend or relative has an allergy, list it on an index card or in a notebook so that you'll have a reminder not to serve fish or another unsafe food to your allergy-prone guest.

❀ **KITCHENEERING HUMOR** ❀

One family has a person severely allergic to nutmeg, which, unfortunately, is in many Christmas cookies. So anyone who brings a nutmeg-containing goodie always puts a small index card on a toothpick and sticks it into the food. The card has the red international "no" sign (a circle with a slash through it) drawn over his name, Billy. That way Billy knows which foods to avoid.

■ **Beverage cooling:** To ice a beverage without diluting it, one of my mother's hints was to put ice cubes into a plastic bag (now I'd

Fire Safety

Always keep a fire extinguisher handy in the kitchen for emergencies. Here are some fire safety facts.

- Baking soda can be used as a fire extinguisher. When thrown on a small fire, it produces carbon dioxide, which helps extinguish the fire.

- Never throw water on a grease fire; it will spatter and spread the fire.

- Don't use flour and cornstarch; they are combustible materials and may even cause an explosion.

- Salt is an old-time remedy that does not do much harm; unfortunately, it doesn't do much good either.

say a zipper bag) and then put the bagged ice into the beverage.

■ **Candles:** One reader wrote that before the arrival of guests, she lit a candle that stood in an artificial wreath centerpiece she had received as a Christmas gift. The entire wreath instantly caught fire and completely disintegrated. Guests and firefighters arrived at the same time! And the story doesn't end: They had a major restoration and cleaning project, which included refinishing the piano. CAUTION: Always check with the florist who delivers such a gift to see if the item is flammable. If there is no tag or if you don't know if it is flammable, then don't light those candles! We all want our parties to be memorable, but not because of a fire.

■ **Friendship cake:** When you send out invitations to a special event such as a golden anniversary, ask each guest to bake and frost a small square cake using their favorite recipe and decorating it as they choose. Then as the guests arrive, piece the cakes together to make a large patchwork cake. What a great hint for a quilters party! Don't forget to take pictures.

■ **Invitations:** Be sure to include a phone number for the location of your party so your guests can give it to anyone who may need to contact them, such as baby-sitters and elderly relatives; not everyone carries a cell phone. Also, if guests get lost en route, they can call to get directions and to say that they will be delayed.

■ **Tablecloth treasure:** For your next holiday or celebration, use a plain tablecloth and a variety of permanent markers, cloth markers, fabric paint, and/or liquid embroidery. Then ask your guests to decorate the cloth—they could draw a picture, sign their name, or even write a poem! CAUTION: Make sure you place a table pad or plastic shower curtain under the tablecloth so that the markers don't bleed through to the table. Be sure to date the tablecloth. Some other ideas are to use a single tablecloth for several occasions, decorating it with a different color each time and embroidering over the signatures to make them more permanent. You will have a table linen history of fun times, which you'll enjoy more each time you use the tablecloth.

Chapter Nine

Just for the Health of It!

Shopping wisely to get the most nutritional value for your money and proper handling and storage of food to prevent food-borne illnesses are two of the keys to good health in the kitchen. In this chapter I've included information on shopping; food storage; safe cooking; kitchen pest control; cooking with less fat, sodium, and sugar; and choosing wisely when eating out.

SHOPPING

Shopping is both more complicated and somewhat easier today than it was in the 1950s and 1960s. For example, it may take extra time to read and understand the comprehensive nutritional labels and the Sell By and Use By dates printed on products, but once this becomes an established part of your shopping routine, you'll discover how much easier it is to make safe and healthy choices than ever before.

Plus I think it is time well spent because you'll get the most value for the money you spend at the supermarket. And although it's not specifically a health issue, the unit pricing that appears in most supermarkets these days makes it easier for you to compare the costs of things—so it's worth taking the time to look at those labels on the products and on the shelves for savings and safety.

Reading the Labels

Most canned, boxed, or otherwise packaged foods carry a number of different labels. Some of the labels are required by law, such as the nutrition facts and ingredients, and others are used by manufacturers to advertise features and benefits of their product.

DATING TERMS

Product dates are most often displayed on items that have a fairly limited shelf life, but they are also stamped onto canned foods and other long-life products.

■ **Sell By** or **Pull Date:** The last day an item should be sold; after this date it should be removed from the grocery shelf.

■ **Expiration Date:** The last day that the item should be sold or eaten.

■ **Freshness Date:** Stamped on the item by the manufacturer to indicate how long freshness is guaranteed; if the item is stale before that date, manufacturers usually refund your money.

■ **Pack Date:** The date the product was packaged or processed by the manufacturer. It does not indicate long the food will stay good, but only when it was processed.

NUTRITION FACTS

The nutrition facts label shows serving size, number of servings per container, and other nutritional information. In addition, most labels provide percentage DV, (Daily Value) which means the percent of the USDA recommended daily allowances of that nutrient provided by the product.

■ **Serving size:** Always compare serving sizes when you are comparing nutritional information. Because manufacturers choose the serving sizes, each brand of the same product may have different serving sizes.

■ **Calories:** The number of overall calories per serving.

■ **Calories from fat/fat calories:** The number of calories derived from fat. The higher this number, the more likely it will be that the food carries health risks.

■ **Total fat:** Fat can account for most of the calories in some products. Some fats, particularly saturated fats and trans fatty acids, are considered bad for you.

Ingredients with large amounts of saturated fatty acids include meat fat, poultry fat, butter, cream, lard, cocoa butter, coconut oil, palm kernel oil, and palm oil.

Any product that lists hydrogenated or partially hydrogenated oils contains trans fat.

Oils with large amounts of monounsaturated fatty acids include olive oil, peanut oil, and canola oil.

Oils with large amounts of polyunsaturated fatty acids include safflower, soybean, corn, sunflower, cottonseed, and sesame oil.

■ **Cholesterol:** A fat-like substance derived from animal products only; high cholesterol levels in the body increase the risk of heart disease. Animal products include egg yolks, meat, poultry, fish, milk, and other dairy products.

■ **Sodium:** Listed as milligrams per serving, sodium is often the hidden component in processed foods that is of particular concern to those with hypertension, heart disease, and other conditions that can be affected by sodium.

■ **Total carbohydrates:** Some manufacturers list all the types of carbohydrates in the product (starch, sugars, and dietary fiber) and others list only the total carbohydrates in grams. For example, a cereal could a total of 23 grams of carbohydrates, of which 5 grams are dietary fiber, 5 grams are sucrose and other sugars, and 13 grams are starch and related carbo-hydrates. If you need to know exact amounts of starch and/or sugars because of a health condi-tion, you might want to buy only products that list those items.

■ **Dietary fiber:** Fiber is considered to have a role in lowering cholesterol and preventing colon cancer. Bran, whole wheat, and other whole grain cereals provide the most fiber per serving. Look for cereals that are low in sugars and sodium and high in fiber. Among the hot cereals, oatmeal and other whole-grain types provide the most fiber. A slice of whole wheat bread has 2 to 3 grams of fiber, whereas a slice of enriched white bread has less than 1 gram of fiber, a dinner role has only 1 gram, and a plain croissant has less than 1 gram of fiber.

■ **Sugars:** Some cereals include less than 1 percent by weight sugar, whereas others have 55 percent by weight. Other foods may have hidden sugars.

■ **Protein:** The American Heart Association gives us the most easily understood explanation of the difference between animal and vegetable proteins. Protein is made up of twenty-two amino acids, and nine of them must be obtained from food because they cannot be produced by our bodies. These nine are called essential amino acids and animal products contain all of the essential amino acids that we need. Each plant food group is missing or low on at least one essential amino acid, so to get all the amino acids that we need from plant foods, we need to eat plant foods that have complementary proteins during the day. Some examples of complemen-tary plant food combinations are rice and kidney beans, salad greens with chickpeas and walnuts, and baked beans and whole wheat bread.

■ **Vitamins and minerals:** Nutrition labels may also include the percentage of certain major vitamins and minerals, including vita-mins A and C and calcium and iron.

INGREDIENT LABELS

As required by law, ingredients are ordered on the product **label by weight from most to least,** although the labels do not show the exact amount of each ingredient. For example, if sugar is the first ingredient listed on a box of cereal, then that cereal has more sugar in it than any other ingredient. Be aware that sugar can be listed as sucrose, glucose, dextrose, fruc-tose, maltose, lactose, sorbitol, or mannitol. Other sources of sugar are honey, corn syrup, corn syrup solids, molasses, and maple syrup.

If you are watching your sodium intake, note that the following ingredients increase the total sodium content of the food: salt, onion salt, cel-ery salt, garlic salt, seasoned salt, monosodium glutamate, baking powder, baking soda, meat tenderizer, bouillon, sodium benzoate, sodium caseinate, sodium citrate, sodium nitrate, sodi-um phosphate, sodium propionate, and sodium saccharin. Remember that many condiments are high in sodium, including ketchup, mus-tard, soy sauce, steak sauce, barbecue sauce, Worcestershire sauce, chili sauce, salad dress-ings, olives, pickles, and relishes.

If a product lists fats or oils first on the label, it is likely to be high in fat content. The USDA currently recommends that you buy margarines that list liquid vegetable oils as the first ingredients and vegetable oils that specify the polyunsaturated or monounsaturated oil by name. Liquid oils tend to be higher in polyunsaturated fats than shortenings, stick margarines, and other fats that are partially hydrogenated. Hydrogenation makes vegetable oils more solid at room temperature. When the ingredient label does not specify which oil the product contains, it may contain coconut, palm, or palm kernel oil.

MANUFACTURERS' LABELS

Manufacturers are permitted to make certain claims on packages, particularly in reference to the content of sodium and fats. It is important to understand exactly what is meant by terms such as **low-sodium, cholesterol free**, and **light**.

Products that make claims for levels of **sodium** must also give the exact sodium content by milligrams per serving.

Sodium free = less than 5 milligrams.
Very low sodium = 35 milligrams or less.
Low sodium = 140 milligrams or less.
Reduced sodium = at least 75 percent reduction from usual levels.
Unsalted, without added salt, no-salt added = no salt added during processing.

Products that give **fat and cholesterol claims** on labels must also carry full nutrition labeling. The terms used give milligrams per serving.

Cholesterol free = 2 milligrams or less.
Low cholesterol = 20 milligrams or less.

Reduced cholesterol = at least 75 percent reduction from original food; both original and reduced amounts must be listed.
Extra lean = no more than 5 percent fat by weight.
Lean, low fat = no more than 10 percent fat by weight.
Light (lite), leaner, lower fat = at least 25 percent reduction in fat from a comparable product.
Ground beef has different terminology. Although fat content labels vary from store to store, ground beef is usually higher in fat than ground chuck, and ground round and ground sirloin are leaner. The fat content can vary from 16 to 28 percent by weight, and some supermarkets label their ground beef regular, lean, and extralean. You need to read the labels or ask the meat manager for the fat percentage.

The Safe Shopper

Along with other legislation on food content, my mother would have welcomed the Sell By and Use By dates on food packages, cans, and other containers. In her day, shoppers had to rely on their own observations of food and, of course, the only way to test for freshness for foods sold in non-see-through containers was to buy the item and open the container to see or sniff for better or for worse. Of course, packaged food has become so much more commonplace today that the guidelines set down by the USDA and other government bodies have become even more important.

Here are some shopping hints.

■ The Sell By or Best Used By dates should be far enough in the future so you don't end up having to discard the food.

■ Check for cleanliness at the meat, seafood, and fresh-food counters. If, for example, cooked shrimp is displayed on the same ice bed as raw fish, it could get contaminated.

■ Buy only Grade A eggs.

■ Determine if a product includes raw or undercooked animal-derived ingredients such as found in some Caesar salad dressings.

■ Dairy products should be pasteurized. Cheese that has been made from raw milk can be sold if it has been aged for more than 60 days. However, people with weakened immune systems should avoid all unpasteurized dairy.

■ Carry raw meat and seafood in individual plastic bags to avoid drips that may contaminate other food.

■ Take groceries directly home and put cold foods in the fridge immediately. Consider keeping an insulated cooler or other container in your vehicle to help keep hot or cold foods at the proper temperature on your way home from the market. Deli hot foods should be eaten, kept hotter than 140 F, or refrigerated immediately.

■ Never buy dented cans; the food inside could be contaminated.

Shopping the Healthy Planet Way

I am a firm believer not only that should we shop safely but also that we should shop with a concern for the environment and for the future.

New packaging materials and techniques used to help preserve freshness plus the proliferation of prepared food products have made our lives easier, but they have also contributed to environmental concerns. While I don't think many of us are prepared to give up the plastic wrap completely, here's a few ways that you can contribute to a healthier planet.

■ **Avoid products with excess packaging** and look for those with recyclable packaging. Then remember to recycle all packaging materials that you can.

❀ **HELOISE HINT:** Take a few minutes to write, call, or e-mail manufacturers to voice your concerns. You could even mail wasteful packages back to the manufacturer with a note explaining that as much as you like their product, you will quit buying it if it continues to be overpackaged. Manufacturers listen when money talks.

■ **Take your own carrier bags** to the supermarket to reduce the number of bags you take home.

■ **Recycle grocery bags** for garbage, storage, and other uses so that you don't have to buy new bags for such purposes. Just remember that it's not recommended to store food items in bags that were not manufactured for food. And if you recycle bread bags with print on them, do not allow the printed outside of the bag to touch food, because there may be harmful substances in the print material.

- **Wrap your lunch in a reusable container** to avoid using disposable products altogether. Reuse yogurt and margarine containers for soft food.

Check with your garbage/recycling company to find out what types of containers are recycled in your area.

- **Aluminum foil** is the only recyclable sandwich wrap, but if you are just going to use the foil once and throw it out, it's better to wrap with something else. The process by which aluminum is made is harmful to the environment.

- **Put lunch juices in a thermos** instead of containers made from products that can't be recycled.

- **Buy canned juice** concentrate instead of juice in polyethylene jugs, which just use a lot of packaging for extra water that you can add at home.

- **Buy milk in polyethylene jugs** rather than in cartons which are made of paperboard-coated with polyethylene; in some parts of the country it is considered too costly to separate the coating from the carton paper and so these are not recycled. To find out what is recycled in your community, call the company that picks up the garbage and/or recyclables in your community.

- **Look for the most food in the least packaging.** A pound of peas in a plastic bag generates less waste than two 8-ounce boxes of peas with inside paper wrappers, because both layers of packaging will end up in a landfill. Buy canned vegetables only if you can recycle the cans.

- **Avoid packaged microwaveable foods** in which special bags or separate trays or dishes are used for cooking; these are usually just marketing gimmicks. If you use quickie products, look for those that allow you to serve right out of the container.

- **Molded pulp egg cartons** are usually made from 100 percent recycled paper. They are a better ecological choice than polystyrene cartons.

STORING FOOD SAFELY

As this book is being written, food safety is a major issue in our country because food-borne microorganisms cause tens of millions of cases of intestinal illness each year in the United States. For most healthy people, distressful vomiting, abdominal cramps, and diarrhea are short-lived, but for people with weakened immunity—such as the very young, the elderly, or those with certain diseases—the symptoms can be severe and the infections can be difficult to treat.

Canned Foods

Most canned foods remain good for 2 years or more and are nutritious much longer under proper conditions according to the Canned Food Information Council. Store canned foods in a dry place at moderately cool, but not freezing temperatures or extreme heat. Storage temperature is the primary factor affecting storage life of canned goods. Avoid storing canned goods near steam pipes, radiators, furnaces, or kitchen ranges. Also avoid dampness, which may cause cans to rust. Rotate your canned goods in storage so that you have a regular turnover of about once a year.

✿ **HELOISE HINT:** If a product has no date marked on it, write the purchase date on the container with permanent marker. You still won't know how long the item has been on the supermarket shelf, but you will know how long it's been on *your* shelf. If you have a question about the product's freshness, call the manufacturer's 800 number, which is usually found on the label or package. Have the package handy so that you read off the product code and any other identification information the customer representative might need.

It's okay to leave leftover food in the can and store it in the refrigerator for a day or two. But don't store acidic foods, like tomatoes, in cans because they may get a "tinny" taste.

Refrigerating and Freezing

Information about safe refrigeration and freezing of specific foods is available from numerous sources, such as cookbooks or from your county extension agent. Generally, the refrigerator should be kept at a temperature of about 40F and the freezer at 0F or below.

- **Refrigerate most raw foods** at temperatures of between 30 and 50F.

- **After cooking,** if food is to be kept and not served immediately, it should be cooled quickly in the refrigerator to below 60F.

- **Food that is to be held and served warm** should be kept at minimum 140F.

Packaging for the freezer must be moisture/vaporproof to preserve the nutritional value of foods and to prevent their drying out. Rigid containers and plastic bags need airtight seals, and wrapped foods should be stored in extra-heavy aluminum foil, freezer plastic, or polyethylene-lined papers. Seal the edges of rigid container lids with freezer tape. Squeeze the air from bags before sealing. *Always* label containers with the name of contents, date of freezing and, if you rent food lockers, include the locker number on the package to make sure your food goes into your locker. Mistakes can happen.

If you have a garden or buy in bulk from farmers' markets to stock up your freezer, always freeze the fruits and vegetables quickly after packing in containers. Either put them in the freezer a few packs at a time as they are ready or keep the packs in the refrigerator until all are ready. If you rent a locker, transfer the packs from your home freezer to the locker in an insulated container.

To refrigerate or freeze hot foods, divide them into small portions for quicker cooling, and allow space around the containers for circulation of cooled air to prevent the refrigerator's or freezer's temperature from rising. Write dates on the containers so that you'll know when the leftovers are too old to eat.

Save space in your freezer by freezing soups and casseroles in loaf pans or square pans. They'll be easier to stack and fit. If you put food into a zipper bags, put the bags in pans, freeze to shape the leftovers, and remove the pans so that you can use them.

Do not attempt to freeze too many items at one time. The heat given off by warm foods can raise the freezer temperature. Try to place warm products away from already frozen ones. (Many upright freezers have a special quick-freeze shelf. See the manual that came with your freezer for more information about your particular appliance.)

REFREEZING SAFELY

Fruits, vegetables, and meats that have not completely thawed and those that have been thawed for only a short time and have been refrigerated, can usually be refrozen safely, but they may have lost some quality and flavor. Refrozen vegetables get tough. Refrozen fruits get mushy and soft, making them suitable for cooking but not for eating raw.

Low-acid foods, such as vegetables and meats, spoil rapidly after completely thawing and reaching 45F; it is *not* advisable to refreeze them as is. You can cook them, then freeze. Acid foods, such as most fruit and fruit products, are likely to ferment after thawing and reaching 45F. A slight fermentation of acid foods can change or spoil the flavor, but the food is usually safe to eat.

In case of a **power failure**, a filled freezer will usually stay frozen for about 2 days; a half-filled freezer may not stay frozen more than 1 day under normal conditions. Not 101F in

Storage Times for Frozen Foods

Beef, roasts and steaks: 6 to 12 months.

Beef, ground: 3 to 4 months.

Bread and yeast rolls: 3 months.

Chicken parts: 9 months.

Chicken or turkey, whole: 12 months.

Chicken or turkey, cooked: 4 to 6 months.

Meat dishes, cooked (such as casseroles or meat loaf): 2 to 3 months.

Dairy (ice cream or sherbet): 1 month.

Fish, cooked: 3 months.

Fish fillets, most types: 2 to 3 months; moderate to high oil content (mackerel, mullet, croaker), 1 to 3 months; low oil content (flounder, red snapper, redfish, trout), 3 to 6 months.

Fruit and fruit juice concentrates: 1 year or less.

Ham: cooked, canned or cured: 1 month.

Lamb: 6 to 9 months.

Liver: 1 to 2 months.

Oysters: 1 to 2 months (removed from shell and frozen in their own liquid).

Pork, cured: 1 to 2 months.

Pork, fresh cooked: 2 to 3 months.

Pork, roast: 4 to 8 months.

Pork, chops: 3 to 4 months.

Shrimp, in the shell: 6 to 12 months (remove the heads, which contain fat that may get rancid).

Shrimp, peeled and deveined: 3 to 6 months.

Processed meats (pork sausage, luncheon meats, bacon, hot dogs): 1 to 2 months.

Vegetables: 8 months.

summer in Texas!. To prevent spoilage, pack the freezer with dry ice. About 50 pounds of dry ice will keep the temperature below freezing in a 20-cubic-foot home freezer for 2 or 3 days, if you act quickly after the power goes off. CAUTION: Do not handle dry ice with bare hands; it burns.

A full freezer will maintain its temperature better than one that's only partially filled. If your freezer isn't full of food, fill it with bagged ice from the supermarket or fill clean plastic milk jugs or plastic soda bottles to about 2 inches from the top with water and put in the freezer. The bonus is that the jugs or bottles can be taken camping or to picnics to cool foods in your cooler and provide clean drinking water as the water thaws.

Freezer Monitor: Before you go on vacation, place a small clear bag of ice cubes in the top basket or shelf of your deep freezer. When you return, if you find the cubes have melted and refrozen into one chunk, you'll know that your freezer has been off for a considerable amount of time and some foods may not be safe to eat.

COOKING SAFELY

Here are some tips for handling and cooking foods safely.

- **Wash hands, utensils, counters, and cutting surfaces** with hot soapy water frequently during meal preparation to avoid cross-contamination of different foods or contamination from raw to cooked foods.

- **When using a meat grinder or similar food machines,** always disassemble and thoroughly wash all parts after blending or grinding raw meat, poultry, eggs, or vegetables.

- **Keep can openers clean and rust-free.** If your hand-held can opener sticks, clean first, then oil the parts with vegetable or mineral oil.

- **Wash all fresh fruits and vegetables** with clean water, using a soft brush if appropriate.

- **Protect any cuts or sores on your hands** with a plastic sealing bandage or plastic gloves. Bacteria from raw meat, poultry, or fish can easily enter the body through open wounds.

- **Drop the lid from canned goods into the can** before disposing or recycling it and it won't cut through the bag.

- **Cook food well.** Temperature is the best gauge for determining food safety. Bacteria grow at temperatures above 40F and below 140F, so use thermometers to test for proper temperatures and promptly refrigerate or cook foods—including vegetables—after you've cut them up. Periodically use a thermometer to check that your refrigerator is

Meat Temperatures

Always test meat temperatures with a thermometer to determine doneness:

- Beef and lamb should be cooked to at least 140F.
- Pork should be cooked to 150F.
- Poultry should be cooked to 165F.

keeping foods at 40F and the freezer is no warmer than 0F.

- **Avoid raw or lightly cooked seafood,** including lightly steamed mussels and snails, oysters on the halfshell, raw clams, sushi, and sashimi, for safest seafood eating. Also, fish should be flaky, not rubbery when cut.
- **Eggs should be cooked thoroughly,** because raw eggs may carry dangerous bacteria.
- **When reheating cooked foods** or partially cooked foods, heat them through to at least 165F.
- **Observe microwave cooking times** and directions about turning or stirring the dish to make sure it is thoroughly cooked.
- **When grilling,** precook meat and poultry in the oven, on the stovetop, or in the microwave.
- **Refrigerate leftovers** in covered containers to prevent cross-contamination.

The best advice for food safety is, **when in doubt, throw it out.** If the food looks or smells suspicious in any way, discard it and make sure no pet or small child can accidentally get at it while it's in the garbage can. Do not taste any food you're not sure of. Don't take a chance!

The USDA recommends that if a consumer or physician believes that a diarrhea episode is related to food from a particular source or restaurant, it should be reported to the local health department or nearest USDA office. Such notification can help others avoid illness.

PEST CONTROL

In some climates, even clean kitchens can sometimes attract unwanted guests like ants, roaches, and other pests. Also we bring some of them in from supermarket packaging. The best defense against pesky bugs is to make your kitchen an less-than-hospitable place for them to thrive.

You will want to pay particular attention to starchy food products such as flour, sugar, and other meals, which are prime breeding ground for insects. Open newly bought starchy foods as soon as you get home from the store to make sure it is not infested. If it is return it without delay. Get into the habit of putting newly bought starchy foods into the freezer for at least 7 days or storing such foods in the freezer or refrigerator; freezing kills the larvae.

Pest Prevention

If you discover insects in your cupboards, getting rid of them is a huge chore, so my best advice is to buy small quantities of staples, enough for a few weeks, freeze them for 7 days, and then store in tightly sealed containers or resealable plastic bags. Here's what to do if you do find bugs:

1. Take everything out of your cabinets and destroy every visibly infested box or bag. It is not wasteful, because in the long run, it's cheaper to throw out infested food than to let new foods get infested. Be sure to care-

fully check every single box of staples, including flour, meals, cereal, dried fruits, spices, pet food, pasta, dried beans, and peas.

2. *Do not skip this step.* Take the boxes that you determine to be pest free and put them into the freezer for 7 days at 0F or into an oven at 150F to 160F for 30 minutes. Freezing or heating will destroy weevil eggs.

3. Scrub the shelves with hot, sudsy water with a stiff-bristled brush. Pay special attention to cracks, crevices, the undersides of shelves, where pests or eggs are likely to be hidden, ready to reinfest everything after you've cleaned up.

4. Before returning anything to your cabinets, spray the shelves, crevices, and cabinet walls with an insecticide that says it kills whatever unwelcome insects have become established in your cabinets. Allow the cabinet doors to remain closed for 3 or 4 hours. The alternative to spraying cabinets is to close up the kitchen, cover all food, get the children and pets out of the house, and set off a fogger-type insecticide according to the directions given on the can.

5. After doing all of the above and before returning any foods to the shelves, put everything into sealable glass or plastic jars and containers. Clear containers will let you see if foods are reinfested and sealed containers will prevent pests from migrating to other places in the cabinets.

Ants munch on any food left out, especially foods containing sugar. Here are some tips for keeping ants out of the house.

- Keep all work surfaces clean and don't leave food out on counters overnight.
- Store food in your refrigerator or freezer or in sealed containers.
- Wash kitchen floors frequently so that spills don't attract food-seeking insects.
- Take the trash out each night or at least keep it near the door so that insects don't get a chance to march through the whole house to get at the garbage.
- Keep the perimeter of your house free of dense plants, wood chips, and other conditions that encourage pests to live and breed.
- Ants are said to dislike mint; plant it around your house perimeter to discourage them. You'll have mint for your tea, too!
- Boric acid will get rid of ants (see below).

❀ KITCHENEERING HUMOR ❀

Home-style recipes and methods for getting rid of kitchen pests do work, but creative substitutions may not. A cafeteria manager tried cucumber peelings as a repellent for ants; they worked very well when left on the kitchen counter overnight. Then a friend suggested that watermelon might be even better so the manger chopped up some and left it on the counter overnight. The next morning the watermelon was loaded with feasting ants. The manager decided to stick with the cucumber peels!

Cockroaches are among the most adaptable kitchen pests. This sounds like a B-horror movie, but it's been estimated that more than ten thousand cockroaches can live and reproduce beneath your refrigerator during a 12-month period, even if the rest of the house is immaculate. To defend against roaches, keep their hiding places clean: sinks; old product boxes; closet water heaters; the insides of all appliances, radios, wall clocks, TVs, and stereos; cupboards and drawers; cracks in plaster; and behind the baseboards. Seal the space around under-sink water pipes with duct tape to keep roaches out. My sources tell me that small brown German roaches often lay their eggs in stacks of grocery-store brown paper bags, and when they hatch, the babies feed on the glue used to manufacture the bags. So you may find a roach infestation where you store the paper grocery bags. I'm told that roaches also like the glue in cardboard cartons, check the areas where you store these items.

As alternative to commercially produced sprays or traps, here are two home-made recipes guaranteed to curb your roach problems. *Note:* Boric acid can be harmful to pets and children if ingested in a large amount at one time or in small amounts over a period of time. Please keep away from little ones!

HELOISE'S FAMOUS ROACH BALL RECIPE

You can set out these "tasty" treats in your cupboards for roaches any time that you suspect infestation. Be sure to keep them out of the reach of children and pets, however. Boric acid can be bought at drugstores, pharmacies, or grocery stores. For larger quantities, buy it from wholesale chemical distributors.

¼ cup shortening or bacon drippings
⅛ cup sugar
8 ounces powdered boric acid
½ cup flour
½ small onion, chopped (optional)
Enough water to form a soft dough

Mix the shortening and sugar together until they form a creamy mixture. Mix together the boric acid, flour, and onion and add to the shortening mixture. Blend well. Add water to form a soft dough. Shape the mixture into small balls (about ½ inch or so in diameter) or break into small blobs. Drop them into open plastic sandwich bags (to keep the balls moist longer). *Label the bag clearly* so everyone in the house knows it's roach poison, and place the bags in out-of-the-way places. Replace the dough when it gets hard.

HELOISE'S FAMOUS DRY POWDER ROACH RECIPE

Mix equal parts of boric acid and flour, cornmeal, *or* sugar. Use the mixture to dust infested areas. Roaches will walk through it and then ingest it when they groom their legs and feelers.

If you don't want to make your own roach killer, use insecticide-containing roach traps instead of sprays, which may contain neurotoxins, such as chlorpyrifos.

Houseflies and other flying insects can spread diseases. Their larvae, called maggots, live in garbage, sewage, soil, water, living or dead plants, and food that's been left out. To avoid or control flies in the house, follow these hints.

- Keep screen doors closed.
- Cover and tightly seal all foods.

- Wrap food well before throwing it out so insects won't be enticed.

- Spritz flying insects with a squirt bottle filled with a mild detergent-water solution. If they are on the window, you'll be washing windows and killing bugs at the same time! Mix about ⅓ cup of dishwashing detergent (the blue type works best) to 1 gallon of water.

❋ **HELOISE HINT:** Hair spray will stop a flying insect in flight.

- To make home-style flypaper, apply honey to yellow paper and hang the paper from the ceiling. The color attracts the insects and the honey holds them. Although it's not an attractive decoration, hang fly paper in the center of the room, because that's where flies gather to mate.

- To make home-style bug traps for your houseplants, smear petroleum jelly on a yellow plastic containers from detergent or other kitchen products; the bugs will be attracted to the yellow color and get stuck. You can wipe the plastic container when needed with a paper towel, and repeat.

As horrible as this thought is, **mice and rats** can live unseen for months in your home, foraging for cereals, crackers, and pet food in your pantry and cupboard. They can enter through a hole as small as ½ inch in diameter, can climb almost any wall or pole, and can drop 50 feet to the ground and still land on their feet, ready to scamper off looking for a free meal in your home. Rats can chew their way through just about anything. Here's how to store food safely.

- Make sure all food is stored in covered containers, especially bulk pet food. Garbage should be kept in sturdy cans with tight-fitting lids.

- To prevent mice and rats from squeezing their way in, be sure all possible crevasses in your home are sealed with steel wool, which they can't chew through.

- Cardboard boxes and cartons are a favorite mouse nesting area. Remove as many boxes as possible from closets and other storage areas.

- Even with protective measures, you may still find signs of rodents in your home or hear them go bump in the night. Rodenticides can be effective, but some can cause the rodents to die slowly within your walls where they will decompose and smell awful until the remains mummify. If your rodent problem is more than just an occasional visiting mouse, you may need to call in a professional exterminator. CAUTION: Rodenticides can be harmful to children and pets; use them with great care.

Silverfish and firebrats snack on materials high in protein, sugar, or starch—such as cereals, flour, paper with glue on it, and starch in clothing and rayon fabrics. Here is a home-style bait recipe. CAUTION: Keep away from children and pets.

SILVERFISH BAIT

1 cup oatmeal, ground to flour in a blender
½ teaspoon granulated sugar
¼ teaspoon salt
1 tablespoon powdered boric acid

Mix thoroughly and put about a teaspoonful each in several shallow boxes near hiding places. Cover each box with a crumpled pieces of paper. It will take 2 to 3 weeks to see results, so be patient.

Because **spiders** feed on all kinds of insects, they are considered helpful. However, we still don't want them in the house. Vacuum webs or brush them away with a broom covered with a pair of old panty hose.

Prevention is the best defense against **weevils**, which are so tiny you can hardly see them. Here's how to keep weevils out of cupboards.

- Before storing foods, check to make sure there are no signs of infestation.
- Store grain products in glass jars or tightly sealed plastic bags to prevent contamination from weevil migration.
- When you bring grain products home from the market, either put them in your freezer for 7 days or place them in an oven set at 150 to 160F for 30 minutes to kill weevil and weevil eggs.
- Buy only enough staples to last a few weeks. Weevils are more likely to invade long-stored products.

■ **A READER RECOMMENDS:**
Several Heloise readers have written to advise putting black pepper, bay leaves, or unwrapped sticks of spearmint gum on pantry shelves to deter weevils. Or poke a few dried bay leaves right into your flours and grains.

EATING HEALTHILY

This section looks at the ways you can eat better, whether you're cooking from scratch, trying to adapt your mother's (or *my* mother's) classic recipes, or simply trying to put a healthy meal on the table from whatever is on hand. Your selection of the right ingredients and cooking methods will go a long way to making your kitchen the healthy heart of the home. And because I know you don't eat all of your meals at home, I've included a few hints for healthy eating when you eat out at restaurants.

Here are a few simple ideas to reduce the fat, sugar, and salt from your recipes.

- **Look for reduced-sodium canned vegetables and soups** or buy fresh or frozen and season with no-salt herbs and spices to taste.
- Look for **reduced-sodium, water-packed** canned tuna, chicken, turkey, and ham for your salads or sandwiches.
- **Use salt substitutes,** which can be found in a number of different flavors.
- **To reduce the salt in canned foods,** discard the liquid that the vegetables are canned in. It will lower the sodium content by one-third and rinsing the vegetables will decrease the salt content even more. This hint is good also for canned tuna and shrimp. *Note:* Rinse shrimp very gently to prevent breakage.
- **To remove fat from canned soups,** refrigerate the can then remove the hardened fat that's risen to the top, or store the can

upside down in the fridge, then you can just pour the broth off the top while the fat clings to the can bottom.

■ **Buy canned fruit packed in its own juice** instead of in heavy syrup. The USDA says that ½ cup fruit canned in juice equals ½ cup unsweetened fruit plus 2 teaspoons sugar. But ½ cup of fruit canned in heavy syrup equals ½ cup unsweetened fruit plus 4 teaspoons sugar.

■ **Canned fruit juices** also contain a lot of sugar, high fructose corn syrup, or corn sweeteners. Many, like juice cocktails, punches, juice drinks, and nectars contain little actual fruit juice. You really need to read those labels carefully to find brands that are really juice so that you get more nutrition for your money. An alternative is to squeeze your own juices or just eat the fruit. Eating whole fruit will also provide more fiber than most juices.

■ If you have to **limit your sugar intake,** try to substitute other flavorings instead of adding sugar. For example, add cinnamon, vanilla, or other extracts to your coffee; add vanilla or fruit (dried or fresh) to plain nonfat yogurt; sprinkle cinnamon on baked apples or in applesauce; sprinkle pumpkin pie spice on sweet potatoes along with a sprinkle of butter substitute; or add chopped dried fruit to your cereal.

■ **To reduce salt** and have something instead of sandwiches for lunch, take along vegetables marinated in Italian or herb salad dressing with a few cubes of Swiss cheese on the side. Swiss cheese is lower in sodium than many other cheeses. Cook your own roast beef, turkey, or chicken for sandwiches. Luncheon meats,

such as ham, are high in sodium, and even deli turkey breast and roast beef have salt added.

■ **Avoid salty condiments.** Get more flavor by adding sliced cucumber, tomato, onion, or radishes to your salads and sandwiches. Also consider adding shredded carrots, bean or alfalfa sprouts, sliced apples, drained crushed pineapple, or grapes to salads or mixes for sandwiches.

Here are some ideas for reducing cholesterol in your recipes from the American Heart Association.

WHEN A RECIPE CALLS FOR:	USE:
Whole milk (1 cup)	1 cup of skim or nonfat milk plus 1 tablespoon of unsaturated oil
Heavy cream (1 cup)	1 cup evaporated skim milk or sour cream or ½ cup low-fat yogurt plus ½ cup low-fat cottage cheese or part skim milk ricotta cheese (thin with low-fat yogurt or low-fat buttermilk, if desired) or 1 can chilled evaporated skim milk whipped with 1 teaspoon of lemon juice, or low-fat buttermilk or low-fat yogurt
Cream cheese	4 tablespoons polyunsaturated margarine blended with 1 cup dry low-fat cottage cheese (add a small amount of skim milk if needed to blend the mixture)
Butter (1 tablespoon)	1 tablespoon polyunsaturated margarine or 1 tablespoon polyunsaturated oil
Shortening (1 cup)	2 sticks polyunsaturated margarine
Oil (1 cup)	1¼ cups polyunsaturated margarine

WHEN A RECIPE CALLS FOR:	USE:
Egg (1 whole)	1 egg white plus 2 teaspoons of unsaturated oil or a commercial cholesterol-free egg substitute.
Unsweetened baking chocolate	3 tablespoons unsweetened cocoa powder or carob powder plus 1 tablespoon (1 ounce) polyunsaturated oil or margarine (reduce sugar in the recipe by one-quarter).

The USDA has these ideas for making desserts healthier.

▪ When baking **fruit breads**, make them with part whole wheat flour and less salt, sugar, and fat.

▪ When **broiling fruit**, add a dash of cinnamon and garnish with a strawberry or mint leaf.

▪ When making **pudding** from a mix, do it with low-fat milk or make pudding from scratch so that you can reduce the amount of sugar along with the fat.

▪ When making **apple crisp topping**, use rolled oats in place of flour to increase dietary fiber; use only half the amount of sugar and fat as called for in the traditional recipe.

▪ **Oatmeal raisin cookies** can be made with less sugar and less fat, just add a few more raisins to boost the flavor and sweetness.

▪ **Pies** can be made with a single crust instead of a double crust to reduce fat and calories, but don't add all the fat back by using a heavy crumb topping. To increase dietary fiber, make your crust with whole wheat flour.

▪ For a **fresh fruit sundae,** top ice milk or low-fat frozen yogurt with crushed unsweetened fresh fruit.

▪ Try **cold or hot fruit compotes** for desserts; flavor with cinnamon. The fruit will taste sweeter if you eat it warm.

When baking desserts, look for recipes that allow you to substitute applesauce for oil in the batter. Usually, you can substitute applesauce for half of the fat in your own from-scratch recipes, but I don't think I'd do my experimenting with favorite recipes when baking for company—I'd try it out for my family first; they are more forgiving. A friend of mine, who is a terrific baker, says she has substituted applesauce for three-quarters of the fat in her favorite recipes with great results, so don't be afraid to experiment. Also, look for a commercial fruit puree product that can be used to replace butter, margarine, oil, or shortening in your favorite recipes or packaged mixes. Follow the instructions given on the label.

Some **sugar substitutes** can be used for baking and some cannot. Please read the labels on your favorite brands to find out which can be used for baking.

Even if you are cutting back on sugar and salt in your diet, **it's not a good idea to reduce the amounts of either ingredient in your traditional recipes when you are home canning fruits or vegetables.** Ingredients such as sugar, salt, lemon juice, and vinegar control spoilage. Instead, get new recipes that allow less sugar and salt but still keep the food safe. To get the latest information about recipes and food preparation, contact your country home economist. Look in the U.S. government section of the phone book, under Agriculture Department.

Try these alternatives to frying.

- **Roast** leaner beef and lamb on a rack in a roasting pan.
- **Broil or grill** quickly and by direct heat in your range broiler or on a grill; extra fats will fall away. Marinades add flavor and soaking meat in an acid solution tenderizes it.
- **Poach** meats or try **no-fat braising**.
- **Stir-fry** meats that have been sliced thinly across the grain; use very little oil or a very small amount of bouillon.

Dining Out

If you are on a special diet for any reason, whether it's allergies, other health problems, or weight control, you can still eat out and enjoy it. Today, most restaurants are used to accommodating special needs. If you find that the place where you are planning to go cannot or will not help you, make reservations elsewhere. If you don't know the restaurant's menu, you may wish to call ahead to discuss your concerns. At the restaurant, if you don't want to discuss your dietary needs at the table, you may wish to talk to your table server privately. Here are some other hints.

- **Request the salad dressing on the side** so that you can regulate how much you eat. Try dipping a corner of the salad pieces into the dressing and putting that corner into your mouth first. It will trick your tongue into thinking there was dressing all over the salad.
- **Get a glass of water** along with whatever beverage you order. Water really does quench your thirst and has no calories! Ask for a lemon or lime wedge to add to your water. Or have a nonalcoholic cocktail of fruit juice mixed with seltzer, club soda, or mineral water. Or try a glass of tomato juice with a twist of lemon or lime.
- **Order cocktails mixed with water or club soda** instead of sweetened mixers. Have a glass of wine instead of a whole carafe or try a wine spritzer (wine and seltzer water) to make the drink last longer.
- **Avoid creamy sauces.** Check out the menu and order vegetables seasoned with lemon, herbs, or spices instead of creamy sauces.
- **Have a baked potato** instead of fries or chips.
- **Order broiled, grilled, baked, steamed, or poached** meat or fish instead of fried meats or those served with a lot of heavy sauce. Choose entrées flavored with herbs and spices instead of smothered in a rich sauce or gravy. If fried foods are the only choice, remove the skin or breading and don't eat the whole serving to avoid fat and sodium.
- If the portion of meat or pasta will be more than you can eat, **ask to take the remainder home** or bring your own carry-out container with you and remove the excess from your plate so that you won't be tempted. Check out the new microwave-safe, tightly sealed

plasticware at supermarkets. You can carry them in a purse. No need to make a fuss or feel self-conscious, a good restaurant should want to please its customers, and good friends won't care.

▪ **Take your own favorite low-cal salad dressing** in a no-leak container when you eat out and order a green salad without dressing.

▪ If you are easily tempted to order things that sound good when others choose them but that are not on your yes list, **ask to order first** and don't let yourself get tempted to change your mind.

▪ **Don't order dessert until after you've finished your dinner.** Then you won't be tempted to eat it even if you are too full to enjoy it. If fruit isn't available, try sherbet, fruit ice, or sorbet. If you just can't resist a rich dessert such as pie, cake, or pastry, get a friend to split it with you. Or just have a cup of tea or coffee instead of dessert. Even if you add a teaspoon of real sugar to satisfy your sweet tooth, you will still add only 16 to 20 calories instead of hundreds or calories from a rich dessert.

It's often difficult to find a **fast-food place** that is right for you. Fast food comes at a price, which is often high calories and low nutrition. Here are some hints for eating at fast-food restaurants when you are cutting back on fats, sugar, and sodium.

▪ **Get the plainest, smallest burger or sandwich available.** Avoid special sauces; let the tomato, lettuce, sprouts, and whatever other salad veggies are offered be the flavoring.

Or substitute mustard, taco sauce, salsa, or diet salad dressing.

▪ **Put light dressings on salads.** Bring your own dressing if the fast-food restaurant you go to often doesn't offer them.

▪ **Order low-fat fruit-sweetened muffins,** such as apple bran, instead of a Danish. Choose a lower-fat bagel instead of a croissant or biscuit.

▪ If you order a **taco salad**, don't eat the shell that holds it. A bean burrito can have as many calories but less fat and saturated fat than an average serving of nachos, but can be salty.

▪ **Top your pizza with low fat choices,** such as mushrooms, peppers, and onion, instead of pepperoni or sausage. And ask for half the amount of cheese.

▪ **Avoid salads with high-fat dressings,** such as potato, macaroni, or cole slaw dripping with mayo and garnished with olives, high-fat cheeses, and real bacon bits.

▪ **Order a baked potato instead of fries.** When you order a baked potato, one pat of margarine provides less fat than such toppings as cheese, chili and cheese, bacon and cheese, and broccoli and cheese. Try topping your potato with diet salad dressing to moisten and flavor it. Add chives or chopped green onion tops if they are available.

▪ **Peel the skin off fried chicken.** The center breast is the leanest part; the fattest parts are the thighs and wings. The drumsticks and side breasts are in the middle range, fat-wise.

▪ Instead of a milk shake, order a **diet soda, plain tea, or coffee.** Or try low-fat milk or fruit juice.

- Instead of a fried pie or other pastry for dessert, have **nonfat frozen yogurt** or nonfat soft-serve ice cream.

- Order a **sorbet or ice** instead of ice cream at the ice cream shop; the smaller sugar cone has fewer calories than the larger waffle cone. Or order your frozen dessert in a cup and eat it with a spoon.

Chapter Ten

Heloise Helps Clean Up

My mother, the original Heloise, passed on many words of wisdom to homemakers—and to me. In one of my favorite quotes from her, she said, "Budget your energy doing only what you can. Life is priceless, so learn to enjoy it. Learn to do things the easy way. Take every shortcut you can find." It is my hope that the collective wisdom gathered here will give you the shortcuts and easy solutions for kitchen tasks that just *have* to be done. So let's deal with those problems pronto!

These hints will help you speed through common kitchen cleaning problems and zap kitchen odors. And since laundry rooms are often an offshoot of the kitchen, and laundry is an ever-present task, you'll also find hints to make the whole process less agitating!

KITCHEN CLEANING

The way I research cleaning hints has changed since my mother began *Hints from Heloise* in 1959. My mother's kitchen cabinet doors were worn from testing various cleaning solutions suggested by readers. But now, with so many different types of varnishes, paints, lacquers, and other finishes available for kitchen counters and flooring, I just can't personally test all of the reader ideas on my own kitchen cabinets. Instead, I call institutes and manufacturers whose research is more extensive than I could possibly do in my own home. The experts can tell me exactly what will clean which types of surfaces. Then I pass that information on to my readers.

Fabrics used for decorating have also changed a lot since my mother's day. So when I get a spot-removal question or hint from a reader, I consult the experts at the various fabric manufacturing and professional cleaning organizations. These experts will tell me what technique is likely to remove spots from certain fabrics and more importantly what solutions may actually damage the fabrics.

The kitchen is one room where we can't ignore the need to clean carefully. Any thing or area having to do with food preparation must be properly scrubbed and disinfected to prevent illness from food-borne bacteria—and that includes your hands. Not only do you need to wash your hands before eating, like Mom said, but you also need to wash hands carefully in between handling different foods, such as meat and poultry and the other components of your meal. Take a hint from the workers in cafeterias who wear plastic disposable gloves to avoid cross-contamination from lots of different foods and to protect their skin from food allergies and hot pepper irritation.

HELOISE'S CLASSIC HOME-MADE CLEANING SOLUTIONS

Vinegar, baking soda, and ammonia were my mother's favorite cleaning products and they have stood the test of time because they are good for most household cleaning jobs and they are cheap!

Also, vinegar and baking soda are kinder to your skin than many harsh commercial products and are safe for most chores. Did you know that the interior walls of the Statue of Liberty were cleaned with baking soda? About 200 tons of it was blasted from a spray gun to get

Caution for Combining Cleaners

Heloise and the Consumer Products Safety Commission warn that you must never combine ammonia or ammonia-based cleaners with chlorine bleach (sodium hypocholrite and sodium chloride) or any product containing bleach when you make home-style cleaners because the fumes from this chemical combination are very dangerous. Always be cautious with any time you combine products. Read labels of detergents and cleaners to identify the ingredients. (Some contain chlorine bleach and other chemicals that can be dangerous if combined with other cleaning solutions or even vinegar!) If in doubt, call the manufacturer; most have 800 numbers. You can get the number by dialing information (1-800-555-1212) and asking for the manufacturer and/or its consumer information line.

rid of 99 years of paint and coal tar. Baking soda was used because it wouldn't hurt the copper! The cleaning of the Statue of Liberty may not have been the biggest cleaning job in the world, but it is certainly a testament to a Heloise favorite cleaner/deodorizer.

Along with vinegar, I probably recommend baking soda more often than any other products—homemade or commercial. Ammonia is stronger and an irritant; it can burn eyes or skin. *Always* read the label precautions on the ammonia bottle before opening it.

CAUTION: Carefully and clearly label all homemade cleaning solutions for safety's sake. Avoid storing cleaning solutions in containers that previously held food. Even when containers are properly labeled, children and preoccupied adults can make mistakes.

Heloise homemade vinegar or ammonia cleaning solutions are good for windows and mirrors and are usually safe on most painted surfaces. Nonabrasive baking soda and borax are generally safe when you need to scrub heavily soiled surfaces. However, it's always best to test any cleaner on an inconspicuous place to make sure it won't harm the surfaces. Mix the solutions in a recycled clean gallon jug and pour into an old pump spray container for spritzing ease. *Note:* Some dishwashing liquids (for hand washing dishes) contain ammonia laureth sulfate and shouldn't be mixed with other solutions. Please check the label.

Baking soda, sprinkled on a sponge, nylon scrubber, or ball-scrubber made from old pantyhose, will clean glass and ceramic surfaces without scratching. Baking soda can clean kitchen appliances, counters, wooden cutting boards, stainless-steel sinks and chrome plumbing fixtures, refrigerator shelves and drawers, cooked on grease and oils on cookware and coffeepots, plastic dishes and utensils, and vacuum bottles. The bonus is that baking soda deodorizes at the same time. You can either sprinkle baking soda on a wet sponge or cloth and scrub as noted above or make a solution of 4 tablespoons of baking soda per quart of warm water. Keep a recycled spice shaker filled with baking soda so it's handy to sprinkle on smelly dishcloths and kitchen sponges or put the solution in a clean, recycled squirt bottle. Make a baking soda paste (just enough water and baking soda to

make a paste-like consistency), apply, allow to set a few minutes, sponge clean, and wipe dry.

Borax heavy-duty scrub: Clean heavily soiled surfaces with half a lemon dipped in borax instead of using abrasive commercial cleaners. Rinse well and dry.

Here are two **vinegar-based cleaners** to use on windows, mirrors and stainless steel.

- Mix ½ cup of white vinegar with enough water to make 1 gallon of cleaner.
- Mix ½ cup of white vinegar, 1 pint of rubbing alcohol, and 1 teaspoon dishwashing liquid (liquid for hand-washing dishes) with enough water to make 1 gallon of cleaner.

Here are two **ammonia-based cleaners**.

Sudsy ammonia contains a little detergent and is good for grease and grime and non-sudsy ammonia is all-purpose cleaner and doesn't streak.

- Mix ½ cup of sudsy ammonia with enough water to make 1 gallon of cleaner.
- Mix ½ cup of nonsudsy ammonia, ½ cup rubbing alcohol, and 1 teaspoon dishwashing liquid with enough water to make 1 gallon of cleaner.

COMMERCIALLY AVAILABLE HOUSEHOLD CLEANERS

The following guidelines are provided by The Soap and Detergent Association. Household cleaners are available as liquids, gels, powders, solids, sheets and pads for use on painted, plastic, metal, porcelain, glass and other surfaces, and on washable floor coverings. Because no single product can provide optimum performance on all surfaces and soils, a broad range of products has been formulated to clean efficiently and easily. While all-purpose cleaners are intended for more general use, others work best under highly specialized conditions.

Abrasive cleaners remove heavy accumulations of soil often found in small areas. The abrasive action is provided by small mineral or metal particles, fine steel wool, copper or nylon particles. Some also disinfect.

All-purpose cleaners penetrate and loosen soil, soften water and prevent soil from redepositing on the cleaned surface. Some also disinfect.

Drain openers unclog kitchen and bathroom drains. They work by producing heat to melt fats, breaking them down into simpler substances that can be rinsed away, or by oxidizing hair and other materials. Some use bacteria to prevent grease buildup, which leads to drain clogging.

Glass and multi-surface cleaners remove soils from a variety of smooth surfaces. They shine surfaces without streaking.

Glass cleaners loosen and dissolve oily soils found on glass and dry quickly without streaking.

Metal cleaners remove soils and polish metalware. Tarnish, the oxidation of metal, is the principal soil found on metalware. Some products also protect cleaned metalware against rapid retarnishing.

Oven cleaners remove burned-on grease and other food soils from oven walls. These cleaners are thick so the product will cling to vertical oven surfaces.

Rug shampoos and upholstery cleaners dissolve oily and greasy soils and hold them in suspension for removal. Some also treat surfaces to repel soil.

Specialty cleaners are designed for the soil conditions found on specific surfaces, such as glass, tile, metal, ovens, carpets and upholstery, toilet bowls, and in drains.

Toilet bowl cleaners prevent or remove stains caused by hard water and rust deposits and maintain a clean and pleasant smelling bowl. Some products also disinfect.

Tub, tile, and skin cleaners remove normal soils found on bathroom surfaces as well as hard-water deposits, soap scum, rust stains, and/or mildew and mold. Some also treat surfaces to retard soiling; some also disinfect.

3 STEPS TO CHOOSING THE RIGHT CLEANING PRODUCT

Our friends at The Soap and Detergent Association offer this helpful advice:

1. Check Out the Soils and Surfaces

The first thing to consider in any cleaning task is: What am I trying to get rid of? Is there grease on the stove, mildew on the shower door, or do you have hard water that leaves mineral deposits on bathroom and kitchen fixtures? Identifying the dirt you see—or maybe don't see, in the case of germs—is the first step in determining the type of cleaning product you need.

Now look at where the dirt is located. In other words, what type of surface is soiled? Today's beautiful surfaces offer many options in home décor, but they also require a bit of thought about how to safely clean them.

2. Consider Your Own Cleaning Needs

Are you a once-a-month, bucket-wielding cleaner who likes to use dilutable powders or liquids to tackle the whole house? Or do you prefer quick, frequent cleanups using spray cleaners? Do you have young children and need to disinfect surfaces regularly? Taking a moment to think about your cleaning needs and preferences will help you decide among the various product types.

3. Read the Label . . .

On the cleaning product:

Product labels are your best source of information for choosing a cleaner. Mildew remover . . . oven cleaner . . . glass cleaner . . . the name itself usually says exactly what the product will do. And if the name doesn't tell you, the back of the label will explain the types of soils the product is formulated to remove and the surfaces it should or shouldn't be used on. Labels provide just about everything we need to know about a cleaning product and its safe and effective use.

On surfaces and appliances:

Fiberglass, no-wax floors, countertop surfaces, ceramic glass cooktops—all have their own characteristics and cleaning requirements. Most surface and appliance manufacturers give instructions for cleaning their products . . . usually on a tag or sticker attached to the product. Or, contact your retailer or the manufacturer for care instructions. These are your best guides to caring for and cleaning new purchases.

Safety First Dos and Don'ts

Household cleaning products are safe when used and stored according to the directions on the label. Follow the label directions carefully, and if you have any questions, call the toll-free number found on most product labels. Here are some simple precautions to help prevent accidents from occurring:

DO:

- Read and follow label directions for proper use, storage, and disposal.
- Store cleaning products away from food and out of the reach of children or pets.
- Store products in their original containers and keep the original label intact. Product use and storage, disposal instructions, precautions, and first aid instructions vary according to their ingredients. It can be dangerous to use a product incorrectly or to follow the wrong emergency procedures.
- Put cleaning products away immediately after removing the amount needed for the job. This will limit accessibility to young children and help prevent accidental spills.
- Keep buckets containing cleaning solutions out of the reach of young children.
- Properly close all containers, especially those with child-resistant caps.

DON'T:

- Mix cleaning products. Products that are safe when used alone can sometimes cause dangerous fumes if mixed with other products.
- Reuse an empty household cleaning product container for any other purpose. The label instructions and precautions for the original product may be inaccurate or dangerous if used for a different product.

Courtesy of The Soap and Detergent Association

HINTS FOR CLEANING AND SIMPLE FIX-ITS

- **Air conditioning/exhaust-fan grills/ ceiling fans:** Wipe often with full-strength vinegar to clean and dust. This also helps to keep fresh air circulation.

- **Aluminum pots and pans:** To eliminate discoloring, fill a pot or pan with water; add 1 tablespoon cream of tartar for each quart of water used. Boil for around 10 minutes. Pour out. Wash and rinse as usual. Or, put 1 cup vinegar and 1 cup water in the pot and boil. Wash as usual, rinse, and dry.

- **Aluminum screens:** To clean up pitted frames, remove the screens and treat them outdoors with a rag dipped in kerosene. Rub both sides of the screen and frame. Wipe off carefully. This acts as a rust inhibitor for older screens. CAUTION: Kerosene is flammable. Do not light up anything while doing this task. Store flammables, clearly marked, in a cool place, away from ANY heat source.

- **Appliances I:** CAUTION: Always unplug electrial appliances before cleaning. Clean fingerprints and smears from shiny refrigerators and other appliances with a solution of half vinegar and half water applied with an old piece of terry towel. See also chapter 1, for more on the care and cleaning of appliances. Small blemishes on white appliances can be covered with white nail polish or white typewriter correction fluid. You can also buy touchup paint in small brush-bottles for this purpose at some home improvement stores and catalogs.

- **Appliances II:** You can wax the outside of enamel refrigerators, freezers, washers, and dryers with car wax. It will help to erase fineline scratches and also make them shine.

■ **A READER RECOMMENDS:**
One reader puts the cheapest type of clay unscented litter-box filler into the grease tray of his barbecue pit to absorb the grease drips. Then all he has to do when he is finished barbecuing is scoop out the lumps, throw them into the garbage, and replace the filler.

- **Barbecue storage:** Be sure to wash the grate of your grill well before storing it for the winter. An unwashed grate sitting all winter can build up bacteria that can contaminate your food and make you sick when you fire up again in the spring. Scrub with a wire brush or grooved scrapers made for grills. Or just scrub with steel wool and a good grease-cutting detergent. Always wear rubber gloves to protect your hands and clean well.

- **Brass and copper:** Tarnish can be removed with commercial cleaners or with some of the home-style cleaners, such as those listed here.

> This one is for brass only: dissolve 1 teaspoon of salt in 1 cup of white vinegar and add enough flour to make a paste. Apply and let stand for about 10 minutes. Rinse extremely well with warm water and polish dry.
>
> Saturate a sponge or cloth with vinegar or lemon juice, sprinkle salt on the sponge

and then lightly rub, rinse, and dry. Or dip a used half of lemon in salt, scrub away then rinse. These methods won't remove burned on stuff from copper-bottomed pans but they will make them shine.

Make a paste of flour, salt, and white vinegar or lemon juice; rub on, rinse, and dry.

Make a thick paste from rottenstone (an abrasive powder available at hardware stores) and oil (such as cooking or salad oil). Wipe off the excess oil after rubbing and polish with a clean cloth.

Brass fireplace tools can be rubbed with a very fine emery cloth, available at hardware stores.

- **Blender:** Rinse out the blender with water, then fill halfway with water and add a drop of liquid dishwashing liquid. Put the lid on and turn on low to agitate. Rinse well.

- **Burned food:** If food has burned onto the bottom of your cooking pot, soak the pot in full-strength vinegar for 30 minutes. Scrub and wash well. Or, add 3 tablespoons baking soda with enough water to cover the bottom. Simmer until gunk comes off.

- **Burn marks:** Burns marks on laminated countertops cannot be removed. Patch the burned area if you have a matching piece of laminate. Or, if possible, cut out the area and replace with a cutting board or decorative tile.

▧ A READER RECOMMENDS:
A long-time Nebraska reader sent this hint for cleaning copper. Spread on regular tomato ketchup, let it sit for a while, and then wash as usual.

❈ CLASSIC HELOISE HINT: For a quick cleaning of copper or stainless steel, use white (non-gel) toothpaste as a polish.

- **Candle soot on white stucco ceiling:** Mix a tiny amount of water with the powdered cleaner trisodium phosphate (TSP), which is available at home-improvement and paint stores, to make a paste. Test a small hidden area first. Blot (don't overwet!) the paste on the stained area only. This may not work on painted surfaces. Check with your local paint or hardware store for specific recommendations for specific paints.

- **Candlewax drips:** If you place candlesticks in the freezer for at least an hour, the wax drips will harden and can be easily picked off with a plastic knife or other nonscratching tool. If you have wax drips on dishes or other kitchenware that can be washed, first gently scrape off large pieces with a nonscratching tool, then rinse or soak in very hot water. Finish by washing in hot sudsy water and, if necessary, scrub with a nylon scrubber. Skin buffing pads that have become too rough for your skin are good for removing wax, sticky goo, and other annoying things from dishes, etc. Just wash the used pads with your laundry detergent and you can reuse them in the kitchen.

- **Ceiling:** To get rid of water stains, *do not* just paint over them because they'll be back to bleed through the paint. First, find out the source of the leak and make sure it's fixed. Then, cover the stain with clear varnish or a product sold in paint stores to prevent stains from coming through. Let dry completely. It may be a good idea to apply 2 coats of varnish or the product before painting.

- **Ceramic tiles (glazed):** Clean with an all-purpose cleaner or a commercial tile cleaner. For the crystalline tiles, use a mild soap detergent. Never use citrus-based cleaners or alkaline cleaners. CAUTION: Citrus fruit and foods containing acid may take the finish off the crystalline tiles. When purchasing tiles, ask the distributor for the proper care and any cautions.

- **Ceramic tiles (unglazed):** Use an all-purpose household cleaner on unglazed tiles, but be sure it is not a high-alkaline cleaner or citrus based. Allow it to stand for 5 to 10 minutes so it can work. Then scrub with a nylon-bristled brush. Rinse well. Commercial ceramic tile cleaners are also available.

- **Chair and table leaf storage:** To prevent marks on walls where you lean folding chairs and table leafs when you store them and to keep them dust free, put an old pillowcase over each chair or table leaf.

- **Chairs, cane-bottomed:** When cane chair bottoms sag, wipe the surface of the seat with a cloth dipped in hot water and wrung out well. Scrub thoroughly, then place the chair outdoors in the sun to dry, the sag should shrink up. Repeat when necessary.

- **Chairs, upholstered seats:** Sometimes minor soil can be removed from fabric if you sprinkle on dry cornstarch, then vacuum it up. Some foam-filled chair pillows can be spot-treated and then hand washed or put into the washer and washed on the delicate or knit setting; check the label. (You did save that label, didn't you?)

- **Chamois cloth:** If you like to use chamois cloth for windows and other cleaning, it will last longer if you wash it after each use in mild soapy water, leaving just a little soap in the cloth to help keep it pliable between uses. After washing, wring it out gently, pull it to its original shape, lay out to dry, but not in direct sunlight or near a heat source. Also, never use a chamois with strong chemicals, oil, grease, or as a sponge when washing the car.

- **China:** For some marks, rub the china with baking soda or cover the piece with liquid or powdered dishwasher detergent and water. Let it sit for several hours or overnight.

- **Chopping-block countertops:** Scrub surfaces with soap and water or a paste of baking soda and water. You can also deodorize by sprinkling the cutting board with salt and then scrubbing with half a lemon or vinegar on a sponge. Be aware that cuts and crevices can hold bacteria. Occasionally, disinfect the counter or chopping block with a solution of 2 to 3 tablespoons bleach to a quart of water. Rinse surface very well. Let dry. Recoat surface with a thin layer of mineral oil (not vegetable oil) and allow it to soak for 30 minutes.

- **Chrome:** Most chromium plating on small appliances, faucet handles, and so forth can be cleaned with sudsy water and buffed dry. If suds don't do the job, rub with baking soda sprinkled on a damp sponge or cloth, rinse and buff dry. Soap and lime buildup rinses off easily if you spray undiluted white vinegar on the fixtures and allow to set for a few minutes. If you remove the faucet aerator and soak it in undiluted white/apple cider vinegar for a while, the lime buildup should dissolve well enough so that you don't have to buy a new aerator. The trick is to remember how it was originally assembled before you put it back on the faucet! You can heat the vinegar for really stubborn gunk.

- **Clay pots:** The noticeable white rings that appear on pots both outside and inside are usually caused by a salt buildup. Wipe pots with a cloth soaked in undiluted vinegar.

- **Cleaning supply holder:** Leave the handle on, but cut out the top side off a large plastic milk jug and you'll have a container to store cleaning supplies, sponges, and scrubbers.

- **Coffeemaker:** It's best to wash a glass coffeepot after each use with soap and hot water so coffee oils don't build up to create a bitter taste. Run full-strength white vinegar through a normal brew cycle to clean the machine too. Then run several cycles of hot water to clear out the vinegar. CAUTION: After running vinegar through the cycle, don't put the machine on autopilot and put coffee in by mistake!

- **Coffee stains:** To get rid of stains in cups and mugs, rub the inside with a mixture of half salt and half white vinegar (or baking soda and hydrogen peroxide), then wash as usual.

- **Cookie sheets I:** To get rid of greasy buildup on regular metal sheets, elbow grease with a scouring powder or fine steel wool should remove it. Or, try oven cleaner. CAUTION: *Do not* use this method on nonstick pans.

- **Cookie sheets II:** To clean up nonstick pans, soak them in hot, sudsy water and use a nylon scrubber. Never use abrasive cleaners or steel wool. *Do not* use metal utensils on nonstick surfaces; use wooden or plastic tools. *Do not* put nonstick pans into the dishwasher. Read the manufacturer's care and cleaning instructions for your particular brand.

- **Cooler storage:** To avoid mildew when you store a cooler, let it dry thoroughly before you put it away, and place a spacer, such as a piece of wood or folded cardboard, between the lid and rim to prevent the cover from sealing tightly and to let air circulate. Sprinkle a bit of baking soda in the bottom of the cooler before storage to prevent that musty odor.

- **Copper:** If the item is lacquered, wipe off the surface with a damp cloth; *do not* use cleaners. If item is unlacquered, drizzle vinegar directly on the object and follow by sprinkling salt from a saltshaker over that and scrub. Or: Sprinkle salt on the sponge, drizzle vinegar over the sponge, then scrub away. Wipe with a paper towel. Rinse well and dry thoroughly. There are commercial cleaners designed specifically to clean copper also.

- **Cork flooring/wall covering:** Because cork is porous, use a floor wax on a regular basis to protect the surface. You can add a sealer as a protective coating. Follow directions carefully. Avoid using water on cork. Wipe up spills ASAP with a damp sponge.

- **Countertops:** Some difficult stains on laminated countertops can be lightened with a paste of baking soda and lemon juice. Let the paste dry; then wipe up with a damp sponge. If that doesn't work on stains such as indelible ink, marking pens, and newsprint, try using a little denatured alcohol on a cotton swab. Be careful since some solvents are extremely flammable. Follow directions on the containers. CAUTION: Do not use acid (citrus cleaners) or alkaline-based cleaners for general daily cleaning. They may corrode, etch, and permanently damage laminates by discoloring them. If you accidentally damage the surface with scouring powder or an abrasive pad, restore the shiny surface temporarily with mineral oil or silicone car polish.

- **Crayon on blackboard:** Use an oil-based lubricating spray to remove marks without damaging the blackboard. Test first on a small spot. Spray and let set for several minutes. Wipe off with a clean dry cloth. You may need to repeat to remove. Then add several drops of liquid dishwashing detergent to warm water. With a clean sponge, wipe down the board with a circular motion to remove any oily residue. Rinse well with warm water. Dry with a clean cloth. Don't use until completely dry.

- **Crayon on painted walls/washable wallpaper:** Spray a multi-purpose lubricating oil on a sponge or paper towel—do not let it drip on the floor—and apply to the stain. Gently wipe with a paper towel or clean white cloth. Dry-cleaning solvent will also work well. If the mark remains, pour a bit of baking soda on a damp sponge and gently rub in a circular motion to remove. If there is any lubricant residue left behind, dampen a sponge with a mixture of several drops of mild dishwashing liquid to 1 cup water. Squeeze extra liquid out of the sponge and apply to stain. Rinse sponge and go over area. Dry with a clean cloth.

- **Crystal chandeliers:** If a wire breaks and the crystals from a chandelier fall off, you can replace the wire with a twist-tie. Scrape the paper off the wire and put it through the opening in the crystal, hang it back on the chandelier. For cleaning, look for a special no-rinse crystal chandelier cleaner in the cleaning supplies department of your supermarket or home improvement store. You need only spray on the cleaner, and let it drip off. You may need to touch the ends of crystal drops with a cloth or paper towel to absorb some of the cleaner drips but you won't have to polish each crystal. *Do* protect furniture and floors from the dripping cleaner with an absorbent towel placed on top of an old shower curtain.

- **Crystal decanter:** If dishwasher detergent and hot water don't get rid of the stains, fill the decanter with full-strength warm to hot white vinegar and soak overnight or for several days, depending on the stain. Scrub with a bottle brush. Wash and rinse as usual.

- **Curtains:** To make curtains crisp without ironing, wash and rinse as usual. Add 1 cup of epsom salts to a sink filled with water, stir to dissolve and rinse the curtains in the solution; hang to dry, no need to iron! Or when you wash sheers or similar fabrics, hang them back up damp and put heavy dinner knives in the hem openings. The added weight helps pull out wrinkles as the curtains dry.

✿ **HELOISE HINT:** Spray-paint rods the same color as the curtains and they won't show through colored sheers.

- **Dishes:** When there's solidified egg yolk on a plate or gooey cheese left from a food like lasagna on a casserole, sprinkle the mess with salt or baking soda. Rinse in cold water before washing and it will come off easily.

✿ **CLASSIC HELOISE:** In my mother's day, hand-washing dishes meant using a dishrag, which you could sanitize by pouring bleach on it and letting it sit overnight in the corner of the sink. The dishrag was replaced by the sponge, which, until recently, we thought could be sanitized by running it through a dishwasher. Now, it's known that these traditional rags and sponges harbor bacteria that are not necessarily destroyed in the dishwasher cycles. *Update:* Look for disposable hand towels or super-strong paper towels to use as substitutes for the dishrag of Mom's day or your old yucky sponge.

■ **Dish drainer, tray, and sink rack:** When these items get mildewed, fill the kitchen sink with about 2 inches of hot water and add a couple of glugs of chlorine bleach. Place the items in the sink and let soak for about 15 minutes. If your hands won't tolerate bleach and you have no rubber gloves, after the soaking time, unplug the sink with barbecue tongs and let the bleach water drain away. Rinse items and let dry.

❀ **HELOISE HINT:** For easy cleaning, best-quality plastic dish drainers, trays, and racks can be placed upside down in the dishwasher and then washed as you would wash dishes, on the normal or light setting. Just be sure that the racks don't block any moving spray arms of the dishwasher.

■ **Dishwasher:** To remove brownish-orange stains, use a lemon or orange powdered breakfast drink. It's the citric acid that works. Put 1 or 2 tablespoons, but no detergent, in the dishwasher cups. Run the dishwasher through the wash cycle. Repeat until all stains are removed. It should look almost new.

■ **Dishwashing by hand:** Adding about a ½ cup of vinegar to dishwater will prevent grease from clinging to dishes, pots, pans, and the sink. Adding a ½ cup of vinegar to rinse water will make crystal and glassware sparkle, too. The bonus is that when you rinse in a pan of clean water instead of under running water, you save water—important if you live in a drought area!

■ **Dishwashing detergent:** When you've used most of the dishwashing detergent in a plastic squirt bottle, add some water, and shake to dissolve the remainder. You'll get a diluted detergent powerful enough to wash eyeglasses or your hands, or to quick-wash dishes, pots, and pans that don't go into the dishwasher. It will rinse off more easily than full-strength detergent and you'll be saving money using up every drop of detergent. This is especially true with ultra and concentrated products.

■ **Door tracks, sliding glass:** Clean stains by spraying or pouring full-strength vinegar into the door tracks. Let it sit for a bit. Rinse out with water and dry.

■ **Drains:** Instead of cleaning drains with harsh caustics, use this preventative hint to keep them clear. Each week, pour ½ cup of baking soda into the drain, followed by 1 cup of vinegar. Let the mixture foam for about a minute or so and then flush the drain with lots of very hot water. *Note:* If you have a clogged drain that can't be opened with a plumber's helper, call the plumber. Caustic chemicals won't unclog a badly stopped-up drain, and if sewage mixed with caustic chemicals backs up into your sink or tub, the surface glaze can be damaged. Then it will stain very easily and seldom look clean unless bleached frequently.

■ **Drawer organizers:** If your plastic silverware organizers slide around in the kitchen drawer, keep them in place with double-sided adhesive tape. Then you can still remove them for cleaning.

■ **Dust brush:** A natural-bristle paintbrush removes dust from nooks, crannies, and knickknacks.

■ **Dust mop:** If you live in an apartment and shaking a dust mop outside makes a mess on your neighbor's porch or balcony—not to mention a mess of neighborly relations—tie a paper or plastic bag around your mop before shaking it to collect the dust. Sometimes when you wash a synthetic-fiber dust mop, all the strands of yarn get tangled up hopelessly. But you can continue to use the mop: Put it into an old pillowcase or make a pocket from an old towel by folding it in half and sewing up the sides, leaving an end open. You can spray the mop pocket with a dust magnet product, dust away, and then launder it so that you always have a clean mop. And when this mop is clean, you can dust walls and remove cobwebs from corners with it.

■ **Dustpan substitute:** If you break a glass, wet the edge of a folded newspaper and use it as a dustpan. The wet paper will gather many shards of broken glass. Used paper plates from dry foods like sandwiches can be cut in half for the same purpose.

■ **Dust prevention:** Cover party crystal and trays with plastic wrap when you store them and they'll stay clean between parties. *Note:* Although this may seem like a waste of disposable wrap, if water is an issue in your area, you will be saving water by not washing everything *before* and *after* each party.

■ **Electrical appliance cords:** To remove food splatters off cords, first unplug the appliance, then dip a sponge into warm sudsy water and run along cord. Do not wet the plug. Dry with a clean cloth.

■ **Enamelware:** Can be put in the dishwasher, but do not scour with powders or steel wool.

■ **Fingernail savers:**

Clip steel-wool scouring pads with a spring clothespin when you scrub with them.

Wear rubber gloves to protect hands and nails from cleaning solutions.

Use those little square plastic clips from bread bags to scrape gunk off of dishes, pots, and pans. It's safe for nonstick surfaces, too.

■ **Floor repair:** To patch a gouge in resilient flooring, finely grate scraps of the flooring with a food grater, mix the grated flooring with clear nail polish, then plug the gouge. This hint is not for dents, but for gouges or holes.

■ **Floor waxing:** Before you put a new coat of wax on linoleum or tile floors, **remove** the old wax. It's a chore but the results are a longer-lasting, better shine. Remove the old wax with a solution of three parts of water to one part of rubbing alcohol. Here are some other waxing hints:

If a highly waxed floor gets dull between washings, mop with a solution of 1 cup fabric softener in about 2 gallons of water.

If you're in the mood to wax the floor and discover that you have no floor wax, substitute a solution of 2 tablespoons of liquid furniture polish and ½ cup vinegar added to a gallon or so of warm water.

You can apply wax to floors with a long-handled paint roller. The bonus is that rollers work fast and will reach under furniture for you.

Buff your newly waxed floor and get your muscles toned at the same time. Wrap an old bath towel around each foot and skate around the floor. Do be careful while you're skating so that you don't fall!

■ **Floors, removing marks:** Shoe heel scuffmarks on resilient flooring can be removed by rubbing them with a pencil eraser or a dry paper towel. You won't believe how well this simple hint works. Crayon marks will come off if rubbed with a damp rag containing toothpaste or silver polish.

■ **Floors, rinsing:** Kitchen floors (and some painted surfaces) can be rinsed with water that contains a splash of vinegar to remove soapy film. *Do not* use vinegar water on marble or terrazzo floors, because it's acidic and will ultimately dull them.

■ **Freezer:** To clean and remove stains, take everything out of the freezer and wipe down with a solution of liquid dishwashing detergent and water or baking soda and water.

■ **Furniture:** CAUTION: Always test furniture polishes on an inconspicuous place before applying them. Different finishes require different types of polish, and the wrong polish can

Floor Cleaning

Whether you have vinyl, wood, linoleum, tile, or any other floor, you need to follow the manufacturer's instructions for cleaning it. It's not just a matter of how the floor looks, but how long its finish will last. Most types of flooring can be cleaned with water and mild detergent or household cleaners, as described below. A couple of cautionary notes: When scrubbing tile floors, avoid soaking the floor with excess water; it can seep into seams and loosen the adhesives that hold the flooring. No-wax floors get dull if detergents or floor cleaners are not properly rinsed off or if the wrong cleaner is used.

• If floors are only slightly soiled, sweep or vacuum, then damp mop with a clean sponge mop and warm water, pressing just hard enough with the mop to remove surface dirt.

• When you wet mop, clean small areas at a time and rinse the mop frequently in a bucket of *clean* water; otherwise, you'll find that you are just smearing the dirt around instead of cleaning it up. Be sure to change the water when it gets dirty, which can mean several times for a large room.

• Flooring manufacturers warn against washing floors with strong soaps, dish-washing liquids, and gritty powders or cleansers. When floors are really dirty, wash with a no-rinse cleaner or general-purpose liquid detergent. *Note:* Read those labels on products to see which floors they are formulated to clean and do follow the label's directions for use!

• Here are the general directions for scrubbing floors with most recommended detergents. You will

continued ...

need two buckets: one for the detergent solution and one for rinse water.

1. Dip the sponge or mop into the bucket.

2. Don't squeeze or wring the mop out before you spread the cleaning solution over a small area.

3. Wait a minute for the detergent action to loosen the dirt. Let the detergent do the work for you.

4. Scrub the area with the mop; then wipe up the liquid.

5. Rinse well, being certain not to leave any detergent on the floor. Changing the rinse water often will yield better results. *Note:* Always rinse floors with clean water even when directions for the floor cleaner say it's not necessary. Not rinsing can result in a sticky film forming on the floor. If a film remains after rinsing, try mopping one more time with a solution of 1 cup or so of white vinegar to a bucket of water.

Before *cleaning wood floors, always* check with a flooring company or flooring specialist for information. Certain treated floorings require specific cleaning methods. Here is a Heloise home-style wood floor cleaner that is generally okay for most floors: Mix ½ cup of apple cider vinegar in 1 gallon of warm water. Wet a soft cloth or sponge mop and squeeze most of the moisture out; then wipe the floor without getting it really wet. Buff after cleaning to bring out the luster.

damage the surface so much that refinishing is the only solution to repairing the surface. The following home-style formulas are Heloise Healthy Planet polishes. Unless otherwise directed, you mix them up, apply with a clean soft cloth, and then polish with another clean, soft cloth. Old socks are terrific for furniture polishing; you can put one on each hand and do double-time.

Cover scratches with colored markers, shoe polish, the meat of a pecan or walnut, or commercially prepared lemon or boiled linseed oil.

Renew a piece of furniture by cleaning it with mineral spirits; read the container for directions and for the surfaces it will not damage. Or use my Heloise furniture polish: Mix together ⅓ cup of vinegar, ⅓ cup of turpentine, and ⅓ cup of boiled linseed oil. Moisten a soft cloth with the polish and rub over furniture; polish with a clean cloth. CAUTION: Never attempt to boil linseed oil; it's highly flammable. Buy it at the hardware store and DON'T store the cleaning rags for long term or near any heat source. (Always clearly label homemade cleaning compounds and keep them away from children and pets.)

Add 1 teaspoon of lemon oil to 2 cups of mineral oil to get a lemon-scented polish. Apply and then buff with a soft clean cloth.

Mix 1 teaspoon of olive oil with the juice of one lemon, 1 teaspoon of brandy or whiskey, and 1 teaspoon of water. This polish must be made fresh each time.

Mix three parts olive oil with one part white vinegar. Apply and polish.

For oak furniture, boil 1 quart of beer with 1 tablespoon of sugar and 2 tablespoons of beeswax. When cool, wipe the mixture on wood, allow to dry, and then polish with a chamois cloth.

❀ KITCHENEERING HUMOR ❀

A reader wrote me that she tried the mayonnaise polish on a low wooden chest. She applied too much so she left the room to get a cloth to wipe off the excess. When she returned, she found her big old tomcat purring happily as he licked off the mayo. She says she sat on the floor and laughed while he finished his snack and saved her the step of wiping off the mayo.

To remove a water white spot from furniture, rub the spot with equal parts of toothpaste (not gel) and baking soda, applied with a soft damp cloth. Rinse out the cloth and wipe off the residue. When the finish is smooth, buff with a clean soft cloth. Restore color and shine by rubbing the spot with the meat of half a pecan, then buff.

To touch-up black-painted metal furniture, cover scratches with a wide felt-tip marker. Then apply wax over the marker to finish.

■ **Glass cooktops:** Let cooktop cool before cleaning. Use a nonabrasive sponge or clean cloth. Apply a paste of baking soda and water to it and wipe surface or use a ceramic glass cleaner. Do NOT use cleaners that contain bleach or ammonia. NOTE: Always follow the owner's manual for your appliance.

■ **Glass cookware:** To get rid of burned-on grease, spray the cookware with oven cleaner and let stand for 30 minutes. Wash and rinse well.

■ **Glass decanter:** To remove stains and mineral deposits from decanters, fill with warm white vinegar and let stand overnight. Then add uncooked rice and shake to remove the stains on the inside that a sponge or brush can't reach. Rinse and dry. Or try about ¼ cup of dishwasher detergent dissolved with hot water. When the water cools, fill the decanter to the top and let soak for a few hours or overnight. A bottlebrush may remove stubborn stains, too, but it may not remove them completely.

■ **Glass vases, lime deposits:** Remove lime deposits by filling the vase with hot water and then drop in a couple of denture tablets. Let soak a few hours and then scrub with a bottlebrush. Rinse and let dry. Or fill with warm vinegar and let stand for several hours; rinse and let dry. *Note:* You can save that vinegar to clean something else or pour it down the drain to freshen it. To avoid lime deposits, use only distilled water, because there can be lime content in the water. This is a good hint for making coffee, too, because if you brew coffee with distilled water, you'll hardly ever need to clean your coffeepot.

❀ **CLASSIC HELOISE HINT:** When a bottlebrush wouldn't fit into a narrow-necked crystal vase, my mother put some broken eggshells into the vase, added a little water, shook until all the film and dust were scrubbed off, and rinsed well.

■ **Glass-top coffee table:** A permanent marker stain should come off with regular glass cleaner and some elbow grease. If that doesn't do it, moisten a cotton ball with full strength household isopropyl (rubbing) alcohol.

■ **Glasses in dishwasher:** To prevent hard water spots from forming on glasses in the dishwasher, be sure to use the right amount of dishwasher detergent. More IS NOT better! Adding a rinsing agent will help make the water run off the dishes faster and speed the drying process, which also helps to prevent spots from forming. When hand washing, don't air-dry glasses (especially fine crystal); dry with a soft, lint-free towel.

■ **Glasses, film:** To try to eliminate foggy film, soak in warm to hot, full strength vinegar and then scrub with a brush or plastic scrubbie. If the film coating persists, the glasses are etched (little scratches). Etching cannot be removed, sad to say.

■ **Glasses, hand washing:** Aside from cutting oneself while cutting bagels, the other common danger that lurks in the kitchen and sends folks to hospital emergency rooms is cutting one's hand when washing glassware and crystal. Instead of putting your hand into the glass to swish around a dishcloth or sponge, wash glassware with a long-handled brush, like a bottlebrush. To avoid water spots, wash with the proper amount of liquid dishwashing detergent and rinse in the hottest water safe for the glasses and your hands, and then dry with a soft lint-free cloth. If you live in an area that has hard water, rinse the glasses in water to which a splash (less than a glug but more than a spritz) of vinegar has been added.

✿ **HELOISE HINT:** When washing crystal and other fine ware, wear rubber gloves. You'll get a better grip and won't let precious items slip from your hands in the soapy water.

■ **Glasses, stuck:** When two stacked glasses get stuck together, put cold water in the top glass and dip the bottom one in warm to hot water. Gently pull the glasses apart. Or pour some baby oil or mineral oil between the glasses, allow to set for a while and then gently pull them apart. Wash in hot soapy water and rinse.

■ **Gold:** To polish a gold tray, wash in lukewarm soapy water, rinse, dry with a soft cloth or polish with a chamois.

■ **Gravy stains (on a tablecloth):** As soon as you see a spill, spoon up as much of it as possible. Blot the stain with paper towels. Put the tablecloth into a sink and soak with a mixture of 1 teaspoon of a mild, colorless detergent to each cup of lukewarm water. If the stain is still there, put a full-strength liquid laundry detergent on the fabric, rub it well, and then launder as you normally do. (See **Grease** following.)

■ **Grease (on a tablecloth):** Spoon off any blobs of grease. Then sprinkle cornstarch or artificial sweetener or talcum powder over the stain to absorb it. When absorbed, brush powder off. Use a prewash spray and wash in the hottest water safe for the fabric. Read the care label. Before putting into the dryer, check stain to make sure it's gone.

■ **Grout:** Clean grout in kitchen or bathroom tiles with a mild bleach solution, about 2 tablespoons bleach to a quart of water. A cotton swab or toothbrush is a handy applicator for the bleach solution.

■ **Hardwood floors I:** Chair legs or furniture feet may mar hardwood floors. You may be able to minimize the damage by filling the dents with shellac or clear nail polish. Apply self-adhesive-backed moleskin to the bottom of chair legs to prevent this damage.

■ **Hardwood floors II:** Wax, polyurethane, or other liquids can seep through the protective finish on the floor and soak into the grain of the wood, causing black spots or dark stained areas. Wipe up spills immediately or the floor can be damaged so it will need refinishing. If black spots are not stained too deep, they can be removed.

On a *waxed* floor, rub the spots gently with fine sandpaper or very fine steel wool. That will lighten the area, so it will have to be restained and waxed to match the rest of the floor.

On a floor with a *polyurethane* finish, the black spots may be due to cracked polyurethane, caused by age or impact. Strip off the polyurethane and sand the spots. Restain to an even color, if you have to. Apply fresh coats of polyurethane.

■ **Ink:** To get ink stains out of leather furniture, dip a cotton swab into a bit of rubbing alcohol or patent leather cleaner and carefully dab at the stain. Then wipe with a damp sponge and recondition the leather.

■ **Iron:** To get rid of the stains on the bottom, first turn off the iron, unplug it, and let it get cold. To remove starch or synthetic fiber buildup or icky brown gunk, wipe the bottom with a cloth soaked in diluted white vinegar. Repeat if you have to. Also, iron cleaner (in a tube) is worth having on hand.

■ **Jewelry:** Do not wear diamonds while doing housework or gardening. Cleaning products can harm diamonds and gold, and a good knock can loosen the prongs that hold a stone in place. Bleach can be harmful to gold and other metals used in jewelry making. *Note:* This includes the chlorine in swimming pools!

✾ **CLASSIC HELOISE HINT:** To avoid having to bend over to wipe up spills, my mother made Heloise mats, and what a nostalgia trip it was for me to visit my friend Judy's parents home and see a Heloise mat on her floor. Here's how to make a Heloise floor mat: Get a couple of old terry-cloth towels or cloth bath mats. Cut them into a small round or oval shape and sew them together to make a two-layer mat. You can zigzag-stitch around the edge, sew on some fringe or put bias tape around the edge to prevent fraying. Toss the mat on the kitchen floor and when there is a spill, simply scoot the rug over with your foot and mop it up. When the mat is dirty, toss it into the washing machine to get clean again. My mother made these for friends and family and everyone loved them! If you don't sew, you could glue the edges of the pieces together with washable fabric glue, but sewing will last through many washings and keep the mat more flexible and absorbent.

■ **Labels, sticky:** To soften gummy glue on glass or plastic jars, put the jar in the microwave with a damp towel over it, set on Low, and check it every 30 seconds or so. The heat softens the glue and you can usually pull the label off easily. You can also soften gummy labels on glass bottles by filling the bottle with very hot water, let sit for a while until you can lift a corner off easily, then carefully peel away the label. Or remove sticky residue from labels with prewash spray or vegetable, baby, or mineral oil. Apply, let set to soften, and rub off with a nylon scrubber. Prewash spray will usually remove labels or sticky residue left by them if you allow the spray to remain for a while to soften and then scrub off with a plastic scrubber. Remove bumper stickers with spray lubricant, following the previous instructions. Acetone or acetone-based fingernail polish will remove sticky residue from glass and some surfaces, but it may also damage some other surfaces and fabrics, and, it will take off your fingernail polish at the same time! Remove stickers and sticky residue from wood or wood paneling by rubbing with mineral oil on a cloth or paper towel. Let the oil set a while and repeat if necessary.

■ **Leather-topped furniture:** To remedy drink spills, first blot up. Then, cover the leather with saddle soap and let it dry totally. If there is a white mark still remaining, match a color of scuff-type liquid polish to the area to see if you can disguise the spill mark. If the piece is antique and valuable, talk with leather experts or ask about commercial leather polishes sold in furniture stores.

■ **Linen napkins/tablecloths:** To remove stains from white damask, try dabbing 3 percent hydrogen peroxide with a cotton tip swab and wait for 24 hours to see if the stain comes off. If they are permanently stained, you can dye them or have them professionally done.

■ **Lipstick:** To remove lipstick from a table napkin, place paper towels under the stained area. Dab a bit of rubbing alcohol on the stained area and gently rub. Keep blotting until the stain is gone. Then launder the napkins as usual.

■ **Marble:** Marble needs to be treated with care. You can clean it with this home-style solution: Mix 1 tablespoon mild liquid dishwashing detergent (that you hand-wash dishes with) with 1 quart warm water and apply to a small area at a time with a sponge to clean. Rinse the marble completely to remove any and all soap residue. (According to the Marble Institute of America, a buildup could damage the stone.) Buff dry with a soft cloth so water will not be left standing; never allow to air dry because water will leave stains.

Do not use any acidic cleaners, such as lemon, vinegar, bathroom or kitchen cleansers, on marble because they will eat into the surface.

If a water ring is only on the surface, try rubbing with a good marble-polishing powder, usually tin oxide, from a hardware store or marble-manufacturing company.

■ **Microwave:** To remove stains, clean up splattered food right after cooking so it won't stick. But if it does, add 2 tablespoons of either baking soda or lemon juice into 1 cup water in a 4-cup microwave-safe bowl. Allow the mixture to boil in the oven for about 5 minutes. Let set 15 minutes to cool. The steam will condense on the inside walls. Then just wipe off the walls, inside of the door and don't forget the door seals.

- **Miniblinds:** To clean greasy metal mini-blinds, wipe with a solution of a teaspoon of mild liquid detergent to 1 quart warm water.

- **Mirrors:** Remove spots with a homemade glass-cleaning solution of 2 cups water with 1 cup isopropyl rubbing alcohol (70 percent) and 1 tablespoon household ammonia. Pour into a clean pump-spray bottle.

OR: For a fast cleanup, pour a bit of vinegar on a paper towel and wipe.

CAUTION: Always put cleaning product onto a clean cloth and then apply to mirror; that way you've kept the cleaning product away from the frame so it's not damaged.

- **Nonstick spray** can build up on some flooring and make it very slippery. It's best to spray pots and pans over the sink.

- **Oil bottles:** Put oil bottles into plastic bags before placing them on the shelf and you won't have to clean bug-inviting oil dribbles on the shelves.

- **Olive oil:** For olive oil–based stains on a tablecloth or napkin, sprinkle any artificial sweetener (from packets) over the oil stain. Let set to absorb the oil. It may pull all of it up. On washable material, apply liquid laundry detergent directly on the spot, then wash as usual in hot water. It may take several times.

- **Oven I:** *Do not* use any cleaning aid in a *continuous-* or *self-cleaning* oven; it could damage or ruin the finish. Instead use liquid detergent and water or window cleaner to wipe up spills. Use a damp sponge to wipe up the ash after cleaning.

- **Oven II:** If the oven is really dirty, wear rubber gloves and have plenty of air circulation when you use commercial oven cleaners. Follow directions carefully. Do not spray the electrical connections, heating elements or lightbulbs. If the oven is only mildly stained, sprinkle baking soda onto a damp cloth and scrub. To make this onerous task easier, clean up spills right after they happen. Pour salt on burned food, let the oven cool and wipe clean.

To prevent spillovers on the bottom of the oven, put a sheet of aluminum foil or a baking sheet under the heating coils to catch and contain the spills.

- **Oven III:** To remove melted plastic from the electric oven—don't ask, it's happened to many people—put a bag of ice on top of the melted plastic to chill it, thus making it more brittle. Gently and very carefully use a razor-blade scraper to lift off the plastic puddle. *Note:* This will not hurt an interior porcelain finish.

- **Oven IV:** To clean the racks, remove them from oven and take outside. Put them inside a big heavy-duty plastic trash bag; spray them with an oven cleaner or put 2 tablespoons ammonia in and close the bag tightly. Let soak overnight. The next day, spray off with a hose (do not let residue run into plants or onto any surface that could be damaged). If any spots or stains remain, use a scrub brush to get them off.

- **Paper towels:** The rule in my house for paper towels is that clean hands get wiped on cloth towels; paper towels are only for messy, icky jobs. Hang a small hand towel or large washcloth on a cup hook near the paper towel roll so you won't always use a paper towel. Recycle paper towels that have been used only to dry clean hands or pots by letting them dry and then saving them for really messy chores. Hang a clothespin bag inside a kitchen cupboard to hold reusable paper towels.

- **Patio umbrella:** To get rid of the mildew, use a solution of 1 gallon water, ¾ cup liquid household bleach, and a squirt of liquid dishwashing detergent. (CAUTION: Avoid using detergents that should not be combined with chlorine bleach. Check the label.) Open the umbrella outdoors and lay on its side. Put on gloves and old clothes and use a soft-bristled brush. Test a bit of the solution under the umbrella for colorfastness. Then scrub each section of the umbrella. Rinse thoroughly with a hose and dry any metal parts. *Note: Do not* use on acrylic prints because bleach will fade colors. Read care label.

A READER RECOMMENDS:

A Virginia reader had a good idea on how to remember the brand name of paper towels when you are testing different ones to see which one you like. Tuck the wrapper inside the roll before you put the roll on the dispenser and when the paper is used up, you'll know the brand name to buy again or not to buy again.

- **Pet food dishes:** If your pet always leaves behind a few bits of food that dry and get almost cemented to the dish, spray the dish with nonflavored, nonstick spray before putting food into it and cleaning will be easy.

- **Pewter:** Rub with a paste made by mixing denatured alcohol and whiting (an abrasive powder available in hardware stores). After the paste dries, wash, rinse, and buff dry with a soft cloth. Corrosion on pewter can be removed by gently rubbing with fine (0000) steel wool dipped in mineral oil. *Note:* To get a duller finish on pewter, make a paste with rottenstone and oil; rub, rinse, and buff dry.

- **Plastic container:** To remove stubborn tomato stains, start with baking soda. Put a small amount on a damp cloth and rub the stains. If stains remain, soak the container for about a minute in a solution of ⅛ cup of liquid bleach and 1 quart water. (Keep solution weak so it does not ruin the finish on the plastic.) Wash and rinse well. These stains may be removed by setting the plastic container in the sun for several hours.

- **Plastic grocery bag storage:** Bend the ends of a hanger all the way up and hang it on a hook, then slip the handles of plastic grocery bags on the hanger ends for neat and orderly storage.

- **Plastic mesh bags:** Recycle plastic mesh bags from onions and other vegetables. Tie them in a ball and use them to scrub pots, pans, car windshields, and anything that you don't want to scratch.

- **Plastic picnicware:** Recycle and save landfill space. Instead of throwing away heavy plastic silverware put it in a mesh bag, secure it to the top rack of the dishwasher and it will come out clean and ready to use again.

- **Plastic pet toys:** Put them into a solution of baking soda and water. Scrub to remove yucky stuff. Rinse and dry.

▪ **Plastic tablecloth:** Using the delicate cycle, wash in warm water with a couple of bath towels for scrubbing action. Dry on warm and take out after 5 minutes or so.

▪ **Pots:** To clean a stained enamel pot, fill it with water and add ⅛ cup of bleach. Allow the pot to soak for 10 minutes, then wash as usual. If stains are really stubborn, you may have to repeat this process several times. To avoid this problem, clean pots well after each use.

▪ **Range burner drip bowls:** It's best to clean them after use if needed with dishwashing detergent and water. Scrub with a plastic scouring pad, rinse, and dry. For heavy stains, soak a paper towel in ammonia and put it on the stained area. Then scrub with a plastic scouring pad. Do not use abrasive cleansers.

▪ **Range-hood filter:** If the filter can be removed and will fit, wash in the dishwasher. If you have to wash the filter by hand, try an ammonia-based window cleaner or detergent specifically formulated to remove grease. Apply the cleaner, let soak, rinse. Repeat if necessary.

▪ **Range top:** Wipe off with hot soapy water right after a spill. Harsh scouring powders can scratch chrome; use metal polishes made for chromium.

▪ **Refrigerators/appliances:** Use a solution of half vinegar and half water on an old clean terry towel to wipe away smears and finger marks.

▪ **Rubber gloves, skin care:** Slather lotion or oil on your hands and slip on cotton gloves before you put on your rubber gloves to wash dishes and you'll be giving your skin a good moisturizing treatment while you work.

▪ **Rubber handles (on appliances):** They may get sticky, but don't use strong cleaners on them. To prevent tacky buildup, wipe handles clean daily; but for stubborn dirt, try one of these methods:

> Mix baking soda and a bit of water together. Rub the paste on the handles (not on black though) to clean.
> Mix mild liquid soap and water. Apply with a clean sponge.
> Use a mild spray cleaner.

▪ **Screws and bolts:** Soak rusty or corroded nuts and bolts in vinegar overnight or longer. Vinegar also can loosen up the mechanism in a padlock.

▪ **Scrubbies:** Recycled old panty hose—whole ones or parts—have replaced my mother's famous nylon net for making scrubbie balls for kitchen fixtures, sinks, and woodwork. They scrape dirt blobs without harming surfaces.

▪ **Scuff marks on floors:** Shoe scuff marks on resilient floors can be taken off by simply rubbing them with a pencil eraser or dry paper towel. Believe me. It works!

▪ **Scuff marks on no-wax kitchen floors:** Black scuff marks should come right off if you rub them with a paper towel. If that doesn't work, sprinkle baking soda on a dampened sponge and scrub. Rinse with water.

▪ **Silver:** Of course, you can use a commercial cleaning product and follow directions or use the following home-style method. CAU-TION: *Do not* use this method on antique, silver plate, or hollow-handled pieces because it may cause damage. Also, only use this old-fashioned method occasionally and be aware that it may remove the "patina" (soft luster caused by tiny scratches that come with frequent use) from intricate patterns.

1. Cover the bottom of a deep plastic or glass pan with a layer of aluminum foil.
2. Pour in 2 quarts of boiling water.
3. Add 2 teaspoons of baking soda and stir well till dissolved.
4. Place silver pieces into solution until tarnish disappears.
5. Rinse in warm water and polish dry.

CLASSIC HELOISE HINT: One of my mother's hints for cleaning charred shish-kebab skewers is to push them through a soap-filled steel wool pad *before* the pad is wet. They get clean in a flash! Wash and rinse as usual.

- **Spills:** To quickly wipe up spills, throw newspapers on them, then let them absorb the mess and throw them away. Because the newspaper ink may stain certain surfaces if left too long, remove and dispose of the newspaper as quickly as possible.
- **Spoon rest:** I get a lot of mail with hints on what to use for a spoon rest at the stove but since anything will hold a spoon, why not put the spoon on something that you'll throw away instead of something you have to wash? Rest your cooking spoon or fork on a paper towel that's only wiped one pair of clean hands, in a food can or on a frozen food box that you've just emptied, or anything else that isn't just more counter clutter.

- **Spray cleaner:** To get those last 2 inches out of the spray cleaner, drop some marbles into the container to raise the liquid level back to where the spray pump works.
- **Stainless steel:** You can remove little rust spots with a silver or stainless-steel cleaner but not all will come off completely. Corrosion occurs when acids, salt, and even normal use removes the protecting coating on stainless-steel items. Avoid rust spots by always rinsing all food residue from flatware so that it doesn't have time to corrode. If you aren't planning to run your dishwasher for a day or two, it's best to wash stainless flatware by hand. I rinse mine before putting it into the dishwasher even when it will be run the same day.
- **Stainless-steel sink:** Baking soda on a wet sponge will scour a really messed up stainless-steel sink; a spritz of vinegar will remove hard water residue; and you can polish stainless steel sinks with any kind of light oil such as lemon oil, mineral oil, or salad oil. You can also buy a stainless-steel polish at most grocery stores that will bring back the luster of stainless steel sinks.

CLASSIC HELOISE HINT: One of my mother's readers said that the women who worked in the kitchen of her church kept a small cloth saturated with butter in the fridge ready for polishing stainless-steel sinks after they were washed with soap and water. Today, I use vegetable oil on a paper towel.

- **Teacups:** To remove tea stains, mix a paste of baking soda and water. Rub it on the stains. Let stand for several minutes and wash as usual.

▪ **Teakettle:** (CAUTION: *Do not* use this method for electric kettles.) To eliminate lime buildup, fill kettle with full-strength vinegar and boil for several minutes, add some marbles to "bounce" and break up the sediment. Allow to stand, then scrub if needed. Rinse well.

▪ **Telephones:** Wipe with an all-purpose spray on a paper towel or use wet towelettes to get rid of makeup or dirt. *Do not* spray the phone directly.

▪ **Television:** Clean screen and cabinet with a soft, clean cloth. CAUTION: Do not use liquid or aerosol cleaners on the screen. As with all appliances, unplug before cleaning.

▪ **Tissue towels:** Attach a toilet-paper holder to the inside of a kitchen cabinet under the sink and buy the least expensive tissue to hang there. Save your paper towels for major wipe-ups and blot up most spills with less expensive, more environmentally friendly paper. It's handy for nose wiping, too. Why waste a whole tissue for each sniffle.

▪ **Toothbrush:** An extra toothbrush is the perfect thing to clean the teeth of a fork when food is stuck on them. It will also clean around the handles of pots and pans; the coffee filter; around the sink rim; the small grooves of silver; the rim of the stove; the rubber around the fridge door; the handles of the stove, oven, and drawers; and any other place where small grooves collect dirt.

▪ **Trash bag storage:** Why waste cupboard space storing plastic bags when you can store them where they are used? After cleaning your trashcan, put the whole roll of plastic bags into the bottom. Draw up the first bag, leaving it

attached to the roll; open it and drape it around the top rim; hold it in place with the elastic from panty hose or clip with a clothes pin. When the bag is full, tie it shut, lift it up, and tear the plastic bag off the roll as you grab the next bag. Then drape the new bag over the rim as before.

▪ **Varnished paneling/woodwork:** To get rid of fingerprints, apply a solution of 1 part vinegar to 2 parts water with a clean cloth and wipe away. Polish with a clean, dry cloth.

▪ **Vinegar:** Keep household vinegar in a squirt or spray bottle, and it will be handy for many of my Heloise Hints.

▪ **Vinyl floor:** For light stains, vacuum or sweep up; then damp mop with warm water. Go over small areas at a time and rinse mop often so you don't smear dirt around. For really dirty floors, use a no-rinse cleaner or all-purpose liquid detergent. CAUTION: *Do not* use soap, gritty powders, or abrasive cleansers.

Darkened or yellowed areas caused by rubber- or vinyl-backed throw rugs placed on top of vinyl floors cannot be removed. That's because there is a chemical reaction between the backing of the throw rug and the vinyl flooring. Scrubbing and bleaching may lighten the stain a bit, but cannot remove it completely. Do not use abrasives because you may damage the finish on the vinyl. Placing other objects on top of this flooring can also cause yellowing. Do not leave any object in one spot on the floor for an extended time. Unfortunately, these stains cannot be removed.

▪ **Vinyl furniture:** Clean with a mixture of mild detergent and water. Rub well to loosen dirt. Rinse and dry with a towel. If this is not successful, use commercial vinyl cleaners for difficult or greasy stains.

To remove *ballpoint ink stains*, dip a cotton swab into a bit of rubbing alcohol and carefully dab at the stain. Then wipe with a damp sponge.

- **Vinyl seat cushion:** Make a baking soda and water solution by mixing 4 tablespoons of baking soda and 1 quart warm water. Use a damp cloth or sponge to apply the solution, rinse, and wipe dry.

Automobile wax can be used to wax vinyl fabrics, which will help repel stains.

- **Waffle iron:** The grids can accumulate burned-on grease. To get rid of it, place an ammonia-soaked paper towel between top and bottom metal grids and leave overnight. If the grids are nonstick, follow manufacturer's instructions. Wash and rinse well.

- **Wall coverings:** You really need to get the manufacturer's care directions when you have wall coverings because there are so many different types: paper, plastic, fabric, resin coated, impregnated materials, and so on. CAUTION: If you don't know the cleaning directions for your wall covering, always test cleaners on an inconspicuous place before proceeding. Colors can bleed, papers can come right off the wall, and anything can happen when you use the wrong cleaner.

Most washable coverings can be gently washed with mild detergent and cool water. Work from the bottom up, using as little water as possible. Work on small areas and overlap as you wash. Rinse with clear water and *blot* dry.

For nonscrubbable coverings, rub gently with an art gum eraser or doughy wallpaper cleaners (available at home improvement and hardware stores). When using doughy cleaners, knead and turn the wad often so that you are using clean surfaces on the wall.

❀ **CLASSIC HELOISE HINT:** My mother's old hint for cleaning lightly soiled wallpaper or nonwashable wall covering by rubbing it with a wadded-up slice of white bread still works.

Spot-clean before spots set. Blot grease spots with paper towels or facial tissue while you press lightly with a warm iron over the towels or tissue. Or apply a paste of nonflammable dry-cleaning solvent and absorbent powder (Fuller's earth, talcum, or cornstarch); allow to dry, then brush off.

Crayon can sometimes be sponged off with dry-cleaning solvent. Pencil marks and smudges can sometimes be removed with art gum or pencil erasers. Always rub gently. The real trick is to be gentle with the "budding artists" who put such stains on the walls! To remove ink stains, diluted bleach or commercial ink remover may work on wallpaper, but either one may also remove the color of the wallpaper. Test first in an inconspicuous place!

To remove grease marks from *washable* wall-paper, apply a baking soda paste to grease stains and allow to dry. Brush off with a clean, soft cloth or brush.

■ **Walls/doors:** To remove sticky tape from painted surfaces, apply petroleum-based prewash spray or mineral oil to the tape. Leave for several minutes and remove. Start at a corner and work the tape loose. If needed, use more spray or oil, particularly if there are layers.

■ **Walls I:** To patch *nail holes in colored walls*, fill with moistened crushed aspirin or white toothpaste and then dab area with watercolor paint to match the color. If you have leftover paint, use it.

■ **Walls II:** To mask the discoloration caused by *nail holes in white walls*, fill with moistened crushed aspirin or white toothpaste; push into holes. Wipe off any excess with clean, damp cloth.

■ **Walls III:** Simply painting over *water and oil stains* will not cover them, even if many coats of paint are applied. The stains will bleed through. First, the stains have to be painted over with a sealer product sold in paint stores. Clear varnish will work, too.

For *small ink stains*, "white" them out with correction fluid to seal, then paint over.

For *water stains* in the ceiling, bleach them with 3 to 5 percent hydrogen peroxide, taking care to avoid any drips. Sometimes it's possible to mask spots with white shoe polish or correction fluid. If it doesn't work, use commercial stain sealer and repaint. (See also **Ceiling.**)

■ **Walls IV:** A bit of foam bathroom cleaner or dry-cleaning solvent will remove crayon marks from semi-gloss or glossy paint. Follow directions on cleaner container labels.

■ **Walls, washing:** Dust walls before washing and wash from the bottom up so that drips won't make their marks. Also, clean small areas at a time, then rinse and dry, before you move on to another area. Here are some other Heloise Hints for best results:

Wash most painted surfaces with soap or mild detergent and water or mild commercial household cleaners. Do look for cleaning information on the paint cans so that you can use the proper cleaner for the type of paint on your walls and woodwork.

To soften soap waters and rinse waters, add 1 tablespoon of borax or a commercial water softener per quart of water.

■ **Waxy buildup on floors:** If you don't own one, start by renting a floor scrubber. Follow these simple guidelines:

Boost the power of heavy-duty general-purpose household cleaner with 1 cup of nonsudsy ammonia.

Working a small area at a time, pour a small amount of the cleaning solution on the floor, let it set a few minutes, and go over it with the floor scrubber. After the entire floor has been scrubbed, go back over it with a damp mop.

After the floor is dry, apply a fresh coat of wax.

CAUTION: If you have no-wax floors, you absolutely need to follow the manufacturer's guidelines for cleaning. It's not the same as with traditional flooring. If you have lost the directions, call a flooring company that sells the flooring you have and/or the products you need. If nothing else, they can give you the number for the manufacturer's consumer or customer service/information line. Most manufacturers have 800 numbers or Web sites.

■ **Wheels:** If the wheels on your chopping block, table, or tea cart have minds of their own and roll when you want them to stay still, try this hint from a reader. Insert wedge-shaped pieces of wood between the wheel and the frame on two wheels, diagonally across from each other to stop the rolling. When you need to move the furniture, remove the wedges, and then put them back in for stability when you have the furniture where you want it to stay.

■ **Window blinds (bamboo):** Dust and clean only with a soft hand brush or brush attachment of vacuum cleaner. Do not wash with water or use citric-based cleaners.

■ **Window blinds (wood):** Put old clean socks on your hands and wipe on both sides of slats to clean dust or remove dust with the brush attachment of vacuum cleaner. Apply furniture polish to the slats or a creamy liquid wax.

■ **Window condensation:** Here's a Heloise home-style way to deal with drippy condensation on windows in the winter: Wipe moisture off the windows and be sure they are dry. Then with a couple of tissues, apply undiluted hair shampoo to the windowpanes. They may look cloudy at first but should clear up. To avoid

Heloise Hints for Busy Families

Heloise fans have sent in many good ideas on how they manage to keep up with jobs, children, gardens, and community volunteer work and still survive with their wits and dispositions intact. It's not easy, and every day is not perfect, but it is possible to organize the workweek so that at least some of what needs doing gets done and you still have some time for family and friends and to recharge your own batteries. Here are some of the best survival hints sent to me:

• Put in a laundry load before leaving for work so that it is ready to start with a push of a button or turn of the dial by the first person who gets home. The next person loads the dryer. Then you will do at least one load of clothes each day.

• Put children's jobs on a list with space on the bottom for add-on jobs. The list eliminates the need to nag, and children check off jobs as they are completed, thus getting the satisfaction of seeing what they've accomplished. If there are no children in your house, adults can have no-nagging-needed job lists, too.

• Teach children to make their own lunches and breakfasts. On weekends make meals so that there are leftovers for Monday and Tuesday and nobody has to cook. Have each family member list his or her favorite foods and make each person's favorite at least once every other week or so to keep everyone happy and cooperative.

• After the dinner dishes are done, set the breakfast table and take out any foods that don't require refrigeration, such as cereals.

continued ...

Heloise Hints for Busy Families, continued

- Keep lunch, bus, or milk money handy in a change bowl near the door. Everyone can drop all loose change into the bowl each night and take what's needed in the morning.

- Few of us can do it all. Hire a local teenager to help clean up once a week or so. Or hire a professional service to do the big jobs every couple of months. You work hard. You deserve a break!

condensation, try to vent the extra moisture from your rooms with kitchen and bath exhaust fans. Too much moisture for too long can cause wood framing to rot or warp and can make paint peel.

■ **Window decal remover:** Some decals will come off if you paint a few coats of vinegar on, let soak for a few minutes, and wash right off. Others come off after applying petroleum-based prewash spray as you would the vinegar. Still others, like bumper stickers on cars, come off if you heat them with a hair dryer before peeling them off.

■ **Window shades:** If the window shades are washable, take them down, unroll, and lay them on a flat surface. Dust with a clean cloth and wash with mild detergent suds and warm water. Rinse well, wipe dry, and hang immediately. If the shades are *not washable*, they should be cleaned by a professional cleaner. A clothing dry-cleaner can recommend someone for you. Or you can buy a dough-type wall

cleaner at a paint or wall-covering store and follow the directions carefully. *Always* test cleaners on an inconspicuous place before doing a whole project.

■ **Windows:** For a quick cleanup, spritz windows with full-strength white household vinegar and wipe with crumpled newspaper or paper towel. Or, make a solution of equal parts of water, isopropyl rubbing alcohol, and non-sudsing ammonia to cut grease. Mix and put in a spray bottle, and be sure to label it clearly. Dry them on the outside from right to left and on the inside, dry them up and down. That way you will be able to determine whether any remaining streaks are inside or out. To make windows sparkle, add ½ to 1 cup vinegar to ½ gallon water. Put solution into a spray bottle and apply to windows. Dry well.

■ **Windows (salty accumulation):** If you live near the ocean, the breezes bring salt that sticks to your windows. Spray full-strength white vinegar on the windows (not on the window frames). Allow it to stand for several minutes and then scrub with sponge covered with nylon net. Dry with paper towels or crumpled newspaper. Yes, you may end up with ink on your hands if you don't wear rubber gloves, but the windows will sparkle!

■ **Windows/storm doors (plastic/vinyl):** Use only a cleaning product formulated for plastics and vinyls. Some household cleaners and/or ammonia could cause a streaking in the plastic.

■ **Windows streaking:** Minimize streaking by waiting until the time of day when the sun is not shining directly on the windows. Heat causes the windows to dry too quickly, which leaves streaks behind. Also, you'll get less streaking if you wipe off surface dirt and dust with a dry cloth before washing.

✿ **CLASSIC HELOISE HINT:** My mother and I used to recommend newspaper for washing windows. *Update:* The type of paper and ink used today is not always the same as when Heloise Hints were first published. Now, not all newsprint is absorbent enough and some of the inks smudge on window casings. You'll have to test your local paper to find out if it's good for window cleaning.

- **Wood kitchen cabinets:** To remove grease—assuming that the woodwork is finished and also washable—use a wood cleaner and follow cleaning directions carefully. Then polish or wax with a soft cloth.

If the cabinets are *unfinished wood*, any kind of a cleaning substance including water could damage the surface, so rub grease off with a soft, dry cloth.

If the cabinets are *wood laminate*, lightly spray with a nonabrasive non-citric all-purpose cleaner. Let it stay on for several seconds, then sponge off.

- **Wood patio furniture:** To remove mildew caused from setting out in weather (non-flood conditions), you will need to use a chlorine bleach and water solution. (*Note:* First, test the solution on a hidden area to make sure it does not discolor the furniture.) Make the solution by mixing ¾ cup of chlorine bleach

and 1 gallon of water. Apply to the furniture and keep wet for 5 to 10 minutes. Rinse well and let air-dry completely.

- **Wood surfaces:** To cover *shallow scratches* or small rings, use the meat of several pecans or walnuts. Break the meat in half and rub it on the scratches with your finger until it feels warm. The scratches should disappear in about 30 seconds. Wood stain that matches the coloring of the paneling can be rubbed into the scratch and then wiped with a clean cloth. Test on a hidden area first.

For *deep scratches or cracks* in wood, use wax sticks made for that purpose. Available at hardware stores, they come in a variety of colors to match most wood finishes. Rub into a crack until the wax is flush with the surface. Heat a putty knife in hot water and then use the flat side to press it across the area to get a smooth surface.

To remove *white rings* on most wood furniture (from hot mugs or wet glasses) try one of the following (CAUTION: *Do not* use on unfinished, lacquered, or antique furniture.):

Apply a mixture of mayonnaise with tobacco ash (cigar is the best) with a clean dry cloth.

Use a non-gel toothpaste and baking soda mix. Rub gently until warm; it may take time for marks to disappear.

Rub furniture wax into the wood with very fine steel wool.

Wax the wood when you have finished.

- **Wood trim:** Clean with a dusting product that can be sprayed on the cloth or directly on the surface. The newer "antistatic" or "electrostatic" microfiber cloths work well. Add shine by applying furniture cleaner or polish to the surface. Wipe with a clean, soft cloth.

✿ **CLASSIC HELOISE HINT:** When a wooden salad bowl gets sticky with oil residue, one of my mother's readers sent in a hint to sand it with a fine grade of sandpaper, with the grain if possible, then finish with a clear waterproof spar varnish, applied lightly. The reader said that the bowls will look like new and there will be no taste from the varnish. *Update:* After sanding the salad bowl, apply mineral oil with a paper towel; mineral oil won't get rancid like salad oil and leaves no taste. Also, a mineral oil rub is faster and less messy than varnishing the bowl, and you'll have no brush to clean afterward. And I'm not so sure I'd like to put food into a varnished container, considering the difference in chemicals used today as opposed to the 1960s.

• **Wooden spoons, reseasoning:** After washing wooden spoons and other wooden cooking tools in hot sudsy water, scrub them if needed and rinse well. Wipe dry and allow to air-dry completely. Then heat some mineral oil (not vegetable oil, which can get rancid in wood) over medium heat. Dip the spoons in it until they are completely coated. Drain on paper towels. To save on paper towels, place one layer of paper towels over several layers of newspapers. When they are cool enough to handle, wipe them off and they are ready to use.

• **Woodwork and wood paneling:** To clean varnished wood surfaces, mix one part vinegar to two parts water to make a solution that cleans fingerprints and mild built-up dirt

from varnished woodwork or paneling. Wring out the rag well and wipe surfaces. After cleaning, polish the wood with a dry cloth to bring out the luster. This solution can also clean some furniture finishes; test first on an inconspicuous place.

KITCHEN ODORS

Life, especially kitchen life, is full of aromas and scents; some lovely, others not. Let's face it: Many of them stink! They always seem to happen when you least expect it or when you expect company! Talk about adding stress to already busy days.

As experience has taught you, it's always best to deal with them right away. If you don't, they only get worse.

Keep Heloise's cheap, home-style odor busters on hand all in one place and ready-to-use in urgent smelly crises. I like products that are environmentally safe, such as baking soda, vinegar, and lemon juice. They do a great job in masking and removing household smells. But there are many other odor solutions in your kitchen cabinets that many readers have shared with me. And now I'm happy to share them with everyone in this book.

KITCHEN ODORS A-TO-Z

• **Air freshener:** Conserve the power of small plastic air fresheners by pulling back the foil only halfway. The aroma will last longer and won't overpower a small room.

- **Air freshener (homemade):** Soak a cotton ball with peppermint, vanilla, orange, lemon extract, or oil of cloves. Place it in a small, clean, glass jar, the lid of which has been punched with holes. Secure tightly. Place in the smelly room out of the reach of small children and pets. CAUTION: Extracts are strong concentrates with high alcohol content. Do not let the extract touch granite, marble, painted surfaces, or wood.

- **Air freshener in a vacuum:** Grab a handful of your favorite spiced tea (loose or in a tea bag) and toss it into the vacuum bag. While you clean, it will give the house a nice spicy smell.

- **Aquarium smells:** Too much algae growth and uneaten fish food can give the tank an odor. Clean out leftover fish food with a turkey baster, used only for this purpose. Monitor the aquarium and clean it on a regular basis to prevent smells.

- **Ashtray:** To deodorize ashtrays, fill them partially with a small amount of clay-type cat-box litter or baking soda. It will help to reduce odor and to extinguish the cigarettes completely.

- **Baby bottle:** Get rid of that awful sour-milk smell by filling bottles with warm water and a teaspoon of baking soda. Let sit overnight. Then wash and sterilize as usual. *Note:* To prevent this from happening, immediately after baby has finished, rinse the bottle with cold water and put a teaspoon of baking soda into it and fill with cold water. Let soak until you need the bottle again.

- **Birdcage:** To keep odors from building up, place several layers of newspaper or grocery store paper bags on the bottom of the cage. Remove and replace with new sheets every other day.

- **Bleach (on hands):** Of course, you should wear rubber gloves to prevent this. But to remove the odor of bleach, wash your hands with soap and water, rinse, and then dab with a little apple cider vinegar, toothpaste, or mouthwash.

- **Bottle/jar deodorizing:** If they have a bad smell after washing, soak them overnight in a mixture of half vinegar and half water. Rinse well. Be sure to wash the lid in hot soapy water and store with the lid off.

- **Breath deodorant:** For a surefire homemade remedy for bad breath, gargle with a solution of 1 teaspoon baking soda to ½ glass of warm water. At a restaurant, eat the parsley. Chew, chew, chew, then wash it down with a big gulp of water—swishing around a bit to get the parsley flakes off your teeth! Parsley is a natural breath cleanser and nutritious, too.

- **Burned food:** Put several slices of lemon or ¼ cup vinegar in a saucepan half-filled with water, bring to a boil, and let cook for a few minutes. (Watch carefully so it doesn't boil dry and create yet another disgusting smell and ruin your pot.)

- **Butcher block deodorizer:** Sprinkle baking soda on the top of the block and scrub with a clean, damp sponge. Rinse well. Or, you can sprinkle it with salt and scrub with a lemon, and then rinse well. To renew the surface, apply a light coating of mineral oil (*not* vegetable oil) and wipe up with a paper towel.

- **Cabbage:** To kill cabbage-cooking stink, try one of these methods:

Drop a whole walnut into the boiling water, shell and all

Put a heel of bread on top

Add a splash of vinegar to the cooking water

Place a bowl of vinegar next to the stove to absorb the odor.

- **Can opener:** Wash a nonelectric can opener in warm, soapy water after every use to get rid of food bits that harbor bacteria and smell bad. Clean the blades or cutters of an electric can opener with an old toothbrush dipped in baking soda.

- **Carpet:** For a quick fix of general carpet odor, sprinkle baking soda over it. Leave on for at least 30 minutes; then vacuum.

- **Carpet (musty):** This may be a sign that the carpet or rug is damp. Be sure to check the underpadding to see if it is damp. Take the rug and padding outside to dry in the sun if you can. If you cannot remove the rug, try to dry it with a fan. If the damp area is small, use a hair dryer set on cool. Turn on ceiling fans, or use box fans. Also, if you have air-conditioning, turn it on to the lowest temperature.

- **Carpet deodorizer:** Sprinkle baking soda, with a flour sifter or your hands, over the carpet that needs freshening. Allow it to sit for at least 20 minutes, then vacuum. If you notice lightly soiled spots, rub a small amount of cornstarch into them, before you vacuum. *Note:* To extend a commercial carpet deodorizer, mix equal amounts of baking soda and the commercial product to double the volume.

- **Cat bedding:** To deodorize, toss a handful of baking soda onto the bedding in between washings and then vacuum. Don't do this if your cat is on a salt-restricted diet because baking soda is sodium bicarbonate.

- **Cat litter box (cleaning):** To eliminate odor, empty all the litter out of the box. Pour about ½ inch of vinegar into the box, add a healthy dose of baking soda, and top off with several inches of water. Stir to mix well. Let sit for several hours, then empty and wash with hot, soapy water. Allow to dry outside if the weather permits. Keep an air freshener in the room where the litter box is.

- **Cat litter box (deodorizing):** To deodorize, before putting cat litter into the box, pour a layer of baking soda on the bottom. This will help to subdue odors until you change the litter. *Note:* Cats are picky and some may not like baking soda. If they are not using the box, don't use baking soda.

- **Cat sprays:** To remove the smell if a cat sprays inside, use an enzyme-based commercial product made for this purpose. It is available at your vet or pet store. If odor remains, mask it with potpourri or a room deodorant spray.

- **Cat urine on carpet:** To remove the smell, use an old, thick towel (one designated for this kind of use) to blot up all of the urine ASAP. Then rinse the area with cool water, and apply a warm detergent solution. Follow with a solution of ⅓ vinegar and ⅔ cool water. Blot between each step with a paper towel. Rinse and blot dry. You can also use a commercial enzyme-based pet stain cleaner. Or, depending on the fabric, treat persistent stains with 3 to 5 percent hydrogen peroxide. Test a small hidden area first. Be careful of bleaching and rinse quickly.

CAUTION: Although professionals recommend using a diluted ammonia solution as a final step, I don't because it smells like urine and may encourage your pet to commit repeat offenses!

■ **Cigarette:** (See also **Smoke.**)

In draperies: Have them professionally cleaned or spray them with a fabric freshener. Depending on the draperies, they can also be placed in the dryer on the "fluff" cycle with a fabric softener sheet to freshen them.

In soft furnishings: Have professionally cleaned or spray them with a fabric freshener.

In wooden cabinets: Clean cabinet first. Put small dishes of either vinegar or baking soda (not combined) on shelves to help absorb odor. This may take several days or weeks. If there's still odor, put a bag of cedar shavings inside to give it a pleasant aroma.

■ **Closet (mildew or musty):** Place a clean coffee can or other container filled with activated charcoal in the back of the closet. Or: Use a closet dehumidifier, which is available at hardware or drugstores.

■ **Closet deodorizer:** To keep a closet sweet-smelling, mix 3 to 4 teaspoons of your favorite spice with a box of baking soda. (I like cinnamon and nutmeg!) Pour the mixture into several clean plastic margarine tubs, punch holes into the lids, and put in the back of the closet or on the shelves.

Leave doors open when possible.

■ **Closet freshener:** Pour several tablespoons of fresh, unused ground coffee into a couple of old clean socks and hang them in the closet to help prevent that musty odor. (See also **Air freshener [homemade].**)

■ **Coffee cup/mug/tumbler:** To prevent odors, rinse out your cup ASAP after use. To remove the coffee smell, pour 1 teaspoon of baking soda into the cup and fill with warm water. Let it stand at least ½ hour or so and then scrub with a brush or sponge. You may have to repeat this process.

■ **Cooking:** To eliminate general cooking odors, boil a mixture of 1 cup water and 1 to 2 tablespoons vinegar in a saucepan on the stove. CAUTION: Watch carefully so the pan does not boil dry. To give the whole house a good smell, add cinnamon (a whole stick or sprinkle of powdered) to the water/vinegar solution.

■ **Cooking (corned beef):** To eliminate that smell, add a tablespoon or so of vinegar to the water while boiling.

■ **Cooler:** Before you store a cooler, sprinkle a generous amount of baking soda into it and stuff with crumpled newspapers to prevent a musty smell. Also, try to store with the lid propped open to allow the air to circulate. When you are ready to use it again, dump the soda into the kitchen sink. Run lots of water, and the drain will be refreshed too!

■ **Cutting boards:** To remove smells like onion or garlic from a wooden cutting board, sprinkle with salt and then rub the surface with a cut lemon or lime. Then wash with warm soapy water, rinse, and reseason with mineral oil if the board is wood.

- **Dishwasher:** First you have to find out where the odor is coming from. Look inside the dishwasher to examine the drain hose and the bottom reservoir for food particles or residues that may be trapped there. Gunk and grease can accumulate. If the water isn't hot enough to wash it away, this stuff can cause the odor. Using a large wad of paper towels, clean out the reservoir. Be careful, because there could be broken glass or other sharp bits.

The odor may be coming from clogged kitchen drainpipes or sewer lines. If you suspect this, call a plumber.

To prevent odors, clean the dishwasher every month or so by pouring either ½ cup bleach or 1 cup household vinegar into the detergent cup and run through a cycle. There are also commercial dishwasher freshener products that can do the job, too. In between use, pour baking soda on the bottom of the dishwasher to help control the odor.

- **Dog bed deodorizing:** Sprinkle a little baking soda over the bed to neutralize odor until washing, which you should do often to keep doggie smells to a minimum. Don't use if your dog is on a salt-restricted diet because baking soda is sodium bicarbonate.

- **Doggie deodorant I:** Dogs can get that stinky doggie smell in between baths. To help eliminate it, rub baking soda into the fur (don't get into eyes); leave on for about 10 minutes and brush out. Your precious pup will be welcome inside again! But don't apply to your pet if it's on a salt-restricted diet as baking soda is sodium bicarbonate.

- **Doggie deodorant II:** Make a doggie spritzer by mixing 32 ounces of water with 2 capfuls of a fragrant bath oil and pour into a spray bottle. Spritz your pet's coat and rub in. CAUTIONS: Be sure to label the bottle of this homemade mixture. Don't spray into dog's eyes or ears!

- **Drains:** Try this homemade mixture to keep drains fresh smelling. (But note that it does not unclog drains): Pour ½ cup baking soda into the drain, and then pour 1 to 2 cups of vinegar down the drain. Let sit and bubble for several minutes; turn on the hot water and let it run for a minute or so and finally flush out the drain with lots of cold water. To kill germs that could be causing the smell, pour ½ cup liquid household bleach or 1 cup vinegar down the drain. Let sit for about 20 minutes, then flush with water.

- **Fart:** Wave your hand to disperse bad odor or use a room deodorant spray. In the bathroom, light a match, then blow it out to get rid of bodily function smells.

- **Fish:** To eliminate the cooking odor of fish in the kitchen, simmer a solution of ½ cup vinegar and ½ cup water in a saucepan on low heat. Or: Put a cup of vinegar in an open container on the kitchen counter.

- **Fish smell on hands:** At home: Squeeze lemon or lime juice over hands and wash well, or pour apple cider vinegar over hands and rub in. A dab of toothpaste or a bit of mouthwash rubbed into your hands will also do the job.

Before you go on a fishing or camping trip: Soak small towels in a mixture of lemon juice and water, then put into resealable plastic bags and store in the freezer. Pop them into the cooler when you head out. By the time you've caught your limit, the towels will be thawed and ready to use.

- **Freezer deodorizer:** Use a solution of 4 tablespoons baking soda in 1 quart of water to wipe the wall and bottom of the freezer then rinse and wipe dry. If you notice a stain that has not been removed, *do not* use an abrasive cleaner because it can damage the surface. Instead, pour baking soda onto a wet sponge and scrub the area. Place an open tub or box of baking soda in the freezer compartment for continuous deodorizing.

- **Freezer food spoilage:** To remove the stench from spoiled food as a result of an electricity failure, first, dispose of the spoiled food. Clean the freezer with soap and water. Then rinse with a solution of about 1 cup vinegar to 1 gallon water. Pour clay-type cat litter in open containers or pour lemon extract on cotton balls and place inside the freezer. Leave closed for several days.

- **Garbage cans:** To prevent odors, place a fabric-softener sheet or perfume sample strip into the bottom of the can before you put the plastic garbage bag inside.

- **Garbage disposal:** Drop in a handful of sliced citrus peels (lemon, lime, orange, or grapefruit), with lots of running water and grind; flush with water. Or, add several drops of peppermint or other extracts along with water to deodorize it.

- **Garlic odors in plastic storage containers:** If they've taken on a garlicky odor, wash in hot, soapy water and then give them a vinegar rinse and dry. Stuff a crumpled sheet of newspaper inside and put the lid on securely. Leave for a day or two.

Versatile Vinegar

Did you know that vinegar has been around for more than 10,000 years? It has been used as a preservative, a condiment, a beverage, and during World War I to treat wounds. It's legend that Cleopatra made a wager that she could consume a fortune in a single meal! How? It's said she dissolved a precious pearl in the vinegar and drank it! Who knows for sure?

- **Glass jars:** Wash well in hot, soapy water and rinse completely. Fill with a solution of half vinegar and half water. Let sit overnight with the lid off. Rinse and dry. You also can fill the jar with crumpled newspaper and let it stand overnight to get rid of smells. Clean the lid with hot soapy water.

- **Hands:** To remove smells on hands, scrub with toothpaste or rinse hands with mouthwash. To avoid smelly hands, wear rubber or thin plastic gloves when working with onions, garlic, or other strong smelling items.

- **Ice cubes:** Automatic maker: First, check the ice-cube bin because the cubes could be picking up odors from the refrigerator. Use activated charcoal (found at pet stores) as a deodorizer for the refrigerator. Put several pieces into a cleaned-out, plastic butter tub, replace the lid, punch holes in it, and place inside the refrigerator. Wash the bin with cool soapy water. Rinse and dry well.

- **Kitchen sink:** Getting rid of odors can be an ordeal. Try these ideas:

The sink area may still smell because there's a buildup of bacteria in the drain. Pour a cup or so of bleach into the sink and allow it to sit for 20 minutes to kill bacteria that may be growing inside. Run cold water for at least a minute to clear the drain.

If you have a garbage disposal, the rubber splashguard may be slimy and need to be cleaned. Run water. Add several drops of liquid dishwashing detergent and use a round brush or a toilet brush (just for this purpose) to scrub the guard well; go up and down and all around to get it clean. Then run more water.

Examine sink stoppers and splashguards; they can get grungy and harbor bad odors. Because they are inexpensive, you can replace them often.

- **Lunch box:** Moisten a piece of stale bread or paper towel with vinegar and place it in the lunch box overnight. In the morning, wash it well and dry. Leave the top open to air out.

- **Microwave:** To clean and eliminate odor, combine 2 tablespoons baking soda with 1 cup of water in a large microwave-safe bowl. Place in the microwave and turn it on high for 2 to 3 minutes. This will soften the spills so you can wipe them up and the smells will be gone! Be careful when you open the door because the steam will be hot.

- **Microwave (burnt popcorn):** Burnt popcorn odor is such a disgusting and lingering smell! Try this: In a large microwave-safe bowl, combine 1½ cups of water, ½ chopped lemon, and 4 to 5 cloves. Bring mixture to a boil. Let it sit in the microwave for 10 to 15

Microwave Magic

To get a pleasant aroma throughout the house, combine 1 cup of water and 2 teaspoons of pumpkin-pie spice—or any combination of spices to your taste—in a large microwave-safe bowl and cook on high until it boils. When it reaches the boiling point, cook for a minute or two. Or, combine 6 whole cloves and a half lemon in a cup of water and microwave on high for 2 to 3 minutes. CAUTION! Always allow the liquid to cool before removing the bowl.

minutes before you remove the bowl. Leave the door of the microwave open to further air it out.

- **Mop (floor):** Soak the mop for several hours in a mixture of 1 quart water and 4 tablespoons baking soda. Rinse well, squeeze out, and hang to dry.

- **Mouse:** A dead mouse or other small rodent can make one putrid odor! Vacuum or sweep the area completely, getting rid of any mouse remnants. (Be sure to wear gloves!) Then wipe down with a diluted solution of bleach or vinegar if safe for the surface. Place air fresheners or fabric-softener sheets in the area. Place a deodorizer near the air-conditioning intake or spray a room deodorizer on the air-conditioning filter and place the air-conditioning on fan. Repeat if needed!

- **Natural gas odor:** If you smell a leak:

1. Look for the source immediately—anything that runs on gas, such as the water heater or pilot lights on the stove.

2. Cut the gas supply and open all the windows so the gas leaves the house, particularly the kitchen.

3. If you can't find the source and the gas odor remains, turn off the main gas valve and open the windows. CAUTION: Do not turn on anything, as an electric charge might cause an explosion. Do not use matches or candles. Leave the house ASAP and call the gas company from a neighbor's home.

FYI: Natural gas is odorless—therefore an additive is added, so if there is a leak, you will smell it.

■ **Odor remover:** Pour some vinegar into a wide mouth large glass jar, add a few cloves and some cinnamon, then microwave for a minute or so. Place the jars where needed. This process seems to remove the odors instead of just covering them like some commercial products and it doesn't put fluorocarbons into the air like some room deodorant sprays.

■ **Onion odor on hands:** If you've sliced or peeled onions and your hands stink, try one or more of these methods:

Dampen your hands with water and sprinkle with salt. Rub the salt in and rinse.

Wet your hands. Fill one palm with baking soda and rub well with the other. Rinse with warm water.

Cover the smelly area with toothpaste or mouthwash. Rinse in warm water.

Rub your hands with the dull side of a stainless-steel knife or stainless-steel kitchen sink.

■ **Oven-cleaner odor:** Remove the smelly residue left over from oven cleaning with these three simple steps:

1. When you've finished cleaning the oven, place a layer of newspapers on the bottom of the oven.

2. Spray warm water on the top and side walls of the oven.

3. Use a clean cloth to dry the oven walls then discard the newspaper.

■ **Oven spills:** Baking food inevitably spills over in the oven. Sprinkle salt on the burned gunk. It will help to eliminate smoke and odors and make it easier to clean up after baking. To prevent spills, put a baking sheet or aluminum foil under things that contain foods that may bubble over or onto the bottom of the oven.

■ **Paint odors:** To remove paint odor, try these methods:

Turn on exhaust fans in the kitchen or ceiling fans elsewhere. Open the windows and doors in the rest of the house.

Add a couple drops of vanilla to a gallon of paint. (If the paint is white or ivory, use one drop of lemon extract per gallon.)

Cut large onions in half and place them in the corners of a newly painted room.

Set out several small bowls of vinegar around the room.

■ **Pet urine in carpets:** First you must soak up the urine ASAP. Use several layers of paper towel or a thick old cloth, and stomp on it to absorb moisture. Be sure to check the padding underneath where the urine may have soaked through. After the urine has been completely removed and the carpet is dried thoroughly, you can sprinkle baking soda over the dried area or place a fabric-softener sheet between the carpet and the underpadding to mask any lingering odor.

- **Plastic food storage containers:** To remove smells, fill the container with a solution of 1 tablespoon baking soda to 1 quart water, or soak small containers in a bucket or sink full of the solution. Let sit, then rinse with clean water and dry.

- **Plastic tablecloth:** If your plastic tablecloth is smelly, soak or wash it in a solution of 1 tablespoon baking soda to 1 gallon of water. Rinse and hang to dry outside.

- **Potpourri:** Heloise wet formula: Mix 2 cups rose petals, 2 cups rosemary, 2 cups mint, 4 cinnamon sticks, ½ cup whole allspice, and 2 whole cloves. Put mixture in a large jar and cover with heated white vinegar. Allow the jar to sit for one week. To release the fragrance, simmer in a saucepan on low heat. (CAUTION: Watch carefully to make sure the pot doesn't go dry.) You can gather other flowers and spices to create your own special potpourri.

- **Potpourri (alternatives and substitutions):** Make any area in your home smell wonderful with these methods:

Simmer wet potpourri in a mug placed on a coffee-cup warmer.
Microwave a bowl of potpourri and water. See CAUTION in **Potpourri** above.

- **Potpourri refreshening:** Add drops of your favorite perfume, perfume samples, or essential oils to jazz up old dry potpourri. Stir carefully and do not get any onto wood or laminate surfaces because it can stain.

- **Refrigerator (meat spoilage):** Remove everything from both the refrigerator and freezer compartments. Sprinkle baking soda on a damp sponge (or mix 1 cup ammonia with 1 gallon water) and wipe the inside completely, including baskets, racks, and underneath vegetable bins. Be sure to check the drip pan for any blood that might have leaked down. After the refrigerator is clean, place a dish of vanilla or lemon extract or an opened box of baking soda inside, or pour dry unused coffee grounds onto several paper plates. Set them on separate shelves. It may take several days for the odor to dissipate.

- **Refrigerator deodorizer:** These tried-and-true methods work:

Put a box of baking soda into the refrigerator or put the baking soda into a plastic margarine tub and poke several holes in the lid and change it at least every 3 months. When you do, pour it down the sink to freshen it or pour it on a wet sponge and wipe out the inside of the refrigerator for extra cleaning. (Note: Do not recycle the baking soda from the refrigerator for use in recipes because the absorbed odors would be transferred to the food.)
Place lemon or lime slices on small dishes and put on different shelves.

Wipe out refrigerator walls with white household vinegar.

If you are moving or putting a refrigerator in storage for a short time, place socks filled with dry coffee grounds or activated charcoal inside to prevent musty odors.

■ **Rodent cages:** To deodorize a hamster or gerbil "aquarium," first empty the aquarium of everything—bedding, toys, and animals—and put it into the shower. Fill with a half-inch or so of water and a couple of tablespoons of baking soda. Scrub the bottom and sides. Rinse with clear water. The smells will be gone and the glass will sparkle.

■ **Room deodorizer:** To make an aromatic pomander ball, make holes in the skin of an orange with a round toothpick then push cloves into the holes. Cover the orange completely or make a design. Wrap with a ribbon and hang.

■ **Room deodorizer (vacuuming):** Put a scented fabric-softener sheet into the bag of your upright vacuum cleaner to create a fresh smell. This should last for several weeks.

■ **Rubber gloves:** To prevent odor, sprinkle the inside of the gloves with baking soda or talcum powder. Or, dry the outside surface while you have them on; then pull them off turning them inside out; hang on a towel rack to air-dry.

■ **Smoke:**

In the home: Getting rid of an overwhelming smoke smell can be especially difficult because the two biggest areas that absorb odors are walls and flooring. First, a quick fix: If a room smells of smoke from a party or the fireplace, open the windows and doors to get it out. Then take a small tea towel and soak it in white household vinegar and water. Wring it out to eliminate excess water and then swing it around the room.

My mother would set out bowls of vinegar or ammonia to eliminate smoke odors. Place a couple around your rooms during the day and see if you notice a difference when you return at night. CAUTION: Don't use ammonia if you have pets or small children.

For serious smoke smells, you'll have to clean the walls. If they can be "wet washed," use a nonabrasive, all-purpose cleaner. If the odor remains, you may have to repaint the walls, being sure to use a sealer first.

If your rooms are carpeted, you can buy special cleaners that can help remove the smoke: dry carpet cleaner with granules that are brushed into the carpet and then vacuumed up; deodorizing cleaners that are sprinkled onto the carpet and vacuumed up; carpet cleaning machines that use detergent and water solutions. As a last resort, call the professionals!

■ **Toaster oven:** To help contain the smell of burnt crumbs and grease, pour a bit of baking soda on the bottom tray. Be sure to clean the tray as often as possible to prevent a fire.

■ **Tobacco smoke:** See **Smoke.**

■ **Towels:** To get rid of the sour smell, wash towels in small loads, using hot water, the normal amount of detergent plus ½ cup baking soda or 1 cup ammonia to the rinse cycle. Put into the dryer right away. You may have to wash them several times.

■ **Trash compactor:** Boy, odors can grow in this handy kitchen appliance. Before you put any trash into the bag, place a thick layer of newspaper on the bottom and cover it with a layer of baking soda. As trash accumulates, keep it odor-free by tossing a handful of baking soda on top.

■ **Vacuum cleaner bag:** Any of the following, added to the bag, will eliminate that musty, dusty vacuum cleaner "exhaust": Carpet freshener, several whole cloves, baking soda, a cotton ball dabbed with almond or peppermint extract or your favorite perfume.

■ **Washing machine hoses and drains:** To freshen, pour a cup of white vinegar into the washer and run a small-load cycle.

■ **Washing machine odor:** Follow these steps:

1. Turn the water-level dial to the highest setting.
2. Set the water-temperature dial to hot and fill the washer tub.
3. Set wash cycle on normal wash and start the cycle.
4. Stop after 1 minute. Add a gallon more of hot water. Do not let the tub overflow.
5. Add 2 to 4 cups household chlorine bleach.
6. Begin the cycle again and allow it to run for several minutes, then stop and let it sit for 15 to 30 minutes.
7. Turn on and let washing machine complete the rest of the cycle. When complet-

ed, open the lid and allow the drum to air out. Also, leave the lid open when not in use.

■ **Wastebasket:** To prevent odors, put a fabric-softener sheet or perfume strips or samples into the bottom of the basket.

■ **Wooden bread box odor:** After receiving so many letters asking what to do about woody odors in wooden bread boxes that are so strong that bread stored in them absorbs the odor, we tried every conceivable method to get the smell out. We had no luck at all! So the only solutions are to return the box to the store and get a refund or just use the box for something other than food. I use mine to store letters.

THE LAUNDRY ROOM

Laundry rooms are attached to many kitchens, and although I wouldn't call them "the heart of the home," you probably find yourself spending a lot of time there. These hints will help you get better results in less time.

Start by enlisting all of the members of your family in keeping the laundry moving. Give each of them a guided tour of the laundry room. Teach them how to do the laundry and what products to use to get their clothes clean. Explain the difference between detergent, bleach, and fabric softener, for example. Keep a sign posted with basic instructions.

■ Often, laundry rooms are so small that space is a precious commodity. Install shelves above the machines to hold laundry products.

■ If you do have the space, set up a counter for sorting and folding clothes as soon as they come out of the dryer.

■ Keep garment racks, clothing trees, an iron, ironing board, and a laundry cart nearby.

■ Hang a few small plastic bins or receptacles on the wall to hold a sewing kit (complete with pre-threaded needles and buttons) and lost-and-found items.

■ Store all washing supplies in a large plastic basket in a cabinet or on a shelf so you have everything you need close at hand (and to keep any spills contained).

■ Keep a notepad with a pen on a bulletin board near your laundry area. This is handy for jotting down the laundry products you need as you run out of them. It's also a good place to leave laundering instructions for family members.

■ If you are waiting for the washer or dryer to stop, use the time to organize. Open any cabinet and reach way in the back to pull out and get rid of five items, such as empty boxes, bottles with a little cleaning stuff left, lint, odd socks, or old rags.

■ Toss a load of laundry in the washing machine before you leave for work—minus water and soap. Whoever gets home first adds the detergent (and bleach if required) and pushes start. (CAUTION: Do not start the washer, dryer, or dishwasher and then leave the house!) Before dinner is on the table, the clean clothes are ready to go into the dryer. A load of clothes can be done each day, so it doesn't build up to a huge task over the weekend.

HELOISE'S LAUNDRY LIST

Keep copies of this list on the laundry room door, and check off items to add to your weekly shopping list.

- ☐ Bleach
- ☐ Bluing
- ☐ Detergent
- ☐ Detergent booster
- ☐ Disinfectant
- ☐ Dryer sheets
- ☐ Enzyme presoaks
- ☐ Fabric finishes
- ☐ Fabric softener
- ☐ Fabric washes for delicates
- ☐ Pre-wash stain removers
- ☐ Sizing
- ☐ Starch
- ☐ Water softeners

Sorting

When it comes to sorting laundry, it helps to have a number of baskets on hand. You can also have receptacles just for towels or heavily soiled work clothes. Of course, the number of bins you set up depends on how much space you have.

■ A READER RECOMMENDS:

One reader purchased three inexpensive plastic hampers in different colors and gave the kids a clothes-sorting lesson. They throw darks into a blue hamper, whites into a white hamper, and mixed colors into a beige hamper. It's easy to do a quick load of laundry, with no need for sorting.

■ Always separate light-colored garments from dark ones.

■ Separate lint-producing garments like bath towels from lint-collecting ones such as synthetic or permanent-press clothes.

■ Use a hamper only for big items like towels and jeans, and a small laundry bag for the small stuff like T-shirts.

■ Buy some light-colored duffel bags and several indelible pens. Write washing instructions—hot, warm, and cold water—on the front of each laundry bag with the pen. Clothes can be put in the appropriate bag.

As we know too well, dark socks all look similar in color when you are trying to match them—and there always seems to be one without a mate! Here are several ways to keep them together:

■ Pin socks in pairs with a nonrusting pin or hold them together with a plastic hook.

■ Buy fabric paint pens. Match up black socks and label them with a letter and pairs of navy socks with a number. Each family member could have a label with different pen color.

■ Presort colored socks before washing and place each "color" in its own zippered mesh lingerie bag.

❀ **CLASSIC HELOISE HINT:** Make about a half-dozen laundry bags out of nylon net (available at sewing and fabric stores). Label each bag or the hook you hang it on: whites, darks, pastels, delicates, towels—whatever laundry categories are appropriate for your family. Then place things in their respective bags as they are used. When the bag is filled, you have a load for the washer.

Nifty Laundry Tricks and Tips

1. Read the care labels, detergent labels, and washer and dryer settings first!

2. Check for fresh and old stains. Read the care labels on the clothing. Determine what the stain is and how to treat it before tossing into the machine.

3. Close all zippers and hook all fasteners before you put them into the washing machine or dryer because otherwise they will snag and possibly get bent or broken.

4. Sew on loose buttons; repair rips and tears before putting into the washing machine or dryer.

5. Check pockets to remove all items before putting into the washing machine.

6. Turn jeans, corduroys, or velveteens inside out when you wash them so they won't fade. Wash in the coolest water and dry on the lowest heat.

7. Wash and dry printed T-shirts and sweaters inside-out to prevent pilling.

8. If you need to use a spray-type laundry stain remover, be sure to turn the stained item inside-out and spray the stain from the back side.

9. Rub a small bit of liquid detergent on stained polyester garments before putting into the washing machine.

10. Test a garment for colorfastness by making a solution of 1 tablespoon 5 percent bleach and ¼ cup water. Using an inside seam, put a drop or two of the solution on it for just 1 minute to see if the color changes. Then rinse and air-dry.

11. Wash same-colored clothing together to avoid fading and bleeding.

12. Use the right water temperature; otherwise you can damage more delicate washables.

13. Put the right amount of detergent into the machine first and not on top of the clothes.

14. After the water and detergent have mixed, put clothing into the washing machine piece by piece. Lay each garment in a circle around the agitator.

15. Do not use chlorine or non-chlorine bleaches together.

16. Do not use bleach on acetates, silk, spandex, or wool.

17. Turn the dryer on the correct setting for the fabric and dry.

18. Remove lint from the dryer filter after the dryer load. Clothes will dry faster and energy will be saved, too.

19. Do not overload a washer or dryer because clothes will not get clean or dry properly. Never add wet items to a partially dried load.

20. When you hang clothes immediately after pulling them out from the dryer, they may not have to be ironed later. Place a hook over the door and keep hangers on it, hang a clothesline, or use a foldable clothes rack.

21. Don't dry some of the "newer" white fabrics in natural sunlight because they contain fluorescent brighteners, which react in the sun and may cause fabric to become yellowed permanently.

22. Do not put wet colored garments into a laundry hamper with white garments; they could bleed color onto them.

Budget Organizing

Recycle the large plastic caps from fabric softener or liquid detergent bottles. They can be used to:

• Store tubes of lipstick or small makeup brushes

• Sort screws and nuts at your workbench

• Use for mixing small amounts of craft paint

Putting Away Laundry

▪ To cut down on time sorting and folding socks, fold them right as you take them off the line or out of the dryer.

▪ After folding clothes (especially towels, sheets, underwear, and T-shirts), place them *under* an existing stack in your drawer or shelf so they will be rotated evenly and the same ones won't be used constantly. This will help the items last longer.

▪ If you have a big household, color-code clothing. Assign each person a different color, and dot the care label or the waist seam of undergarments. That will make identification easier.

▪ A READER RECOMMENDS:

One reader, while folding laundry, folds the bras and undies together to make sure she has five sets. That way she's set for work for the whole week.

STAINS

Dealing with stains is probably the most frustrating part of doing laundry. And it can be expensive to replace stained clothing! I believe that there's usually a remedy for every stain. Some might demand a little bit of imagination. Others will need a lot of patience. And, you'll even see in these pages an entry called "When All Else Fails," which asks you to accept the inevitable . . . the stain will always be with you but you can learn to live with the stain—or sew on a patch to hide it. Be as creative as you can.

The best way to conquer any stain is to have knowledge and a plan. In the following pages I'll give you tried-and-true stain removal guidelines, information about types of stains and the kinds of cleaners plus a host of invaluable, home-tested hints and tips. If the solution to your problem isn't in the pages of this book, I hope that you will contact me at the address or e-mail provided and share your favorite stain stories. Perhaps we can find the solution together or another reader will have found the remedy that we can pass on. (Contact me by fax at 1-210-HELOISE or visit my my website at www.Heloise.com.)

THE 3 RULES: SOON, SLOW, SEVERAL!

Always keep these rules in mind when you take on any stain.

1. As SOON as possible—ASAP. Attack the stain as SOON as you can. The more time left on the fabric, the more difficult it will be to remove!
2. Lift the stain SLOWLY. Some stains take time to get out.
3. Repeat these steps for stubborn stains. You may have to do them SEVERAL times.

8 STEPS TO EFFECTIVE STAIN REMOVAL

Sometimes it just takes one quick step to get the stain out. Sometimes you need to be more diligent and patient.

1. Read First, Act Later—but not too late: Read the care label and follow the instructions precisely.
2. Gentle to Hard: Trying the least drastic stain removal first may do the job.
3. Flush: Flush or soak the stained areas ASAP with cold water. Many times this gentlest of methods will remove the stain. But watch for delicate fabrics that may be damaged by water.
4. Protect and Absorb: Placing a paper towel—or several layers to be extra safe—underneath a stain before treating will absorb any stain that's going through the fabric.
5. From the outside in: Work from the outside toward the center of the stain to prevent it from spreading.
6. Blot, don't rub: Except where otherwise instructed, *blotting*—dabbing firmly with an absorbent cloth—is better than *rubbing*—using a circular motion to gently scrub the

area. Be aware that rubbing may spread the stain and damage the fabric.

7. Time heals all: Give your stain remover enough time to work before rinsing or washing. Don't rush it or you may have to repeat it.

8. This is a test: Always test a small hidden area first just in case your cleaning method proves to be as damaging as the stain. This is especially important if you don't know what the fabric is.

WHAT KIND OF STAIN IS THAT, ANYWAY?

Where do these stains on our clothing come from? Thin air it seems! When we're at work or play, we suddenly notice a spot or stain. To most of us, they are mystery stains. I like to think of myself as the Stain Detective. And, I hope that with the help of this book you, too, can become the Sherlock Holmes or Nancy Drew of the stain world.

Like any good detective, you need to understand everything about the perpetrator and the victim.

It's key to know what kind of a stain you have in order to treat it properly and with the right product. Here are the three basic types you need to know:

■ **Grease and oil:** Butter, candle wax, chocolate, and crayon are a few of the major culprits that cause these stains. Washables are best treated with warm or hot water. But remember that many greasy food stains also contain protein and/or sugar.

■ **Protein:** Baby formula, blood, cheese, egg, ice cream, urine, yogurt, and grass. Use cold water to wash blood- or egg-stained items and cool to warm for other stains of this kind.

■ **Sugar:** Since sugar hides in so many foods from fruit and juices to chocolate, you have to be careful because heat may set sugar stains. A greasy stain may require hot water, but a sugar stain should be treated with cool water first.

FABRICS: A STAIN FIGHTER'S GLOSSARY

Knowing the rules for stain removal and understanding the major types of stains that can cause you grief are the first two parts of your education in effective stain removal. It is equally important to know the types and styles of fabrics that you are trying to clean since so much depends on it. But be sure to always read the care instructions if they are attached to the item. If not, you'll have to figure out what kind of fabric you are working with and consult the following list from the International Fabricare Institute:

■ **Acetate:** A synthetic fiber that is used for luxurious fabrics such as taffeta and satin. It is often blended with rayon.

■ **Acrylic:** The generic name for a synthetic fiber derived from polyacrylonitrile. Acrylic is typically used as a substitute for wool.

■ **Angora:** A hair (wool) fiber from the Angora rabbit. It may be blended with rayon or wool fibers for a novelty effect.

- **Aramid:** A generic name for a synthetic fiber that is very strong and highly flame-resistant. Trade names are Nomex and Kevlar.

- **Bias:** The diagonal of a woven fabric between the warp and the filling (crosswire) threads. This part of the fabric has the greatest amount of stretch and can easily be distorted in the cleaning and pressing process.

- **Bleeding:** The running of dyes that aren't colorfast in solvent or water. When the color runs it can stain other materials.

- **Blend:** A fabric made from two or more fibers that will have the performance characteristics of both fibers (i.e., a cotton and blend).

- **Boucle:** A rough, fairly thick, stubborn yarn that gives a fabric a tufted or knotted texture.

- **Brocade:** A heavy jacquard weave fabric with a design, such as leaves and flowers, woven into it. Metallic threads are often used in brocades.

- **Bugle beads:** Tube-shaped beads, originally made of glass although often man-made. They are sewn on dresses and blouses as decoration. These beads may contain a coating on the inside that can be removed in dry cleaning, giving the bead a translucent appearance, or can discolor during long-term storage.

- **Cashmere:** A fine, soft wool obtained from goats native to Kashmir and Tibet.

- **Cellulose:** Fibers that come from a plant source, such as cotton, linen, ramie, and rayon.

- **Chenille:** From the French word for caterpillar, a fuzzy pile yarn that resembles a caterpillar or pipe cleaner. Commonly found in rugs, bedspreads, and bathroom accessories, but also used in sweaters, blouses, and dresses.

- **Chiffon:** A sheer, lightweight, drapable, woven fabric originally made of silk but today usually made from man-made fibers.

- **Chintz:** Any closely woven, plain weave fabric with a shiny lustrous finish, often printed in bright floral designs.

- **Colorfast:** A term that implies that the color in a fabric will not be removed in the recommended cleaning procedure and will not wash out or fade upon exposure to sunlight or other atmospheric elements.

- **Corduroy:** A pile-corded fabric in which the rib has been sheared or woven to produce a smooth, velvet-like nap.

- **Crepe:** A fabric with an overall crinkled surface that is made from yarns with such a high twist that the yarn actually kinks.

- **Denim:** A twill weave fabric with a colored warp and white filling thread.

- **Faille:** A woven fabric that has a very narrow, crosswire rib.

- **Fake (fun) fur:** A common term for synthetic fabrics used to imitate animal pelts.

- **Felt:** A fabric made from wool, fur, or hair fibers that mesh together when heat, moisture, and mechanical action are applied.

- **Flocking:** A term used to describe small pieces of fiber glued or bonded to the surface of a fabric.

- **Fusible:** A fabric with an adhesive coating that can be attached to another fabric by applying heat, moisture, and pressure.

- **Interfacing:** A fabric used to give additional body and strength to certain parts of garments. Some areas that usually contain interfacing include front opening edges, collars, and pocket flaps. Some interfacing material may not be compatible with the shell fabric and may cause a bubbling or puckering of the shell fabric.

- **Jersey:** A single-knit fabric with plain stitches on the right side and purl stitches on the back. The word *jersey* is often used to describe any knit.

- **Knit:** A method of making fabrics through the interlacing of yarns. These fabrics tend to mold and fit body shapes and are marked by their ability to stretch and recover to the original size.

- **Lace:** Knotted, twisted, or looped yarns that produce a fragile, sheer fabric, usually with intricate design patterns.

- **Metallics:** Man-made mineral fibers composed of metal, plastic-coated metal, metal-coated plastic, or a core completely covered with metal. Metallic fibers are primarily used to create shiny, decorative yarns.

- **Nap:** A fuzzy or soft downlike surface produced by brushing the fabric, usually with wire brushes.

- **Non-woven:** Fabrics made from fibers that are held together in a web by mechanical or chemical means or through heat. Some examples include felt and Ultrasuede.

- **Oxford:** A fabric woven in a basket weave and made of cotton or a cotton blend. It often has a thin, colored warp and a thick, white filling.

- **Pile:** A woven fabric containing an extra set of yarns woven into the base of the fabric to produce the hairlike surface texture. Velvet, velveteen, corduroy, and fake fur are the most common pile fabrics.

- **Pilling:** The tendency of fibers to pill or roll up. Pilling occurs when the loose end of a fiber is rubbed and collected on the surface of the fabric. The length of the fiber and twist of the yarn will affect pilling.

- **Rayon:** The generic name for a cellulose-based, man-made fiber. Rayon has characteristics similar to those of cotton, linen, and ramie.

- **Satin:** Fabrics that are characterized by yarns that usually float over four to seven yarns before being interlaced with yarns laid in the opposite direction. The floating yarns along the surface reflect light, which gives the fabric its luster. Satin fabrics can be made from silk or man-made fibers like acetate or polyester.

- **Shell:** The outer fabric of a garment or household item.

- **Silk:** A natural filament fiber produced by silkworms when spinning their cocoons.

- **Sizing:** A term for materials used to give a fabric stiffness, luster, or firmness. Different types of material are used on different fabrics.

- **Velvet:** A fabric with a short, closely woven pile. It is usually made of rayon, acetate, silk, nylon, or a blend of these fibers.

- **Weave:** Yarns interlacing at right angles. There are three basic weave types: plain, twill, and satin. All other weaves are variations of these. Some of the more common variations include basket, rib, and jacquard.

- **Woolen:** A wool fabric made from loosely twisted yarns that has a somewhat fuzzy surface.

- **Worsted:** A wool fabric with a clean, smooth surface made from tightly twisted yarns.

- **Yarn:** A continuous strand spun from short (staple) fibers or long (filament) fibers. Yarns can be of low twist (lofty) or high twist (tight).

LAUNDRY PRODUCTS: A PRIMER

Knowing the different products and their ingredients helps you select the right product for the cleaning job. The following list, courtesy of The Soap and Detergent Association, gives you the general types of cleaners available.

■ **Laundry detergents and laundry aids** are available as liquids, powders, gels, sticks, sprays, pumps, sheets, and bars. They are formulated to meet a variety of soil and stain removal, bleaching, fabric softening and conditioning, and disinfectant needs under varying water, temperature, and use conditions.

■ **Laundry detergents** are either general purpose or light-duty. General-purpose detergents are suitable for all washable fabrics. Liquids work best on oily stains and for pretreating soils and stains. Powders are especially effective in lifting out clay and ground-in dirt. Light-duty detergents are used for hand- or machine-washing lightly soiled items and delicate fabrics.

■ **Laundry aids** contribute to the effectiveness of laundry detergents and provide special functions.

Overflow!

Have you ever added too much soap to the washing machine and suddenly suds are flowing out everywhere? Grab a saltshaker and sprinkle salt on the suds; they will dissipate immediately.

• **Acetone:** This highly flammable, colorless liquid is used to dissolve fats, oils, and waxes.

• **Ammonia:** Cuts heavy soil and grease when added with detergent. CAUTION: DO NOT EVER combine ammonia with chlorine bleach or products containing chlorine bleach because mixed together they create hazardous fumes.

• **Bar soap:** Bathroom and laundry bar soaps and powders can be used to pretreat serious stains or soiling before laundering. They can be helpful when you need to wash hand-washable lingerie. Bars do a good job removing perspiration and tobacco stains.

■ **Bleaches** (chlorine and oxygen) whiten and brighten fabrics and help remove stubborn stains. They convert soils into colorless, soluble particles that can be removed by detergents and carried away in the wash water. Liquid chlorine bleach (usually in a sodium hypochlorite solution) can also disinfect and deodorize fabrics. Oxygen (color-safe) bleach is gentler and works safely on almost all washable fabrics.

■ **Bluings** contain a blue dye or pigment taken up by fabrics in the wash or rinse. Bluing absorbs the yellow part of the light spectrum, counteracting the natural yellowing of many fabrics.

■ **Boosters** enhance the soil and stain removal, brightening, buffering, and water softening performance of detergents. They are used in the wash in addition to the detergent.

■ **Borax:** Boosts laundry cleaning. (Available in the detergent section of your supermarket.)

■ **Cleaning solvent (dry-cleaning fluid):** Removes cosmetics, grease and gum stains. Use also on dry-cleanable clothing.

- **Enzyme presoaks** are used for soaking items before washing to remove difficult stains and soils. When added to the wash water, they increase cleaning power.

- **Fabric softeners**, added to the final rinse or dryer, make fabrics softer and fluffier; decrease static cling, wrinkling, and drying time; impart a pleasing fragrance and make ironing easier.

- **Hydrogen peroxide (3 percent):** As a mild, slow-acting oxidizing bleach, it lifts bloodstains and whitens lace.

- **Isoamyl acetate:** Called banana or pear oil, it dissolves paint and lacquer.

- **Oxalic acid crystals:** Used for bleaching and cleaning.

- **Oxygen bleach:** Applies to all types of colors and fabric. The powdered version provides detergent and an all-fabric bleaching action good for stain and soil removal.

- **Prewash soil and stain removers** are used to pretreat heavily soiled and stained garments, especially those made from synthetic fibers.

- **Starches, fabric finishes, and sizings** used in the final rinse or after drying give body to fabrics, make them more soil-resistant, and make ironing easier.

- **Water softeners** added to the wash or rinse, inactivate hard-water minerals. Since detergents are more effective in soft water, these products increase cleaning power.

A SHOPPING LIST OF LAUNDRY SUPPLIES

Here's a quick checklist of the laundry supplies you might want to have on hand.

Ammonia
Baking Soda
Bleaches:
Chlorine and oxygen
Dishwasher powder or liquid
Fabric color remover; or substitutes such as lemon juice
Club soda
Detergents:
enzymes and presoaks
heavy-duty powder
liquid and light-duty liquid for delicates
Cleaning fluids:
amyl acetate or acetone, an odorless, fragrance-free ingredient in nail polish remover
dry-cleaning solvent/fluid
nail polish remover
rubbing alcohol
Glycerin
Oxalic acid
Rust-stain remover
Spot-and-stain remover
White bar soap
White vinegar

CLOTHING STAINS A-TO-Z

- **Acetate (triacetate):** Check the label to find out if the item needs to be dry-cleaned. If not, wash in warm water in a washing machine on the gentle cycle. Never twist or ring when wet. Use fabric softener to reduce static electricity. Always iron on a low setting or use steam.

- **Acne medications/skin creams:** These may contain bleaches, like benzoyl peroxide, which can discolor fabrics. Let medications dry completely after applying and before putting on clothing. Wash hands well and dry completely after applying so none will get onto clothing. If it does, the stain or discoloration may be permanent.

- **Acrylic:** Use warm water in machine washing and tumble dry.

- **Adhesive tape:** Apply ice or freeze the sticky residue by putting the garment into the freezer. With a dull knife blade, carefully scrape off the hardened gummy residue. Pretreat area with a petroleum-based prewash spray and launder as usual.

- **Alcoholic beverages:** Use cool water to soak or sponge the stain immediately. Then pour a bit of white household vinegar on a sponge and apply to the stain. Rinse. If any stain remains, gently rub liquid laundry detergent into it, then launder as usual. (See also **Wine**.)

- **Antiperspirant/deodorant:** Salts from perspiration can eat away at fabrics. (Antiperspirants that contain aluminum chloride can cause fabrics like rayon to turn yellow.) When these stains happen, get to them ASAP. CAUTION: Ironing may set the stains.

Fresh and light stain: Rub liquid laundry detergent or prewash stain remover into the stained area. Use the hottest water safe for the fabric and wash. If stains remain, apply white household vinegar and let sit for 30 minutes. Then wash the garment using an enzyme detergent or oxygen bleach.

Heavy stain: Place the stain facedown on a paper towel and sponge the back of the stain (outside of garment) with a dry-cleaning solvent. Let dry and rinse. Rub in liquid laundry detergent and launder in the hottest water safe for the fabric.

Older stain: Apply undiluted white vinegar, rinse, and launder as usual.

To help prevent stains, let deodorant dry completely before you dress.

To prevent buildup, do not wash garments repeatedly in cold water because it may not break down the deodorant or perspiration buildup, but be sure to:

Wash the clothing after every wearing and don't put it away without cleaning.

Rub liquid laundry detergent onto the underarm area of the garment, and after every third or fourth wearing, use the hottest water safe for the material.

- **Artist's oils:** While turpentine will remove oil paint, it also will discolor some fabric. Use bar face soap to remove artist's oil paint from clothing.

Note: Bar soap can also be used to clean brushes. Apply soap and brush under warm running water. Rub the brush into the soap, moving from side-to-side. With your fingers, rub soap through the bristles until paint is gone. Rinse with clear warm water.

- **Baby formula:** Soak clothes in cold water ASAP, and then rub liquid laundry detergent into the stain or treat with an enzyme presoak or prewash spray. Launder in the hottest water safe for the fabric. If the stain persists, sponge it with dry-cleaning fluid and launder a second time before putting into the dryer.

As a last-ditch try for white, chlorine-bleachable clothing, use a large non-aluminum container or your kitchen sink. Fill with 1 gallon hot water; add ½ cup dishwasher detergent and ¼ cup bleach and nothing else. Stir until detergent is dissolved.

Add clothes and let soak for 15 minutes or a little longer if still stained. For fabrics that can't be washed in hot water, such as nylon, let mixture cool before placing clothes into it. *Note:* If formula stains are left to set, they will become permanent and no amount of bleach will remove them!

■ **Baseball caps:** Test cap for colorfastness first by using a small amount of detergent and water on a hidden spot. Blot area with a white cloth. If any dye comes off on the cloth, it might not be a good idea to try to clean it. If dye does not come off, hand wash with laundry detergent, rinse, and air-dry. To clean the sweatband, use the kind of spot remover that you spray on that dries to a powder. Follow directions carefully. Use a clean toothbrush to brush off powder. Or, put a small amount of this homestyle solution using 1 tablespoon hair shampoo to ½ cup of water onto the band; scrub it in with the toothbrush. Rinse carefully and let air-dry.

Baseball cap forms are available in sporting good stores and they will help keep the shape of the cap when drying. Putting caps into the dishwasher or washing machine could damage the brim.

■ **Beer:** Rinse with cool water, then sponge stains with white household vinegar.

■ **Berry:** See Fruit/fruit juice/berries.

■ **Blankets (cotton, rayon, or other synthetics):** For heavily stained or soiled blankets, prespot and presoak. Wash 4 to 6 minutes in cold or warm water (depending on the care label) on the delicate cycle with detergent and an oxygen bleach (if label says okay). Dry on gentle cycle or line dry. For a quick freshening, put into dryer on air setting with a fabric softener sheet.

■ **Blood:** Treat the stain ASAP. Do not use hot water because heat may set protein stains.

Get the stained item into cold water and soak for 30 minutes. Then apply a prewash stain remover. If stain remains, rub it with liquid laundry detergent or bar soap. Still a problem? Make a solution of 1 tablespoon ammonia and 1 cup water and apply to the stains. Rinse and launder following care-label instructions. Check garment before putting into dryer. If the stain is still there, pour a small amount of 3 percent hydrogen peroxide on the stain (always test this on a hidden area to see if the 3 percent hydrogen peroxide affects fabric color). Launder again.

Unseasoned meat tenderizer is also effective in getting rid of fresh bloodstains. Dampen the area with cold water then sprinkle on unseasoned meat tenderizer and let sit.

When All Else Fails!

In spite of your best efforts, some stains are permanent. But you can get around that by sewing or ironing on an appliqué design patch over that hopeless stain or scorch mark. It just may be your fashion statement!

Repeat to remove all of the stain; then the garment can be laundered.

If stain has dried, soak in warm water with an enzyme-based product. Then launder as usual.

- **Breast milk:** Soak clothes in cold water ASAP, and then rub liquid laundry detergent into the stain or treat with an enzyme presoak or prewash spray. Launder in the hottest water safe for the fabric. If the stain persists, sponge it with dry-cleaning fluid and launder a second time before putting into the dryer.

- **Butter/margarine:** For washable fabrics, pretreat with a heavy-duty liquid laundry detergent or a prewash spray. Then launder as usual. For heavy stains on washable fabrics, put stained areas facedown on paper towels. Apply dry-cleaning solvent to the backside of the stain; replace towels frequently. Let dry; rub in liquid detergent. Rinse and launder. Nonwashables need to be professionally dry-cleaned. If you're out and about and spill grease or oil on your favorite article, don't fret. Simply pat on some flour, talc, or even white artificial sugar onto the grease spot. When absorbed, brush off and then wash or take to the cleaners as soon as possible. It may be necessary to pretreat with a stain remover and wash in the hottest water safe for the fabric.

- **Candle wax:** Use a plastic card or your fingernail to lift off as much of the wax as you can. (Even the dull side of a knife may damage certain fabrics, so do this step with care.) Then, put paper towels on each side of the stained area. Use an iron, turned to a low-to-medium setting, depending on what's appropriate for the fabric. Check the care labels on the fabrics and your iron to determine the temperature. For example, linen and cotton can tolerate high temperatures better than polyester or other synthetic fabrics. Press the stained area until wax comes up and replace the towels often to absorb it. If there's still a stain, make a mixture of 1 tablespoon mild white dishwashing liquid, 1 teaspoon household ammonia, and 1 cup of water and treat it. Then wash in the hottest water safe for the fabric (check the care label). Or, to remove the stain, you can apply full-strength liquid laundry detergent, allowing it to set, then washing as usual.

- **Candy (other than chocolate):** Use cold water and a small amount of liquid detergent on the stain; then rinse. If the stains are red, soak the garment in a strong laundry detergent and a bit of bleach (if it's okay for the material) or apply a prewash spray.

- **Carbon paper:** Dampen the area and rub liquid laundry detergent into the stain. Hand wash the garment in warm, soapy water. Rinse and repeat steps if needed.

- **Cheese:** As soon as possible, soak clothes in cold water and then rub liquid laundry detergent into the stain or treat with an enzyme presoak or prewash spray. Launder in the hottest water safe for the fabric. If the stain persists, sponge it with dry-cleaning fluid and launder a second time before putting into the dryer.

- **Chewing gum:** Put the garment in the freezer to harden the gum. CAUTION: Don't put the garment into a plastic bag. Then remove residue by scraping very carefully with a dull knife or credit card. If you still see residue, sponge dry-cleaning fluid on the area or treat with prewash spray and then launder.

▪ **Chocolate:** Scrape away any chocolate you can. Try these methods: Soak the garment in cold water for 30 minutes. While the fabric is wet, rub liquid laundry detergent into the stain. Rinse. If a greasy stain remains, sponge it with dry-cleaning fluid. Rinse. Launder in warm water.

Or: Blot the spot with cool water. Then presoak with a powdered laundry detergent with enzymes. Follow the label directions. Launder as usual.

Treat with a solution of 1 teaspoon household ammonia diluted in 1 cup water.

(CAUTION: *Do not* use this on wool or silk blends). Launder as usual.

▪ **Christening gown:** When you buy the gown, check the care label to know in advance how the dress can be cleaned. A gown decorated with lace or pearls may be difficult to clean at home and most likely need to be professionally cleaned. As soon as possible after the christening, take the dress to be dry-cleaned by a professional—even if it looks clean! It may have spots from the baby, which you can't see. There also could be stains that will oxidize and show up as brown/yellow spots later.

▪ **Clay:** Sports or gardening stains of this nature can be difficult to remove but give this a shot. First, eliminate any dry dirt; shake or brush off. Combine powdered detergent (that contains no bleach) and enough household ammonia to make a paste and apply to the clay stains with a white cotton cloth. Let set for about 10 minutes and then launder in the hottest water safe for the fabric. You may have to repeat the process.

▪ **Cloth diapers:** Scrape off any residue. Rinse diapers in cool water so stains don't set. Wash in hot, soapy water. Add a little bleach every 2 or 3 washes to remove stubborn stains, but run diapers through a second and final rinse, adding ½ cup vinegar to remove any bleach or soap residue. *Note:* Do not use fabric softener in every wash because it will cause the diapers to be less absorbent.

▪ **Coffee/tea:** Rinse in cold water ASAP and then rub in several drops of mild, white dishwashing liquid. Rinse well and then treat with a solution of 1 part white household vinegar and 3 parts water. Rinse again then launder as usual. *Note:* If you have used cream in your coffee, you may need to sponge the stain with dry-cleaning fluid.

▪ **Cola:** Stains on 100 percent cotton, cotton blends, and permanent-press fabrics can be removed, if sponged with undiluted white vinegar within 24 hours. Then launder or dry-clean according to manufacturer's directions.

▪ **Collar and cuff:** To get out body oil stains, pretreat by rubbing liquid laundry detergent, hair shampoo, or a prewash stain remover into the stain. Launder as usual.

▪ **Corduroy:** Check the care label to make sure these are machine washable. Turn garments inside-out and wash in warm or hot water. Hang and line dry; brush up nap.

▪ **Correction fluid:** Because most correction fluids are latex based, this kind of stain usually needs professional care. Let your dry cleaner know exactly what and where it is.

▪ **Cough syrup/tummy medications:** Scrape off any sticky stuff. Soak garment for 15 minutes in a mixture of water, liquid detergent, and several drops of white vinegar. Then launder with appropriate bleach for the fabric. Sponge the affected area with dry-cleaning fluid.

- **Crayon I:** Scrape off excess wax with a dull knife or spoon. Place several layers of paper towel under the stained area and dab with dry-cleaning fluid until the crayon color is gone and no longer bleeding through to the towels. Using plenty of detergent, wash in the hottest water appropriate for the fabric.

- **Crayon II:** *If fabric has gone through the washer*, rub the stains with liquid laundry detergent then wash the garment with cold water and detergent. After the wash cycle, stop the washing machine and let the garment soak overnight. Next day, complete the wash cycle.

- **Crayon III:** *If fabric has gone through the dryer*, spray both sides of the new stain with a petroleum-based, prewash stain remover and rub into the fabric. Let sit for a while and then wash as usual. If stains remain on a bleach-safe fabric, follow directions. (If there is crayon wax on the dryer drum, dampen a small cloth with the spray and then wipe out the drum. Be sure to then clean with a damp cloth.)

- **Crayon IV:** *If a crayon has gone through a whole load of clothes*, wash everything again with hot water, laundry soap, and 1 cup baking soda. If any color still remains, wash bleach-safe clothes with chlorine bleach or oxygen bleach in the hottest water that's safe for the fabric. Then launder as usual.

- **Cream:** Soak clothes in *cold* water ASAP, and then rub liquid laundry detergent into the stain or treat with an enzyme presoak or prewash spray. Launder in the hottest water safe for the fabric. If the stain persists, sponge it with dry-cleaning fluid and launder a second time before putting into the dryer.

- **Curtains:** To whiten sheers, use a whitener and brightener powder that's made for the washing machine. It's available in grocery or sewing stores in the section with fabric dyes. Follow directions exactly.

- **Deodorant:** See **Antiperspirant/deodorant**

- **Down (comforters, jackets, and vests):** First read the care label instructions. If the garment can be machine washed, use a mild detergent on a gentle setting. Then put into the dryer on a low heat setting with a clean tennis ball to help redistribute down as it fluffs. You may want to take the item out and fluff by hand periodically during the drying process. If these garments have a musty smell, put them in the sun for a while. Some colored garments might need to be in the shade.

- **Dye transfer:** Use a packaged color remover to try to eliminate color from other fabrics that may have been transferred to white fabric. Follow label directions. Then launder. If dye remains on non-colorfast fabrics, soak in oxygen bleach then launder.

- **Easter egg dye:** Soak stain for at least 30 minutes in a prewash stain remover. Then launder as normal.

- **Egg:** Using a dull-edged knife, scrape off as much residue as possible. Wet the area with cool water; pour on full-strength liquid laundry detergent and scrub the stain with a toothbrush. When the stain is gone, wash in the hottest water safe for the fabric.

■ **Evening clothes (gowns, prom dresses):** Fancy clothing that is heavily beaded or sequined may not be able to be washed or cleaned at home. Read the care instructions. Some garments can be spot-cleaned but others, like taffeta, cannot. Take these to a dry cleaner for consultation. But be aware that some beads (plastic) will dissolve when they come in contact with some dry-cleaning solutions or spot removers.

■ **Fabric-softener sheets:** If fabrics are stained by contact with a fabric-softener (dryer) sheet, dampen the stained area and rub with white bar soap. Rinse and launder as usual. Or, use liquid laundry detergent directly on the area, let set then wash in hot water. Check before drying to make sure the stain is gone.

■ **Feces/stool:** Remove solid residue from the fabric. Soak the garment in warm water and an enzyme detergent. After all traces of the stain are removed, launder as usual.

CAUTION: Always wear gloves when cleaning fecal matter.

■ **Flood-stained fabrics:** If clothes have been soaked in muddy flood water, first get rid of as much dirt and residue as you can by shaking or brushing ASAP. Prewash fabrics in cool water with powdered laundry detergent. (Do not use hot water because it may set stains.) If garments have sewage, blood, or grass stains, add an enzyme presoak to the prewash. For garments affected by motor oils or other heavy soils, use a prewash soil-and-stain remover. Use powdered detergent, which is more effective in getting rid of ground-in dirt and clay. Allow detergent to dissolve before adding clothes to the washer. Wash in small loads with a full water level. Use the hottest water safe for fab-

rics. *Note:* If clothing has been contaminated with sewage, be sure to add a disinfectant to the wash, such as liquid household bleach, if it's safe for the fabrics. There are many commercial products, which also can sanitize and control odors. Check the care labels. You may have to wash many times to get clean. Check the rinse water: If it's dirty, wash again; if it's clean, the clothes should be clean. CAUTION: If there's iron in the soil deposits or water, bleach will make rust stains appear on fabrics. Don't put clothes into the dryer until the stains are gone. Heat will set them.

■ **Fruit/fruit juice/berries:** Get to them as fast as you can. Try one of these methods:

Soak the stained area in cold water for about 30 minutes. Rub liquid laundry detergent into the wet area if there are remaining stains. Launder with detergent and warm water. If there are still stains, apply hydrogen peroxide to bleach-safe fabric, then rinse well.

For washable fabric, soak in cold water. If stains are still there, dab white vinegar on them and rinse. If they are stubborn, apply hydrogen peroxide to bleach-safe fabrics.

For "dry clean only" fabrics (read the care label), sponge with dry-cleaning fluid.

Soak in cool water; wash. If stain remains, cover area with a paste made from oxygen-type bleach, several drops of hot water, and a few drops of ammonia. Wait 15 to 30 minutes; then wash as usual.

■ **Fruit stains:** To remove stains from hands, pour lemon juice on your hands and rub well. Rinse with water and dry.

- **Gloves:**

Gardening: Shake off clay or dirt but leave gloves on to wash with soap and water. Remove and hang to dry.

White cotton: Wash in a mild detergent then hold them under the faucet and run hot water into them just for several seconds. Rinse, let all water run out, and dry flat.

Winter gloves and mittens: To dry, slip them over the tops of clean empty soda bottles. Read care label for cleaning instructions.

- **Glue:** To get quick-drying glue out of fabrics, first, attempt this home remedy: Wet a clean cloth with hot soapy water and put it on top of and underneath the spot where the glue spilled. Repeat every 15 minutes. Keep cloth hot (put into microwave for 10 to 15 seconds to heat). The hot cloth should soften the glue, which then can be peeled off the fabric. If this does not work, commercial solvents found at hardware stores will.

CAUTION: Read the directions before you use a commercial solvent and test on a small inconspicuous area to make certain it will not hurt the clothing.

- **Grass, flower, and foliage:** Use the following methods:

For washable fabrics: Treat stains with prewash spray or apply liquid detergent into them. Using an enzyme detergent, wash in the hottest water designated for the fabric. Or, apply rubbing alcohol to the stained areas before laundering as usual.

For dry-cleanable only fabrics: It may be safe to apply alcohol or sponge with dry-cleaning fluid but be sure to test on an inconspicuous spot first.

For acetate fabrics: Sponge stains with nonflammable dry-cleaning solvent.

- **Gravy:** Use a spoon to scrape off all of it that you can. Blot the stain with white paper towels; then sprinkle cornstarch, salt, talcum powder, flour, or artificial sweetener over the area and let set to absorb the grease. Brush off. Then treat with a laundry detergent and wash in the hottest water allowed for the fabric.

- **Grease (motor oil, salad dressings, cooking oils):** Try one or more of these methods:

To absorb oil, rub in cornmeal, cornstarch, or talcum powder and let set. Brush powder away. If fabric is washable, launder as above.

For washable fabrics, pretreat with a heavy-duty liquid laundry detergent or a prewash spray. Then launder as usual.

For heavy stains on washable fabrics, place stained areas facedown on paper towels. Apply dry-cleaning solvent to the backside of the stain; replace towels frequently. Let dry then rub in liquid detergent. Rinse and launder. (See also **Suede.**)

- **Hair dye:** These stains on fabric can be tough, if not impossible, to remove. Read the care label first and then dab area with appropriate bleach. Launder as normal. *Do not* use on silk or wool; instead apply a dab of hydrogen peroxide to the stain and watch to see if it starts to fade. CAUTION: Test on a hidden area first. Launder as usual.

These Old Wives' Remedies Really Work!

For white washables, dissolve 1 tablespoon of borax in hot water and add to the rinse water. Clothes will get whiter.

For black washables, add several glugs of white household vinegar to the clear water rinse; it will help remove soap residue that causes black clothes to look dull.

For ink spots on clothing, soak them in warm milk before they dry. If the stains have dried, press table salt into them and drizzle lemon juice over them.

*What is a glug? You get a glug of something when you lift the container up and tip it for just a second. As the liquid comes out, the air in the bottle causes a "glug" sound and voilá—that's a glug!

- **Ice cream:** Soak in cold water and then hand wash in warm soapy water. Rinse. If the ice cream was chocolate, or a greasy stain remains, sponge it with cleaning fluid. After all the stain is gone, launder as usual.

- **Ink (ballpoint, felt-tip, liquid):** Some of these stains may be impossible to remove, but first give pretreating a try with these methods:

  For *dried stains,* gently rub with isopropyl alcohol until the stain comes out. CAUTION: Do not apply to highly colored material.

  For *spot removing,* sponge the area around the stain with commercial dry-cleaning fluid. Then put the stain facedown on several layers of clean paper towels and apply cleaning fluid to the back of the stain. Rinse completely with water; launder as usual.

- **Iodine:** Rinse with cool water from the backside of the stain. Soak in a solution of color remover, rinse, and launder as usual.

- **Jeans:** Acid-washed or other distressed jeans (with bleach) may yellow because chemicals used to create the look may not have been completely rinsed out or were exposed to strong heat or light. The yellow will not come out. Take them back to the store where you bought them or to the manufacturer for a refund or replacement.

- **Leather:** Read care labels. Use special soaps, such as saddle soap that can be applied and removed with a moist cloth. For serious cleaning, take to a specialty professional dry cleaner.

- **Leather boots:** To prevent winter salt or chemical stains, along with water and snow, treat boots with a commercial protect-all or water- and stain-repellent spray *before* you wear for the first time. If they get stained, use specially made products, available at shoe-repair shops or in supermarkets.

- **Linen:** To remove yellow spots that have set on washable linen, soak in a commercial whitener and brightener, found alongside dyes in the grocery store. Then wash as usual.

- **Lingerie:** To get rid of yellowing in washable cotton, nylon, or silk, soak for 30 minutes in a solution of 2 to 3 ounces of 3 percent hydrogen peroxide for each gallon of lukewarm water. Rinse and launder following care label instructions. You may have to repeat this process.

- **Lipstick:** ASAP put the stained area on several layers of absorbent towel and saturate the garment with rubbing alcohol. CAUTION: Test a hidden spot for colorfastness. Then dip a cloth into rubbing alcohol and dab the area. Or, use a prewash spray on both sides of the fabric and work it in with a small brush. Rinse and launder as usual.

- **Makeup/foundation:** Because water-based or powdered types of makeup are nongreasy, they can usually be removed by dampening the stained area; rubbing with white bar soap; rinsing and laundering as normal. Treat oily makeup stains with a prewash spray or liquid laundry detergent. Then dampen the area; rub to work the stain out. Rinse and launder in the hottest water safe for the fabric.

- **Mascara:** To remove water-based mascara, moisten the area and rub with liquid laundry detergent or white bar soap. Rinse and wash as usual. To remove oil-based mascara, apply prewash spray to the back of the stain, allow to set for several minutes then machine wash. Repeat if necessary.

- **Mayonnaise:** Get to this ASAP. Check the care label and pretreat with a prewash stain remover. Wash as usual. Check to make sure the stain is gone before putting into the dryer.

- **Meat juice:** Soak first in cold or warm water with an enzyme presoak. Then wash as usual. Or soak in cold water and sprinkle *unseasoned* meat tenderizer on the stain and let it sit. Repeat if necessary and then wash.

- **Mildew:** Take the garment outside. Brush the mildew stain with a stiff brush to remove mold spores.

For bleachable fabrics, soak for 15 minutes in a solution of 1 tablespoon chlorine bleach and 1 quart water. Rinse and launder, adding ½ cup chlorine bleach to the wash cycle.

For nonbleachable fabrics, flush the stain with a solution of ½ cup lemon juice and 1 tablespoon salt. Dry the garment in the sun to "bleach out" the mildew stain. After all traces of stain are removed, launder as usual.

CAUTION: Some new white fabrics may have an optical brightener infused in the material and consequently the sun will turn them yellow.

- **Milk:** ASAP soak clothes in cold water and then rub liquid laundry detergent into the stain or treat with an enzyme presoak or prewash spray. Launder in the hottest water safe for the fabric. If the stain persists, sponge it with dry-cleaning fluid and launder a second time before putting into the dryer.

- **Mucus:** Remove the residue from the fabric. Soak the garment in warm water and an enzyme detergent. After all traces of the stain are removed, launder as usual.

- **Mud:** Allow the stain to dry completely. Using a stiff brush, brush away the dirt. Rub some liquid laundry detergent or prewash spray into the remaining stain. Launder as usual. If the stain is heavy, pretreat with an enzyme detergent.

- **Mustard:** First, dampen the area and then rub liquid laundry detergent into the stain. Rinse and then soak in hot water with detergent for several hours. Use an enzyme detergent for final laundering.

- **Mystery stains:** Always check clothing for spots and stains before you store. Deal with spots and stains when you find them. If caught early, these stains may be soluble in water, so flush the stain ASAP with cold water. Put prewash spray on the stain and rub. Launder as normal after all traces of the stain are gone.

If stains are old and yellowish, they may have been created by spills from light-colored sugary drinks like apple juice, soda pop, and white wine or even from oils such as body lotion, mayonnaise, and salad dressing. If not noticed and the clothes are stored, the heat in a warm closet may have caused them to turn yellow or brown. They are difficult to remove.

For washable fabrics, try to lighten by using a heavy-duty detergent and all-fabric bleach for color or household chlorine bleach for bleachable whites.

For oil-based stains (you may notice jagged, irregular edges), set the temperature for the hottest water safe for the fabric. If you're uncertain, use warm water.

- **Nail polish:** Use one of these methods: Sponge the stain with pure acetone *after testing a hidden area for colorfastness.* Launder as usual. *Note: Do not* use acetone on fabrics containing acetate or triacetate because it will dissolve them. For acetate fabrics, use amyl acetate, which is safe.

Or: Put the stain facedown on several layers of paper towel. Sponge the backside with nail polish remover, which is fragrance- and color-free and contains no additives. Replace the towels, as needed, and repeat until stain is gone. Launder as usual. *Note:* Do not use nail polish remover on acetate; it will do damage. Instead, send to dry cleaner.

- **Needlepoint:** Cleaning will depend on type of thread (wool or synthetic) and canvas used. Some colors are not safe to wash. First, try to lift off dust and dirt with a vacuum. Use the brush attachment and hold ½ inch above needlepoint; do not touch the thread because it may be fragile. If there are other stains, check with your local arts and crafts store or dry cleaner before you do anything else.

- **Oil/grease/butter/margarine:** Greasy or oily stains need pretreatment with a prewash spray. Then rub liquid laundry detergent into the dampened stain. When the stain is gone, launder with plenty of detergent in the hottest water safe for the fabric.

- **Orange-colored stains:** French salad dressing or spaghetti sauce can leave orange stains on garments. Dampen a cotton napkin with water then moisten with a squeeze of lemon juice or small amount of white vinegar. Blot the stain until it disappears. Rinse in clear water. Use this method on synthetic fiber, cottons, and drip-dry clothes, but do not use on silk.

- **Paint:** Don't let the paint dry on fabrics if possible. Scrape off any fresh paint, and then get to stains immediately. Treatment differs based on type of paint but always check the care label first:

Oil-based or varnish: If the fabric is color-safe, use a bit of turpentine or paint thinner, then rinse well in water. Rub with a paste of powdered detergent and water; wash as usual. Or, sponge with nonflammable drycleaning solvent. Launder.

Paint thinned with solvents: Dab some of the solvent onto the stained area. After the area is wet with solvent, work a bit of liquid laundry detergent into it and soak in hot water. Launder as usual.

Water-based: Often will wash out with just soap and water. But if the paint has set and dried, it will be more difficult to remove. Rinse stain in warm water to flush out paint; launder as usual.

- **Pencil lead:** Use a clean pencil eraser to gently erase as much of the lead stain as you can. Rub liquid laundry detergent into the remaining stain and then launder as usual.

- **Perfume:** Use cool water to soak or sponge the stain immediately. Then pour a bit of white household vinegar on a sponge and apply to the stain. Rinse. If any stain remains, rub liquid laundry detergent into it and launder as usual.

- **Perspiration:** Rub area with bar soap; then launder in hottest water safe for fabric. If stains remain, wash again with enzyme detergents or oxygen bleach in hottest water safe for fabric. Note: If a perspiration stain has affected the color of the fabric, sponge a bit of white vinegar on the stain. Then rinse and launder again.

- **Plastic ("rubber" baby pants):** Use the delicate cycle and wash on warm. Always protect small items by putting into a mesh bag. Dry on warm and take out after 5 to 10 minutes.

- **Play putty:** Rub liquid laundry detergent into the spot and then scrub it from the underside of the fabric. Treat stain with diluted

hydrogen peroxide (test in an inconspicuous area first) and then wash in the hottest water safe for the fabric.

- **Ring around the collar:** Rub liquid laundry detergent or prewash spray or hair shampoo into the area and let this work on the stain for 30 minutes. Or, rub area with white bar soap on a damp sponge and launder in the hottest water safe for the fabric.

- **Rubber cement:** Use an ice cube or ice pack to harden the cement. Or: Put garment in the freezer, and then scrape off with a dull knife. Saturate the area with a prewash stain remover. Rinse and launder as usual.

- **Rust:** Commercial rust removers found in the fabric dye section of your grocery store will do the job. Follow the label directions exactly. Never use the rust remover near or inside a washer because it can remove the glossy finish on the porcelain outside or inside the machine.

Alternatively, you can give white vinegar a try, but NEVER use bleach on rust stains. For a small rust stain, sprinkle it with salt and rub with half a lemon. Set out in the sun to help "bleach" it out. *Note:* Some white fabrics should not be put into the sun. Read care label.

- **Rusty discoloration on white fabric:** Use phosphate detergent (if available) in wash, along with 1 cup enzyme detergent or oxygen bleach. If stains persist, dissolve 1 ounce oxalic acid crystals per gallon of water in a plastic container. Soak clothes for 10 to 15 minutes. Rinse and launder.

- **Salad dressing:** Remove as much of the liquid as you can. Sponge area with cleaning fluid to get rid of the grease; then treat remaining stain with a prewash product. Launder as usual with appropriate bleach, if needed. Read care label and test on hidden area of fabric first.

■ **Sap:** It may be possible to remove tree sap from washable garments by using a stain remover that contains dry-cleaning solvent, but read the directions first and test an area for colorfastness. Then put the stained area face-down on several layers of paper towel and apply the solvent from the back.

Alternatively, make a paste of powder or liquid laundry detergent (without bleach) and ammonia. Apply to the spot and let it sit for 30 minutes, then launder. Repeat paste step if needed.

■ **Scorch marks:** Heavily scorched fabric cannot be returned to its original state. Try one of these removal methods but always read care labels first:

> For *bleachable fabrics:* Launder with chlorine bleach.
> For *nonbleachable fabrics:* Soak in enzyme detergent or oxygen bleach and the hottest water safe for fabric and then launder.
> For *colorfast fabrics:* Always test a hidden area for colorfastness first then use a clean white cloth to dab 3 percent hydrogen peroxide on the scorched area to fade light scorch marks on fabrics. You may have to apply several times, but scorch marks will lessen.
> For *delicate fabrics:* Rub scorch marks lightly with a clean white cloth dampened with white vinegar. Wipe with a clean, dry cloth.

■ **Semen:** Pretreat with a laundry product containing enzymes. Launder with oxygen bleach.

■ **Shoe dye/polish:** To remove shoe dye or polish from off-white hose, soak the discolored section of the hose in rubbing alcohol and wash as usual. If you need to use a color-remover, treat the entire hose because it may change the overall appearance. *Note:* To keep dye from bleeding on hose, spray the inside of shoes several times with a fabric-protector spray and repeat occasionally.

■ **Shoe polish:** Some shoe polish, especially liquid, may not come out. But try these methods:

> For *liquid shoe polish,* pretreat with a paste of powder or liquid detergent and water. Then launder as normal. Or, apply cleaning fluid to the stain; then wash the garment in detergent and warm water.
> For *paste shoe polish,* use a dull knife and scrape residue off. Pretreat with a prewash stain remover and rinse well. Launder using a color-safe bleach.

■ **Silk fabric:** CAUTION: Silk: First, read the care label to see if the item can be hand- or machine-washed. Use warm to cool water and wash gently. Lengthy soaking can damage colors; chlorine bleach and excessive rubbing will damage delicate silk fiber. Iron on low or steam settings.

Never try to remove spill stains on silk by rubbing the area because silk fibers break easily. Blot instead.

> *Beverage spills:* These may disappear when the fabric dries, but sugar in some drinks may create a yellow stain that appears later. Take silk garments to the dry cleaner

as soon as possible. Let the counter person know exactly what was spilled where.

Perspiration/body oils: These are silk's worst enemies. Maintain silk garments with regular dry cleaning or hand-washing.

■ **Sour cream:** ASAP soak clothes in cold water and then rub liquid laundry detergent into the stain or treat with an enzyme presoak or prewash spray. Launder in the hottest water safe for the fabric. If the stain persists, sponge it with cleaning fluid and launder a second time before putting the clothes into the dryer.

■ **Sticky residue:** This gluey stuff left behind from gummed stickers can be removed by carefully dabbing the area with a petroleum-based prewash spray or cleaning fluid, depending on the care label.

■ **Suede I:** Surface dirt stains can be removed by gently rubbing the material with an art gum eraser or lightly buffing the spots with the fine side of an emery board. Or: Pat cornstarch or flour into a minor oil-type stain to soak it up, brush off, then, wipe the surface with a damp, clean cloth. Let it dry and then brush with a clothes brush to bring up the nap. Stubborn or difficult stains should be removed by a professional dry cleaner that deals with suede and leather.

■ **Suede II:** To treat grease or other heavy stains effectively, the only solution is to take the garment to a specialty professional dry cleaner.

For an *emergency treatment,* pat talcum powder or cornstarch onto the fabric to absorb grease. Brush off excess then sponge out the grease with a cloth dipped in white vinegar. Use a suede brush to restore the nap. CAUTION: Test vinegar on a hidden spot before sponging it on the fabric.

Maintain suede with regular brushing using a special suede brush. If it gets dusty, wipe with a damp cloth. Do not store suede in plastic bags because it needs air circulation.

■ **Suede (imitation):** Launder in a washing machine set on delicate cycle, cold water, and use a mild detergent. Line dry.

■ **Sunscreen/suntan lotions:** Some contain oil to make them moisture-resistant and this oil is not easy to remove. Read the manufacturer's directions before applying. Make sure the products are dry before you put on your clothes and wash your hands after you have applied lotions before you touch clothing. If you do get any on a garment, check the care label and pretreat the stain ASAP. Launder as usual. Or: To lift greasy sunscreens, sprinkle a bit of cornstarch on the stains and let sit for several minutes. Brush off gently and then launder as usual.

For a stain on the neckline of white clothes, treat with a solvent (spot remover) or prewash spray because many sunscreens contain oil. Wash as usual using the warmest water safe for the fabric. Don't put into the dryer unless you are certain that all of the stain is gone. Repeat the process if necessary. If the stain has not been removed, take the garment to a dry cleaner.

■ **Sweaters:** Read the care label first in determining how to remove a stain; it will depend on fiber type. Some can be hand-washed and then blocked-dried; others can be machine washed on the gentle cycle. Be sure to use the laundry detergent indicated for the fiber. If the label says dry clean only, take to a cleaner or use an in-dryer kit, which can remove light soil and odors.

Check for colorfastness on a hidden spot before you use stain removal methods.

- **Swimsuit:** To prevent fading/fabric damage from pool-water chlorine, buy chlorine remover for aquarium water, which is available at pet stores. Soak your bathing suit after each swim in a solution of 1 drop anti-chlorine formula in 1 gallon water. Don't rinse out.

- **Tar:** For washable fabrics, first remove any residue of tar. Wash with detergent as usual. Or, use a cleaning fluid; place stain face-down on paper towels to absorb the tar. Launder in hottest water safe for fabric.

- **Tea:** On washable fabric, rinse area and soak with cold water. Then use a prewash spray to treat the stain. Wash as usual. Because tea contains tannin, the stain may come back. Treat again and wash as usual. Nonwashables will need to be professionally dry cleaned.

- **Tennis shoes:** To remove stains from white rubber shoes, use a whitewall tire cleaner. Follow directions on the label.

- **Ties:** To prevent serious stains, before you wear a tie the first time, spray it with a fabric stain-repellent. To treat stains on silk ties see **Silk fabric**. Read the care label for cleaning instructions. Dry cleaning may be the only answer.

- **Tobacco:** Dampen stain and rub with bar soap. Rinse. Then soak in enzyme detergent or oxygen bleach. Launder. If stain still remains, launder again with chlorine bleach, if it's safe for the fabric. Check care label.

- **Tomato ketchup/barbecue sauce:** Scrape off any stain excess and then soak the garment in cold water for a half hour. While the item is still wet, rub white bar soap or liquid laundry detergent into any remaining stains. Launder in warm water and detergent.

On 100 percent cotton, cotton blends, or permanent press, within 24 hours sponge undiluted white vinegar to remove stain. Then launder or dry-clean as the manufacturer recommends.

- **Toothpaste on fabric:** CAUTION: Do not use this treatment on silk or delicate fabrics as the rubbing motion could break the fibers. Put a cloth underneath the fabric and work with a damp cloth to remove the toothpaste; then blow-dry garment with a hair dryer.

- **T-shirt/washable shirt:** To remove underarm stains, before laundering, sponge the stained area with white household vinegar and allow to sit for a couple of minutes. If you still see stains, apply a paste of water and an enzyme laundry detergent or an enzyme presoak. Let soak for several hours and then wash garment in the hottest water safe for the shirt's fabric.

- **Urine:** Soak the stained area in warm water. If any stain remains, sponge the area with a solution of half white household vinegar and half water. (This also helps to neutralize any leftover odor.) Rinse well and launder as usual.

- **Urine residue:** Flush the stain as soon as possible and then soak in warm water with an enzyme detergent. For bleachable fabric, launder as usual and add chlorine bleach to the wash load. For other fabrics, add an all-fabric

Dryer Hints

Did you know that dust and lint buildup in dryers is a leading cause of home fires? So, for safety's sake, clean the lint filter after each load and the exhaust duct of your dryer on a regular basis.

If you leave clothes in the dryer too long, put a big damp towel in the dryer with the wrinkled clothes. Set the dryer for 15 minutes and when it's done, take it out right away. Presto, wrinkles are gone!

bleach to the wash load to help eliminate any remaining stain.

- **Velvet:** To eliminate water stains on velvet, hold the wet area over steam spouting from a teakettle for just a few minutes. Shake garment and let dry. Brush up nap.

- **Velveteen:** See **Corduroy**.

- **Vomit:** Get rid of any solid residue from the fabric. Soak the garment in warm water and an enzyme detergent; you can add baking soda to the rinse too. After all traces of the stain are removed, launder as usual.

- **Wedding dress:** When you buy a wedding dress, ask about the cleaning care and get written care instructions. Read the care label *before* you buy. The fabric and trims may be difficult to clean. You will want to preserve this special-day garment and pay attention to how you can do that when you purchase. For example, because wedding dresses often have trims of beads, embroidery, seed pearls, appliqué, or sequins that have been glued on, the adhesives

are soluble and might dissolve in dry-cleaning solvent.

Polystyrene buttons, beads, and imitation pearl beads also may dissolve in the solvent. Some imitation pearl beads are polystyrene with a hard shell covering. Polystyrene will dissolve in perchloroethylene, which is the most common dry-cleaning solvent. So the beads will disappear and leave just the enamel shell. However, if the pearl bead is glued on rather than sewn on, often the glue or adhesive is not resistant to solvent.

Sequins that are held on with adhesives rather than being sewn on are not resistant to solvent either. In some cases sequins can shrivel or curl if exposed to heat or moisture used in cleaning. Glitter is very fragile, and if it's been glued on, it may come off during cleaning. Metal or glitter trim can also corrode, oxidize, or change color.

Silk, taffeta, brocade, chiffon, and organza fabrics require special care. As soon after the wedding as possible, take the dress to be dry-cleaned by a professional—even if it looks clean! It may have spots from perspiration, body oils, perfume, or hairspray, which you can't see. There also could be food or beverage stains that will oxidize and set in later. Be sure to tell the dry cleaner about any cleaning method you already have tried. Point out any stains and let the dry cleaner examine the gown carefully. Also have them make any repairs of small tears.

If you are wearing an heirloom or antique gown, follow these hints: Take the dress to a dry cleaner who specializes in restoring antique fabrics. Tell the dry cleaner how old the dress is and what the fabric is. Show the cleaner the stained areas and point out any weak fabric or loose trim.

- **White fabrics turned gray:** Dissolve 1 tablespoon borax in a cup of hot water and add to the final rinse to help whites become white again. An old-fashioned bluing agent that you add to laundry or a whitener and brightener may work, too.

- **White nylon, polyester (durable press turned yellow):** Soak garment overnight with enzyme detergent or oxygen bleach. Then launder in the hottest water safe for fabric with detergent and bleach-safe for these fabrics. Or: Launder with enzyme detergent or oxygen bleach added to regular detergent and in the hottest water safe for fabric. Do not dry these modern fabrics in the sun because they may contain fluorescent brighteners, which react badly to the sun.

- **White silk (turned yellow):** If the garment is washable, soak it in a plastic container or sink for 2 or 3 hours in a mixture of 1 gallon warm water with 2 ounces of 3 percent hydrogen peroxide. Remove, rinse in warm water. Dry on a plastic hanger.

- **Wine:** Soak stained area in cool water. If the material is bleach-safe, use bleach (follow washing instructions) or electric dishwasher detergent (make a paste with a bit of water) and scrub with an old, clean toothbrush. After spot treating, wash in the hottest water possible for the fabric. For 100 percent cotton, cotton blends, and permanent press, sponge stain with undiluted white vinegar within 24 hours; then launder or dry-clean according to the manufacturer's instructions.

- **Woolens:**

For hand washables, wash in cool water with a mild soap or bleach-free detergent. Soak for 3 to 5 minutes. Rinse several times in clean water. Gently squeeze—don't ring—out excess water. Lay out flat to dry and do not put in sunlight or in direct heat.

For machine washables, use a mild, bleach-free detergent on the warm, gentle cycle. Add detergent to the machine as it fills to dissolve before putting garment in. Hang to dry.

Index

Underscored page references indicate boxed text.

Index

Index

Index

Index

About the Author

Heloise is the world's most famous name in lifestyle advice. Her daily column, "Hints from Heloise®" was begun by her mother, the original Heloise, in 1959, and has been running ever since. In 1977, the current Heloise, schooled at her famous mother's knee, took over the column that is now syndicated in more than 500 newspapers worldwide. "The high priestess of household hints" (as the *New York Daily News* called her) also writes a monthly column for *Good Housekeeping* magazine and has a radio show, "Ask Heloise," broadcast on the Liberty Broadcasting Network. She has written eleven books with millions of copies in print. Visit her website at www.Heloise.com.